Visions from Abroad

Mona Khazindar

Visions *from* Abroad

Historical and Contemporary Representations of Arabia

Introduction by
Philippe Cardinal

ithra | SKIRA

Cover
Anonymous
Arabie, seventeenth century
Courtesy of the Bibliothèque nationale
de France

Editor
Paola Gribaudo

Art Director
Marcello Francone

Design
Luigi Fiore

Editorial Coordination
Vincenza Russo

Editing
Anna Albano

Layout
Paola Ranzini Pallavicini

Translations
Johanna Kreiner and Sara Heft
for NTL, Firenze

We would like to express our deep gratitude to Ithra and, in particular, to Mr Mohammed Khoja, Sponsorships and Partnerships strategist.

First published in Italy in 2019 by
Skira editore S.p.A.
Palazzo Casati Stampa
via Torino 61
20123 Milano
Italy
www.skira.net

Printed and bound in Italy. First edition

ISBN: 978-88-572-3946-0

Distributed in USA, Canada, Central & South America by
ARTBOOK | D.A.P. 75 Broad Street Suite 630, New York, NY 10004, USA.
Distributed elsewhere in the world by Thames and Hudson Ltd., 181A High Holborn, London WC1V 7QX, United Kingdom.

www.skira.net

Note to Readers

A modern and simplified transcription has been systematically adopted for Arabic terms, particularly for proper nouns. From one author, era, and language to the next, transcriptions may vary greatly: the name of the city of Jeddah, for example, has been spelled Djuddah, Djeddah, Djedda, Jedda, Gedda, Geddah, Dsjidda, etc. The same applies for the city of Mecca—spelled Meccah, Mekke, etc.—and for most names transcribed from Arabic. When they appear in the texts cited in this publication, these different transcriptions have been consistently replaced by the most common forms used in contemporary English: Jeddah, Mecca, Yanbu, Medina, etc. The text of this work is peppered with a great many citations taken from the books of explorers, Orientalists, geographers, historians, and adventurers who traveled in Arabia and/or wrote about it—in different languages, but mainly in Arabic, English or French. Translations of some of these works are more accessible than the original text and in those cases, citations have been retranslated back to their original languages from the aforementioned translations, resulting in a version that diverges slightly from the original text.

A book conceived by
CULTURAL PROJECTS PAL&TE ART PUBLICATIONS

Contents

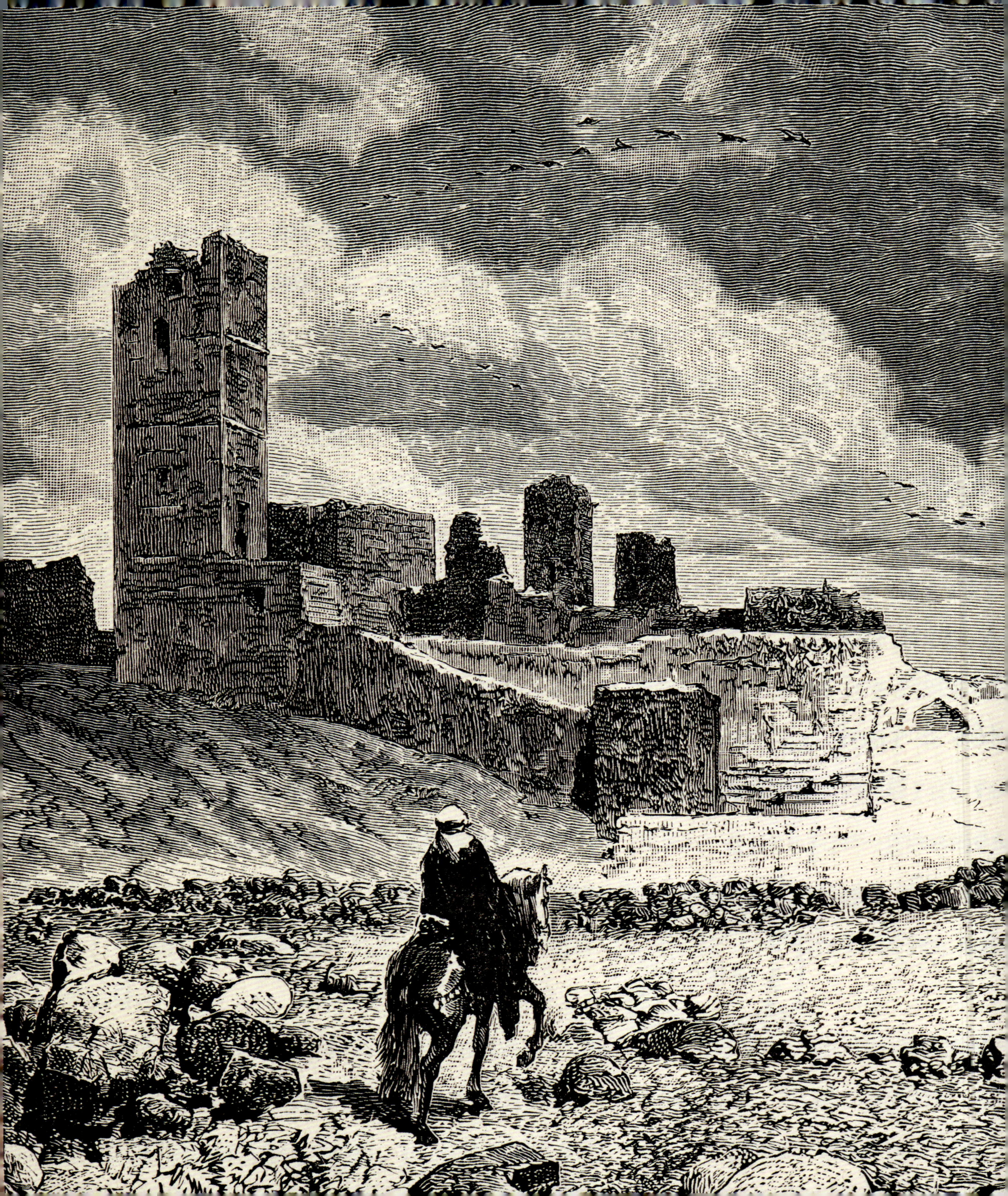

Introduction

Alongside visual representations from about a hundred different artists, the text of this work seeks to demonstrate how a whole series of images of the vast territory that is Arabia, long considered one of the most obscurely secretive parts of the world, have gradually emerged in books and travel accounts inspired by the region. It should be noted that all of these artists and authors are foreigners to the peninsula.

Arabia's reputation for impenetrability, and the mystery that this has created, might be retraced to antiquity: in the early second century, during the reign of the Roman emperor Trajan and his successor Hadrian, the Limes Arabicus was established, a strategic fortification some 1,500 kilometers long, consisting of forts, fortresses, and watchtowers running from Syria through the deserts of northern Arabia. One hundred and fifty years earlier, despite their dominant position in the world, the Romans had failed miserably to take over the caravan trade in southern Arabia, the source of the peninsula's wealth.

Dismissed from the milestones of knowledge, this Arabia then ceased to be of any concern for Europeans. But while Europe was in the midst of the Middle Ages, a number of Arabic-language authors wrote travel books and geographical compendia providing accounts of Arabian realities. It would take many centuries, however, for the works of Ibn Hawqal, penned in the eleventh century; Ibn Jubayr, from the twelfth century; or of Ibn Battuta and Abulfeda, from the fourteenth century—to name just a few—to be translated and printed in European languages. Of Arabia, these authors first recounted the context in which the pilgrimage to Mecca and visits to the city of Medina were carried out—a context encompassing a great many episodes of the Muhammadan act and the beginnings of Islam. Consequently, for these authors, Arabia most often tended to be limited to the expanse of Hijaz, and the political situation was not necessarily treated.

Hijaz has nevertheless always played a substantial role in terms of influence for every Muslim power neighboring Arabia, which over time included the Abbasids of Baghdad; the Fatimids of Cairo; the Ayyubids of Cairo and Damascus; and later, the Ottomans. Overseen by the dominant power of each era, the organisation of the pilgrimage was extremely complex to carry out: it called for logistics and resources made all the more substantial in the face of the Bedouin tribes of the lands and deserts that had to be crossed to reach the holy cities, who continually seemed to make every effort to disrupt the well-oiled choreography of the caravans. Under those circumstances, it was nevertheless impossible to build a fortification modelled after the Romans' Limes Arabicus to ward off the Bedouins, because they happened to be on their home turf!

Quite evidently, European curiosity about Arabia took time to emerge: Ludovico di Varthema, the first from the continent to undertake the voyage to Medina and Mecca, only did so at the dawn of the sixteenth century. In other words, his journey took place two centuries after those of Marco Polo, and one century after those of Niccolo de' Conti—other Italians drawn to faraway lands. He followed in the wake of the journeys of the great discovers, Magellan, Vasco de Gama and Christopher Columbus, at a time when America was attracting attention.

It is not exactly clear, however, why Ludovico di Varthema, who figures in several chapters of this publication, one day decided to leave his hometown of Bologna to travel to the Near East, to Damascus, where he managed to be recruited as a Mameluke officer, joining the escort service of some fifty men tasked with protecting the caravan bound for the holy cities—and in whose ranks he had to fight Bedouin armies, he asserted. Following stays in Medina, then Mecca, where he cast off his mercenary attire, Varthema continued his journey onward to Yemen, then India, which clearly illustrates that Hijaz represented but a leg of his journey.

Following Varthema, it took more than a century and a half for another European to make the journey

Anne Blunt
Melakh
Woodcut by Gaston Vuillier
after a watercolor by Anne Blunt
From *Voyage en Arabie. Pèlerinage au Nedjed, berceau de la race arabe (A Pilgrimage to Nejd, The Cradle of the Arab race)*
Paris, 1882
Courtesy of the British Library

to Mecca and Medina, cities from which non-Muslims were banned—a ban which, depending on the era, could more or less apply to the whole of Hijaz. A few exceptions applied to this ban: until the eighteenth century, it could happen that notables undertook their pilgrimage openly accompanied by Christian servants or slaves. This was most likely facilitated by the fact that the status of a slave in Islam was quite similar to that of a child, in that they were not held responsible for some of their actions. A pilgrimage completed by a child or a slave was consequently not considered as valid. This was the case for the pilgrimage completed towards the end of the seventeenth century by a young Englishman who fell into slavery, John Pitts, in the company of his North African master; he also features in the pages of this book, and narrates this episode of his life in a work devoted to his fifteen years in captivity.

It was necessary to wait until the late eighteenth and early nineteenth centuries for a true interest in the holy cities of Hijaz to develop—an interest that inevitably clashed with their particular status in the eyes of Islam. Nevertheless, while the ban on their presence there was perceived by some of these travelers as something of a challenge to be met, most of them always managed to demonstrate great respect for Islam and the pilgrimage rituals. This was already the case for Varthema, who rather remarkably and unexpectedly, for a man of his era, demonstrated a true sense of moderation in his descriptions. This was also the case for Pitts, of whom the twentieth-century historian Jacqueline Pirenne wrote: "Believe us in saying that nobody has described with such comprehensive objectivity the religious attitude of those who made the pilgrimage to Mecca."

As for these later authors who have just been mentioned, and who, over the course of the nineteenth and in the early twentieth centuries, devoted works to their sojourns in the holy cities—including Ali Bey El Abbassi, Léon Roches, Richard Burton, John Fryer Keane, Christiaan Snouck Hurgronje, Jules Gervais-Courtellemont, Étienne Dinet, and a few others—they appear to have all shown extreme deference towards their subject of observation. Even those who were open about their lack of concern for religion in general demonstrated sincere respect in their writings. This is the case for the spirited British explorer Richard Burton, who, in the presence of the Masjid al-Haram, wrote "Sublime it was, and expressing by all the eloquence of fancy the grandeur of the One idea which vitalised El Islam, and the strength and steadfastness of its votaries." It is true that this was noted on the occasion of a night visit under the light of the *Dhu al-Hijjah* moon. Burton subsequently devoted years of his life to a translation of *The Arabian Nights*, still recognised as the best English-language version of this work. He had himself buried in a tomb shaped as a Bedouin tent.

To some extent, these nineteenth and twentieth century European authors unveiled to their readers—practically under a seal of secrecy—this very part of Arabia, described in the works of the aforementioned Muslim geographers and travelers, and which millions of pilgrims over the course of the centuries were already familiar with. There were also other authors, and European travelers who directed their curiosity toward other themes. The discipline of archaeology was emerging at the time in Europe, where old stones had already long been a source of interest. As Arabia was situated in the vicinity of some of the world's richest territories in terms of ancient civilisations, the quest for such discoveries was naturally undertaken there, encompassing an entirely different host of authors, to whom fate was not always kind: Johann Ludwig Burckhardt, Ulrich Jaspar Seetzen, Charles Montagu Doughty, Charles Huber, Antonin Jaussen, Raphaël Savignac, and a handful of others.

Burckhardt was certainly the one best able to describe the radical prejudice held by the region's populations against all explorers, archaeologists and epigraphers in search of discoveries: "It is very unfortunate for European travelers that the idea of treasures being hidden in ancient edifices is so strongly rooted in the minds of the Arabs and Turks," wrote the Swiss explorer, who discovered the ancient city of Petra. He added that this detestation was even more solidly rooted in the minds of Bedouins, who immediately took any traveler curious about ruins or old stones for a magician out to steal treasures: "[…] nor are they satisfied with watching all the strangers' steps; they believe that it is sufficient for a true magician to have seen and observed the spot where treasures are hidden (of which he is supposed to be already informed by the old books of the infidels who lived on the spot) in order to be able afterwards, at his ease, to command the guardian of the treasure to set the whole before him."

One day or another, every traveler with a passion for archaeology thus faced animosity elicited by their curiosity. They were sometimes imprisoned, often harassed, continually insulted—circumstances that might seem merely anecdotal in nature, had they not cost the lives of a few, including the German Seetzen and the Frenchman Huber, who were murdered.

Waclav Seweryn Rzewuski
Arab village in the desert of Nejd,
1817–19
From *Impressions d'Orient et d'Arabie. Un cavalier polonais chez les bédouins*
José Corti / Muséum national d'histoire naturelle, Paris, 2002

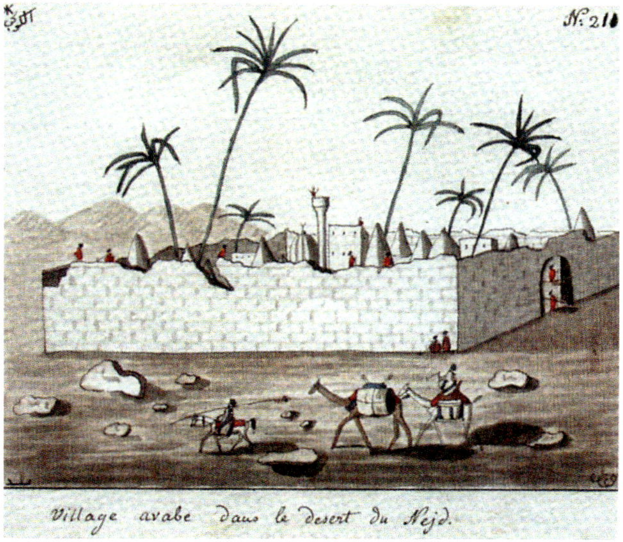

The late eighteenth century also saw the famous Danish expedition—the only group scientific expedition ever bound for Arabia—with archaeology as only one focus among many, and from which the cartographer and mathematician Carsten Niebuhr alone returned. Upon landing in Jeddah, the scientists set out to avoid going into Hijaz and headed south, where they got to work immediately. But their endeavors came to a sudden end. Niebuhr surprisingly grasped the reason for the demise of his comrades, the philologist Frederick Christian von Haven, the doctor Christian Carl Kramer, the naturalist Peter Forsskål and the draughtsman Georg Wilhelm Baurenfeind, who died for wanting to continue to "live in the European manner" on Arabian soil; and as he had the opportunity to write upon his return, "We ourselves were the cause of maladies against which other people could easily protect themselves."

Still other visitors conducted their journey under different auspices, such as the members of a more restricted circle including Waclaw Seweryn Rzewuski, Carlo Guarmani, Anne and Wilfrid Blunt and a few others, who set out and faced the tribes, combing the Arabian deserts in search of purebred horses. Perhaps it was unsurprising that the Pole, the Tuscan, and those Brits, of duly aristocratic descent, got along fine with the Bedouins, so intent on origins. The interest of these visitors for their horses could only be a source of flattery for the latter; or at any rate, they accepted it more readily than the highly suspicious curiosity that others displayed for half-faded inscriptions carved into the stone of some ruined edifices. They were thus welcomed without any problems. At times, even, with open arms.

Such was the case for example, for one of these surprising travelers, Count Waclaw Seweryn Rzewuski. A remarkable horseman and peerless Arabist, reputed as a resourceful gentleman, he traveled to Arabia to procure horses for the stud farms of Queen Catharina of Württemberg and Tsar Alexander I of Russia. Considered by the Bedouins "as the great emir of the Northern tribes, in the kingdom of Skandar"—none other than Alexander I, Tsar of Russia and King of Poland—he appears to have enjoyed great prestige among the tribes, although he most likely exaggerated his own merits somewhat: "I was compared to the favorite hero of the Arabs, the celebrated Antarah. My praises were sung in verse by the tribes, and this is how my name spread across the desert to the very ends of Arabia, as I later learnt, where all is novel, and where, under the spell of language, each person adorns truth with the marvellous offerings of an ardent imagination."

Still others placed humans at the heart of their intentions, forming yet another distinguished and heterogeneous assembly that included Laurent d'Arvieux, George Forster Sadleir, Maurice Tamisier, Georg August Wallin, William Gifford Palgrave, Harry St. John Bridger Philby, and a few others. They held a century-spanning dialogue among anthropologists (before the term was coined), eminent diplomats, and authorised spies. Among them was the young Laurent d'Arvieux, nephew of the French consul in Sidon, in whose home he had been raised, and who, due to his fluency in Arabic and Turkish, had been tasked with a dangerous mission "by order of the late French King Louis XIV [...] to the Camp of the Grand Emir Chief of the Arabs, known under the name of Bedouins". The title of his later, highly relevant work alluded to this, representing the first dissertation ever devoted to "the rights, customs, of the Bedouins." This group also included the highly renowned Finnish Orientalist Georg August Wallin, who undertook an extended sojourn among Bedouins in central Arabia around the mid-nineteenth century, displaying astute understanding and solicitude towards his hosts.

The captain Forster Sadleir was also among this group, tasked by the English government with transmitting a message to Ibrahim Pasha, leader of the troops sent by Mohammed Ali to Arabia. Sadleir left from Qatif, a port on the Arabian Gulf, and only reached Ibrahim at the last minute, after a forced march, in Yanbu on the Red Sea, as the latter was preparing to sail back to Egypt. Sadleir was thus the first European to cross the entire peninsula from end to end, from coast to coast, and from east to west, nearly without realizing it. He even wrote a book in which he recounts how he undertook this long journey in unfamiliar lands, scrupulously noting the distances traveled, although this failed to inspire much

Anne Blunt
Reception at the emir castle in Ha'il
From *Voyage en Arabie. Pèlerinage au Nedjed* (A Pilgrimage to Nejd)
Woodcut by Gaston Vuillier after a watercolor by Anne Blunt, Paris, 1882
Courtesy of the British Library

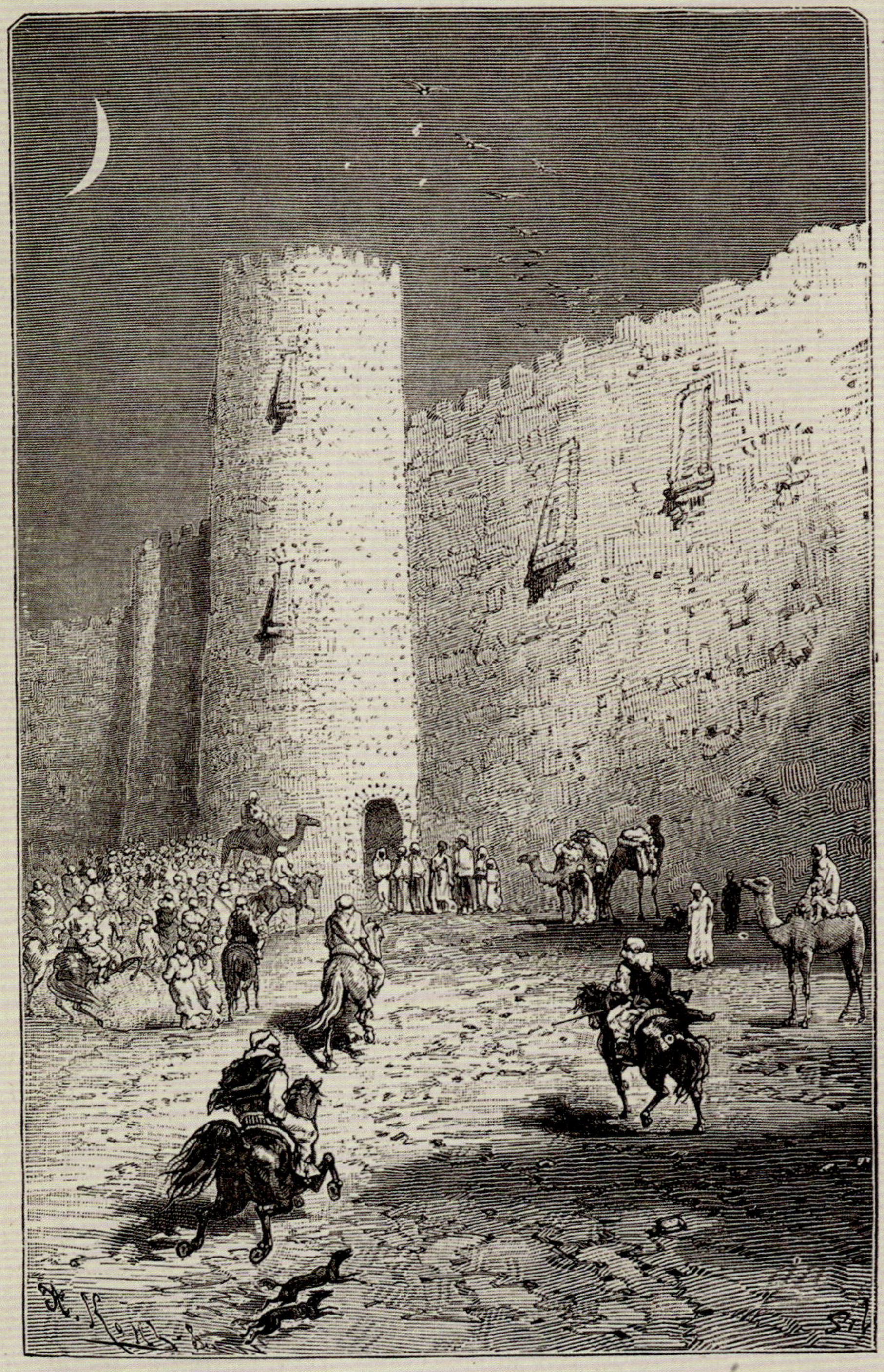

Entrée chez l'émir, à Haïl.

of anything in him—quite the opposite of D'Arvieux, who, after visiting the territory of a single tribe, wrote a whole book about Bedouin society.

Others, in contrast, gave themselves over to their fertile imaginations: the clever British Jesuit, William Gifford Palgrave, for example, a likely spy for the French emperor Napoleon III, who crossed central Arabia disguised as a Syrian doctor in 1862–63, plotting from the court of one emir to the next. The rather sensational account that Palgrave later provided of his adventures in Nejd nevertheless appeared eminently dubious.

And lastly, to conclude, there was the tight circle of the more recent travelers—Bertram Thomas, Wilfred Thesiger, and a few others—who came to brave the deserts, or rather, the largest desert of all, the desert of deserts: Rub' al Khali, the "empty quarter". Ultimately not really so empty, this expanse—this "grandiose void," in the words of Philby—is the ancient womb of Bedouin culture, as observed by these last explorers. A true sense of urgency drove Thesiger to spend about five years of his life there, from 1946 to 1950, traveling across it repeatedly from one end to the other. Thesiger was aware that he was both one of the first and one of the last observers of a way of life on the verge of extinction. "All that is best in the Arabs has come to them from the desert," he wrote, fully aware that this immutable world would soon cease to exist.

What sets these last authors—including Thomas, Thesiger and Philby—apart from those who preceded them is this awareness that they were seeing one world come to an end. All of those who preceded them on Arabian soil had believed that this society would endure for a thousand years to come, as it had existed for millennia. But from the early decades of the twentieth century, the intrusion of modernity—particularly of modes of transport: trains, automobiles, and airplanes—very quickly jeopardized Bedouin society, largely rooted in camel transport and the caravan trade, ultimately leading to its demise. Just as this decline was being observed, the discovery of oil and the creation of a petroleum industry allowed for another society to replace the old one, made possible by hydrocarbon revenues—a society that allowed the peninsula's inhabitants to stand on equal footing with technological progress.

For some eighty years, this new society has dominated foreign perceptions of Arabia, despite the fact that it has remained highly diverse. Thus, while Arabia continues to assert this diversity, the present publication has the merit of holding up a mirror to it, in which the array of approaches proposed by artists, travelers and writers are made visible, like so many reflections.

It is only natural for the author of such a publication to be Saudi Arabian, and essential that she has a sense of belonging to different cultures, in order to be able to successfully see it to fruition. Born in the United States, Mona Khazindar completed her secondary studies in Saudi Arabia, and her university studies in France, at the Sorbonne. Schooled in three different continents, her professional career has been concentrated in a single country, France, and a single international institution, the Institut du Monde Arabe, where she arrived upon completing her studies, and only left some twenty-five years later, after having served as director general. This exceptional path, wholly devoted to the art and culture of the Arab world, made her the ideal candidate to treat a subject never before addressed as extensively as it is in this publication.

What emerges from the pages of this book, in the context of its thematic approach to Arabia, is the quality of many of its perceptions, in particular, those of d'Arvieux, Niebuhr, Burckhardt, Wallin and a few others. These perceptions were clearly animated by curiosity, as well as a sense of mystery, undoubtedly religious, but also anthropological, surrounding an Arab culture that scholars such as Jacques Berque and Maxime Rodinson had extensively researched, without even successfully accounting for the "fascination" it held for Europeans. As a century-old cycle comes to an end for this region of the world, who will be able to say whether the mystery has not been renewed, the fascination still intact?

Philippe Cardinal

نمونهٔ بندر جده

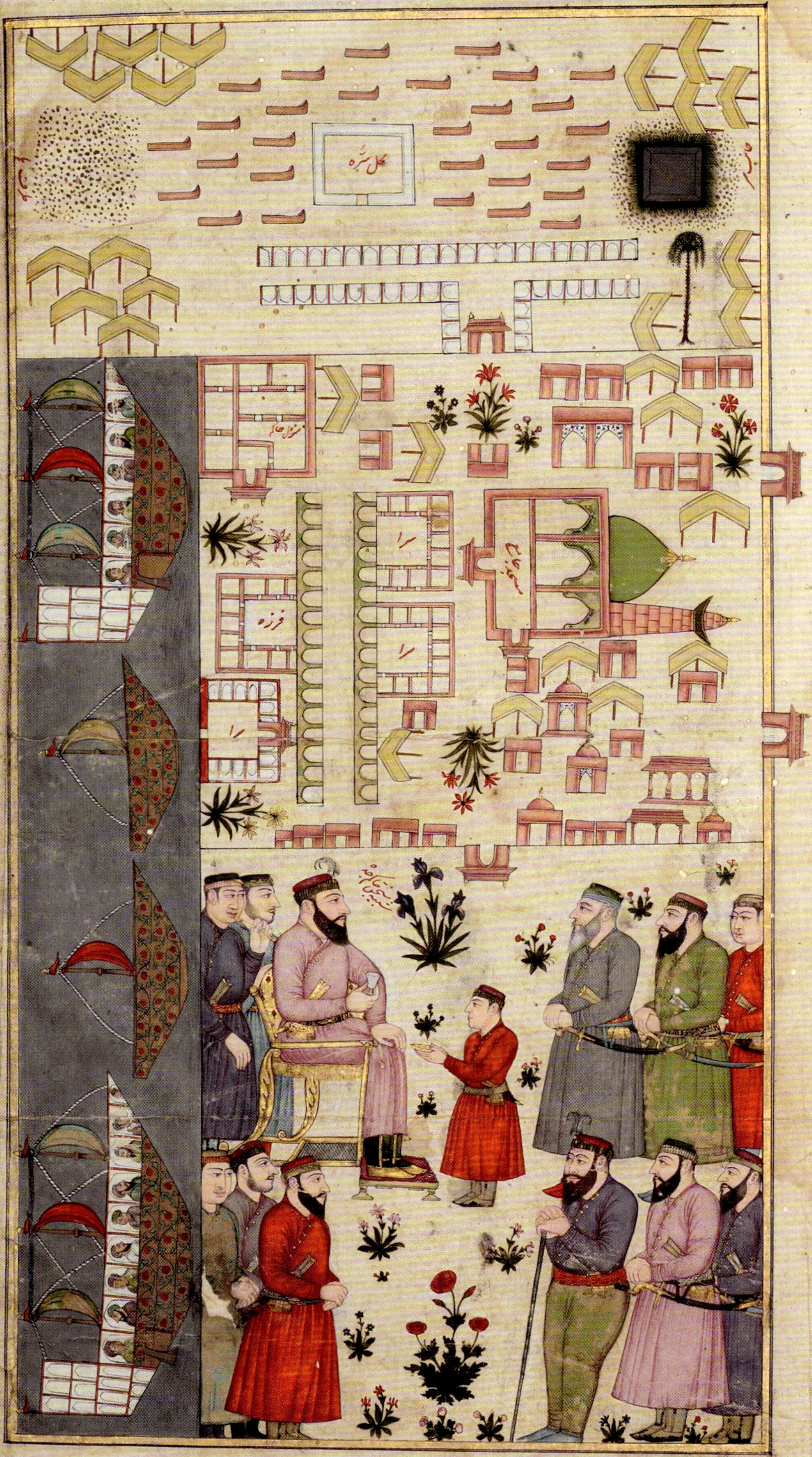

The Gates of Arabia

Since the beginnings of Islam, the Red Sea city of Jeddah, on the western coast of Arabia, has been the main gateway to the holy cities, the Hijaz region, and the peninsula as a whole, despite the bordering Arabian Gulf to the east and Indian Ocean to the south. It was chosen in the 26th year of Hijrah by the Caliph Uthman to replace the old port city of al-Shu'ayba as the main access point for those traveling to Mecca, located less than a day's walk away. Jeddah thus took on the eminent role of "Gateway to Arabia," which it has held ever since.

Nevertheless, reaching Jeddah by a maritime route has never been simple. Red Sea navigation was always extremely perilous, at least until the emergence of steam-powered vessels in the mid-nineteenth century. Prior to that, the voyage was undertaken only in large traditional sailing vessels: two-masted *sambuks* or smaller *dhows*, sometimes with a single mast. "This sea is one of the most difficult known to mankind: cut and crossed in all directions by submarine currents, bristling with reefs and banks of coral, it lies wide open to violent squalls which the proximity of coast and mountain makes very frequent and very sudden; thus shipwrecks are common occurrences," wrote Charles Didier in 1854, after surviving a storm while crossing the Gulf of Aqaba. After boarding a Jeddah-bound *sambuk* in Suez, the French writer then headed to Ta'if to meet the Sharif of Mecca, as the title of his work, *Sojourn with the Grand Sharif of Makkah*, indicates quite clearly.

"We were favoured with a very fair wind all day long, and soon rounded Ras Muhammad, the farthest cape of the Sinai Peninsula. In the evening the wind, though still fair for us, rose to a worrying degree of violence, and the sea was so rough that we were cruelly tossed about in our cockle-shell," Didier continued. Red Sea navigation never occurred at night, when boats anchor, "but this time," he explained, "it was impossible. We had reached the Gulf of Aqaba, all of which had to be crossed before we could find shelter, or even an anchorage; we therefore had to go on sailing at night, despite the ever-increasing fury of the waves and the roughness of the wind."

The ship pursued its tormented course: "At the impact of each wave, the *sambuk* made a cracking sound as though her timbers were opening, and she heeled so violently, first on one side and then on the other, that there seemed no chance she could right herself again; I expected from one moment to another to see her capsized bottom uppermost." The writer's miseries were far from over: "This mortal extremity lasted all night, a long winter night, and the breaking

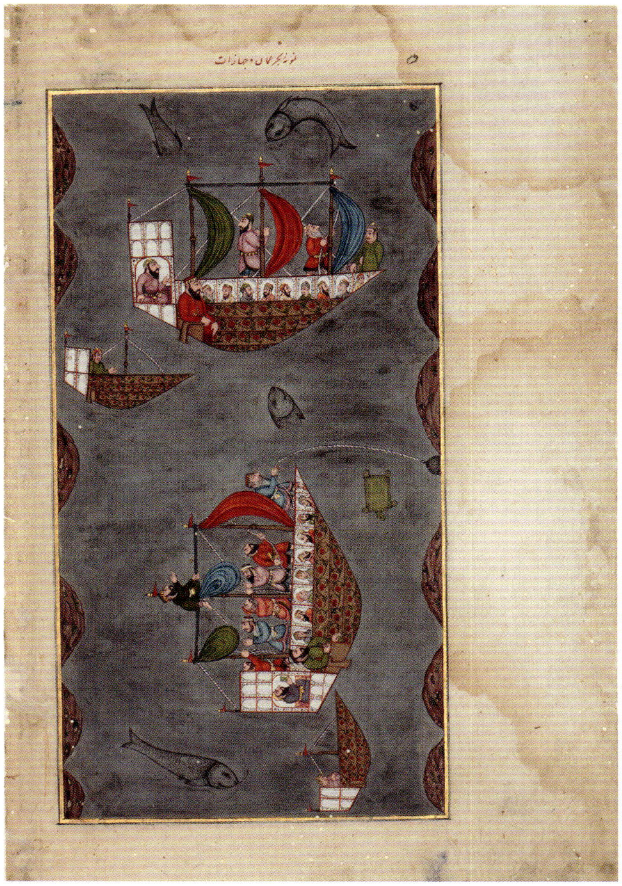

Safi ibn Vali
The Port of Jeddah, c. 1677–80
Folio 22b from the *Anis al-Hujjaj* (The Pilgrim's Companion)
by Safi ibn Vali
India, possibly Gujarat
Ink, watercolor, and gold on paper
33 × 23.2 cm
Nasser D. Khalili Collection of Islamic Art, London

This illustration is a map showing some of the landmarks of Jeddah. Ameen Rihani wrote describing the port of Jeddah, in *Around the Coasts of Arabia* (1930): *"Jeddah is still the main gateway to the Kaaba—the same ancient Jeddah that was cursed by the pilgrims of Granada for its harbor, which for two miles is a tangle of reefs and shoals; for its water, which, when found, is more precious than ottar of roses; for its trade—people who were more mercenary in those days than the infidels of Aragon and Castille; for its* motawwifin *(guides) who were as rapacious as the Berbers of Africa, and for the Beduin bands, waiting outside the Mecca-gate. Exciting times they had, those pilgrims of old."*

Safi ibn Vali
Crossing the Sea, c. 1677–80
Folio 3b from the *Anis al-Hujjaj* (The Pilgrim's Companion)
by Safi ibn Vali
India, possibly Gujarat
Ink, watercolor, and gold on paper
33 × 23.2 cm
Nasser D. Khalili Collection of Islamic Art, London

Some pilgrims traveled by boat crossing the Red Sea, the Mediterranean, the Arabian Sea, or the Indian Ocean. They faced many dangers such as the frequent ocean storms that would overtake the pilgrims and the vessels, as well as attacks by pirates.

of the day, far from putting an end to it, did no more than extend it, for the weather was even worse and the storm lasted till nightfall. Only then did we enjoy a brief respite."

The account by the pilgrim Ali Bey El Abbassi, a Spanish officer known by the name of Domingo Badia y Leblich, and dubiously claiming to be an Abbassid prince, bears a strong resemblance to that of Didier: "The navigation of the Red Sea is dreadful. We sailed almost continually between banks and rocks, above and under water; so that we were obliged to have a guard of four or five men upon the prow, who examined the course attentively, and who cried to the steersman to steer to the right or left. But should they commit an error, or discover the shoal too late, or too near the ship; or should the steersman, who cannot see them, not keep far enough off; or, in keeping too far, strike the ship upon a neighbouring bank, which had not been observed, and should he misunderstand the cry, as sometimes happens; or should the wind or current prevent him from changing his direction, during the interval which takes place between the discovery of the rock and the arrival of the vessel at the place of danger; the ship would be dashed to pieces, and all would be lost. What chances to run between life and death, at every instant, in this hazardous navigation!" Ali Bey concluded: "It is on these accounts that there are so many shipwrecks every year in this sea."

Ali Bey himself was a victim of one, as he recounted in describing his pilgrimage, carried out in 1805: "Terrible day! About midnight a furious storm arose. The wind increased in such a manner that at two in the morning it blew with double force, so that in a few minutes the cables of four anchors were broken. The vessel, being left to itself, and the mercy of the wind and waves, was driven upon a rock, upon which it struck with dreadful violence." Panic broke out on board, leading Ali Bey to leap into a lifeboat to escape and ultimately save his life.

While not all travelers experienced such storms, they all grasped the dangers of Red Sea navigation. According to the young Englishman Joseph Pitts, who fell into slavery and undertook the pilgrimage with his North African master around 1685: "There is no safe sailing in this sea by night, because of the multitude of rocks (tho' I don't observe that the maps describe those rocks) which are so thick that we were always in sight of some or other of them, and sometimes in the midst of a great many of them, and sometimes so near as to be able to throw a stone to them. Some of the rocks are much bigger than others, some look like islands, others just appear above water, and some are to be seen a little under water." The extent of these dangers was well summarized by the German geographer Carsten Niebuhr, member and sole survivor of the scientific expedition commissioned by King Frederick V of Denmark, which reached Jeddah in 1762: "No other journey in the world is riddled with as many dangers."

Concerning the aforementioned travelers, it should be noted that they undertook the ordinary journey, from Suez to Jeddah, via coastal navigation—hugging the coast over some thirty days, dropping anchor every night. But over an extended period stretching from the mid-tenth century to the mid-thirteenth century—initially due to political troubles and subsequently due to the Crusades, in particular the seizure of Aqaba by the Franks in 1115—both caravan travel overland from Egypt and navigation in the northern Red Sea were impossible.

Consequently, and for nearly three centuries, both the transit of pilgrims from Egypt and North Africa and that of merchandise had to be rerouted, toward the Egyptian port of Aydhab, located nearly across from Jeddah, on the opposite coast of the Red Sea. This route forced pilgrims to travel up the Nile from Cairo to the city of Qus, or even beyond to Aswan, from where they subsequently crossed the eastern Egyptian desert, and going via Wadi Allaqi, reached the port of Aydhab, located on today's Egyptian-Sudanese border.

This journey was much longer, and also unsafe due to the fact that this part of the Egyptian desert was infested with aggressive tribes and furthermore forced pilgrims to face the open sea during their crossing to Jeddah. Various celebrated travelers had to take this route, starting with the geographer and chronicler Ibn Hawqal, who, around the mid-tenth century, found only a handful of rows of huts in Aydhab, as he recounted in *The Face of the Earth*. A century later, the poet and scholar Naser Khosrow, hailing from Balkh, in Khorasan, described the locality as "a small town". All of this soon changed, according to the Andalusian writer Ibn Jubayr in 1183, for whom Aydhab was then nothing less than "one of the most frequented ports of the world." Indeed, alongside the pilgrims, Egyptian cereals bound for Hijaz went through Aydhab, and in the Fatimid and Ayyubid eras, the city became the Egyptian entryway for all spices, where ships sailing from Yemen and India landed.

Van de Z. W. Zyde
Vue de la ville de Jambo du côté du S.O. (View of the city of Yanbu from the southwest)
Vue de la ville de Dsjidda du côté de l'O. (View of the city of Jeddah from the west)
From *Description de l'Arabie d'après les observations et recherches faites dans le pays même*
Carsten Niebuhr
Paris, 1779
Engraving
25 × 34 cm
Nasser D. Khalili Collection of Islamic Art, London

Yanbu shares with Jeddah the title of "Gate of the Holy City," wrote Richard Burton in *Personal Narrative of a Pilgrimage to Al-Madinah and Meccah* (1855). Yanbu is also spelled Yanbu'a, Iambia, or Jambo and is the port of Medina, while Jeddah is the port of Mecca.

Jules Gervais-Courtellemont
Commerçants indiens de Djedda (Indian merchants of Jeddah), 1869
From *Mon Voyage à La Mecque* (My Trip to Mecca)
Paris, Librairie Hachette, 1897
Engraved after a photograph by the author
Bibliothèque nationale de France, Paris

The distance from Suez to Jeddah is 634 nautical miles (1,174 kilometers). Jules Gervais-Courtellemont reached Jeddah three days after departing from Suez. In *Mon Voyage à La Mecque*, he wrote that due to the coral reef, boatmen used small landing boats to transfer the passengers to the docks. The captain of his ship cast anchor several kilometers away from the land to avoid the coral reefs that run parallel to the shore and which were a perpetual threat to the ships. The Arab pilots of the Red Sea are known to be very capable, wrote Gervais-Courtellemont, but "God's intentions are inscrutable" said the boatmen who led the passengers to land.

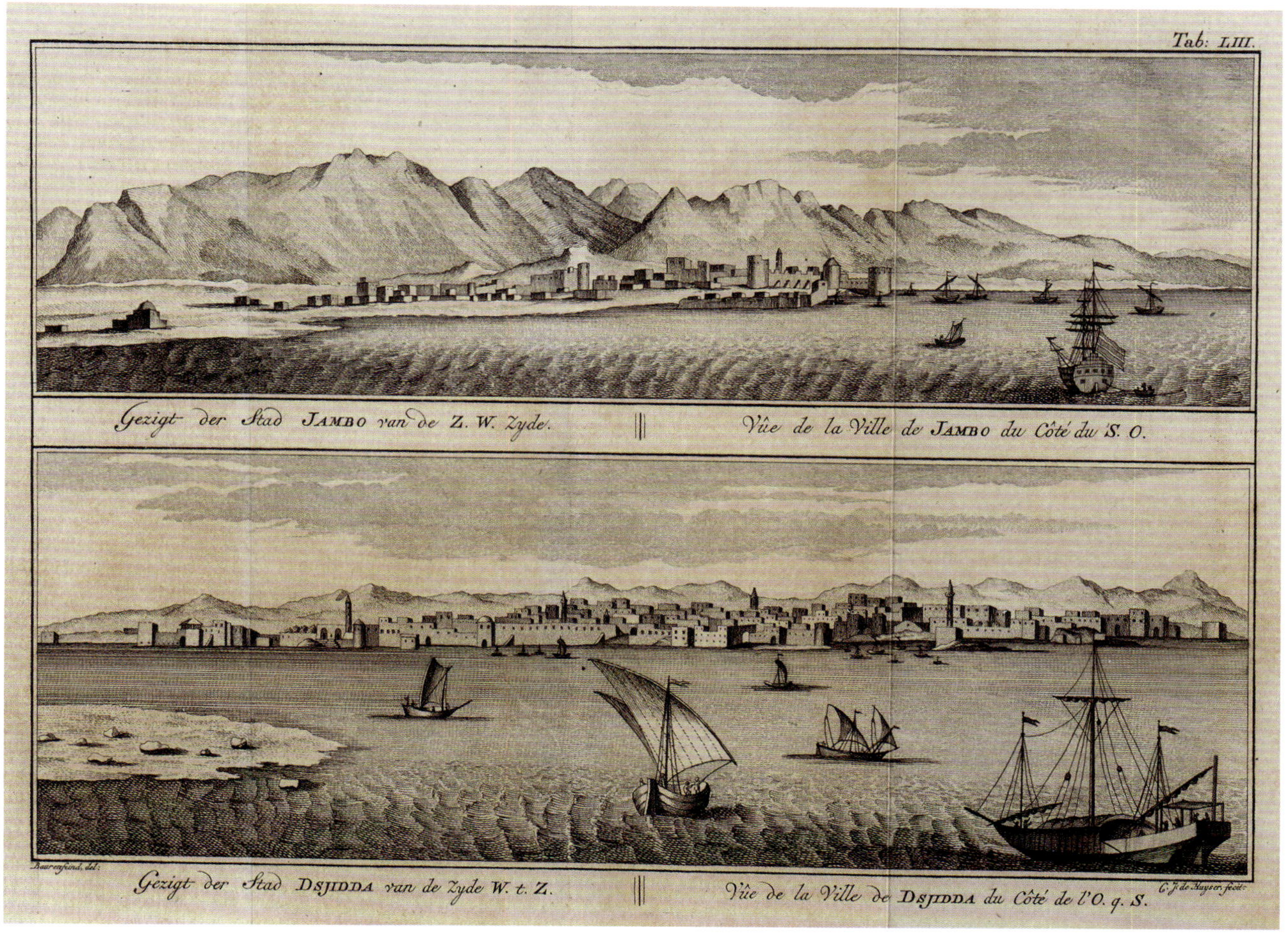

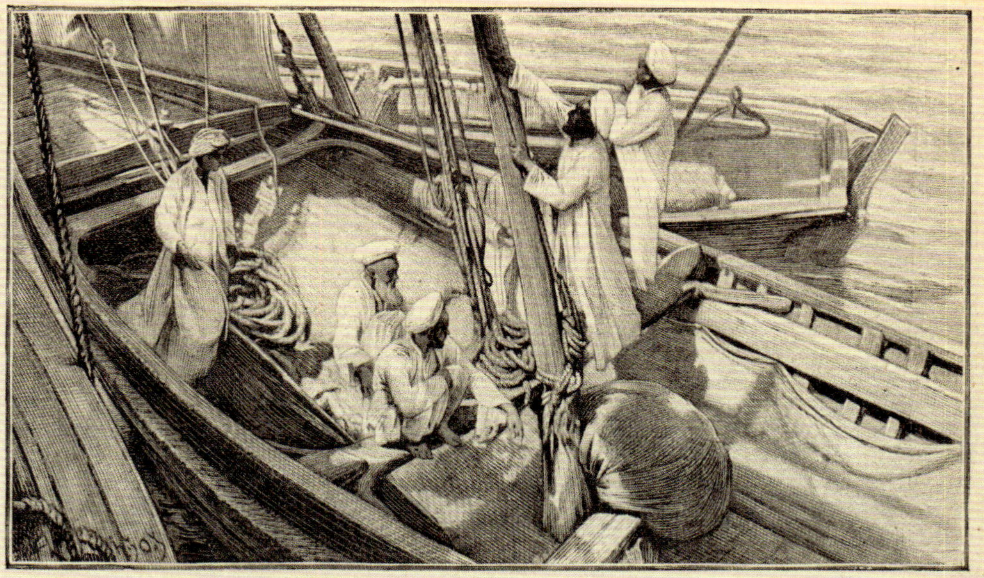

COMMERÇANTS INDIENS DE DJEDDA.

And yet, according to Ibn Jubayr, "The people of Aydhab use the pilgrims most wrongly. They load the *jilab* with them until they sit one on top of the other so that they are like chickens crammed in a coop. To this they are prompted by avarice, wanting the hire. The owner of the craft will exact its full cost from the pilgrims for a single journey, caring not what the sea may do with it after that." He added, with uncharacteristic vehemence in this regard: "This is the country of Islam most deserving a *hisbha*, and the scourge employed should be the sword." While waiting for such retribution to rain down, "a sojourn in that accursed town is the greatest snare on the road of the pilgrims to the Ancient House (the Kaaba)," he wrote, incensed, enumerating all of the vile acts and abominations of which the people of Aydhab were guilty, and declaring, "the best for him who can is not to see it."

But he still had to cross the Red Sea and reach Jeddah. His boat naturally endured a violent storm: "We passed that night in a storm which drove us to despair, seeing one of the famous storms of the Pharaonic Sea."

Ayyubid's and Mameluke's victories over the Crusaders allowed the overland caravan to be organized once again, thriving as it never had before, in particular, thanks to the introduction of the *mahmal*, a ceremonial palanquin established by the Mameluke Sultan Baybars in 1266 and intended to lead the pilgrimage. Later on, in 1422, it fell to another Mameluke sovereign, Barsbay, who fulfilled Ibn Jubayr's wish by destroying the city of Aydhab to punish its inhabitants for their wrongdoings.

Just as the traditional Egyptian caravan route was reopened, navigation in the northern Red Sea also become possible once again, and the *sambuks* could once again carry pilgrims every year between Suez and Yanbu—the port of Medina—and Jeddah, by the thousands and even tens of thousands.

Ludovico di Varthema—the first European, with the exception of the Andalusians, of course—to provide an account of his journey in Arabia, undertaken in 1503, was struck by the intensity of the trafficking of merchandise in Jeddah: "From India there comes a great many jewels and all sorts of spices, and part comes from Ethiopia," the great traveler from Bologna noted. He continued: "So that in this city there is carried on a very extensive traffic of merchandize, that is, of jewels, spices of every kind in abundance, cotton in large quantities, wax, and odoriferous substances in the greatest abundance." Some two-and-a-half centuries later, Niebuhr was struck both by the scope of the trading and the pusillanimity of Turkish sailors, who refused to face the open sea and came from Suez to Jeddah "to load coffee brought by the Arabs of Yemen, the cloth, spices, and incense transported there by the Indians and the English, hailing from Surat, Madras, and Bengal."

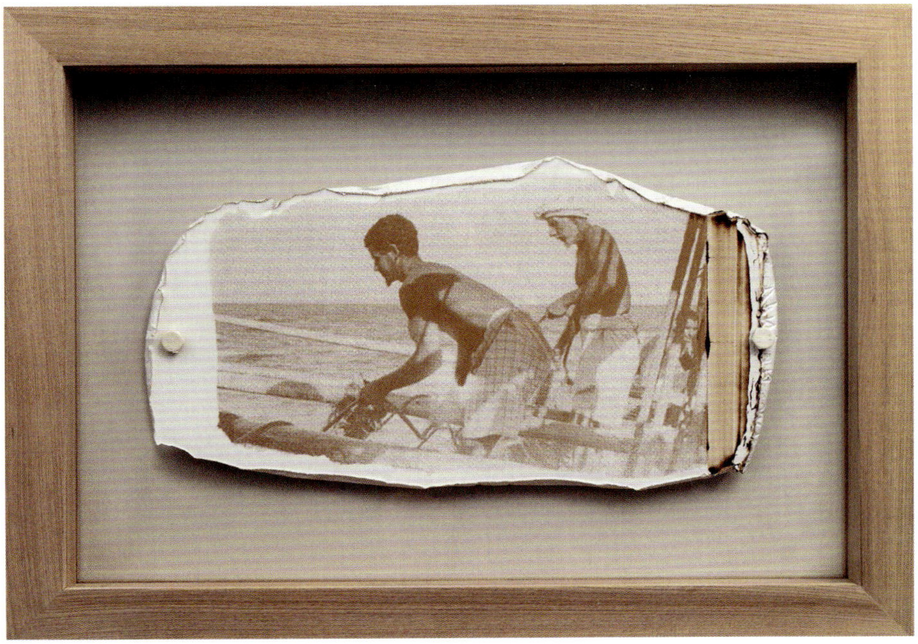

Piers Secunda
Pearl Divers, 1938
2017 Dammam No. 7
crude oil and varnish
on industrial floor paint,
with cast-paint nuts and bolts
49 × 70 × 6 cm
Courtesy of the artist

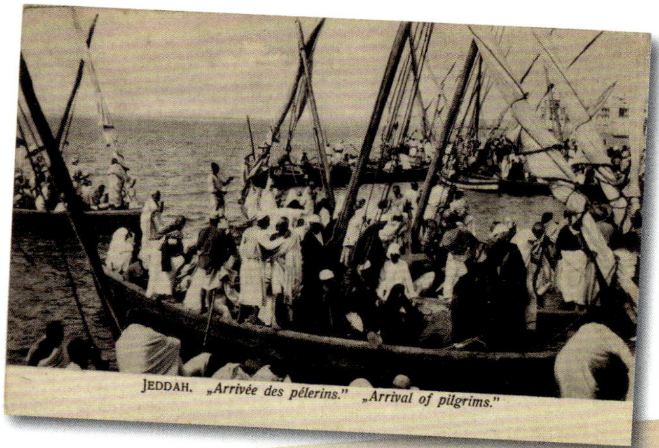

Postcard
Arrival of the pilgrims in Jeddah,
postmark dated 21/12/09
Nasser D. Khalili Collection
of Islamic Art, London

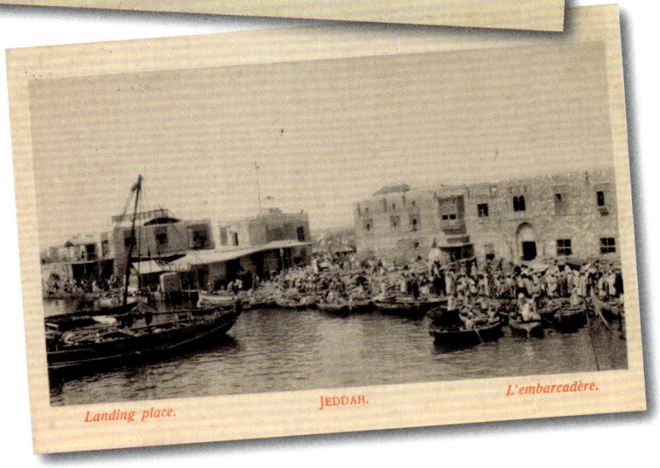

Postcard
The Landing place in Jeddah
Nasser D. Khalili Collection
of Islamic Art, London

Pilgrims arriving in Jeddah would disembark at the Quarantine pier.

For Ali Bey El Abassi, in the early nineteenth century, Jeddah was the center "which may be considered as the mart of the interior commerce of the Red Sea." He specified: "There are, it is said, about a hundred coasting vessels that trade from Jeddah to Suez, and the same number which go to and from Mokha"; adding, "A year never passes without several being lost upon the rocks in the Red Sea." Hardly ten years later, the great Swiss explorer Johann Ludwig Burckhardt, discoverer of Petra, made a somewhat similar calculation: "The number of ships belonging to Jeddah is very great. Taking into account all the small vessels employed in the Red Sea trade, two hundred and fifty perhaps may be calculated as belonging either to merchants of the town or to owners who navigate them."

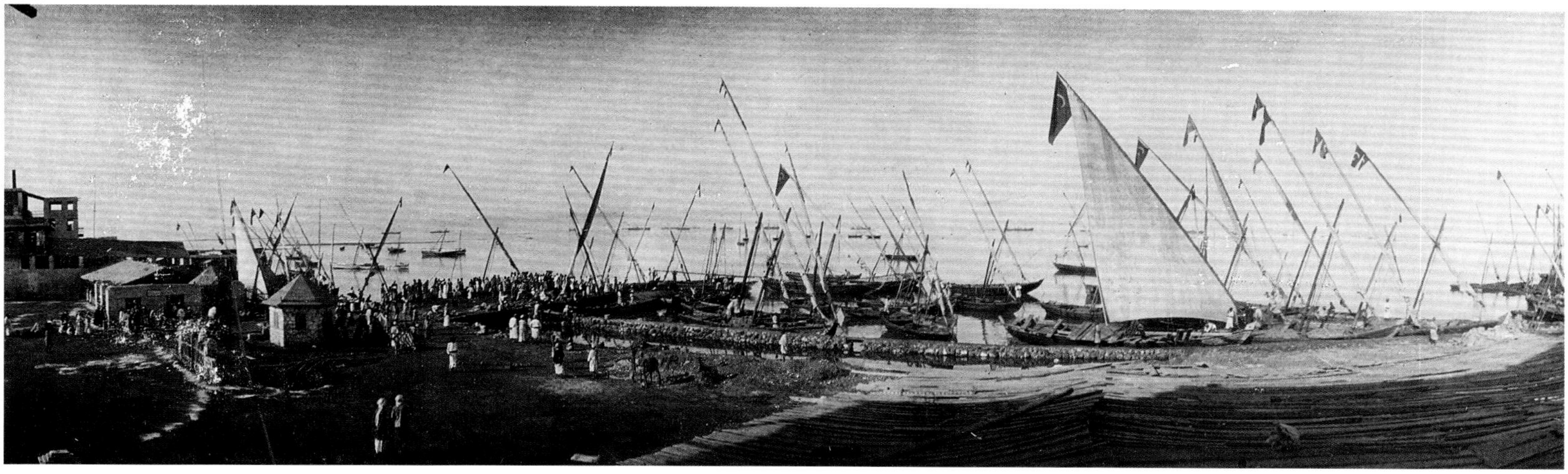

Khedive Abbas Hilmi II
Jelbas in the harbor of Jedda, 1909
Courtesy Mohamed Ali Foundation and Durham University Library, Dublin

The *jelbas* (also spelled *jalbut*) are small passenger-carrying crafts measuring 7 to 10 meters long. It is believed that the name "jalbut" is derived from the Royal Navy's "jolly boat," a boat used to ferry people between shore and a large ship. Jelbas were employed to shuttle pilgrims between the Red Sea ports of Suez, Tor, Kosseir, Suwakin, Moka, Yanbu, and Jeddah.

Burckhardt also noted, "The ships are navigated chiefly by people from Yemen, from the Somali coast, opposite to Aden, and by slaves, of which the latter three or four are generally found in every ship." For the desire of materials, "No vessels of any kind are now constructed at Jeddah, so scarce has timber become," he explained, adding, "Suez, Hodeida, and Mokha, are the only harbours in the Red Sea where ships are built."

While Burckhardt's sojourn in Hijaz occurred at the same time that Muhammad Ali's campaign in Arabia was in full swing, the Swiss explorer nevertheless observed some "forty or fifty ships" daily in the port of Jeddah, attesting to substantial commercial activity, which appeared not to have been impacted either way by this upheaval. "Being obliged to anchor in the roadstead," as Burckhardt explained, "small boats came to unload the cargo carried by large ships." A high-ranking Egyptian government official, Saleh Soubhy, made similar observations. Having twice accompanied the pilgrimage, in 1888 and 1891, as part of a mission to improve pilgrims' sanitary conditions, he recounted, "All of the ships are obliged to anchor at a distance in the sea: Passengers and merchandise come ashore on small sailboats. Known as *sambuks* in the region, these boats are skilfully steered by the natives, zigzagging extensively to reach the port. It is impossible to take a straight path, as this harbour, which would be so beautiful at the cost of a few sacrifices, is strewn with coral reefs and sand bars, seaweed, and stony islets."

Travelers could thus delight in the daytime at the view of dozens and hundreds of sails shimmering on the horizon, and many did, appreciating the constant back-and-forth and intricate arabesques of the *sambuks* and *dhows* on the waves. As noted by French Orientalist painter Étienne Dinet during his 1921 pilgrimage, "The *sambuks* with sails alone are able to handle this labyrinth of sharp reefs." When night fell, the songs and music of sailors and boatmen rang out from the decks of the finally-still *sambuks*, and could be heard in the heart of the city.

Alongside the *sambuk* ballet in the port of Jeddah, another show was presented by the city itself. Hence, Maurice Tamisier, a young French Saint-Simonian enlisted in one of the armies and sent to Arabia by the Egyptian Wali Muhammad Ali, observed in 1833, upon reaching Jeddah on a boat used to transport pilgrims, that "the pilgrims' eyes are bathed in tears." They most certainly experienced great emotion upon arriving in these places that would see them commence their pilgrimage rituals, following weeks of grueling navigation; but it is most likely that this emotion could very well be heightened upon glimpsing the extraordinary city of Jeddah. The lines of a true

HENRY DE MONFREID

Henry de Monfreid had an insatiable appetite for adventure and claimed that all he longed for was "the sea, the wind, the virgin sand of the desert, the infinity of far-off skies in which wheel the numberless hosts of the skies... and the dream that I became one with them."

Henry de Monfreid was also a prolific writer, painter, and photographer who became recognized for his journeys on the Red Sea and the Horn of Africa. He once ventured across the Suez Canal, reaching the southernmost tip of the Arabian Peninsula on his sailboat. De Monfreid aspired to explore Africa and he engaged in his business dealings to fund his travels. He would turn to a life of crime, however, due to the lucrative prospects of being a gunrunner and a smuggler. His unconventional lifestyle led to multiple near-encounters with Royal Navy coast-guards, whom he managed to evade multiple times.

In 1911, de Monfreid traveled aboard "L'Oxus" to the French colony of Djibouti, where he began to trade in coffee. He took a camera and glass plates. He also used a stereoscopic camera and regularly sent his photo plates to France. He was passionate about photography and would carefully pack the plates in a box to mitigate the risk of them breaking. He captioned many of his photos with a great deal of precision using a signatory purple ink. An example can be seen in the photo of the *dhow* in the Red Sea reproduced on page 19. After spending 18 months in Africa, he wrote to his father that he planned to buy a new camera, a Gaumont with a Zeiss lens. He also wrote to him about his disdain for the colonizers and his preference to socialize with the local population. He learned their language and began incorporating their habits into his life.

In 1912, he bought himself a six-ton *dhow* called the "Sahala". He made adjustments to the boat in order to flexibly navigate the Red Sea. In 1920 he acquired a large *dhow*, named the *Altair* ("the soaring eagle"). De Monfreid gave his travels priority over his family, whom he often abandoned for extended periods of time.

De Monfreid mentioned in his writings that he had Muslim women traveling for the Hajj ride aboard with him. This allowed him to travel from Obock to Jeddah with a boat full of contraband without being stopped by the Aden Royal Navy. Those sailors would not dare search a boat transporting pilgrim women.

Another renowned traveler, Wilfred Thesiger, mentioned in his book *Arabian Sands* that he contemplated buying one of de Monfreid's *dhows* in Djibouti. Thesiger admired de Monfreid's "lawless and free way of life" and was inspired by reading his book *Aventures de Mer et Secrets de la Mer Rouge*.

Prior to World War I, the French were aware of the importance of consolidating knowledge over the far south of the Red Sea. At the time, the southernmost points, which included the Bab el Mandeb Straits, were

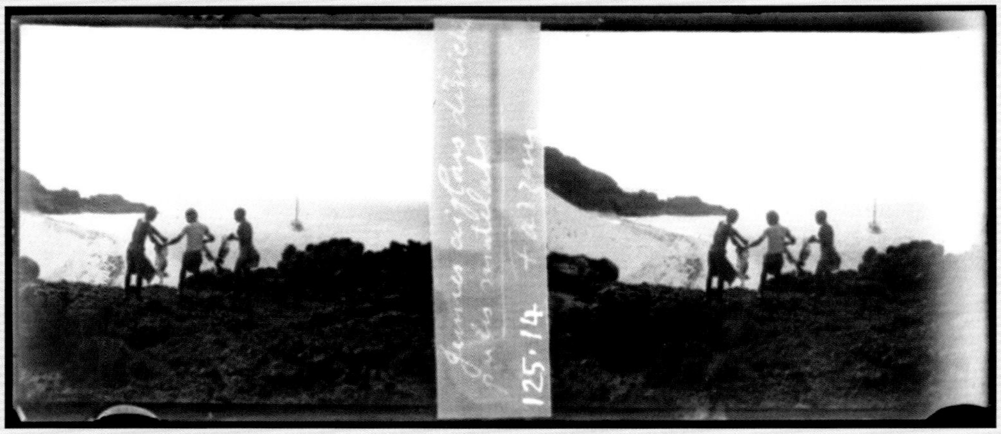

Henry de Monfreid
Baby eagles picked up by the seamen in the Farasan island,
1917
Stereoscopic image
Courtesy Société de Géographie/ Bibliothèque nationale de France
©Adagp, 2018

Henry de Monfreid described in *Trilogie de la mer Rouge* (Trilogy of the Red Sea), the Farasan island as being covered with vegetation sufficient to nourish many herds of goats and wild donkeys. He wrote that an important oil source emerges at low tide in the southern part of the island and that at present this source is only exploited for extracting naphtha that is used to coat boats.

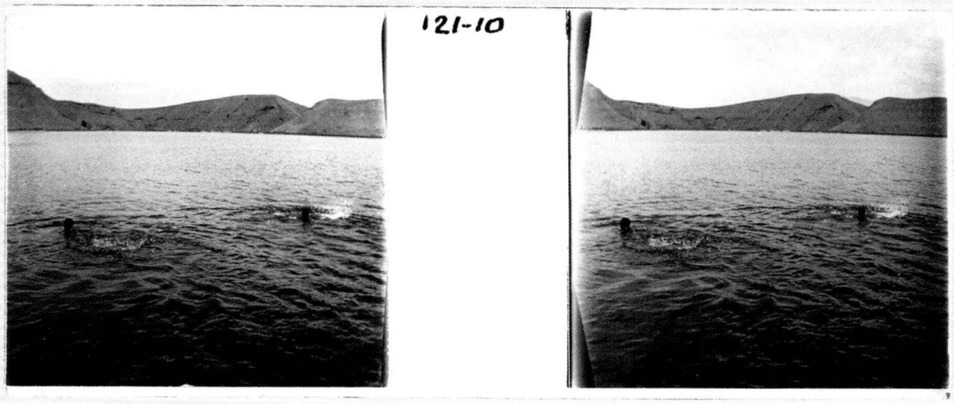

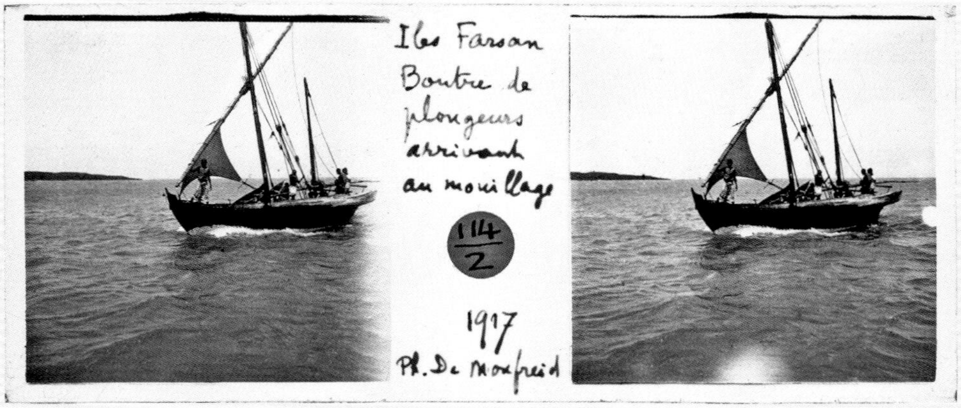

Henry de Monfreid
Diver's dhow arriving at anchor in the Farasan Islands, 1917
Stereoscopic image
Courtesy Société de Géographie/Bibliothèque nationale de France
©Adagp, 2018

Henry de Monfreid traveled from Djibouti to Farasan Island on board his *dhow* the *Fat el-Rahman* and accompanied by two *sambuks*: the *Sahala* and the *Rengileh*. He hired crew and divers and took provisions for six months: rice, dates, butter, doura, sugar, biscuits, etc. Farasan is a mountainous island located in the Red Sea in the south of the Arabian Peninsula. Its water is very transparent to the point, wrote Henry de Monfreid in *Trilogie de la mer Rouge* (Trilogy of the Red Sea), that he would sometimes have the impression that he was hovering over a fantastic forest of multicolored corals. *"Thanks to the calm climate of the archipelago of Farasan, the waters have conserved this beautiful transparency, indispensable to divers*," he wrote.

Henry de Monfreid
Pearl fishing in the Farasan island, June 1914
Stereoscopic image
Courtesy Société de Géographie/Bibliothèque nationale de France
©Adagp, 2018

Henry de Monfreid wrote in *Aventures de mer* (Adventures of the Sea) that in 1910 there was much talk about pearl farming, which he followed with great interest. Tired of trading in leather and passionate about the sea, he decided to find a solitary area in the Red Sea where he could work in peace and live his way. He chose the Farasan Island, which at the time was under Turkish control. He wrote that there on the island, thousands of indigenous people in boats sought pearls and oysters, known as *bilbil*, and each year, about two million pound sterling worth of these items were sold in Aden, Bombay, and Massaoua. Henry de Monfreid used to go hunting for pearl oysters and he also tried to trade in pearls, but unable to compete with the brokers, he abandoned that activity.

controled by the Ottomans. In order to explore that region, the French needed a reliable captain with a boat as the indigenous people were viewed to be untrustworthy. Henry de Monfreid proved to be the perfect candidate for this mission as he had the intrinsic motivation to explore for his personal gains and was equipped to interact with the locals. His connection to the indigenous people would allow him to strategically extract information from them. The journey would be long and arduous, but Henry de Monfreid never shied away from a challenge.

In January 1914, de Monfreid left Djibouti for Cheikh Said, an Ottoman- controled fortress located in the Bab el Mandeb Strait. At the time the Ottomans were allied with the Germans, making this expedition increasingly risky for de Monfreid. In the city of Moka, he was summoned by the Turkish governor, who revealed his knowledge of the photographs and who referred to the Frenchman as both his prisoner and his guest. Henry de Monfreid mentions in his journal that he managed to escape this situation. He also succeeded in keeping the original photos by duping the governor, who requested that he forfeit all photographic evidence, with a box of unused photo plates. This mission enabled de Monfreid to gather information on the sea, the coasts and the conditions of navigation.

In his book *Secrets of the Red Sea*, de Monfreid wrote that, around the year 1914, the pearl oyster banks took him south of the Red Sea to the Farasan and Duhuluk islands. As part of his fishing expeditions, he sailed the Red Sea with his *dhow* and camped on the islands for weeks. This job was both challenging and perilous. Henry paid for the services of two divers who used snorkels to dive dozens of meters deep in search of oysters. He learned of the many strategic benefits of the Farasan Islands, especially their location along the Indian road. Henry de Monfreid knew that the British would take interest in this island so he was quick to plant a French flag, despite the French government's protest against it.

In 1931, de Monfreid met the renowned French writer Joseph Kessel, who was reporting on the slave trade in the Red Sea. Kessel read his journals and encouraged him to publish them. Monfreid followed his friend's advice and his books went on to become bestsellers.

At the conclusion of the war, he returned to France, where he retired in a small village. He spent the remainder of his days playing piano, writing, painting, and tending to a garden, which he transformed into an opium poppy plantation. He produced about seventy books in a span of thirty years.

In 1974, de Monfreid passed away at the age of 95, a few days after stating, "I have lived a rich, restless, magnificent life."

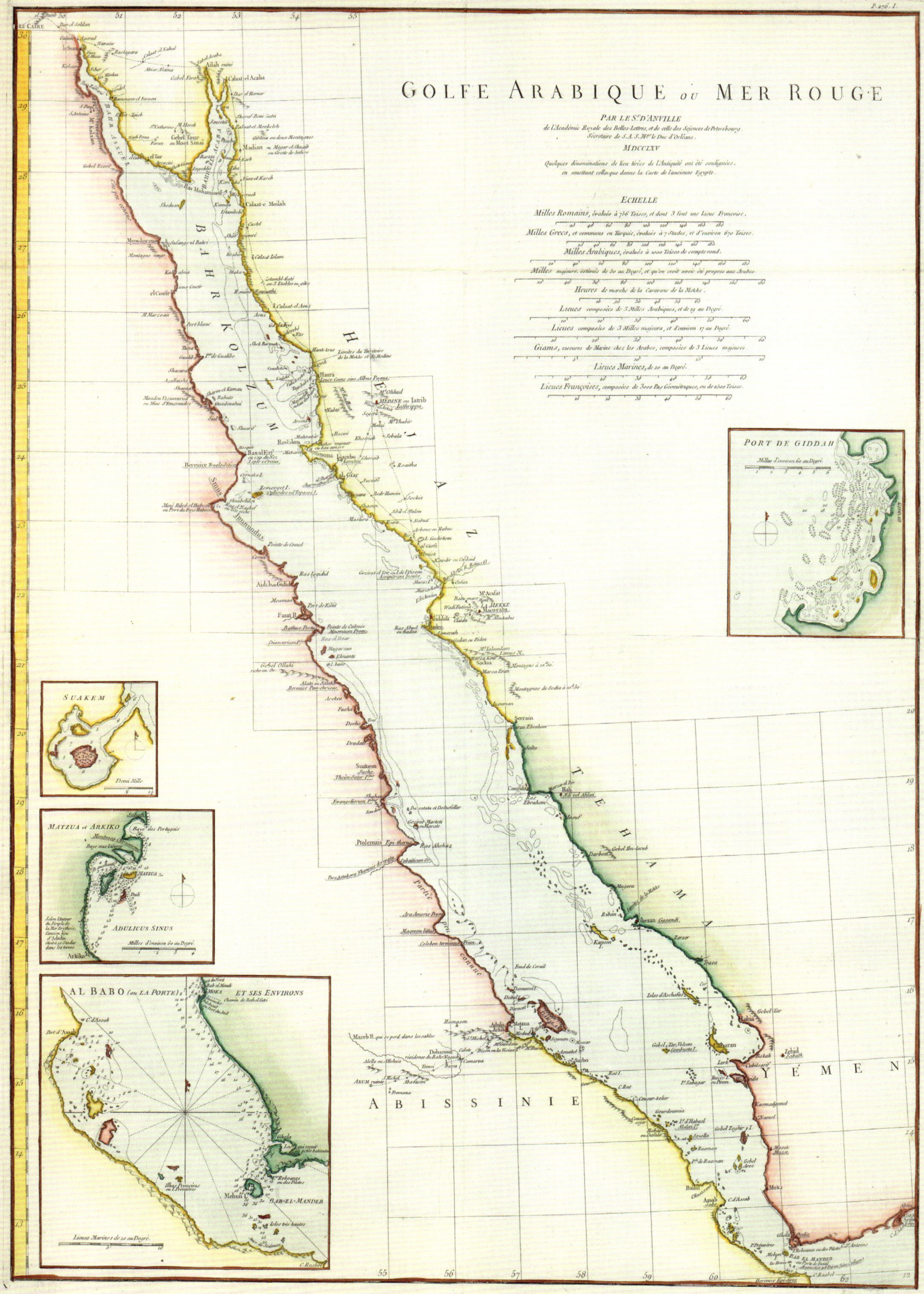

P. 276. I.
GOLFE ARABIQUE ou MER ROUGE
PAR LE S.r D'ANVILLE
de l'Académie Royale des Belles-Lettres, et de celle des Sciences de Petersbourg.
Sécretaire de S. A. S. M.gr le Duc d'Orléans.
MDCCLXV
Quelques dénominations de lieu tirées de l'Antiquité ont été soulignées, en omettant celles que donne la Carte de l'ancienne Egypte.
ECHELLE
Milles Romains, évalués à 756 Toises, et dont 3 font une Lieue Françoise.
Milles Grecs, et communs en Turquie, évalués à 7 Stades, et d'environ 670 Toises.
Milles Arabiques, évalués à 1000 Toises de compte rond.
Milles majeurs, estimés de 50 au Degré, et qu'on croit avoir été propres aux Arabes.
Heures de marche de la Caravane de la Mekke.
Lieues composées de 3 Milles Arabiques, et de 19 au Degré.
Lieues composées de 3 Milles majeurs, et d'environ 17 au Degré.
Giams, mesures de Marine chez les Arabes, composées de 3 Lieues majeures.
Lieues Marines, de 20 au Degré.
Lieues Françoises, composées de 3000 Pas Géométriques, ou de 2500 Toises.
PORT DE GIDDAH
SUAKEM
MATZUA et ARKIKO
ADULICUS SINUS
AL BABO (ou LA PORTE) ET SES ENVIRONS
BAB-EL-MANDER
BAHR KOLZUM
HEDJAZ
TEHAMA
YEMEN
ABISSINIE
MEDINE ou Iatrib
MEKKE
Suakem
Matzua
Moka

Jean Baptiste Bourguignon d'Anville
Golfe Arabique ou mer Rouge
(Arabian Gulf or Red Sea), 1765
From d'Anville's *Atlas*
Copperplate engraved with hand coloring
67 × 48.5 cm
Nasser D. Khalili Collection of Islamic Art, London

Varthema wrote in *The Itinerary of Lodovico di Varthema of Bologna from 1502 to 1508* regarding the Red Sea that *"this sea is not red, but the water is like that of any other sea. In this sea we sailed one day until the setting of the sun, because it is not possible to navigate it during the night-time. And every day they proceeded in this manner until they arrived at an island called Chamaram (Kamaran). After this island you can proceed in safety. The reason why it is not possible to sail during night is that there are many islands and many rocks, and it is necessary that a man should always be stationed on the top of the mast of the ship in order to see the route, which cannot be done during the night-time, and therefore they can only navigate during the day."*

Malin Basil
From the Arabian Gulf, 1980
Acrylic on canvas
60 × 90 cm
Mrs. Lubna Al-Olayan Collection, Riyadh

Watchtowers were built as observation and protection posts in strategic locations in Arabia. They were built with circular bases and could accommodate only a small number of men.

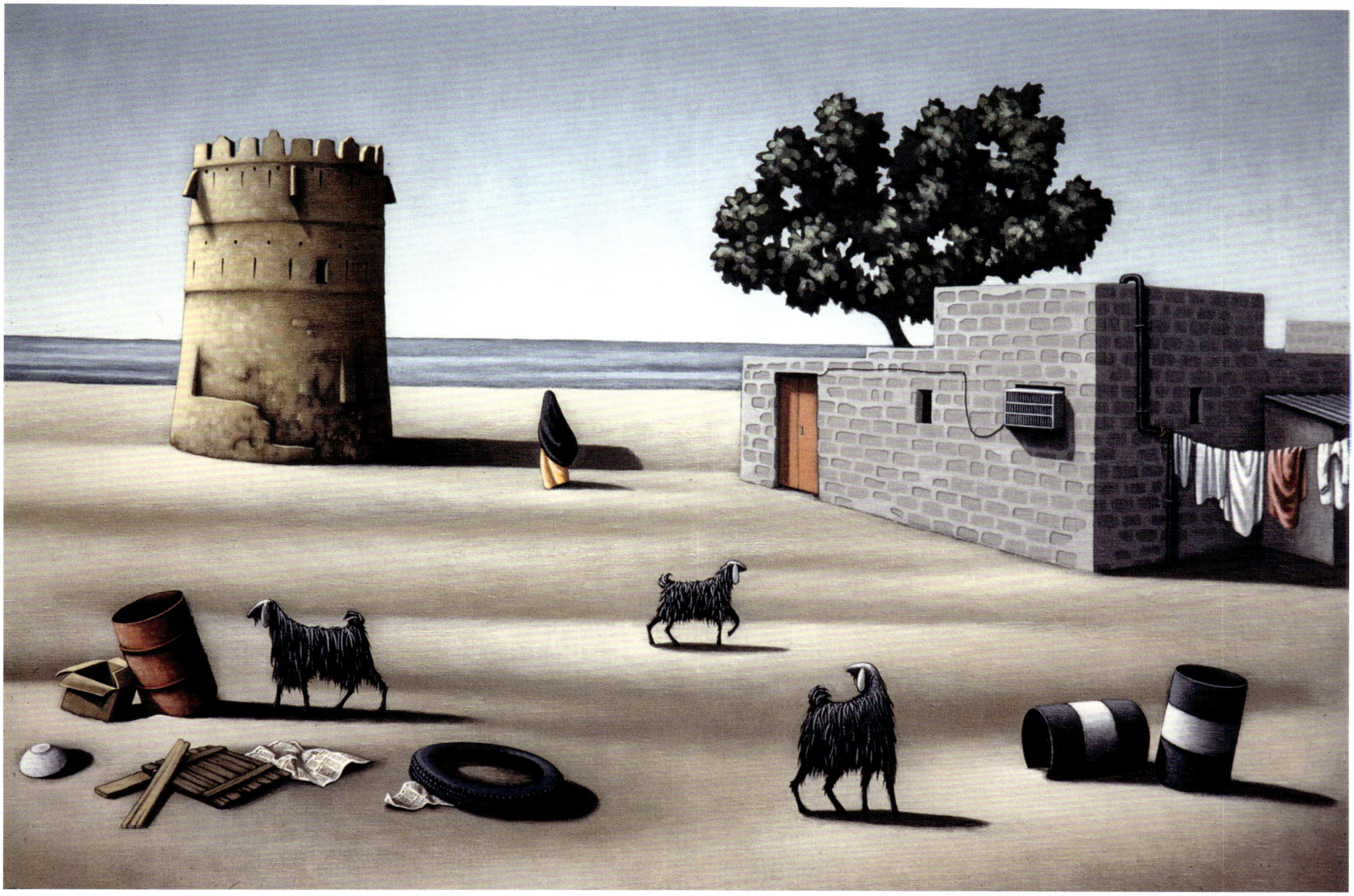

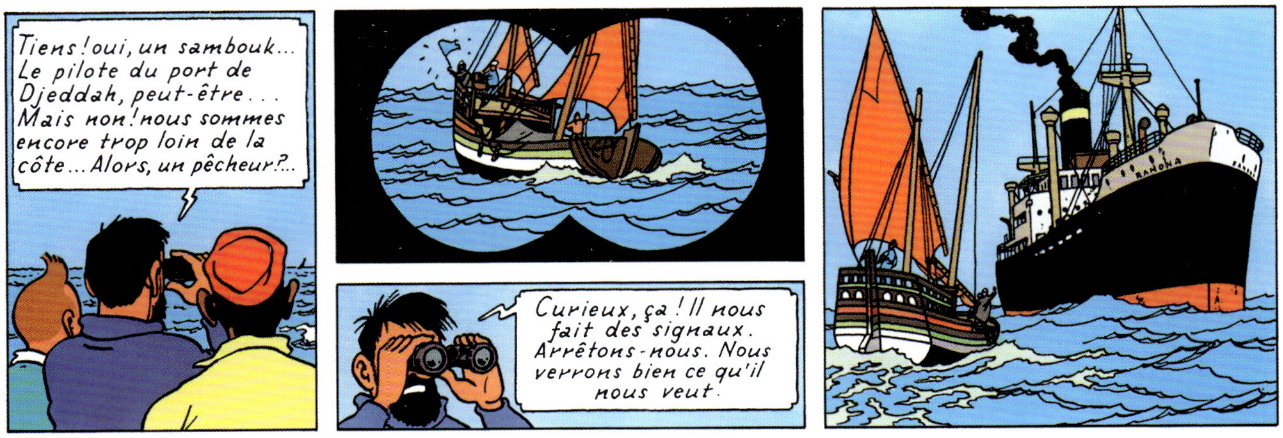

Hergé
Coke en stock (The Red Sea Sharks), 1958
From the series *The Adventures of Tintin*
Published by Casterman
Courtesy Hergé/Moulinsart 2018

"Hey! Yeah, a sambuk... the pilot from the port of Jeddah, perhaps... but no! We are still too far from the coast... a fisherman then? exclaims Captain Haddock Weird!! He's sending us signals. Let's stop. We'll find out what he wants".

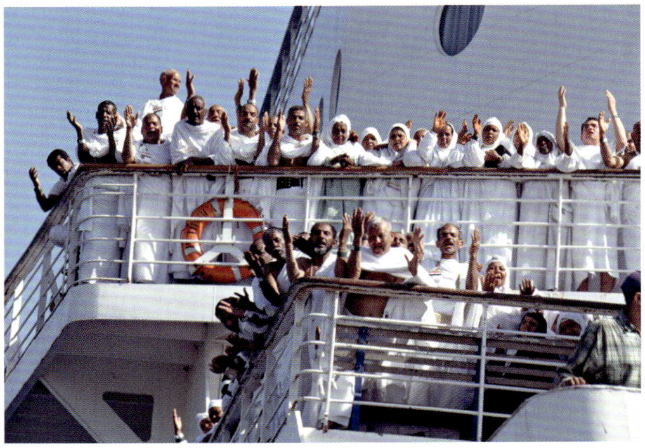

Kazuyoshi Nomachi
Pilgrim's ship in Jeddah

The introduction of steam navigation during the 1830s and especially its development after the opening of the Suez Canal in 1869 changed the nature of the pilgrimage drastically and revolutionized its economy. Not only did it contract the time of the journey but the number of pilgrims increased substantially thanks to larger vessels. After reaching Jeddah, the pilgrims had to travel another 90 kilometers by road before reaching Mecca.

author allow for appreciation of this discovery: "The built city of Jeddah is stunning in appearance," wrote the great journalist Albert Londres, in his 1931 novel *Pêcheurs de Perles* (Pearl Fishermen). He continued: "Fantastic palaces are all the nobler in their dilapidation. The simplest house looks like a castle built by lace-makers. Imposing in their structure and five stories, their facades carry the graces of countless loggias small and large, balconies and wooden canopies, enchantingly sculpted. You feel that you are strolling in the most impressive illustration of the *One Thousand and One Nights*."

This city, which can be seen "rising graciously, all white, between the greyness of the distant mountains and the blueness of the tides beneath a sky radiant with light," in the words of Saleh Soubhy—this "unexpected city," in the words of Albert Londres—thus faced the *sambuks* dancing over the waves. Between the two, such as a theater curtain before a stage that might very well lie on either side, was a fortification that rose and fell from one era to the next. Among the first travelers to have provided accounts of their passage through Jeddah were Palestinian geographer Al-Maqdisi, in the late tenth century, and Naser Khosrow, in the mid-eleventh century, who found in front of them a city "surrounded by a strong wall," in the words of the latter. In contrast, Ludovico di Varthema wrote in 1503, with apparent surprise, that "this city is not surrounded by walls".

Just a few years later, the traveler from Bologna seems to have found Jeddah encircled by an imposing wall with six towers. Its erection was ordered by Mameluke Sultan Qansuh Al Ghuri in 1511 and it was said that all residents participated in the construction, which was completed in six months, due to the dangers posed to the city by Portuguese squadrons who had recently appeared in the Red Sea. The fortification dissuaded the Portuguese from attacking, but once the danger had been removed and some time passed, it was apparent that the fortification was poorly maintained. After his 1762 visit to the city, Carsten Niebuhr wrote: "Jeddah is surrounded by walls which are still standing, but are now so ruinous that a person may, in many places, enter over them on horseback."

Nevertheless, other troubles—which brought Muhammad Ali's armies to Hijaz—soon resulted in the reconstruction of the wall, as observed by Ali Bey El Abbassi in 1805: "The town is surrounded with a good wall, which has irregular towers." This was confirmed in 1814 by Johann Ludwig Burckhardt, who implied that the towers had increased considerably in number: "At every interval of forty or fifty paces, the wall is strengthened by watchtowers." But the situation quickly deteriorated, because in 1833, Maurice Tamisier observed: "In the east, the city wall is protected

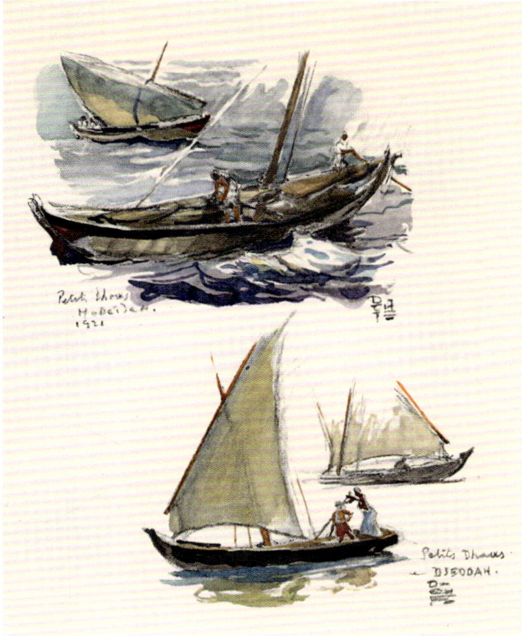

Charles Dominique Fouqueray
Dhows at El Wadi, 1921
Lithograph
12 × 21 cm
From *Escales d'Asie*, Claude Farrère
Laborey, Paris, 1947
Courtesy Musée national de la Marine/A. Fux

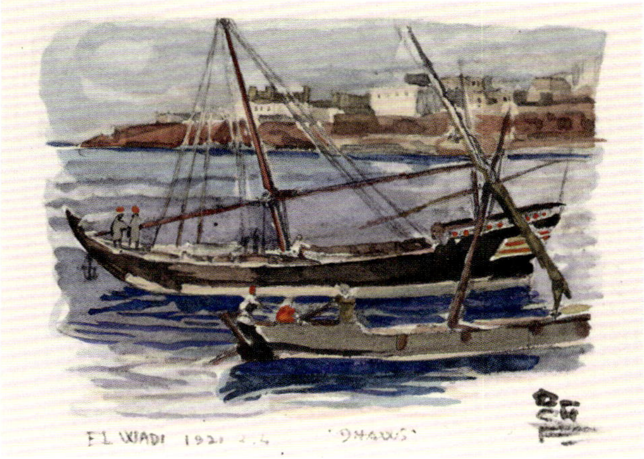

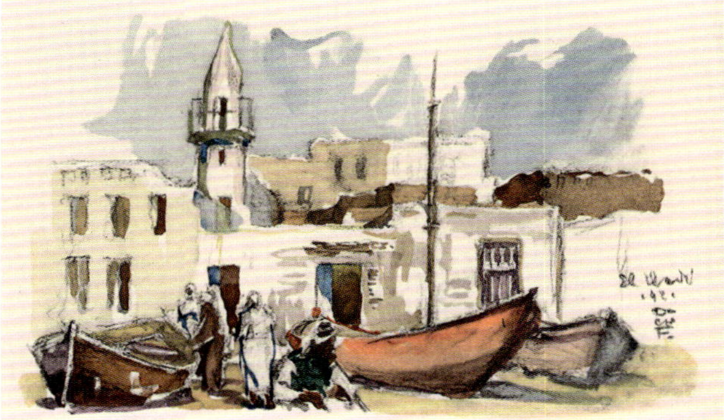

Charles Dominique Fouqueray
Small dhows in Jeddah, 1921
Lithograph
11 × 21 cm
From *Escales d'Asie*, Claude Farrère
Laborey, Paris, 1947
Courtesy Musée national de la Marine/A. Fux

Dhow is the English spelling of the Indian word or more precisely of the word in the Swahili dialect designating "small and medium boats". Today, the word *dhow* is rarely remembered or used by Arabs. Arabs, Wilfred Thesiger wrote in 1959, were once a great sea-going race, sailing their *dhows* around the coast of India to East India and perhaps farther. *Dhows* were the last trading vessels in the world that made long voyages entirely by sail.

Charles Dominique Fouqueray
El Wadi, 1921
Lithograph
12.5 × 21 cm
From *Escales d'Asie*, Claude Farrère
Laborey, Paris, 1947
Courtesy Musée national de la Marine/A. Fux

Claude Farrère in *Escales d'Asie* wrote that as good sailors, the crews of the *dhows* beautify their boats by applying a coat of coconut oil on the waterline. The repeated application of the oil endues it with a rich reddish-brown color that is apparent in Fouqueray's *dhow* paintings.

Charles Dominique Fouqueray
Dhows at Yanbu al Bahr, 1921
Lithograph
13 × 25 cm
From *Escales d'Asie*, Claude Farrère
Laborey, Paris, 1947
Courtesy Musée national de la Marine/A. Fux

Yanbu al Bahr, meaning Yanbu of the Sea, was described in *Sailing Directions for the Red Sea* by Robert Moresby and T. Elwon in 1841 as being *"situated on a low sandy shore, on the northern side of a capacious inlet of the sea. Its high houses and mosque can be seen 13 miles distant, and the approach to it is not dangerous."*

Charles Dominique Fouqueray
Dhows at Yanbu al Bahr, 1921
Lithograph
12 × 20 cm
From *Escales d'Asie*, Claude Farrère
Laborey, Paris, 1947
Courtesy Musée national de la Marine/A. Fux

Escales d'Asie describes a sailing voyage around the coast of Arabia. Starting in Suez, Claude Farrère traveled down the Red Sea to Aden, then to Muscat and up towards the Arabian Gulf to Basra. Claude Farrère wrote that *dhows* have one mast or two, rarely three.

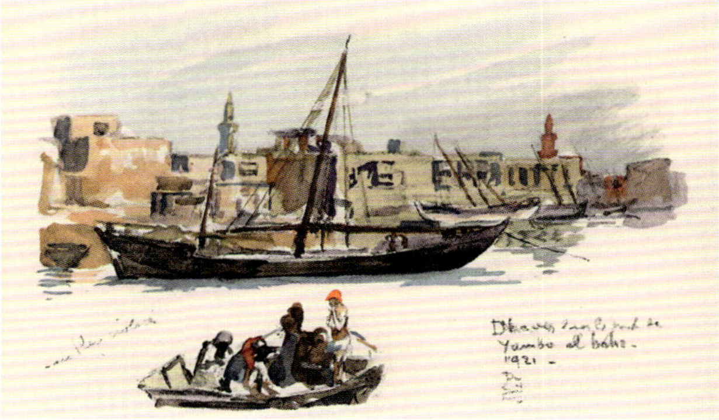

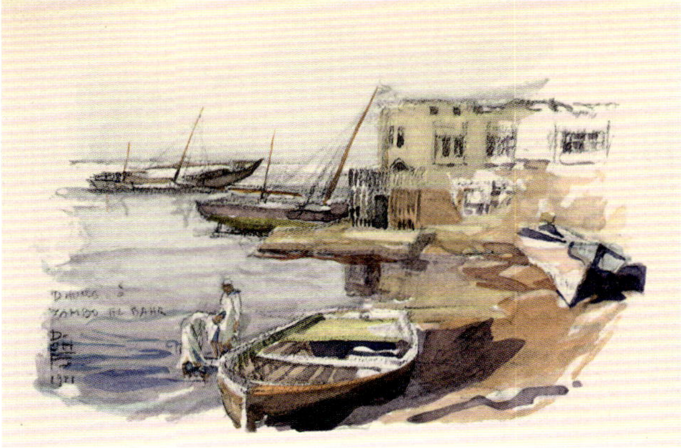

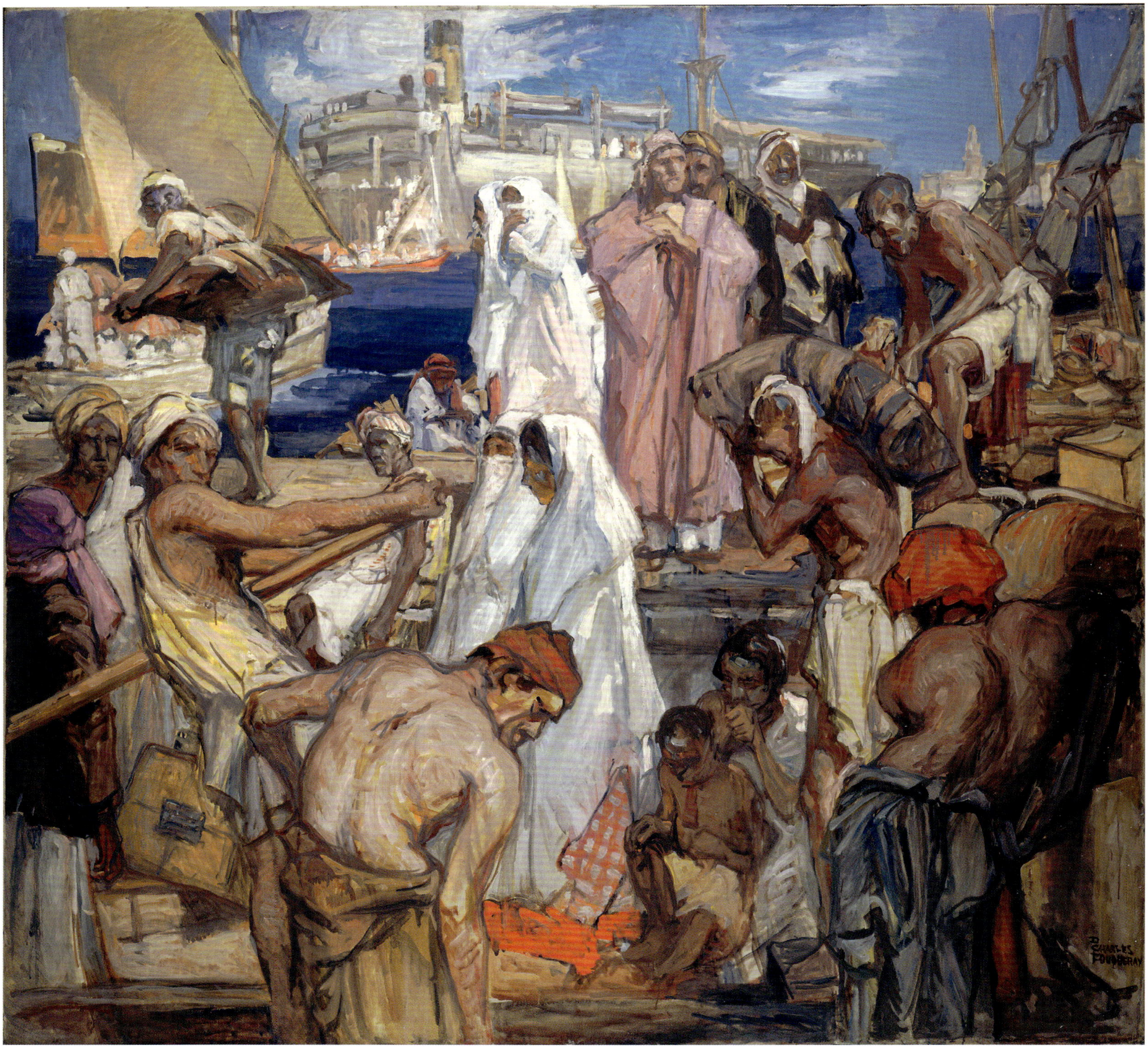

Charles Dominique Fouqueray
Pilgrims in Jeddah, 1921
Oil on canvas
200 × 220 cm
Gift of Mr. Garnier, 1985
Musée du Quai Branly – Jacques Chirac, Paris
Courtesy R.M.N. – Grand Palais/ Jean Gilles Berizzi

Richard Burton wrote in *Personal Narrative of a Pilgrimage to Al-Madinah and Meccah: "The ships of the Red Sea—infamous region of rocks, reefs, and shoals—cruise along the coast by day, and at night lay-to in the first cove they find: they do not sail when it blows hard, and as in winter time the weather is often stormy and the light of day does not last long, the voyage is intolerably slow."*

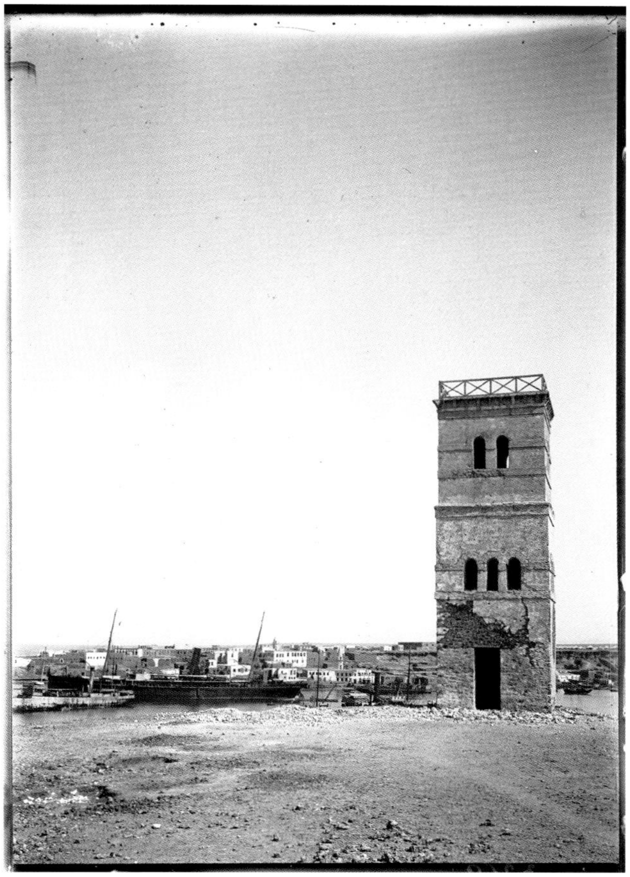

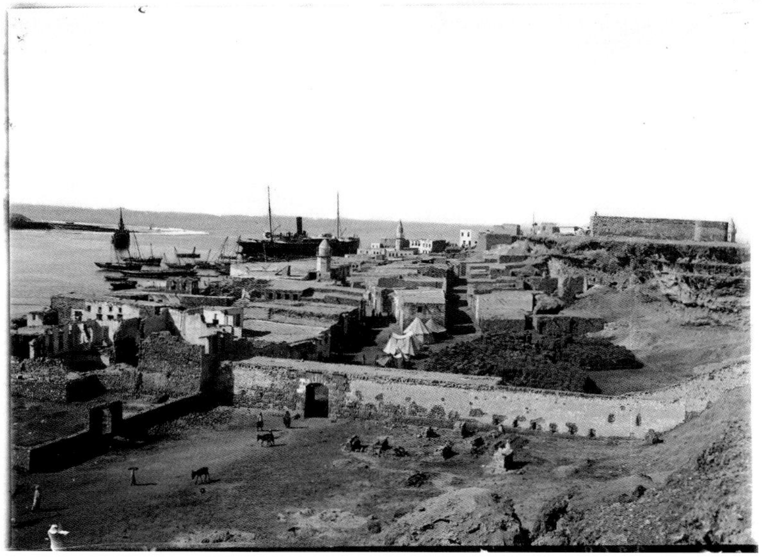

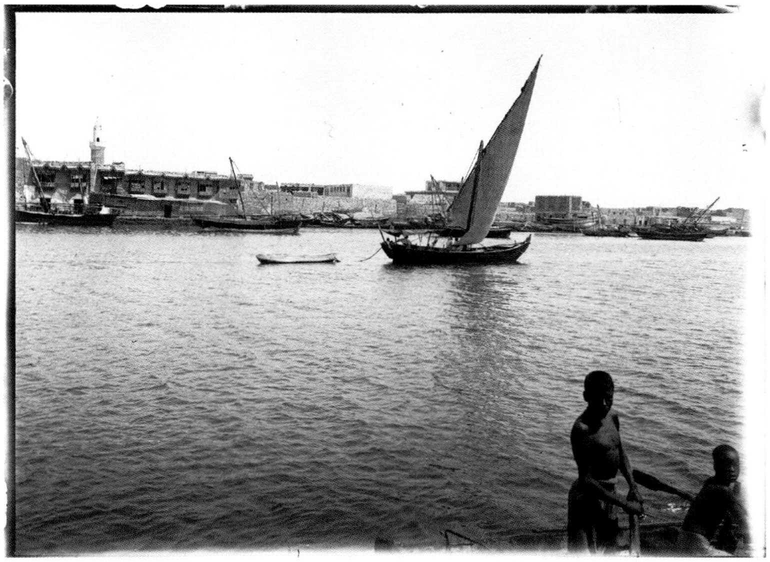

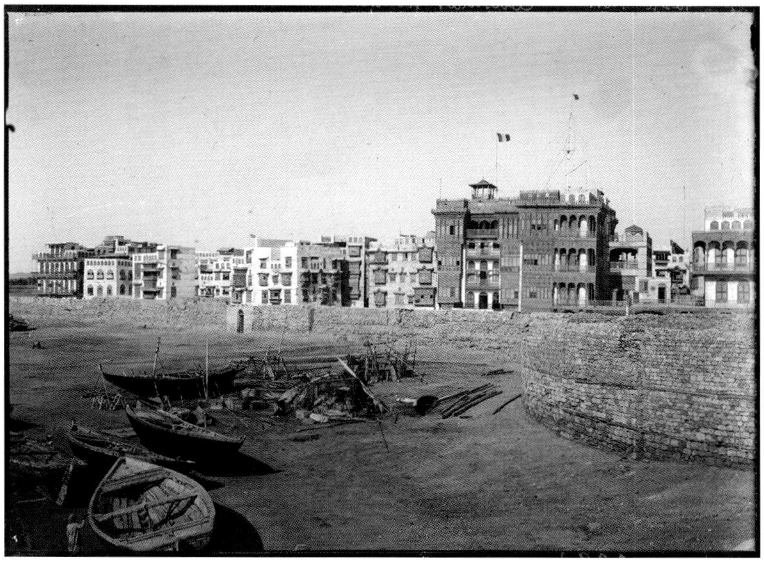

Jaussen and Savignac
Watch tower located south of the port of Al Wajh, 1917
French Biblical and Archeological School of Jerusalem

Rice was imported and arrived at the port of Al Wajh from where it was sent to other cities of Arabia. Ameen Rihani wrote in 1930 describing Al Wajh: "*Al Wajh breathes an air of prosperity.*"

Jaussen and Savignac
Al Wajh, 1917
French Biblical and Archeological School of Jerusalem

The city of Al Wajh and its stony shore viewed from the southeast. In the background can be seen the minarets of its two mosques.

Jaussen and Savignac
Partial view of the port of Yanbu, 1917
French Biblical and Archeological School of Jerusalem

Richard Burton wrote, "*Yanbu also boasts a 'Hammam' or hot bath tenanted by an old Turk, who with his surly Albanian assistant, lives by 'cleaning' pilgrims and travelers.*"

Jaussen and Savignac
The maritime wall of Jeddah, the French consulate and the telecommunication center of the French military mission, 1917
French Biblical and Archeological School of Jerusalem

Consulates and other foreign missions were located beside the harbor in order to assist the pilgrims as soon as they disembarked. Pilgrims were obliged to have their passports stamped in their consulates. John Keane wrote in *Six months in the Hijaz, Journeys to Makkah and Madinah 1877–1878* that the pilgrims "*landing in Jeddah were helpless and gullible and before landing, each one is required to pay a Turkish Customhouse official one rupee and after landing, they have to pay duties based on the weight of their baggage.*"

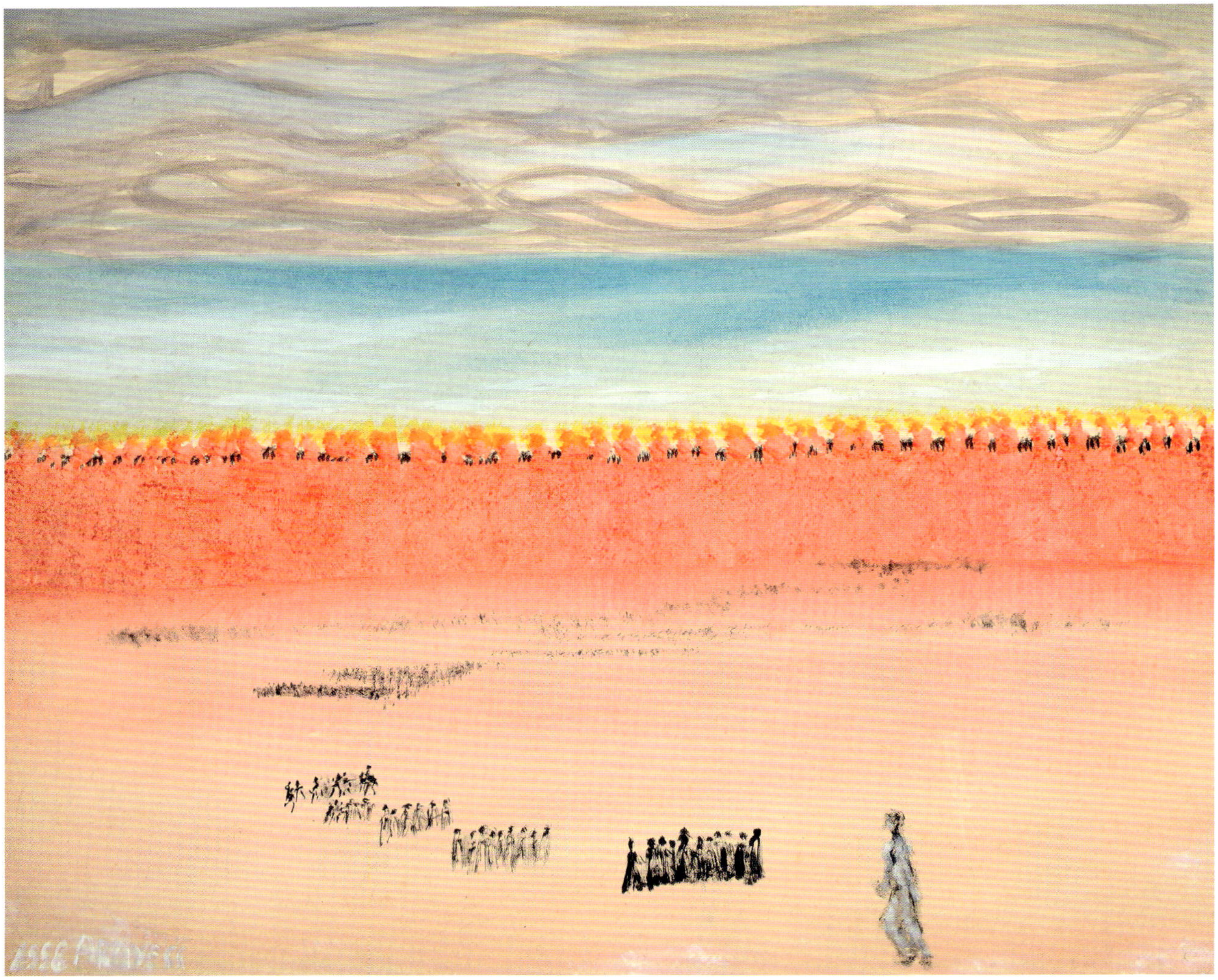

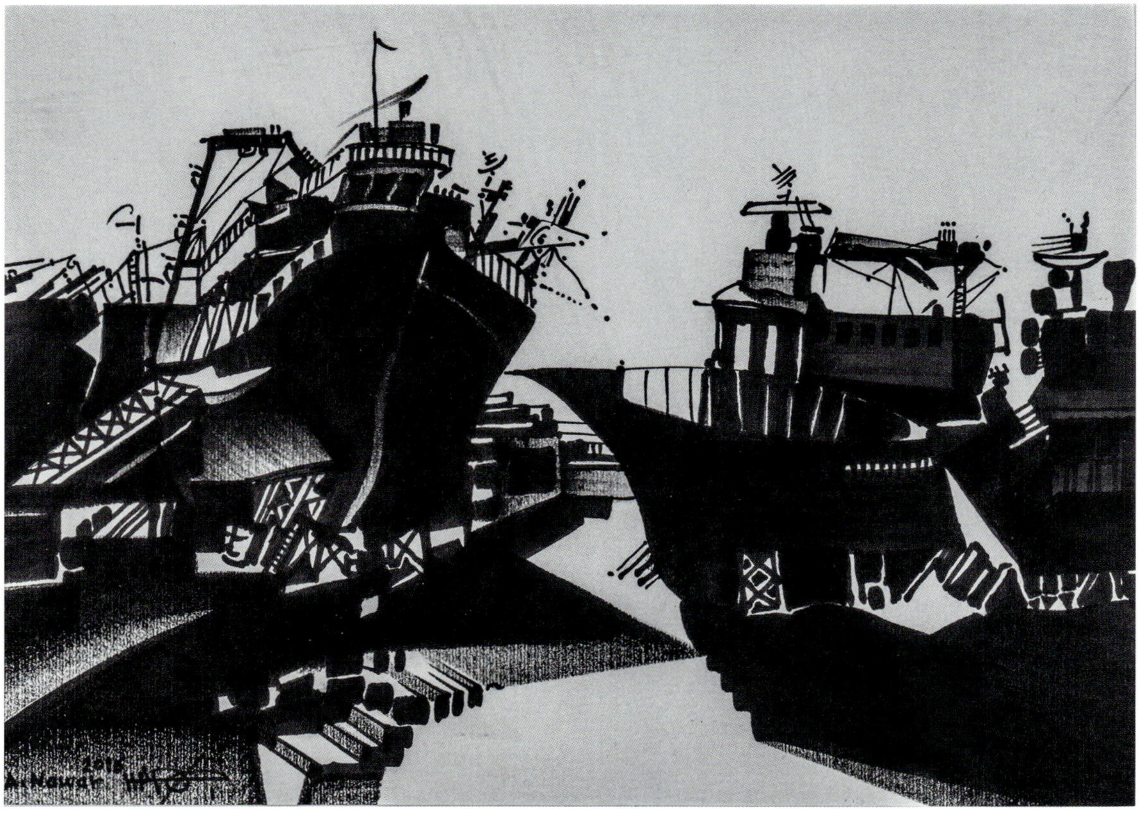

Aref El Rayess
Untitled, c. 1982
Mixed media on panel
55 × 70 cm
Courtesy Saleh Barakat, Beirut

"It is difficult to speak of routes in Arabia, and to determine their direction: excepting the great pilgrim-routes there are no certain roads followed in the desert; no soil is impassable for the camel; and the daring Bedawy, who knows his land and its wells, and is inured to the hardships of hunger and thirst, chooses his way wherever he likes," wrote Georg Wallin in *Travels in Arabia*.

Ahmad Nawar
Hijaz: Inspiration from the Holy Land (23), 2016
Flo-master ink drawing
26.5 × 41.5 cm
Courtesy of the artist
and Hafez Gallery, Jeddah

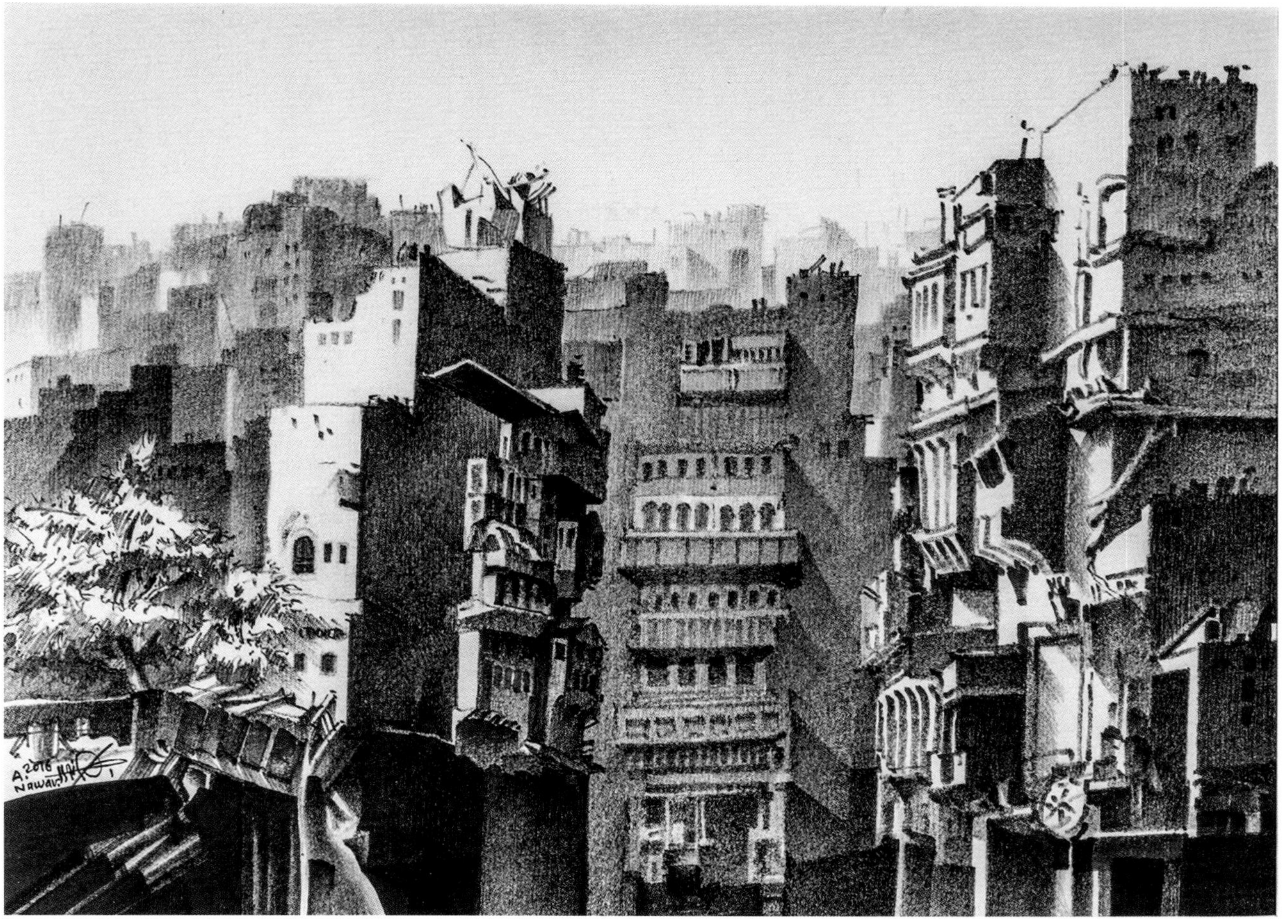

Ahmad Nawar
Hijaz: Inspiration from the Holy Land (27), 2016
Flo-master ink drawing
26.5 × 41.5 cm
Courtesy of the artist
and Hafez Gallery, Jeddah

Ahmad Nawar's artistic approach in this series is very nostalgic. He seeks inspiration from the past to evoke the present. His Flo-master pen drawings resemble the wood engravings practiced by the German artists in the beginning of the nineteenth century.

by a rather well-preserved trench; it is, however, ruined in the south and the north." When the French pilgrim Jules Gervais-Courtellemont visited the city in 1896, things had gotten even worse: "A fortified wall surrounds the city, once protecting it from the assault of Bedouin tribes in the days of revolt," he observed in his travel account, deploring that "the wall is breached everywhere and in some places along the southeast side only piles of rubble mark where it once stood."

The curtain thus rose, dropped, and rose once again! The fortifications were demolished once and for all in 1946, and with it large swathes of the old city disappeared at the same time. Nevertheless, over many centuries, pilgrims and travelers landing in Jeddah were impressed by the splendors of this unequalled city, fascinated by its décor, the sophistication of its architecture and dazzling whiteness of its stone.

Like an "oasis of stones, lost on this appallingly sterile coast," as described by Jules Gervais-Courtellemont, Jeddah was no less than "a nice city, well-built, well-designed, well-populated, lively, animated, perfectly deserving, from all points of view, its present role of port of Mecca," in the eyes of Charles Didier, who went on to describe its wide streets, "opening from time to time on spacious squares." Maurice Tamisier was equally struck: "Jeddah is much better laid out than Egyptian cities; roads are wide, quite well aligned, and remarkably clean, especially during Ramadan." And according to Ali Bey El Abbassi: "Jeddah is a pretty town. Its streets are regular. The houses are fine, built of stone, and are two and three stories high."

These "beautiful houses, as is the custom in Italy" aroused the admiration of Ludovico di Varthema and impressed visitors. "The houses of merchants on the seaside are mostly made of coral stone, practical in terms of construction and beautiful in appearance," according to Carsten Niebuhr. They were "high, constructed wholly of stone, brought for the greater part from the seashore, and consisting of madrepores and other marine fossils. Almost every house has two stories, with many small windows and wooden shutters. Some have bow-windows, which exhibit a great display of joiners' or carpenters' work," noted Johann Ludwig Burckhardt with his typical precision.

This "display of 'joiners' or 'carpenters'" mentioned by Burckhardt, and these "countless loggias

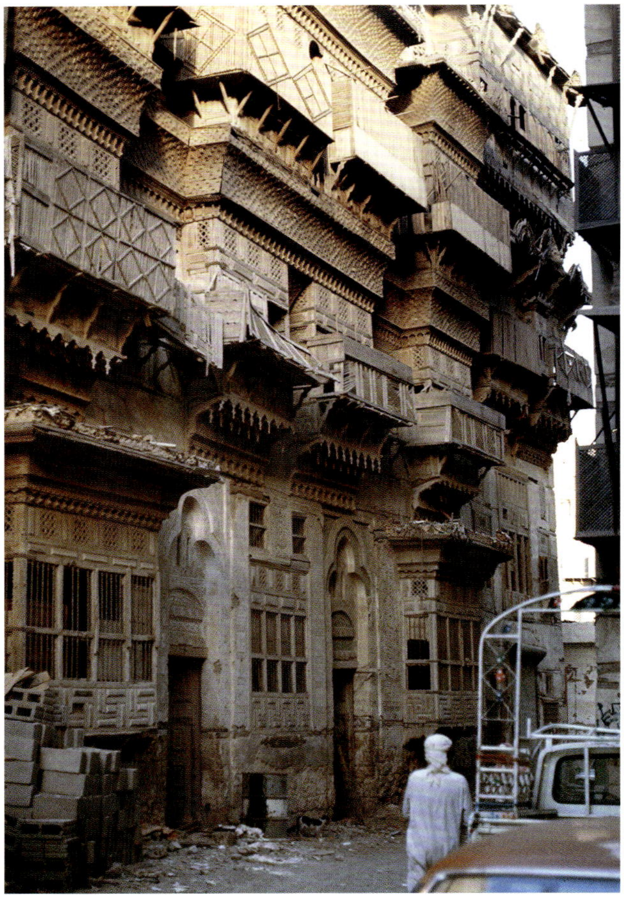

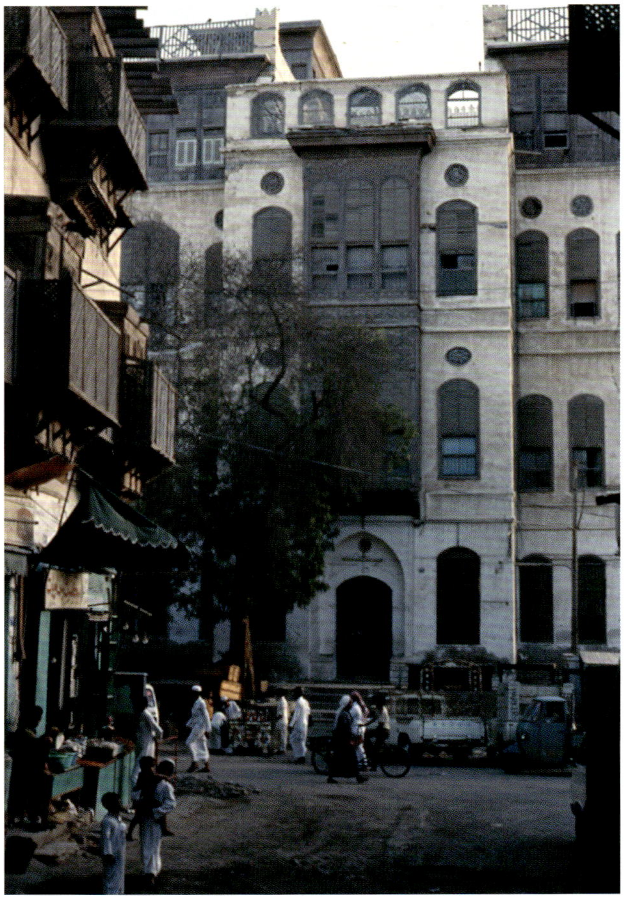

Fouad Elkoury
An alley in Jeddah's downtown, 1973
Courtesy of the artist

Fouad Elkoury
Jeddah's traditional architecture, 1973
Courtesy of the artist

Thanks to its outstanding reflection of the Red Sea architectural tradition, "Historic Jeddah" was listed in the UNESCO Heritage World list in 2014, becoming the third site in Saudi Arabia to be honored by UNESCO. The other sites are the Al-Hijr archeological site, Mada'in Saleh (2008) and Al-Turaif district in Al-Dir'iyah (2010).

small and large, balconies and wooden canopies, enchantingly sculpted," as described by Albert Londres, clearly include the sumptuous *musharabiyas* that adorned the facades of homes, as described in detail by Saleh Soubhy: "The facades of each dwelling feature some sort of wooden kiosks, called *musharabiyas*, with full-sized windows and latticework, and mats and cushions inside. Those not exposed to sunlight are occupied more often. These *musharabiyas* can be of extremely great value. I have seen several made of wood from the Indies, adorned all over with sculptures of unmatched graciousness and delicateness." Maurice Tamisier noted as well: "There are some houses whose *musharabiyas* and doors are sculptured with the most delicate taste; these ornaments embody a grace and an elegance encountered nowhere else in Arabia."

"Built with madrepores extracted from the sea," in the words of Tamisier, or, in those of Charles Didier, "of conchyliotypoliths, stones encrusted with shells, which are very common along the shores of the Red Sea," these houses seduced travelers, even dazzled them, quite literally: "when the sun is shining, the dazzling whiteness of the walls can be harmful to the eyes," lamented Carsten Niebuhr in this respect. Referred to as "coral stone" by Londres, "madrepore" by Tamisier, "madreporite" by Burckhardt, or even "conchyliotypoliths" by Didier, "the stones whiten by weathering," further specified Tamisier, "and confer to the houses an air of elegance," which was widely appreciated.

Despite the administrative hassles that disturbed the beginning of his stay in Jeddah, the painter Dinet did not fail to appreciate with his artist's gaze "the city's appearance, with its tall white houses with *grey musharabiyas*." Indeed, the contrast between the white stone and the dark sculpted wood of the *musharabiyas* undoubtedly enchanted travelers. In the elegant words

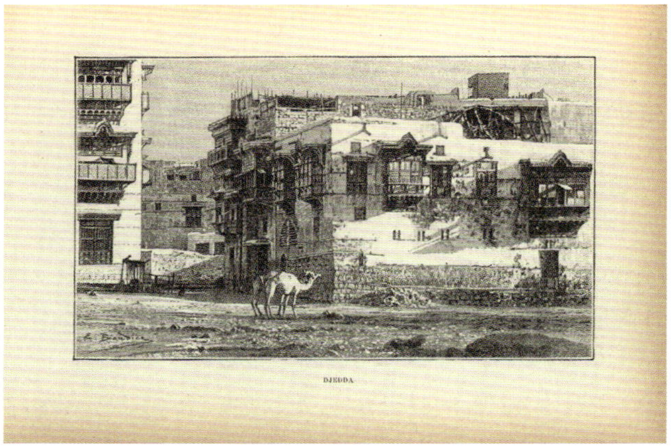

Jules Gervais-Courtellemont
Djeddah
From *Mon Voyage à La Mecque*, 1896
Engraving modeled after the photograph of the author
Paris, Librairie Hachette
Bibliothèque nationale de France, Paris

Jules Gervais-Courtellemont arrived at Jeddah three days after departing the port of Suez. He described the city in *Mon Voyage à La Mecque*: *"The city is built by the seaside on a low and sandy plain; not the smallest hillock, not the least pleat in the land, a true burnt and arid beach. ... Legions of mosquitos attack you night and day, the water is bad, the heat humid and oppressive, and not the least greenery enlivens this sad landscape that surrounds it."*

Anne de Henning
Beit Nassif in Jeddah, 2011
Courtesy of the artist

Nassif house, located on Al Alawi street in Jeddah's downtown and beside the old souk, was once the tallest palace in the city with its five stories. It is also one of the best-preserved houses and was purchased by the government and open for visitors.

Anne de Henning
Beit Bujunaid in Jeddah's downtown, 2011
Courtesy of the artist

This house bears the family name of its owners, the Bujunaid family. It is famous for its carving, fretwork, lattices, and verandas. The wood used in the houses in Jeddah was imported from India, Java, and other locations. The carvings were done by Indian craftsmen.

Ronan Olier
Musharabiyas in Jeddah, 2010
Gouache
65 × 50 cm
Courtesy of the artist

Jeddah's downtown houses are famous for their latticework balconies and *musharabiya* or *rawashin*, as they are commonly called in Hijaz.

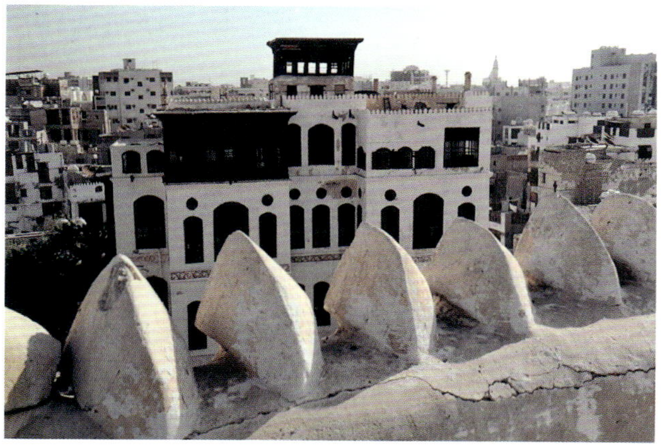

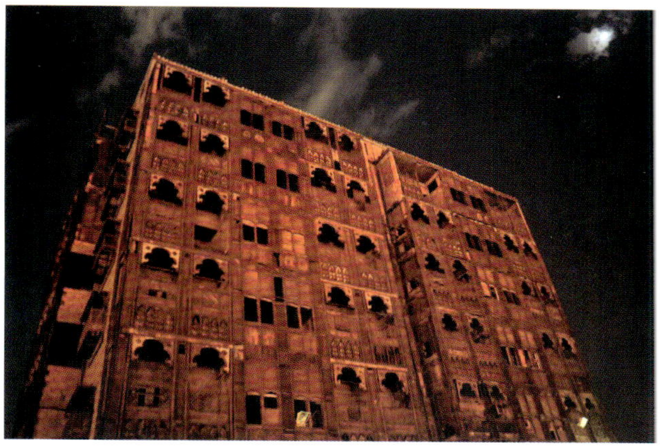

of Albert Londres, the sight "of these fantastic houses of Jeddah makes one wonder if they emerge from the ground or from an extravagant dream."

"The city has an appearance of wealth," wrote Tamisier, and as previously mentioned, was "the centre of extensive trade," observed Gervais-Courtellemont. The city's souks were consequently the best proof of its continual prosperity, which dated back to the tenth century and the decline of the Abbasids of Baghdad, and subsequently remained steady. As early as the eleventh century, Naser Khosrow extolled the quality of Jeddah's souks; in the mid-nineteenth century, Charles Didier found them "well stocked with all sorts of merchandises, mostly imported, and locally-produced or exotic foodstuff: Damascus, Baghdad, Iran, Egypt, and mainly India are all represented by their natural or manufactured products." Over the course of a millennium, in every era, pilgrims and travelers painted such flattering portraits.

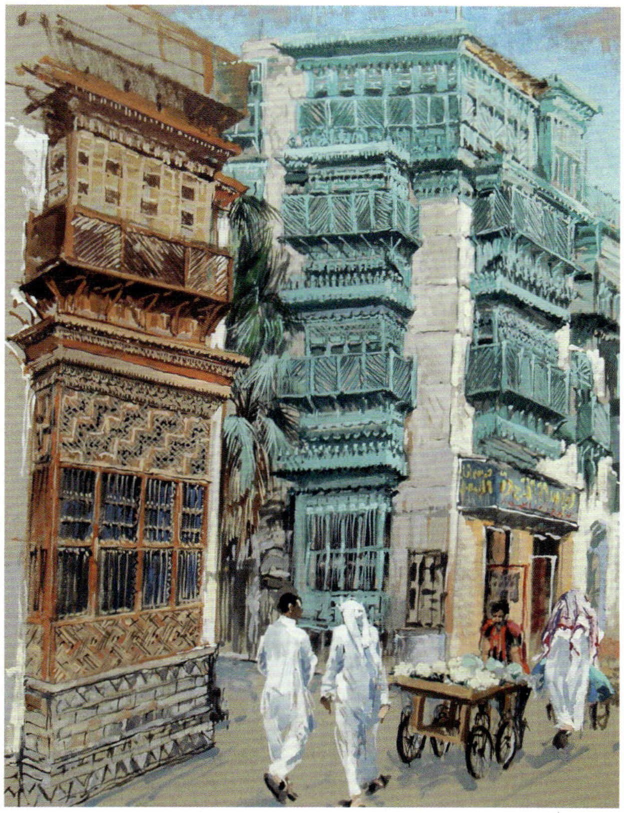

Burckhardt was certainly the figure who undertook this exercise with the greatest skill and rigor, providing such a meticulous description of Jeddah's bazaar in the early nineteenth century that his readers were able to find in his book more information about Jeddah than they could find elsewhere about almost any other city in Europe, as noted a century and a half later by the historian Jacqueline Pirenne in her work, *À la Découverte de l'Arabie* (In Search of Arabia). "Concerning trade, the information provided by Burckhardt is inexhaustible," she wrote, "starting from the most general observations to the examination of the smallest shops: their number, what they sell, the exact nationality of the merchants in each speciality; he notes the prices, their variability, the total revenue of large companies, the mechanisms of the increases and decreases of prices." Awed by such precision, readers quickly get a sense of the crowd of buyers and merchants bustling about in the thirty-odd pages Burckhardt devoted to the Jeddah bazaar in his *Travels in Arabia*, which also shed light on their tastes, customs, and practices.

In this way, Burckhardt focused alternately on "thirty-one tobacco-shops," "twenty-five coffee-shops," "twenty-one butter-sellers," "eight date-sellers," "five bean-sellers," "ten or twelve stands where bread is sold," "eighteen vegetable or fruit-stands," and more. For each of these trades, the Swiss traveler described the conditions of its operation and the customers to which it catered. Those of the café business, composed mainly of shopkeepers "of the third class" and "sea-faring people, [who] make it their constant resort," we thus learned, made immoderate use of the dark brew (see *Cities of Yesterday and Tomorrow*) and tobacco. Burckhardt describes the different types of pipes used in these establishments; provides their names and those of their various parts; indicates the materials used; tells how the tobacco should be prepared; notes the different varieties of tobacco and where they come from; and more. Then comes the information on fruits, their varieties, their origin, their quality; the lemons, for example, are "of the smallest size," pomegranates "of middling quality," grapes "of the best kind," water-melons "small but of good flavour," quinces "have not the harsh taste of those in Europe, and may be eaten raw". One had to be leery of fruit hailing from Ta'if—so delicious when eaten there—due to the fact that "for having been packed up at Ta'if in an unripe state, it acquires a factitious maturity by fermentation during the journey." As for plants: "the usual kinds are me-loukhye, bamye, portulaca, eggplants, or badingans, cucumbers, and very small turnips, of which the leaves are eaten, and the root is thrown away as useless."

Burckhardt continued: "Three shops where wa-ter-skins are sold and repaired," "five sellers of sweet-meats, sugar-plums, and different sorts of confection-ary," "four pancake makers," "eleven large shops of corn-dealers," "eleven clothes shops," "four barbers' shop," and more. We thus learn that the best water skins were those from the port of Sowakin, "in great re-quest, being very light, and sewed with much neatness. A Sowakin waterskin will last, in daily use, about three to four months." In the chapter devoted to barbers, we learn that "the mustachios are always cut closely, and never allowed to hang over the lips; in this they differ from the northern Turks, who seldom touch their thick bushy mustachios with scissors."

The list goes on: "one watchmaker," "eighteen druggists," "eleven shops where small articles of Indian manufacture are sold," "six large shops of Indian piece-goods," "five makers of *nâl*, or sandals," "three sellers of sweet-oils or essences," "seven money-dealers, or *sarrafs*," and more. Burckhardt mentioned that the watchmaker was Turkish. He also recounted, "All the Jeddah merchants wear watches, many of which are of good English manufacture; they are brought either from India, or by the *Hadjys* from Constantinople." Burckhardt notes that the latter often need "money in the Hijaz; they are sometimes compelled to dispose of their most valuable articles; the watch is always the first, then the pistols and sabre, and lastly the fine pipe,

Ronan Olier
The Souks in Jeddah
Gouache
50 × 56 cm
Courtesy of the artist

John Keane wrote in describing the souks in Arabia, "*The shops are of the ordinary Eastern description. A low platform facing the street, on which samples of the wares are exposed.*"

Postcard
Textile and Gold souk
Nasser D. Khalili Collection of Islamic Art, London

For centuries, Jeddah was Saudi Arabia's commercial center and its window to the world. Philby, who lived in Jeddah around the same time the photo featured on this postcard was taken, described its souk in *The Heart of Arabia. A record of Travel and Exploration* as being vast and busy and reminded him of the business quarters of the great cities of India.

Ronan Olier
Textile Souk in Jeddah
Gouache
60 × 70 cm
Courtesy of the artist

Traditional souks are still very popular today, not only in the small towns but in the major cities as well. John Keane refers to Jeddah as being polyglot. Natives of every country may be seen in its crowded bazaars, and the products of the same can be bought in its shops.

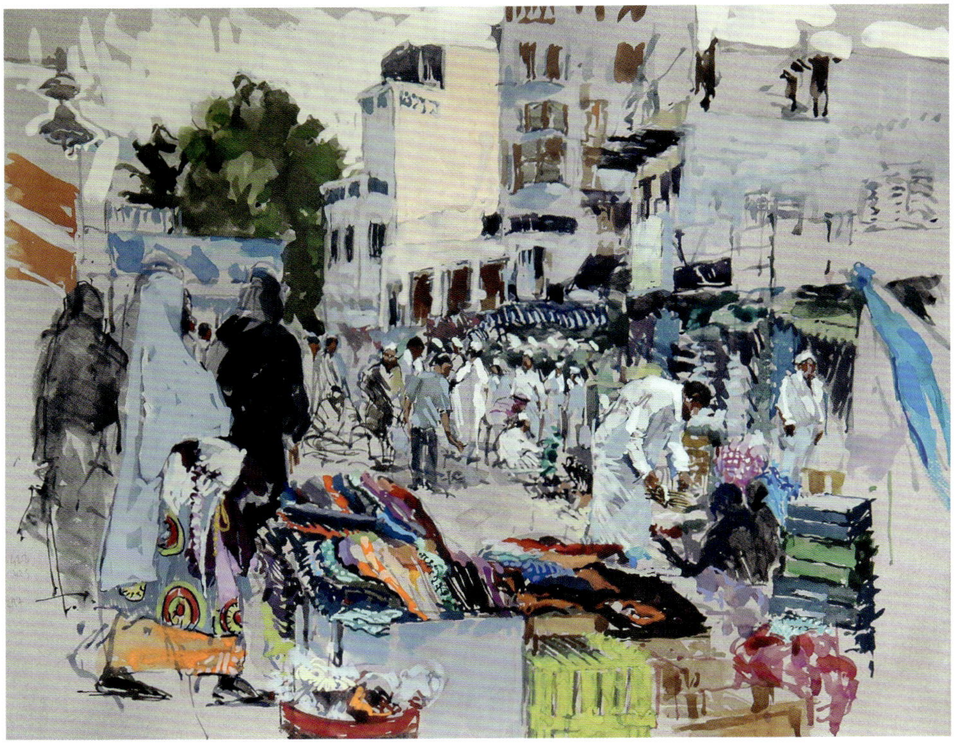

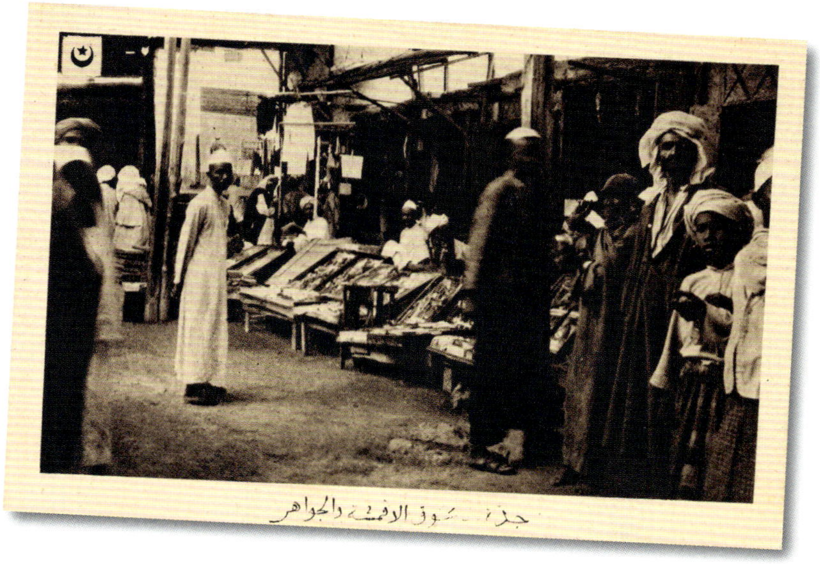

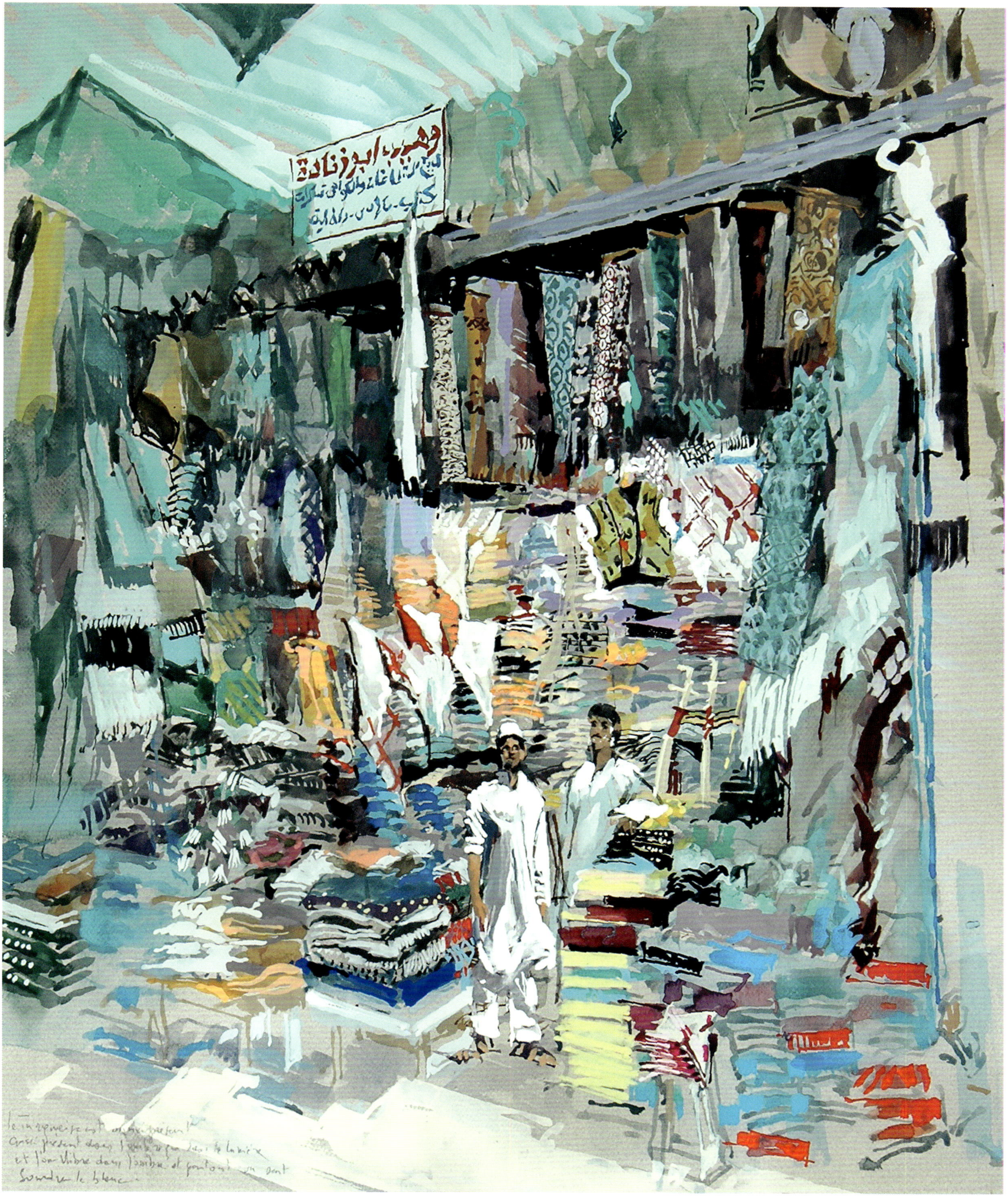

Malin Basil
The Gold Souk, 1980
Acrylic on canvas
100 × 75 cm
Private collection

Gold souks are very popular and are found in almost all the cities and towns in Saudi Arabia. Philby in *The Heart of Arabia. A record of Travel and Exploration* described souks writing: "*At the first sound of the call to the prayer, the shops are closed down, the crowd vanishes to perform its ablutions … the shops reopen when the prayer finishes and once again the souk is filled with the clamor of men. And so they alternate between noise and silence the livelong day.*"

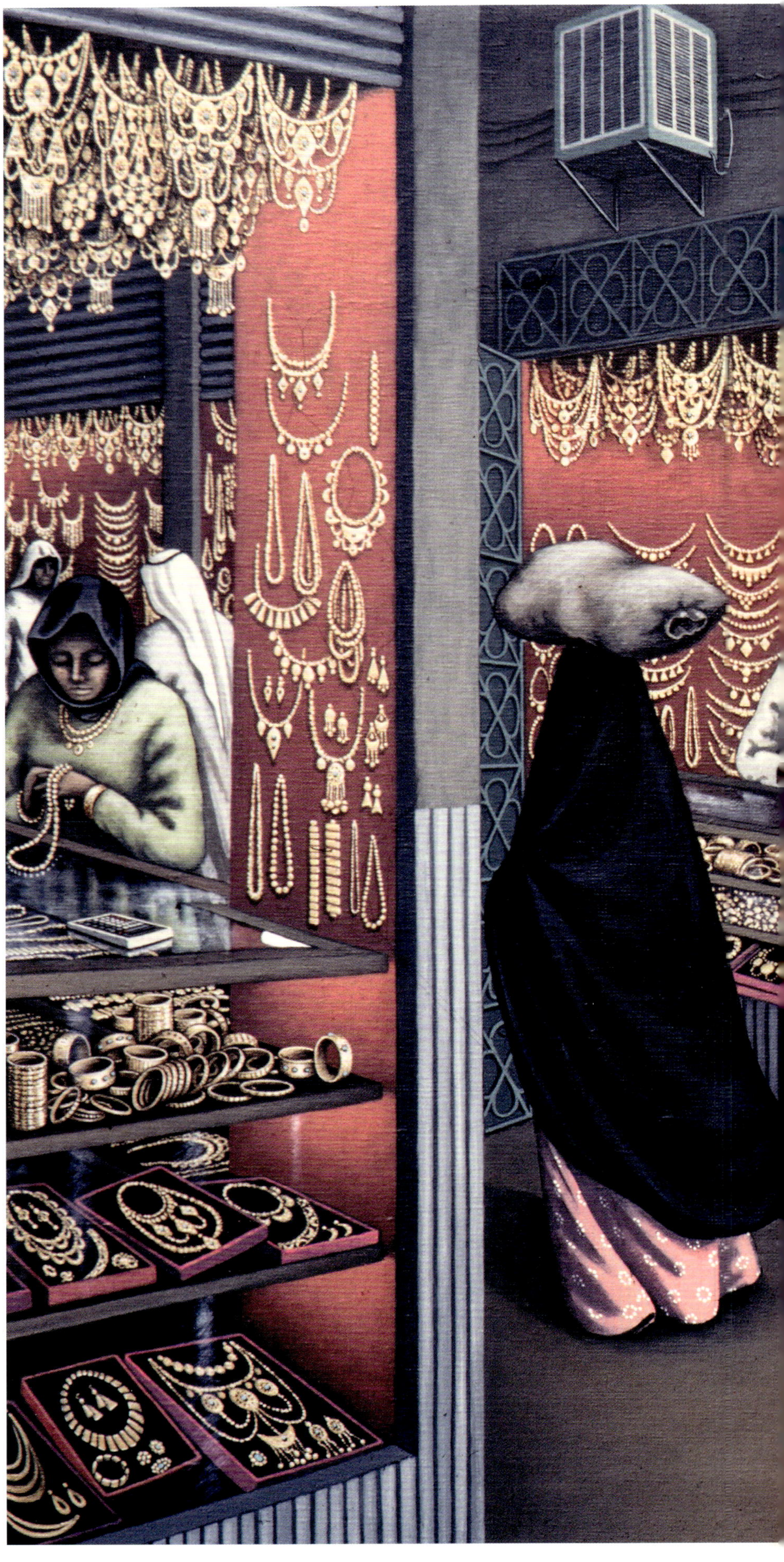

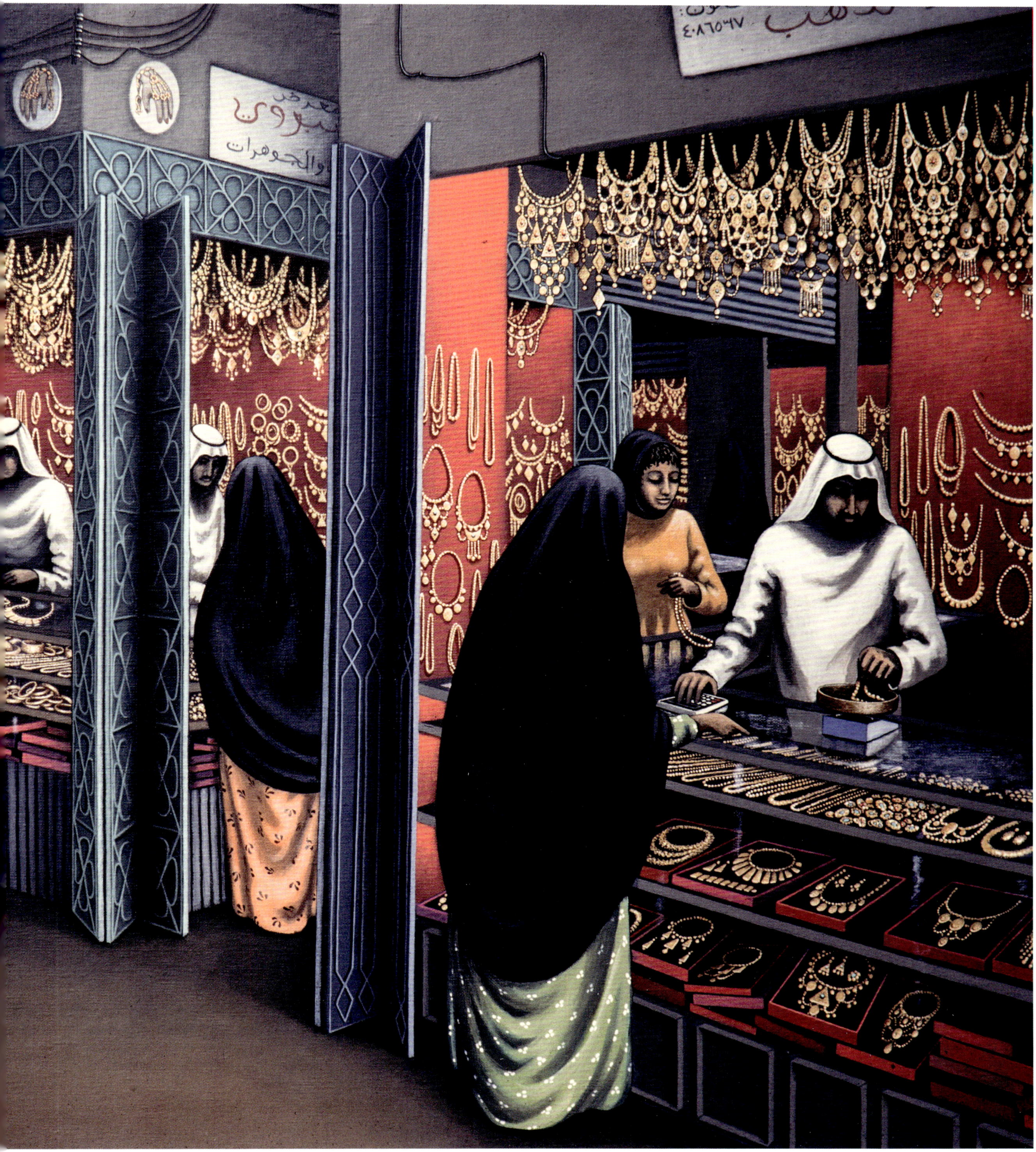
معرض
٤٠٨٦٥٦٧

and the best copy of the Koran." All of these things, he concluded, end up "in the auction-markets of Jeddah."

On the subject of changers, or *sarrafs*, Burckhardt writes: "The value of money changes here more rapidly than in any part of the East with which I am acquainted. The price of dollars and sequins fluctuates almost daily, and the *sarrafs* are always sure to be gainers." He also reported, "The *para*, or smallest Turkish coin (here called *diwany*), is current all over the Hijaz, and in great request," going on to note that "forty *paras* make a piastre; but in the time of the Hajj, when small change is necessary for the immense daily traffic of the pilgrims, the *sarrafs* gave twenty-five *paras* only in change for the piastre."

With notations, remarks, and comments, Burckhardt listed more than forty different activities, professions, and trades; and if we count the many shops, workshops, boutiques, and dispensaries mentioned, this number increases to more than 300! A few decades later, Charles Didier, during his brief stay there, had a similar impression of the city, albeit one that was inevitably much more superficial: "The only business of Jeddah's inhabitants is commerce that is carried out on a cash-only basis and on which they generally become rich."

But who really are these inhabitants of Jeddah, Burckhardt seemed to wonder. In the same manner that he perceived that "three Koreysh families only, descendants of the ancient tribe of that name, are found in Mecca," Burckhardt inferred from his extensive observations that "the inhabitants of Jeddah, like those of Mecca and Medina, are almost exclusively foreigners," and, "those who can be truly called native are only a few families of sherifs, who are all learned men, and attached to the mosques or the courts of justice." Some twenty years later, Maurice Tamisier reached the same conclusion: "Today in Jeddah, there are only around twenty Arab families that have been there for many generations."

The historic population of Jeddah was replaced by another, as Burckhardt noted, due to the fact that "the descendants of the ancient Arabs who once peopled the town have perished by the hands of the governors, or have retired to other countries." Excepting the handful of families of sherifs that made up the intellectual and religious elite, "all the other Jeddawys (people of Jeddah) are foreigners or their descendants." It may be tempting to wonder where they came from—and Burckhardt responds: "The most numerous are those from Hadramaut and Yemen; and to these may be

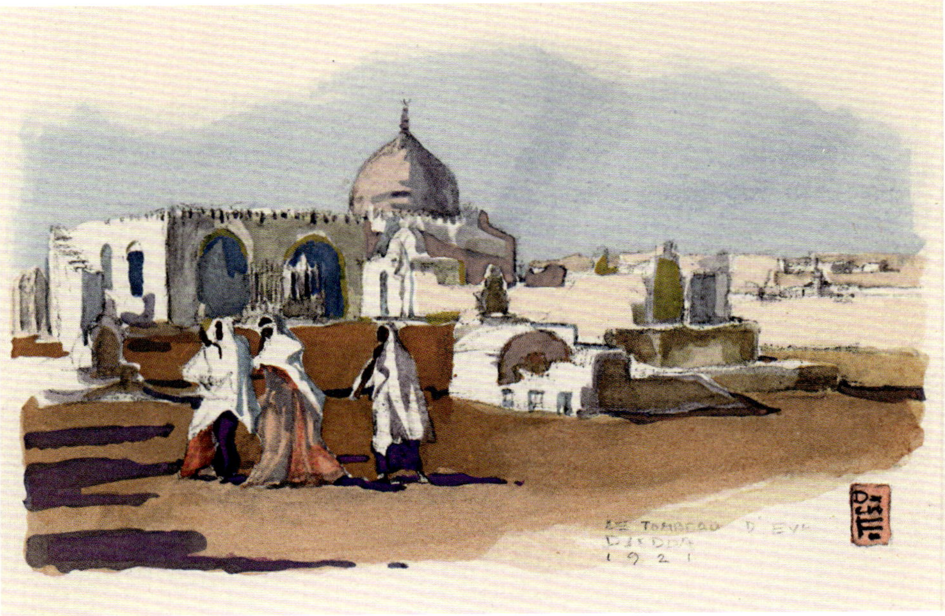

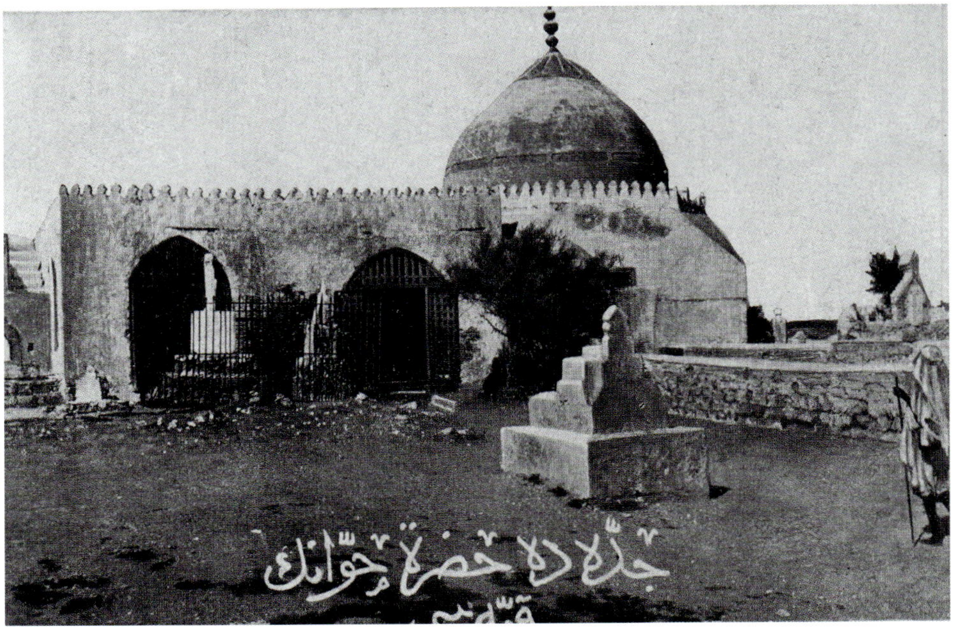

Charles Fouqueray
The Tomb of Eve, 1921
Lithograph
14 × 20 cm
From *Escales d'Asie*, Claude Farrère
Laborey, Paris, 1947
Courtesy Musée national de la Marine/A. Fux

The name "Jeddah" means grandmother in Arabic. It is said that the city was named Jeddah due to the fact that Eve was buried there. Many authors who visited Jeddah mentioned the existence of the tomb of Eve. As early as the twelfth century, Al-Idrisi wrote in his *Geography*: "*It is said that Eve went there after the exit from Eden, and it is there that her mortal remains are buried.*"

Postcard
Eve's tomb in Jeddah
Publisher kh/m
Nasser D. Khalili Collection of Islamic Art, London

The first documented mention of the existence of Eve's tomb in Jeddah was made by Hamadani (tenth century) who wrote, "*It has been related that Adam was in Mina when he felt a yearning to see Eve… that Eve had come from Juddah, and that he knew her on Arafat.*" Ameen Rihani wrote that the tomb is in an enclosure, outside the city wall, containing other tombs. The women of Jeddah visit it every Thursday.

Ursula Schulz-Dornburg
From Medina to Jordan Border, 2002–03
Courtesy of the artist

Several attempts were made in the 1960s, 1970s, and 1980s to reconstruct the Hijaz railway. The project was ruled out due to the excessive cost of its reconstruction as well as the development and expansion of the road network and air travel.

Ursula Schulz-Dornburg
From Medina to Jordan Border, 2002–03
Courtesy of the artist

The Hijaz railway continued to maintain service throughout World War I despite frequent raids due to the Turks' capacity to repair the damages quickly.

Ursula Schulz-Dornburg
From Medina to Jordan Border, 2002–03
Courtesy of the artist

The city of Medina and its railway station remained under Ottoman control after the signature of the armistice of Mudros in October 1918. It was only on January 10, 1919, when a group of officers mutinied Fakhri Pasha, that the city surrendered and the Hijaz railway was brought to an end.

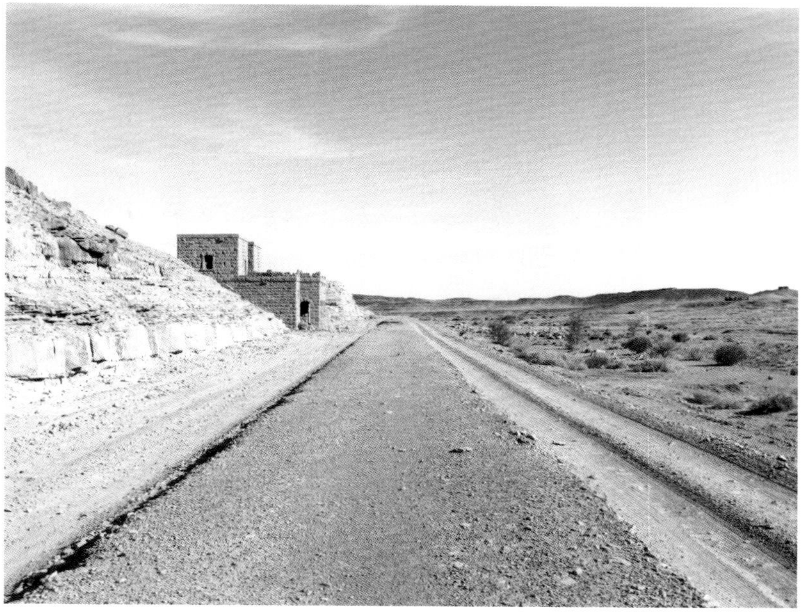

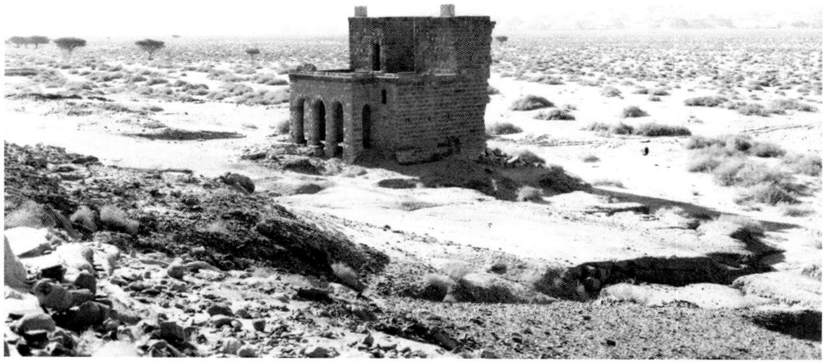

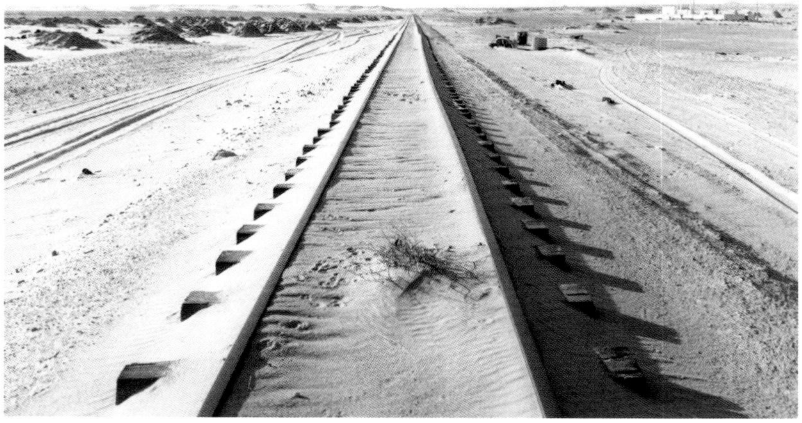

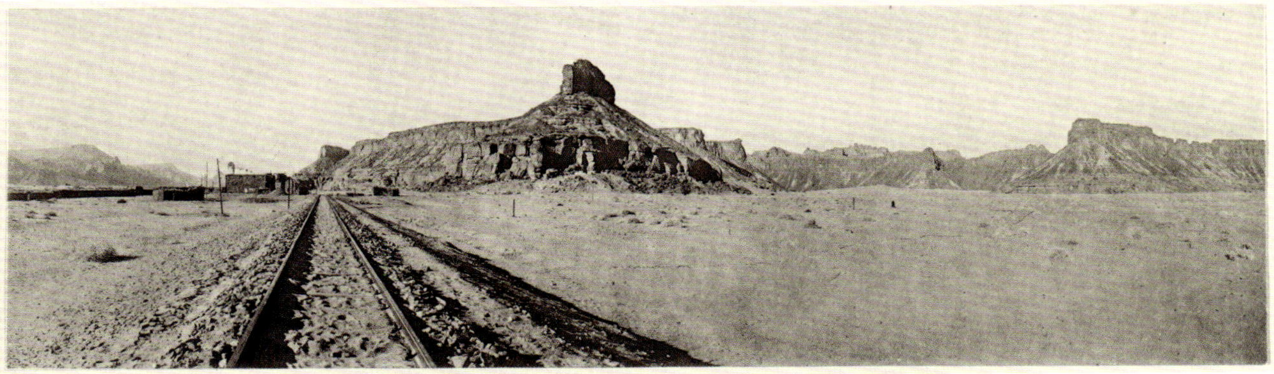

Bernhard Moritz
Al-'Ula valley located 1 km south of the train station, 1916
Plate 60a from the *Bilder aus Palästina, Nord Arabien und dem Sinai*
Dietrich Reimen, Berlin, 1916
Library of Congress Prints and Photographs Division, Washington, D.C.

The 'Ula station was inaugurated on September 1, 1907.

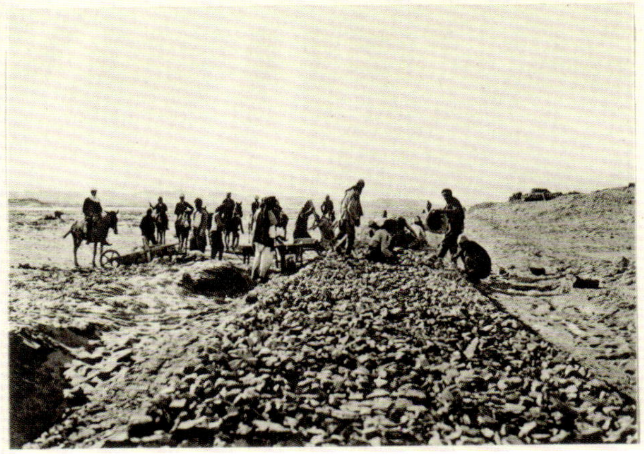

Bernhard Moritz
Ballasting the rail tracks during the construction of the Hijaz railroad, 1906
Plate 55 from the *Bilder aus Palästina, Nord Arabien und dem Sinai*
Dietrich Riemen, Berlin, 1916
Library of Congress Prints and Photographs Division, Washington, D.C.

A 1,320-kilometer project, the Hijaz railway was designed to provide pilgrims with cheap and fast transport as far as Medina. The construction started on September 1, 1900, the fourth anniversary of Sultan Abdulhamid II's accession to the throne, and finished in 1908.

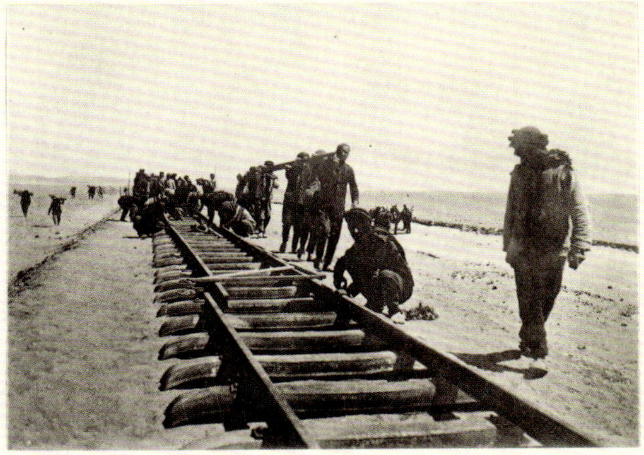

Bernhard Moritz
Construction of the Hijaz railroad: laying the rails near Tabuk, 1906
Plate 56 from the *Bilder aus Palästina, Nord Arabien und dem Sinai*
Dietrich Riemen, Berlin, 1916
Library of Congress Prints and Photographs Division, Washington, D.C.

In 1909, quarantine facilities for the railroad were established at Tabuk. The center was capable of processing up to 4,000 pilgrims at a time.

added some Malays, people of Maskat, Indians," as well as "the settlers from Egypt, Syria, Barbary, European Turkey, and Anatolia," and others still, "of Persian origin, Tatars, Bokhars, Kurds, Afghans; in short, of almost every Mohammedan country in the world." However, "there are no Christians living in Jeddah"; and as for Jews, who until recently were still active in Jeddah's money trade, exercising the profession of *sarraf*, "they were driven out, about thirty or forty years since, by the predecessor of the current sherif, and they all retired to Yemen or to Sanaa."

How did such a change come about? Quite gradually, as the consequence of the fact that "in every Hajj, some of the pilgrims remain behind," as Burckhardt noted. He continued: "The mixture of races in Jeddah is an effect of the pilgrimage, during which rich merchants visit the Hijaz with large amounts of goods: some of these, not being able immediately to settle their accounts, wait till another year; during this period, they cohabit, according to the custom of the country, with some Abyssinian slaves, whom they soon marry; finding themselves at last with a family, they are induced to settle in the country. Thus every pilgrimage adds fresh numbers to the population not only of Jeddah, but of Mecca also, which is indeed very necessary, as in both towns the number of deaths is far greater than that of births." The newcomers all maintain links with their countries of origins, bonds that will form the basis of their future ventures.

This significant change was nevertheless none too apparent, due to the fact that "in the Hijaz, most of the foreign visitors change their native costume for that of the people of the country"; and Burckhardt went on to note that "the Indians offer an exception to this general rule ; they form a distinct colony, and retain their native language, which the children of other strangers usually forget, their mothers being in many instances Arabs, natives of Mecca."

Burckhardt also specified that "the trade of Jeddah and Mecca are closely linked," and went on to provide details of the colossal fortunes of certain merchants, observing that "every town-inhabitant, not excepting even the *olemas*, or learned men, endeavours to employ whatever capital he possesses in some advantageous traffic, that he may live without much bodily exertion." From bulk to retail, on land or sea, trade in all of its forms existed in Jeddah, whose prosperity was based on various factors. The first of these, an endlessly replenished inherent advantage, clearly lay in the holding of the pilgrimage. Every year, the city's

Anonymous
The Hijaz railroad probably around Mada'in Saleh
Photograph from an official album of photos on the Hijaz railway
Nasser D. Khalili Collection of Islamic Art, London

The railway station complex at Mada'in Saleh has been rebuilt. Today, there is a restored 1906 German train at the station.

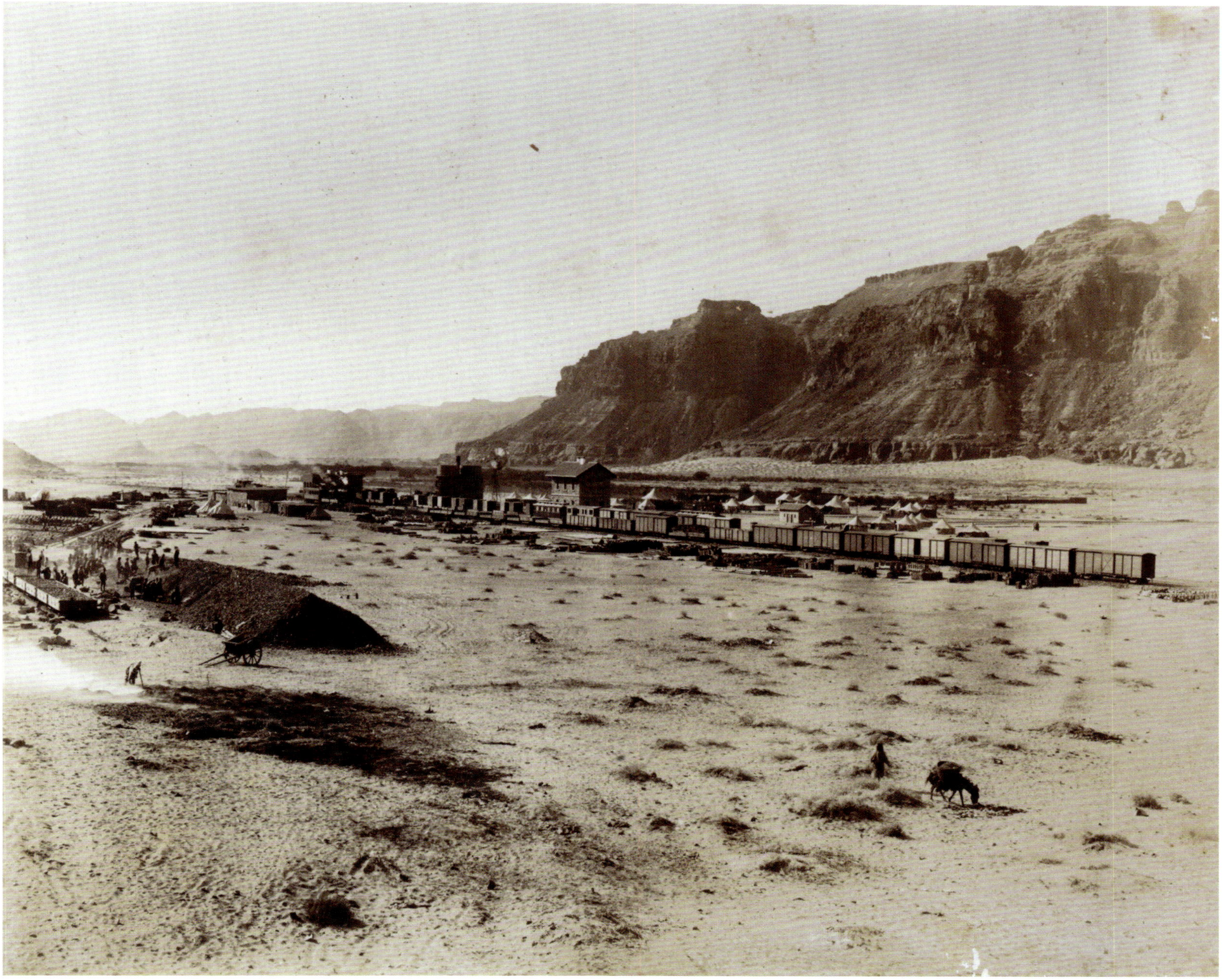

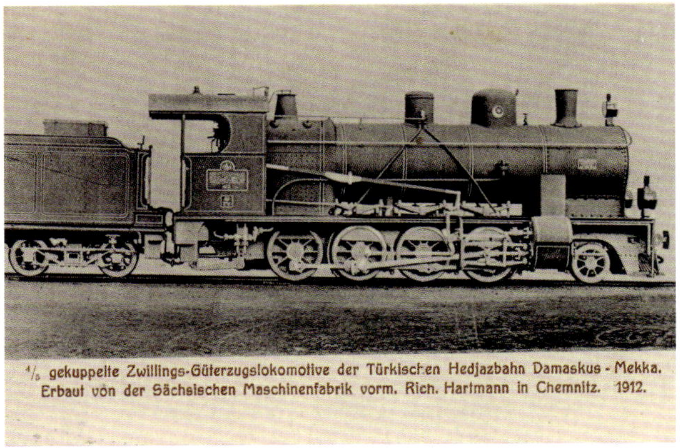

Postcard
A German-made locomotive Hartmann 2-8-0 on the Hijaz railway, 1912
Postcard printed by Verlag V. Rich Liebold, Germany
Nasser D. Khalili Collection of Islamic Art, London

Constructed in 1907, this locomotive is the same model as the one currently standing derelict at Buwair station, 90 kilometers north of Medina.

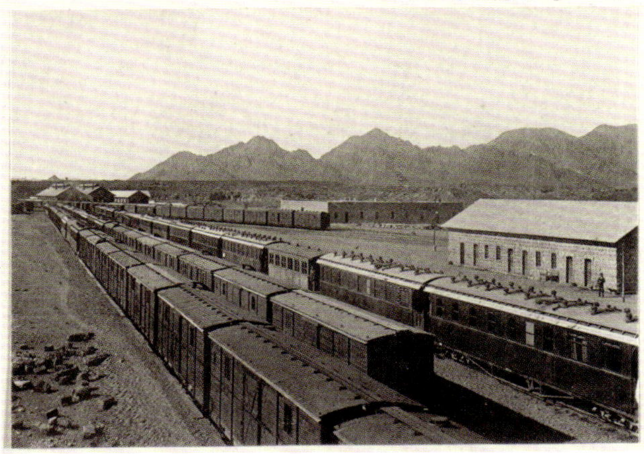

Bernhard Moritz
Freight rail and garages at Medina station, 1916
Plate 66 from the *Bilder aus Palästina, Nord Arabien und dem Sinai*
Dietrich Riemen, Berlin, 1916
Library of Congress Prints and Photographs Division, Washington, D.C.

In the years preceding World War I, the number of pilgrims traveling to Medina by train was more than double than that of the old caravan route.

population increased considerably, tripling or quadrupling due to the constant passage of pilgrims during a period stretching from the month of Shawwal to the month of *Dhu al-Hijjah*; that is to say, at least sixty days or so. In this respect, it is clear that "to provide food, during their stay, for an influx of population amounting to sixty thousand human beings, and for twenty thousand camels, together with provisions for their return homewards, is a matter of no small moment," as the Swiss traveler wrote in understated terms. In this context, he went on to explain, whoever possesses "a few dollars, lays them out in the purchase of some kind of provision, which, when the Hajj approaches, he transports upon his ass from Jeddah to Mecca."

What would be a fortune in any other city in the world, given the heavy taxes paid by pilgrims and the expenses integral to their stay, was but one source of wealth among others in Jeddah. "During the interval of the Hajj," resources could be used in different ways, Burckhardt observed, as "there is considerable trade with the Bedouins, and especially with the inhabitants of the towns of Nejd, who want India goods, drugs, and articles of dress"—not to mention grain speculation, of course. On this subject, he somberly noted: "It is a traffic peculiarly attractive to the smaller capitals, as, the prices being very variable, it is a lottery by which money may sometimes be doubled in a short time."

But the major business lay in international trade, as "Jeddah derives its opulence not only from being the port of Mecca, but it may be considered as that of Egypt, of India, and of Arabia; all the exports of those countries destined for Egypt first pass through the hands of the Jeddah merchants." Burckhardt first analyzed the workings of the coffee trade, in which Jeddah held a central, pivotal position, with shipments arriving from Yemen partially intended to supply Hijaz, while the rest was sold to Egypt and Turkey. However, coffee prices fluctuated so widely that this trade was limited to those "who have large capital at their command, and who can bear occasionally great losses."

"Much safer" but "equally profitable" was "the trade in India goods" that major Jeddah merchants set out to resell, particularly to Egypt. This trade was furthermore carried out with unsettling simplicity and "with less intrigue and fraud, than anywhere I have seen in the Levant," Burckhardt observed, noting: "In Syria and Egypt it is the work of several days, and the business of three or four brokers, to conclude a bargain between two merchants to the amount of a thousand dollars. At Jeddah, sales and purchases are made of entire ships' cargoes in the course of half an hour [...] and the next day the money is paid down." No sooner had the Indian ships time to enter the port of Jeddah, "charged with spices, rice, sugar, tea, grains, and precious stones," than "the goods when sold in Mecca, during the Hajj, yielding a clear gain of twenty to thirty per cent, of fifty per cent when sold in retail."

All of this sheds light on the breadth of the profits that were made in Jeddah. "Of all the Red Sea ports, this is where people come to purchase merchandise first-hand," noted Burckhardt, who accurately surmised that "this city is probably richer than any town of the same size in the Turkish dominions." An ethnologist ahead of the discipline's time, the Swiss explorer strove to describe Jeddah in such a way that—in the words of Jacqueline Pirenne—"is as far as possible from an anecdotal, superficial account that anyone passing through could have provided," far surpassing those that many other travelers had already left. He painted a portrait that provides a detailed perception of this highly singular city, unique in its kind, as it may have been slightly over two centuries ago—thus allowing a better insight into the city as it stands today.

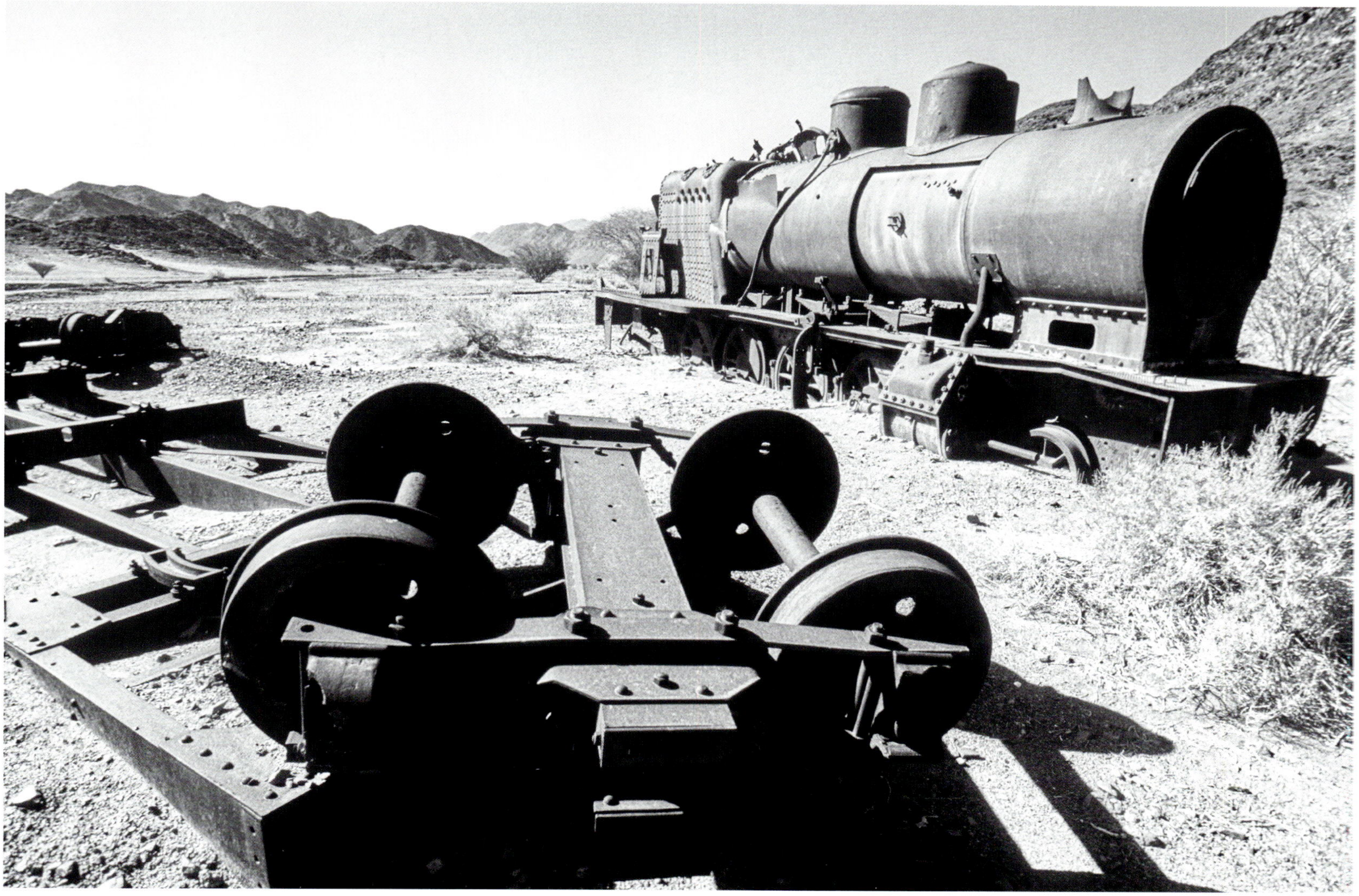

Olivier Couppey
An abandoned locomotive
Courtesy of the artist

There are currently four locomotives abandoned on the deserted Saudi stretch of railway.

Postcard
Map showing the Hijaz railway line with the different stations on the route
Printed in Tunis and captioned in Arabic and French
Nasser D. Khalili Collection of Islamic Art, London

Autographed postcard inscribed in French addressed to Madame Rollin. The postcard reads, *"When you recover, we shall travel to Mecca, with the Arabs, barefoot on the sand of the desert."*

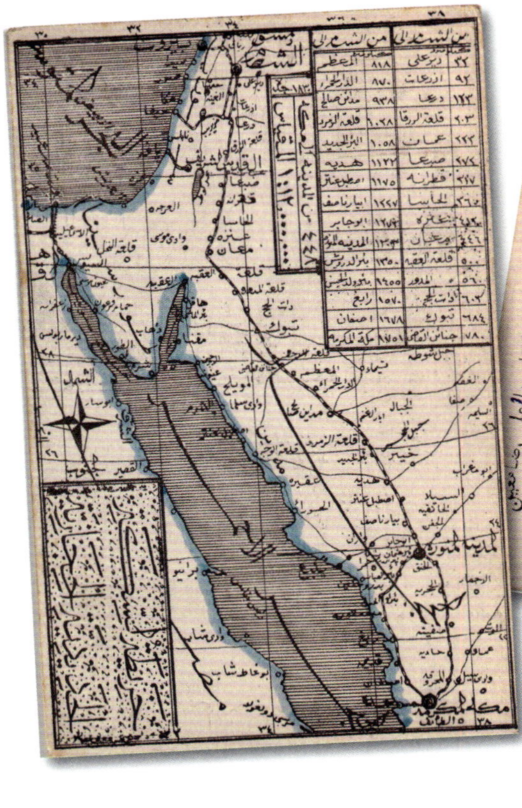

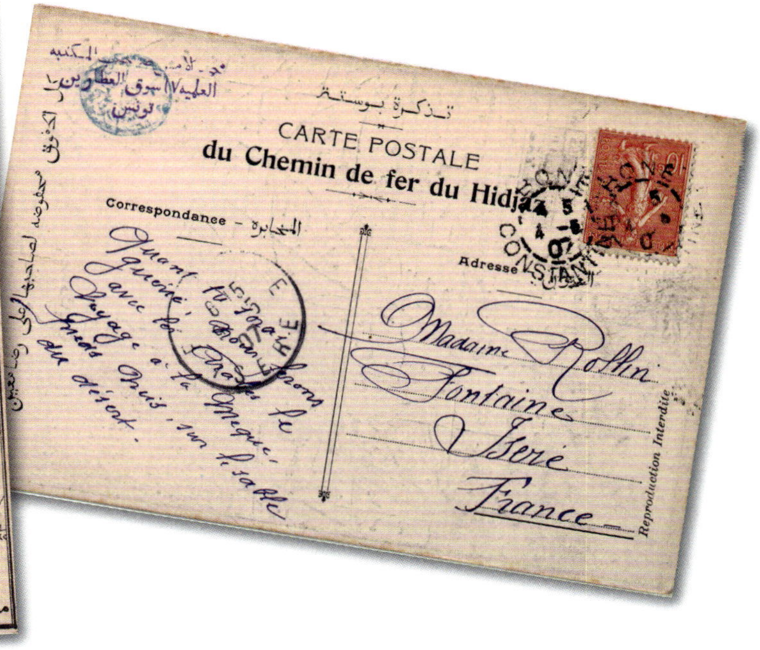

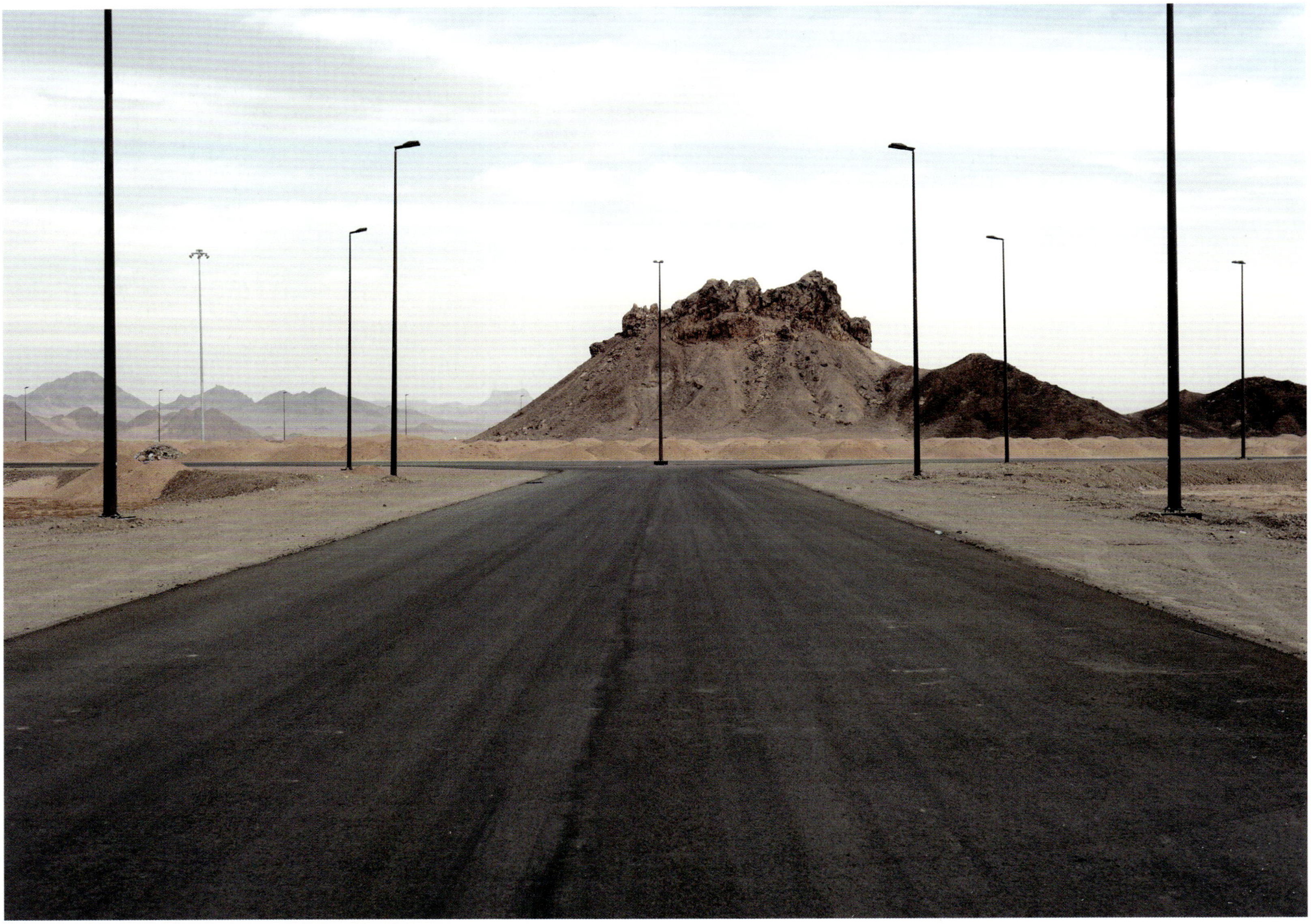

Yann Gayet
From the series *Lisières*, 2013–14
Courtesy of the artist

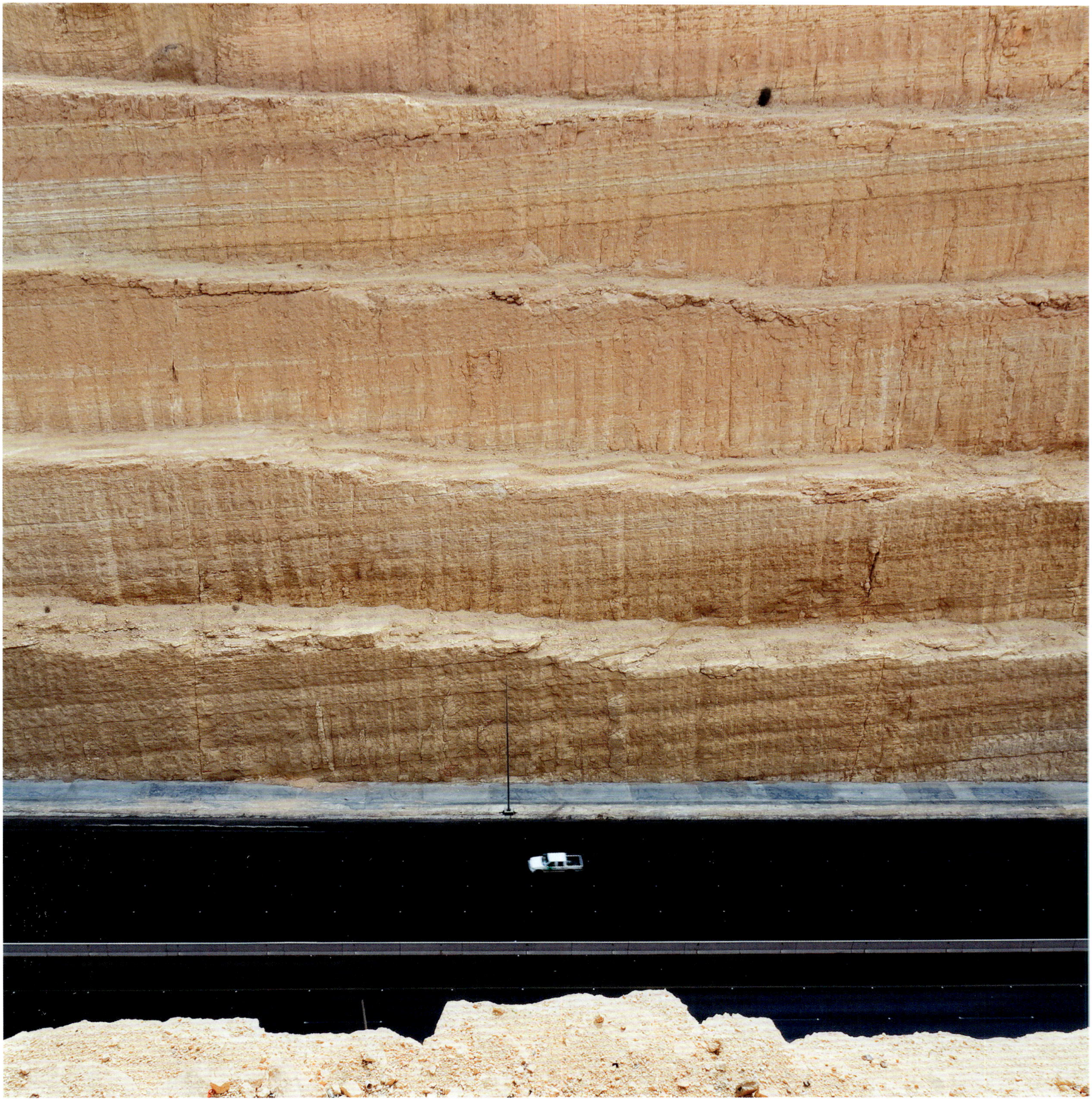

Roger Grasas
A road in Arabia crossing the desert
From the series *Min Turab*, 2007–2016
Courtesy of the artist

ثم ابين تعرف بها محاريب البلاد وصفة كل استقبال الى الكعبة المشرفة
وقد تقدم صفة استخراج المحاريب وصفة كل استقبال البلاد في الطول

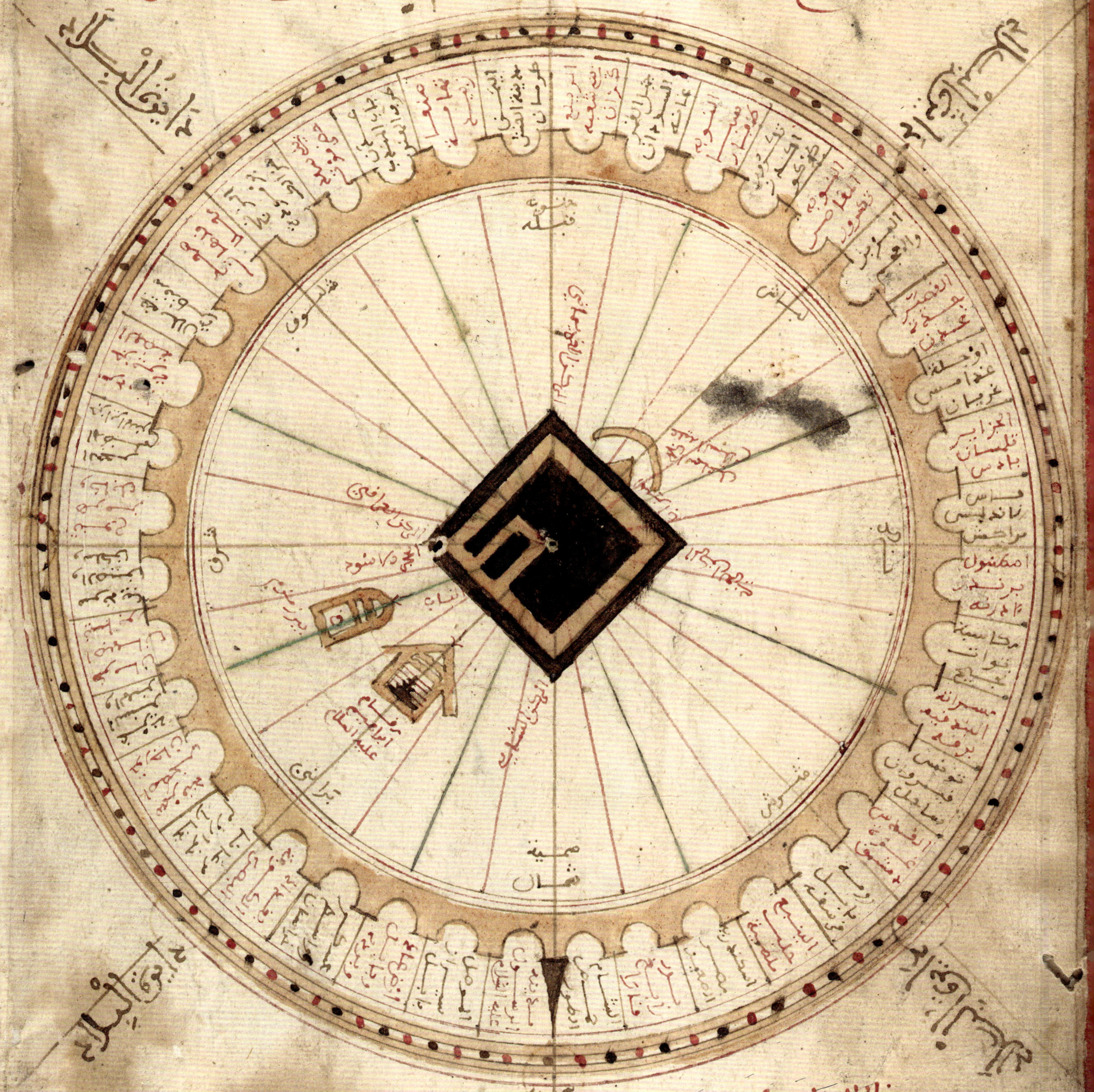

قال الله العظيم في محكم كتابه الحكيم وحيث ما كنتم فولوا وجوهكم شطره

The Center of the World

For Muslims the world over, Mecca has always represented the center of the world—it was simply a matter of being able to reach it.

It was only quite recently, thanks to modern modes of transport—steamboats, trains, cars, planes—that what was once an extremely long journey fraught with dangers has become a trip that one can now take knowing that in all likelihood the return home is guaranteed.

For most pilgrims, hailing from countries from which access to the ports of the Red Sea's western coast—principally Jeddah, but Yanbu as well—was impossible, the only option for reaching Hijaz was traveling overland by caravan. This is why, over the thirteen centuries from the establishment of the Islamic pilgrimage until the emergence of the aforementioned modern modes of transport, many tens or even hundreds of thousands of pilgrims made the choice, year in and year out, to face any number of equally dreadful dangers. To name just a few, these included getting lost in the desert; dying of thirst; falling victim to a sandstorm; being swept away in a sudden torrent; being attacked by bandits; or succumbing to an epidemic, which was a frequent event until the early twentieth century.

Despite this frightening catalogue, these dangers, while well-known, were never enough to dissuade pilgrims from undertaking a journey that was also so costly that they sometimes had to sacrifice a fair portion of their wealth or their life savings. In the eighteenth century, the cost of this journey, from Damascus to Mecca and back, was estimated at four hundred piastres—the cost of a house in that city at the time. Over the course of these thirteenth centuries, the conditions surrounding the pilgrimage caravans remained constant. That is, discounting those departing from a point on the Arabian Peninsula, the caravans always left from the same three starting points of Cairo, Damascus, or Baghdad. There was also a caravan that left from Istanbul, of course, but it ultimately joined the Syrian caravan in Damascus. Likewise, a small Palestinian caravan joined the Egyptian caravan around Aqaba. For those pilgrims who did not reach Jeddah and Hijaz by sea route, it was imperative that one of these three caravans arrived in Mecca. Organized and overseen by the large Muslim countries—Egypt, Syria, Iraq, the Ottoman Empire—these caravans were headed by a major dignitary, provincial governor, or high-ranking military official, the *Amir al-Hajj*; escorted by soldiers; and consisted of convoys carrying tens of thousands of camels, and just as many pilgrims, in each one.

Ali ibn Ahmad ibn Mohammed al-Sharafi al-Safaqusi
Nautical atlas, 1571–72
Drawing on paper
26.8 × 20.7 cm
Bodleian Library, Oxford

The Kaʿba is placed in the center of this map, which shows a series of cities in a ring around it. The Maqam Ibrahim, which is the stone Ibrahim used for climbing when building the Kaʿba, Hijr Ismail, and the well of Zamzam, appear on the map as well. The text above the map reads: "*A circle for ascertaining the right direction towards Mecca for each country and a guide for facing Mecca.*"

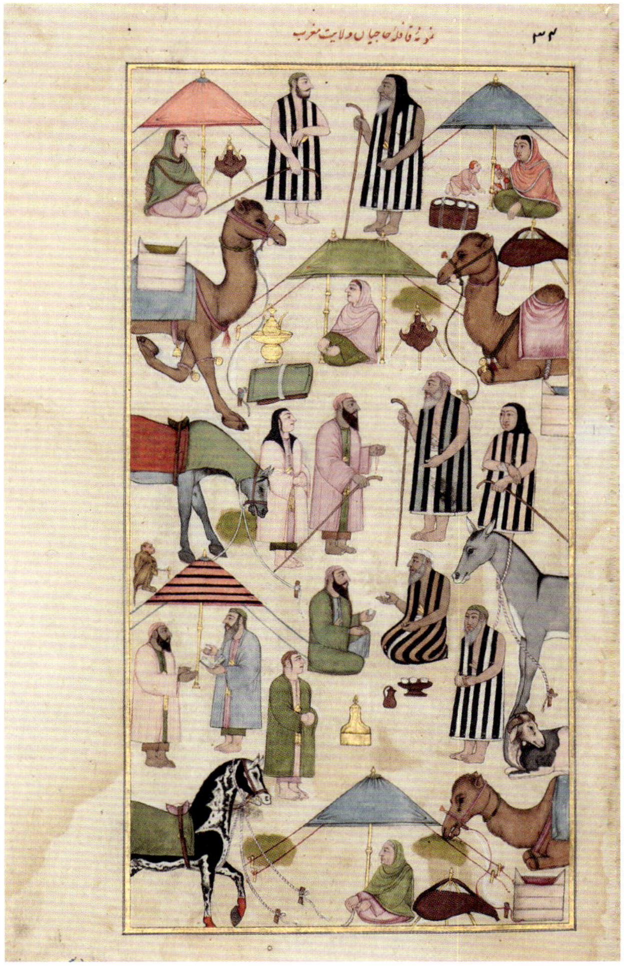

Safi ibn Vali
The camp of the caravan of the pilgrims from the Maghreb, c. 1677–80
Folio 15a from the *Anis al-Hujjaj* (The Pilgrim's Companion)
India, probably Gujarat
Ink, watercolor, and gold on paper
33 × 23.2 cm
Nasser D. Khalili Collection of Islamic Art, London

The camps at the Hajj are composed, as much as possible, of pilgrims speaking the same language or coming from the same country.

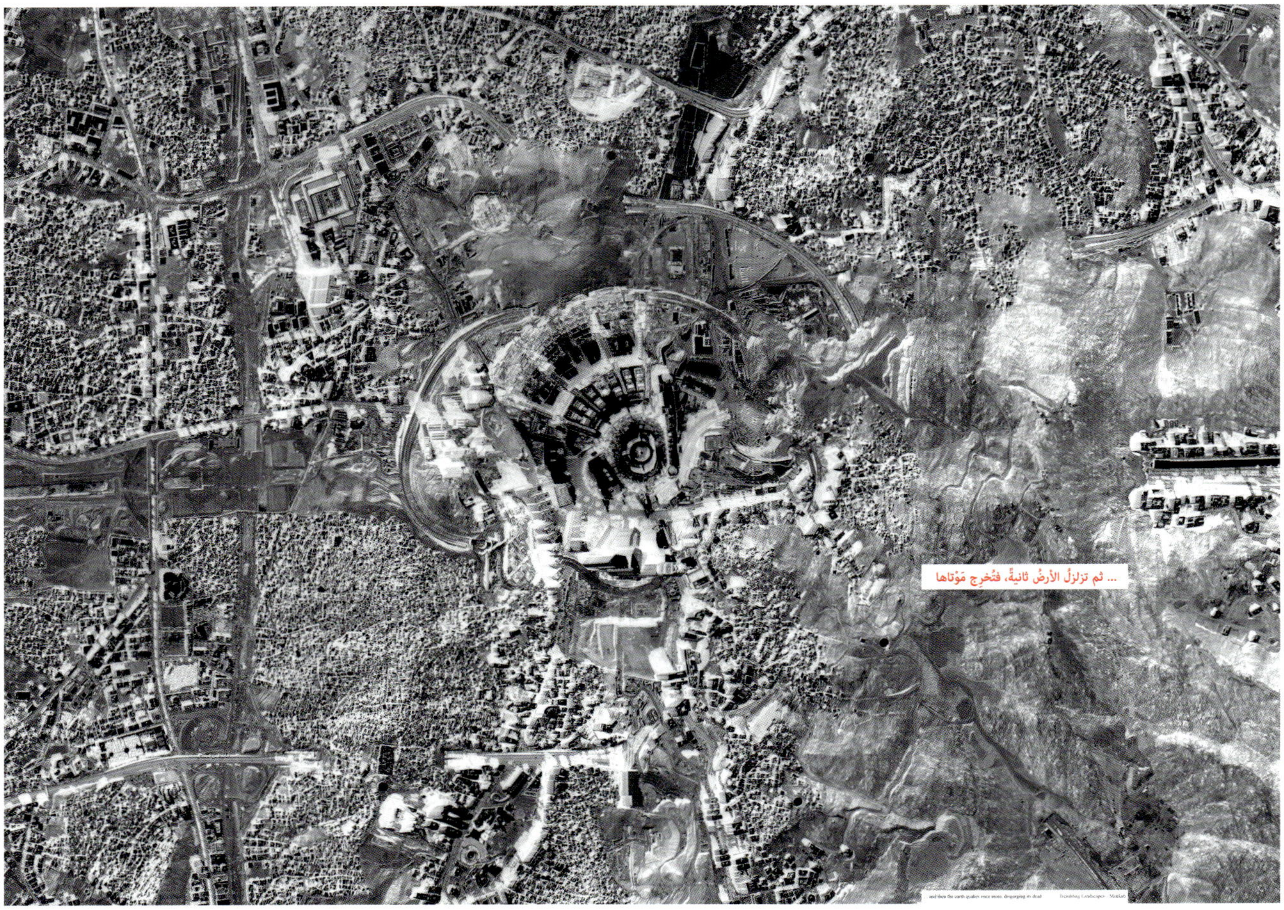

Ali Cherri
Mekkah
From the series *Trembling Landscapes*, 2016
Lithographic print with ink stamp
Courtesy of the artist and the Imane Farès Gallery, Paris

Trembling Landscapes is an ongoing project in which Ali Cherri investigates the effects of catastrophes, both manmade and geological, on cities situated on active fault lines. The text in Arabic reads: "*Then the earth will shake a second time, and the dead shall come forth.*"

The Bolognese Ludovico di Varthema, who was the first European to provide an account of such a trip, undertaken in 1503, recounted that the caravan he was accompanying as part of the Mameluke escort numbered 40,000 pilgrims and 35,000 camels upon departure from Damascus. Upon arrival in Mecca, he wrote: "We found the caravan from Cairo, which had arrived eight days before us. [...] In the said caravan there were sixty-four thousand camels and one hundred Mamelukes."

Later, during the final decades of the eighteenth century and as illustrated by Turkish fiscal documents, the number of travelers joining the Damascus caravan each year fluctuated between 70,000 and 100,000. Circumstances further in the past had dictated even larger caravans. In 1253, for example, during the pilgrimage undertaken by the mother of the last Abbasid caliph, al-Musta`sim bi-llah, her caravan, which set off from Baghdad, included no fewer than 120,000 camels.

Some years, the caravans gathered much smaller numbers of pilgrims, as English traveler Richard Burton observed in 1853, after disembarking at Yanbu and joining the Mecca-bound Damascus caravan in Medina. He wrote: "From what we could see, it amounted to about seven thousand souls, on foot and horseback, in carriages and mounted on the magnificent camels of Syria." This was about the same number as in 1876, when another British traveler, Charles M. Doughty, joined the Damascus caravan to Mada'in Saleh: "The hajjāj were this year 6,000 persons; of these more than half are serving men on foot; and 10,000 of all kinds of cattle." In 1814, due to political troubles afflicting Hijaz, nearly all of the Egyptian pilgrims chose to reach the peninsula through the port of Jeddah. For the same reasons, there was no caravan leaving from Baghdad that same year. Consequently, of the three major caravans, only the one leaving from Damascus was somewhat substantial. According to Swiss explorer and orientalist Johann Ludwig Burckhardt in his *Travels in Arabia*, it "consisted of four or five thousand persons, including soldiers and servants, [and] it had fifteen thousand camels."

The great Egyptian historian Maqrizi recounted that the Abbasid caliph al-Mahdi spent some thirty million dirhams during his 776 pilgrimage, developing and marking out the route from Baghdad to Mecca, having caravansaries built at each stop and equipping them lavishly. Over the centuries, a great many caliphs, sultans, and princes allocated substantial subsidies for the protection of caravans, the development of routes, and

Mahmud Husayn Malik Al-Shu'ara'
A view of the Ka'ba and surrounding buildings in Mecca, 1876–77
Watercolors on paper
49.2 × 59.2 cm
Museum of Islamic Art, Doha

This painting was commissioned by the Qajar prince Farhad Mirza to celebrate his return from the Hajj in 1876–77.

Ziad Antar
Mecca Tower
From the series *Expired*, 2005
Gelatin silver print
Courtesy of the artist

In 2000, using a 1948 Kodak SLR camera and black-and-white medium-format films that had expired in 1976, Ziad Antar began photographing contemporary buildings that reflected futuristic architectural gestures such as Burj Khalifa in Dubai and the Clock Tower of Mecca featured in this photograph.

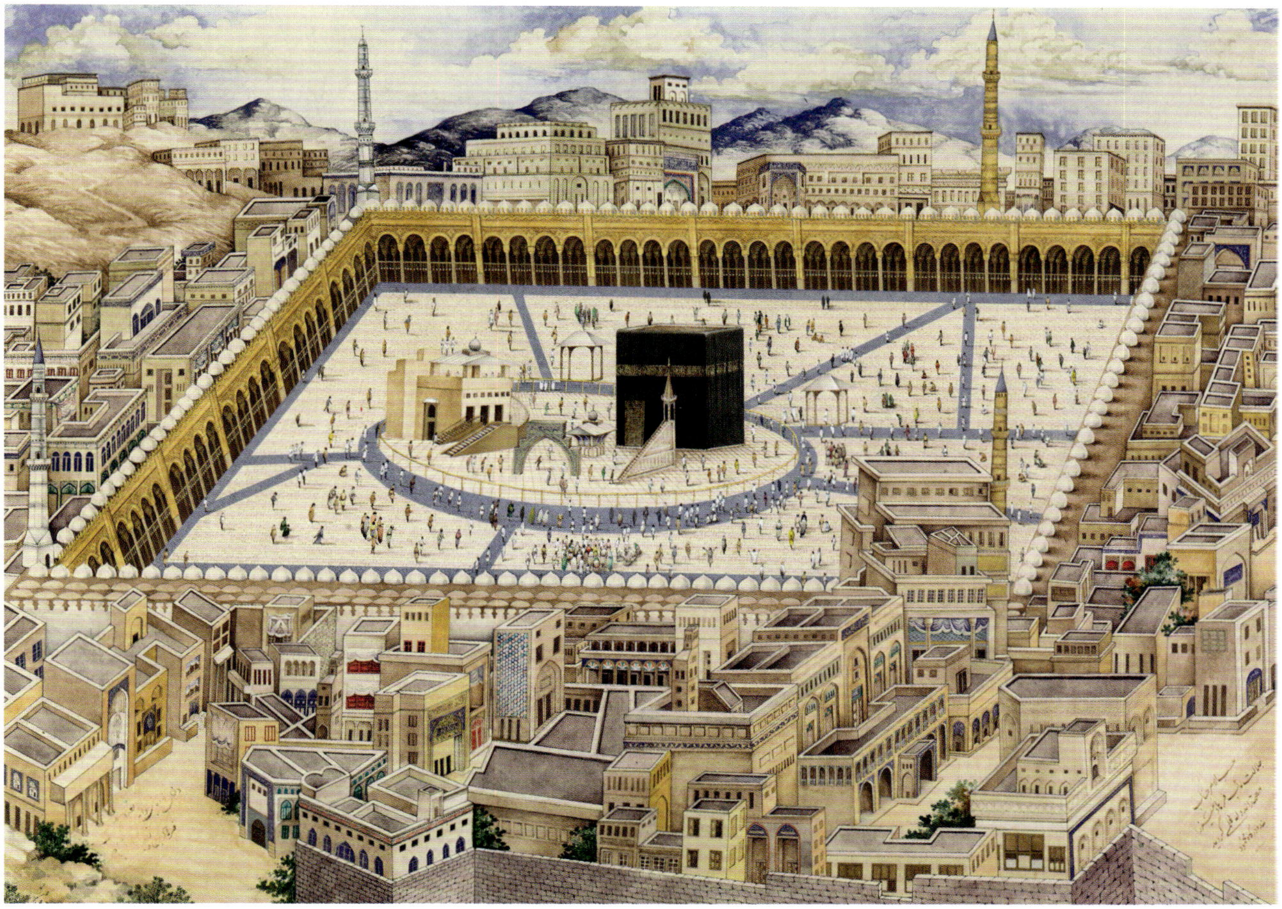

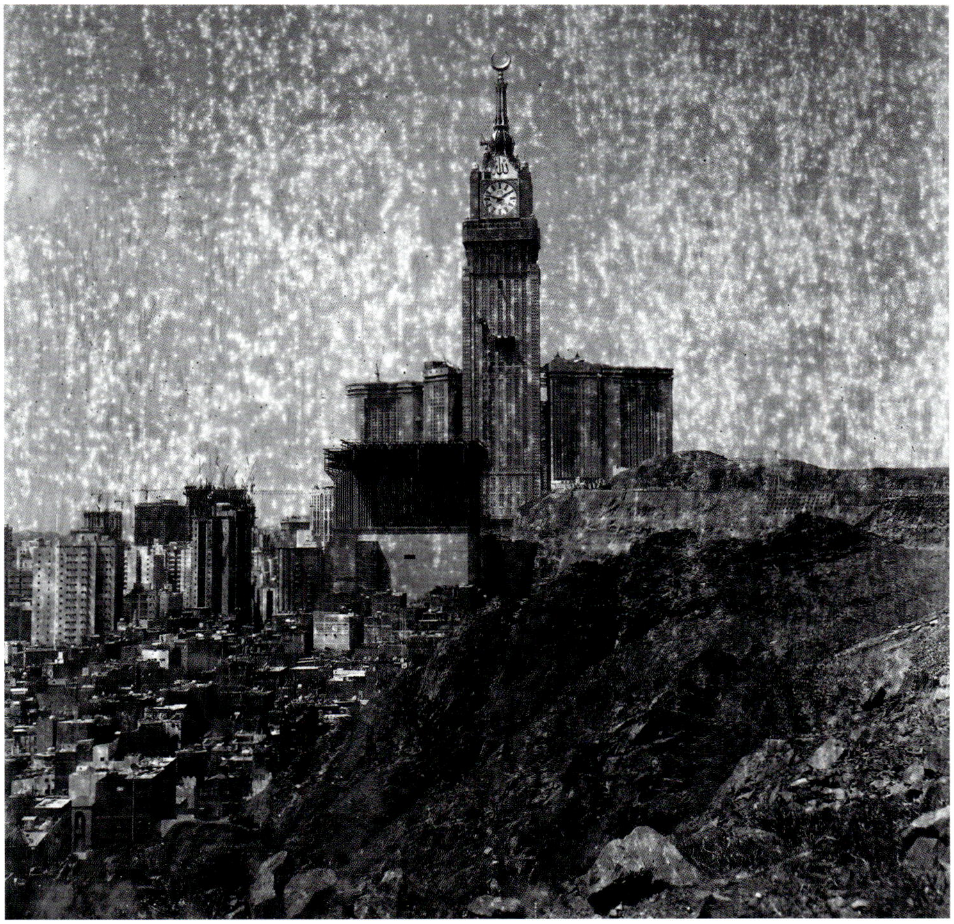

the construction of *ribats* to house poor pilgrims—and *maristans* to care for them in the holy cities. For centuries, Egyptian rulers also had a major portion of the wheat crop from Upper Egypt sent to Hijaz in order to provide for the subsistence of pilgrims.

Despite these sustained efforts, and despite the "funds" (*surra*) that served to remunerate the Bedouin chiefs of the territories through which the caravans traveled to buy the protection of tribes, the pilgrimage routes remained consistently dangerous until the early twentieth century.

The Egyptian caravan took a little over one month to proceed from its Cairo departure point to Mecca, traveling more than 1,600 kilometers with thirty-one stopover points. The journey was slightly longer from Damascus: it took twenty-seven days to Medina and ten more to reach Mecca. More precisely, "Reaching Mecca from Damascus, in Syria, takes 490 hours by foot," estimated Turkish pilgrim Mehmet Edib Mehmet, author of the 1682 *Journey from Constantinople to Mecca*. Long segments of these two routes, like the one between Baghdad and Mecca, were completely devoid of water supplies, taxing the needs represented by such a great number of people and animals. It is thus

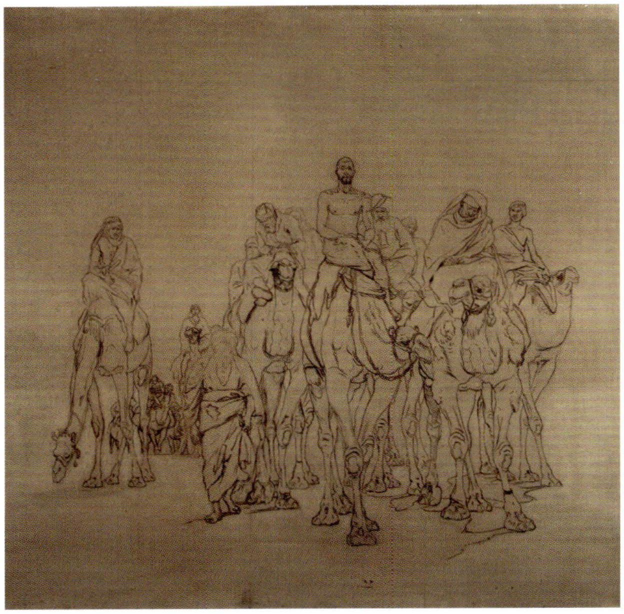

understandable that the issue of water so preoccupied pilgrims without exception, even becoming an obsession. This is why the problem raised by the "scarcity of water"—in Mehmet Edib Mehmet's specific terms—recurs with astonishing regularity in the writings of all pilgrims, from the Andalusian Ibn Jubayr to the North African Ibn Battuta, and with even more prevalence in the accounts of European travelers.

When the direct route from Baghdad to Mecca was impassable, as happened frequently, pilgrims were forced to go through Damascus, which meant a journey of "seven hundred and eighteen hours by foot," as experienced by the Kashmiri nobleman Abd al-Karim in 1741, who went so far as to specify, in his *Journey from India to Mecca*, that "equipped with a European watch, I verified this count myself."

The pilgrims leaving from Constantinople faced an even longer journey. "The number of days between their departure from Constantinople to their arrival in this capital comes to two hundred and sixty," according to Mehmet Edib Mehmet. Of course, this duration included the stays in Mecca and Medina, as well as the long stopover in the city of Damascus both on the way and on the return.

It is not difficult to grasp the exhaustion of many pilgrims, who were often of an advanced age, commented numerous authors: "The trek through the desert is extremely tiring, especially given the great distance between stops," wrote the Kashmiri Abd al-Karim. He went on to note somberly that "one of our travel companions perished of consumption in the Khaybar desert, and we buried him in the sand."

According to this same author, "The fatigue would be bearable, were it not for the ongoing worries inspired by the Bedouin Arabs." This constant fear of bandits coming to rob or kill him equaled and perhaps even surpassed that of thirst, and appears to have plagued the pilgrims. Of all the inconveniences of the journey, this climate of permanent insecurity seems to have been the most difficult to tolerate. In his *Journey*, for example, in speaking of one stopover or another, Mehmet Edib Mehmet often mentions that "this route, too, is infested with thieves." During another stopover, three days to the south of the city of Maan, he refers to an event from a few years prior, laconically writing that "this is where the caravan was plundered."

"We could not cross the desert without a strong escort," Abd al-Karim continues in his account, "and even when the caravan is best guarded, and there are a great many pilgrims, anyone who strays a bit is inevitably plundered by the Bedouin Arabs, who harass them incessantly. Despite the presence of the group, despite "all of the precautions taken by the *Amir al-Hajj*—the commander of the caravan—these wretches could not be stopped from robbing and assassinating three of our travel companions with three pistol shots," the Kashmiri wrote, extremely distressed by the Bedouins' wrongdoings. He devoted about five pages of his short volume to recounting "some of their most common tricks" in minute detail—notably, how one of his friends was robbed of a belt containing 300 gold pieces as he prayed. "Another day," he continued, "the Bey of Shiraz was performing his ablutions, when an Arab

Léon Belly
Pilgrims Going to Mecca, 1861
Wash drawing and ink mounted on canvas
88 × 92 cm
Musée Quai Branly – Jacques Chirac, Paris
© R.M.N.– Grand Palais

Léon Belly
Pilgrims Going to Mecca, 1861
Oil on canvas
161 × 242 cm
Musée d'Orsay, Paris
© R.M.N.–Grand Palais

This painting was exhibited at the Paris Salon of 1861 and was awarded the "First class" medal. In *Pilgrims Going to Mecca*, Léon Belly superbly depicts the furnace heat of the desert and its sun-bleached sky.

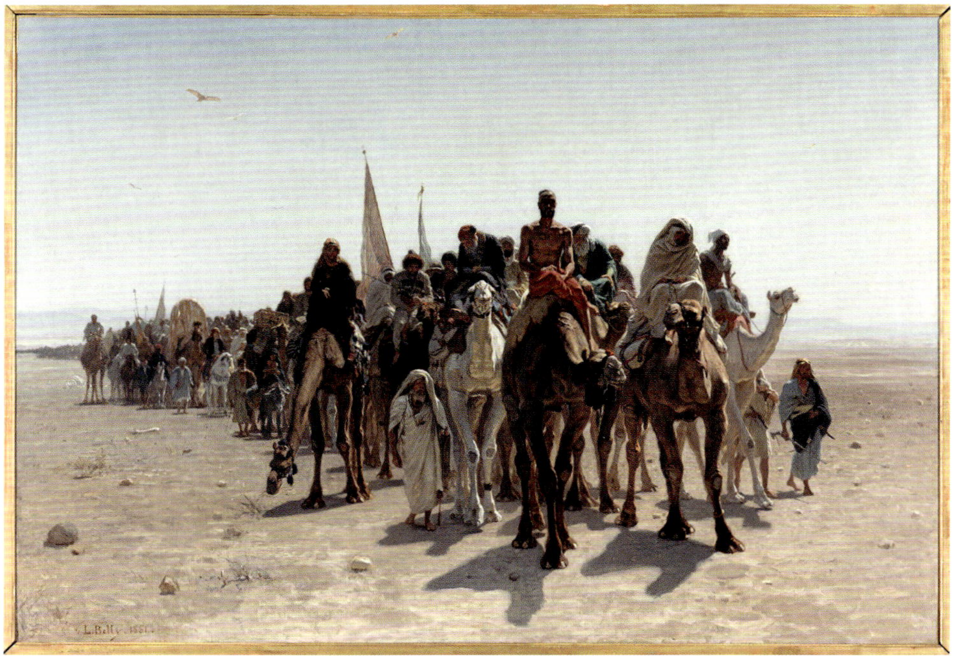

Anonymous
The March of the Grand Caravan from Cairo to Mecca
From *A New and Complete System of Geography: containing a full, accurate, authentic and interesting account and description of Europe, Asia, Africa, and America, as consisting of continents, islands, oceans, seas, rivers, lakes, promontories, capes, bays, peninsulas, isthmuses, gulphs &c. with their strange ceremonies, customs, amusements, &c. &c.*
Charles Theodore Middleton
London, 1777
Engraving
Nasser D. Khalili Collection of Islamic Art, London

The pilgrimage caravans were highly organized and were described and functioned as "small moving cities". They were led by the *Amir al-hajj*, who was responsible for the security of the pilgrims. He had officers, soldiers, medics, cooks, Bedouin guides, judges, imams, muezzins, and pilgrims under his authority. Due to the insecurity of the roads and frequent attacks by bandits, caravans traveled in long processions.

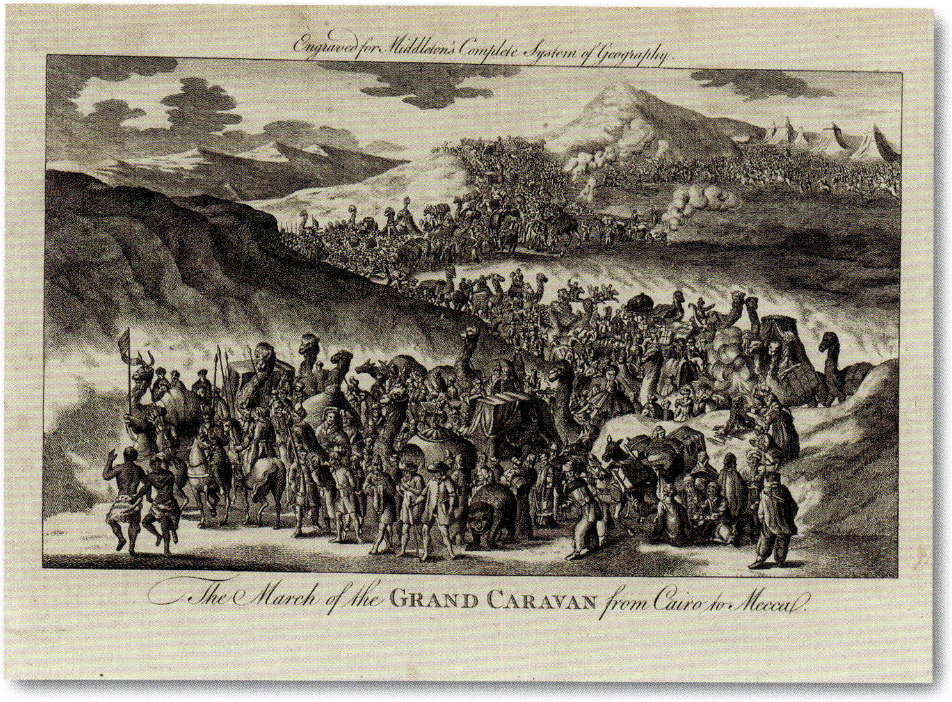

Anonymous
Pilgrims en route to Mecca
From *The Illustrated London News*, Nov. 1, 1879
Nasser D. Khalili Collection of Islamic Art, London

At the rear of the caravan procession were camels equipped with litters that were provided for richer pilgrims to protect them from the sun and the heat. Some poor pilgrims ran short of supplies during the travel and were obliged to interrupt their journey to work. They resumed their journey afterwards.

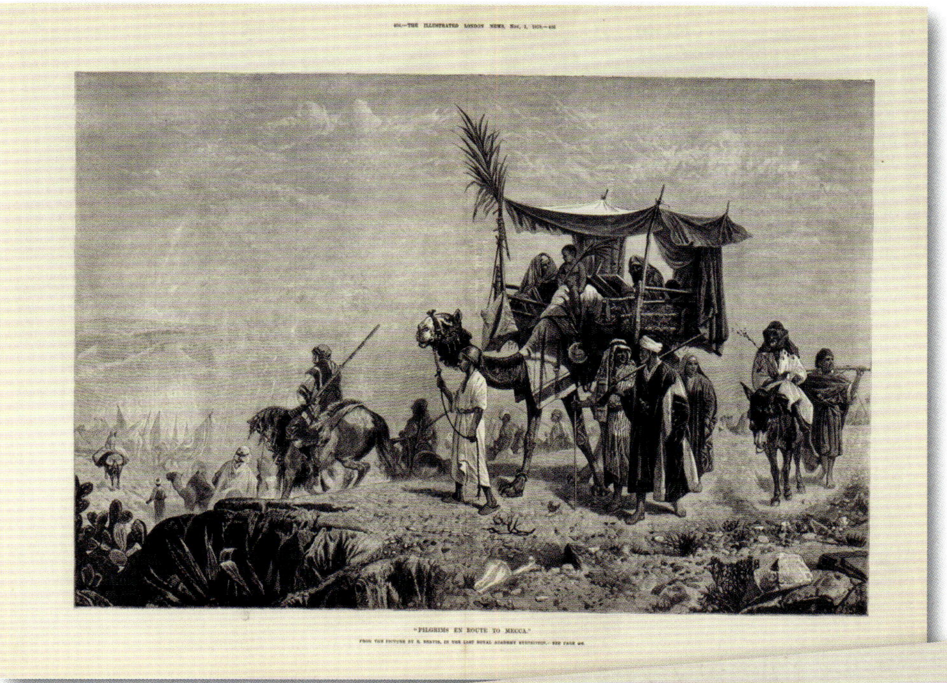

Charles Cousen
The Mecca Caravan, c. 1849
Tinted steel engraving
From *Forty Days in the Desert*
William Henry Bartlett
A. Hall & Co., London, 1856
Nasser D. Khalili Collection of Islamic Art, London

The *Amir al-Hajj* of the caravan stops at every town he passes through so that the persons who wish to go to the pilgrimage can join the caravan.

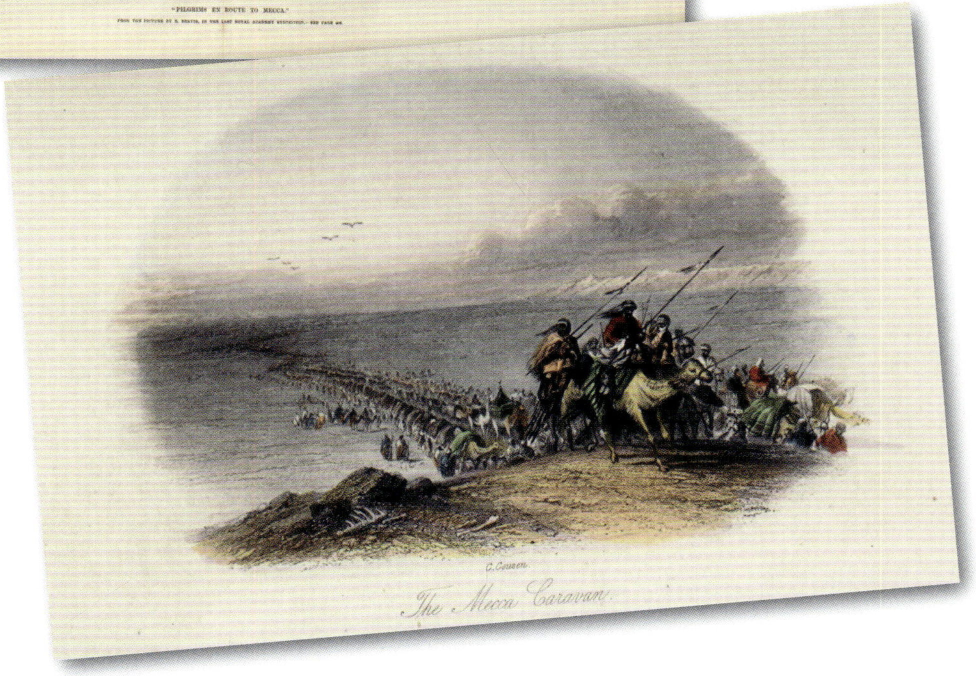

IN THE CENTER OF THE CENTER

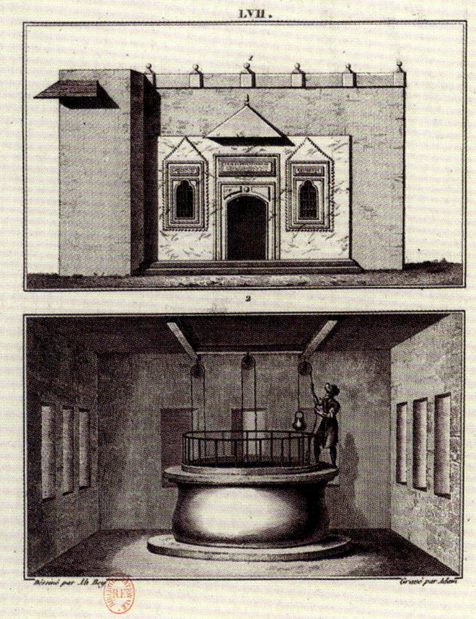

Hailing from Balkh, in Khorasan, the renowned scholar, poet, and traveler, Naser Khosrow, provided an account of the four pilgrimages that he made to Mecca in the first half of the eleventh century, in a celebrated work entitled *Safarnama* (Book of Travels). In these pages, he provided a highly detailed description of the interior of the Ka'ba.
The door of the Ka'ba "is toward the east," Khosrow wrote, and is positioned "higher than the courtyard," so that "a man of average height, when standing on tiptoe, can reach the threshold." Two large silver rings are attached to the door "too high for anyone to reach," and "two other silver rings, smaller than the first two, are attached much lower so that anyone could reach them." In these "lower rings is fitted a large silver lock," in such a way that "the doors cannot be opened without removing it". To enter the edifice, therefore, "a wooden staircase wide enough for ten men abreast has been constructed so that one can get inside the house of God."
The edifice is empty, as we know, entirely empty. It contains only "three pillars positioned within, which support the ceiling and are made of teak. They are all square, except for one, which is round," Naser Khosrow observed. Nevertheless, the ground, walls, and ceiling were decorated according to the orders of various Abbasid caliphs of Baghdad, one of whom had sent one hundred blocks of white marble which were sawed on site by artisans from Iraq in order to redo the floor slabs; another caliph had the walls covered "to the ceiling with slabs of coloured marble adorned with arabesques"; and another one had affixed to the wall "on the western side, six silver *mihrabs*, each of which is as tall as a man."
Here also could be found "two planks affixed to the wall with silver nails, which are said to come from Noah's ark," Naser Khosrow noted, further explaining to his readers, "In the northern section of the Kaaba there is an elongated slab of red marble on the floor: it is said that the Prophet used to pray here, and all who have learned about this feature strive to conduct their prayers on this same spot."
What Naser Khosrow failed to specify in his work were the days of opening, when pilgrims and visitors could gain access to the inside of the Ka'ba. This absence of information is most likely due to the fact that at the time, the edifice was open quite frequently. The Andalusian traveler

Ali Bey El Abbassi
Main façade of the little house where the Zamzam well is located and view of the Zamzam well
Plate n° 57 in *Atlas: Illustrations de Voyages d'Ali Bey el Abbassi en Afrique et en Asie pendant les années 1803, 1804, 1805, 1806 et 1807*
Didot, Paris, 1816
Bibliothèque nationale de France

At the time of Ali Bey El Abbassi's voyage to Mecca, the Zamzam well had a building over it, roofed by a large cupola and a small dome. Men were employed without pay to draw the water. The men roped leather buckets to a small wheel; one would come up full while the other went down empty. Richard Burton, who took the pilgrimage in 1853, described the taste of Zamzam water as being nauseously bitter, while John Keane, whose pilgrimage occurred in 1877, wrote that he performed his ablutions with the water of Zamzam. He also drank from it and described it as tasting like a weak solution of Epson salts and having medicinal value.

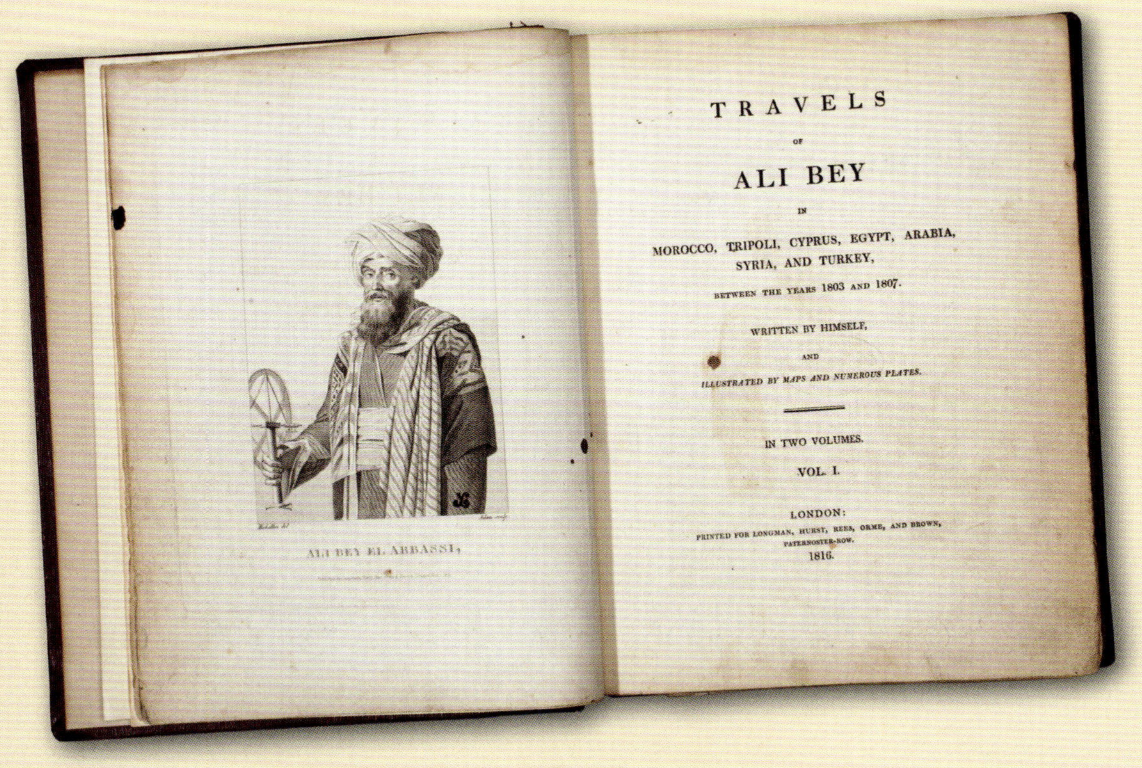

Ali Bey El Abbassi
Front page with a portrait of Ali Bey El Abbassi from *Travels of Ali Bey in Morocco, Tripoli, Cyprus, Egypt, Arabia, Syria, and Turkey, between the years 1803 and 1807*, London, 1816
Nasser D. Khalili Collection of Islamic Art, London

Ali Bey El Abbassi started his travels from Gibraltar to Tangiers, and from there he reached Tripoli, Alexandria, and then Cairo. He left Suez on December 23, 1806 on a *dhow* and arrived in Jeddah on January 13, 1807, after a terrible crossing.

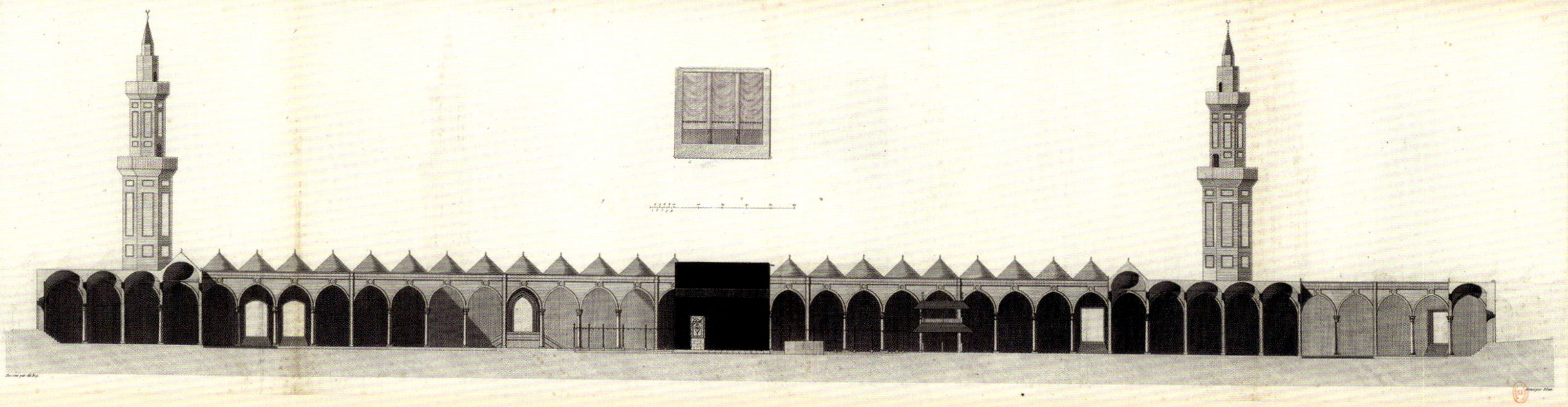

Ali Bey El Abbassi
Profile of the temple of Mecca, 1814
Plate n° 54 in *Atlas : Illustrations de Voyages d'Ali Bey el Abbassi en Afrique et en Asie pendant les années 1803, 1804, 1805, 1806 et 1807*
Paris, Imprimerie de P. Didot
Bibliothèque nationale de France

The Ka'ba, positioned in the center of the Holy Mosque of Mecca, is called *Bayt Allah* (House of God). According to the Koran, it is the first temple erected for mankind. It is enclosed within four arched colonnades or arcades. The arcades feature a row of little domes, thirty-six on the long side and twenty-four on the short side.

Ibn Jubayr, who completed the pilgrimage in 1183–84, and was in Mecca about a century and half after Naser Khosrow, observed that the door of the Ka'ba was open every Tuesday and Friday, and every day during the month of *Rajab*. Some 140 years later, when the North African geographer Ibn Battuta completed his first of many pilgrimages, he wrote, "The noble door is open every Friday following prayers; it is also open on the day of the Prophet's birthday."
Ibn Battuta then narrated the sequence of the visit, after the positioning in front of the door of "a platform similar to a pulpit, with steps and wooden legs, where four pulleys are adjusted to help the platform roll." As the custodianship of the Ka'ba was entrusted to the Bani Sheyba family, of the Quraysh tribe, it was thus the head of this family who opened the door, "holding the illustrious key in his hand". Ibn Battuta continued: "He afterwards kissed the illustrious threshold, and entered the sanctuary alone," where he performed prayers and prostrations, the interior of the Ka'ba being the only place in the world where these could be performed in all directions. He was then joined by the other members of the Bani Sheyba family present there, who in turn performed their devotions. Next, "the door was opened, and people rushed to enter." As could be observed, opening days gradually grew less frequent over time. And the visit to the interior of the Ka'ba, which the vast majority of pilgrims, in the past, had the right to claim, became a privilege. This is how at the end of the seventeenth century, the Turkish pilgrim Mehmet Edib Mehmet counted the edifice's opening days: "The temple opens at various times of the year: on the *Ashura* (the tenth day of the month of *Muharram*), from morning till noon; on the twentieth day of the same month, for the sweeping of the temple; the Ka'ba is also open on the day of the Prophet's birth; on the day of the commemoration of the Prophet's Night Journey and Ascension; on the first Friday of the month of *Rajab* and on the first Friday of the month of *Ramadan*."
A century later, Carsten Niebuhr, the sole survivor of the famous Danish expedition to Arabia, wrote: "Save extraordinary circumstances, the door of the Ka'ba opens only twice a year; and even then, only eminent figures are allowed to enter, and those in their entourage." It was thus quite natural that the pilgrim Ali Bey El Abbassi subsequently took pride in having been invited to visit the interior of the Ka'ba twice in the space of a few days, although these respects were due to a princely title that was in all likelihood usurped.
He wrote: "Saturday the 24th of January 1807, the 15th of the month *Doulkaada*, in the year 1221 of the *Hegira*, they opened the door of the Ka'ba, which is shut the whole year, except three days." He explained that one day was reserved for men, the second for women, and the third was "appropriated to washing and purifying the house of God."
"I was carried to the temple on those days," Ali Bey recounts, "and as there was an immense crowd, they made me sit down in a kind of bower belonging to the guard, which is composed of black eunuchs." Then, "The crowd being a little diminished, my guide and some guards conveyed me to the Ka'ba. They took great care to make me put my right foot upon the first step in ascending."
Having accomplished his devotions within the edifice, Ali Bey continued his account: "I kissed the silver key of the Ka'ba, which one of the Scherif's children, who was seated in an armchair, held for that purpose. After this I withdrew, escorted by the eunuchs, who made their way through the crowd, by striking people with their fists."
Between this first visit—during which he was treated with a certain consideration, in particular, with guards who ensured that his path was clear—and the second, Ali Bey was received by the Sherif of Mecca, which allowed him to be invited to the inside of the temple once again, and to participate in the purification rituals held there. Ali Bey indeed participated alongside the sherif in the operation that first consisted in washing the floor, with water mixed with rosewater, small brushes in each hand: "I began my duty by sweeping with both hands, with an

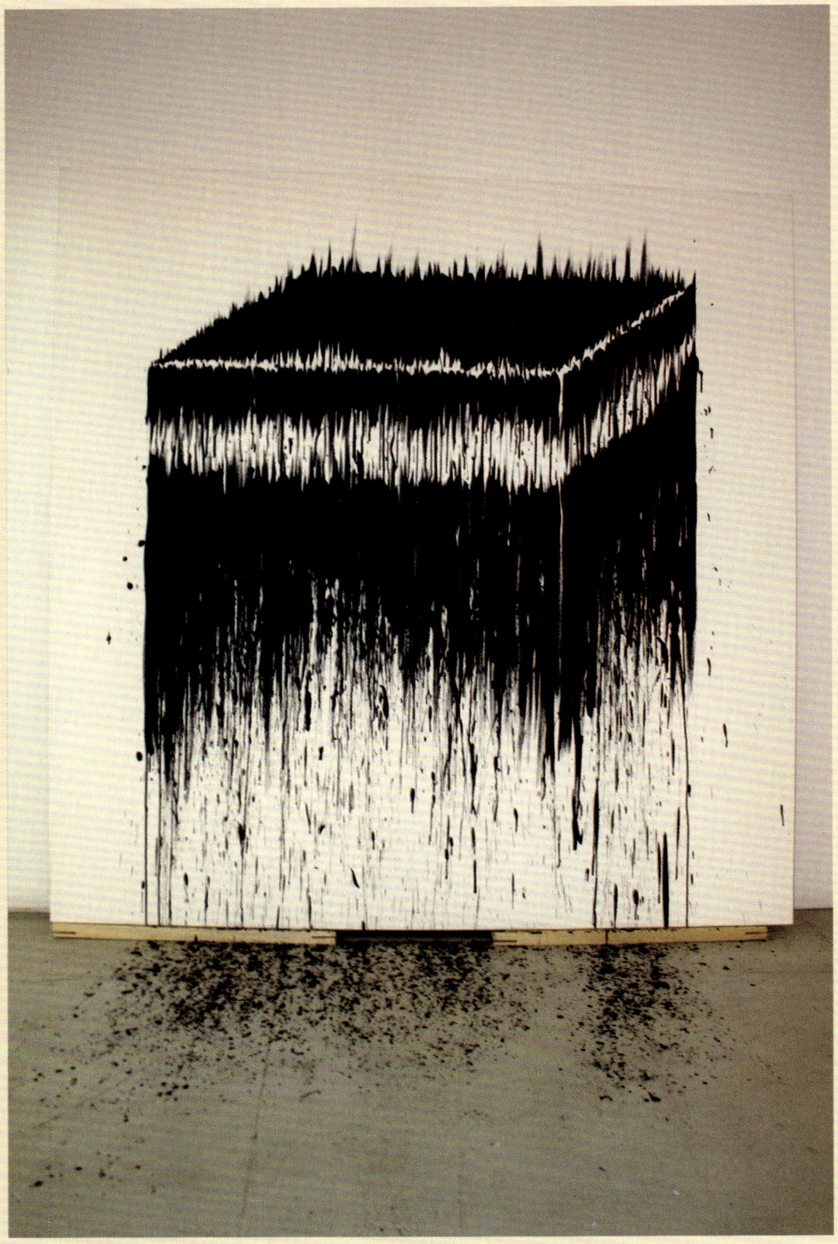

Kader Attia
Black Cube II, 2005
Oil on canvas
200 × 200 cm
Courtesy of the artist and of
Nagel Draxler Gallery, Berlin

This painting is one of a series that Kader Attia created, inspired by the form of the Ka'ba, considered the center of all things. The tenth-century historian Al-Mas'udi wrote: *"The Ka'ba with respect to the inhabited parts of the world is like the center of a circle with respect to the circle itself. All regions face the Ka'ba, surrounding it as a circle surrounds its center, and each region faces a particular part of the Ka'ba."*

ardent faith, although the floor was quite clean, and polished like glass." He was then handed a small carafe of this water used for washing, which he was careful to drink and sprinkle on himself, "for although this water is very dirty, it is a benediction of God."

The cleaning efforts continued: "They gave me afterwards a silver cup, filled with a paste made of the sawdust of sandalwood, kneaded with essence of roses that I spread upon the lower part of the wall, which was encrusted with marble, under the tapestry which covered the walls and the roof; and also a large piece of aloe wood, which I burned in a large chafing-dish, to perfume the hall." Once this undertaking was completed, the sherif proclaimed Ali Bey "Khaddem-Beit Allah el Haram, or Servant of the blessed House of God," and Ali Bey concluded, "and I received the congratulations of all the assistants".

All the while, the crowd of pilgrims, amassed before the edifice, piously collected the water that had been used for washing the floor, "which, flowing out at a hole under the door," they sprinkled on themselves, while the guards, "with cups, and with their hands, threw it in quantities over them". Similarly, the small brushes that had been used to clean the floor were broken into a thousand pieces that were thrown to the pilgrims, who then preserved these bits as sacred relics.

The Italian Giovanni Finati, who came to Arabia with Muhammad Ali's army and wound up in Mecca hardly ten years after Ali Bey, provided a whole new story of the same circumstances. In his account, no more crowds of pilgrims jostled to penetrate the temple's interior.

"Once in the year, and once only, this holy of holies is opened, and as there is then nothing to prevent admission, it appears surprising at first to see so few who are willing to go into the interior, and especially since this act is supposed to have great efficacy in the remission of all past sins," Finati noted. For him, this lack of haste was explained by the implicit conditions binding those who entered the house of God, until the end of their days. Such a person, he wrote, would "exercise no gainful trade or pursuit, nor to work for his livelihood in any way whatever; and next he must submit patiently to all offences and injuries, and must never again touch anything that is impure or unholy."

"Since it is not easy to find in the same person sufficient competence, with sufficient forbearance at the same time, and self-denial to fulfill these conditions," Finati continued, "the number who enter the Ka'ba is very limited." On this subject, other arguments were provided by British explorer Richard Burton, who completed the pilgrimage in 1853. Burton also observed that "there is no lack of pilgrims who refuse to penetrate within the house of God." But Burton attributed this abstention to much more pragmatic motives: for him, pilgrims did not enter the Ka'ba "because, among other obligations, this entails those of never again walking barefoot, never

Ahmad Nawar
Hijaz: Inspiration from the Holy Land (5), 2016
Flo-master ink drawing
26.5 × 41.5 cm
Courtesy of the artist
and of Hafez Gallery, Jeddah

This drawing represents the ceremony of the changing of the *kiswa* of the Ka'ba, which takes place every year on the ninth day of the month of *Dhu al-Hijjah* (the last month of the Arab calendar), the day pilgrims leave for the plains of Mount Arafat.

Kazuyoshi Nomachi
The Ka'ba
Courtesy of the artist

The Ka'ba is covered with a heavy black cloth, named the *kiswa*. According to Ibn Jubayr, the *kiswa* is usually made up of thirty-four pieces. The black ground is damasked with shiny black chevron designs and Koranic verses.

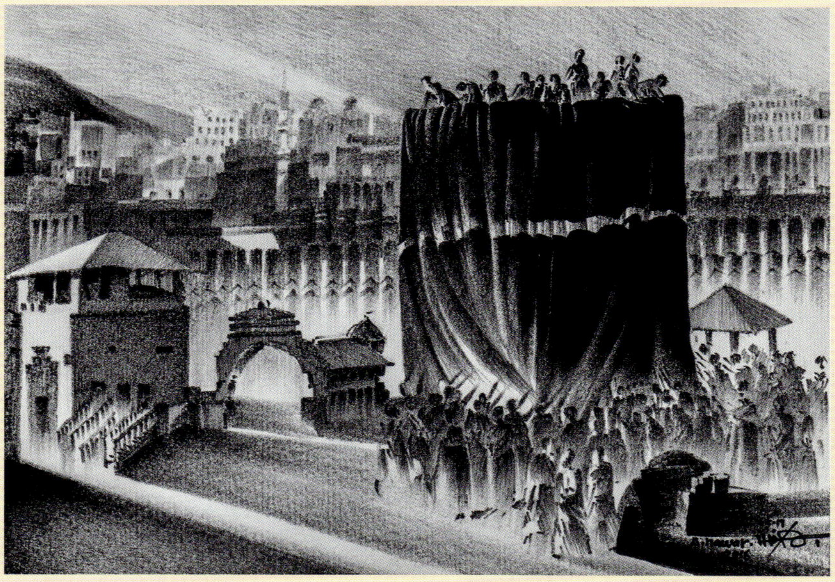

again handling fire with one's fingers, never again telling lies."
In his book, entitled *Six months in the Hijaz* in which he recounts his stay in the city in 1877–78, another Brit, John Fryer Keane, also addresses this subject of the interior of the Ka'ba , and seems to have been strongly impressed by the recommendation made to him, before he entered, to never look up: "Nobody is supposed to look up while in this chamber," he wrote. "You are told that the only man who ever did so was struck blind."
It is unknown whether the intrepid traveler attempted to peer into the upper part of the chamber. It seems that he respected the order, and refrained from doing so: "All that could be see were the hangings of the walls and ceiling embroidered in gold," he assured, "and the three pillars supporting the flat roof." He also stated that "the place was very dark".

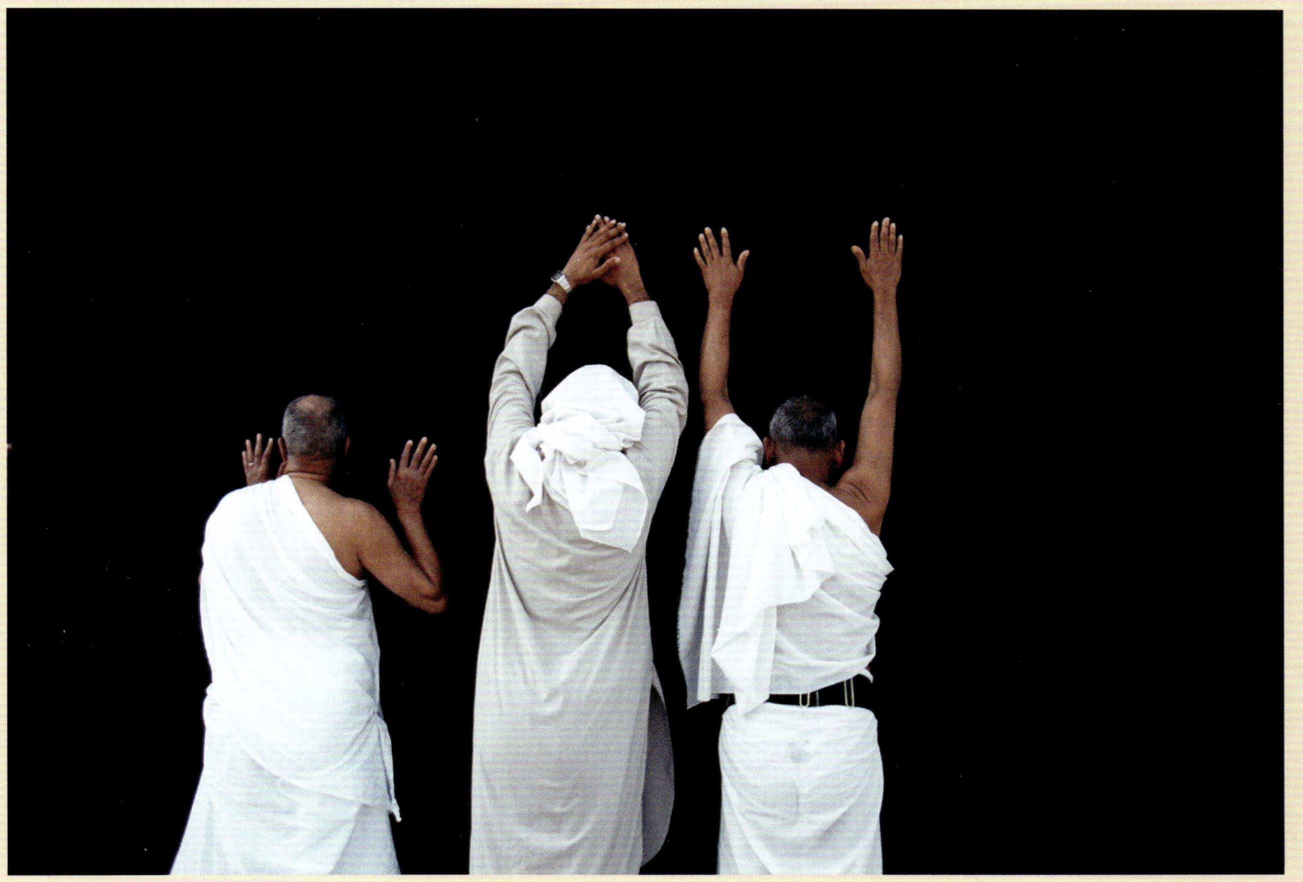

came up behind him, seized his ewer and vanished!" Abd al-Karim concluded this enlightening passage by attesting to the fact that "Bedouins run with great speed!"

Like an ever-shifting city, the substantial size of the caravan was both its strength and its weakness. It was so immense that it was difficult to capture, although it could be entirely devastated, as the Turkish pilgrim recounts. While strictly organized, with its sections, its armed guards, and its hierarchy, it was impossible to fully protect every part, every minute of the day. It was thus frequently subjected to raids and attacks. On various occasions, Ludovico di Varthema had to face different attacks from Bedouin hordes, which he was able to dispel with the other Mameluke escorts (cf. chapter *The Flora of the Peninsula*). These violent incursions consistently left a few victims in their wake among the pilgrims, and it was necessary to conduct a makeshift burial in the middle of the desert before setting off again.

All of the pilgrims who traveled with these caravans were struck by the strict scheduling and rigorous order that was characteristic of them. The young Englishman Joseph Pitts—who fell into slavery and accompanied his North African master on the pilgrimage in about 1685—was able to observe the Egyptian caravan's orderly progress following the first day, when the pilgrims seemed to have trouble understanding where they should stay and what was expected of them. "After everyone hath taken his place in the Caravan, they orderly and peaceably keep the same place. They travel four camels in breast, and the camels are all tied one after the other, like as in Teams. The whole Company is called a caravan, which is divided into several *cottors*, each *cottor* hath its name, and consists, it may be, of several thousand camels, and they move one *cottor* after another like distinct troops. In the head of each *cottor* is some

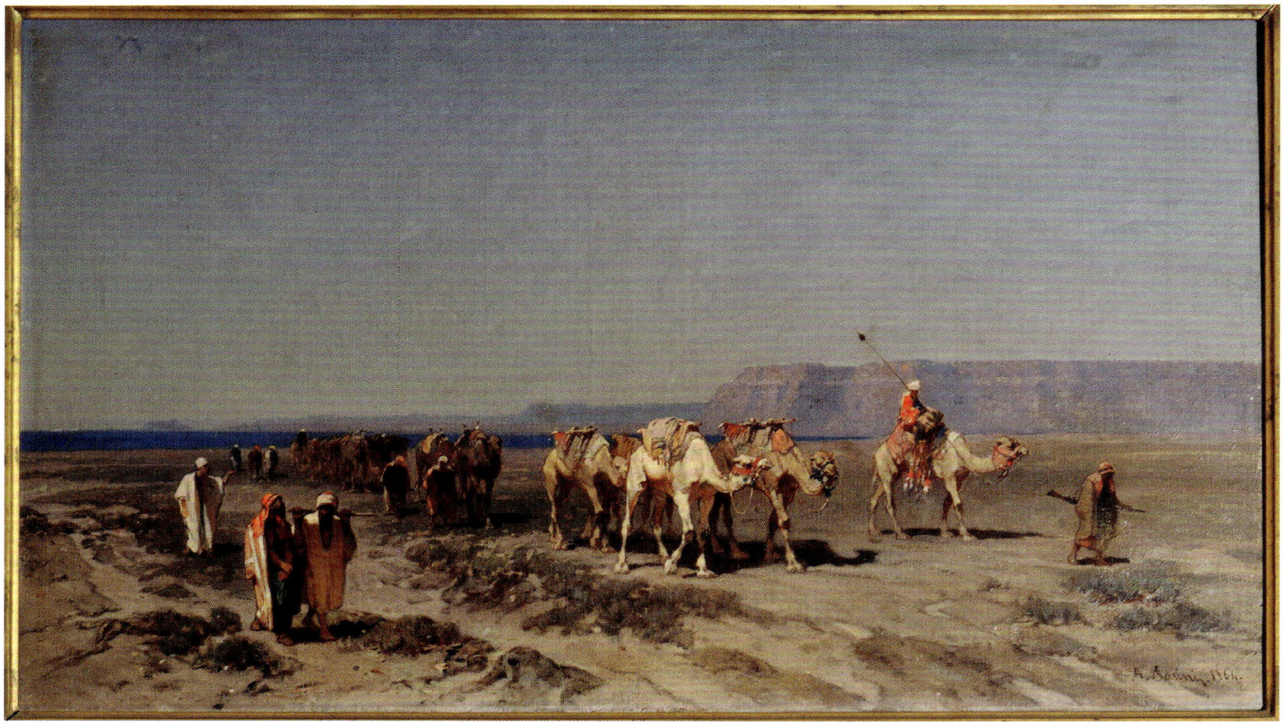

Alberto Pasini
Caravan alongside the Red Sea, 1864
Oil on canvas
37 × 64 cm
Courtesy of Palazzo Pitti, Galleria d'Arte moderna, Florence

In this painting, Pasini depicts the long and monotonous procession of a caravan of camels with its drivers. The oppressive sun is blazing in this immense and perfectly mastered scene. The man who is walking ahead of the caravan is weakened; his back is bent and his head bowed. The camels are unbridled so that they can eat whatever they can find on their route in this sterile land.

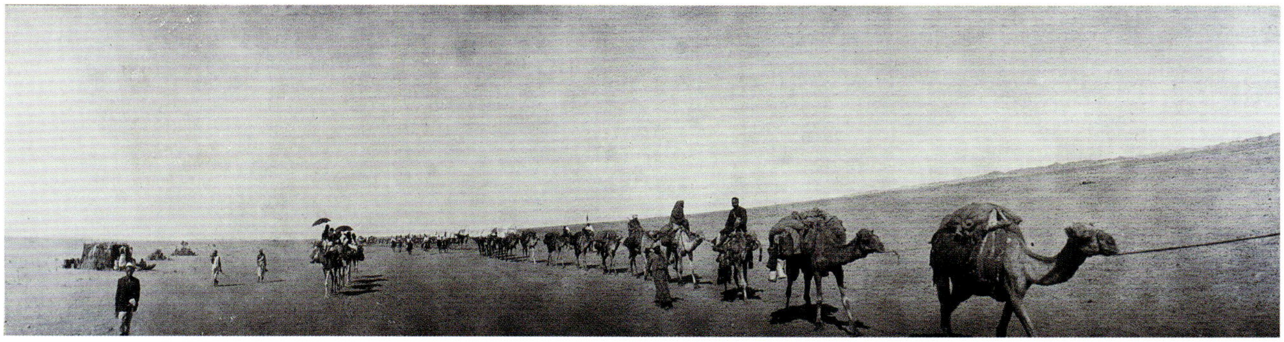

Khedive Abbas Hilmi II
Caravan of Pilgrims, 1909
Courtesy of Durham University, Durham

Traditionally the caravans departed on a Friday after the noon prayer. Poorer pilgrims could not afford to rent a camel and were obliged to make the trip by foot.

Jan Peeters
View of Mecca, 1665
Pen and brown ink, with brush and gray wash, over traces of black chalk, on cream-laid paper, laid down on board
20 × 41.3 cm
The Leonora Hall Gurley Memorial Collection
The Art Institute of Chicago/Art Resource New York

Jules Gervais-Courtellemont wrote in *Mon Voyage à La Mecque*: "*Beyond the East known to Europeans, there, far into the heart of Arabia, within the mystery of the deep deserts that surround it, the Holy City of Islam, Makkah, hides at the bottom of a wild valley hemmed in by two steep and barren mountain ranges. It seems that nature itself wanted to be an accomplice to the Muslim Faith in hiding from the profane these jealously guarded secrets.*"

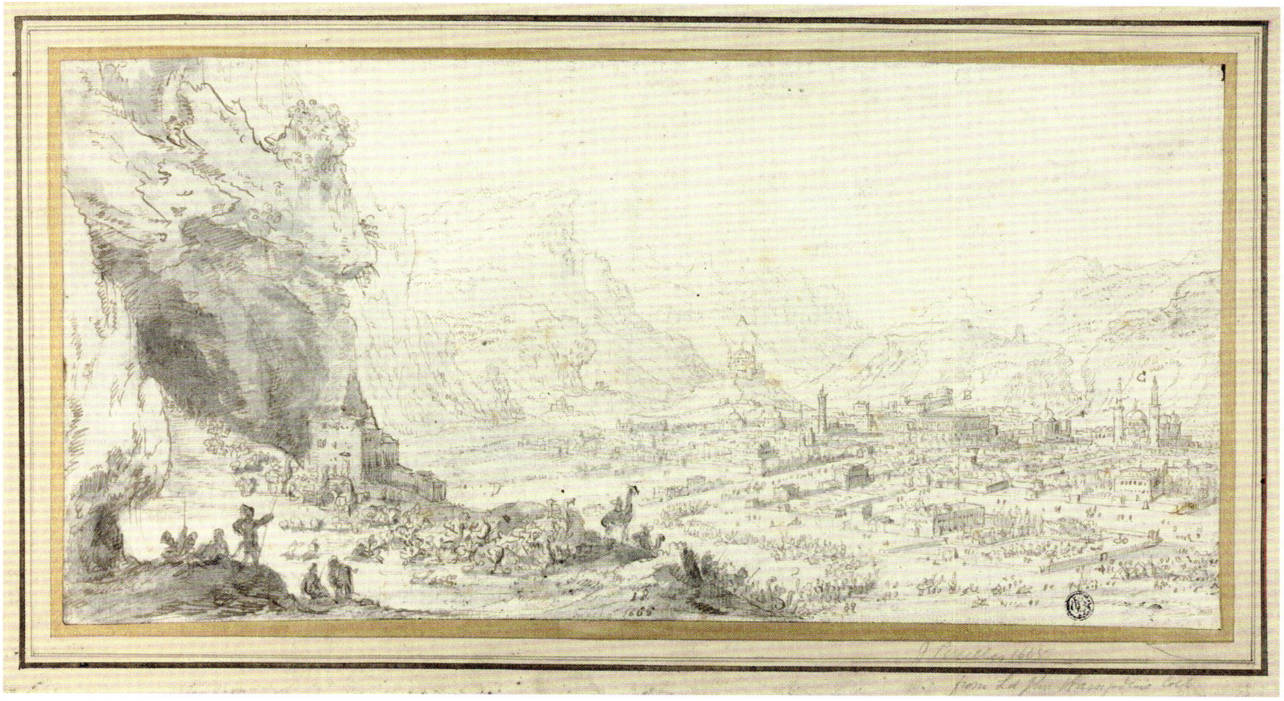

great gentleman or officer, who is carried on a thing like an horse-litter, born by two camels. If the said gentleman or officer hath a wife with him, she is carried in another of the same."

The Kashmiri Abd al-Karim made similar observations: "Everyone must keep to their assigned position in the caravan and not stray from this during the whole journey." Burckhardt in turn provided a similar description of the Syrian caravan in 1814: "On the route, a troop of horsemen ride in front, and another in the rear, to bring up the stragglers. The different parties of *hadjis*, distinguished by their provinces or towns, keep close together; and each knows its never-varying station in the caravan, which is determined by the geographical proximity of the place from whence it comes. When they encamp, the same order is constantly observed; thus the people from Aleppo always encamp close by those of Homs, &c. This regulation is very necessary to prevent disorder in night-marches."

These are more or less the same words used by Pitts: "Were it not for such organisation, one could

Gaspar Bouttats
Mecha in Arabia, 1672
From a collection of fourteen etchings (Views from Arabia, Judea, Chaldea, Syria, Jerusalem, Antiochia, Aleppo, Mecca, etc.)
Etching after Jan Peeters
11.8 × 26.3 cm
Published by Jacobus Peeters, Antwerp
Nasser D. Khalili Collection of Islamic Art, London

This is an imagined scene of a caravan arriving in Mecca with the principal sites marked in Dutch in the bottom of the image. Joseph Pitts, in *A true and faithful account of the religion & manners of the Mohametans in which is a particular relation of their pilgrimage to Mecca*, described Mecca in the late seventeenth century as a town in a valley surrounded by many little hills with no walls or gates.

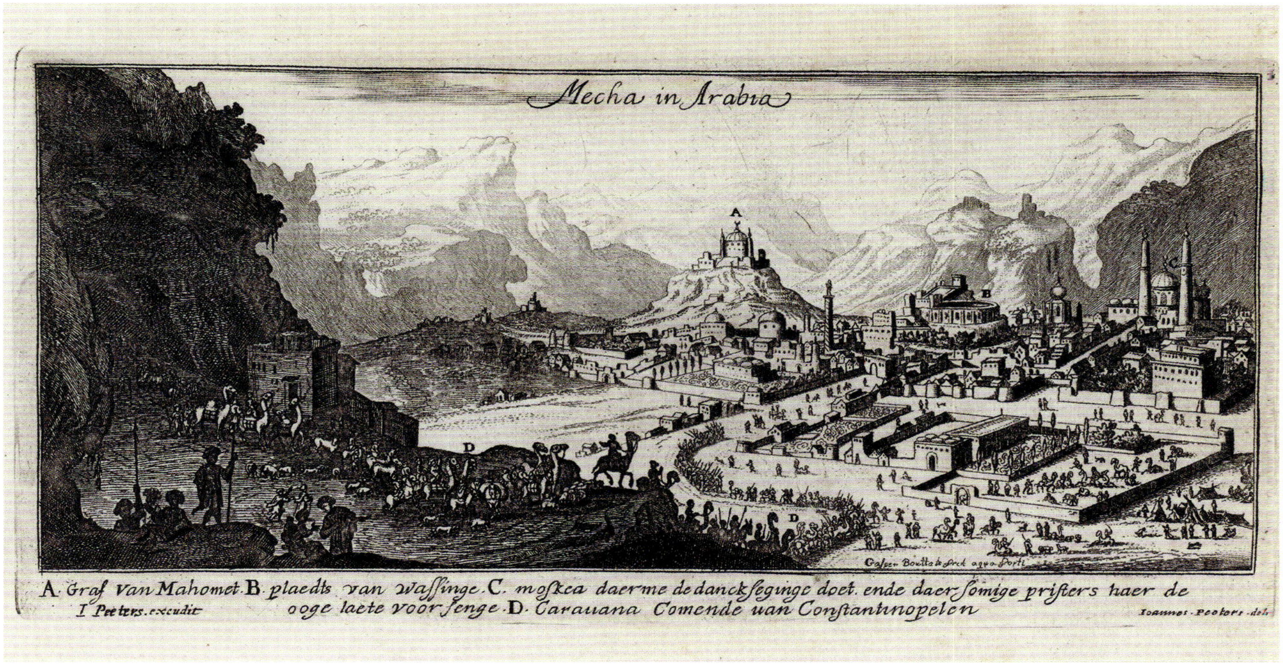

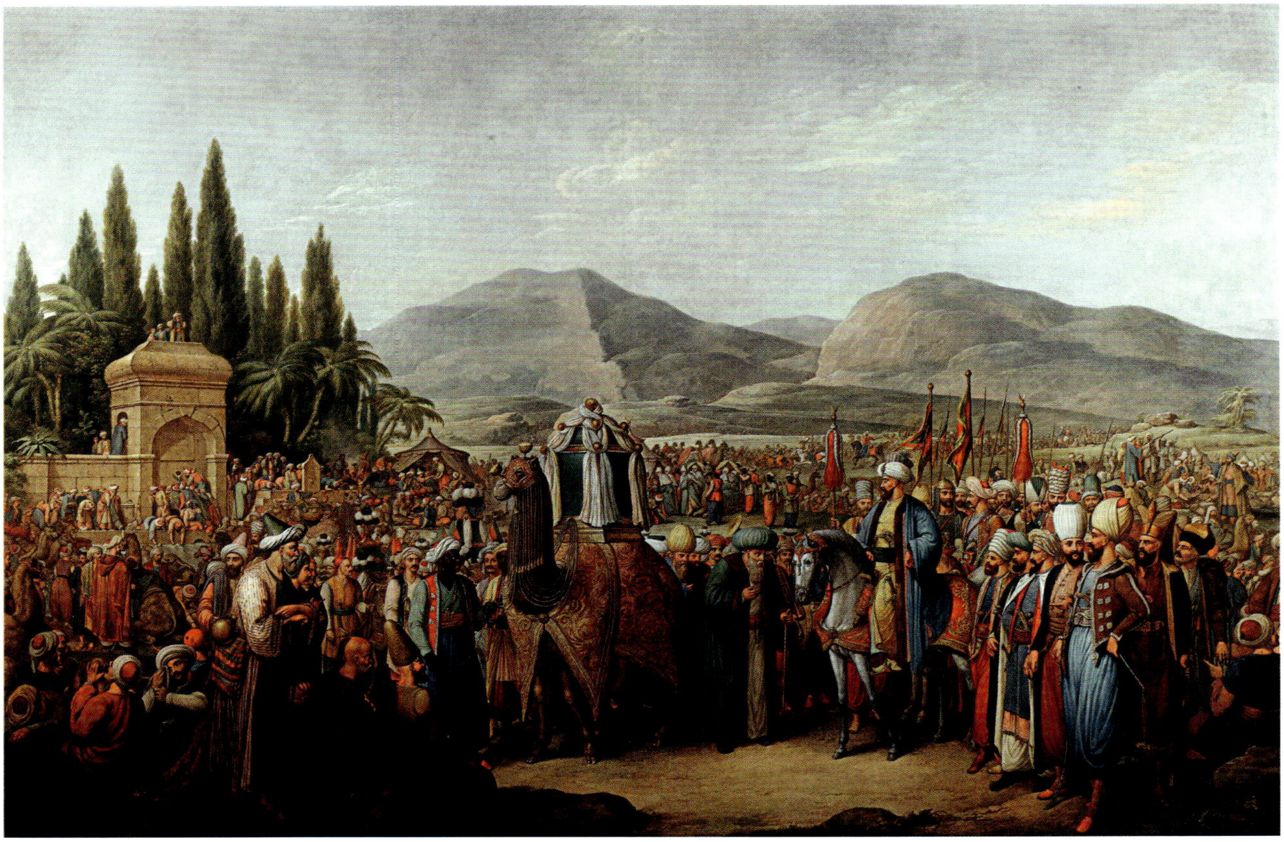

Georg Emanuel Opitz
The arrival of the mahmal *at an oasis en route to Mecca*, c. 1805–25
Oil on canvas
165.5 × 253 cm
Orientalist Museum, Doha
Image courtesy of Sotheby's

This spectacular painting reproduces with minute details the life and composition of the caravan accompanying the *mahmal*. The scene features a meeting between an ottoman official and a religious leader. On the right side of the painting are Ottoman dignitaries and soldiers carrying banners. In the center of the painting, a lavishly decorated camel carries the *mahmal*. On the top left side of the painting, a muezzin is calling for the prayer while some pilgrims are performing the ablutions and women are dismounting their camels.

imagine the confusion that would reign among a multitude such as that." The young Englishman continues: "They have lamps to give light by night belonging to each *cottor*, which are carried on the tops of long poles to direct the *hagges* their march. These lamps are differently figured and numbered, so that every one knows by the lamps which *cottor* he belongs to. These lamps are also carried by day, not lighted, but yet, by the figure and number of them the *hagges* are directed to what *cottor* they belong, as soldiers are by their colours where to rendez-vous. And without such directions it would be impossible to avoid confusion in such a vast number of people."

Most of the journey took place at night, as Burckhardt also specifies: "At night, torches are lighted, and the daily distance is usually performed between three o'clock in the afternoon, and an hour or two after sunrise on the following day." The caravan thus moved forward, day after day, night after night, along its long path, as described by Joseph Pitts: "In the head of every *cottor*, the camel hath two bells hanging one on each side, the sound of which may be heard a great way off. Some other of the camels have bells about their neck, some about their legs, which make a pleasant noise, and makes the journey pass away delightfully."

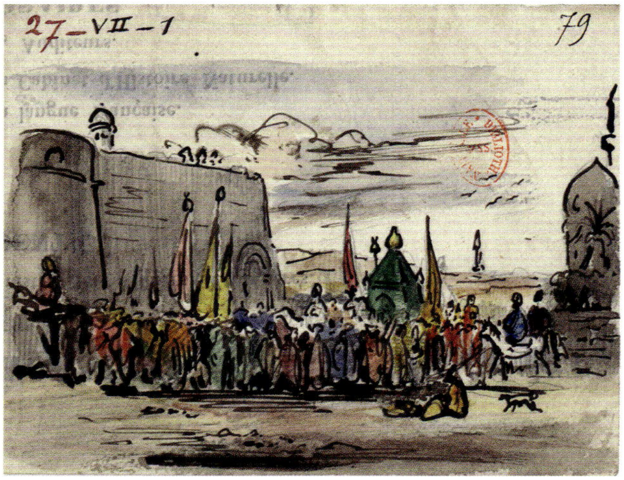

Émile Prisse d'Avennes
Return of the caravan conveying the sacred carpet of Mecca, 1858
Watercolor on paper
29 × 39 cm
Bibliothèque nationale de France, département des manuscrits

The *mahmal* was brought back by the returning caravan. The oldest surviving *mahmal* is yellow and is conserved in the museum of the Topkapi Palace in Istanbul. It was made for the mameluke sultan Qansuh al-Ghouri (d. 1516).

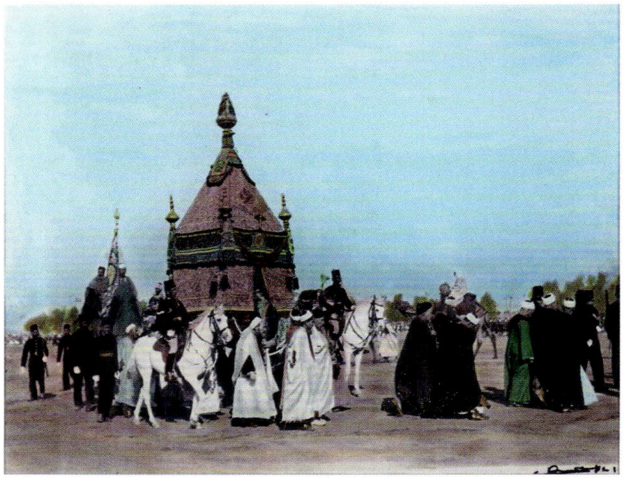

Osama Esid
The mahmal *in procession*, 2017
Silver gelatine print, hand-colored black-and-white photograph with Chinese transparent pigments
Courtesy of the artist and Hafez Gallery, Jeddah

For centuries, the Egyptian caravan carried with it every year the new *kiswa* (the brocade cloth covering the Ka'ba). Caravans from Damascus and Cairo continued to convey *mahmals* to Mecca until after World War I.

Prosper Marilhat
The departure of the sacred carpet to Mecca, first half of the nineteenth century
Oil on paper mounted on canvas
46.5 × 35.2 cm
Musée des Beaux-Arts de Lyon

In *A Photographer on the Hajj: The Travels of Muhammad 'Ali Effendi Sa'udi*, Farid Kioumgi and Robert Graham reported that Muhammad Sa'udi, who in 1904 accompanied the Amir al-Hajj, General Ibrahim Rif'at Pasha, and acted as assistant to the treasurer of the *mahmal*, wrote that the treasury chest then contained 23,000 Egyptian pounds, a sum equivalent to US $5 million today. The caravan included around 1,800 pilgrims and more than 500 soldiers. The plan was to spend about sixty days in Arabia, where they had to hire camels, acquire camp followers, pay bribes, and retain a war chest to pay off hostile tribes.

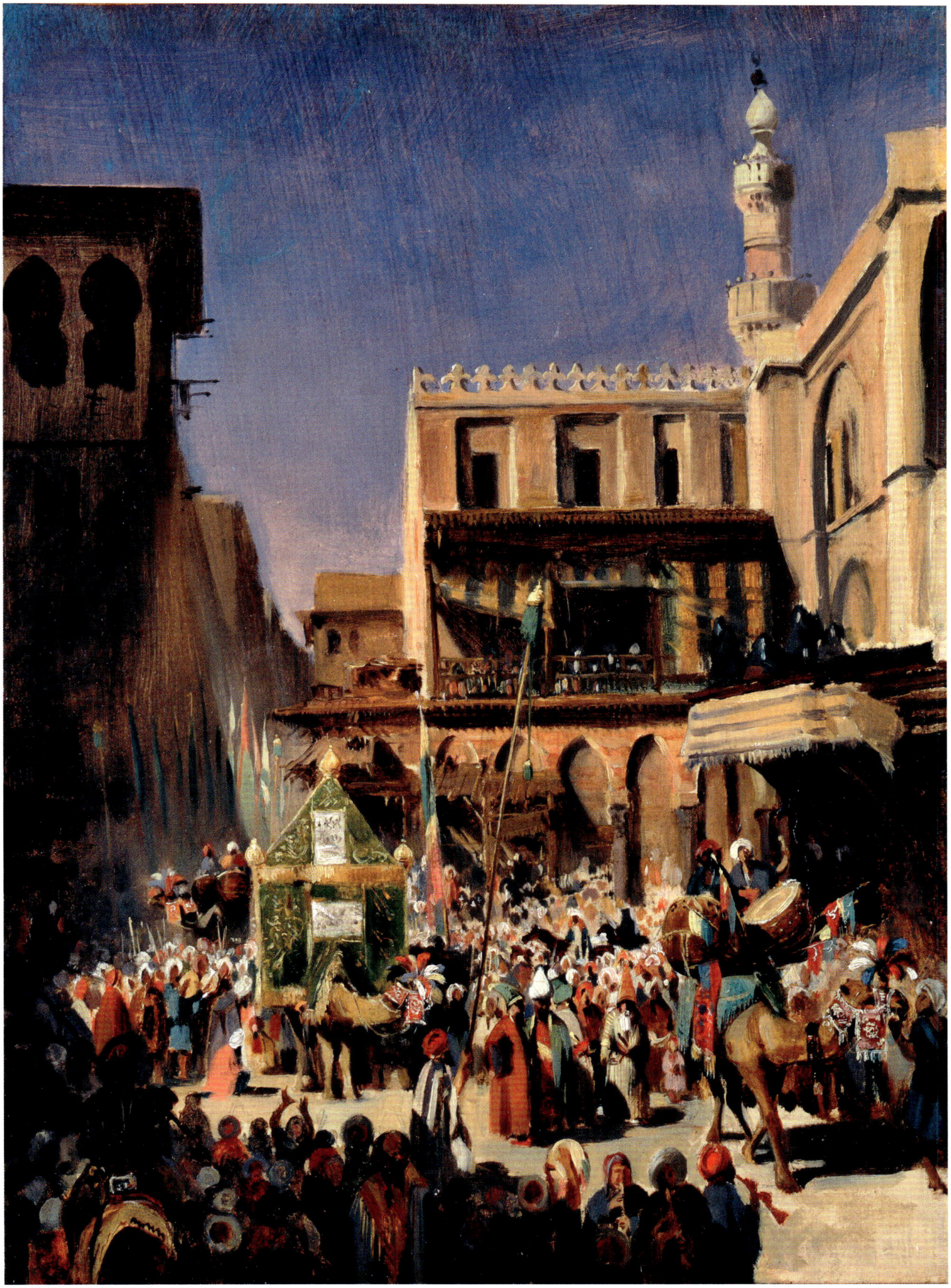

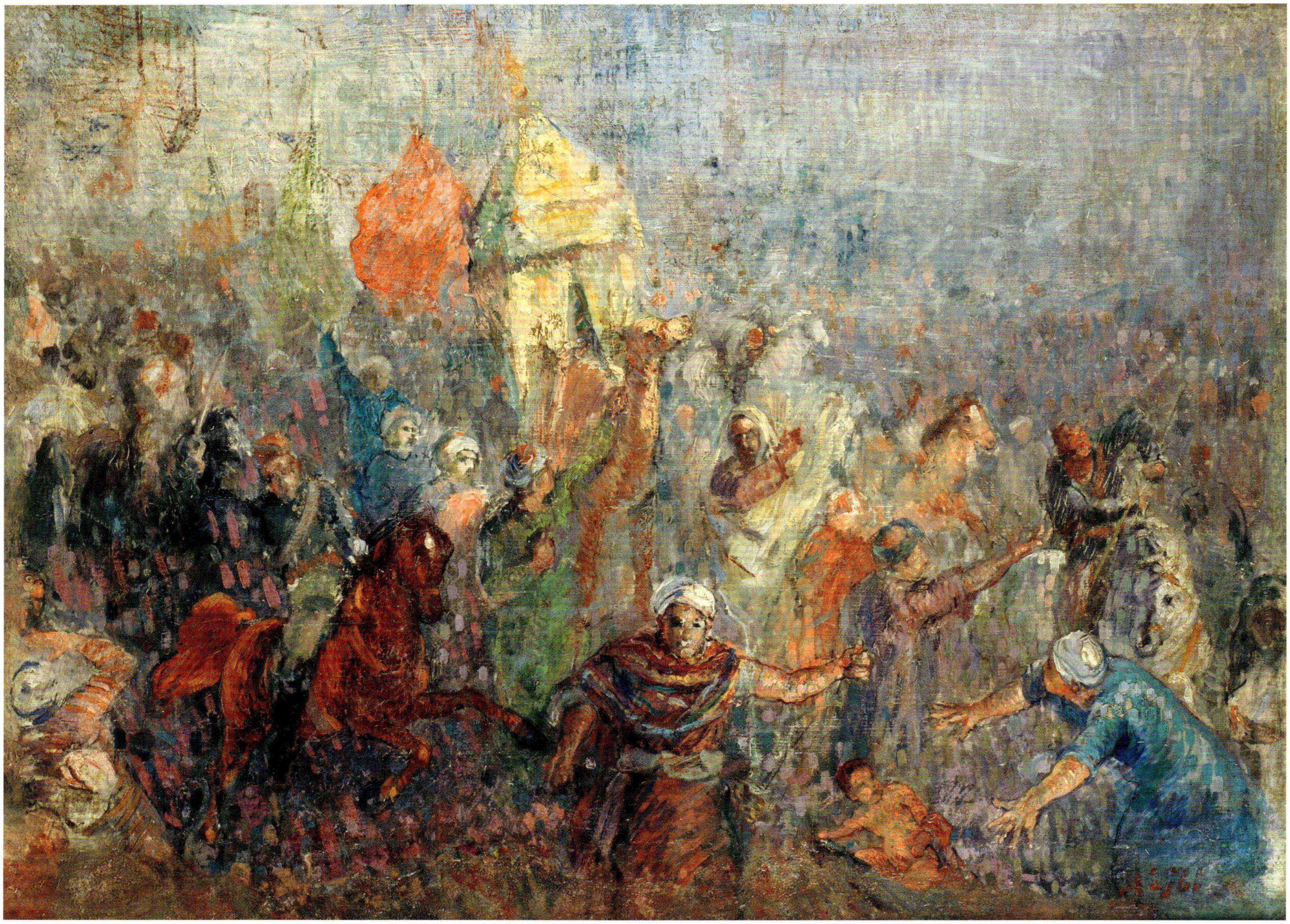

Mohamed Naghi
The mahmal *in procession*, first half of the twentieth century
Oil on canvas
65 × 92 cm
Ramzi Dalloul Collection, Beirut

From the thirteenth century onward, the Egyptian caravan was accompanied by a *mahmal*, a wooden litter sumptuously decorated, about four feet high, and covered with red or green cloth. It had lots of bells hanging on its front side, which made a great jangling at every step of the camel.

Postcard
The arrival in Mecca of the caravan carrying the "suré"
Autograph postcard inscribed in French, dated March 14, 1911
Nasser D. Khalili Collection of Islamic Art, London

Abu Subhi Al-Tinawi
The mahmal, second half of the twentieth century
Reverse glass painting
60 × 70 cm
Private collection, Damascus

The technique of reverse glass painting was developed 600 years ago in Europe. In the foreground of this painting, a dromedary carrying the *mahmal* is followed by a second dromedary transporting the standard bearer. The medallion in the upper left side of the painting features the bust of the governor of Damascus. The caravan arriving from Damascus conveyed with its *mahmal* the new *kiswa*, required for the tomb of the Prophet.

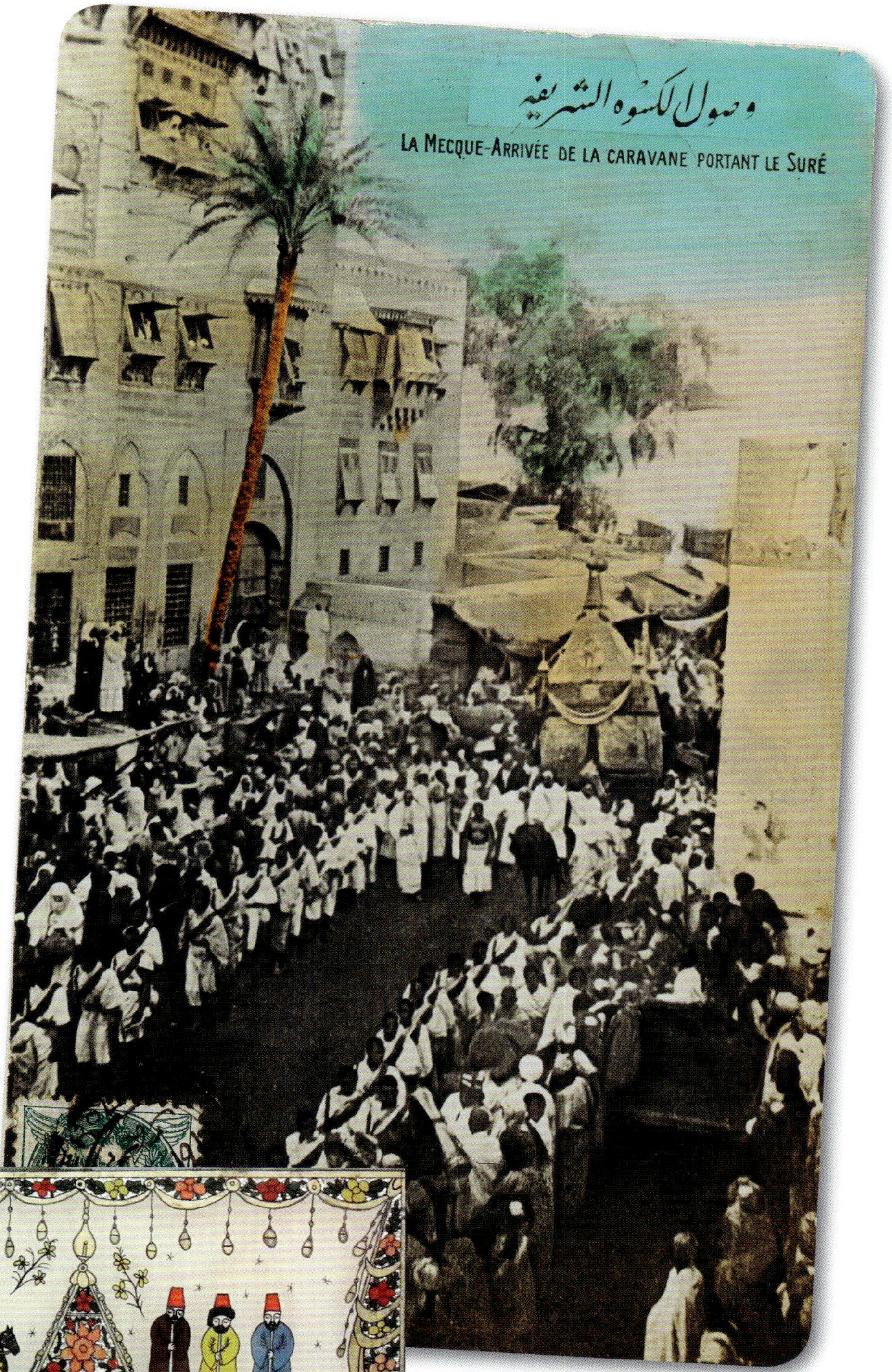

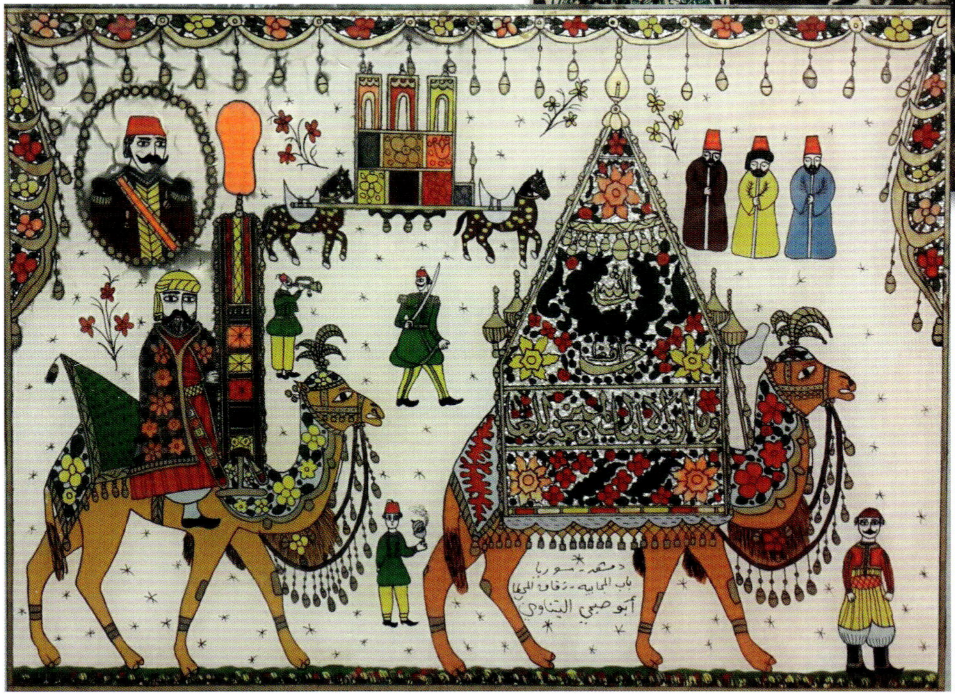

Like Joseph Pitts, Abd al-Karim appreciated these songs and lights: "The journey is also pleasant, with the great many lights spread throughout the caravan forming a wandering illumination. Each camel carries a lamp; the song of their drivers delights the pilgrims and enlivens the animals."

In these conditions, pilgrims could simply drift along. According to Burckhardt: "The *hadjis* usually contract for the journey with a *mekowem*, one who speculates in the furnishing of camels and provisions to the Hajj. From twenty to thirty pilgrims are under the care of the same *mekowem*, who has his tents and servants, and save the *hadjis* from all fatigue and trouble on the road: their tent, coffee, water, breakfast, and dinner are prepared for them, and they need not take the slightest trouble about packing and loading. However great may be the want of provisions on the road, he must furnish his passengers with their daily meals." Of course, this convenience was only available to some of the pilgrims, as Burckhardt clarifies once again: "Those pilgrims who can travel with a litter, or on commodious camel-saddles, may sleep at night, and perform the journey with little inconvenience; but of those whom poverty induces to follow the caravan on foot, or to hire themselves as servants, many die on the road from fatigue."

With the clear exception of the desolate stretches of the route, the caravans were celebrated everywhere they went, as seen in Burckhardt's description of the caravan leaving Istanbul for Damascus: "In its passage through Anatolia and Syria, it collects pilgrims of Northern Asia, until it reaches Damascus, where it remains for several weeks. Every care is taken for the safety and convenience of the caravan; at every station caravansaries and public fountains have been constructed by former Sultans, to accommodate it on its passage, which is attended so far with continual festivities and rejoicings." Fireworks were frequently lit, and musicians sometimes joined the caravan for the duration of a stopover.

It is undoubtedly difficult to take full measure of the inconveniences and dangers that pilgrims could face over the course of the exceptional undertaking represented by the caravan pilgrimage, and the joys that they could encounter in this act. It is certain that in the

Hamra Abbas
Kaaba picture as a misprint 1, 2014
Archival pigment print mounted on Dibond
137 × 110 cm
Courtesy of the Lawrie Shabibi Gallery and the artist

Kaaba picture as a misprint is a series that explores how reorienting objects distorts how they are read. In this print, the artist breaks down the iconic image of the Ka'ba into its simplest, yet still recognizable form—two rectangles, one placed atop the other.

Hamra Abbas
Kaaba picture as a misprint 2, 2014
Archival pigment print mounted on Dibond
137 × 110 cm
Courtesy of the Lawrie Shabibi Gallery and the artist

This series, wrote Hamra Abbas, deals with the different ways in which religion may be understood and experienced—how even when undergoing the same series of events, people may mentally process events in a plethora of ways.

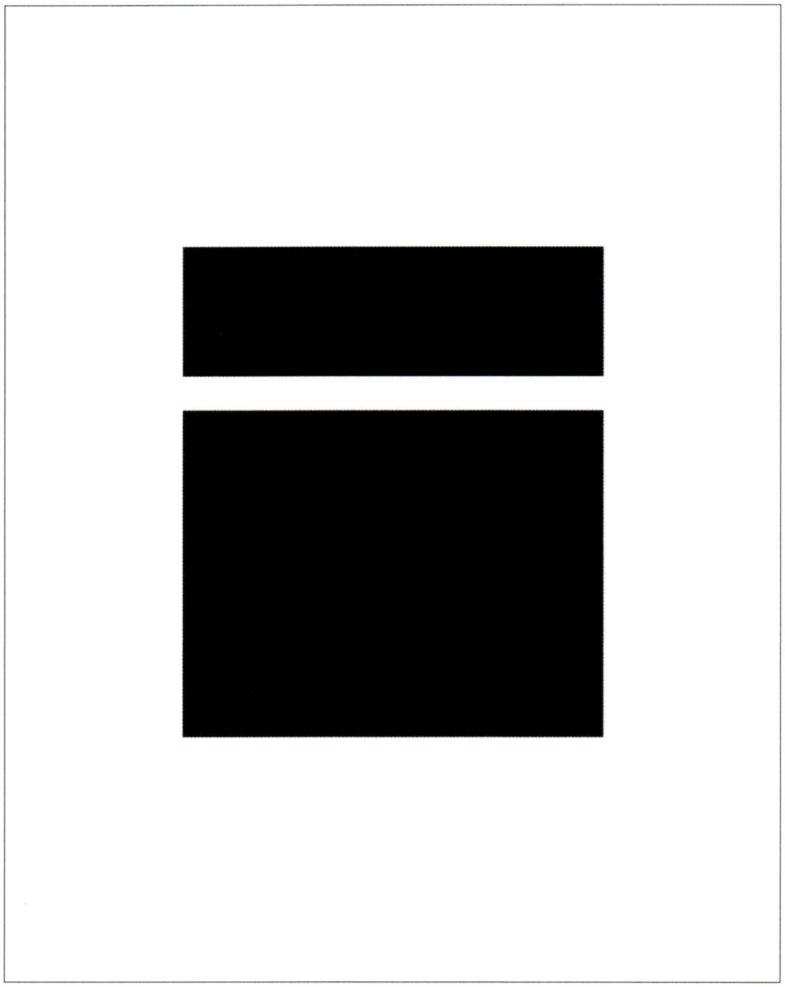

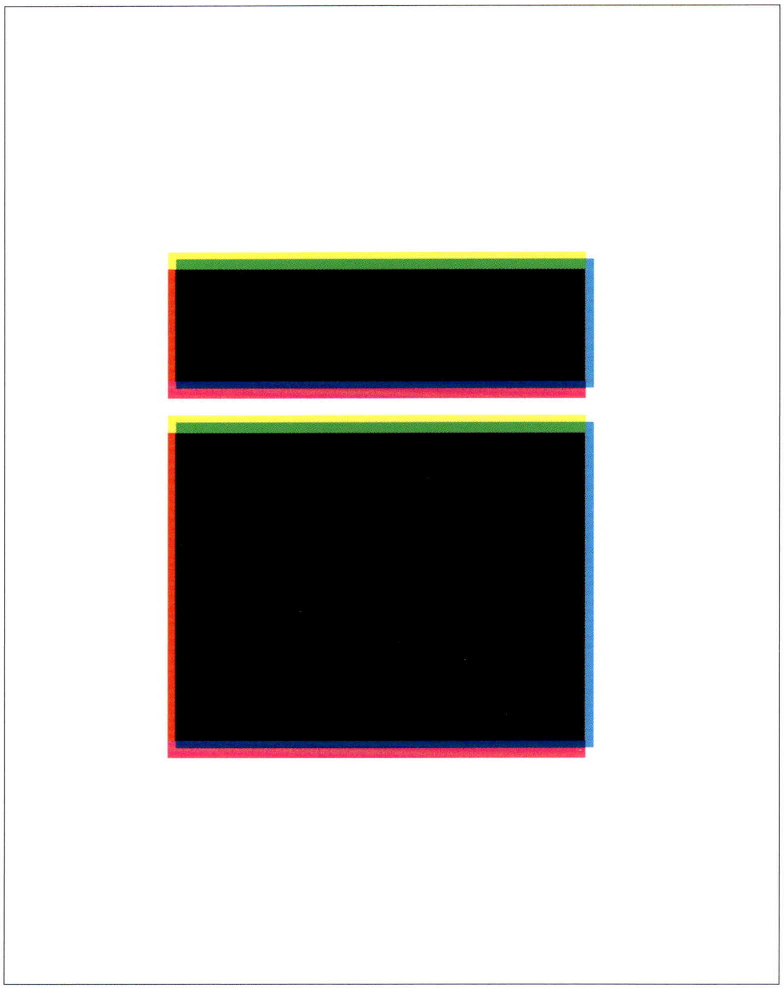

Walid Siti
From the series *The White Cube*, 2012
Charcoal and crayon on paper
71 × 100 cm
Courtesy of the artist

Walid Siti wrote: "*The White Cube is a transparent open space. It reflects the spatial and emotional life of spiritual and physical formation. Inspired by images of the pilgrimage to the Holy Place, it creates an arrangement that offers individual devotees the opportunity to feel a direct and personal closeness with a sacred site.*"

Walid Siti
From the series *The White Cube*, 2012
Charcoal on paper
71 × 100 cm
Courtesy of the artist

The White Cube evokes the perpetual motion of the pilgrims around the Ka'ba.

Walid Siti
From the series *The White Cube*, 2012
Charcoal on paper
71 × 100 cm
Courtesy of the artist

Walid Siti wrote: "*Based on the principle of the relationship between the center and the periphery,* The White Cube *shows the center as the metaphysical source of values, binding the peripheries to it by stringent physical and moral codes.*"

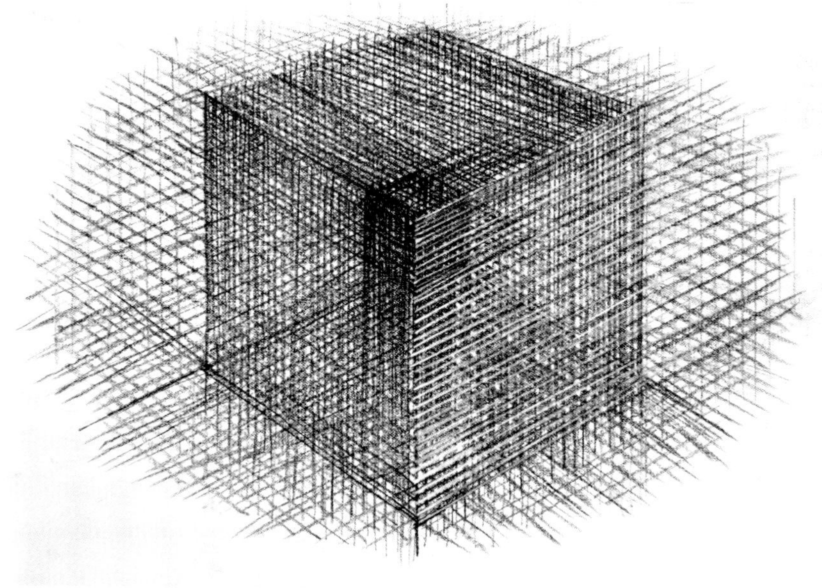

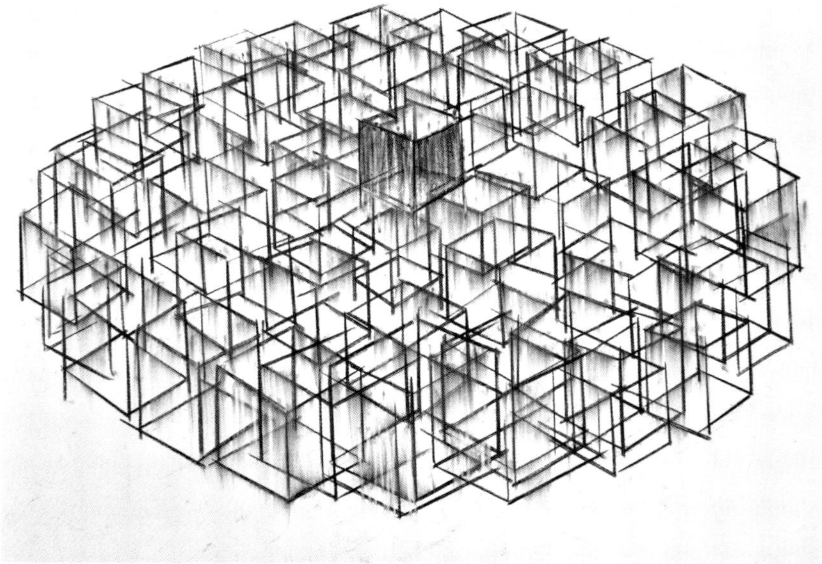

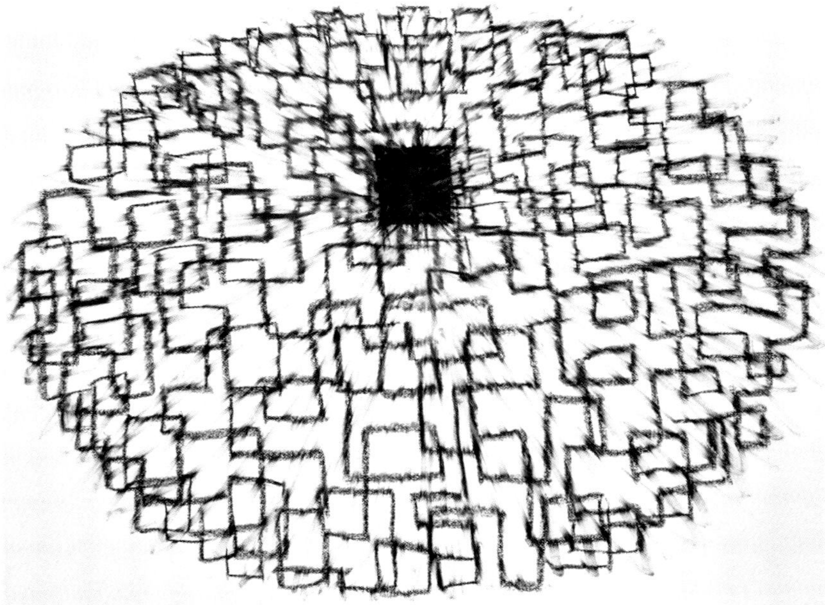

MUHAMMAD SADIC BEY

"No one before me has ever taken such photographs," noted Muhammad Sadic Bey in his diary.

The first known photographs of the holy sites are dated January 1861. They were taken by Colonel Sadic Bey. Muhammad Sadic was a man of numerous significant titles: a general, an author, and a photographer.

An Egyptian army engineer, he made three journeys to the holy cities of Mecca and Medina between 1861 and 1881, writing his observations and taking photographs. His first trip was in January 1861. He was directed to explore the area between the Red Sea port of al-Wajh and the holy city of Medina, and report back on the routes, climate, and overall circumstances of the region. During this trip, Sadic picked up the camera for the first time when he laid eyes on the walls of the city of Medina. That moment marked the first photograph taken of the holy mosque. On photographing Medina, he wrote: "I took a picture of al-Madina al-Munawwarra with the light-rays instrument which is called photography, with the cupola over the grave of the Prophet Muhammad, and I took a point from where I had a view over Medina from the roof of the arsenal (Tupkhana), as I considered to be suitable as it allowed me (to take) part of the residential part (al-Manakha) also. I took the noble cupola from inside the mosque, also with the said instrument. No one had done this before me at all," wrote Sadic Bey in *Summary of the Exploration of the Wajh-Madinah Hijaz Route and its Military Cadastral Map*.

Sadic returned to Hijaz in 1880 as the treasurer of the caravan of the Egyptian *mahmal* and once again in 1884. During his second trip, Sadic wrote that he took many photographs of Mecca, Medina, Mina, the cemetery of al-Baki' in Medina as well as that of al-Ma'ala in Mecca. Sadic created a panoramic image of the holy mosque at Mecca by joining two photographs together, giving the impression of one full image.

Photography was invented in France and Great Britain in 1839–40, and very soon it spread and began to be used in the Arab countries. Sadic owned a device known as a wet-plate

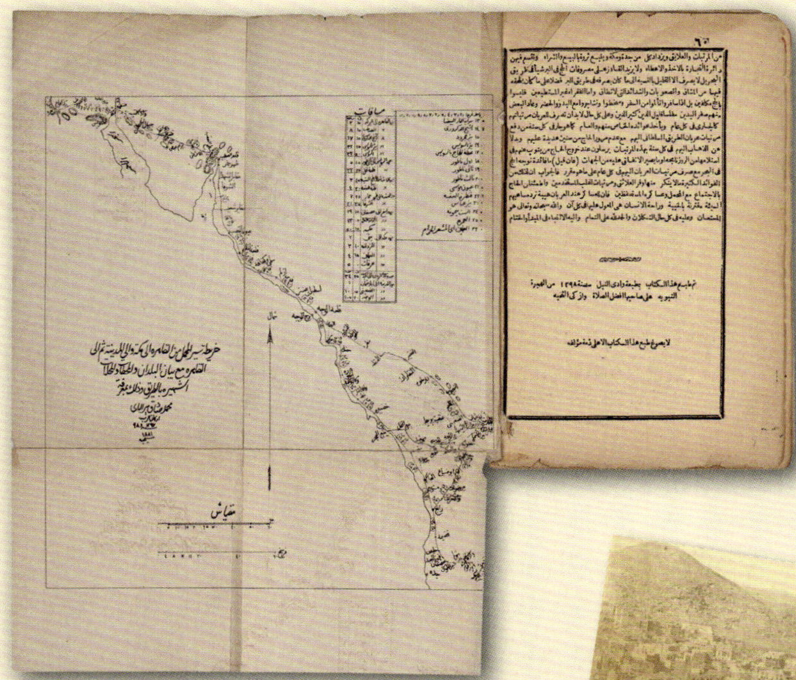

Muhammad Sadic Bey
From *Mash'al al-Mahmal, Risalah fi sir al-Hajj bira min yaum Khurujah min misr …sana 1297* (The Torch of the *mahmal*. A letter on the journey of the *mahmal* from the day it departed from Egypt, 1297), 1880–81
24 × 26 cm
Printed in Cairo
Nasser D. Khalili Collection of Islamic Art, London

Folding map illustrating the route taken by the *mahmal* from Cairo to Mecca, to Medina and back to Cairo.

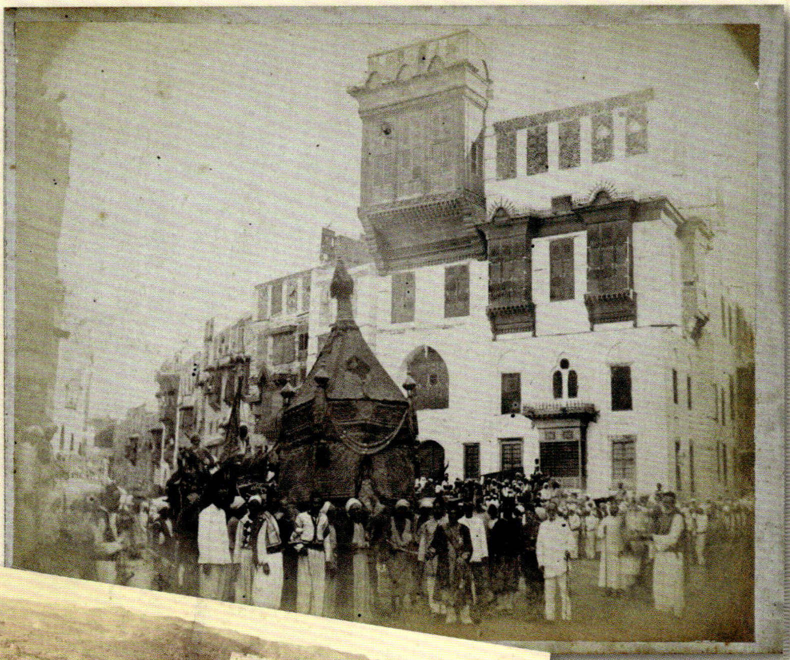

Muhammad Sadic Bey
Mecca, the arrival of the Egyptian mahmal, c. 1880–81
Albumen print
17.6 × 21.4 cm
Qatar National Museum, Doha

Sadic Bey was the first photographer to photograph Hijaz and the pilgrimage. The camel carrying the *mahmal* containing the *kiswa* of the Ka'ba was always chosen among the finest thoroughbreds. Joseph Pitts wrote: "*The* kiswa *is carried upon two camels and those two camels do not do other work at all the year long it is sent out of Egypt*." In other sources it was reported that the camels that carry the *kiswa* are dispensed from doing any work for the rest of their lives.

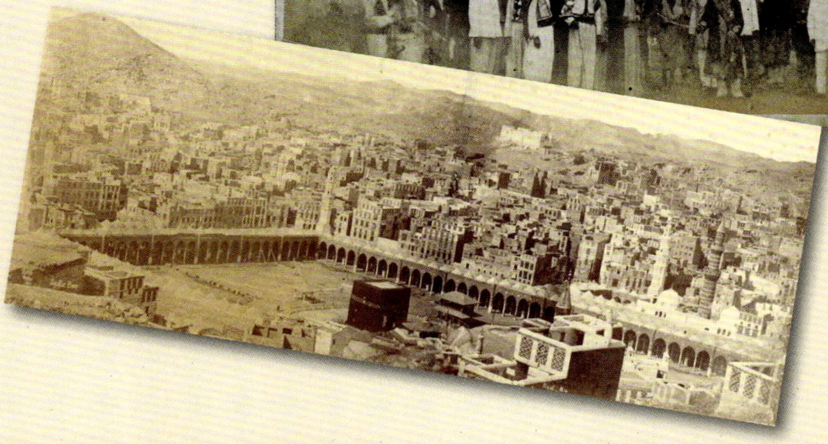

Muhammad Sadic Bey
Panoramic view overlooking the sacred Haram of Mecca and its surroundings, c. 1881
Albumen print
King Abdulaziz Public Library, Riyadh

During the day, pilgrims sit under the shade of the arcades reading the Koran and waiting for the call to prayer.

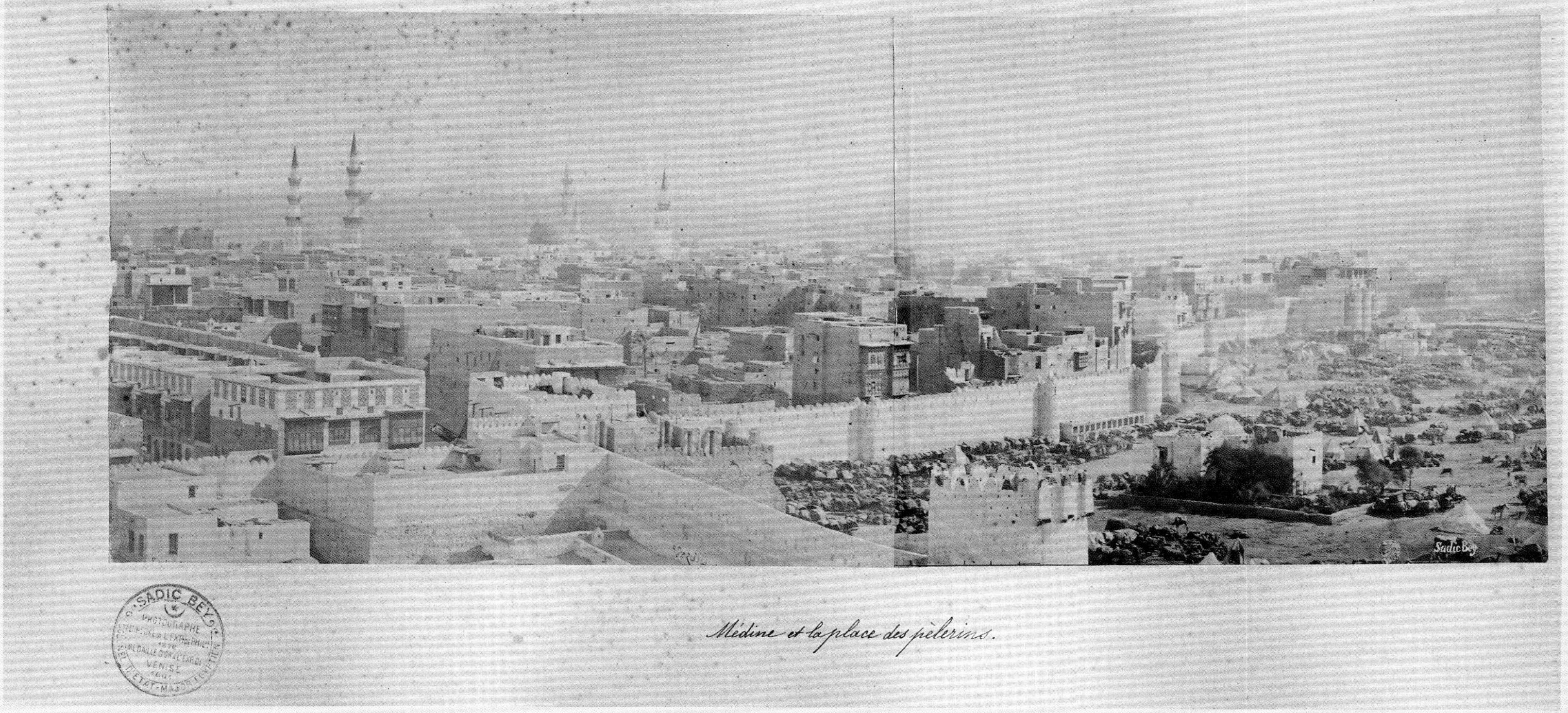

Muhammad Sadic Bey
Medina and the place of the Pilgrims, 1880
Albumen print
King Abdulaziz Public Library, Riyadh

This photo, taken during Sadic Bey's second visit to Medina, features *al-Masjid al-Nabawi* (the Prophet's mosque) and tomb with its prominent dome in the background. Outside the walls, on the right, are the camels and tents of pilgrims.

collodion camera that he brought along with him on his journey, in addition to his measuring instruments. This camera mounted with humid collodion plates used glass plate negatives which proved more robust than paper negatives and also resistant to the harsh climate of the desert. The photographs could be reproduced on albumen-coated paper. Sadic was fully aware of the historical moment he was living in.

He meticulously documented his surroundings by drawing and interviewing. It is believed that his writings, maps, and photographs fulfilled military and strategic goals. The title of his first book contains the wording "military map". He also took interest in the documentation of buildings and fortifications. He photographed landscapes such as mountains and valleys, specifying the distances, the location of the tents of soldiers, the water wells, etc. The Arabian Peninsula was one of the Egyptian authorities' primary military concerns. They recruited European officers who occupied commanding positions in the Egyptian army. The military maps of Hijaz and Nejd produced by these officers were not precise. Sadic was therefore commissioned to produce them.

Furthermore, Sadic's official status as the treasurer of the caravan accompanying the *mahmal* gave him great freedom of movement.

Sadic published several books that brought him exceptional recognition. In 1877, he wrote *Summary of the Exploration of the Wajh-Madinah Hijaz Route and its Military Cadastral Map*. In 1881, he published *Mash'al al-Mahmal* (The Torch of the Mahmal), which contains his collection of photographs, the history of the *mahmal* and the *kiswa*. After his third trip to the holy cities, in 1885 Sadic published *Kawkab al-Hajj fi safar al-mahmal bahran wa sayrih barrani* (The Apogee of the Pilgrimage in the travel of the *Mahmal* by sea and by land), in which he described the celebrations following the arrival of the *mahmal* to Jeddah, Mina, and Arafat. His most famous book was *Dalil al-Hajj* (The Guide to the Hajj for Its Universal Arriving Visitors) published in 1895. The volume is a detailed documentation of the pilgrimage to the holy city of Mecca, from the first step to the last. Sadic explains the difficult traveling conditions and the dangers of the pilgrimage.

In March 1882, an anonymous article in *The Graphic* magazine, recording John Keane's journey to Hijaz, included two engravings of Mecca and Medina, each captioned "from the first photograph ever taken." Henceforth photographs provided a visual illustration of the literary accounts of the holy cities. Later publications on the holy cities often used Sadic's photographs, including Muhammad Labib al-Batanuni's *The Journey to Hijaz*, Saleh Soubhy's *Pèlerinage à La Mecque et à Médine*, and Christiaan S. Hurgronje's *Mekka in the latter Part of the 19th Century*.

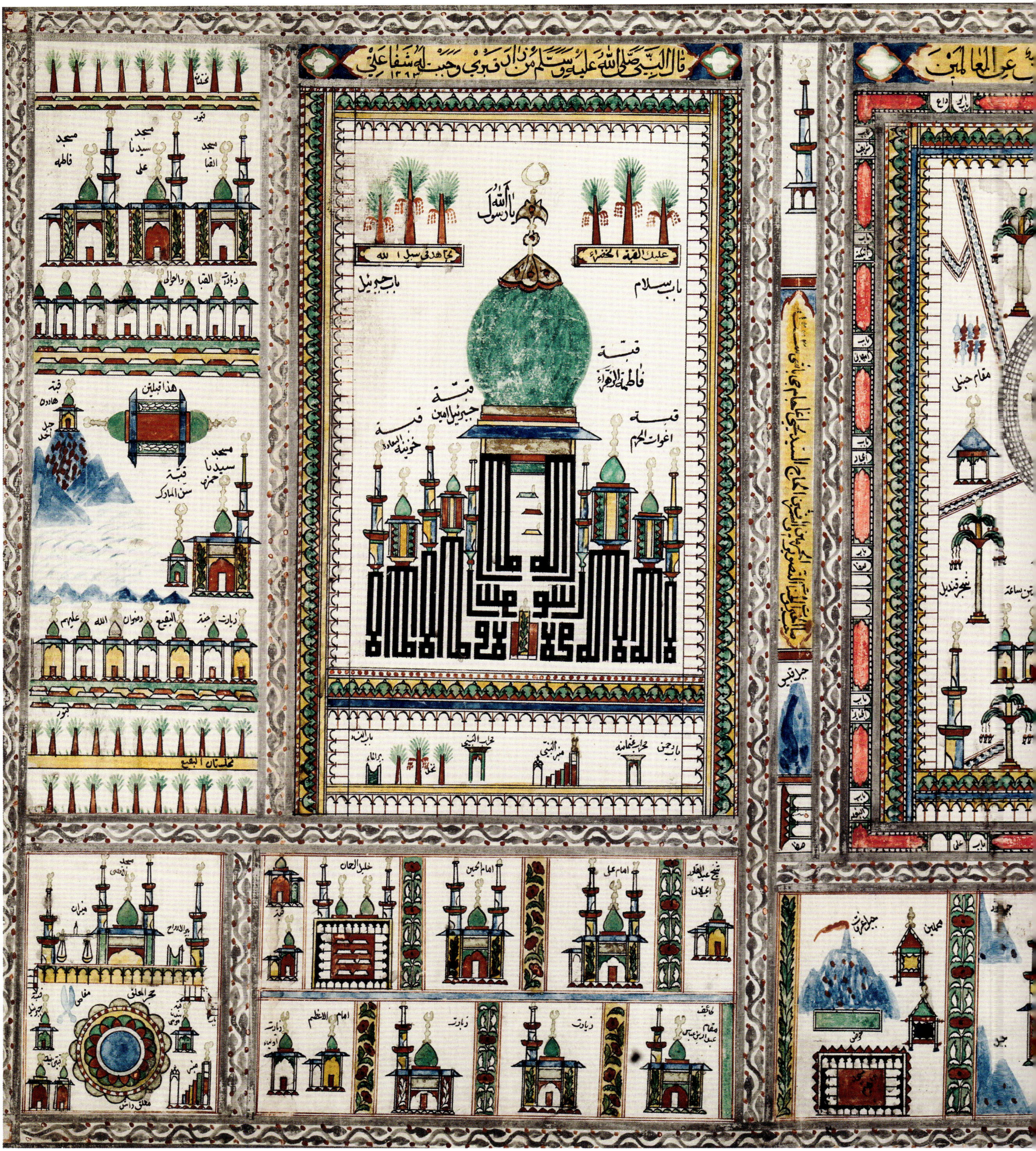
قال النبي صلى الله عليه وسلم من زار قبري وجبت له شفاعتي
يا رسول الله
باب جبريل
باب سلام
قبة فاطمة الزهراء
مقام جبل

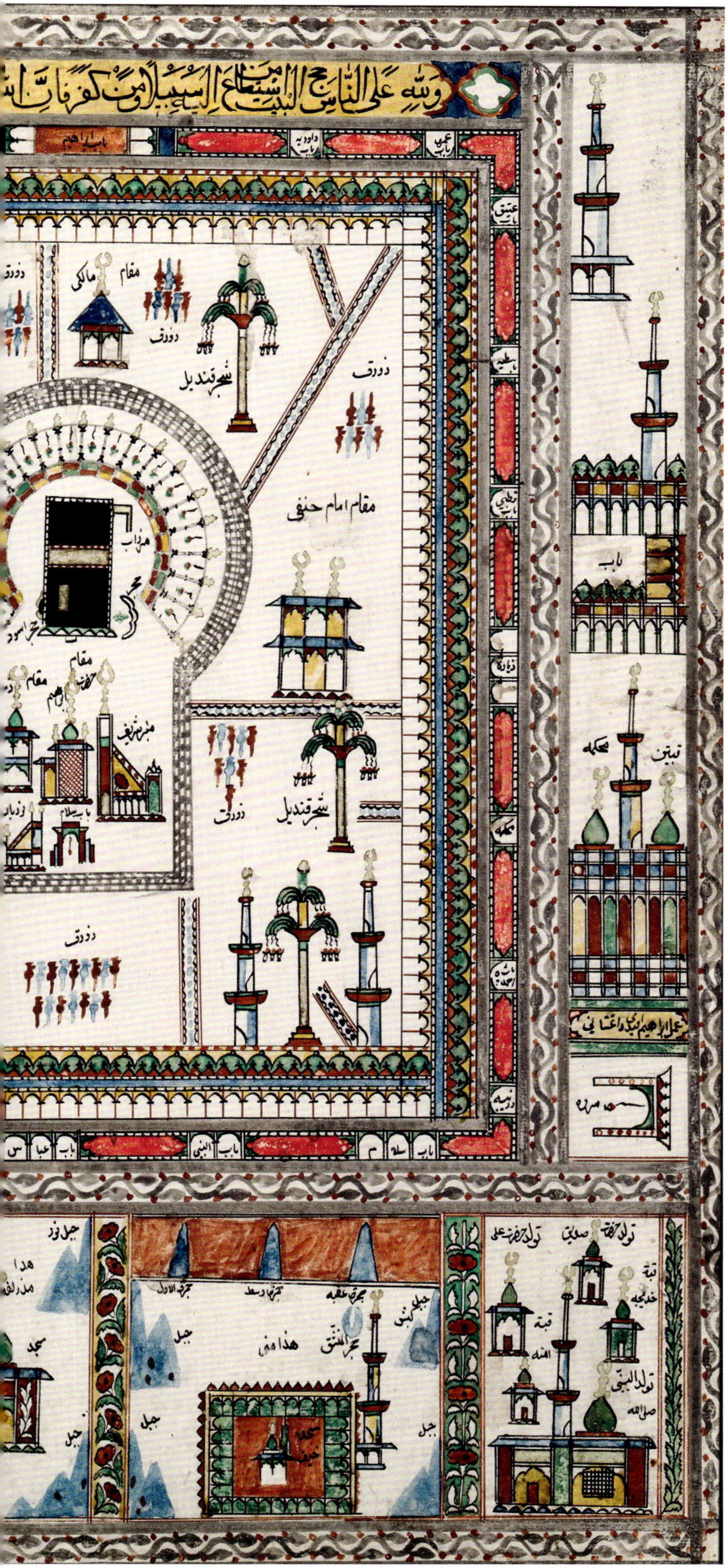

Hajj certificate
Hajj map of Mecca and Medina, 1808
Ink and gouache on paper
South India
56.3 × 78.8 cm
Museum of Islamic Art, Doha

This painting might be a Hajj certificate commissioned by Hajj Yahya (whose name is inscribed in the middle) from the Indian painter Ibrahim. The painting depicts the holy mosque of Mecca and the Ka'ba (on the right-hand portion of the image) and the mosque of Medina with its green dome on the left side. Burton wrote in *Personal Narrative of a Pilgrimage to Al-Madinah and Meccah* that there is a popular proverb that says: *"He who patiently endures the cold of Al-Madinah and the heat of Meccah merits a reward in Paradise."*

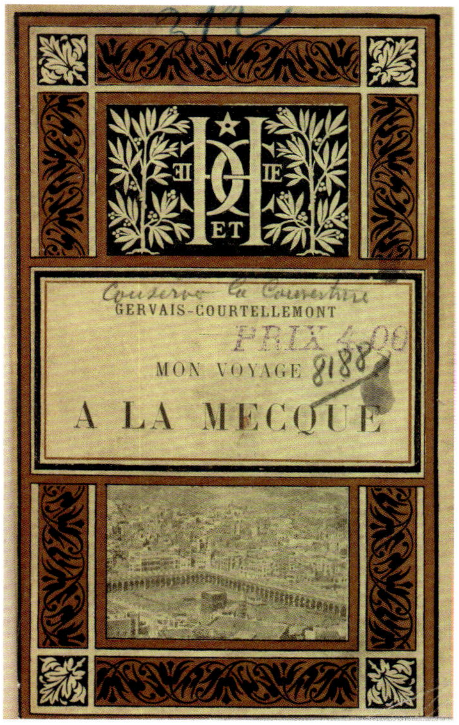

Jules Gervais-Courtellemont
Frontispice de *Mon Voyage à La Mecque*, 1896
Photograph of the Holy Ka'ba by Jules Gervais-Courtellemont with decorative borders
Paris, Librairie Hachette et Cie
Bibliothèque nationale de France

Jules Gervais-Courtellemont wrote that, he traveled to Mecca in 1896 driven by the desire to penetrate the mystery of the holy city and to enrich his knowledge of the Muslim Orient. He was equipped with his camera and recounted his trip in *Mon Voyage à La Mecque*, which he illustrated with the photographs he took during his journey.

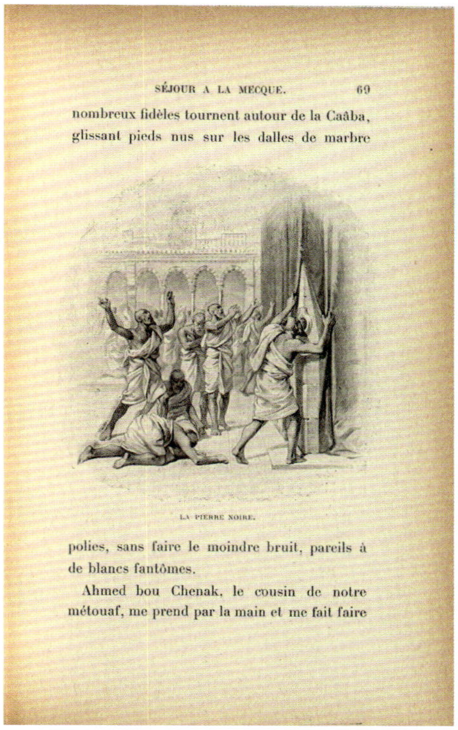

SÉJOUR A LA MECQUE. 69

nombreux fidèles tournent autour de la Caâba, glissant pieds nus sur les dalles de marbre

LA PIERRE NOIRE.

polies, sans faire le moindre bruit, pareils à de blancs fantômes.

Ahmed bou Chenak, le cousin de notre métouaf, me prend par la main et me fait faire

Jules Gervais-Courtellemont
The Black Stone, 1896
From *Mon Voyage à La Mecque*
Paris, Librairie Hachette et Cie
Bibliothèque nationale de France

The *Hajar el Aswad*, or Black Stone, is fixed in the southeastern corner of the Ka'ba, four to five feet off the ground. Pilgrims performing the circumambulation attempt to kiss the Black Stone or at least touch it if they are impeded by the crowd. It is said that the stone was originally white, but has become black as a result of man's sins.

view of many, the difficulties of the journey tended to heighten its merit, as illustrated by the resistance that sometimes met the development of new modes of transport in the service of the pilgrimage, which ultimately led to the caravans disappearing.

When pilgrims had survived all of the dangers represented by the caravan, upon reaching Mecca they fell prey to all of the pilgrimage professionals—residents of the holy city whose first and foremost livelihood depended on profits earned from pilgrims: guides, lodging-house keepers, merchants, brokers, and intermediaries of all types. In Mecca, pilgrims' lives were not in danger, but their resources were.

Nevertheless, these worries, and all of the rest, were overshadowed by the fact of having reached the "Navel of the world"—Mecca and its *Masjid al-Haram*. "It was as if the poetical legends of the Arab spoke truth. [...] I have seen the religious ceremonies of many lands, but never—nowhere—aught so solemn, so impressive as this spectacle," wrote the Englishman Richard Burton, recalling the moment when he contemplated the temple for the first time.

Next came the highly anticipated moment when the traveler performed the pilgrimage rituals with fervor, for days at a time, surrounded by vast and dense crowds: "I have entered into a sort of hypnosis that makes me insensitive to fatigue, hunger and thirst alike," wrote the Frenchman Jules Gervais-Courtellemont upon completing his pilgrimage, undertaken in 1896. Pilgrims had to take a few days to regather their strength before facing the return journey. Sometimes they chose to stay in the holy city for a few weeks, or even to reside there for a few months, becoming a "mujawir" and leading an existence of ascetic and religious contemplation in Mecca.

For all of these pilgrims, it is clear that the caravan journey represented an experience outside of time. Beyond the faith driving them, these highly particular circumstances reveal another reason for which, over many centuries, and despite the dangers faced, so many people were willing to face such perils. All the more so, the sojourn in Mecca was viewed as a special experience in many ways. Johann Ludwig Burckhardt perceptively observed: "Except those of a very high rank, the pilgrims

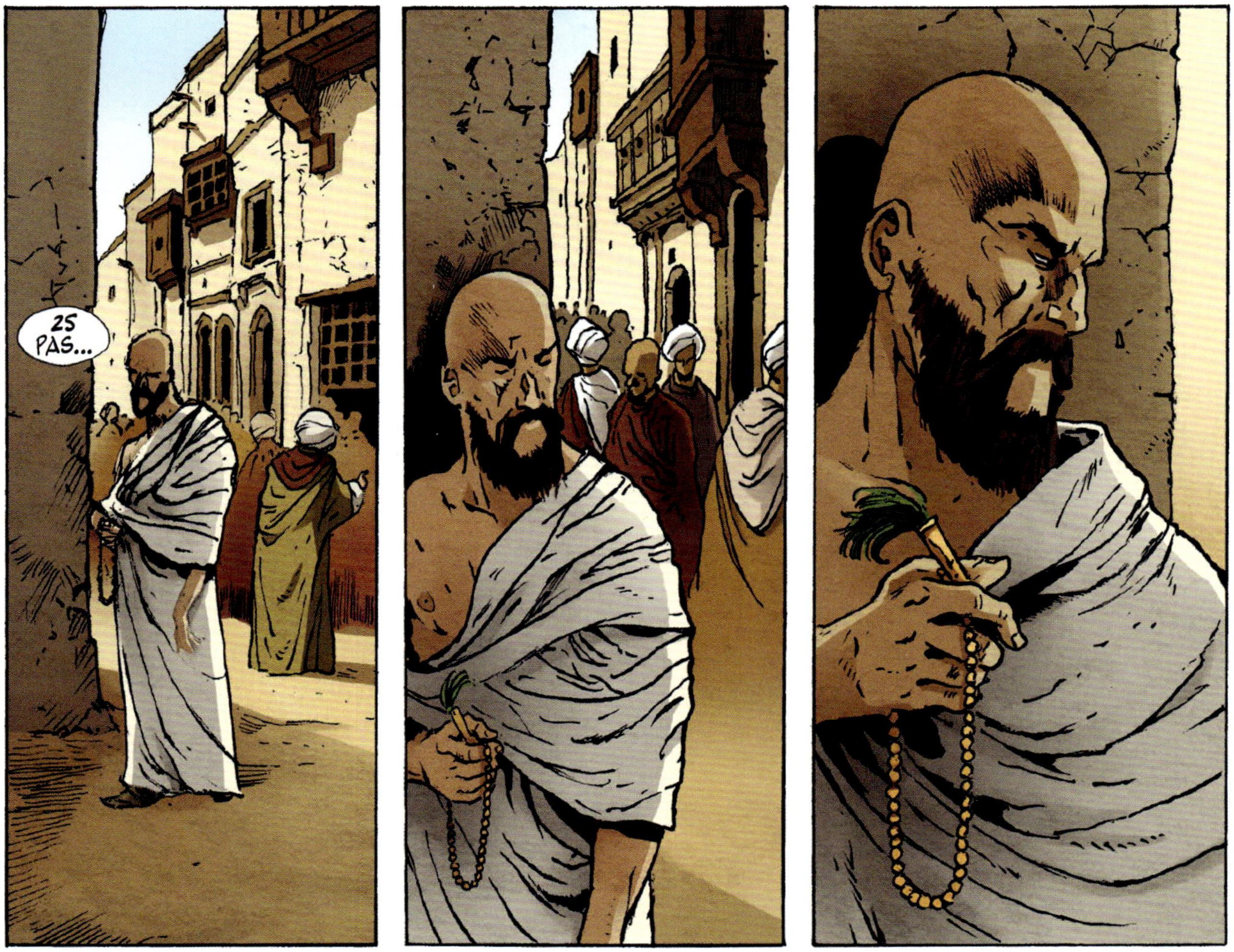

Lionel Marty
From *Captain Sir Richard Burton – Le voyage à La Mecque*, 2013
Scenario by Christian Clot and Alex Nicolavitch
Published by Glénat, Paris

When Richard Burton traveled to Arabia, he took with him a diary made for him by a Cairene: "*It was a long thin volume fitting into a breast-pocket, where it could be carried without being seen.*" He wrote that he began to write notes in Arabic characters, but his journal was afterwards kept in English. The traveler, he wrote, "*must, beware of sketching before the Badawin, who would certainly proceed to extreme measures, suspecting him to be a spy or a sorcerer.*"

Anne Blunt
Hajj camp at Birkeh Jemasneh,
February 20, 1879
Watercolor
Courtesy of the British Library

Birkehs were created to provide water for the pilgrims. Basically, they were tanks or reservoirs for collecting rainwater. Water was channeled into these tanks and stored there until the time of the Hajj, when the pilgrims could make use of it. Many of the old pilgrimage *caravanserais* (khans) and forts were built in places where the winter rain was collected in large *birkehs* (cisterns). These walled cisterns could hold considerable quantities of water.

Postcard
Zamzam
Colored postcard
Nasser D. Khalili Collection
of Islamic Art, London

The original location of the well of Zamzam was east-northeast of the Black Stone. Ameen Rihani recounted in *Around the Coasts of Arabia* how some of the pilgrims, *"in an ecstasy of devotion, would throw themselves sometimes in the well of Zamzam, believing it to be the quickest and safest way to eternal bliss—a short-cut to Paradise"*. It was then decided to cover the well with an iron net. Afterwards and before the expansion of the sacred mosque, the well of Zamzam was enclosed with a parapet wall within a large building. After the 1979 expansion of the mosque, this building was removed. Instead, a large underground hall was built to house the well and drinking fountains were provided for the pilgrims, allowing more space for the circumambulation around the Ka'ba.

Richard Burton
The Pilgrim
From a *Personal narrative of a pilgrimage to El Medinah and Meccah*, 1855–56
Lithograph by C. F. Kell
Royal Geographical Society,
London

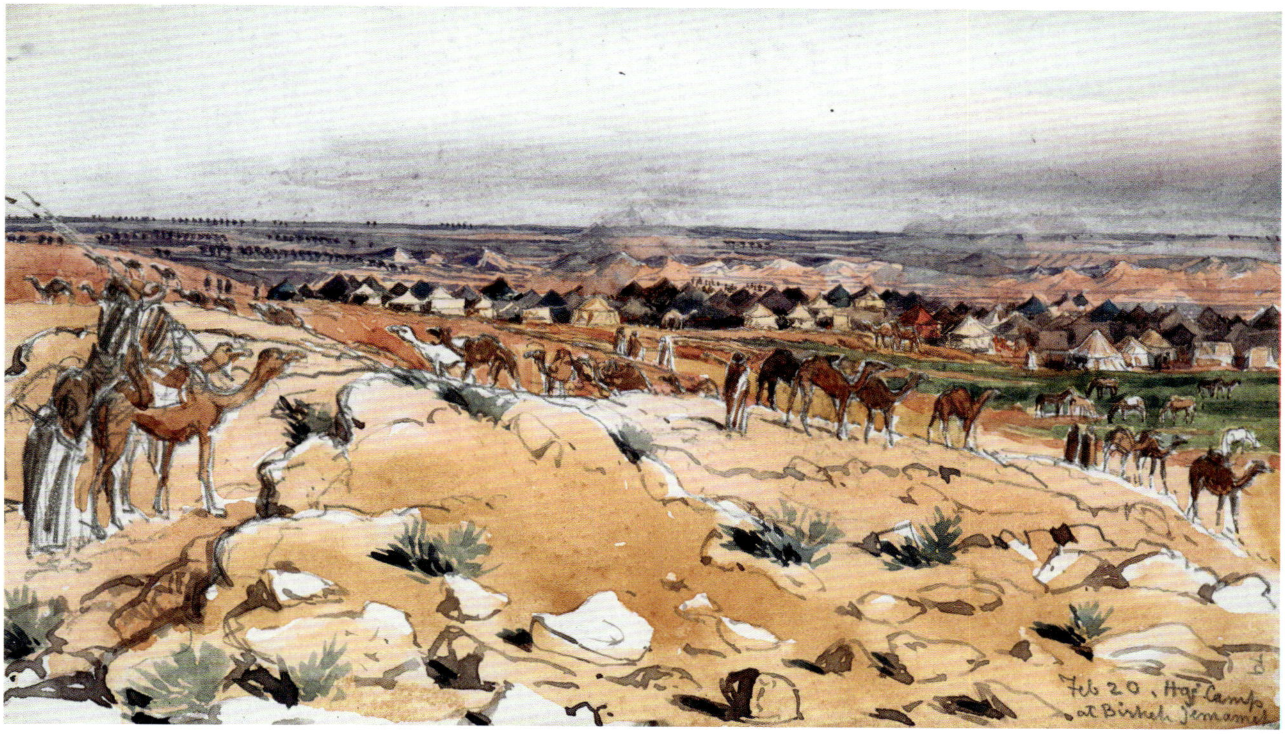

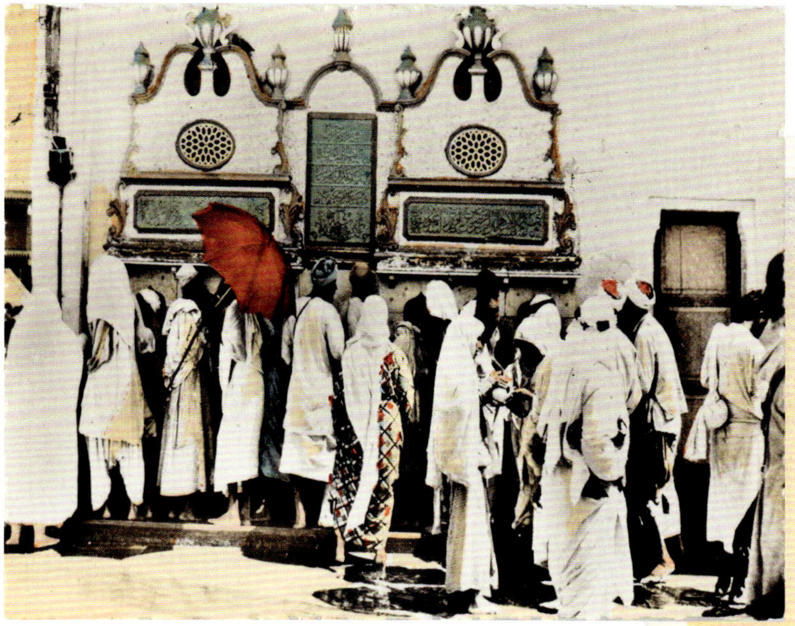

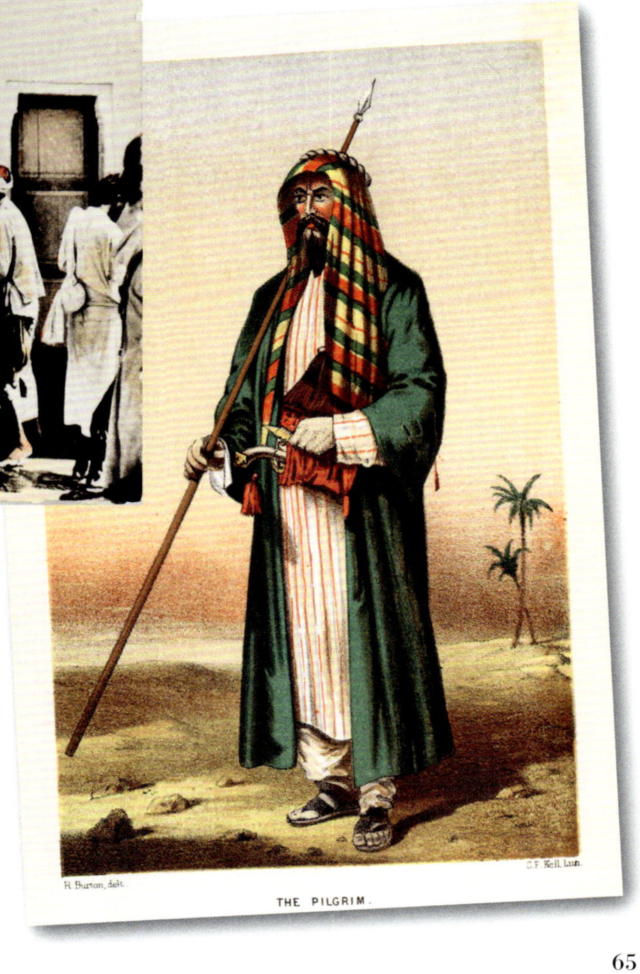

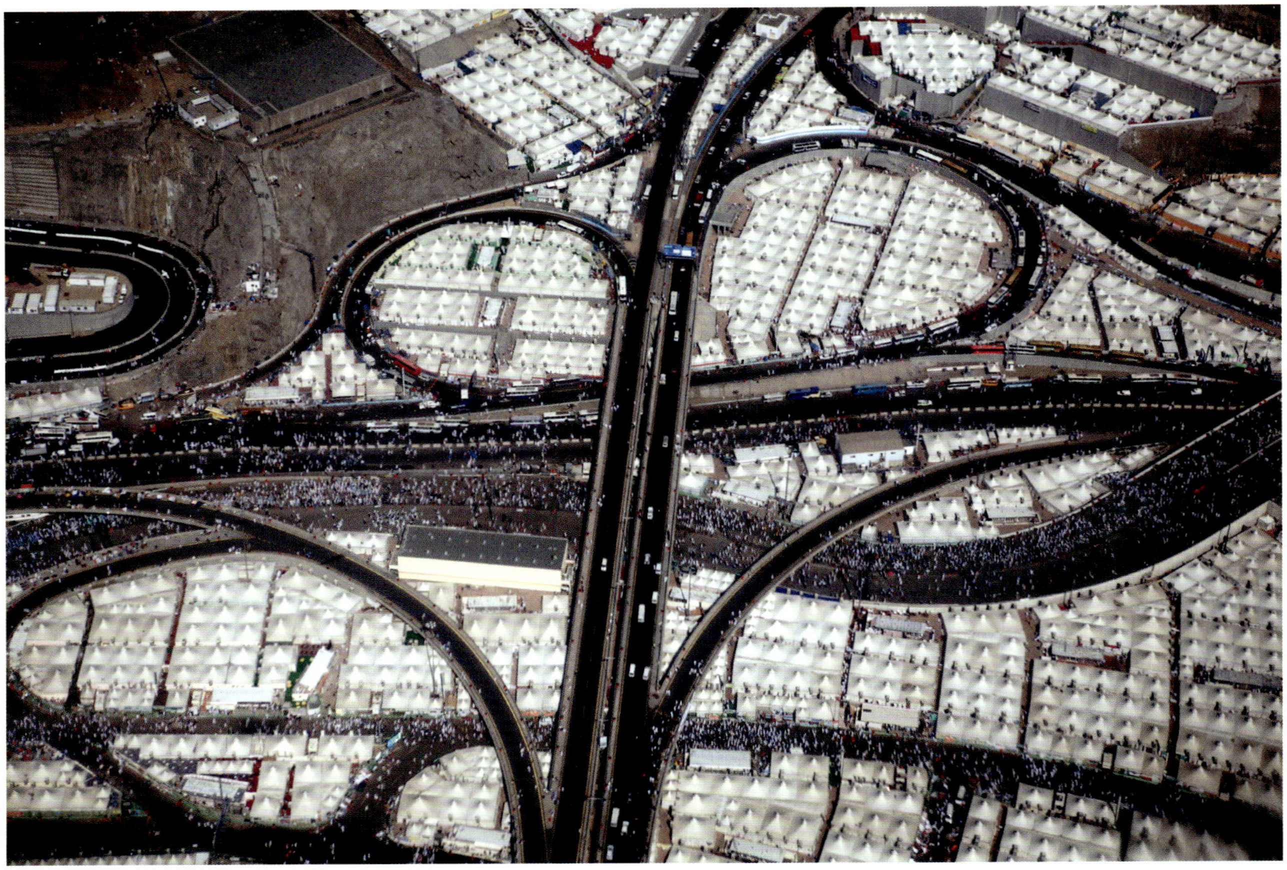

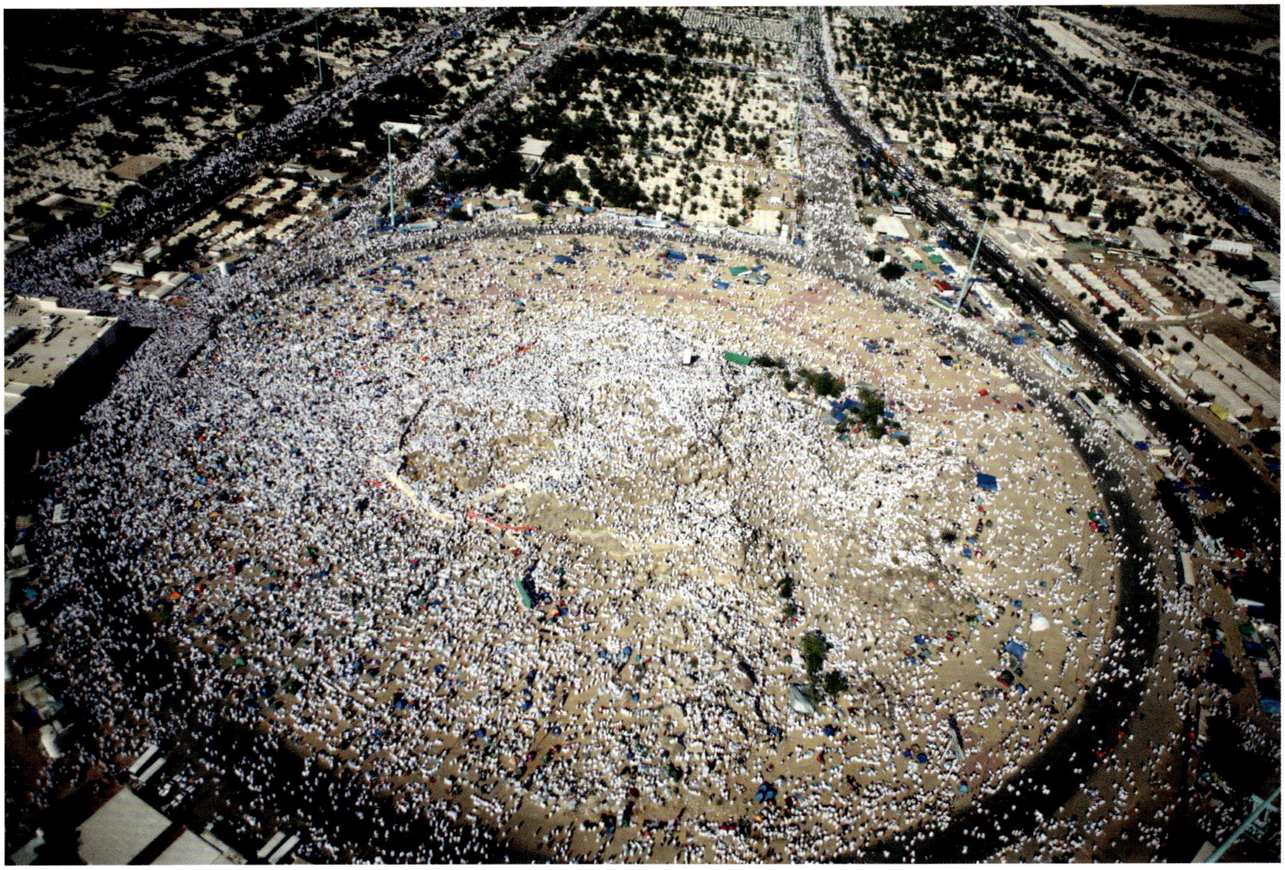

Newsha Tavakolian
An aerial view of the tents used to shelter pilgrims on the sides of the highway at Arafat, 2008
Courtesy of the artist

Newsha Tavakolian
Aerial view of the pilgrims gathering at mount Arafat, 2008
Courtesy of the artist

Arafat is a large plain surrounded by mountains, located 22 kilometers southeast of Mecca. In 1807, Ali Bey described the standing at Arafat, writing: "*No, there is not any religion that presents a spectacle more simple, affecting and majestic*."

Newsha Tavakolian
Pilgrims leave their tents, often depending upon the season, following a chilly night on the rocks and move towards mount Arafat at the crack of dawn, 2008
Courtesy of the artist

Evliya Çelebi, who performed the Hajj in 1672, wrote in his *Book of Travels: "To put on the pilgrim's robe is to separate oneself from all but God."*

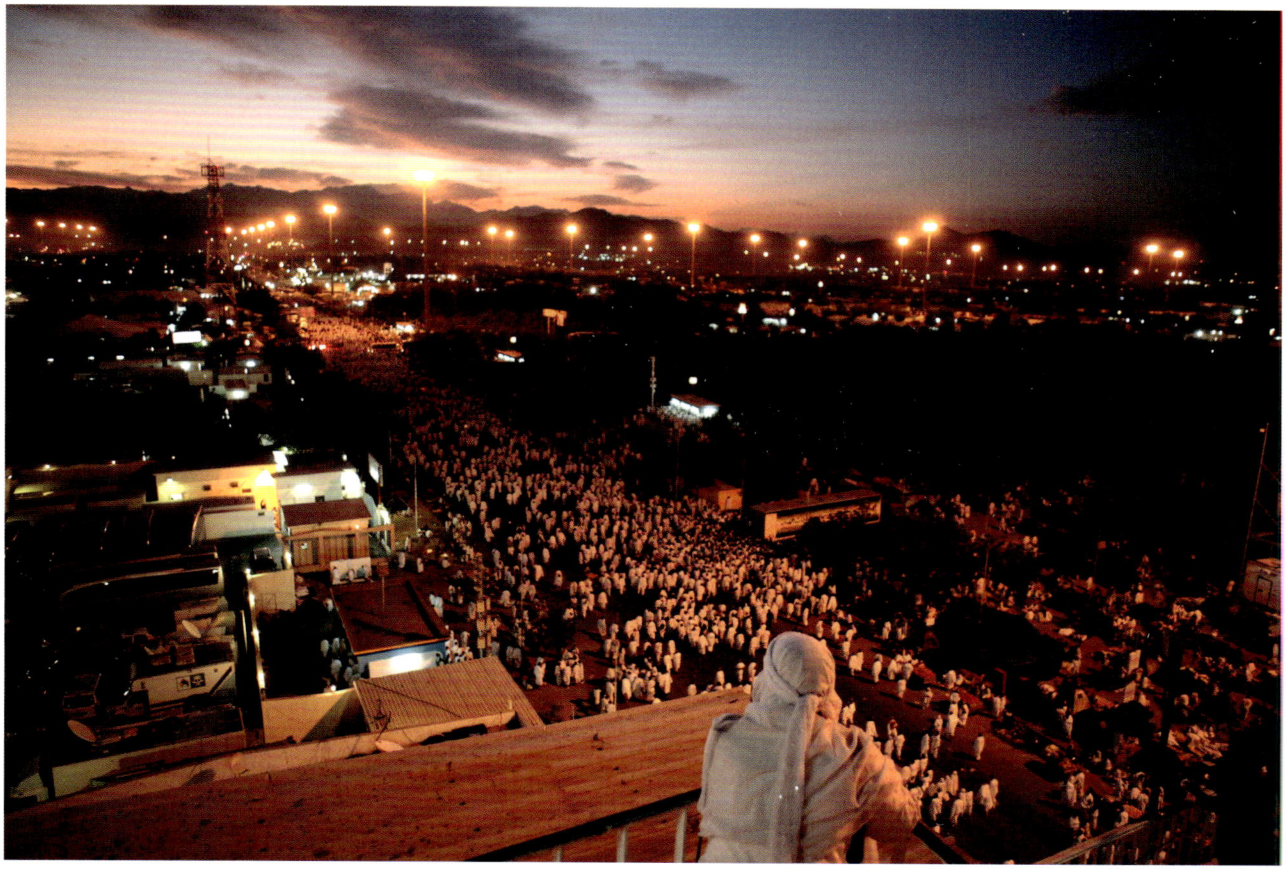

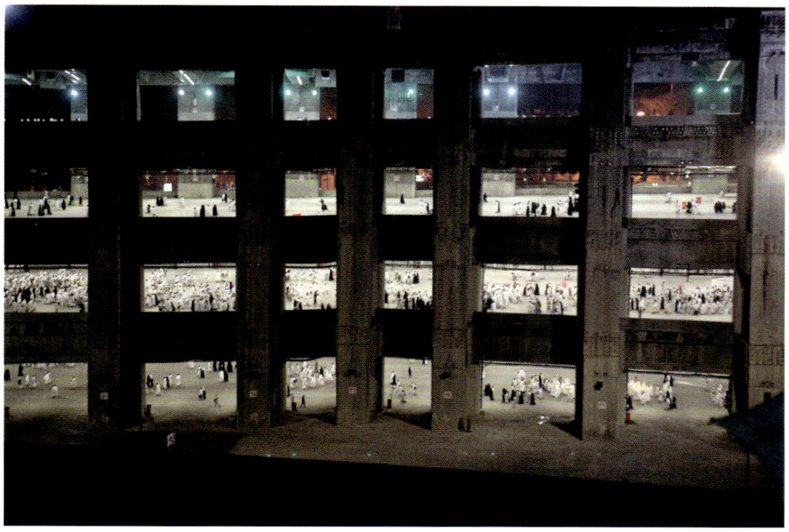

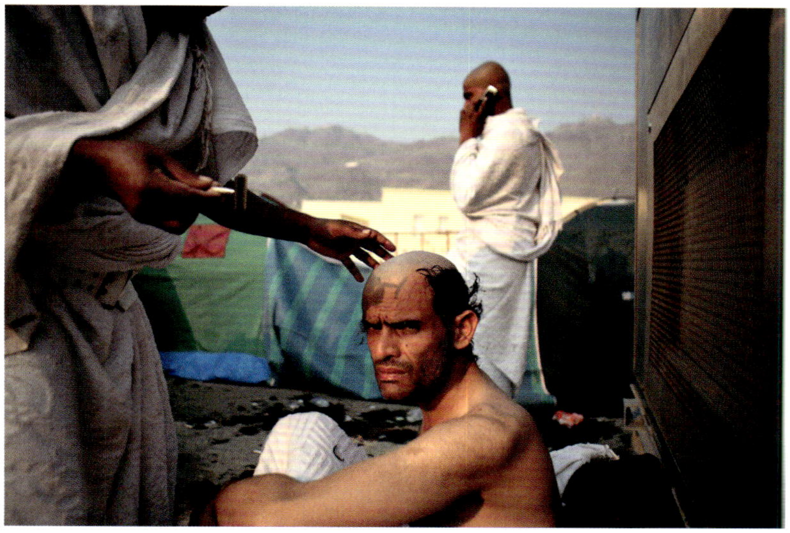

Newsha Tavakolian
The new multi-leveled Jamarat *building*, 2008
Courtesy of the artist

In response to the pressure of rising numbers of pilgrims in recent years, the *Jamarat* has been expanded from its original single level to a large multi-level structure. Each level of this structure can serve north, south, east, and west with twelve entrances. The building contains the *Jamarat* pillars where the pilgrims perform the ritual of stoning the pillars—symbolically thrown at the devil.

Newsha Tavakolian
Eid al-Adha (Feast of Sacrifice), 2008
Courtesy of the artist

The final ritual, on the Eid al-Adha, the tenth day of the pilgrimage, is the shaving of men's heads, after the sacrifice. For women, it is proscribed that the length of a fingertip be trimmed. This act symbolizes the end of the consecrated state and frees the pilgrim from some of the commitments inherent in wearing the *Ihram*.

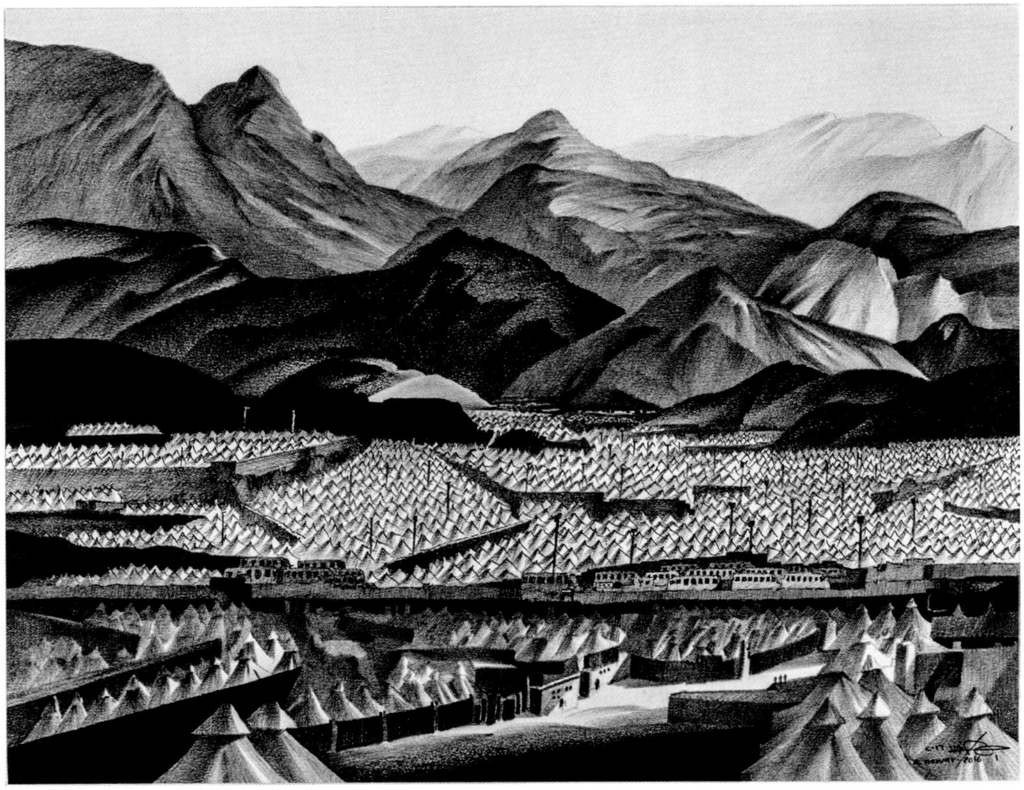

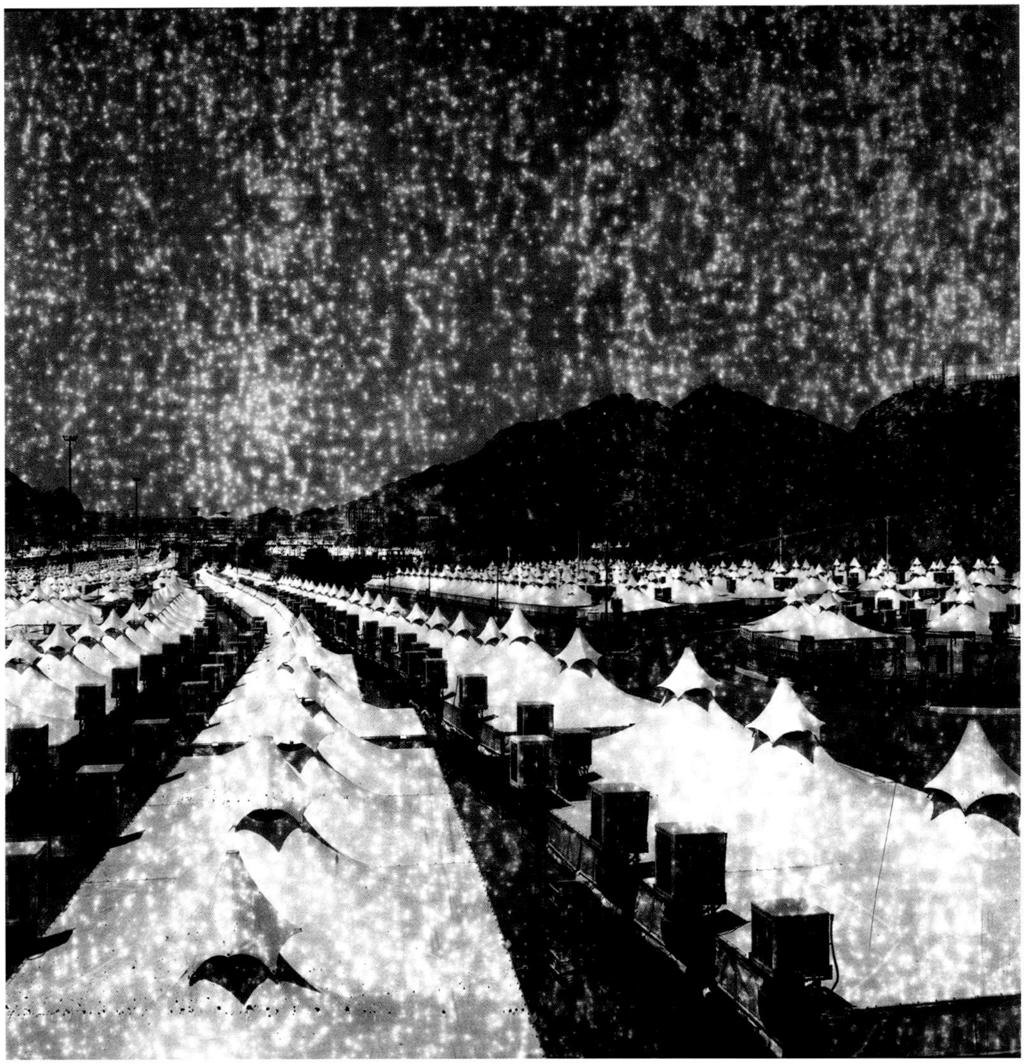

Ahmad Nawar
Hijaz: Inspiration from the Holy Land (6), 2016
Ink drawing
46 × 61 cm
Courtesy of the artist and of Hafez Gallery, Jeddah

In *The Sacred Journey*, Ahmad Kamal described Arafat: "*Here by the mountain, the pilgrim will pass what should be, spiritually and intellectually, the noblest hours of his life. The tents of the faithful will cover the undulating valley as far as the eye can see. This immense congregation with the sacred mountain at its center is the heart of Islam. This is the day of true brotherhood.*"

Ziad Antar
Hajj Tents
From the *Expired* series, 2005
Gelatin silver print
Courtesy of the artist

Ziad Antar's approach to photography is far from being classical or documentary. Instead of embracing the technological advances in photography, the artist chooses to experiment with obsolete and expired material. The result is pictures that recall an indistinct memory.

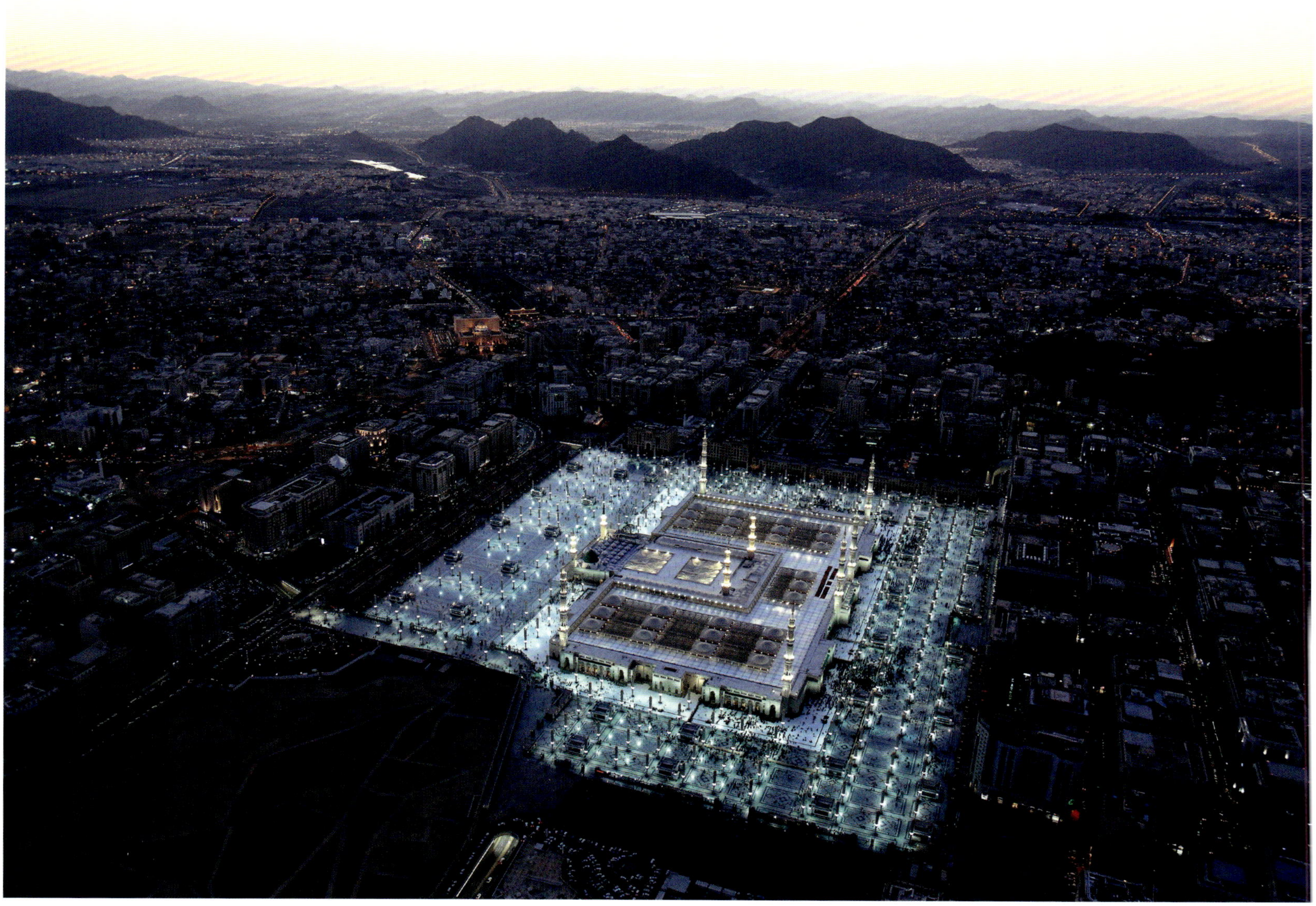

Kazuyoshi Nomachi
Aerial view of Medina, 1990s
Courtesy of the artist

Medina is known in Arabic as *Al-Madina al-Munawwarra* (The Illuminated City). It is the second holiest site in Islam and the city where the Prophet immigrated with his disciples in the year 622 (the first year of the Islamic calendar). He was buried in Medina ten years later. The Masjid Al-Nabawi, or the Prophet's mosque, is one of the Haramayn—the "two sanctuaries" of Islam. The first one is the Masjid al-Haram in Mecca. Unlike the pilgrimage to Mecca, the visit to Medina is not a mandatory stop during the Hajj, but many pilgrims visit it to pay homage to the Prophet.

live together in a state of freedom and equality. They keep but few servants: many, indeed, have none, and divide among themselves the various duties of house-keeping, such as bringing the provisions from market and cooking them, although accustomed at home to the services of an attendant." According to him, for pilgrims, these moments of sharing, like the time spent on the caravan journey, represented "a period of enjoyment; and the same kind of happiness results from their residence at Mecca, where reading the Koran, smoking in the streets or coffee-houses, praying or conversing in the mosque, are added to the indulgence of their pride in being near the holy house."

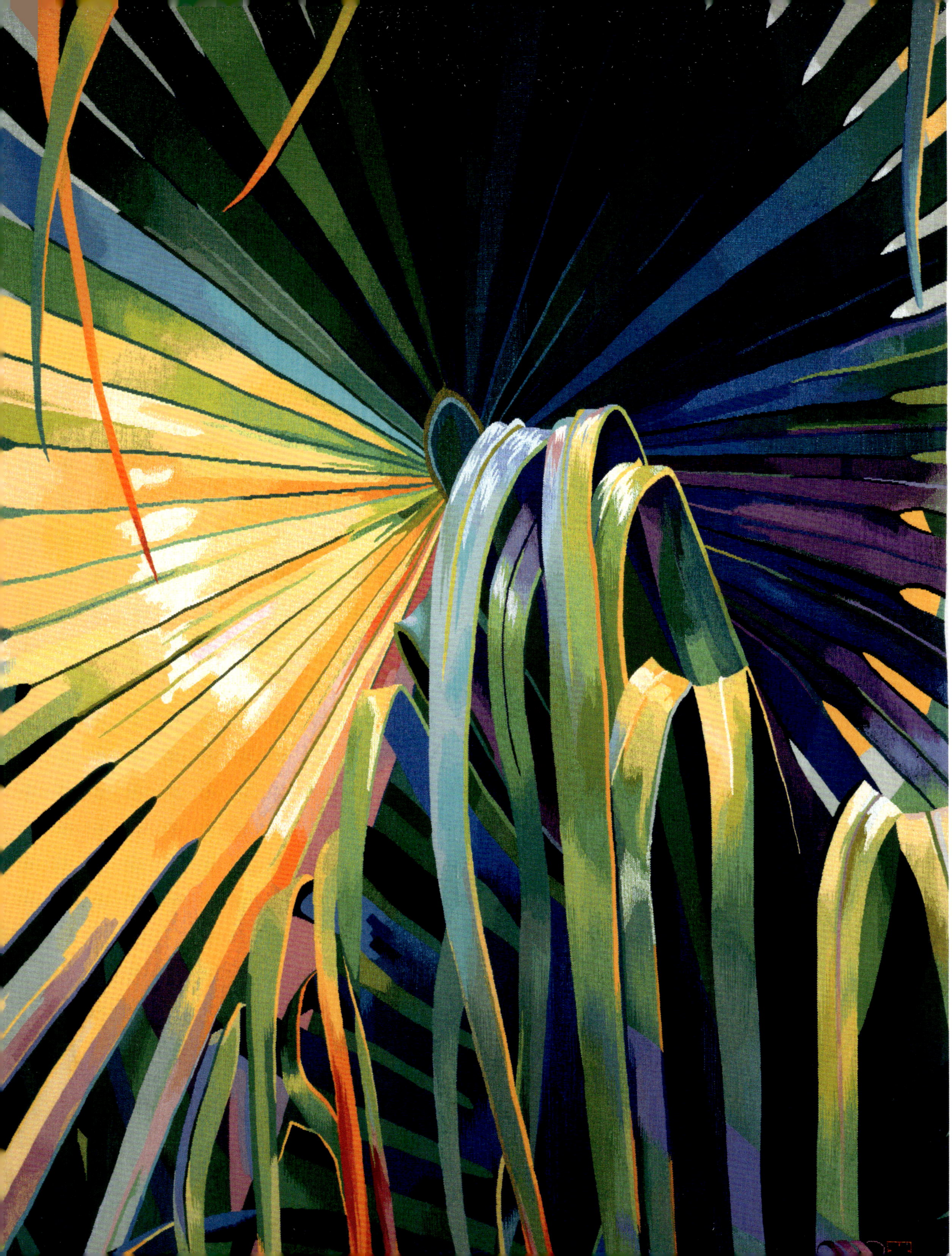

The Flora of the Peninsula

To say that the first authors to leave us an account of their travels in Arabia were not terribly interested in the surrounding landscapes and vegetation would be a falsity. Reaching their goal after a trying journey on camelback, they were struck by the aridity and barrenness of the surroundings—left, in the wake of this long trip, with the desert as a backdrop day in and day out, week in and week out, leg after leg, with a strong sense of monotony.

Day after day, when the caravan came to a rest, the eternal question was that of water, to quench the thirst of many tens of thousands of pilgrims and nearly as many camels—although the latter could at times refrain from drinking. The writings of Ibn Jubayr, and subsequently, Ibn Battuta, provided details of the presence or absence of wells and springs at each stopover of their long journeys. It is clear to readers that the question of water was rightfully at the heart of their concerns.

At times, however, the Damascus caravan left these desert settings behind to pass through a less arid valley and set up camp near a village, some of which are concisely described by Ibn Battuta. "It is a village containing a series of palm gardens and a bubbling spring with a stream flowing from it," he noted of the small locality of Badr, situated on the route from Medina to Mecca—here, and whenever the opportunity arose preferring to dwell on the epic scope of this famous site of the Mohammedan tale.

Nevertheless, the specifications and details that Ibn Battuta chose to share with his readers regarding the surrounding natural environment were often quite brief. During one last stopover in Batn Marra the day before finally reaching the city of Mecca, Ibn Battuta expressed gratitude for this "blessed valley" whose fruits, vegetables, and other assorted herbs are intended to supply the holy city's markets, we are told.

As will be seen later on, Ibn Battuta was not alone in delighting in these fruits—hailing from valleys near Mecca and especially from the region of Ta'if—which he savored over the course of his stay in Mecca: "Here, I ate fruits, grapes, figs, peaches, and dates, the likes of which are found nowhere else in the world. The same can be said of the melons brought here: no other variety can rival their aroma and sweetness." With similar rapture, and undoubtedly a bit of exaggeration, he goes on to note that "every novel and good item is sent to Mecca, and fruits of all varieties are brought in here".

His enthusiasm for the center of Islam deprived him of his better judgment at times. He could not heap enough praise on the city of Mecca and its inhabitants, who seemed to him to represent the best of humankind, "by their beneficence to the humble and weak, and by their kindness to strangers". Regarding the latter, Ibn Jubayr had proven much more severe in his judgments some 150 years earlier.

Similarly, the first European travelers were interested only in the central and sole reason for their journey—the pilgrimage. Given their concern for providing

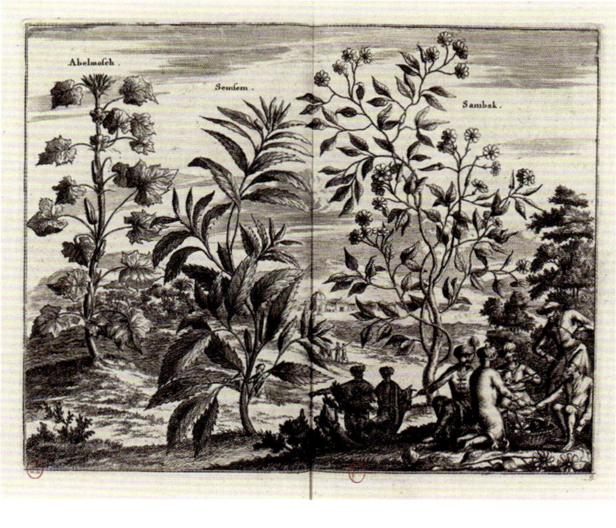

Sheila Hicks
Palm Tree, 1984–85
Tapestry
Wool, cotton, rayon, silk, and linen
365 × 274.5 cm
Manufactured by Atelier Philippe Hecquet Aubusson
Courtesy of the Metropolitan Museum and Art Resource Center

This tapestry was handwoven by the artist using the traditional weaving methods established at the Aubusson workshops in the early sixteenth century. It is the prototype for a larger hanging made for King Saud University in Riyadh.

Pieter van der Aa
Plantes d'Arabie (Plants of Arabia)
From *La galérie agréable du monde, où l'on voit en un grand nombre de cartes très exactes et de belles tailles douces, les principaux empires, roïaumes, républiques, provinces, villes, bourgs et forteresses… les îles, côtes rivières, ports de mer… les antiquitez, les abbayes, églises, académies… comme aussi les maisons de campagne, les habillemens et moeurs des peuples… dans les quatre parties de l'univers*, 1729
Divided in LXVI volumes, Leiden
Bibliothèque nationale de France

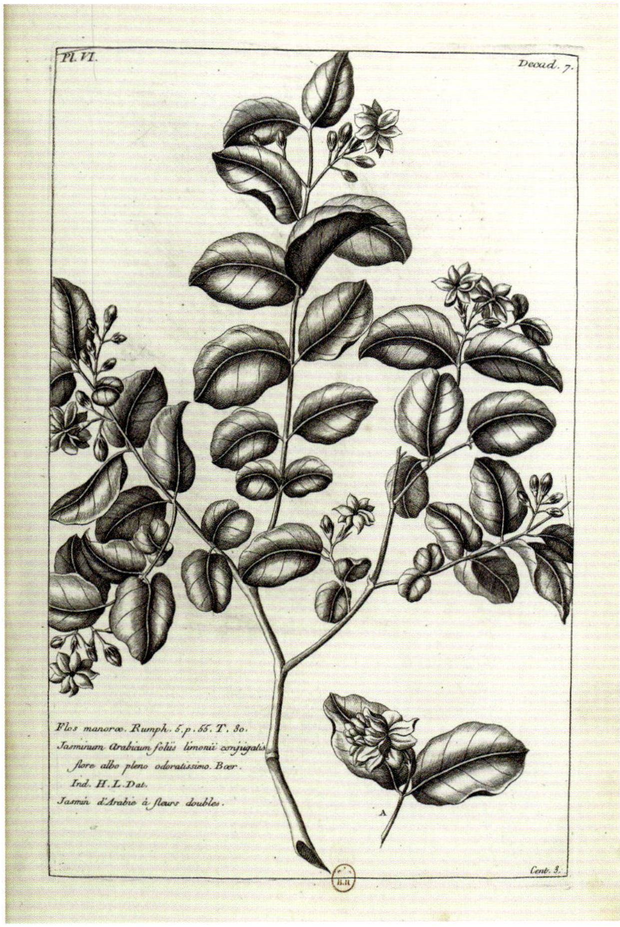

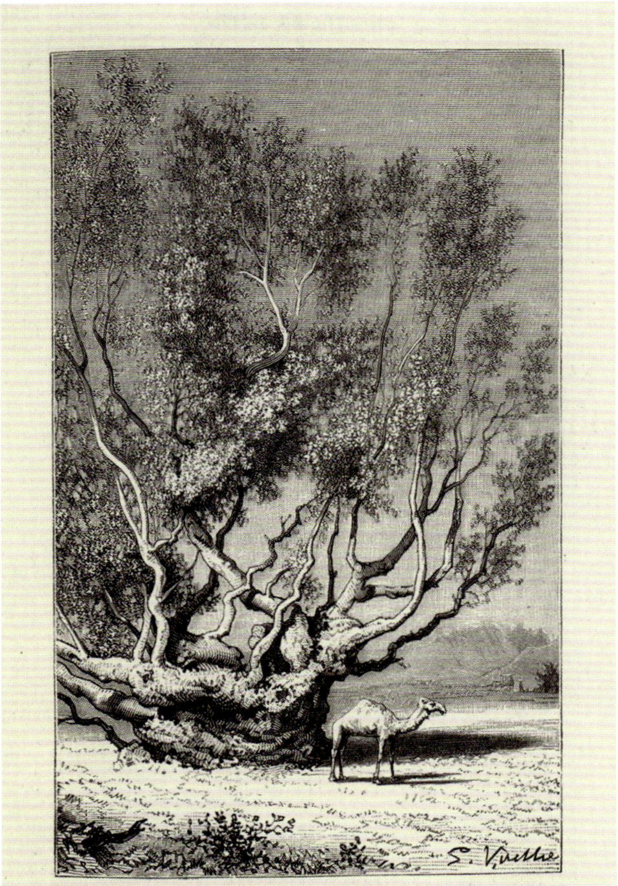

Bouquet d'ithels.

Pierre-Joseph Buc'hoz
Jasminum Sambac / Jasmin d'Arabie
From *Histoire Universelle de végétaux*, 1771–74
Bibliothèque nationale de France

Anne Blunt
Bouquet d'ithels
From *Voyage en Arabie. Pèlerinage au Nedjed, berceau de la race arabe* (A Pilgrimage to Nejd, The Cradle of the Arab race)
Woodcut by Gaston Vuillier after a watercolor by Anne Blunt
Paris, Librairie Hachette, 1882
Courtesy of the British Library

Ithel or *Tamarix aphylla* is a species of pine which is found mainly in the northern regions of Arabia near Tabuk and Mada'in Saleh. It is frequently cultivated by the inhabitants of Nejd for its timber, used in building. Street doors were generally made of a single *ithel*. Its trunk was also used for wooden plates.

accounts that were as detailed as possible, their observations generally proved exact, and more often than not, devoid of the contempt that might be expected in the writings of Europeans addressing the topic of Islam in the sixteenth and seventeenth centuries. This is what notably emerges in *The Travels of Ludovico di Varthema in Egypt, Syria, Arabia Deserta and Arabia Felix, in Persia, India, and Ethiopa, A.D. 1503 to 1508*, the work left to posterity by the Bolognese Ludovico di Varthema, who, as a Mameluke soldier, was part of the armed guard tasked with escorting and protecting the Damascus caravan in 1503. Even more than Ibn Jubayr or Ibn Battuta, Varthema constantly expressed his worry concerning the water supply for his caravan, which "counted 35,000 camels and around 40,000 persons." But what worried him above all, in a wholly professional manner, were the attacks by Bedouins seeking to rob and plunder the pilgrims: "Afterwards we found a little mountain, near which was a well, whereat we were well pleased. We halted upon the said mountain. The next day, early in the morning, there came 24,000 Arabs, who said that we must pay for their water. We answered that we could not pay, for the water was given by God. They began to fight with us, saying that we had taken their water. [...] The caravan counted 300 armed men and us Mamelukes overseeing them, numbering 60. We soon began to fight. One man and one lady were killed by bows on our side, and they did us no further harm. We killed of them 1,600 persons. Nor is it to be wondered at that we killed as many of them: the cause was that they were all naked and on horseback, without saddles."

There is certainly a fair amount of exaggeration in Varthema's accounts of the skirmishes of this sort, at various points of his journey, when the "armies" of Bedouins, in his words, opposed him. Even if, as he believed, "the Mamelukes' bravery is unmatched," it is difficult to believe his claim of having put to flight a column of some 24,000 Bedouins with the help of his 60 peers alone on the outskirts of the village of Badr; he furthermore seemed unaware that this very spot was the theater of a different battle—a founding one, at that!

While Varthema gave free rein to his imagination in turning mere skirmishes into military feats, he also demonstrated true curiosity and an assured sense of moderation—rather remarkably, and unexpectedly, for an early sixteenth-century man—in his descriptions of the cities of Medina and Mecca, and the pilgrimage rites. It is as though the adventurer that he truly was felt the weight of the responsibility of being the first man to provide Renaissance Europe with the details of a ritual essential to the understanding of Islam. This same sensibility is apparent in the writings of another traveler, one who did not choose to perform the pilgrimage of his own free will. That young Englishman, Joseph Pitts, captured by privateers from Algiers in 1678, when he was still a teenager, and resold several times as a slave, had been converted to Islam by one of his masters who subsequently brought him along to Mecca. These unfortunate circumstances did not hinder Pitts from demonstrating true empathy for his newfound coreligionists—to the extent that the historian Jacqueline Pirenne wrote of him: "Believe us in saying that nobody has described with such comprehensive objectivity the religious attitude of those who made the pilgrimage to Mecca."

His account of the pilgrimage—several decades after the fact, once he had regained his freedom—is the first to have been written in the English language. And yet, a search for descriptions of the nature and flora of Arabia is in vain. He merely notes, at the end of the long return journey, that he subsequently undertook from Mecca to Cairo a "fourty days journey. And in all this way there is scarcely any green thing to be seen; nothing but sand & stones."

It was undoubtedly necessary to wait for the century of the Enlightenment and the Encyclopaedists for Europe to develop a more rational, comprehensive curiosity regarding Arabia. In the entourage of a pacifist and educated ruler, King Frederick V of Denmark, an ambitious project was born, later known as the Royal Danish Arabia Expedition, which gathered five men versed in

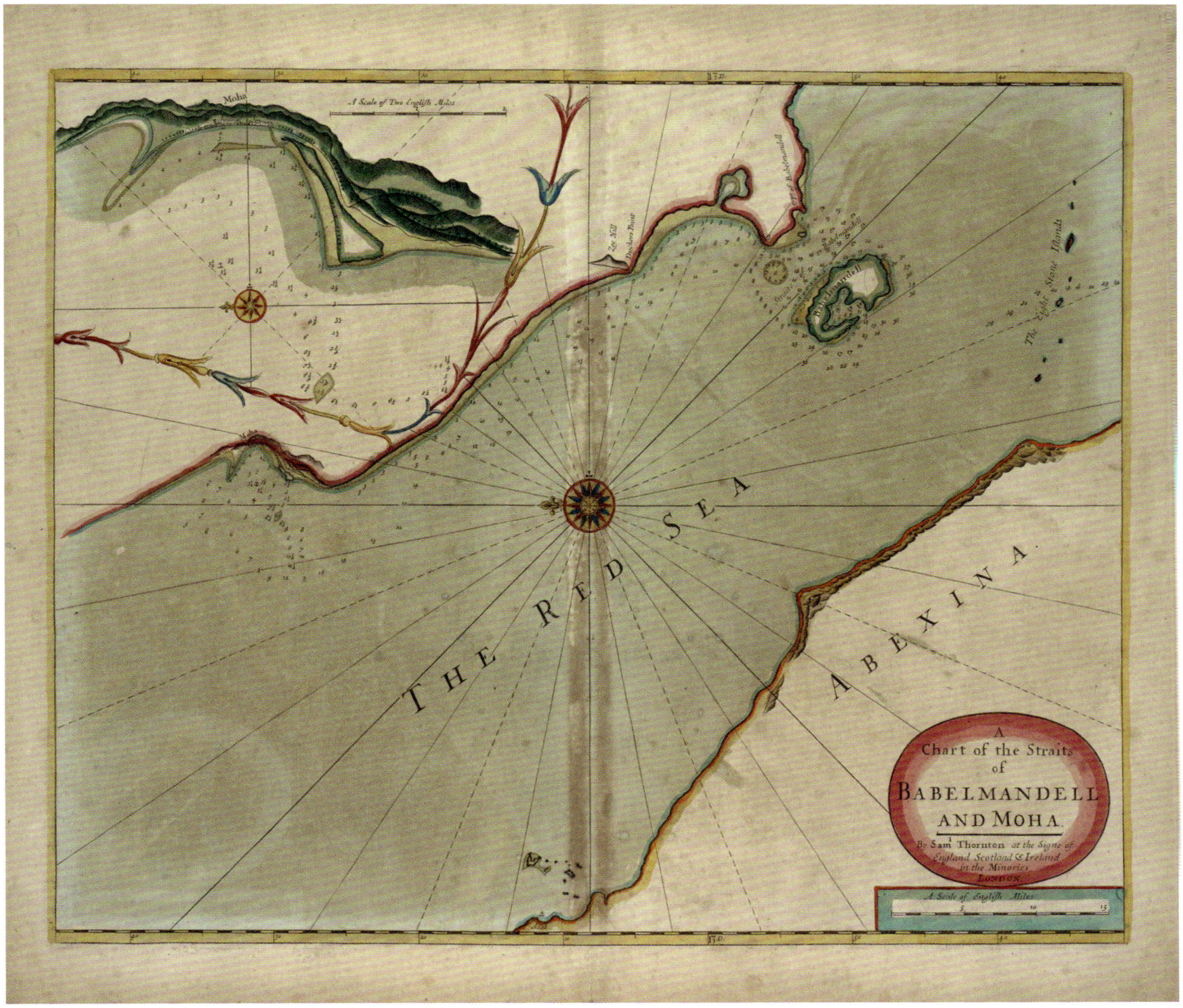

Samuel Thornton
Red Sea, 1702–07
A hand-colored nautical chart of the straits of Bab-el-Mandeb and Moha, incorporated in a sea atlas containing hydrographical description of most of the seacoasts of the world.
Courtesy of the New York Public Library

Richard Burton wrote in *Personal Narrative of a Pilgrimage to Al-Madinah and Meccah*: *"Trade was carried mainly in Jeddah where cargos exported goods to Suez. The exports consisted mainly of coffee and gum-arabic which came from Al-Yaman and Hijaz, mother-of-pearl from the Red Sea, cloves brought by Moslem pilgrims from Java, Borneo and Singapore. Other articles include ginger, cardamoms, Eastern perfumes, such as aloes-wood, attar of rose, attar of pink; senna leaves from Al-Yaman and Hijaz."*

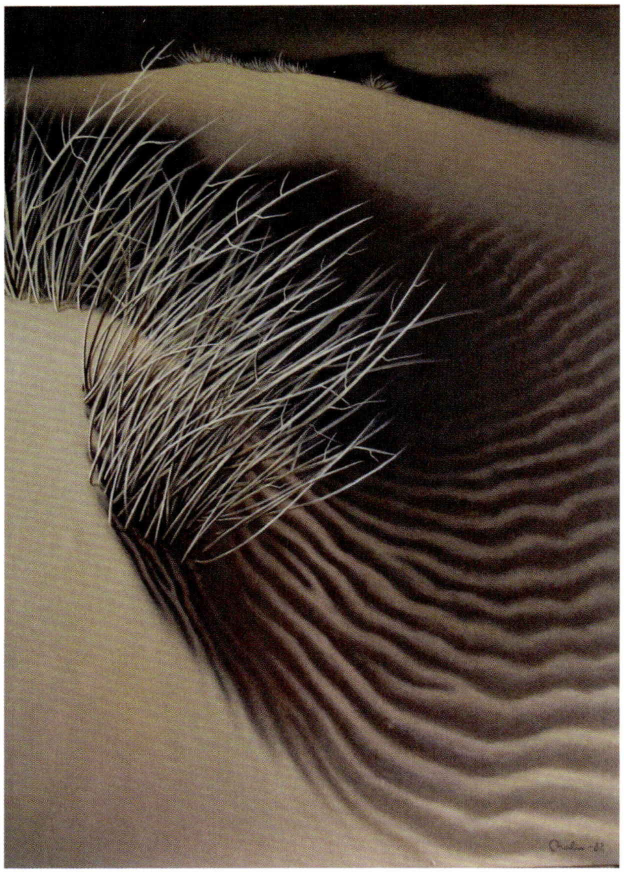

Malin Basil
Sandscape, 1983
Acrylic on canvas
100 × 75 cm
Private collection

John Keane wrote that *"the desert is never completely bare. In some areas there are broom-like growths that are good grazing for camels."*

the arts and sciences, hand-picked from the most prestigious universities of the time: a mathematician and geographer, Carsten Niebuhr; a doctor, Christian Carl Cramer; a philologist, Frederik Christian von Haven; a draughtsman, Georg Wilhelm Baurenfeind; and a botanist, Pehr Forsskål, whose presence would seem to indicate that soon, more light would be shed on the flora of the peninsula.

The scope of the project was such that prior to departure, its members devoted some eighteen months wholly to the preparation of their trip, the fine-tuning of their knowledge, and the acquisition of new insights into the fields and sciences that could help them better carry out their mission. Leaving from Copenhagen in early 1761, they brought with them a long list of questions relating to Arabia and Yemen that had been submitted by the most eminent figures from the universities and academies of the era. These encompassed subjects ranging from religion to climate, and natural history to habits and customs, and represented very nearly every existing discipline, from astronomy to zoology, grammar, cartography, and more. The five men were tasked with finding answers to all of these questions, insofar as possible, in order to allow Europeans to gain a more accurate idea of a part of the world of which almost nothing was known at the time.

Before arriving in Arabia, a stay in Constantinople was planned in order to allow them to grow familiar with Muslim society, and in Egypt, to improve their language skills, where they stayed for nearly two years in all. It is clear that nothing was left to chance.

Finally, one day in October 1762, the small group of six people—they were accompanied by a Swedish servant, Lars Berggren—embarked from Suez on a ship that brought them to Jeddah, after a brief stopover in Yanbu. Worried about how they would be received by the natives, its members were pleasantly surprised to be warmly welcomed. As Taylor Bayard described in his *Travels in Arabia*, "The inhabitants, it seemed, were already accustomed to the sight of Christian merchants in their town, and took no particular notice of the strangers, who went freely to the coffee-houses and markets, and felt themselves safe so long as they did not attempt to pass through the gate leading to Mecca." After spending six weeks in a house provided to them by the Turkish pasha of the city, the group was reassured, and decided to leave Jeddah and head south.

Traveling along the Arabian coast in short stages, sometimes overland by donkey, sometimes aboard worn boats, they reached Tihama and the Yemeni port of Hodeida. The members of the sole group scientific expedition that had ever set out for the Arabian Peninsula got to work enthusiastically from day one, collecting plants, minerals, and insects; taking notes and measurements; haggling over the purchase of manuscripts; and crossing the country while making an effort not to draw too much attention. The activity was strenuous—perhaps too strenuous: after ten months on the peninsula, they hastily, even urgently, made the decision to board the "last vessel sailing that year from Mokha to India," in this part of the world dogged by monsoons. But it was too late: two of them, von Haven and Forsskål, had died a few days apart, in the previous weeks. And on the boat, Baurenfeind died off the coast of the island of Socotra, followed by Berggren. Shortly after their arrival in Bombay, it was Cramer's turn to depart this world.

What exactly happened? Nothing, it might seem—or at least nothing major, judging by the account of the expedition's sole survivor: "Although death almost destroyed our association, no one need to be frightened on that account, nor fear to undertake the voyage to Arabia." Niebuhr added: "It would be a mistake to suppose that my companions died of contagious

Claire Rivier
Acacia, 2006
Ink on paper
20.5 × 22 cm
Courtesy of the artist

Acacia provides food to camels and shelter from the sun to men. Its timber is used by woodworkers, wrote Charles M. Doughty, to make saddle trees, for the burden camels.

Claire Rivier
Acacia, 2006
Pastel on paper
34.5 × 17.5 cm
Courtesy of the artist

Charles Doughty wrote that *"acacias give up to the air a hardly sensible wholesome sweetness; its little yellowish flower-tufts are seen in all the midsummer months. [...] Its leaves are pleasant for the taste and a little gelatinous, it will refresh the parched mouth; the gum, say the Arabs, is very good and cooling to eat."*

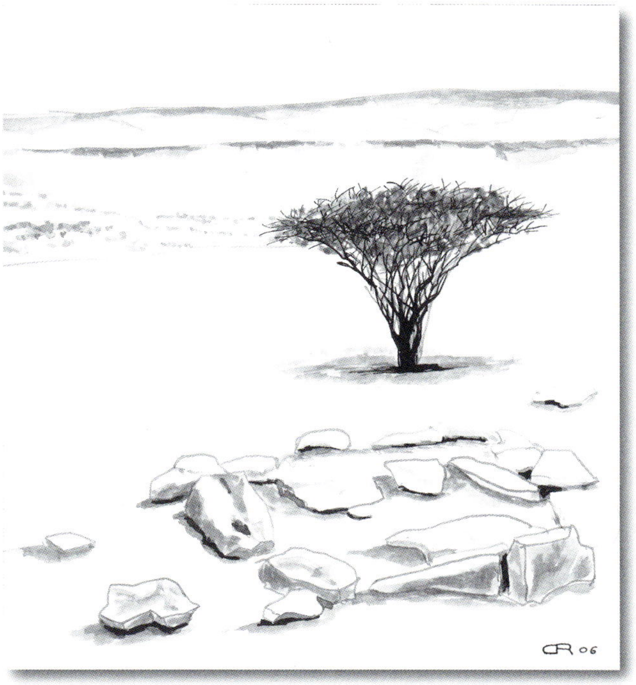

diseases, because they were carried off so quickly one after the other. Rather I believe that we ourselves were the cause of maladies against which other people could easily protect themselves."

No tragedy caused the demise of his comrades; Niebuhr's great merit was that he understood that one ought not attribute the causes of their deaths to the nature of the country. If a reason must be found to explain their deaths, for him, it lay in the haste with which they set out to discover the land; the oppressive heat and excessive fatigue; and the European habits they preserved, including eating too much meat—"an unhealthy habit in hot lands," wrote Niebuhr. He continued: "We found the evening coolness so pleasant after the heat of day that we overexposed ourselves." He lamentingly added, "I, too, wanting to live like my comrades, in European manner, in their time, endured a number of severe illnesses."

In this analysis, Carsten Niebuhr demonstrated remarkable perceptiveness in admitting how they were the cause of their own misfortunes. As he wrote, "Our company was too numerous to allow of our accommodating ourselves at first to the mode of life of the country." Left on his own, "surrounded only by orientals," he fully embraced the lifestyle of the natives, which allowed him to remain in good health for the full three years left of his remarkable journey.

In the name of traveling across Arabia and Yemen without too many inconveniences, Niebuhr pinpointed another error committed by his comrades and himself during the first part of the journey: that of seeking "the acquaintance and protection of the governors of the provinces" and other important figures. But far from ensuring their safety, this keeping of the company of people in high places represented a dual disadvantage, as it drew the attention of all to themselves, due to the fact that "the inhabitants fancied that we were persons of quality and wealth" and required the expenses that went along with such practices. "On my return I scarcely ever presented myself to people in high places and fared very well," he concluded in this regard.

Niebuhr also highlighted the importance of speaking the language, noting that "they have that

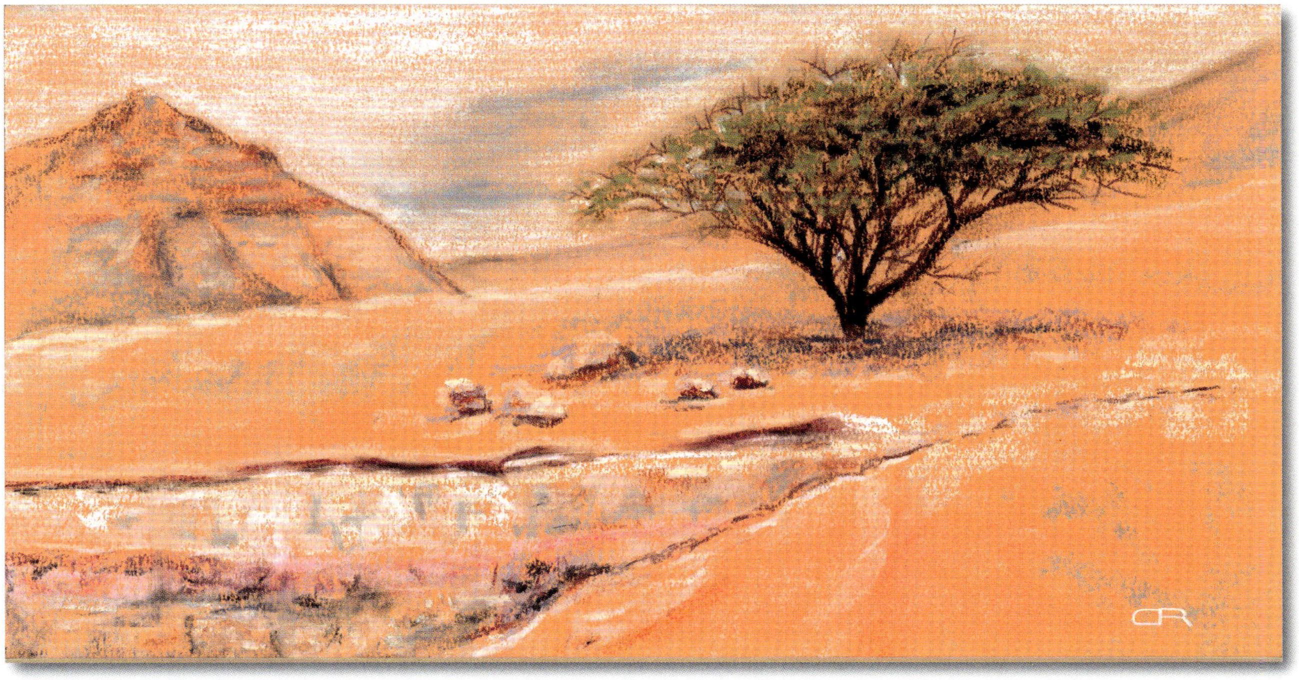

DATES

French writer Charles Didier's first encounter with Arabia came during a brief stopover in Yanbu in 1854, on his way to Ta'if to meet the Sherif of Mecca, at the latter's invitation. If "you overlook the whole of the town, there is nothing much to write home about. Several hundred houses, of which many are half in ruins, are thrown down pell-mell around a square. At one end of the square stands a rectangular fortress, flanked with towers," he observed sternly in his journal. But he delighted in "dates of superior quality" from Medina, "reputed the best in the world".
These same dates had been savored by the great British traveler Richard Burton one year earlier, during his stay in Medina. "I cannot say that the dates of Al-Madinah are finer than those of Mecca, although it is highly heretical to hold such tenet," he wrote following his visit to a palm grove located at the gates of the city, which caused him to wax lyrical: "Presently the Nakhil, or palm plantations, began. Nothing lovelier to the eye than the rich green waving crop and the cold shade. A perfumed breeze, nothing more delightful to the ear than the warbling of the small birds." The quality of dates from Medina had already been noted by Turkish pilgrim Mehmet Edib Mehmet, around 1680: "The fruits of the palm tree here offer a great variety [...] of which the following are unique to the Medina area: the *yerni*, *sultani*, *ajwa*, *halwah*, *sihani*." This richness and diversity were certainly at the root of their renown: "The date trees of Al-Madinah merit their celebrity," wrote Burton, continuing: "Their stately columnar stems, here, seem higher than in other lands, and their lower fronds are allowed to tremble in the breeze without mutilation," contrary to the extremely common and widespread practice of cutting the lower fronds. "These enormous palms were loaded with ripening fruits; and the clusters, carefully tied up, must often have weighed upwards of eighty pounds,"

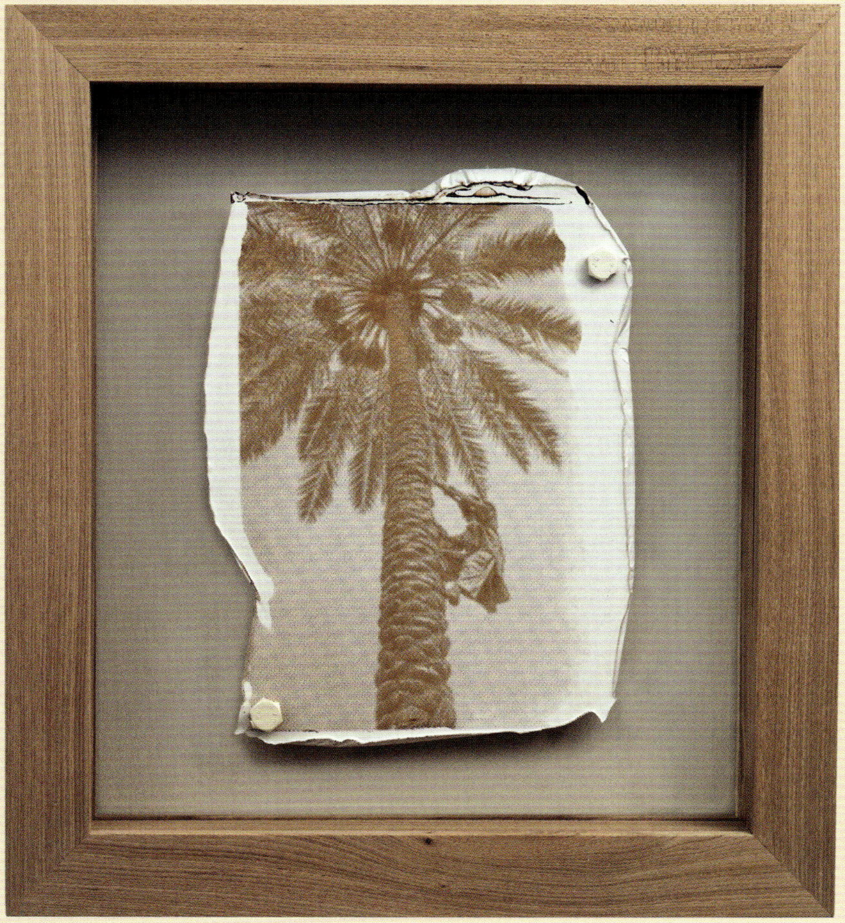

Piers Secunda
A date picker, 1938–2017
Dammam well n° 7
Crude oil and varnish
on industrial floor paint
with cast paint nuts
and bolts
49.5 x 45 x 6 cm
Courtesy of the artist

Charles Doughty wrote in *Travels in Arabia Deserta*: *"The Arabians inhabit a land of dearth and hunger, and there is no worse food than the date, which they must eat in their few irrigated valleys. The fruit is overheating and inwardly fretting under a sultry climate; too much of cloying sweet, not ministering enough of brawn and bone."*

Ilo Battigelli
A date picker, c. 1950
Courtesy of the Pitt Rivers Museum, University of Oxford

The date palm is grown primarily for its fruit and the date harvest is a time of celebration in the lives of the people of the desert. Other products supplied by the date palm include wood for building and fibers that are used for local crafts.

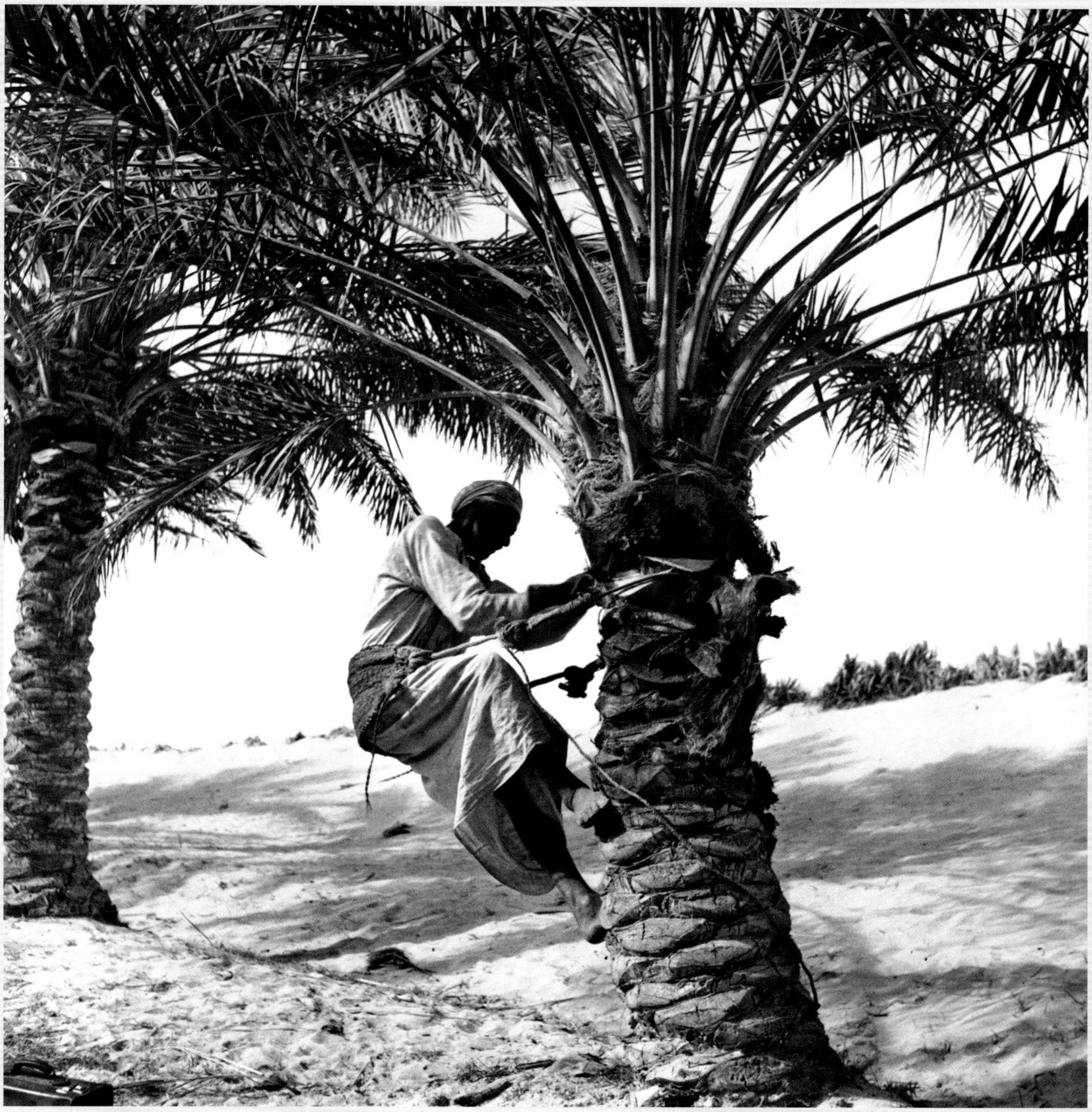

the Englishman further observed, drawing from scholarly works enumerating "a hundred and thirty-nine varieties; of these between sixty and seventy are well known, and each is distinguished, as usual among Arabs, by its peculiar name. The best kind is the *shalabi*." The *shalabi* used to be wrapped in palm fronds or small woven baskets, "and sent as presents to the remotest parts of the Moslem world. The fruit is about two inches long, with a small stone, and has a peculiar aromatic flavour and smell; it is seldom eaten locally on account of the price." Burton then turned his attentions to "another variety, the *ajwa*," which, as he noted, should not be mistaken "for date paste," commonly known as *adjoue* (see below): "The *ajwa* date is eaten, but not sold, because a tradition of the Prophet declares, that who so breaketh his fast every day with six or seven of these fruits need fear neither poison nor magic."

Burton continued: "The third kind, the *hilwa*, also a large date, derives its name from its exceeding sweetness" (*halw*, in Arabic, means sweet). Burton then listed varieties including the *birni*, mentioning its reputation for curing illness, the *wahshi*, the *sayhani* and the *khuzayriyah*, which, he noted, stayed green even when ripe: "the *jabali* is the common fruit; the poorest kinds are the *laun* and the *hilayah*." He also stated that "the date is also left upon the tree to dry, and then called 'balah'". Lastly, the English explorer observed that: "the Arabs delight in speaking of dates as an Irishman does of potatoes. They eat them for medicine as well as for food." Undoubtedly because the date was a fruit unfamiliar in their home climates, it particularly appealed to European visitors. After a tasting in the gardens of Al-Jawf, where he stayed in 1845, the eminent Finnish Orientalist Georg August Wallin wrote, "I noted no less than fifteen varieties, which are regarded as of superior flavour." Over the year (1862–63) that he spent in Najd, English adventurer William Gifford Palgrave, meanwhile, counted a "dozen kinds of dates, each perfectly distinct from the other," and added, "I doubt not that a longer acquaintance might have enabled me to reckon a dozen more."

For Wallin, the best were incontestably those from Al-Jawf and Tayma. Charles Huber shared his opinion, writing: "The dates from Tayma are the best in all of northern Arabia, with the exception of two or three varieties that exist in small quantities in Al-Jawf and Ha'il." For Palgrave, no dates were superior to those from the Al-Hasa oasis, of which "the *khala* is the perfection of the date." But "the *manasif*" was not to be omitted, according to British explorer Charles Doughty, who noted, "one side of the fruit is ripe while the other side is half-ripe". Indeed, the fruit has two colors—dark brown on one side, dense yellow on the other—and two textures, at once firm and tender.

The quality of the fruit, of course depended on how the plantations were irrigated and how the palm trees were watered. Burton observed that "the date-tree can live in dry and barren spots; but it loves the beds of streams and places where moisture is procurable. One of the reasons for the excellence of Medina dates is the quantity of water they obtain." But what held true for Hijaz and in Nejd could not be the case in Al-Jawf: "While the inhabitants of Nejd act upon the principle that the more the palms are watered, the more sugar the dates will contain, and consequently put them under every day, the people of Al-Jawf only irrigate theirs once in three or four days," wrote Wallin. For him, this parsimony explained the extreme quality of the dates produced there—in particular, the celebrated "*helwet Al-Jawf*" that Anne Blunt wrote about in 1878: "At all houses we were fed and entertained, having to drink endless cups of coffee flavored with cloves *(heyl)*, and eat innumerable dates, the '*helwet Al-Jawf*', which they say here are the best in Arabia; they are of excellent flavour, but too sweet and too sticky for general use."

It may also happen, infrequently, that palm trees grew on their own, with no need to be watered. This was observed by Charles Huber in 1880 in Khaybar: "The old Arabic proverb, 'to bring dates to Khaybar', which is equivalent to the French proverb 'to bring sand to the beach', still holds true. The palm trees of Khaybar are almost countless, and you can see how they are able to multiply, given that they need no care and that water is overly abundant. But as is often the case when nature is generous, humans take advantage of this. Having very little to do, the people of Khaybar have preferred to cease all activity, and due to negligence, their palm trees have declined to such an extent that they only give the smallest and most mediocre of fruits most likely found in all of Arabia."

In his description of Jeddah's souk, the Swiss Johann Ludwig Burckhardt (see chapter *The Gates of Arabia*) observed, in 1814, that no fewer than eight shops exclusively devoted to the date business were located there: "The importation of dates is uninterrupted during the whole year. At the end of June, the new fruit comes in; this lasts for two months, after which, for the remainder of the year, the date-paste, called *adjoue*, is sold." This paste is obtained "by pressing the dates, when fully ripe, into large baskets so forcibly as to reduce them to a hard solid paste or cake, each basket weighing generally about two hundred pounds; this is how the Bedouins bring it to the market, where it is cut out of the basket and sold by the pound. This *adjoue* forms a part of the daily food among all classes of people. In traveling, it is dissolved in water, and thus affords a sweet and refreshing drink. There are as many as twelve different sorts of *adjoue*," Burckhardt wrote with his typical precision, even specifying that the best *adjoue* was produced in the city of Taraba, east of Ta'if.

Dates could thus be consumed year-round. And "of all eatables used by the Arabs, dates are the most favourite," Burckhardt affirmed. Didier echoed his observation: "The date is the preferred food of the Bedouins, who feed their horses on it"; as did Englishwoman Anne Blunt, who wrote: "The people of Al-Jawf live almost entirely on dates; not, however, on the '*helwet*', which are not, by any means, the common sort. There are as many varieties here of dates as of apples in our orchards, and quite as different from each other."

Nevertheless, it seemed that immoderate consumption of this fruit did not always have positive effects, according to Doughty: in 1877, he observed the tooth decay of some poor populations of the Nejd forced to adopt a diet consisting only of dates and lukewarm groundwater and having access to nothing else. Very fortunately, this only concerned an extremely marginal population of the most disadvantaged individuals, among those who were courageous enough to live in a land of such great scarcity.

Every year, however, the whole population rejoiced when it came time to harvest the fruits. Doughty noted once again that "the date harvest is a time of excitement in the lives of the people of the desert," the time for paying homage to this extraordinary plant, whose absence would make life in the region impossible. Its stalk, which can reach a peak of twenty-five or thirty meters, used to be used for construction and heating, and its fibers to produce various basketry items needed in daily life.

Caroline Havers
Dates #3 (Harvest)
From the series *Sand & Serendipity*, 2014
Mixed media on canvas
150 × 180 cm
Courtesy of the artist
and of Naila Gallery, Riyadh

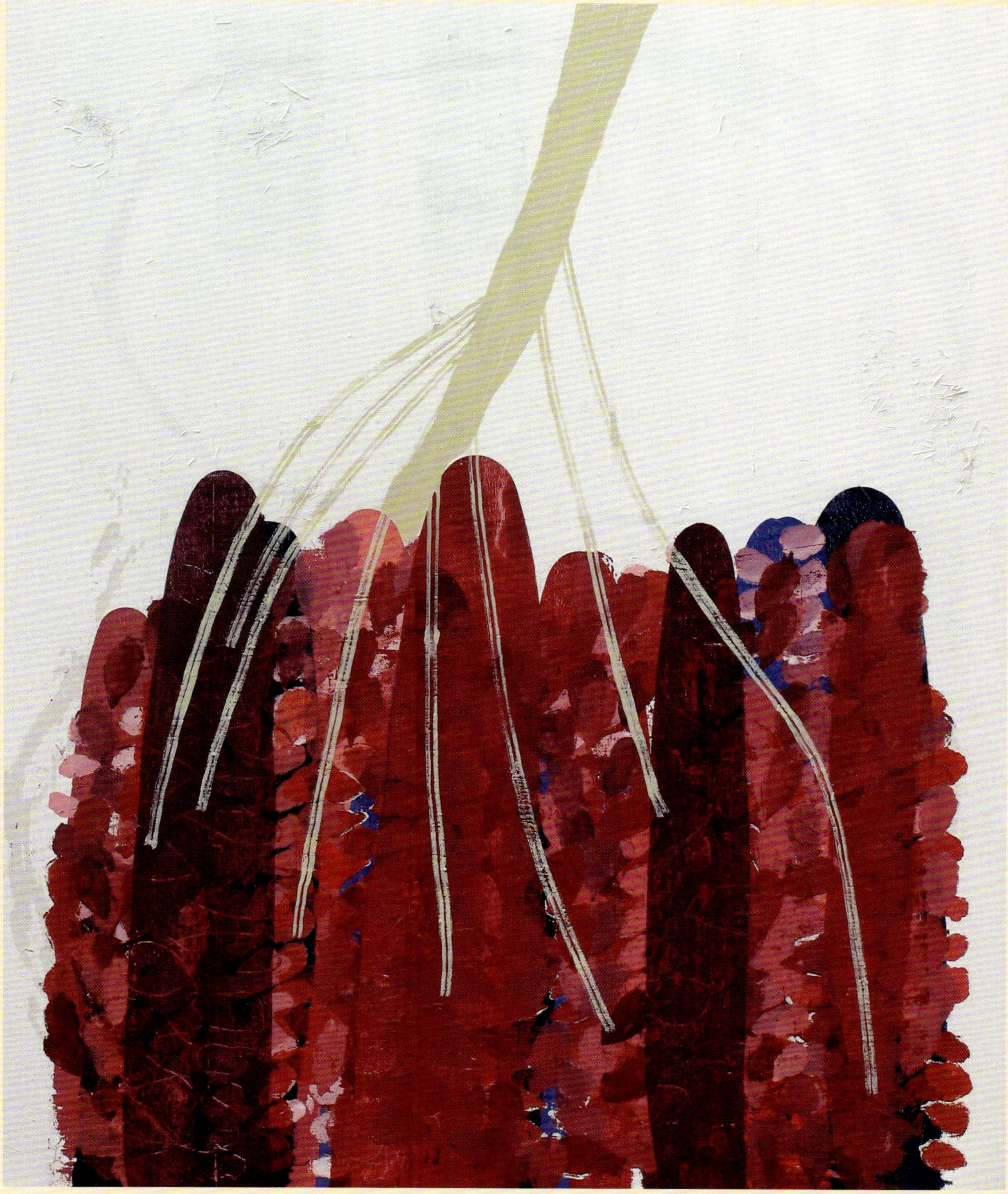

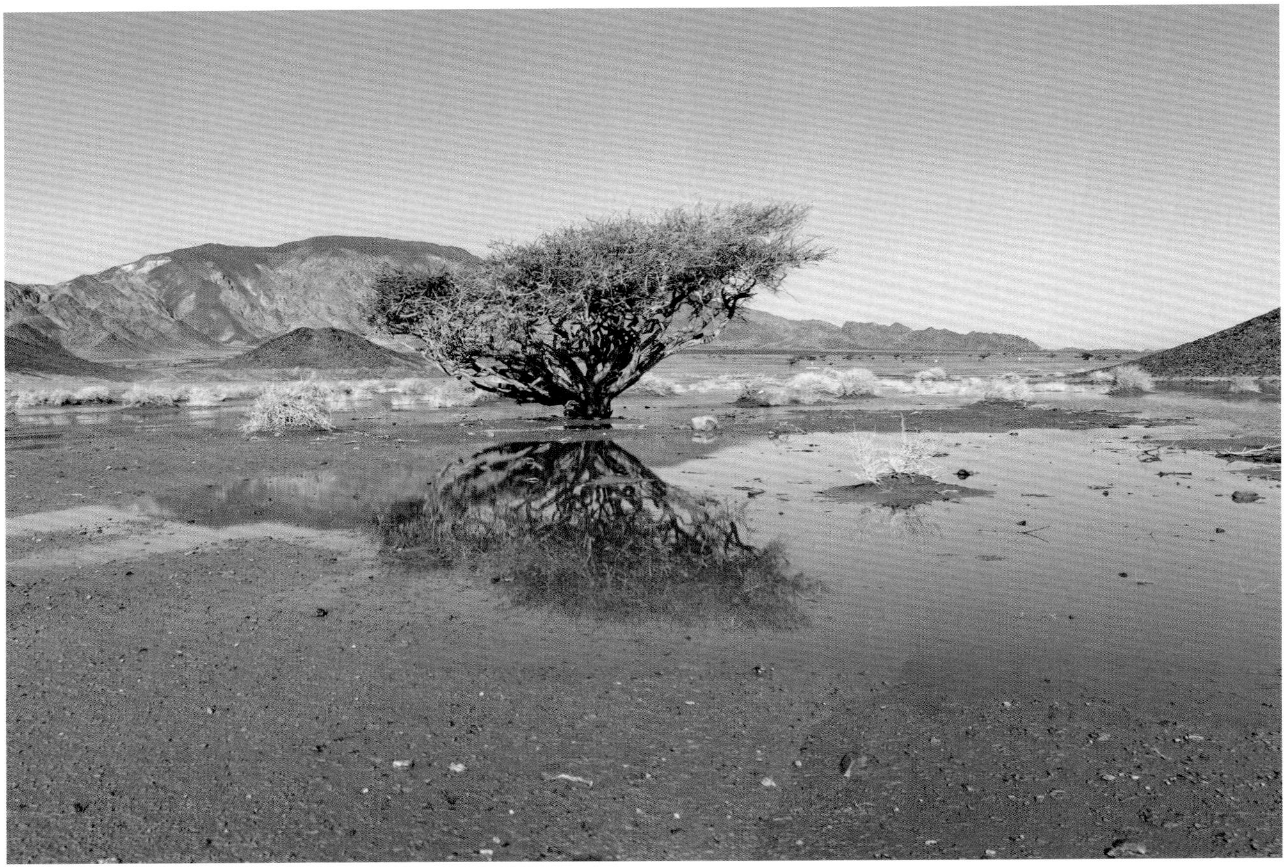

Yann Gayet
Adenum Obesum
From the series *Ruwaydan*, 2010
Courtesy of the artist

Caroline Havers
Cistanche Tubulosa #1
From the series *Sand & Serendipity*, 2014
Mixed media on panel
60 × 120 cm
Courtesy of the artist
and of Naila Gallery, Riyadh

Caroline Havers became fascinated by the exotic beauty of the desert plants that she discovered during her sojourn in Riyadh. The flora of Arabia became one of the recurrent themes in her artwork.

excellent habit, which assuredly does not exist among all the nations of Europe, of trying to assist a stranger who endeavours to speak their language, and never laugh at him if he expresses himself badly." He also noted that the good graces of the locals could be won "by speaking to them of science, as Arabs, unlike Turks, are unashamed to learn things from Europeans." However, it was necessary to demonstrate tact, as "no more should he try to gain the Arabs by flattery: they like sincerity and are aware they have faults, but they like as little as other nations to be rallied about them."

While over the course of their travels, he and his comrades may well have had grounds for complaint about the natives, as he wrote, Niebuhr nevertheless constantly sought understanding, and soon objected: "In our ignorance of the country and its dwellers, we often thought ourselves justified in complaining, forgetting that even in Europe one does not always travel agreeably." This is why he judged that "if an Arab were to travel in Europe he would often have squabbles with the innkeepers, posting masters, postilions, and custom-house officers: he might even have as many causes to be offended at the greed of Europeans as Europeans have at the outrages of Arabs. But he would be mistaken if he were to paint all Europeans to his fellow countrymen as greedy and unpolished because he had been badly received by some of them."

Thus, prior to making judgments and growing offended, Niebuhr sought to understand the people he encountered. He displayed the same respect for the King of Yemen as he would for his own sovereign. Even the highwaymen, because "certainly there are to be found in Arabia, especially in the desert, thieves" who were able to find grace in his eyes, due to the fact that "they rarely killed those they plundered". Contrary to common practice in Europe, "they are even hospitable towards those they have robbed; they leave them with some supplies and some old clothes; they even go so far as to accompany them on their journey, for fear that they will perish in the desert."

Given such wisdom, it is lamentable that this undertaking was cut short, and that the ambitious project in the making, to give the world a "Description of Arabia," was brutally interrupted. The work would undoubtedly have been less rich and extensive than the one later produced by a brigade of French scholars in Egypt, but it was carried out in a similar spirit—the spirit at the heart of eighteenth-century European humanism. We do not know whether von Haven, Forsskål, Baurenfeind, and Cramer shared the same lofty ideas

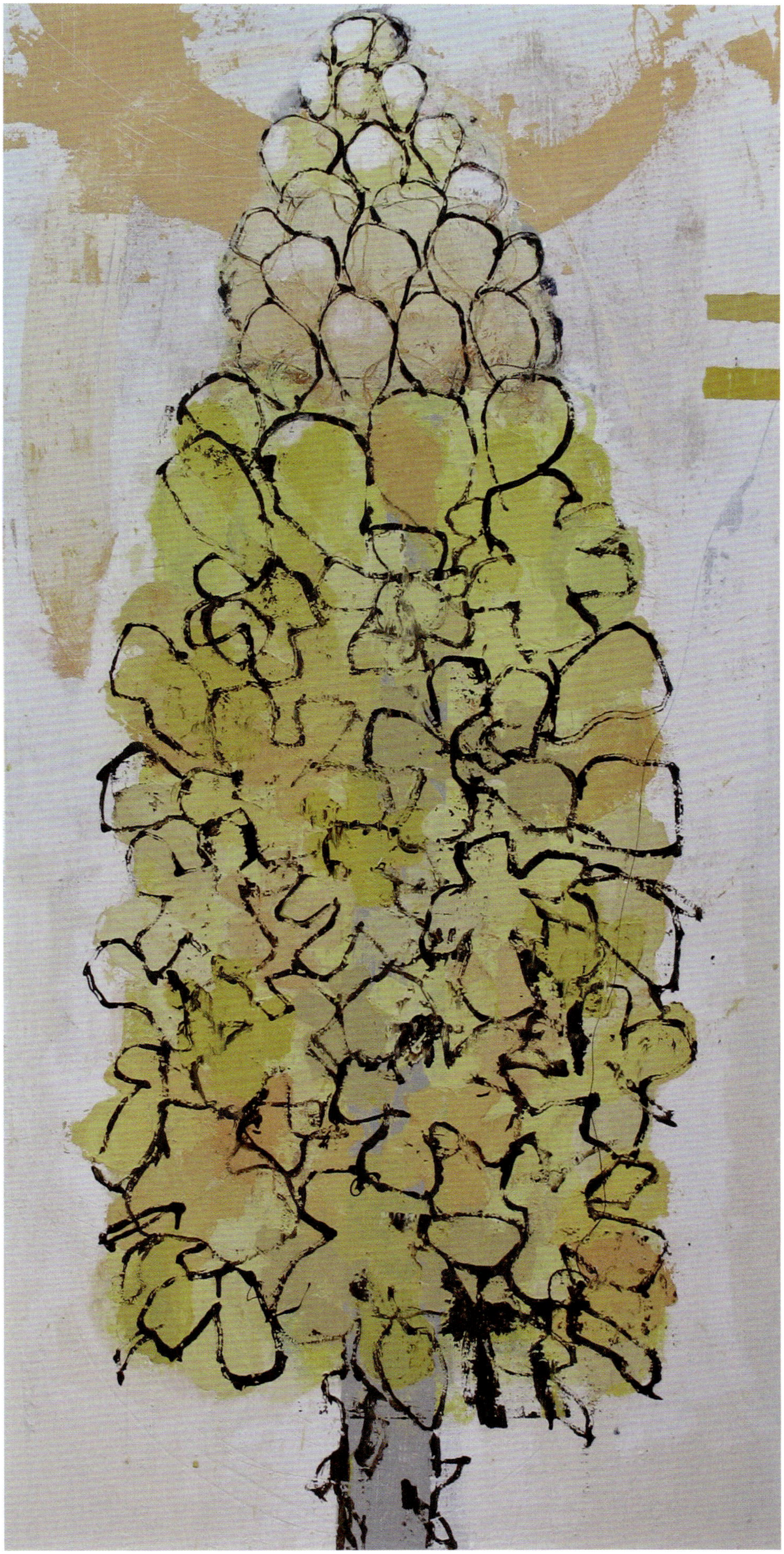

as Niebuhr, but we would like to believe that they did, and imagine the great work that they could very well have completed had their sojourn not been cut short—had they returned home and had the opportunity to use the material collected together to produce such a publication.

Carsten Niebuhr's account remains, of course, the subtlety of which comes across in the few sentences cited here, not strictly limited to the chronicle of an unfortunate team. These few volumes have long been considered a classic not only of the geography, but the ethnology and archaeology (although these sciences did not exist as such at that time) of the places where he spent time in Arabia and beyond. Indeed, after more than a year in India, Niebuhr carried on his journey, traveling extensively in Persia, Iraq, Syria, and Palestine; ultimately, his stay in Arabia was but one episode of an extremely long voyage. He reached Constantinople, finally returning to Denmark from there in late 1767, seven years after his departure.

His book, *Travels through Arabia, and Other Countries in the East*, was published five years later in Copenhagen, in German. It contains a host of new information on the peninsula—its climate, social and political organization, tribes, customs, clothing, food, universities, Koranic schools, etc. Niebuhr strove to provide answers to the multitude of questions that had been submitted by academies, sometimes using the notes left by his comrades, and always stating when this was the case; he had made every effort, despite the obstacles in doing so, to repatriate these notes to Denmark, alongside the collections amassed by each member of the group. He also published the works of the expedition's botanist, his friend Pehr Forsskål, gathered in a book entitled *Flora Aegyptiaco-Arabica*, published in Latin in 1775.

That publication contained the lists of plants studied by Forsskål—classified according to the principles of the great naturalist Carl von Linné, his instructor—and places where they had been observed, in Anatolia, Egypt, Arabia, and Yemen. Unfortunately, ordinary readers will not gain insight into the peninsula's landscapes in the pages of this scholarly and austere opus. But over the course of the nineteenth century, other travelers went to Arabia, showing interest for regions that had never before been the object of substantial description—Shammar, Nejd, Qasim, Al-Hasa, Asir and more—and determined to reveal their great diversity. Only in the twentieth century

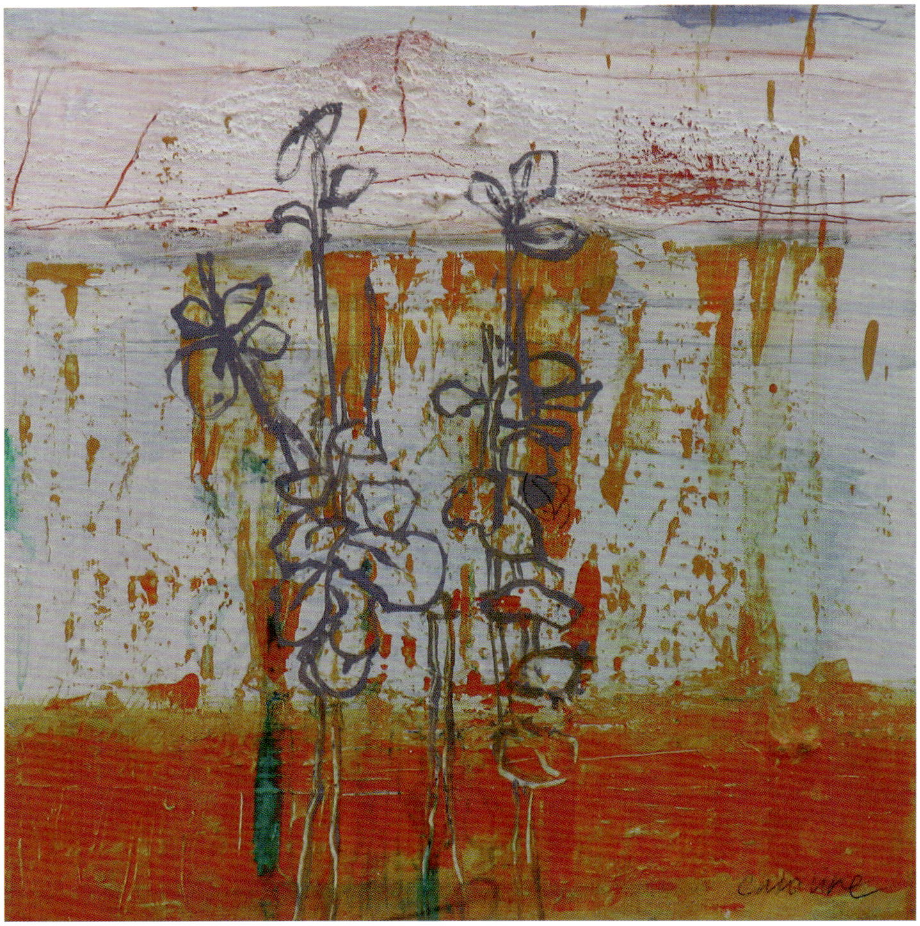

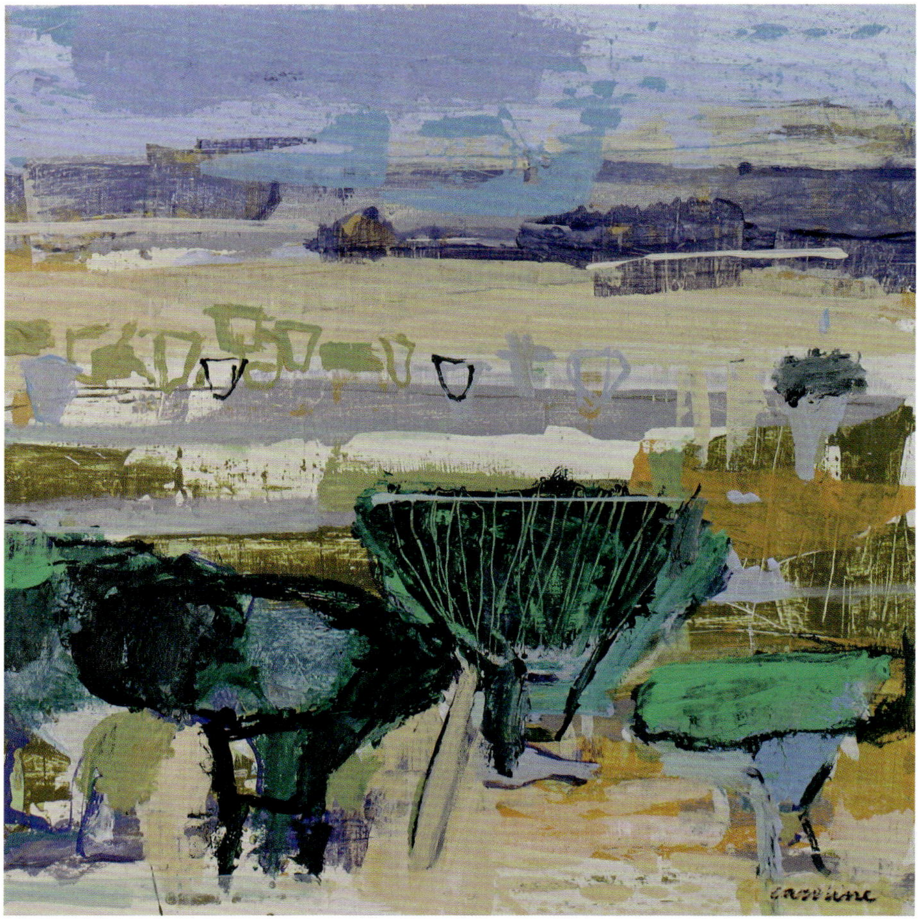

Caroline Havers
Calotropis Procera
From the series *Sand & Serendipity*, 2014
Mixed media on panel
30 × 30 cm
Courtesy of the artist
and of Naila Gallery, Riyadh

Calotropis Procera (*Uthar* in Arabic) is a perennial evergreen desert shrub found in sandy soils. Its height ranges from two to five meters. The branches of the plant secrete a milk that is used in traditional medicine for the treatment of arthritis.

Caroline Havers
Acacia #4
From the series *Sand & Serendipity*, 2014
Mixed media on panel
45 × 45 cm
Courtesy of the artist
and of Naila Gallery, Riyadh

Acacia with its various types is the most commonly found tree in the desert regions. It is a principal source of resins and incenses that were traded via the ancient trade routes. Camels pasture on the thorns and leaves of the acacia tree.

Caroline Havers
Mary's Palm / Kaff Maryam #3
From the series *Sand & Serendipity*, 2014
Mixed media on panel
4 pieces of 45 × 45 cm each
Courtesy of the artist
and of Naila Gallery, Riyadh

Kaff Maryam (Selaginella pilifera) is also called a Jericho Rose. It's a small gray annual herb. *Kaff Maryam* literally means "palm of Maryam" because its leaves are shaped like a clutched hand that resembles the hand of the Virgin Mary during childbirth, according to Arabian folklore.

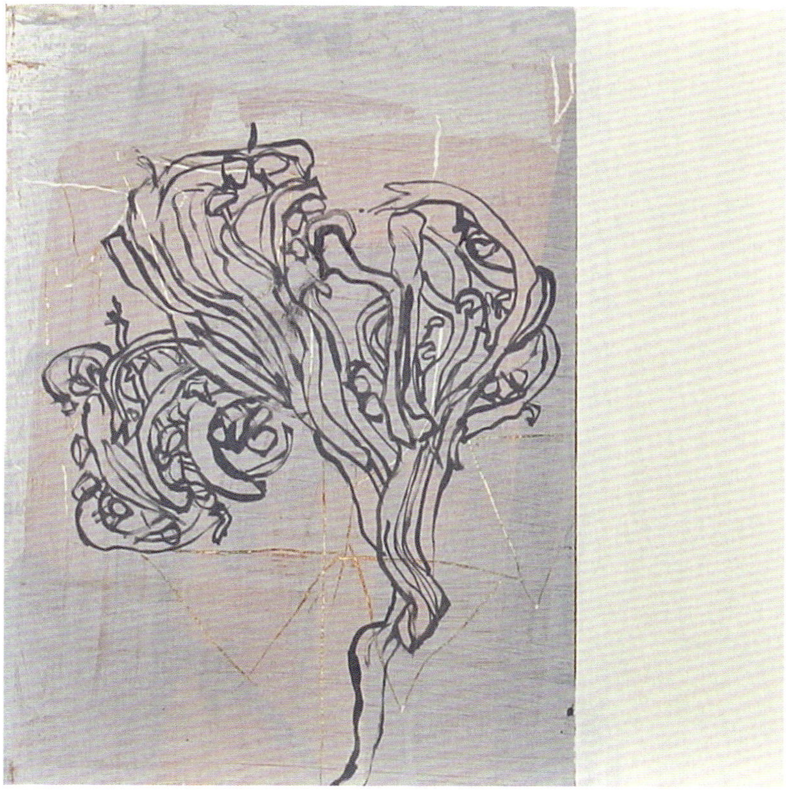

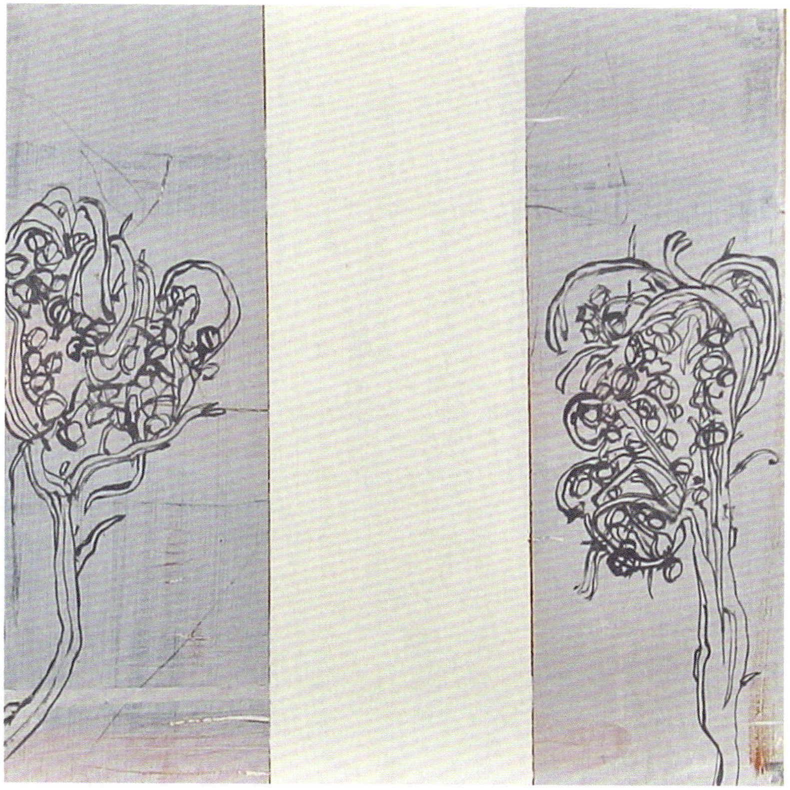

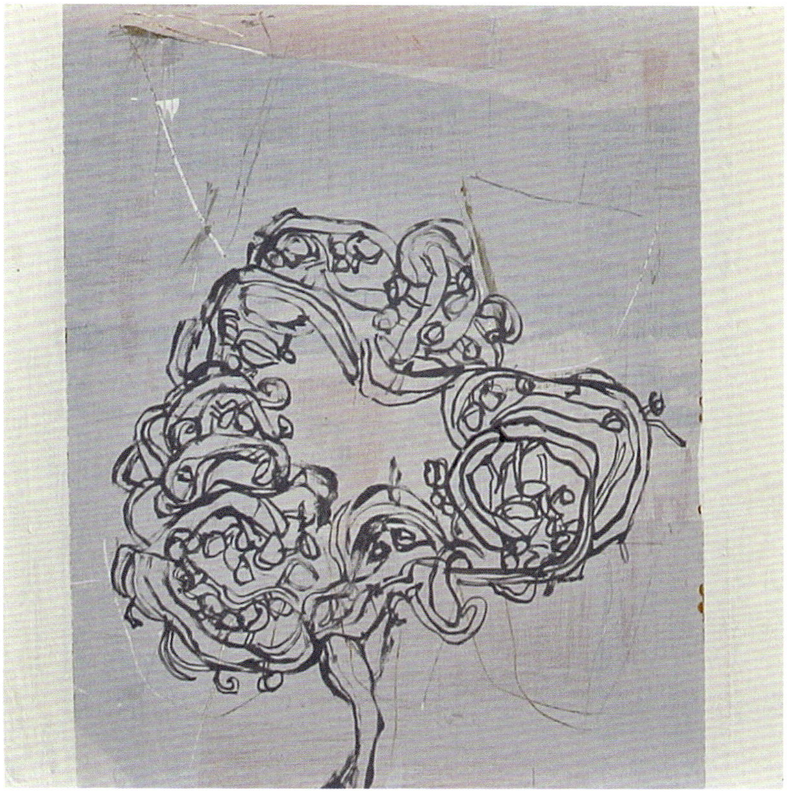

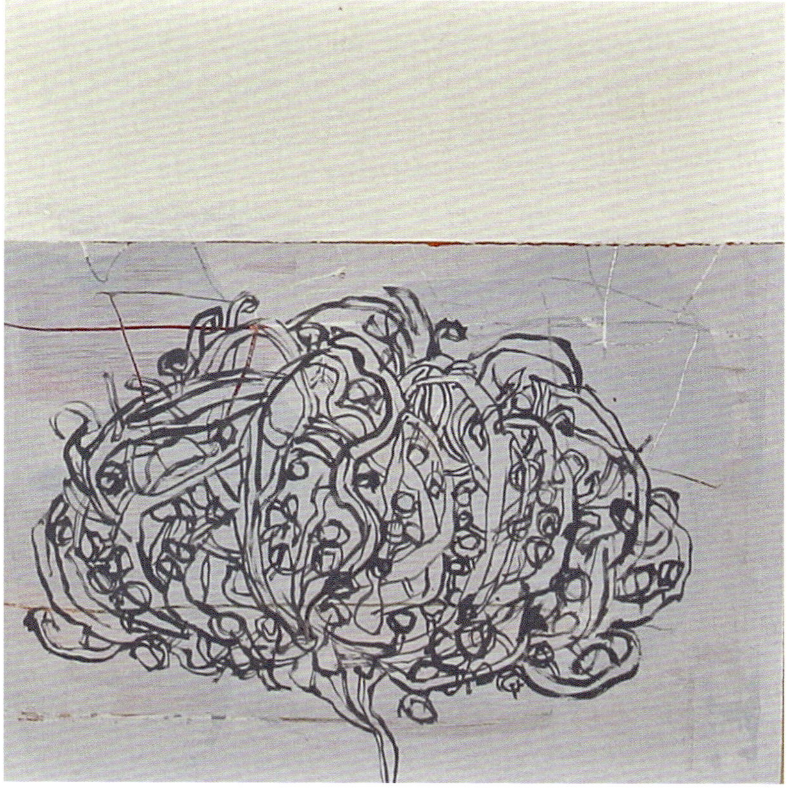

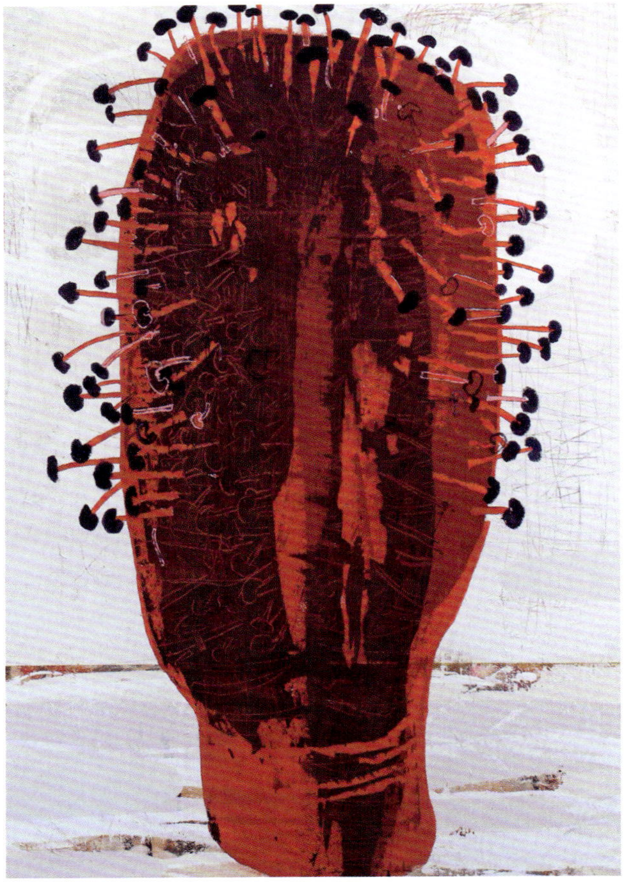

did a few daring Europeans—Bertram Thomas, in 1930, St. John Philby, in 1932, and Wilfred Thesiger, in 1946—travel the peninsula from end to end, revealing to the world the last of these territories, the foreboding *Rub' al-Khali*.

The first travelers to have undertaken the journey to Arabia were first struck by its extreme aridness and barrenness. Subsequently, some were nevertheless able to observe that within Hijaz, there were verdant landscapes and lush nature, in particular around the city of Ta'if.

The encounter with Ta'if happened, we might say, well before travelers even got there. Upon arrival in Arabia—indeed, upon disembarking in the port of Jeddah—they could taste grapes and watermelon, apricots and peaches, figs and pomegranates from there. Simply enough, "all the fruits come from Ta'if," as the Swiss Johann Ludwig Burckhardt noted in a description of utmost precision that he gave of the souks of Jeddah and the eighteen fruit and vegetable merchants that he counted there (cf. chapter *The Gates of Arabia*).

In the event that visitors decided to go there, the trip took two days from Mecca, on steep paths easier to climb on donkey than on camelback. "To those who have only known the dreary and scorching sands of the lower country of the Hijaz, this scene is as surprising, as the keen air which blows here is refreshing," wrote Burckhardt on the subject of this "unrivalled" place, where it snows "every five years or so". Indeed, "this delicious city, so extolled by the Arabs," in the words of Maurice Tamisier, a young French Saint-Simonian recruited in Cairo as medical secretary for one of Muhammad Ali's armies sent to Arabia, lies at an altitude of some 1,600 meters. Seduced by the "magnificence" of Ta'if, he went on: "Travellers who have been burnt by the ardent sun, those whose eyes have grown used to contemplating the parched mountain streams, sandy plains, and stony mountains of this land, will delight in the appearance of the many gardens surrounding the city and their body, released from scorching temperatures, will sweetly savour the delicious sensations of a cooler environment."

"The whole world has heard of Ta'if, the garden of Mecca, whose fruits enjoy a widespread and well-deserved reputation," attested Saleh Soubhy, an Egyptian public health official twice tasked by his government with accompanying the pilgrimage caravan to Arabia in the late nineteenth century. Burckhardt added, "The gardens of Ta'if are renowned also for the abundance of their roses, which are transported to all parts of the Hijaz." Upon approaching, this "plain planted with mimosas, whose green and vigorous tone appears to announce that Ta'if, which the Arabs call the garden of Arabia, is near," in the words of Tamisier, "the air becomes light, refreshing," according to the

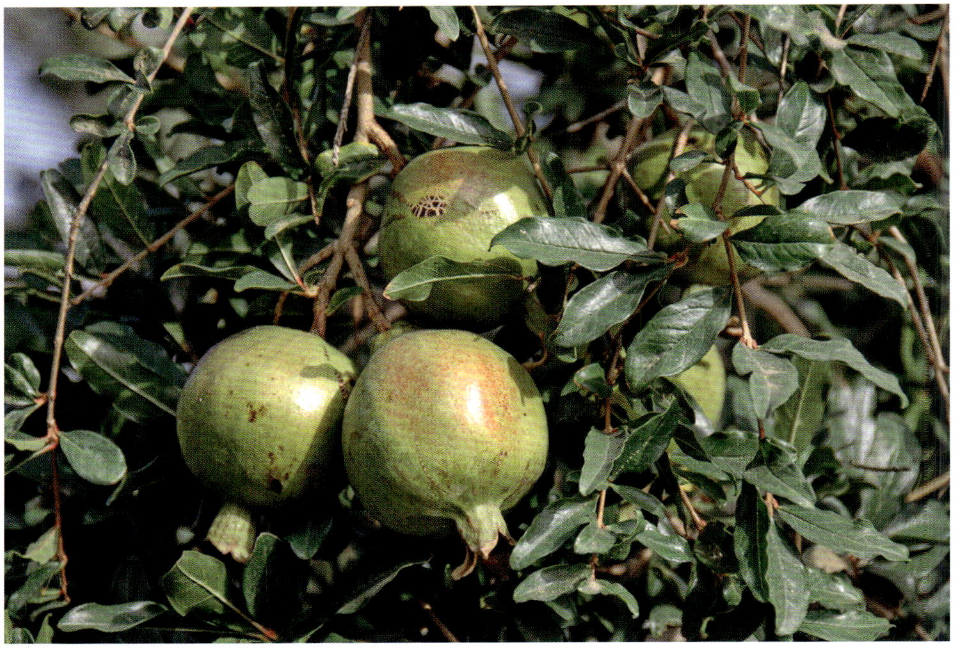

Caroline Havers
Tarthuth #2
From the series *Sand & Serendipity*, 2014
Mixed media on panel
60 × 60 cm
Courtesy of the artist and of Naila Gallery, Riyadh

A burgundy parasitic plant with nail-like seed heads, *Tarthuth* (*Cyanomorium coccineum*) appears in Arabia during the spring. It has been harvested in the desert for thousands of years, it is very appreciated by camels, and it is also used in Bedouin medicine.

Olivier Couppey
Pomegranates in Ta'if
Courtesy of the artist

John Keane wrote in *Six months in the Hijaz, Journeys to Makkah and Madinah 1877-1878* that *"the pomegranates of Arabia are perhaps the best in the world. One kind of pomegranate has the seeds so soft that they may be eaten with pleasure. A much-worn green dye is procured by a simple process from the skin of pomegranate."* Both Ta'if and Medina are famous for their "Rubb Rumman," a thick pomegranate syrup drunk with water during the hot weather and considered cooling and wholesome, wrote Richard Burton.

Colbert Held
Proud of their produce, 1963
Courtesy the Middle East Institute / Colbert Held Archive, Washington, D.C.

Two farm laborers proudly show off onions and cabbages harvested from an irrigated field in Hofuf, the largest Saudi oasis.

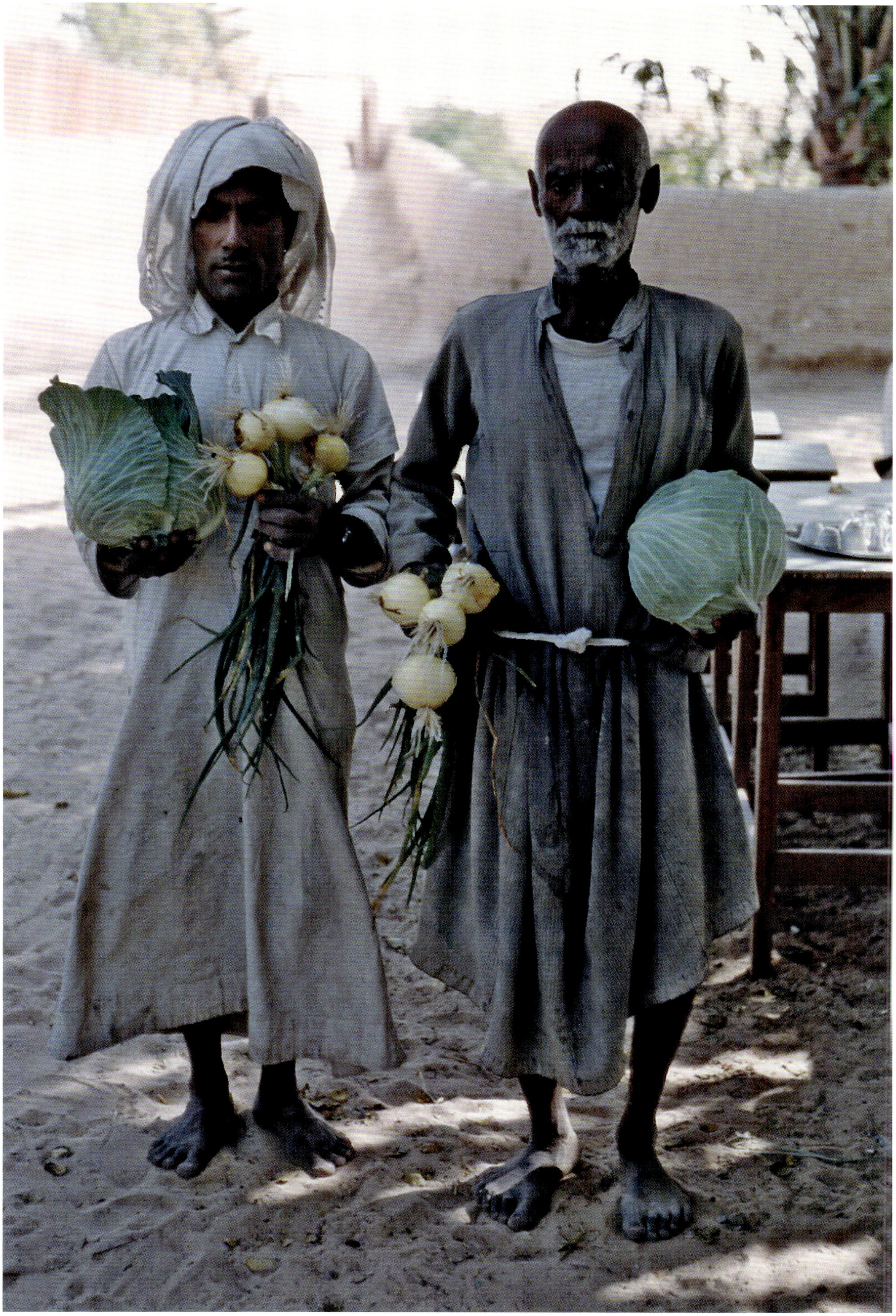

Italian adventurer Giovanni Finati, deserter of both the Napoleonic and Turkish armies, also enrolled in Muhammad Ali's army as a simple infantryman. He added that "from a distance, you can smell the fragrant plants from the gardens of the city." Burckhardt, meanwhile, observed: "Every leaf and blade of grass was covered with a balmy dew, and every tree and shrub diffused a fragrance as delicious to the smell as was the landscape to the eye."

This idyllic place, which one would hardly expect to find so close to Mecca, was already a summer destination for wealthy Quraysh merchants at the time of the Prophet of Islam. Some twelve centuries later, Tamisier could observe that "in the beginning of June, wealthy proprietors from Mecca leave their city to come enjoy the coolness of Ta'if," and more specifically, the gardens which "at the foot of dry mountains, surrounded the barren plain where the city stands, forming a circle of delightful sanctuaries," as the historian Jacqueline Pirenne described this "precious setting".

She continued: "Behind the earthen walls that blocked indiscreet gazes, an abundance of trees and greenery, where irrigation waters flowed, sheltered homes and arbours where the master of the house and his wives came to enjoy the coolness of this favoured spot. Each estate contained a farm, and the owners were always sheriffs or doctors from Mecca, officials serving the Kaaba or wealthy merchants."

Each one of these small spots of paradise had a name and, so it was said, possessed a specificity and a character that made it distinctive, among all the others.

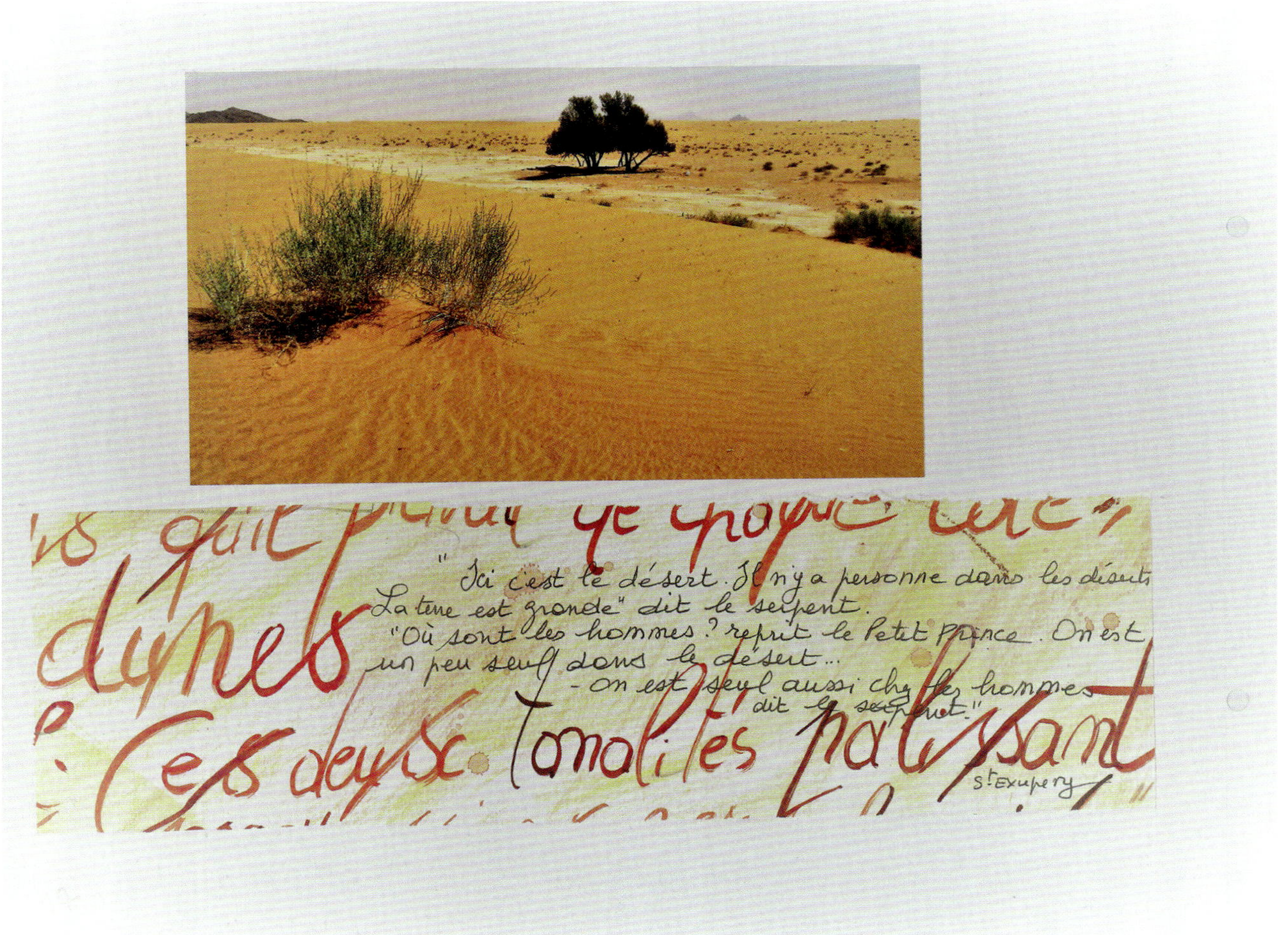

Édith Ortoli
La terre est grande
From *Esprit du désert*, 2017
Artist book, single copy
Mixed media
26 × 32 cm
Text by Antoine de Saint-Exupéry
Courtesy of the artist

John Keane wrote in *Six months in the Hijaz, Journeys to Makkah and Madinah 1877-1878*: *"Though the general appearance of the country is bare rock or sandy desert, there is no part absolutely without a little vegetation. In some places there are large savannahs of coarse grass like long stubble, and in others small jungles of gorse and broom-like growths."*

Carsten Niebuhr
Description de l'Arabie, d'après les observations et recherches faites dans le pays même, 1773-1776
Vol. II, Paris, Librairie Brunet
Nasser D. Khalili Collection of Islamic art, London

Among the five members of Carsten Niebuhr's Danish-sponsored expedition to Arabia in 1762–63 was Swedish botanist Pehr Forsskål, a physician with extensive knowledge of botany. He was fluent in Arabic and during the trip he collected seeds and took botanical specimens. Pehr Forsskål was stricken with malarial fever to the extent that he had to be tied to his camel so he would not fall off. He died in Yarim and his notes and specimens were sent to Copenhagen by Niebuhr, the sole survivor of the expedition, who in 1775 published Forsskål's research as *Flora Aegyptiaco-Arabica*.

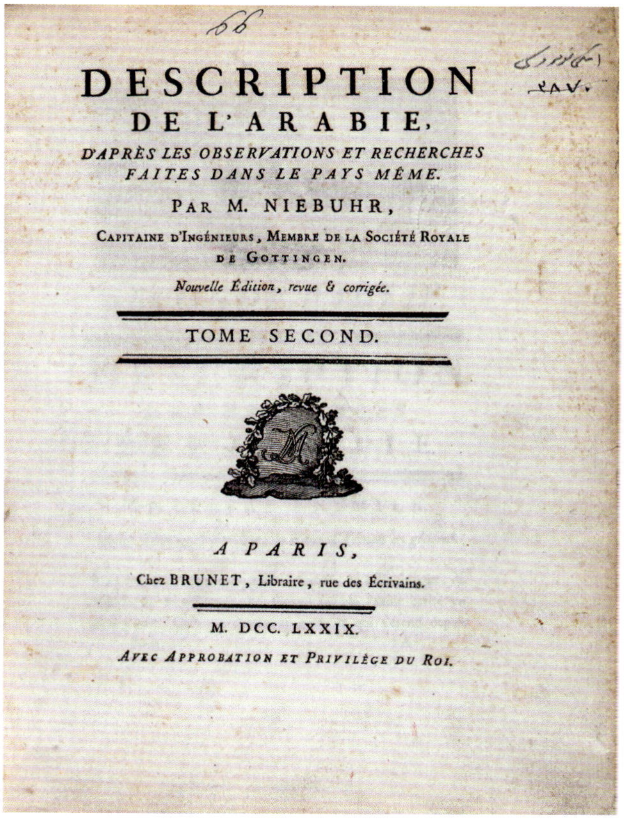
DESCRIPTION
DE L'ARABIE,
D'APRÈS LES OBSERVATIONS ET RECHERCHES FAITES DANS LE PAYS MÊME.
PAR M. NIEBUHR,
CAPITAINE D'INGÉNIEURS, MEMBRE DE LA SOCIÉTÉ ROYALE DE GOTTINGEN.
Nouvelle Édition, revue & corrigée.
TOME SECOND.
A PARIS,
Chez BRUNET, Libraire, rue des Écrivains.
M. DCC. LXXIX.
AVEC APPROBATION ET PRIVILÈGE DU ROI.

Édith Ortoli
L'orgueil des arbres
From *Esprit du désert*, 2017
Artist book, single copy
Mixed media
26 × 32 cm
Poem by Eugène Guillevic
Courtesy of the artist

The poem reads: *"The role of the sentinel is entrusted to the trees."*

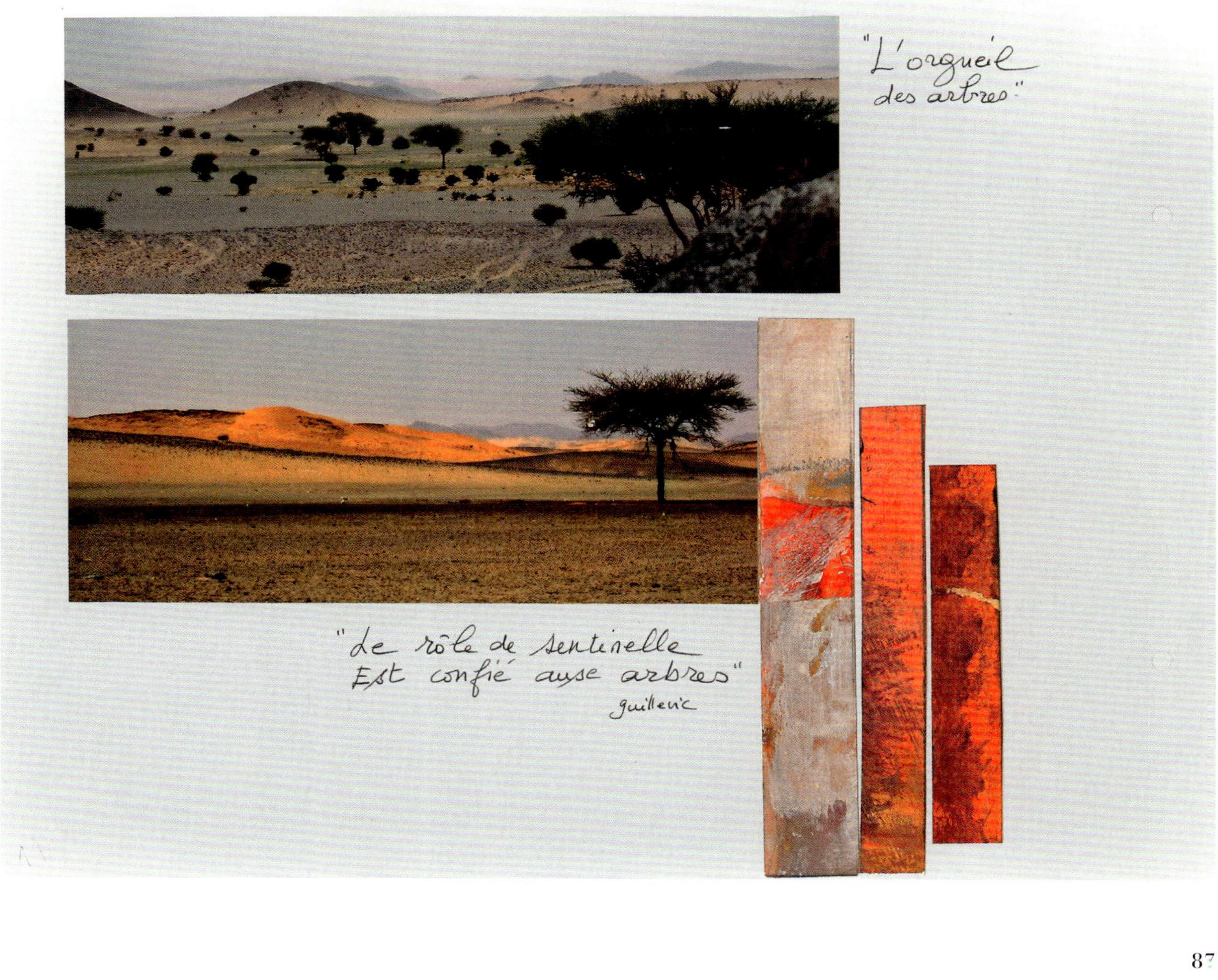

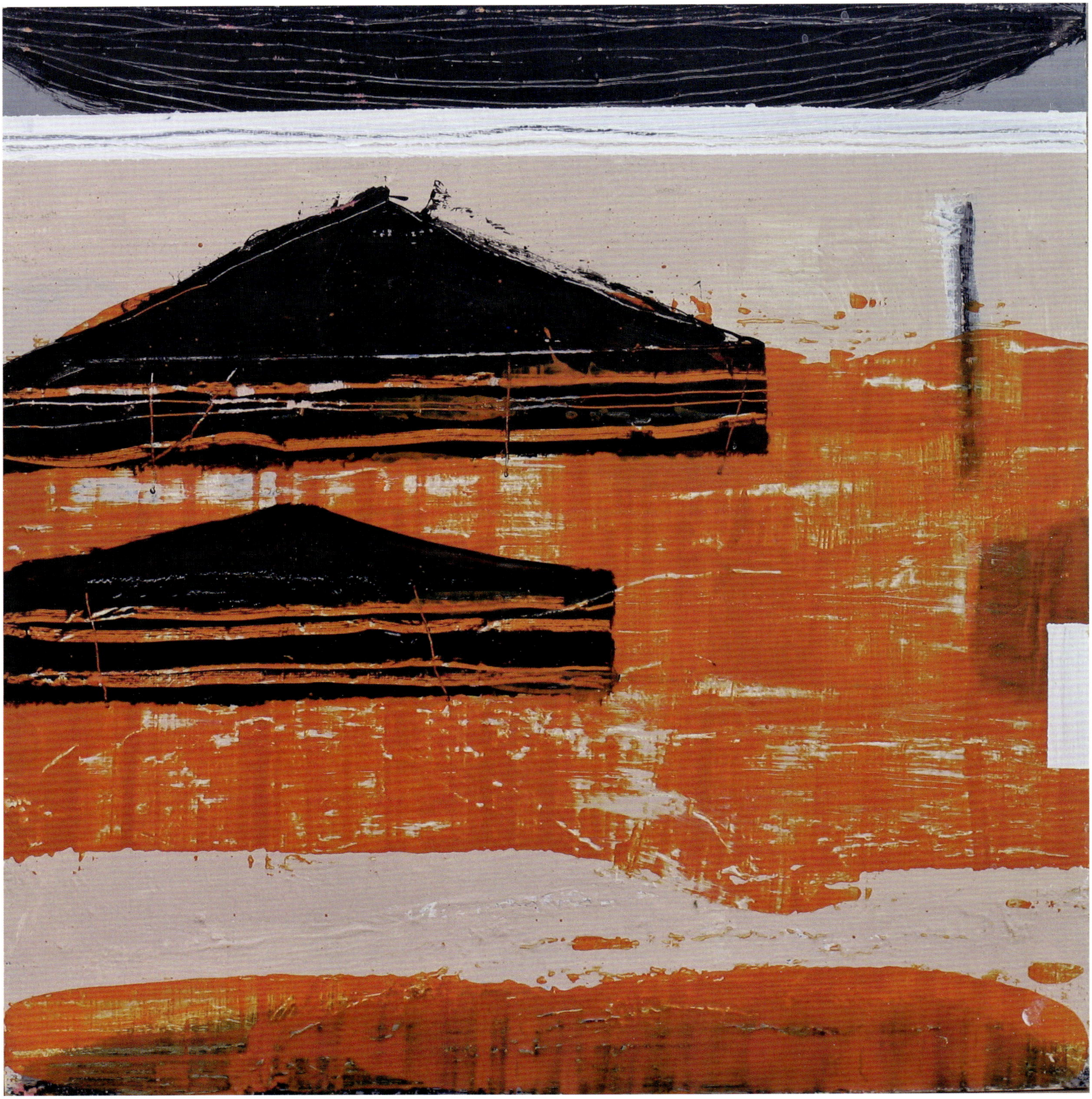

The People of the Sands

Until the first half of the twentieth century the Bedouins posed a paradox to the European travelers. They personified and adhered to some of the highest universal values—generosity towards the destitute, a sense of hospitality towards all beings and an aspiration for liberty and courage. However, they simultaneously engaged in conflicting behaviors—brigandage, pillaging and all forms of theft that would appear to be radically contradictory with their values.This paradox, however, together with the men who incarnated it, has disappeared today. This does not mean that the Bedouins were overcome by force. In this regard, the prediction announced by Carsten Niebuhr at the end of the eighteenth century would prove to be as true as the motto set forth in these terms: "Bedouins cannot be completely dominated by foreigners and never will be."

Neither the restless sands, nor the desert wind (the terrible simoom), with which they came to terms throughout the centuries, led them to disappear. No, if these "free men, who accept no yoke," as Jules Gervais-Courtellemont defined them, are no longer there today, the reason is that the very conditions of their existence have surreptitiously disappeared, undermined by technological progress. Technological progress has reduced to zero, or close to zero, the tremendous dimensions of the desert vastness within which they had always evolved. Technological progress has reduced the camel's unchanging pace, which until then had been the unity of measure that ticked off the beads of their lifetime, to the level of a simple recollection. Technological progress, which made their way of life unfeasible, signed their death warrant.

It is to the abruptness of this evolution, to this deplorable end, that Wilfred Thesiger, the last of our great explorers and one of the few to have completed the crossing of Rub' al-Khali (the Empty Quarter), referred when he observed that "nowhere in the world has there been such continuity as in the Arabian desert. Many civilizations rose and fell around the Arabian desert; they lasted a few hundred years and vanished, new races were born and then disappeared, religions rose and fell, but the nomad bedouins in the desert lived on with the same pattern of life over an enormous span of time. However, in forty years, less than a man's lifetime, all was changed." Thesiger also expressly identified the culpable factor: "The most terrible change for the desert dwellers occurred with the introduction of mechanical transport."

Before this fatal disappearance could take effect—during the course of the twentieth century—the Bedouins were there in force, populating all the desert spaces of the Arabian peninsula: "Like the simple but vigorous plants that fill the most sterile of the cracks in the rocks," wrote Maurice Tamisier on the matter, "they are satisfied in this desolated land and have multiplied over the centuries in those places where we would inevitably perish from hunger if we were guided by our destiny alone." Allowing his frank admiration to transpire, the young follower of Saint-Simon added: "One can hardly believe that beings organised as we are can live in such a harsh natural environment and yet these men are more attached than we to the earth of their homeland and they suffer more than we do in exile."

It may also seem that the natural environment of his homeland—where the Bedouin is, in a certain sense, confined—is also the origin of his unique temperament: "The nomad of the Arabian interior is the hardest of those known among the peoples consolidated by custom and religion. The more his isolation impoverishes him by external friction, the more he relies on his originality," exclaimed the French writer Léopold Derôme. Wilfred Thesiger made the same observations in *Arabian Sands*: "Shut off from the outside world by the desert and the sea, the inhabitants of Arabia have kept their

Caroline Havers
Tents #2
From the series *Sands & Serendipity*, 2014
Mixed media on panel
45 × 45 cm
Courtesy of the artist
and of Naila Gallery, Riyadh

Black tents are named *Bayt al sha'r*, which translates to "house or booth of hair". In Arabic, the word *bayt* designates a tent as well as a house.

Humberto da Silveira
From the series *Bedu*, 1994
Courtesy of the artist

Doughty wrote that the "*Bedouin body is as a light-timbered ship which may lie stranded till the spring-tide, when with one great eating, he may replenish his fainting nature.*"

Humberto da Silveira
From the series *Bedu*, 1994
Courtesy of the artist

Thesiger wrote that he was "*humbled by those illiterate herdsmen, who possessed, in so much greater measure than [he], generosity and courage, endurance, patience and light-hearted gallantry.*"

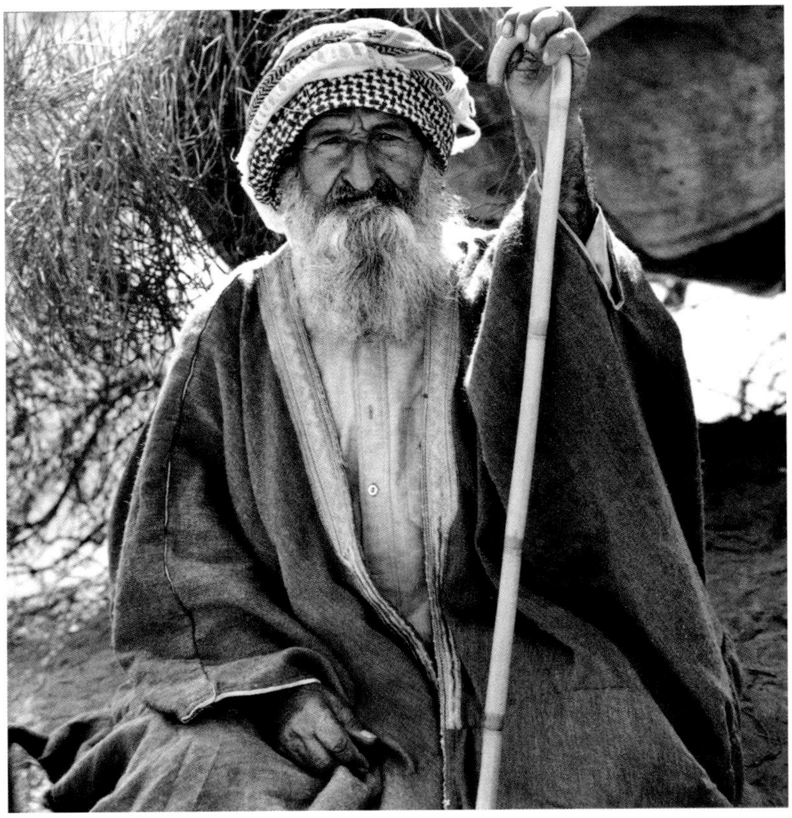

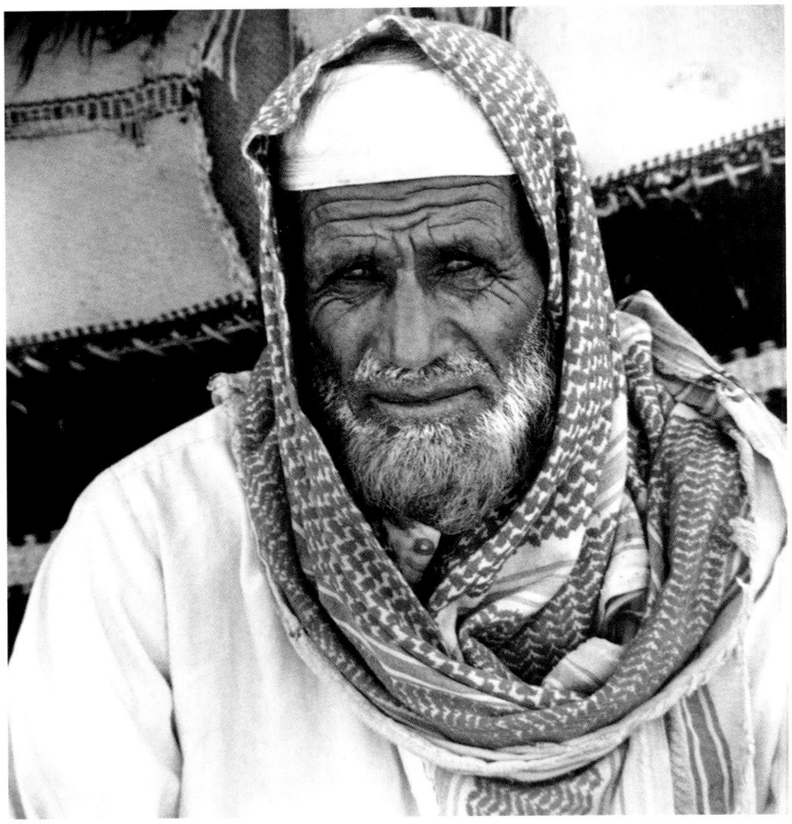

Humberto da Silveira
From the series *Bedu*, 1994
Courtesy of the artist

G. A. Wallin wrote: "*There are two ways of getting on with the Bedouins; either give them sugar and sweet words, or treat them with severity and manly seriousness; I have found the second method the better one.*"

Humberto da Silveira
From the series *Bedu*, 1994
Courtesy of the artist

Wallin wrote that "*nowhere in the world have I seen children more sensitive, good-natured and obedient as the Bedouin children towards their parents.*"

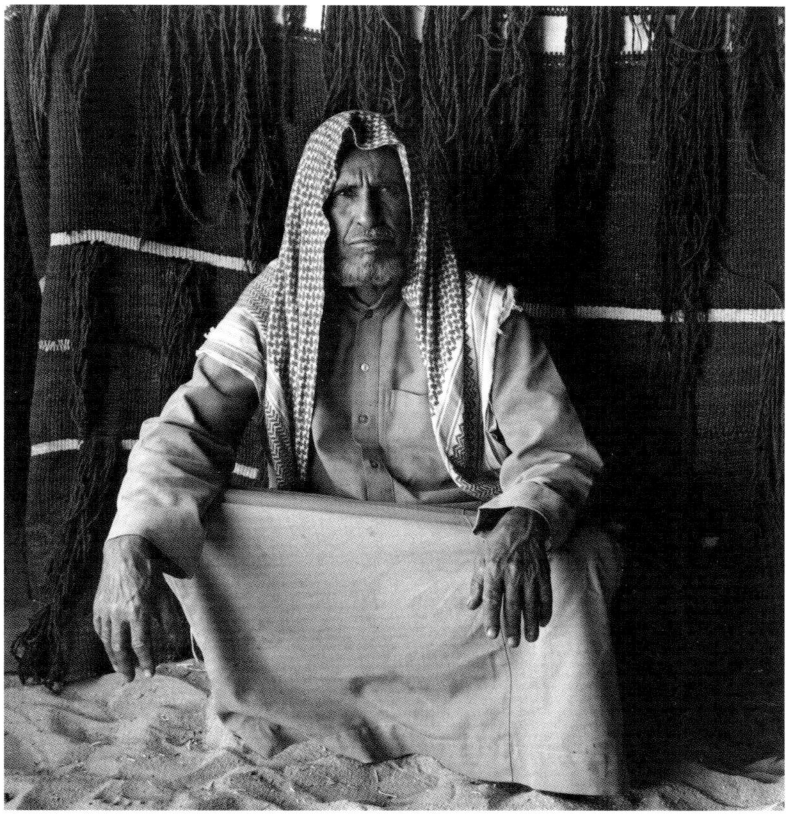

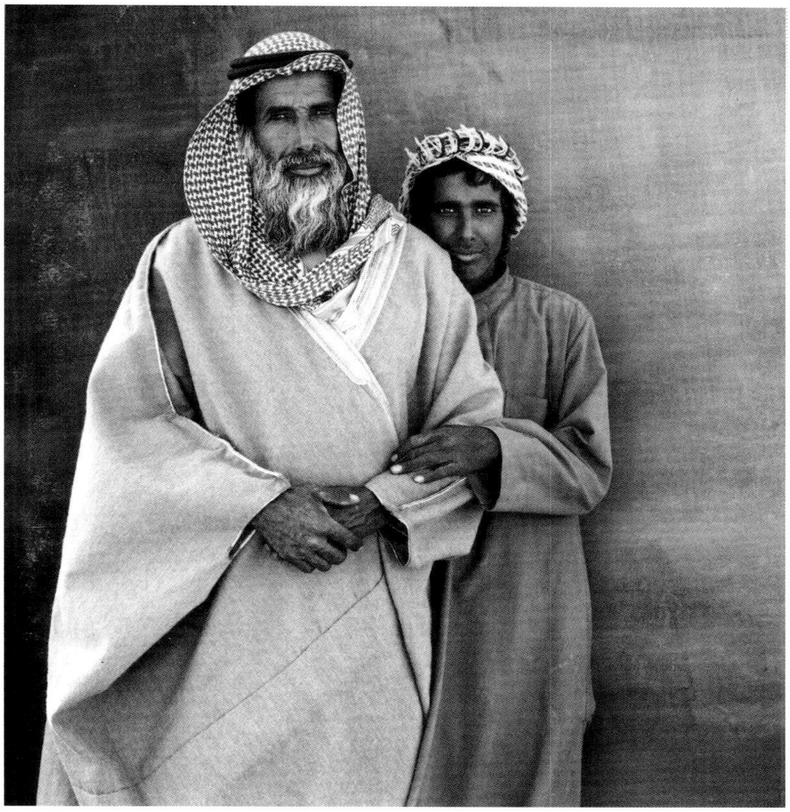

Humberto da Silveira
From the series *Bedu*, 1994
Courtesy of the artist

Anne Blunt noted that it was *"customary in Arabia that the sheykh should receive illustrious strangers in a special tent set up for the purpose."*

concerned to outshine "those who have never seen the Arabs but upon the high-ways, and know 'em only by their robberies".

This reserve, which the Bedouins always conserve, as Laurent d'Arvieux maintained, may depend on the fact that "during the fatigue of traveling in the heat of summer, much talking excites thirst, and parches up the palate," as Johann Ludwig Burckhardt commented. However, the latter observed, that in intimacy, the Bedouin "is free, sprightly, jocose, and decent, in his

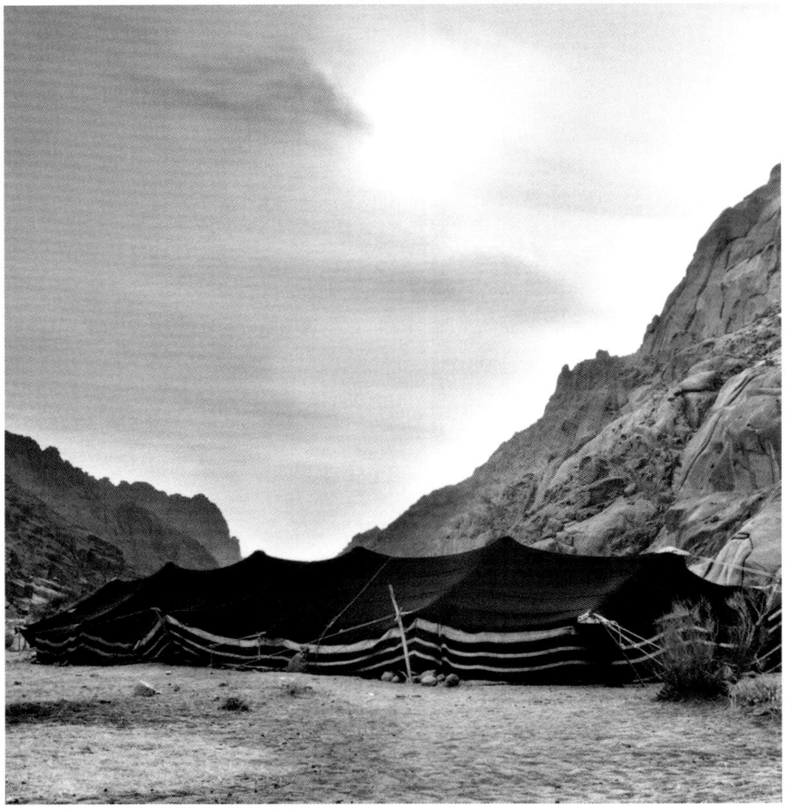

familiar conversation," adding that "when they assemble under their tents, a very animated conversation is kept up among them." He remarked that above all, "they have certainly more wit and sagacity than the people who live in the towns; their heads are always clear, their spirit unimpaired by debauchery." Burckhardt concluded: "The Bedouins are as much distinguished from other Arabs by the purity of their language, as they are by that of their manners."

Burckhardt traced the profile of a man whose "social character is truly amiable. His cheerfulness, wit, softness of temper, good-nature, and sagacity, which enables him to make shrewd remarks on all subjects, render him a pleasing and often a valuable companion. His equality of temper is never ruffled or affected by fatigue or suffering." He is also very resistant to pain, he observed: "The fortitude with which Bedouins endure evils of every kind is exemplary" while revealing a sharp sense of self-irony: "In that respect they are as much superior to us as we exceed them in our eager search after pleasing sensations and refined enjoyments!"

This force of character is due to what "the Bedouin learns at an early period of life, to abstain and to suffer, and to know from experience the healing power of pity and consolation," wrote the Swiss traveler, who added: "He pities and supports the wretched, and never forgets the generosity shown to him even by an enemy." While always ready to help others, on the other hand, "a Bedouin is always too proud to show discontent, or much less to complain," and above all, "he never begs assistance, but strives with all his might, either as a camel-driver, a shepherd, or a robber, to retrieve his lost property."

A strong feeling of pride makes him "fully conscious that his own condition is far preferable to any other that can be his lot," Burckhardt noted, because "the Bedouin exults in the advantages he enjoys; and it may be said, without any exaggeration, that the poorest Bedouin of an independent tribe smiles at the pomp of a Turkish Pasha; and, without any philosophical principles, but guided merely by the general feelings of his nation, infinitely prefers his miserable tent to the palace of the despot."

What can be the origin of this feeling of superiority? Laurent d'Arvieux proposes an explanation for this question. The Bedouins, he says, have a strong sense of tradition that describes them as the descendants of Abraham's eldest son, Ishmael. Arabia was thus eligible for a legacy that was much greater than the small land of Canaan that was assigned to the descendants of Isaac. Consequently, their entire existence would depend on the consciousness of their Ishmaelite ascendancy. "This illustrious descent, which they extremely glory in, does not suffer 'em to exercise the mechanic arts, or take upon 'em the toils of husbandry; they never work at all; their employment is riding, feeding their flocks, and going upon the high-ways," d'Arvieux wrote.

Whatever the thefts for which they were otherwise guilty, the Bedouins would never offer hospitality that was less than scrupulous, the French diplomat observed: "A stranger is no sooner come to their camp than he is receiv'd into a tent; an Arab can only give him a mat to sit and lie on [...] but there's nothing wanting for his good entertainment. He is at no manner of

Charles M. Doughty
Encampment of Billi Aarab (under the harra)
Sketch by Doughty from *Travels in Arabia Deserta* Volume 1, Dover Publications, Inc., New York, 1979

Doughty noted that "*the Bedouins of the same tribe camp their tents together and their tents are pitched in length.*"

expense; his servants and his equipage are treated with the same care, without costing him any thing more for acknowledgment than a God-restore-it-you when he is taking his leave to be going."

Burckhardt's comments strike a very similar chord. "The guest who enters an encampment of the Nejd Bedouins usually alights at the first tent on the right side of the spot where he entered the dowar, or circle of tents. If he should pass that tent and go to another, the owner of the slighted tent would think himself affronted." Even if the latter is absent, the stranger will be received with the same regard, because "it is a received custom in every part of the Arabian Desert, that a woman may entertain strangers in the absence of her husband. Some male relation then does the honours, representing the absent owner of the tent."

The hospitality enjoyed by the stranger is governed by ancestral rules that are very precisely codified, so that "if the stranger's business requires a protracted stay, for instance, if he wishes to cross the desert under protection of the tribe, the host, after a lapse of three days and four hours from the time of his arrival, asks him whether he means to honour him any longer with his company. If the stranger declares his intention of prolonging his visit, it is expected that he should assist his host in domestic matters, fetching water, milking the camel, feeding the horse, &c. Should he even decline this, he may remain, but will be censured by all the Arabs of the camp: he may, however, go to some other tent of the *nezel* (camp), and declare himself there a guest. Thus every third or fourth day he may change hosts, until his business is finished, or he has reached his place of destination."

In a word: "To be a Bedouin is to be hospitable," Burckhardt summarized and then developed this assertion: "The condition of the Bedouin is so intimately connected with hospitality that no circumstances, however urgent or embarrassing, can ever palliate his neglect of that social virtue." Nonetheless, the life of a Bedouin is such that he often may have nothing, or almost nothing to offer. It is in these circumstances that he can show the authenticity of his generous nature: "No stronger proof of hospitality can be given than to state that, with very few exceptions, a hungry Bedouin will always divide his scanty meal with a still more hungry stranger, although he may not himself have the means of procuring supply; nor will he ever let the stranger know how much he has sacrificed to his necessities," continued the Swiss traveler.

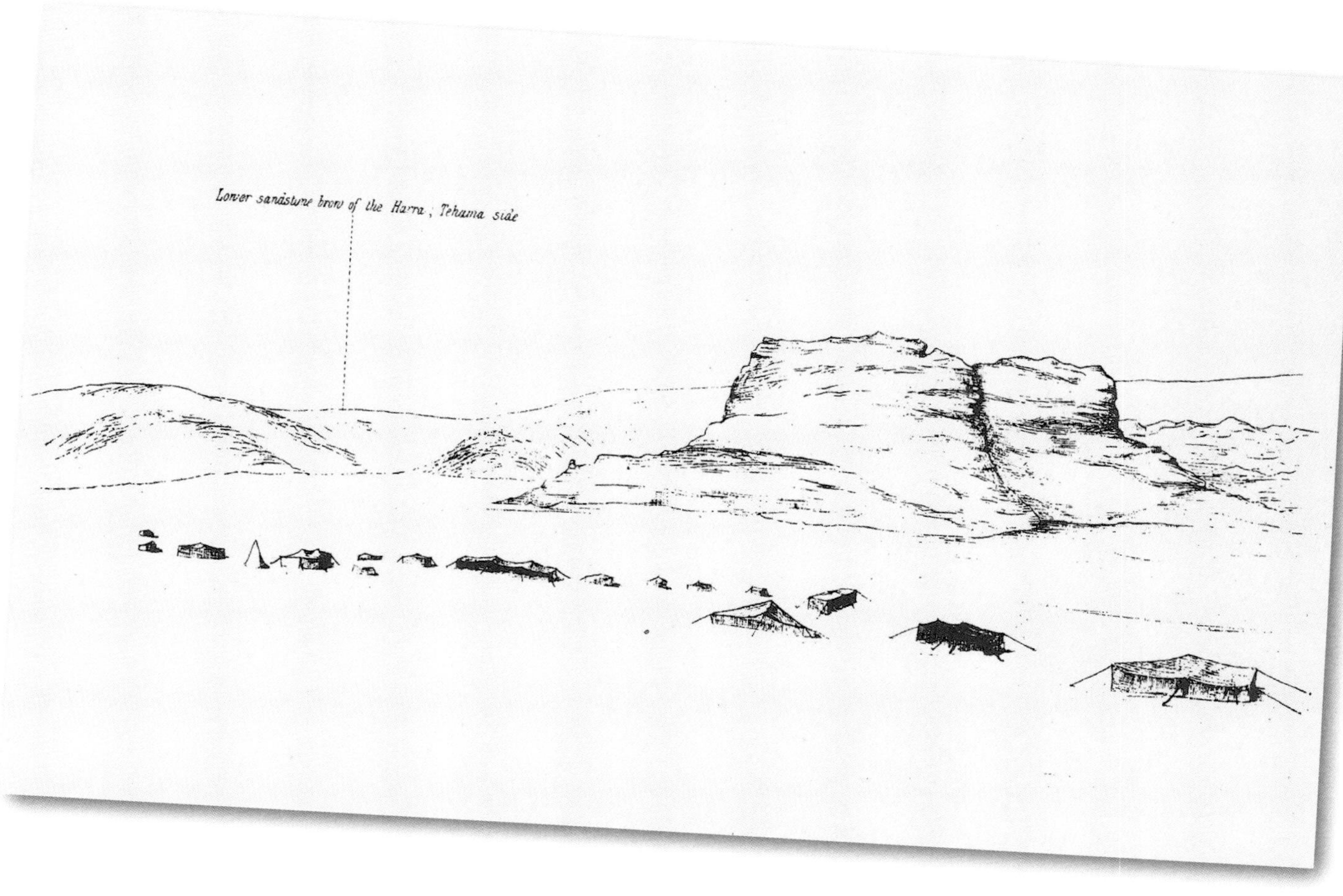

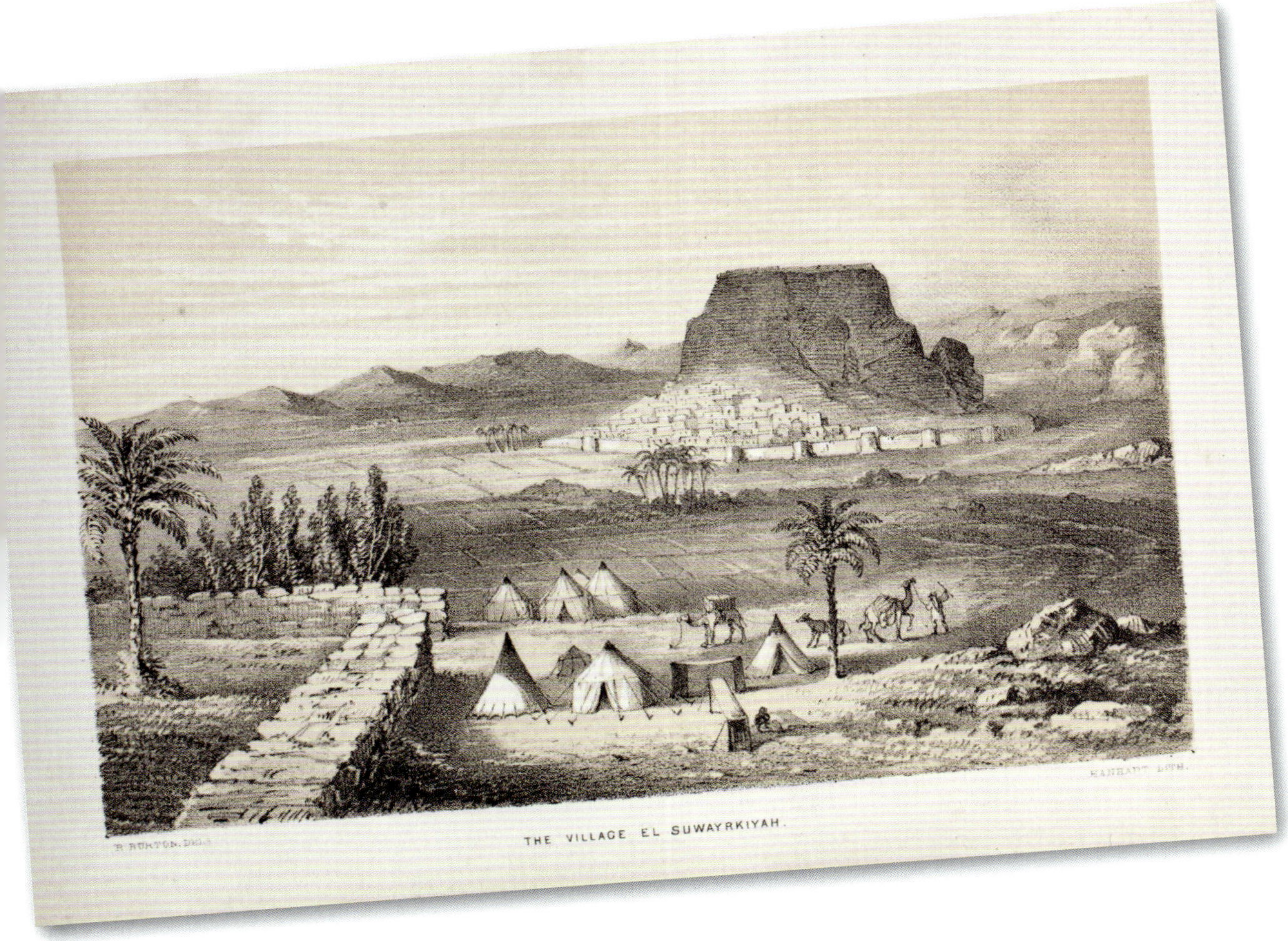

Richard Francis Burton
The Village of El Suwayrkiyah,
1853–54
From *A Personal Narrative of a Pilgrimage to Al-Madinah and Meccah*
Nasser D. Khalili collection of Islamic Art, London

On his way from Medina to Mecca, Richard Burton spent the night in the little village of El Suwayrkiyah. He wrote: *"For the most part it is a haggard land, a country of wild beast and wilder men, a region whose very fountains murmur the warning words, 'Drink and Away', instead of 'Rest and be thankful'".*

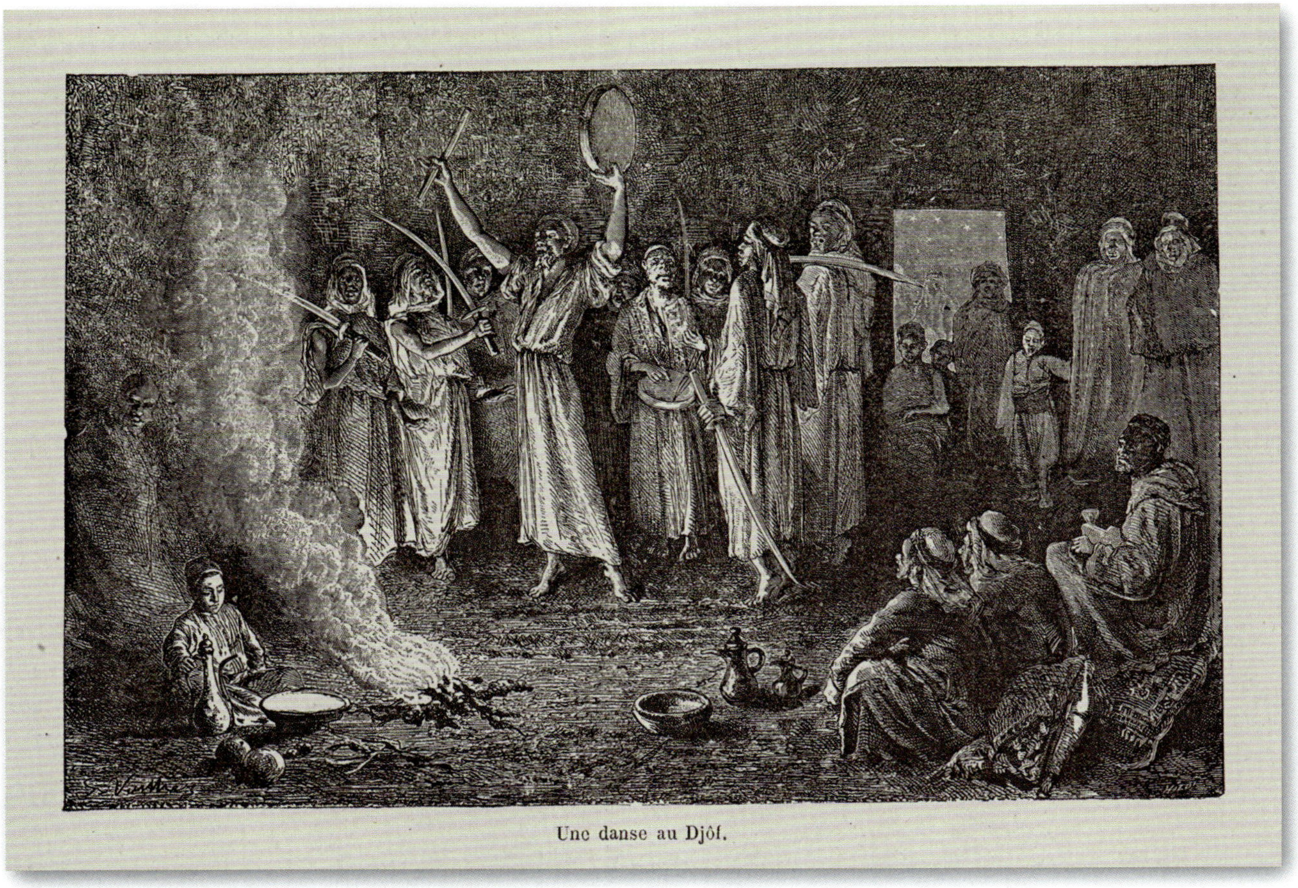

Anne Blunt
Une danse au Djôf (A dance in Al-Jawf)
Woodcut by Gaston Vuillier after a watercolor by Anne Blunt
From *Voyage en Arabie. Pèlerinage au Nejed, berceau de la race arabe* (A Pilgrimage to Nejd, The Cradle of the Arab Race)
Paris, Librairie Hachette, 1882
Courtesy of the British Library

The national dance in Arabia called the 'Ardah is compared to a war dance. Anne Blunt wrote: *"It is a sword dance with a performer beating on a drum made of palm wood and horse hide. The rest hold their swords over their shoulders and chant in solemn measure, dancing as solemnly."*

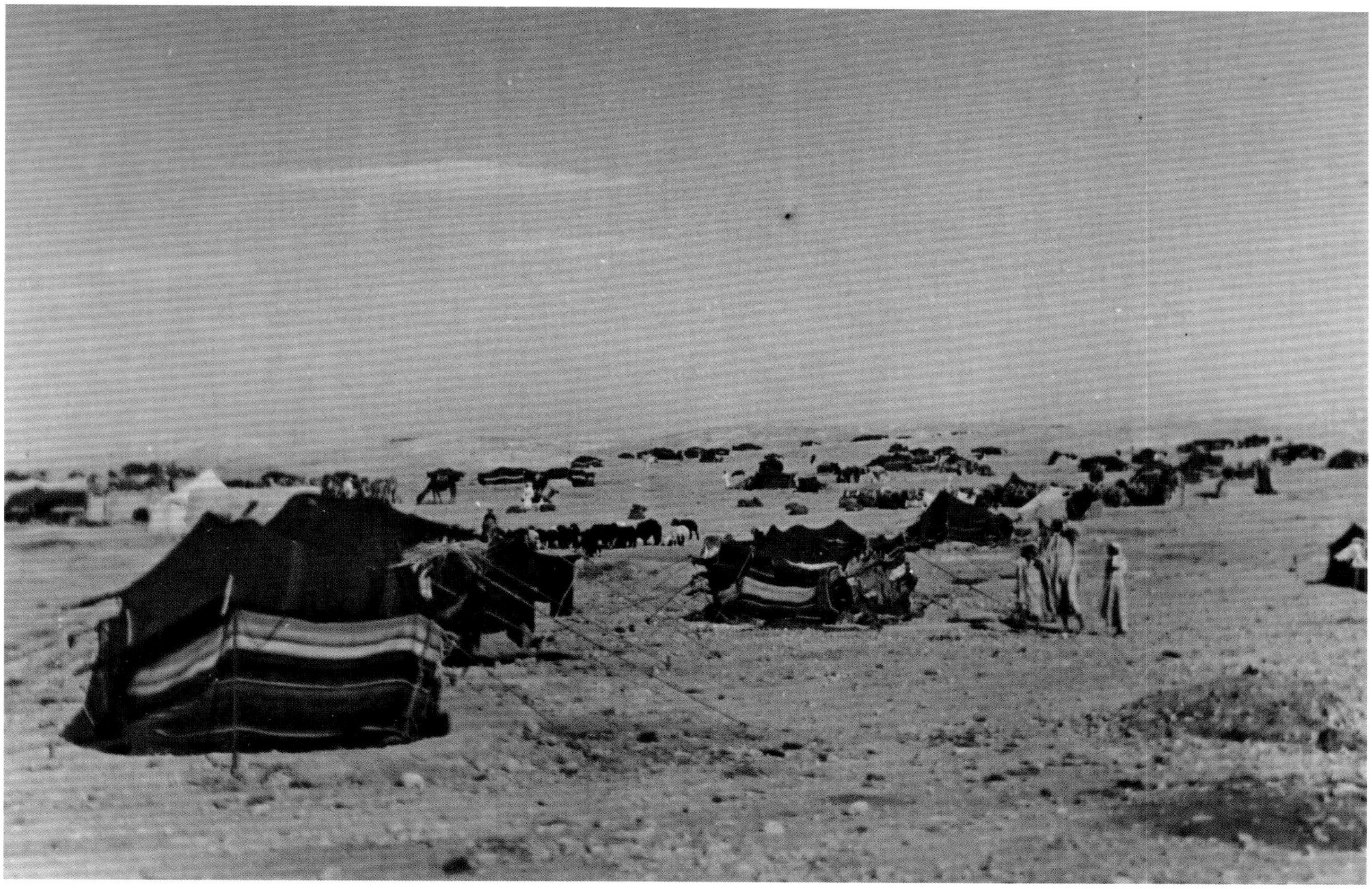

Gerald de Gaury
Bedouin encampment outside Riyadh, c. 1934–35
Courtesy Royal Geographic Society, London

Classic Arab literature, just as many travelers' accounts, love to tell the tale of a Bedouin reduced to a dreadful plight, obliged to sacrifice the last dromedary he still owns, which is still crucial for transporting his family, or his beloved mare, in order to receive an unexpected visitor with dignity. As exaggerated as they often appear to be, these stories do illustrate the great importance of hospitality and the impossibility of abandoning these principles. At a secondary level, they also illustrate the exceptional hardship of life in the desert, about which T. E. Lawrence would write, in *Seven Pillars of Wisdom*: "Bedouin ways were hard, even for those brought up in them and for strangers terrible: a death in life."

The Bedouin, according to d'Arvieux, used this hardship as an excuse for the others, for all the others: "the Bedouin Arabs think themselves ill dealt with, and make themselves amends as much as they can upon the posterity of Issac and all the rest of the world in general." So well, he continued, that "their robberies make all nations their enemies." The Bedouins ransom and pillage the caravans, hold up "passers-by who venture into the desert without a safe-conduct," carry off the cargoes of ships run aground off their coasts, and do not hesitate "to help them get lost in the dangerous passages of the Red Sea, when they are not offered something with good will," wrote Jacqueline Pirenne. But, for them, she emphasizes, there was no war there: "they don't attack 'em when they see 'em in a condition making a defence." When they were not at it, "they retire into the deserts, [where] it is impossible to overcome 'em," Laurent d'Arvieux pointed out.

In all these undertakings, the Bedouins never seek to kill. Rather, they offer hospitality even to their victims and are undoubtedly, according to the German, Carsten Niebuhr, "the most civilised thieves in the world," as readers discovered in chapter *The Flora of the Peninsula*: "A European, belonging to a caravan which was plundered, had been infected with the plague upon his journey. The Arabs, seeing him too weak to follow his companions, took him with themselves, lodged him without their camp, attended him till he was cured, and then sent him to Basra." For d'Arvieux, "It be no crime amongst them to rob and strip passengers, no more than it is for Europeans to go a hunting"; this is a matter of their own vocation, what was due to the descendants of Ishmael. A century later, the French diplomat Niebuhr used another comparison: "Every grand sheikh justly

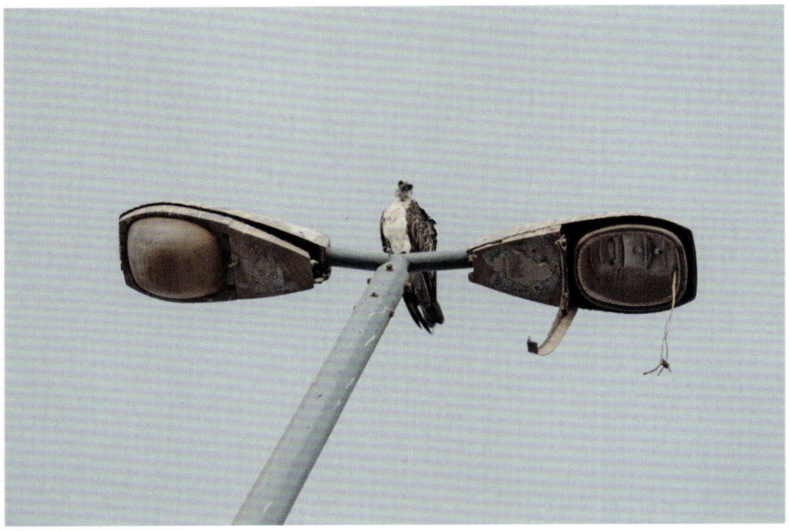

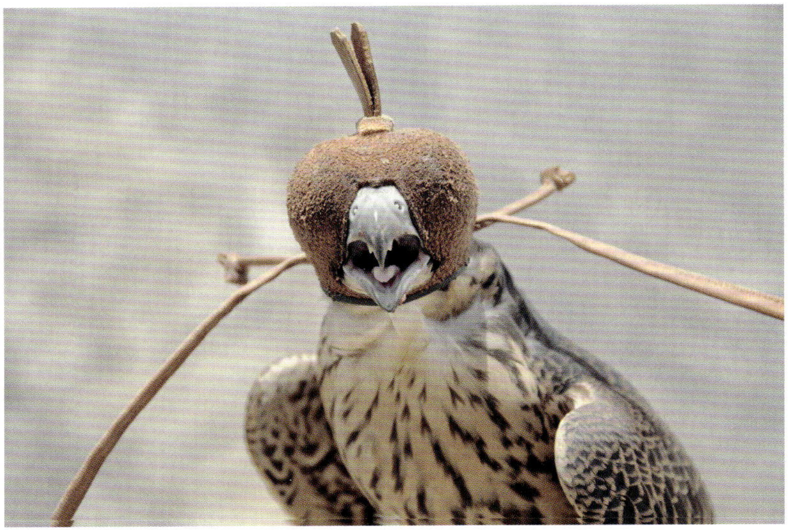

feels the right he possesses to remain the sole master of the solitude he inherited from his ancestors, where the custom reigns, where he makes it be respected." The French writer continued his line of reasoning: "The fact of crossing the desert, in terms of the custom, involves the legitimate confiscation of the stranger's possessions. The stranger is violating the territory. He had only to provide himself with a safe-conduct, which the tribal chiefs do not refuse to those who pay or have earned their confidence."

This manner of proceeding, which "gave the nomads such a bad reputation among travellers and tradesmen," is customary, in his analysis. However, this "is not a fantasy, the effect of a chief's whim or of the greed of those who obey him." The countries of Europe did not act any differently, as Derôme observed, when during a war they took action to seize, in their own territory, the property of the states with whom they were in conflict or that of their citizens. "This custom," he continued, "is much more effective than a law. The latter change[s] constantly, with the result that they have little authority."

But, asked Derôme: "Where does the custom come from? It is older than written history and memory," he responded, "it is an oral tradition in the land of the oral tradition." Custom regulated the pastoralist way of life of shepherding in Arabia—"it is both the legacy of a long history from the past and the natural way in the desert," he supposed again. To this custom and the code of honor that descends from it, the Bedouins are profoundly attached because they guarantee their independence, their liberty, which they value above all else: "The pure nomad has conserved the patriarchal traditions of his people among which a carefree attitude, love of liberty and hospitality remain at the forefront. These three virtues, in fact, form a single virtue, the love of independence. That is the foundation of the nomad's temperament," wrote Derôme, "he rejects the yoke. He prefers misery and hunger, when in need, to obedience."

Custom emanates this independence, this full and encompassing liberty, so complete and immense that the Bedouin holds it above everything, and that he cannot enjoy, he senses confusedly, anywhere else but in the desert, and certainly not in cities. "All that has resulted to the Bedouins from their intercourse with towns is an increase of wants and a decrease of virtues," Burckhardt commented in that regard. Whatever the difficulties and the hardships of his life, the Bedouin is proud of the life he leads, which he would not wish to change for anything in the world, paying much more attention to his liberty than to all the riches here on earth.

Yann Gayet
From the series *Contresens*
Courtesy of the artist

Yann Gayet
From the series *Contresens*
Courtesy of the artist

Thesiger wrote in *Arabian Sands*: *"I was told that in England it takes fifty days to train a wild falcon while in Arabia, it takes them a week to three to train one. This is due to the fact that the Arabs never separate from their falcons. The man who trains a falcon carries it almost everywhere with him. [...] He constantly strokes it, speaks to it, hoods and unhoods it."*

Humberto da Silveira
From the series *Bedu*, 1994
Courtesy of the artist

Thesiger wrote in *Arabian Sands* that he was glad for having hawked in the traditional way as opposed to hunting from cars as is the case nowadays in Nejd.

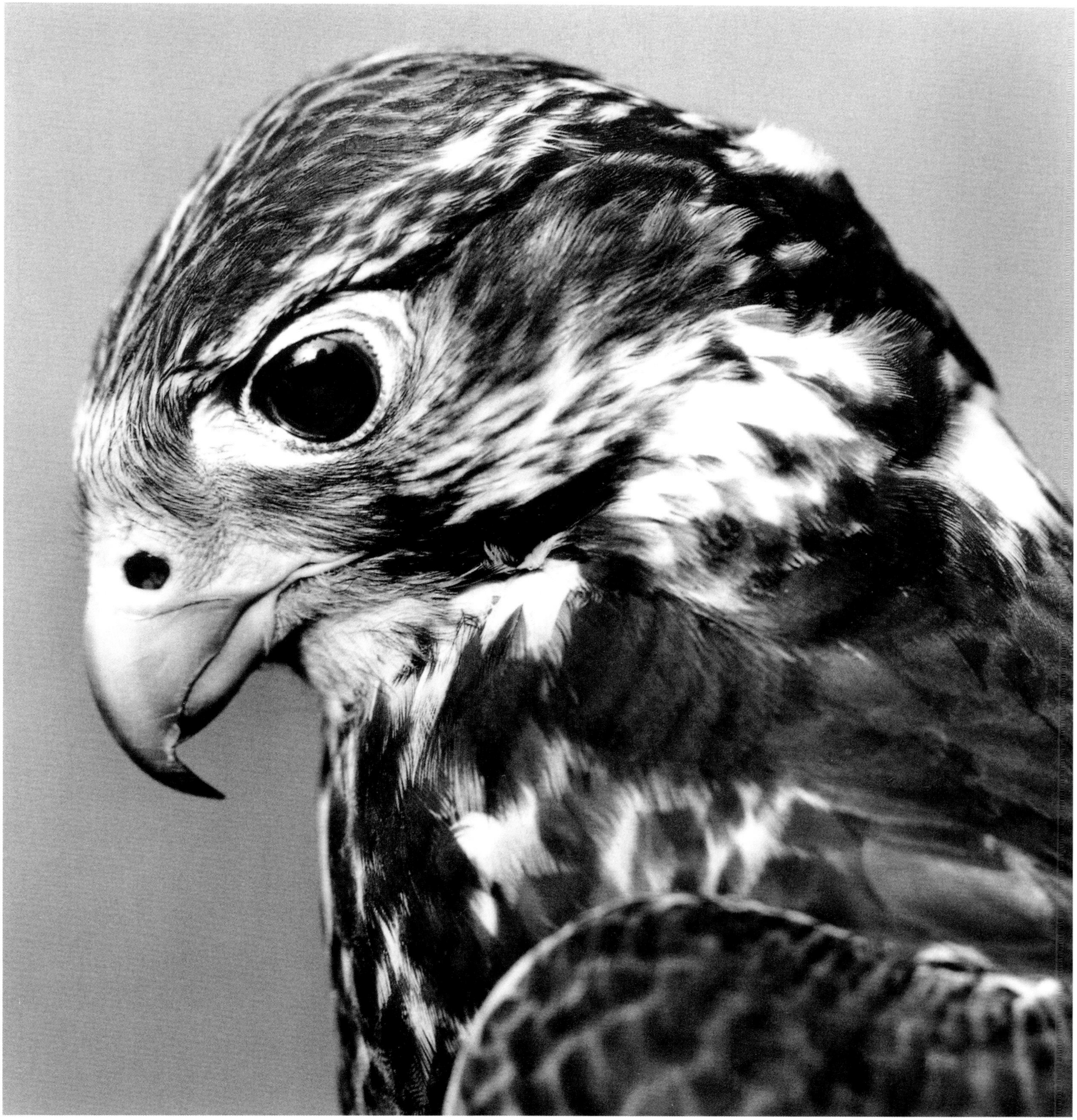

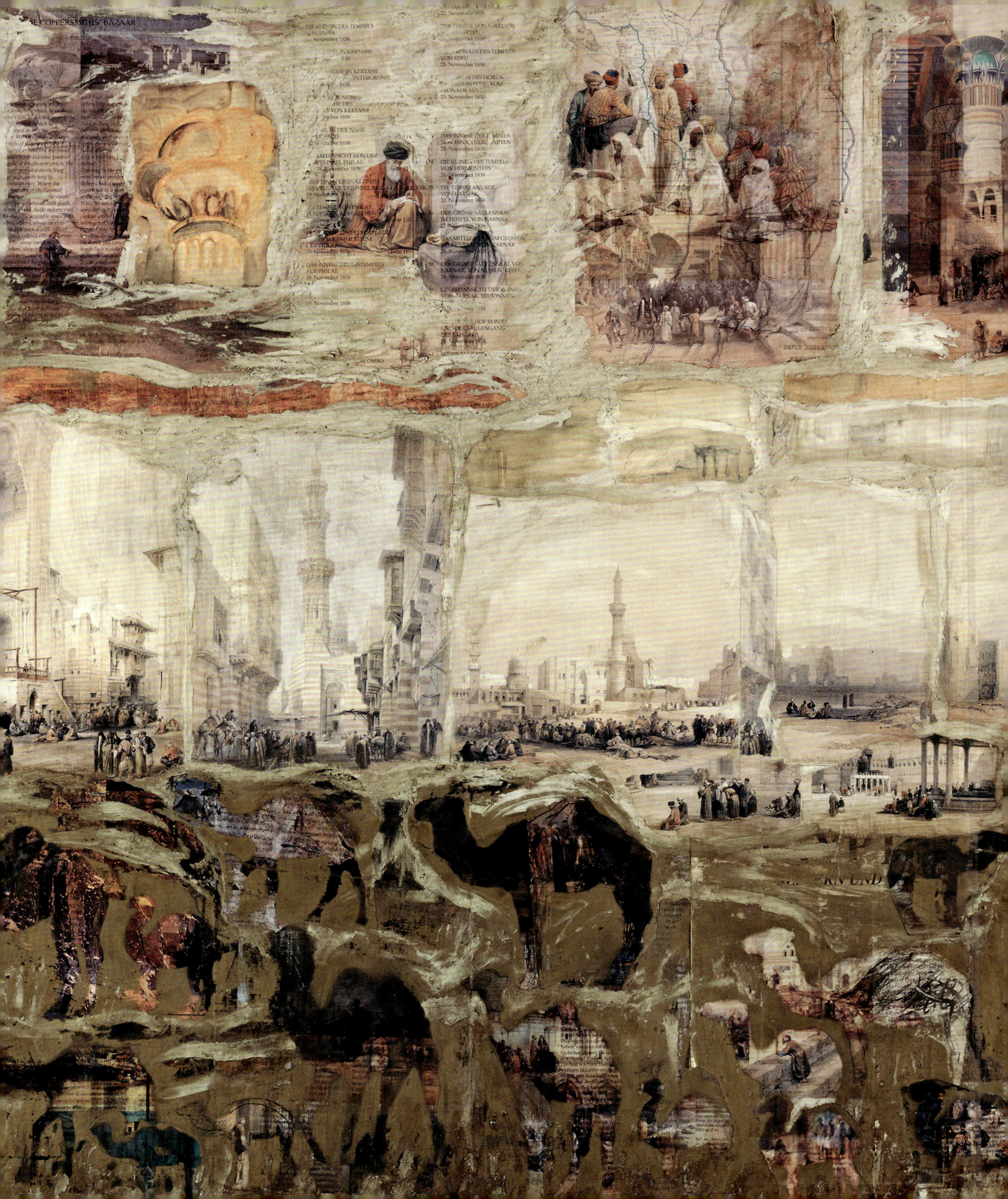
COPPERSMITHS' BAZAAR
DIE RUINEN DES TEMPELS
November 1838
VON EDFU
23. November 1838
23. November 1838

Ship in the Dunes

Is it possible to imagine Arabia without the camels—or rather, the dromedaries—that populate, inhabit, and embody it in the same way as the Bedouins? Certainly not, ascertained Elian-Joseph Finbert, an animal writer who was a camel driver himself at one stage of his life and is also the author of *La Vie du chameau* (Life of a Camel). "If the Bedouins were able to resist and survive in the arid steppes of Arabia," he wrote, "if they were able to create there a human community, it was thanks to the camel, the sole creature capable of thriving there and traversing those steppes. Without this animal, they would have lived only in their oases, as in a jail."

The camel's role was essential and central. Without the camel, there would be no culture, let alone a civilization in the desert. The relations of the Bedouins with this difficult world, "could not have been established if it was not through the camel," wrote Finbert.

The Bedouin is proud of his horse, this magnificent steed which surpasses all others, the possession of which is his pride and his prestige (see chapter *The Arabian Horse*). Nonetheless, the camel offers them greater advantages: "the sense of their existence and their Arab consciousness," Finbert wrote.

The camel guarantees the subsistence of the Bedouin. From the camel the Bedouin gets his food and his garments. The camel gives him freedom, transportation, and above all else, the tools to exist. Owning a herd of dromedaries "is not only a sign of fortune," added Finbert, "it is also a rank of honour and a sign of power."

This praise of the camel that Finbert knowingly elaborated on has the ring of truth. To man, the camel offers everything: its wool and its hide, which the Bedouin uses to clothe himself; its milk and its blood, which he consumes sometimes; and its meat, which provide his nourishment. The Bedouin, in return, offers it his love, because "the camel is part of a man's heart," according to an Arab saying that the Finnish Orientalist, Georg August Wallin, invoked on this topic. Of all the European travelers who dedicated themselves to the discovery of Arabia, according to the historian Jacqueline Pirenne, Wallin is undoubtedly the one who best understood the relation that binds a Bedouin to his camel: "he admires the way the master uses a special language to speak to the camel, caresses it, or scolds it," she stated. Pirenne also mentioned this comment by Wallin: "In general, one has to encounter the man as well as the animal in their own country and with their own entourage to be

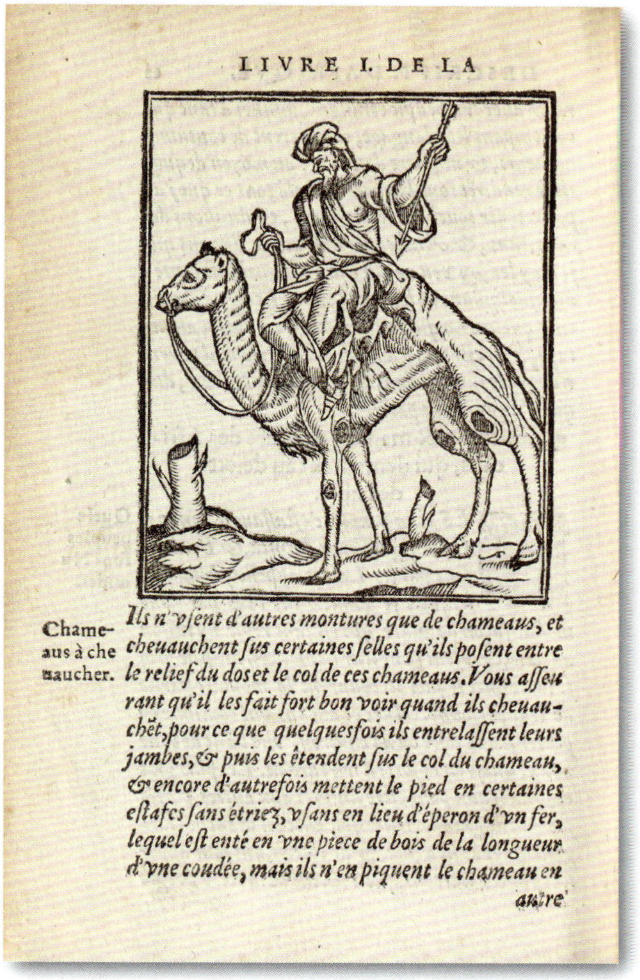
LIVRE I. DE LA

Chameaus à cheuaucher.

Ils n'vsent d'autres montures que de chameaus, et cheuauchent sus certaines selles qu'ils posent entre le relief du dos et le col de ces chameaus. Vous asseurant qu'il les fait fort bon voir quand ils cheuauchẽt, pour ce que quelquesfois ils entrelassent leurs jambes, & puis les étendent sus le col du chameau, & encore d'autrefois mettent le pied en certaines estafes sans étriez, vsans en lieu d'éperon d'vn fer, lequel est enté en vne piece de bois de la longueur d'vne coudée, mais ils n'en piquent le chameau en autre

Ezio Gribaudo
Terra Santa, 1995
Mixed media and collage on paper
70 × 100 cm
Private collection

Maurice Tamisier wrote in his *Voyage en Arabie: séjour dans le Hedjaz, campagne d'Assir* (1840): *"A traveler without a camel in the large desert is like a sailor whose ship sinks in the middle of the sea."*

Al-Hasan ibn Mohammad al-Wazzan, known as Leo the African
Arab riding a dromedary
From *A Geographical Historie of Africa*, 1556
Engraving
5.7 × 5 cm
Paris, C. Plantin,
Bibliothèque nationale de France

Man's companion in the Arabian Peninsula for four thousand years, the camel is used for battle, for transport, and as a source of milk, hair, and meat.

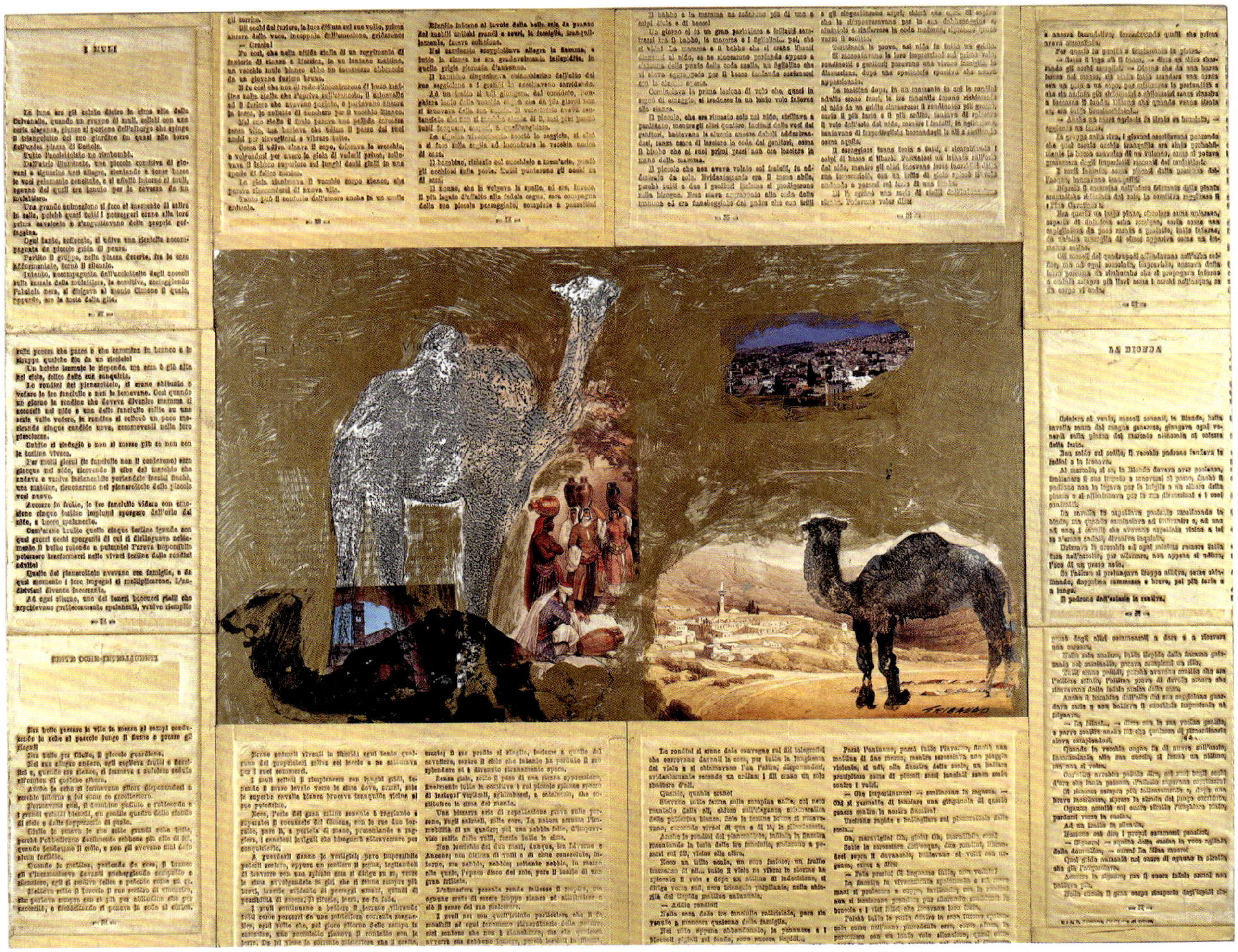

Ezio Gribaudo
Terra Santa XIII, 1995
Mixed media
76 × 58 cm
Private collection

Philby wrote in *The heart of Arabia, a record of travel and exploration* (London, 1922) that *"the normal age of a camel is around fifteen to twenty-five years. A young camel that is offered to a man as his bride's dowry is expected to be still under his ownership on the occasion of his son's marriage."*

able to love them," which he considered to be "one of the golden rules for the comprehension among men."

This very great closeness of the Bedouin with his camel certainly stems from the particularly arid nature of the climate as well as that of the land, that they both inhabit: "Accordingly, the Arab consoles himself with his camels for the sterility of his native land, and the camels, who seem to comprehend the isolation of their masters, give them back this love as much as their organization can allow," wrote the Frenchman and young Saint-Simonian, Maurice Tamisier.

In his dream for the Orient, Tamisier first joined the theoretician and leader of the Saint-Simon ideology, Prosper Enfantin, in Cairo in 1833, who was then attempting to accomplish ambitious projects in Egypt, including dams on the Nile and a canal connecting the Mediterranean to the Red Sea. While there, Enfantin introduced Tamisier to another Frenchman, Joseph Seve, alias Soliman Pacha, the highest-ranking general in the Egyptian army. The latter recruited him as a secretary to the commanding medical officer of the army, who was preparing to depart for Arabia. That is how Tamisier found himself, on a camel, engaged in the Asir campaign. This is why he had plenty of time to discover the country, and to observe this mount, which was utterly new to him, and noticed that "Arabia is one of the countries of the world where the relations between men and animals are most intimate: they have both understood that they must love and assist each other because the dry, burnt earth rejects their embraces."

Bedouins themselves are aware of the important position that camels occupy among them: "God had not made the camel; Nejd, they say, had been without inhabitant," reported the British writer, Charles M. Doughty. Ali Bey El Abbassi added that "the camel is the proper beast for the desert: it is the great gift of God to its inhabitants, and to travellers." Confirming its value was Wilfred Thesiger, who wrote, "The Bedu know the camel's worth 'Ata Allah', or 'God's Gift', they call her." Thesiger crossed the most daunting of all deserts, the Rub' al-Khali, on its back.

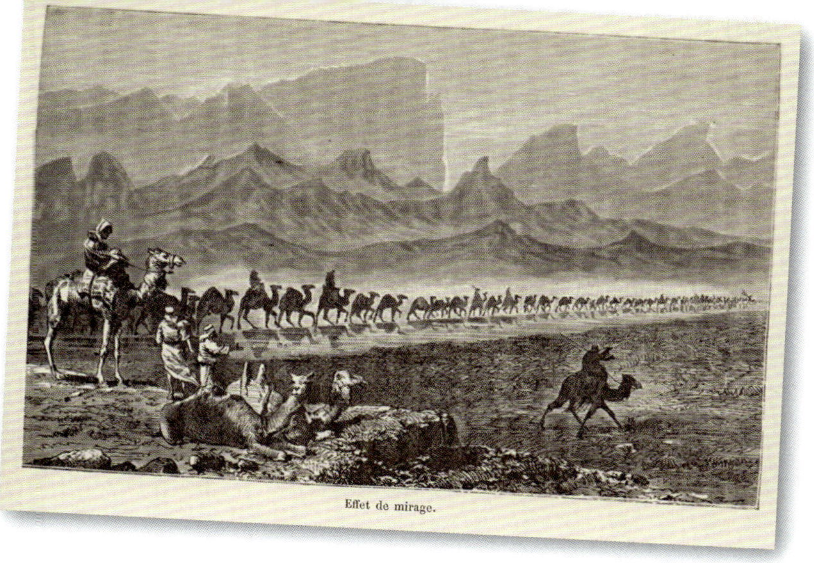

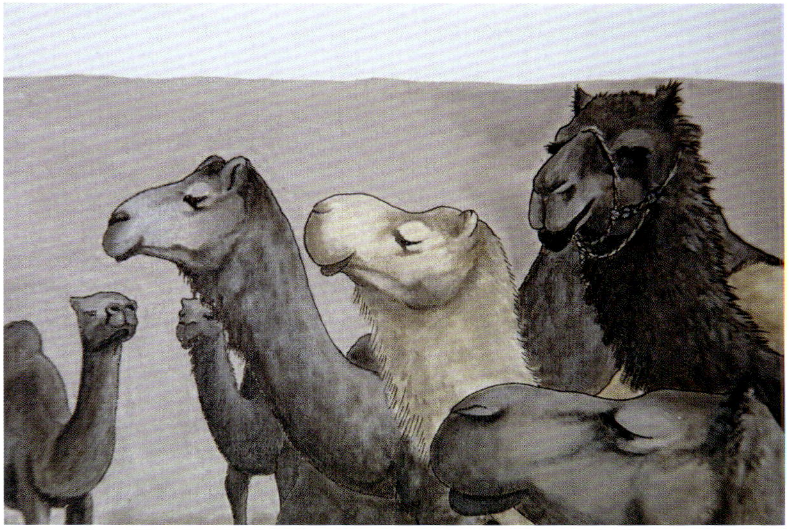

Anne Blunt
Effet de mirage (Mirage effect)
Woodcut by Gaston Vuillier
after a watercolor
by Anne Blunt
From *Voyage en Arabie, Pèlerinage au Nedjed, berceau de la race arabe* (A Pilgrimage to Nejd, The Cradle of the Arab race)
Paris, Librairie Hachette, 1882
Courtesy of the British Library, London

Malin Basil
Camel heads, detail
of the *Waterhole*, 1971
Acrylic on canvas
65 × 100 cm
Private collection

A camel can lose up to forty percent of its body water and still survive. It can drink ten to twenty liters of water a minute and often consumes more than 100 liters at one time.

The French pilgrim, Jules Gervais-Courtellemont, used roughly the same terms in 1896 when he offered the following portrait of the camel, full of tender affection: "an ultimate mount, in these desolate and arid regions, the silly camel, the recalcitrant camel, whose attitudes are grotesque but whose heart is good, the camel that is always complaining, when it is loaded, when it is unloaded, when rising or settling down, but always walking without eating or drinking, a providential animal, made for the desert."

"The Arabs consider the camel as one of the greatest gifts of heaven," remarked Tamisier, as "they perfectly understand that without the camel, their country would be uninhabitable; only the camel is responsible for carrying the fortune and the family of its master to their destination. The camel accompanies him to the battlefield and often saves them from an almost certain death." In other words, and as also confirmed by Thesiger: "The Bedu's existence depends upon the welfare of his camel." Thanks to "its tireless activity, it supports an infinity of families and maintains them in abundance, families who regard the camel as a second father because it is by dint of its work and sobriety that they owe their well-being," observed Tamisier. "The grateful Arab does not consider the camel as an enslaved

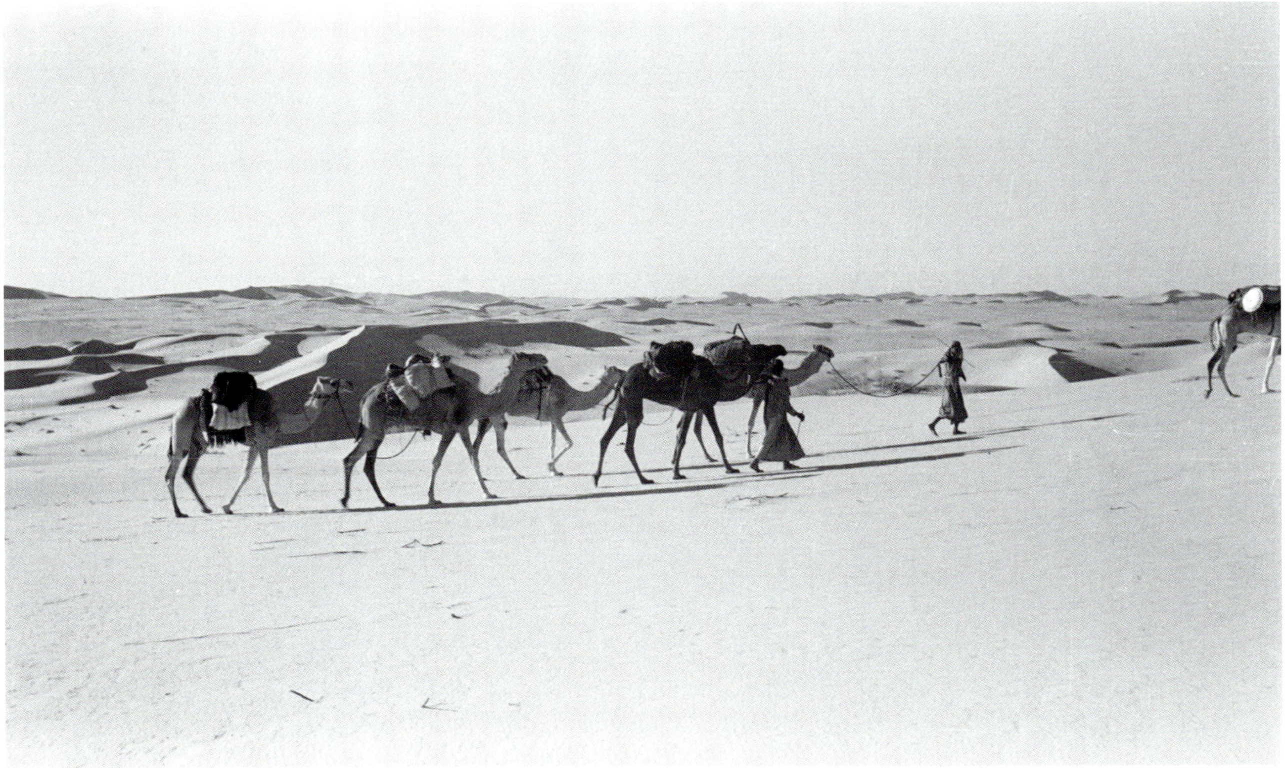

Wilfred Thesiger
View of Wilfred Thesiger's travelling party trekking in the Bani Ma'arid sands of the Empty Quarter (Rub' al-Khali), January 1948
Film negative 35mm
Courtesy Pitt Rivers Museum, University of Oxford

Thesiger reported in *Arabian Sands*, the camels that the bedouins rode were females while, in Sudan and other parts of the Sahara, they always rode on bulls because the females were kept for milk and never ridden. The bulls in Arabia are used as pack animals for tribes that carry goods for hire.

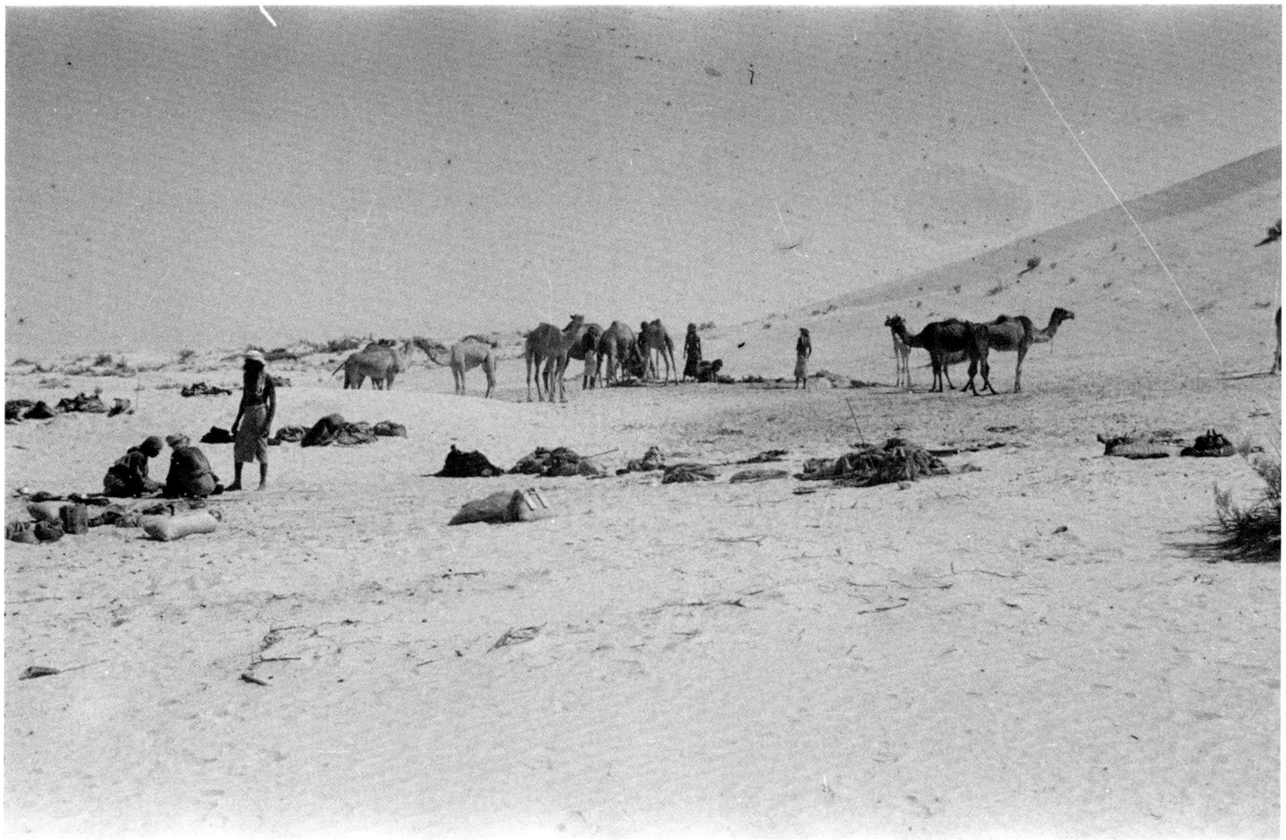

Wilfred Thesiger
Wilfred Thesiger's party at the Khawr bin Atarit well, north of Mughshin in the Ghanim sands, November 1946
Film negative 35mm
Courtesy of the Pitt Rivers Museum, University of Oxford

Thesiger wrote that most of the riding camels were heavily laden when traveling long distances between wells with goatskins filled with water.

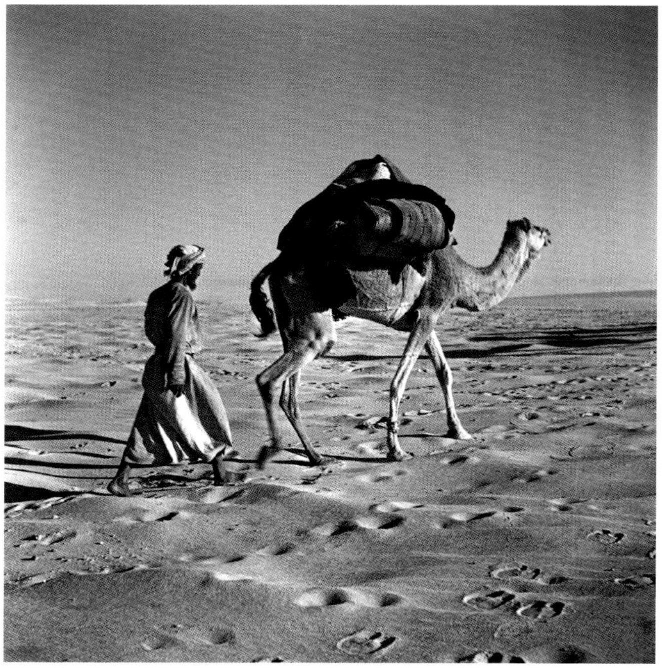

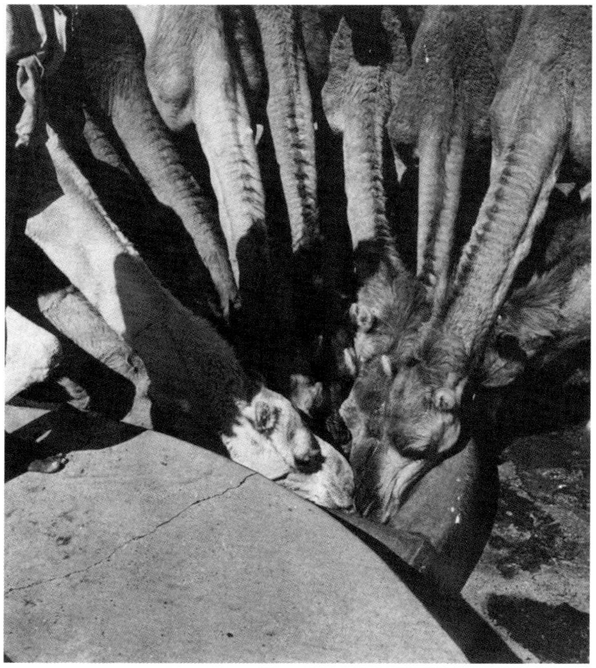

Ilo Battigelli
Dromedary rider, late 1940s
Courtesy of the Pitt Rivers Museum, University of Oxford

Carlo Guarmani wrote in 1866, in *Northern Najd, A Journey from Jerusalem to Anaiza in Qasim*, that *"a dromedary must be of pure breed and sufficiently advanced in age; this last condition is indispensable for a long and dangerous journey, for a well-bred dromedary of full age never lets his voice be heard and, therefore, does not show the enemy the resting-place by night."*

Bob Landry
Herds of camels quenching their thirst, early 1940s
Courtesy of Saudi Aramco

Harold Corsini
Camels and side of a sand dune in Al-Kharj (Nejd region), 1947
Gelatine silver print
32.4 × 26.4 cm
Gift of Standard Oil
Courtesy of the Art Institute of Chicago / Art Resource Center, New York

Philby wrote in *The heart of Arabia, a record of travel and exploration* (1922): "*The freshness or not of the tracks can further serve to date the passage of the animals which made them. The Al-Murra tribe of the Empty Quarter are capable of telling the color of the camel by its tracks.*"

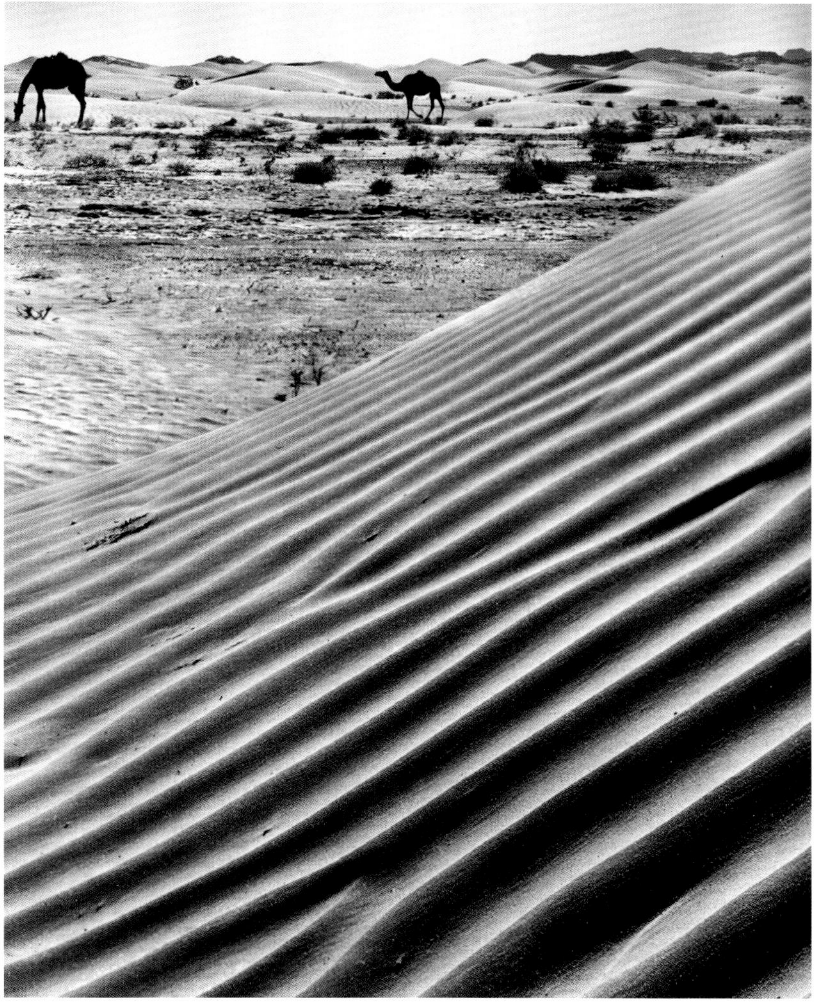

Samer Mohdad
Bedouin camp at Mada'in Saleh, 2002
From *Assaoudia*, Actes Sud, 2005
Courtesy of the artist

Philby wrote that "*as he rides the Bedouin has his eyes constantly on the ground, seeking fodder for his mount, and at sight of a clump or tuft of any favorite herb, he is happy that the camel he rides has food though he be without himself.*"

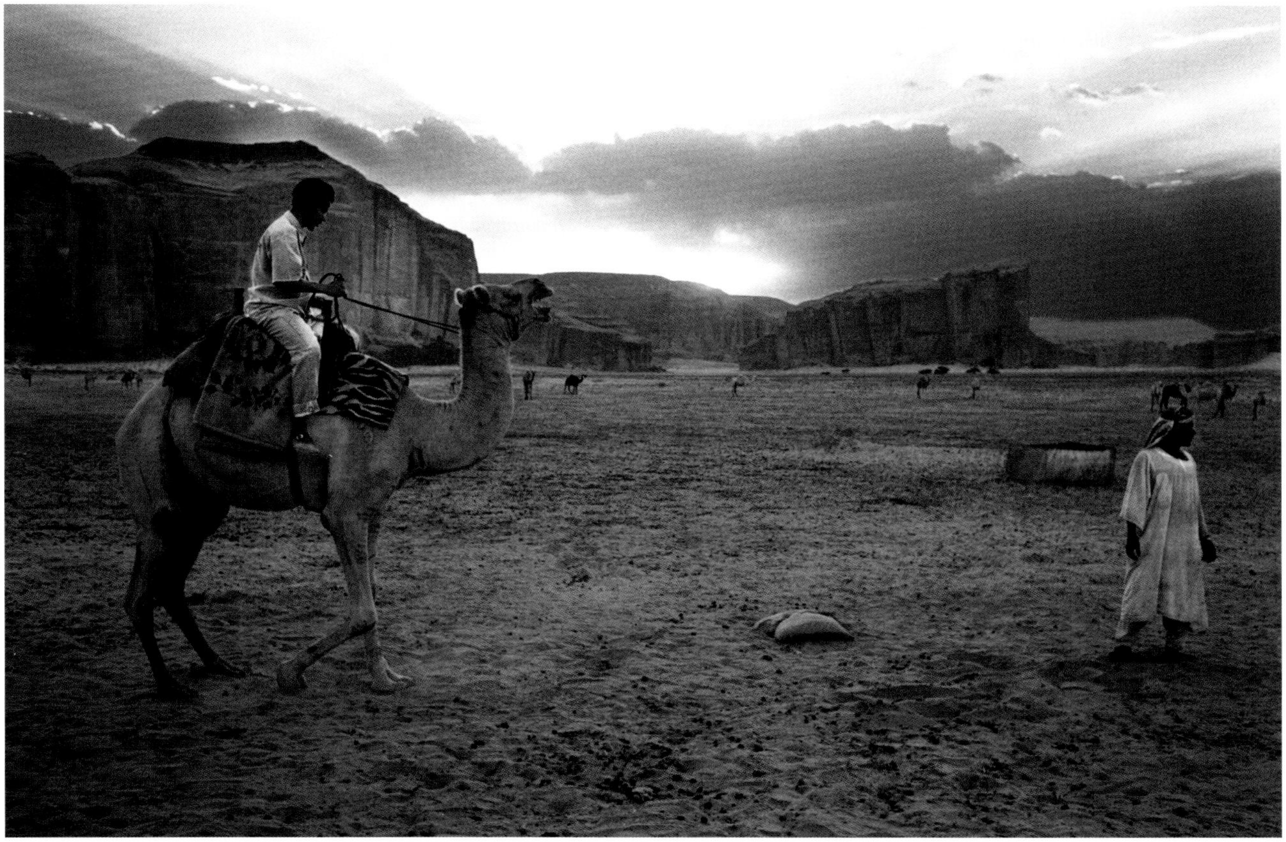

Ezio Gribaudo
Terra Santa, 1995
Mixed media and collage
on paper
70 × 100 cm
Private collection

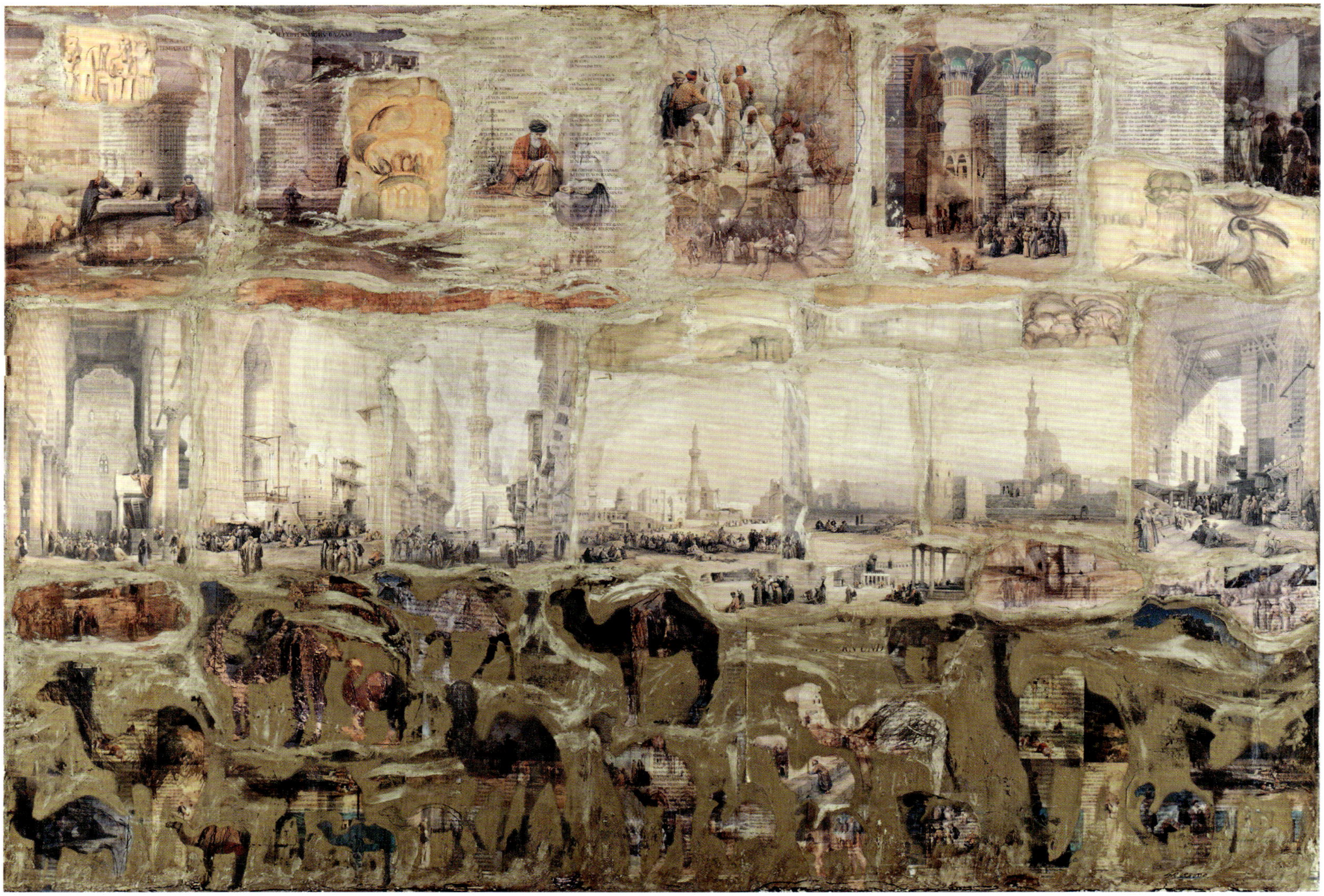

LITTERS AND PALANQUINS

The very first European to mention these little "wooden houses" as he called them was, once again, Ludovico di Varthema. In 1503, this Mameluke born in Bologna accompanied a caravan from Damascus to the holy cities. Needless to say, he made the journey on horseback. However, he observed that among the pilgrims "men ride on camels in certain wooden boxes, in which they sleep and eat." After disembarking in Jeddah exhausted, having suffered through a tempest, Ali Bey El Abbassi found himself a place inside one of these little "wooden boxes" to complete the short distance that remained to reach Mecca: "I set out for Mecca on Wednesday the 21st of January, at three o'clock in the afternoon. I travelled in a machine made of sticks, and covered with cushions, of the form of a sopha or cabriolet, roofed with boughs upon arches, which they placed upon the back of a camel," he wrote. It cannot be said that his description of this "machine made of sticks" was absolutely clear. But at least he had learned its name: "This machine called *schevria* was very convenient, as [it] enabled to sit up or lie down in it; but the motion of the camel, which I felt for the first time in my life, completely exhausted me, in the feeble state that I was in." On this occasion, Ali Bey discovered that one suffers from seasickness while traveling, seated or lying down in such a device, on the back of a camel. John Fryer Keane, aged twenty-two when he disembarked in

American Colony (Jerusalem)
Camel caravan of pilgrims en route to Mecca, c. 1910
Print from glass dry plate negative
Matson Photograph Collection
Library of Congress Prints and Photographs Division, Washington, D.C.

Caravans required tens of thousands of camels, which were gathered outside Damascus, Cairo, and Baghdad. Ropes were tied to link the lines of the camels in the procession.

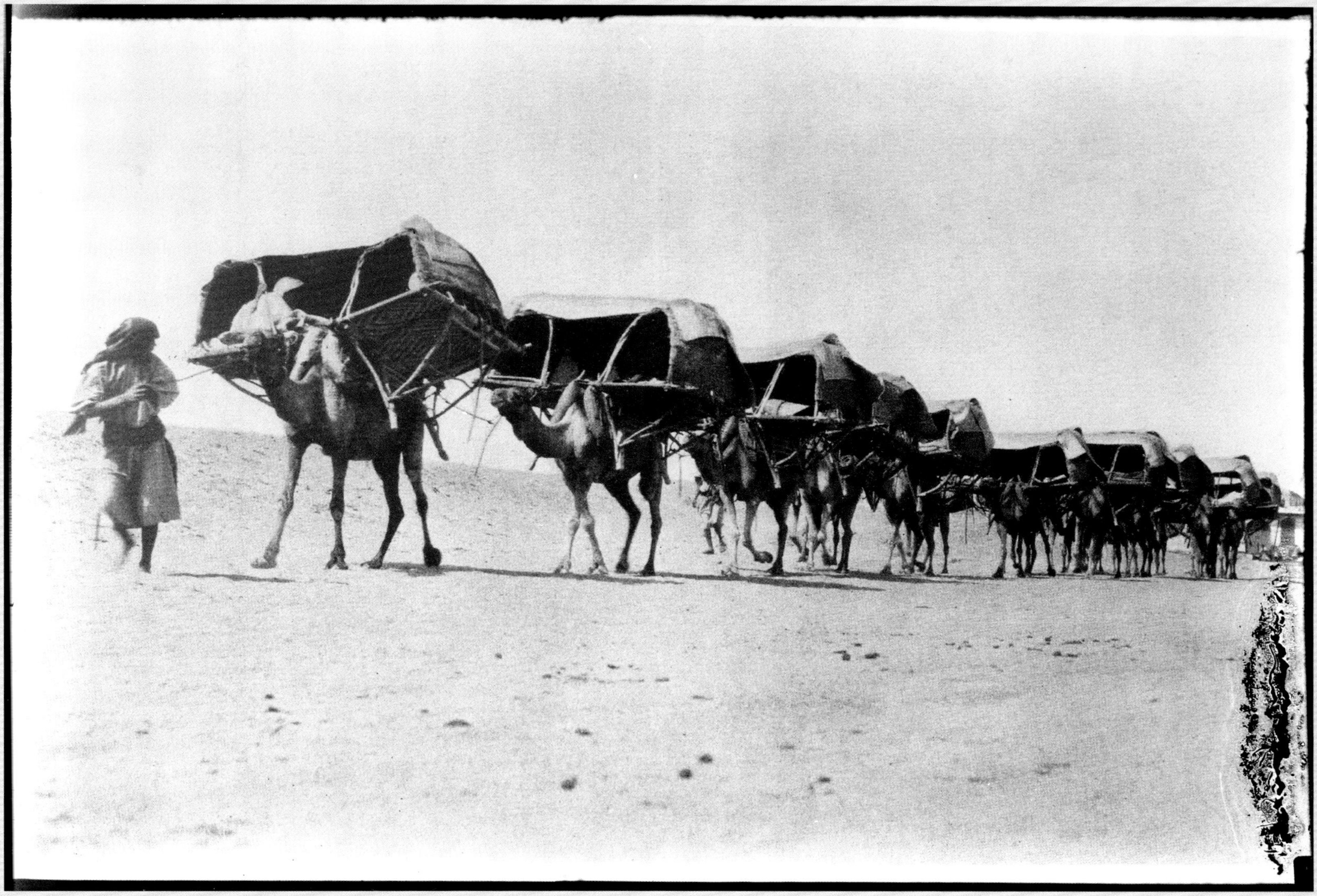

Arabia one day in 1877, who had spent ten years of his life on ships, also discovered to his great surprise the first time he was perched on the hump of a camel that "the pitching of the desert-ship could not find its equal afloat; so that I, old sailor as I was, became exceedingly sick, a thing which had not happened to me for many years while at sea."

Just as Ali Bey suffered from exhaustion when he disembarked at Jeddah, the British explorer Richard Burton was hardly more spry when he arrived in Yanbu. The humid atmosphere of the boat in which he had made the crossing had reawakened the injury in his foot that he had been dragging along since the start of his voyage and he could hardly walk. Although Burton had also opted for one of these very practical, little "wooden boxes," to travel to Medina, it did not inspire his confidence: "My *shugduf*, perched upon the back of a tall strong animal, nodded and swayed about with his every motion, impressing me with the idea that the first step would throw it over the shoulders or the crupper," he wrote, without concealing his apprehension. The main difficulty was getting in: "The camel-man told me," he explained, that "I must first climb up the animal's neck, and so creep into the vehicle." But Burton could not decide whether to do so, "my foot disabling me from such exertion," he claimed. Despite the risks inherent in such an operation, he demanded that they "bring the beast to squat, which they did grumblingly because it often strains the camel to rise with a full *shugduf* on his back, besides which the motion is certain to destroy the vehicle in a few days."

Burton eventually grew accustomed to and appreciated this "vehicle," particularly because it allowed him to draft the notes in his diary in perfect solitude. Many travelers before and after him have appreciated the true value of the comfort this strange "machine" could provide them. This was certainly the case for Saleh Soubhy, a senior civil servant, who performed the pilgrimage twice at the end of the nineteenth century and who noted: "If the camel must transport pilgrims, they place two *chouqdoufs* (one on each side), which are large baskets of palm leaves covered by a cloth that will give travellers relief from the heat of the sun and humidity of the night."

Nonetheless, reading these different authors, or certain others, one cannot be quite sure of the name of this "machine made of sticks" as Ali Bey called it, or this "wooden box," as Varthema did, and what shape it had. As is often the case, it was the Swiss traveler, Johann Ludwig Burckhardt, with his customary precision, who resolved the predicament. Thanks to him, we learn that indeed there was not only one type of these vehicles, but several. He began by explaining that "the name of *shebrye* is given to a kind of palanquin, having a seat made of twisted straw, about five feet in length, which is placed across the saddle of the camel, with ropes fastened to it. On its four sides are slender poles, joined above by cross bars, over which either mats or carpets are placed, to shade the traveller from the sun." To this satisfactory and clear description, Burckhardt added this note: "This among the natives of Hijaz is the favourite vehicle for travelling, because it admits of their stretching themselves at full length, and sleeping at pleasure."

The explanation became slightly more complicated when Burckhardt added the description of a variant: "Similar machines of the palanquin kind, but on a shorter and narrower scale, are placed lengthways on both sides of the camel's saddle, and then called *shekdef*. One person sits in each of them, but they do not allow of his stretching out at full length. Both of these *shekdefs* are covered, likewise, with carpets thrown across." Then, Burckhardt added a final word: "This vehicle is principally used for the conveyance of women."

Finally, he mentioned the existence of another type of palanquin: "Different from that is the *taht roan:* a litter carried by two camels, one before, and the other behind. In this kind of vehicle the great pilgrims travel." Burckhardt went on to say that "it is more frequently used by the Turks than by the Arabians." Burton produced a sketch of this strange vehicle that shows two dromedaries decked out in their best, with this caption: "The Grandee's Litter". Joseph Pitts, a young Englishman who was reduced to slavery and performed the pilgrimage with his Maghribi master in about 1685, saw similar devices used for overlords, notables, and their wives in the caravan that took them from Mecca to Cairo (see chapter *The Center of the World*).

These different palanquins all had different characteristics, as we have noticed. The Andalusian writer, Ibn Jubayr, crossed the Egyptian desert in the direction of the port of 'Aydhab at the end of the twelfth century and had the opportunity to experience the comfort of the *shuqduf* (plural: *shaqadif*): "Across this desert no one will journey save on camel, by reason of their endurance of thirst. The best and most comfortable camel litters used on them are the *shaqadif*," he noted before specifying that "they are like the travelling seats. Two of them are bound together by stout ropes and put across the camel. They have supports at each corner, and on these rests a canopy. The traveller and his companion in counterpoise will thus be veiled from the blaze of the midday heat."

Here, then, is the description of the object, and how one could live and organize himself inside this device. "With his companion he may partake of what he needs of food and the like, or read, when he wishes, the Koran or a book; and who so deems it lawful to play chess may, if he wish, play his companion, for diversion and to

Richard Francis Burton
The Grandee's Litter, 1853–54
From *Personal Narrative of a Pilgrimage to El-Madinah and Meccah*
London, 1855–56
Royal Geographical Society, London

On his journey from Yanbu to Medina, Sir Richard Burton hired camels for which he paid after "abundant bargaining" three dollars each—half in ready money and the rest to be paid after arrival. He also bought a *Shugduf* or litter, used by richer pilgrims and carrying two passengers. He wrote in *Personal Narrative of a Pilgrimage to El-Medinah and Meccah* that *"it is a vehicle appropriated to women and children, fathers of families, married men and to those who are too effeminate to ride. My reason for choosing a litter was that notes are more easily taken in it than on a dromedary's back."* *Shugdufs* are also used by travelers to sleep within them.

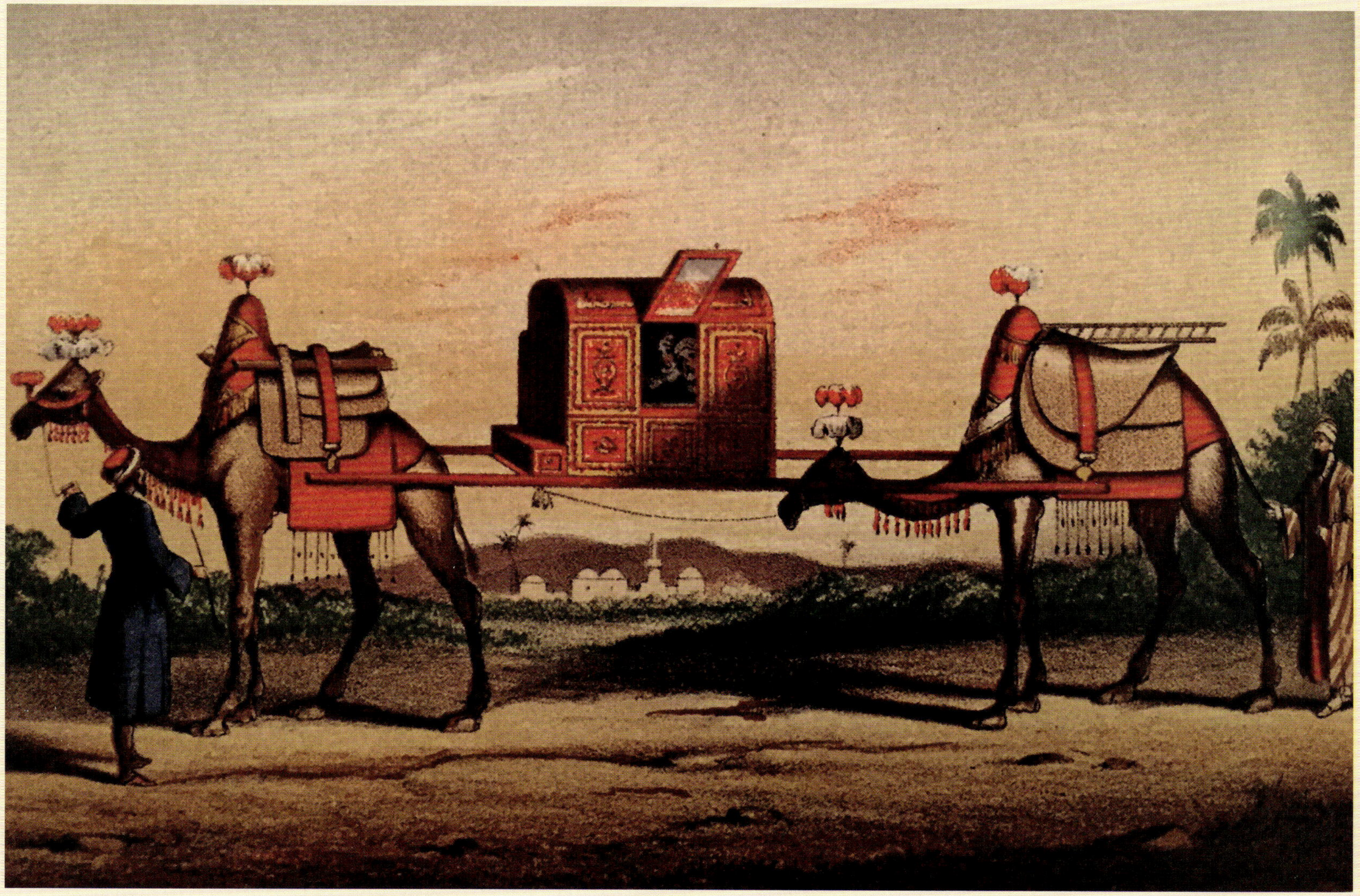

relieve the spirit," wrote Ibn Jubayr, before concluding, "To be short, it eases the hardship of travel."
Such comfort can become dangerous at times. This is what Joseph Pitts recounted on the occasion of his return from Mecca to Cairo after his pilgrimage. The caravan was under constant surveillance by brigands and it happened that during the night, "When they see a *hagge* fall asleep (for it is usual for them to sleep on the road) they loose a camel before and behind, and one of the thieves leads away the camel with the *hagge* upon his back asleep and another of the thieves, meanwhile, pulls on the next camel to tie it to the camel from whence the halter of other was cut." The camel on which the unfortunate pilgrim was still sleeping, with his baggage forming his counterweight, was led away, and "when they had gotten the stolen camel, with his rider at a convenient distance from the caravan, and think themselves out of danger," Pitts continued: "they awake the *hagge*, and sometimes destroy him immediately, and at some other times, being a little more inclin'd to mercy, they strip him naked, and let him return to the caravan."

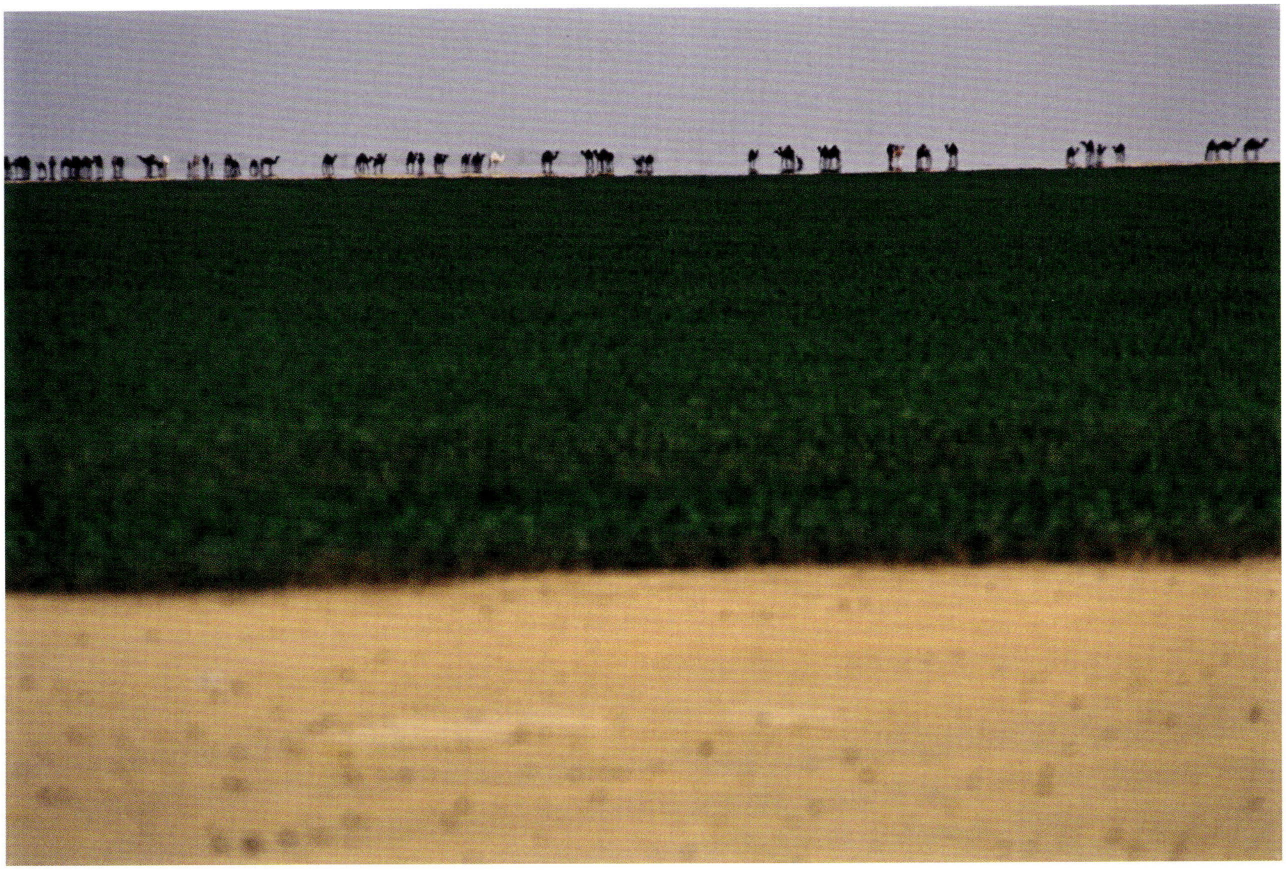

George Steinmetz
Mirage alongside a circular field, Wadi Al-Ghiran, 2002
Courtesy of the artist

Claire Rivier
Dromadaires, 2003
40 × 30.5 cm
Dry pastel on paper
Courtesy of the artist

"Bedus can recognize camels much farther off than they can distinguish human beings," wrote Thesiger in *Arabian Sands*.

animal which he can use or abuse as he wishes." He went on to say that "he considers the camel as a friend that he loves and venerates."

"It is no surprise," therefore, "that they often fondle and kiss them whilst they murmur endearments," reported Thesiger. Details of these effusions are also to be found in the words of Tamisier: "The Bedouin assures his camel that it will be the first among all his camels, that he will see to its marriage, that he will provide it a fate worthy of envy, that he will neglect nothing that will yield it happiness and, during the conversation, he never forgets to call the camel his friend, his brother, and other names of great endearment. During such moments of gaiety, the Arab sings his camel songs of love or war which the camel listens to attentively; and to demonstrate the pleasure it feels, the camel will clamp its jaws, gnash its teeth, and turn its head toward the person singing to it, in order to confer him the greatest attention. In that moment, absorbed by this savage harmony, the camel seems to forget the load it is carrying and crosses incredible spaces of which the masters transmit the memory to their descendants." On the other hand, the Bedouin "does not insult his camel. When he is irritated with it, he only wishes it to be taken by the enemy," noted the archaeologists Jaussen and Savignac, in 1914.

Nearly all travelers describe this special understanding that binds a Bedouin to his camel. All…? The one apparent exception was this malicious debasement of the camel: "He is from first to last an undomesticated and savage animal, rendered serviceable by stupidity alone. One passion alone he possesses, mainly revenge." Those were the beliefs of the British adventurer, William G. Palgrave—too hastily, no doubt. However, it is by the pen of the same author who curiously also offers an

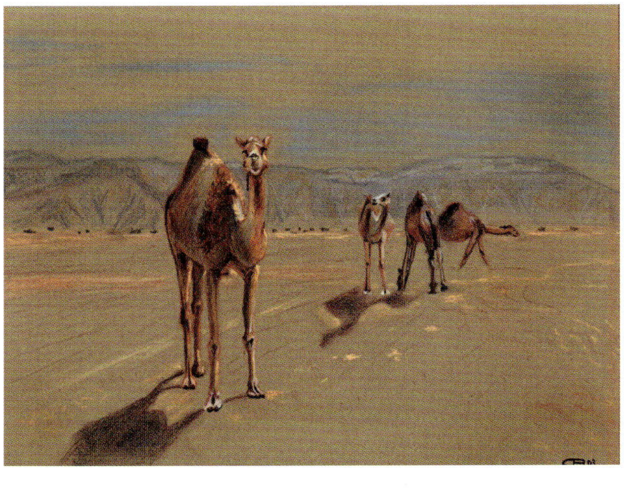

Anne Blunt
Birkeh of Abdallah,
14 February 1879
Watercolor
Courtesy of the British Library, London

After their stay in Ha'il, the Blunts traveled to Baghdad with the returning Persian pilgrim caravan. They followed the Zubeida route, named after the celebrated wife of caliph Harun al-Rashid, who is said to have built caravanserais and wells along this road. This *birkeh* (pool), wrote Anne Blunt, "*is located in the route of the hajj caravan. The inside descends in steps for the convenience of those who come for water.*"

indirect confirmation of the attachment that binds man to his camel. Palgrave mentions several times that "every man held a short crooked stick for camel-driving in his hands," also observing that in the formal and solemn context of a reception at the palace of an emir and in the presence of the emir himself (see chapter *Cities of Yesterday and Tomorrow*), all the men were, in any case, holding "the riding stick or wand." About its use, he wrote, "The inseparable companion of every true Arab, whether Bedouin or townsman, rich or poor, gentle or simple, is to be retained in the hand, and will serve for playing with during the pauses of conversation."

Palgrave had undoubtedly understood that the presence of this staff, in all circumstances, reveals the nature of the bond that unites man to the animal. It is as if this staff, whenever the Bedouin is separated from his mount, becomes the symbol of its presence beside him, an homage rendered to the merits and the inexhaustible abnegation of the creature that the Bedouin considers his twin in the animal world.

This intimacy, this resemblance, so intense, did sometimes amuse some travelers, as was the case of Ali Bey El Abbassi, in this little scene that he described: "It appeared interesting to me to see the camels eat. The driver placed a mat of a circular form, about six feet diameter, upon the ground, upon which he laid a pile of brambles and herbs, cut very small: he then permitted the camels to approach, when they immediately squatted themselves upon the ground all round it, at regular distances, and began to eat with a sort of politeness and order which gave me pleasure. They each eat the herbs that were before them by a little at a time; and if either of them left his place, his companion at his side appeared to scold him in a friendly manner, which made the other feel his fault, and return to it again. In a word, the camels' table is a faithful copy of their masters'."

This amiable picture demonstrates the even temper that camels reveal most of the time. Tamisier, who turned out to be a real connoisseur, stated: "This animal is gifted with extremely sweet manners; it easily becomes quite attached to its master." He also treated it with great regard. "The Bedu are very considerate of their camels, always ready to suffer hardship themselves in order to spare their animals," Thesiger assured, adding that "a Bedu never strikes or ill-treats a camel" arbitrarily. With a fragile constitution despite its

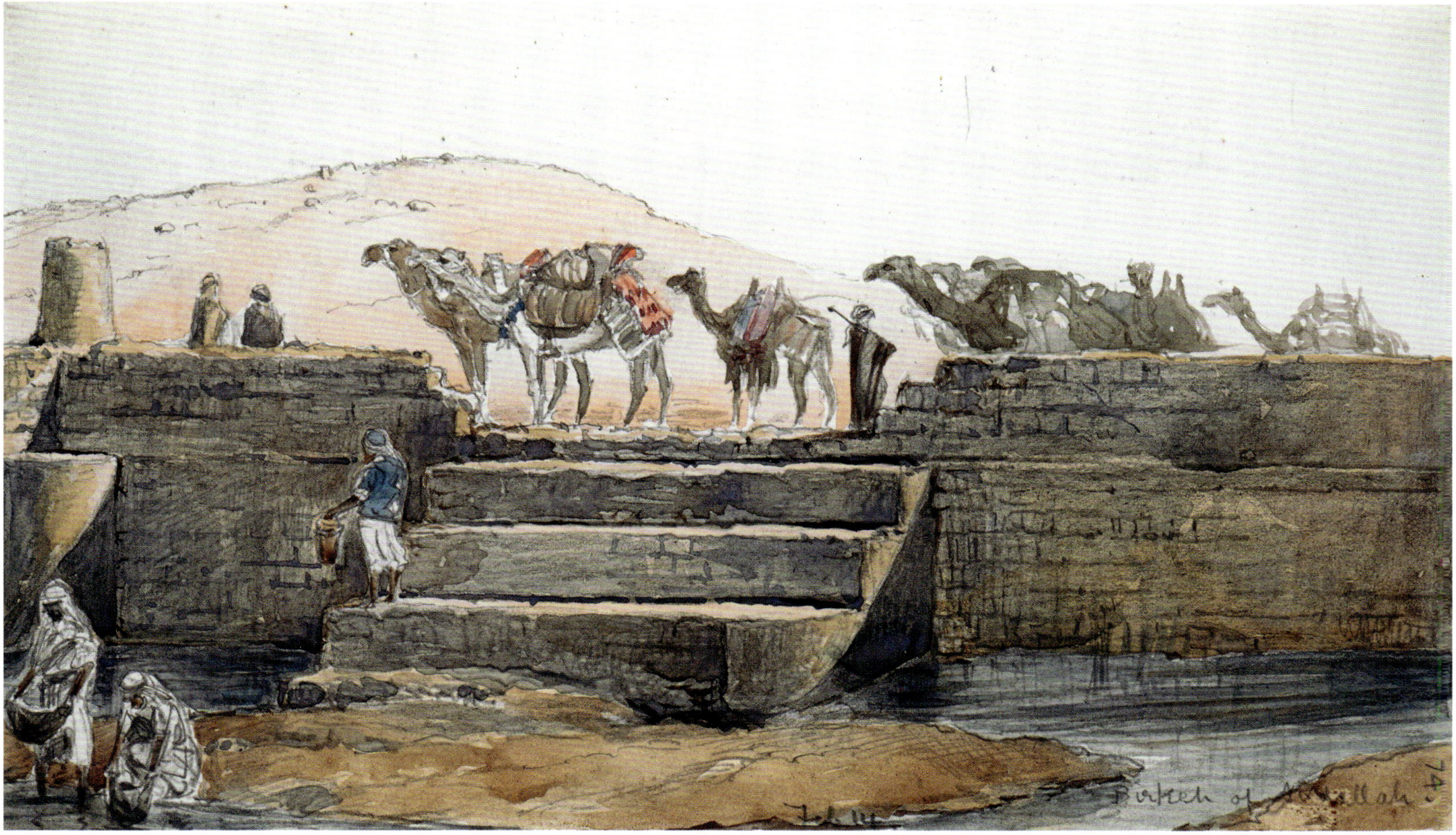

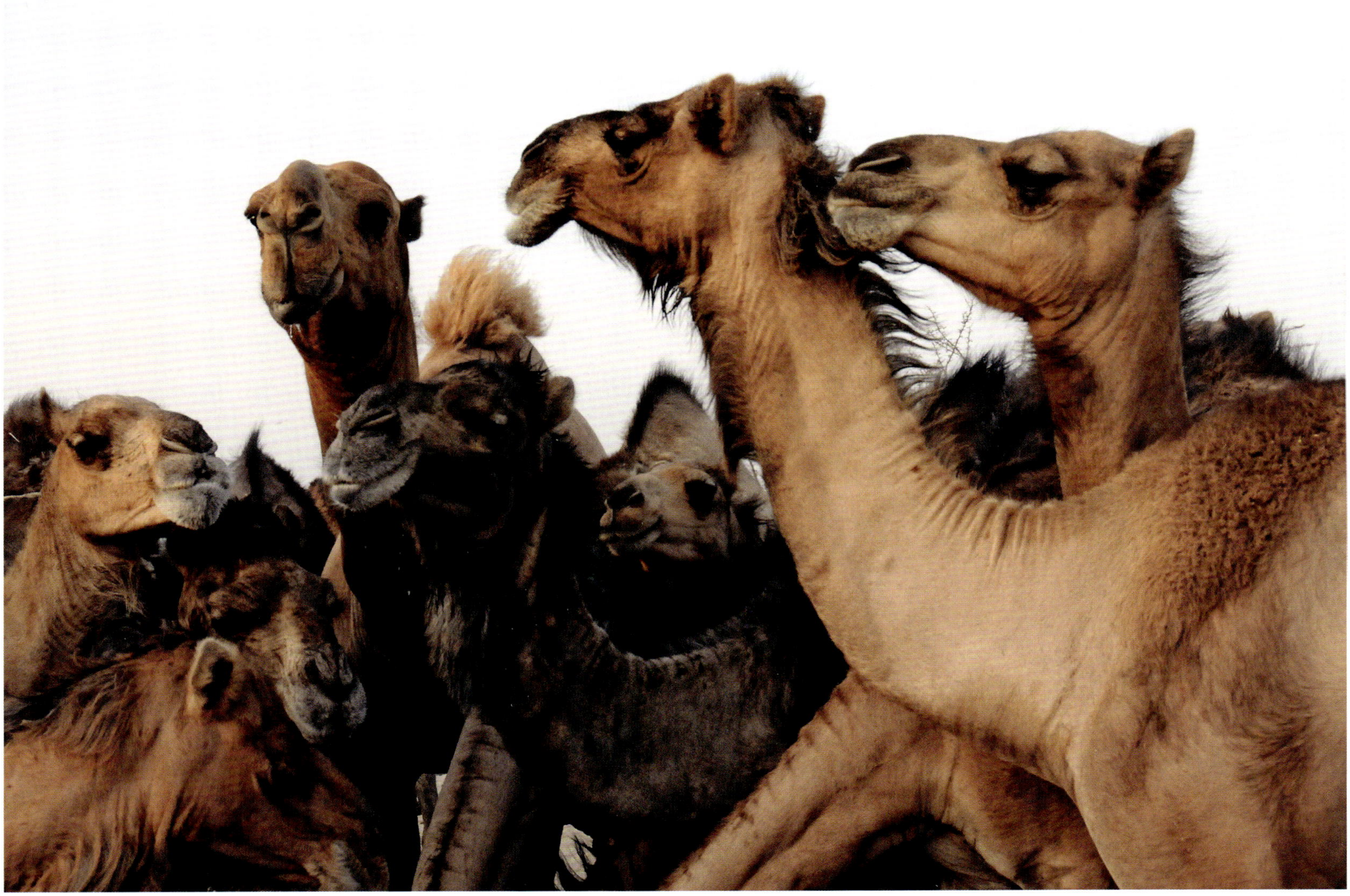

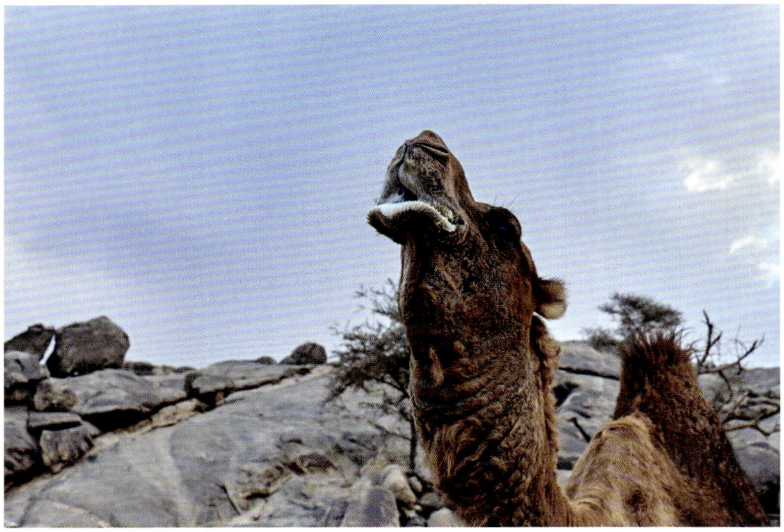

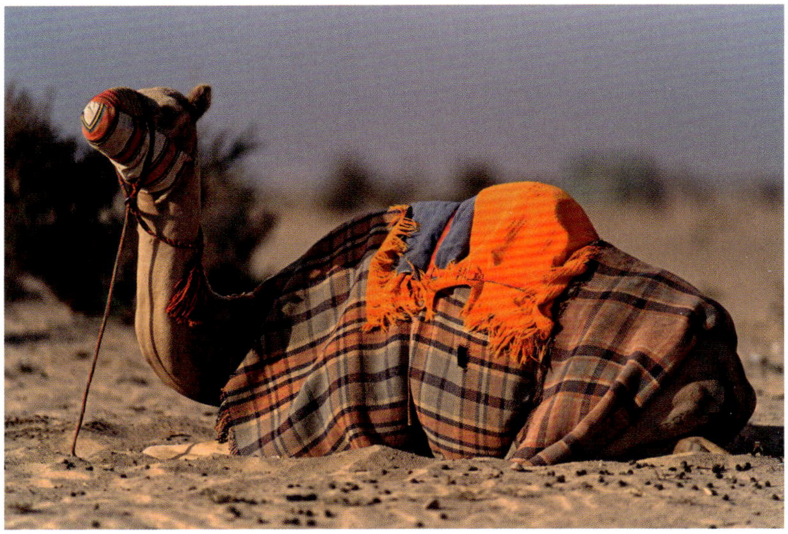

Olivier Couppey
Dromedaries in Arabia
Courtesy of the artist

Olivier Couppey
Camel's Bleat
Courtesy of the artist

"Bedouins derive great pleasure from looking at a good camel as some Englishmen get from looking at a good horse," wrote Thesiger in *Arabian Sands*.

Olivier Couppey
Camel at Rest
Courtesy of the artist

Camels play an important role in the Bedouin's life. They also occupy an important place in the poetry of the desert.

Olivier Couppey
Proud Cameleer
Courtesy of the artist

Bedouins refer to the camels as *'Ata Allah* or "God's Gift".

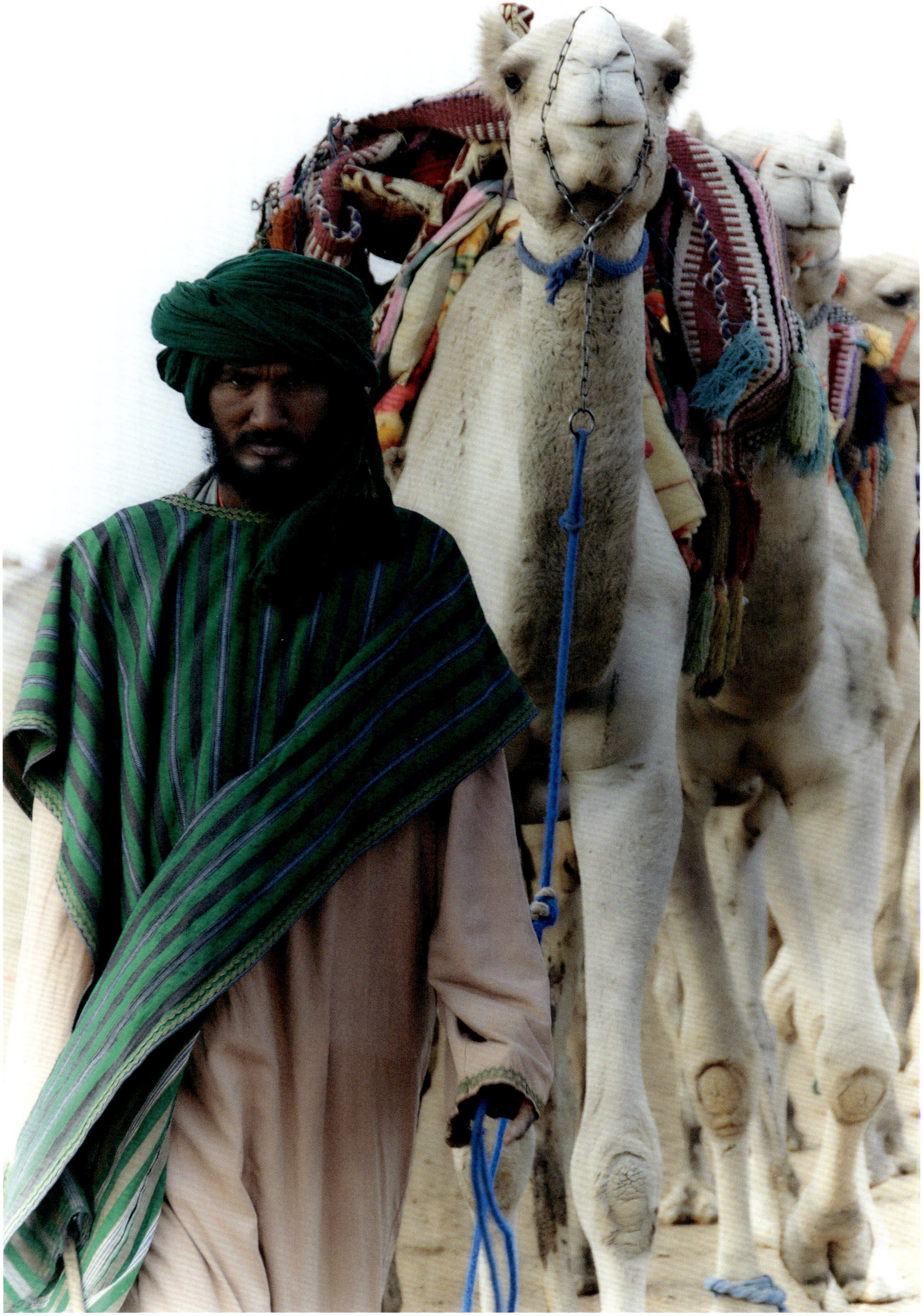

extraordinary endurance, the camel "does not like to be beaten unjustly. If you hit it on the head, that may kill it; on the shoulders, will ruin it: this part of its body is extremely sensitive, so that the simple rubbing of the rider's foot is enough to punish any small errors it may have committed," noted Tamisier. In any case, "the dromedary is usually willing to march according to the will of its master," he goes on. "If it is pressed too hard, it will double its speed and take all the flight it is capable of. If beaten in this moment, the camel will make a new effort and continue its run until it succumbs to exhaustion."

It is a pact for life and for death that unites the man and his camel: "It is not hunger nor is it thirst that frightens the Bedu; they maintain that they can survive riding in cold weather for seven days without food or water. It is the possible collapse of their camels which haunts them. If this happens, death is certain," wrote Thesiger.

The nomad takes all necessary precautions to avoid such a dramatic outcome. "Let us take the example of a Bedouin who is setting out for a long and dangerous trip through a region with no water" and let's follow him, with Tamisier, as he makes his preparations. "He will saddle his dromedary himself; he will attach a *ghirba*—a large leather goatskin—to the flank of the camel, in which he can store water sufficient for ten or fifteen days; a small flask, called *zemzémié* (named after the Haram source in Mecca), attached to the pommel by a hook, containing the provision for one day so that he can detach it and drink at ease without having to stop his course at all." Our author continued: "*Khourdj* or bags with beautiful falling tassels are placed on the saddle; they contain flour, butter, dried dates, a small packet full of coffee, some rice, and a casserole to make the pilaf; so much for the nourishment of the Bedouin, while his bed consists of a carpet and a woollen cover; a rifle in a bandolier hangs from the rear pommel, the sabre hangs from the one at the front; his spear is always in his hand and also serves to catch hold of the halter rope if he lets it drop."

With a touch of mischief, Tamisier finishes this picture: "A dromedary equipped in this way is not overloaded, however it is carrying everything a man might need during a fortnight: his divan, his buffet, and his arsenal!" Thus, the nomad is ready to depart, to take on bad weather and the blows of destiny. The "fine dromedary," for its part, is ready to "cover nine miles in forty-five minutes and ninety miles in ten hours by forced march," explained Tamisier; "while travelling," he added, the dromedary can remain "at times up to forty-eight hours without eating and four days without drinking" without affecting its speed.

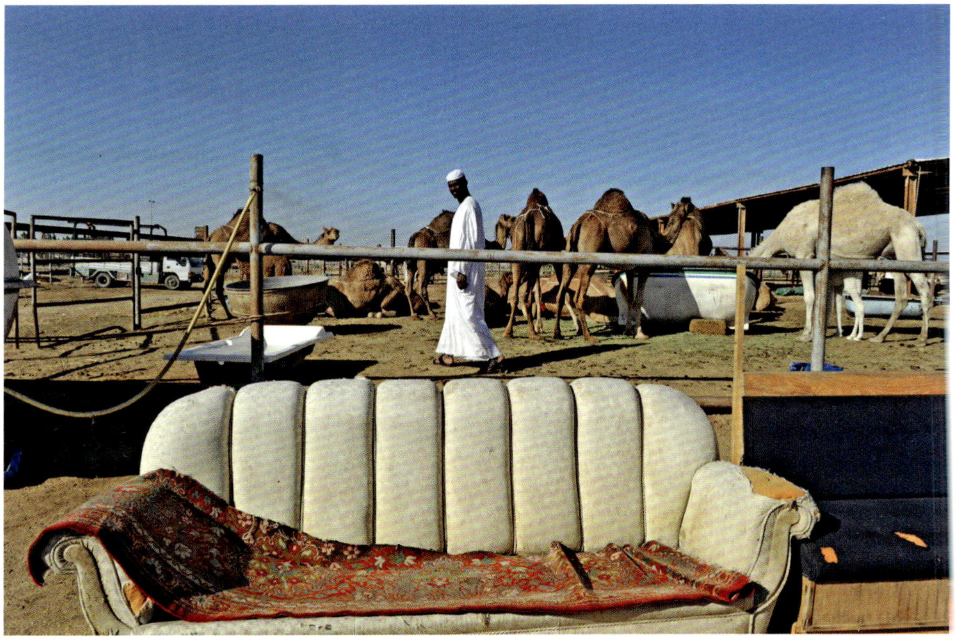

Anne de Henning
Camel market in Jeddah, 2011
Courtesy of the artist

At the time of Wallin's sojourn in Arabia, the average price of camels ranged from 10 to 40 Spanish dollars, whereas horses varied from 20 to 3,000.

Édith Ortoli
Les Chameaux blancs
(The white camels)
From *Esprit du désert*, 2017
Artist book, single copy
Text by René Caillé
Mixed media
Courtesy of the artist

According to Orientalist Joseph Van Hammer, there are 5,744 names and epithets that refer to the camel in the Arabic language.

According to Johann Ludwig Burckhardt, "The richest region for camels is without a doubt Nejd." The Swiss explorer also noted that "the ordinary load of an Arabian camel is four to five hundred kilos for a short trip, and only three to four hundred kilos for a longer voyage." He also reported that "among the Bedouins, female camels are more highly valued and more expensive than the males," because "they support thirst better than the males."

In addition to their sobriety, Maurice Tamisier also admired the ease with which camels walked on the steepest terrain: "They pass the most abrupt of slopes, the highest peaks and along the edge of precipices, challenging the surefootedness of the flocks of goats and sheep. The first time I saw them perched in this way, I could hardly believe my eyes, and I could not imagine how they could manage to disengage without mishap." The French adventurer describes the Bedouin as being well-settled into his saddle, as if he was comfortably installed in a bed. Separated from the horizon, the Bedouin is directed only by the reassuring pendulum formed by the head and neck of his camel. To his camel, the Bedouin speaks, telling him stories, making promises, and singing songs.

On the neck that is swinging regularly in front of him, the Bedouin himself hangs several objects. At first, "to protect their camels from the evil eye,

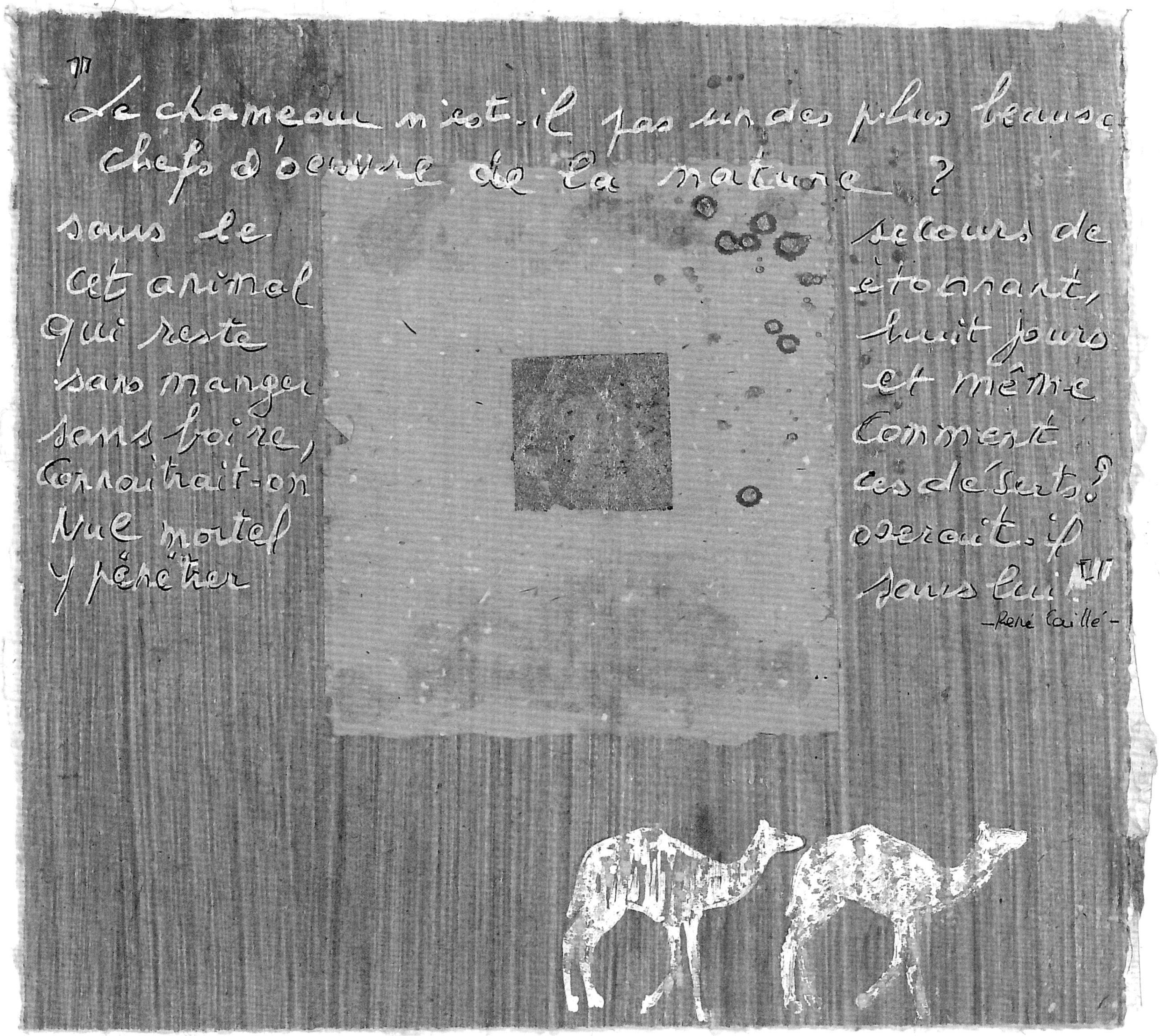
"Le chameau n'est-il pas un des plus beaux
chefs d'oeuvre de la nature ?
sous le secours de
cet animal étonnant,
qui reste huit jours
sans manger et même
sans boire, Comment
connaitrait-on ces déserts?
quel mortel oserait-il
y pénétrer sans lui!"
-René Caillé-

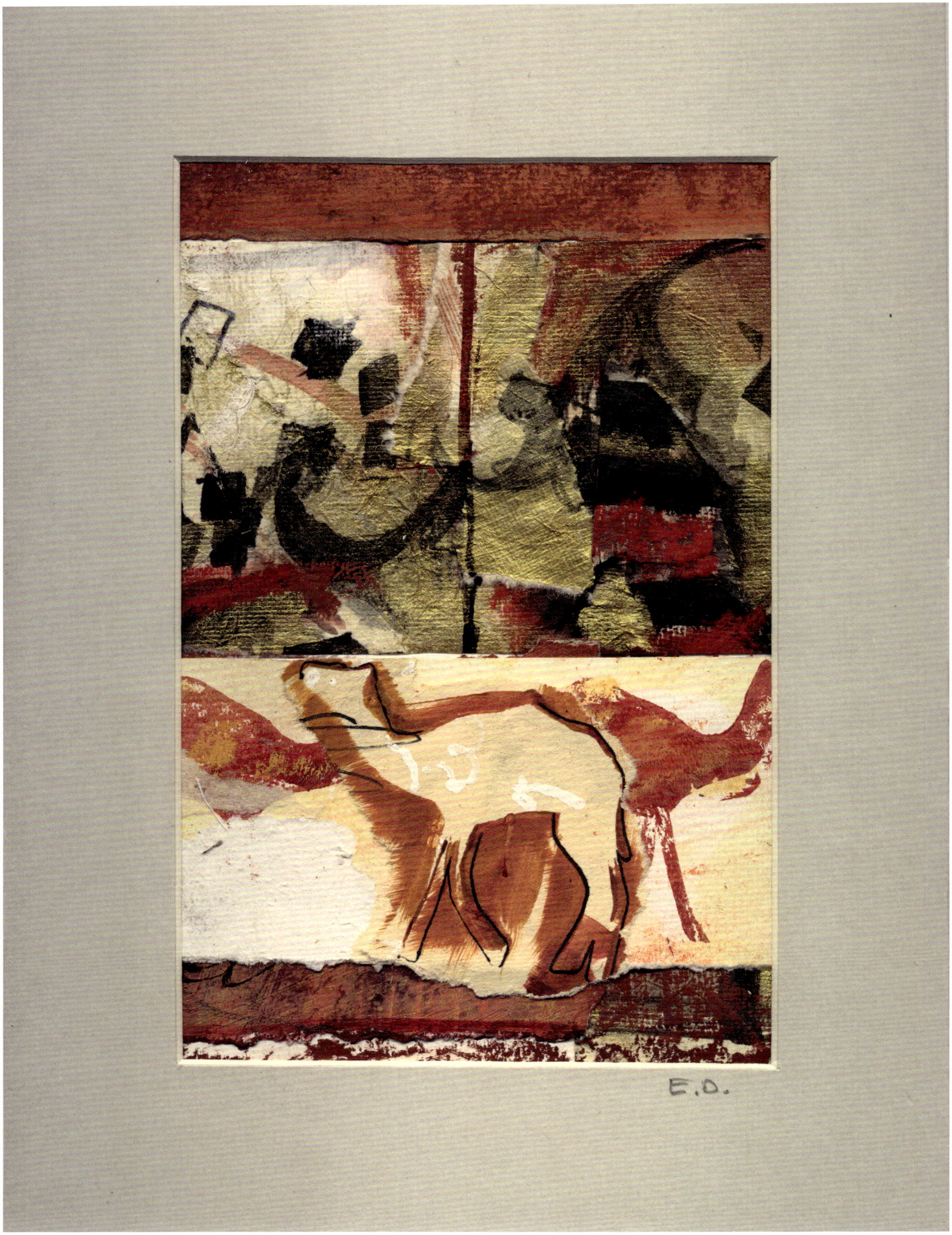
E.D.

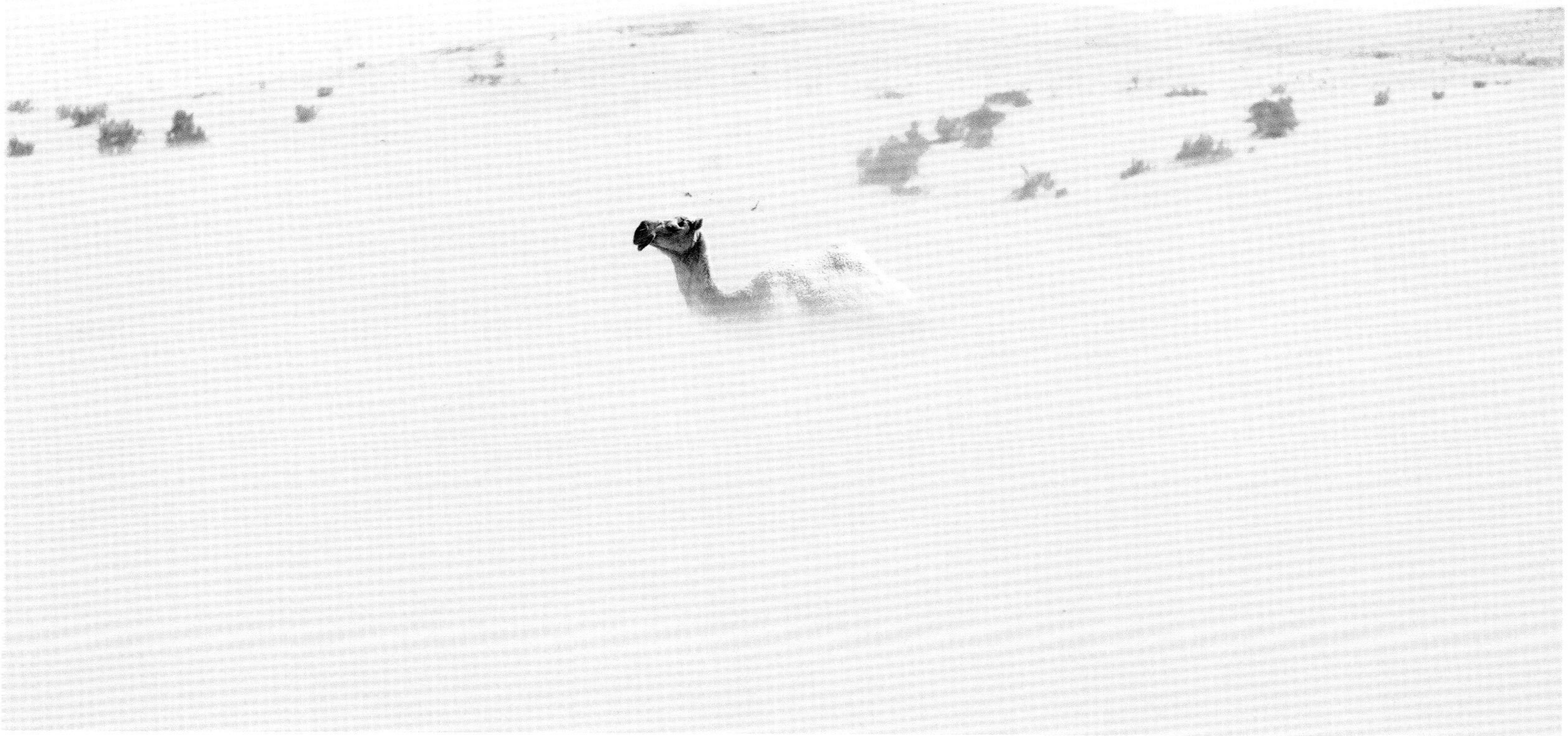

Édith Ortoli
Graphisme Ocre 2
(Ocher Graphism 2), 2007
Mixed media
21 × 16 cm
Courtesy of the artist

Anne Blunt wrote that "*The pilgrims do not care for the welfare of their camels and will not let them graze as they go, because riding a camel which eats as it goes is rather tiresome. Then in the evening the tents have to be pitched in some spot where a large camp can stand altogether, irrespective of considerations of pasture.*"

Yann Gayet
From the series *Contresens*
Courtesy of the artist

Camels are anatomically adapted to the desert climate. Their eyelids are translucent, enabling them to see with closed eyes in a sandstorm.

the Arabs purchase amulets that they hung on their necks." In addition, "while travelling, the Arabs always have a little bag that they attach to the neck of their camel, where they collect the wool that the camels lose while marching, and when they return to their group, they give it to their wives, who use it to make the tents or other textiles they need," reports Tamisier. This small pouch is certainly another indication of the respectful care and attention that the nomad devotes to his mount.

The long neck also carries something else: a red-hot iron brand marked on the animal's hide which allows its identification in case of wandering or theft. This *wasm* is that of the tribe, the clan, or the sub-clan. In 1884, the French epigrapher Charles Huber, who, it seems, was very likely the first to have shown an interest in this detail, noticed that such a mark "was generally composed of several different signs, which are therefore true coats of arms that can be read." Establishing the first list of these signs, Huber noticed that many of them were based on the alphabets of the ancient South Arabian languages, including Himyaritic, Thamudic, and Lihyanic. Later, in 1952, the American anthropologist, Henry Field, drafted a very complete catalogue of those brands.

It was well-settled in their saddles and peering over the head of a dromedary, that travelers discovered Arabia. They were able to affirm that undertaking the voyage on the back of a camel was not disagreeable nor even uncomfortable, and certainly much less tiring than on horseback. This was the opinion, in any case, of French writer Charles Didier, who stated: "Of the variety of ways of travelling that I have tried on land and at sea, I know of none that is pleasanter..."

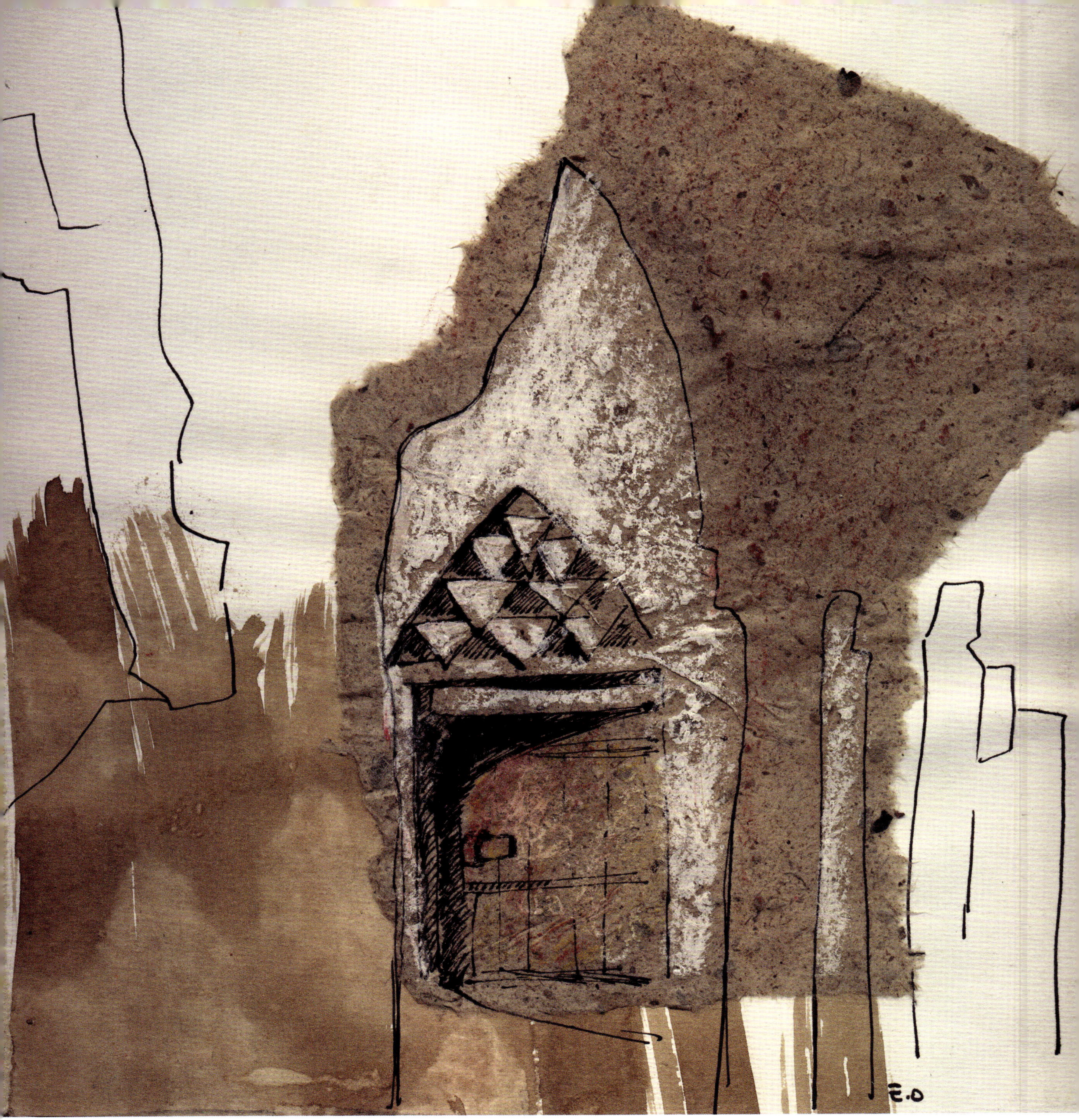
E.O

The Desert of Deserts

Édith Ortoli
La porte du désert
(Gate of the desert), 2007
Mixed media
25 × 25 cm
Courtesy of the artist

Richard Burton wrote in *Personal Narrative of a Pilgrimage to Al-Madinah and Meccah*: "*In the desert the wildness and sublimity of the senses around you stir up all the energies of your soul—whether for exertion, danger, or strife. Your morale improves; you become frank and cordial, hospitable and single-minded: the hypocritical politeness and the slavery of civilization are left behind you in the city. Your senses are quickened: they require no stimulants but air and exercise.*"

Even today, it is possible to view the ruins of a series of small Roman forts all along a line that runs from the north of Syria to the south of Palestine for a total of approximately 1,500 kilometers. Most often they are perched atop natural mounds and were built by Rome at the start of the second century A.D. This line, marked off in equal increments by military boundary stones with Latin inscriptions, constituted the borderline between Roman possessions on one side and Arabia on the other. This borderline, or rather this *limes* ("limit" in Latin), faced the desert.

The strategic shield constituted by the presence of these fortifications would have been perfectly useless if the desert on the edge of which they were erected had been uninhabited. However, wrote historian Jacqueline Pirenne, "That was not the case: there were men living in these stretches that were so apparently inclement; they were Bedouins, that is, inhabitants, of the steppe (*badiat* in Arabic, origin of the adjective *bedouy*)." It was obviously for this reason that these Bedouins were used to making incursions outside the spaces that were supposed to contain them, sometimes so massive that the Romans chose to protect themselves from them.

Over the centuries, this immense territory of steppe and desert did not offer any hold to conquerors. Throughout the course of history, excluding the conflicts that arose within the Middle East itself, there are very few examples to be found of attempts to conquer, and they all ended in bitter defeats. One of the first was certainly the expedition sent from Egypt, ordered by the Roman emperor Augustus, which invaded southern Arabia to take command of the caravan trade: it failed miserably in 24 B.C. Twelve centuries later, in 1182, Raynald of Châtillon, the unruly lieutenant of Baldwin IV, the Latin king of Jerusalem, menaced Medina and Mecca, and attacked pilgrims. His troops were harshly defeated by Adil, the Ayyubid governor of Cairo and brother of Saladin. Later taken prisoner during the battle of Hattin, Raynald of Châtillon was beheaded by order of the latter. At the beginning of the sixteenth century, the Portuguese whose ships had entered the Red Sea attempted to lay siege to Jeddah, but eventually retreated and were finally driven out by the Ottomans beyond the straits of Bab el-Mandeb.

The desert nature of the peninsula was undoubtedly a major factor in making it difficult to conquer. However, Arabia does not consist solely of deserts. There are a great variety of landscapes. In many places there are fields of barley and wheat, even in Nejd. Also, in Hijaz, there are various areas that have long been suitable for the cultivation of fruits and vegetables. This is especially the case for Wadi Fatima, near Jeddah, where melons, legumes, and vegetables are cultivated. Other such localities include Badr and Khulays, near Medina, and Batn Marra, near Mecca, known for their orchards; and the city of Ta'if, the gardens, fruits, and roses of which have been famous throughout all Arabia for more than a thousand years. Other regions of Arabia, such as the Asir region, have had an agricultural tradition for centuries. All of this is true even without considering the cultivation of coffee, practiced in many places in the southern and southwestern areas of the peninsula.

These few examples can certainly be expanded. They help to reveal that Arabia is made of contrasts and a great diversity of soils and landscapes. Nonetheless, it is useful to know that less than two percent of the territory, of its two-and-a-half-million square kilometers, are effectively farmable. This number shows the exact measure of what Arabia really is: a land mainly composed of rocky landscapes, plains of gravel or gypsum, crystalline plateaus, lava fields, stretches covered with flint as far as the eye can see, and basalt rocks.

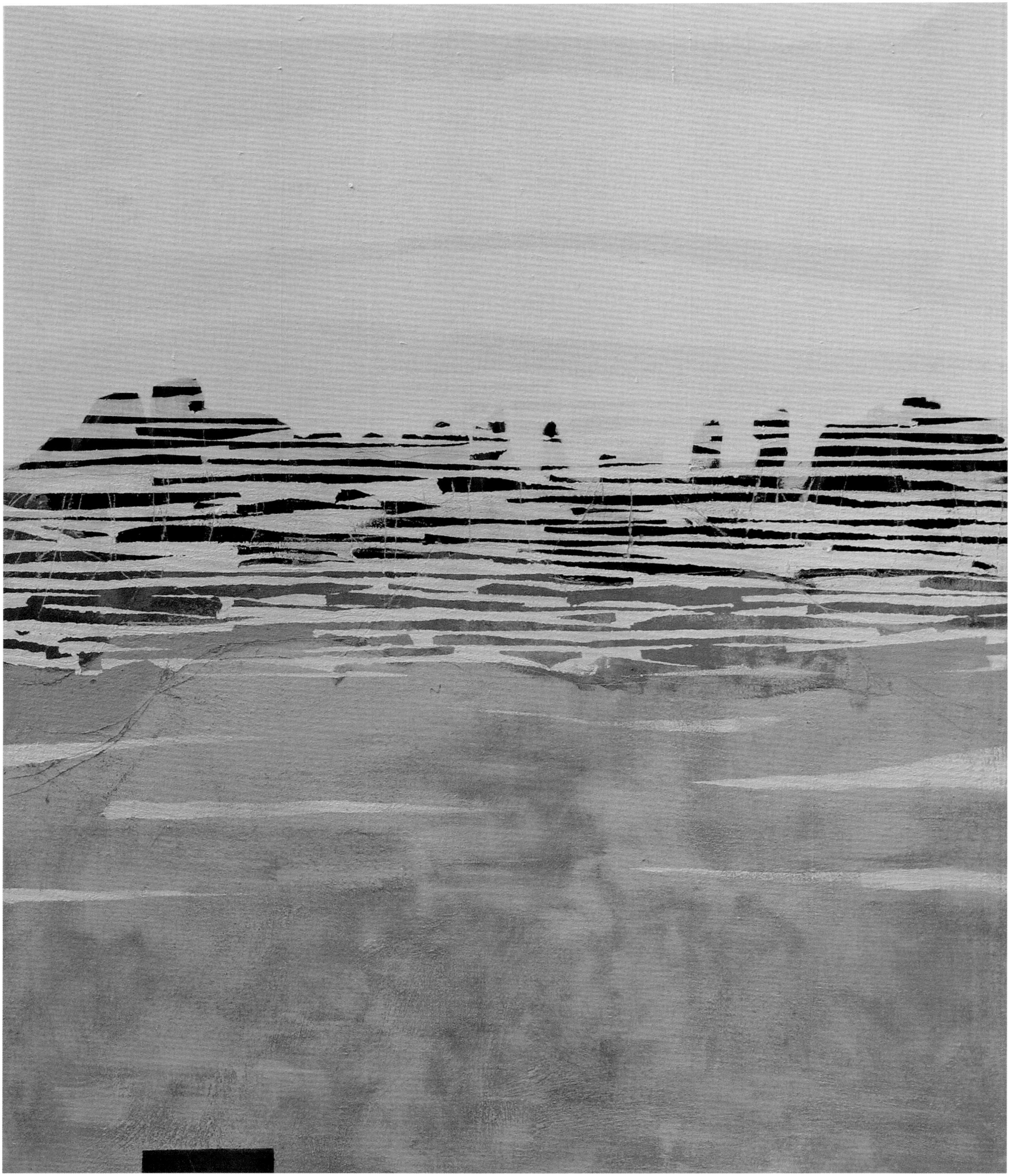

Caroline Havers
Escarpment in dust storm, 2014
From the series *Sand & Serendipity*
Mixed media on paper
180 × 150 cm
Courtesy of the artist and Naila Gallery, Riyadh

John Keane wrote in *Six months in the Hijaz, Journeys to Makkah and Madinah 1877-1878*, describing sandstorms:
"Of all the many other interesting workings of Nature on an unusual scale in this country, I have seen a sandstorm, by forming drifts, alter a landscape in a few hours."

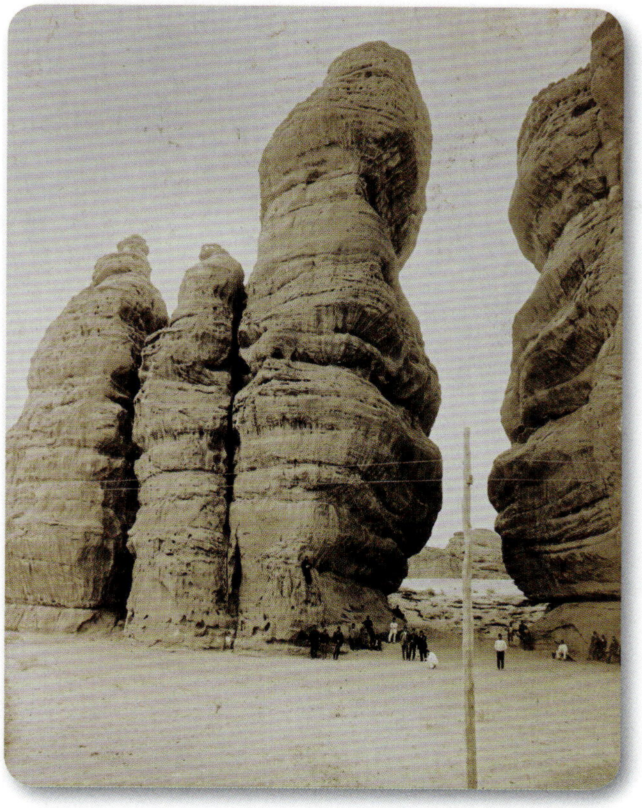

Postcard
In the foreground, the telegraph line between Damascus and Medina in Al-Ula (Dedan). The huge stone monoliths in the background are part of the Mabarak al Naga escarpment.
From the official album of photographs of the Hijaz railroad
Nasser D. Khalili collection of Islamic Art, London

The oasis of Al-Ula is located about twenty kilometers south of Mada'in Saleh (Hegra).

All of these areas are either entirely or predominantly desert. However, the desert, properly speaking—the true desert of sand—the absolute desert, is mainly limited to three areas on the map of Arabia. The first area, the whole south of the peninsula, is occupied by the terrible Rub' al-Khali with its 650,000 square kilometers, it is the equivalent of the combined areas of Germany and Italy. It was not until the 1930s that travelers from outside this part of the world would succeed in crossing it in the same conditions as the natives. Next, in the north, there is the no less awesome Nafud—or the Great Nafud—an oval area with a decidedly smaller area, about 70,000 square kilometers, about the size of Ireland. Finally, the third of these great spaces is situated between the first two and consists of the ad-Dahna desert. This corridor of sand, more than 1,200 kilometers in length, with width varying from twenty-five to one-hundred kilometers, links the Rub' al-Khali to the Great Nafud. Its northernmost segment is sometimes called the small Nafud.

Not many voyagers were drawn to Arabia solely for its desert. The British explorer, Richard Burton, explained that the pilgrimage was his primary intention for visiting Arabia in 1853. He also planned to claim the title of the first foreigner to have crossed the great Rub' al-Khali desert from north to south. Most likely, Burton had hardly considered the difficulties and the dangers of such an expedition in their true measure. This is what stands out in reading his report of the trip when, on the way from Medina to Mecca he faced, for the first time, the desert territories: a few days that seemed infinitely longer to him.

Burton was abruptly shocked by the nature of the landscape: "We travelled through a country fantastic in its desolation—a mass of huge hills, barren plains, and desert vales." Gradually, as he proceeded in the midst of a group of pilgrims, the surroundings struck him as being more and more grandiose and terrifying: "Vast clefts seamed like scars the hideous face of earth; here they widened into dark caves, there they were choked with glistening drift sands. Above, a sky like polished blue steel, with a tremendous blaze of yellow light, glared upon us without the thinnest veil of mist cloud." Later, he continued: "For most part it is a haggard land, a country of wild beast[s] and wilder men, a region whose very fountains murmur the warning words, 'Drink and Away', instead of 'Rest and be thankful'." And also: "It was a desert peopled only with echoes—a place of death for what little there is to die in it." It was there that he had a close brush with death when the group of pilgrims with whom he was advancing was attacked by a horde of brigands. At the very last moment, they would be saved, if not by the cavalry, at least by a detachment of Wahhabis anxious to restore order and send off the Bedouins in rout. This adventure undoubtedly contributed to Burton's decision to abort his project to cross the great desert. His words do seem to reveal a lasting regret: "In the desert, the wildness and sublimity of the scenes around you stir up all the energies of your soul—whether for exertion, danger, or strife."

During the course of the second and final thirds of the nineteenth century, a few intrepid travelers did nonetheless make the choice to take on Arabia by crossing, if not the Rub' al-Khali, as Burton had planned to do for some time, at least the Great Nafud desert. There was a handful who resolved to undertake the crossing along its north-south axis, and for the entire distance from Al-Jawf, in the north, to Jobba and then Ha'il, in the south, they were conscious that this would allow their journey to acquire a powerful symbolic charge from the outset. They are listed here in chronological order: beginning with the Finnish Orientalist, Georg August Wallin (1845); the British adventurer, William Gifford Palgrave (1862); the Tuscan horseman, Carlo Guarmani (1864); the

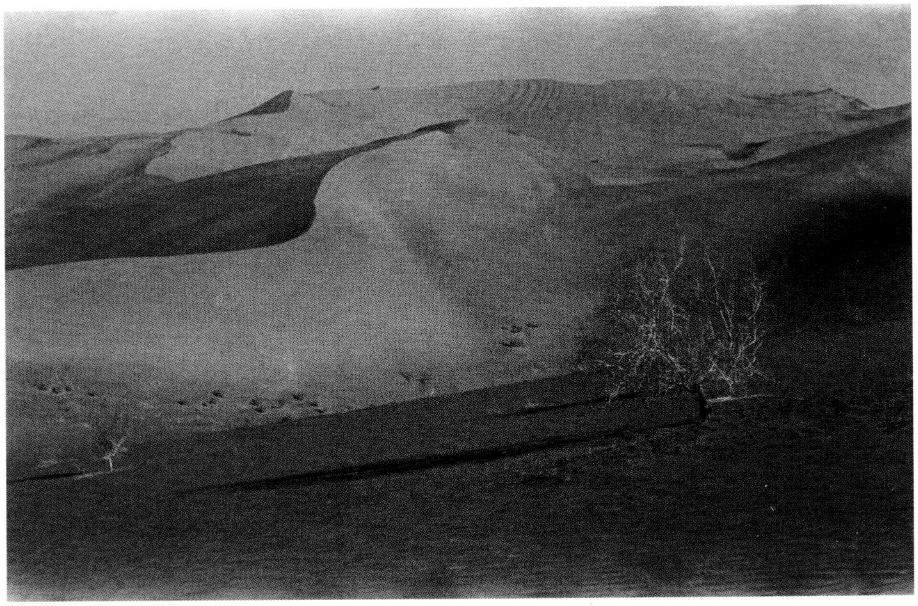

Wilfred Thesiger
Landscape in the Uruq ash Shaybah sands in the Empty Quarter (Rub' al-Khali), December 1946
Courtesy of the Pitt Rivers Museum, University of Oxford

Thesiger described in *Across the Empty Quarter* the crossing of the Uruq ash Shaybah sands, some of the highest dunes in the Empty Quarter, writing: "*The peaks were steeper and more pronounced, rising in many cases to great pinnacles, down which the flowing ridges swept like draperies. The sands were very soft, cascading round our feet as the camels struggled up the slopes. [...] I wondered how much more these camels would stand, for they were trembling violently whenever they halted.*"

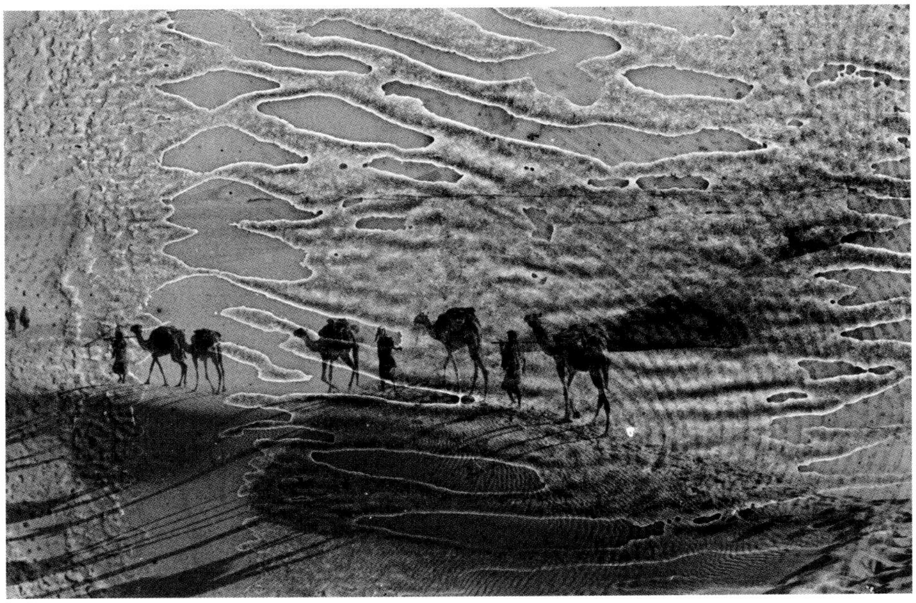

Wilfred Thesiger
View of Wilfred Thesiger's party travelling from Khawr bin 'Atarit well in the Ghanim sands to the Ramlat al Ghafah in the Empty Quarter, November/December 1946
Courtesy of the Pitt Rivers Museum, University of Oxford

The Empty Quarter, covering an area larger than France, lies in the southeast of Arabia. It is the largest continuous sand desert on earth, with dunes stretching for hundreds of kilometers.

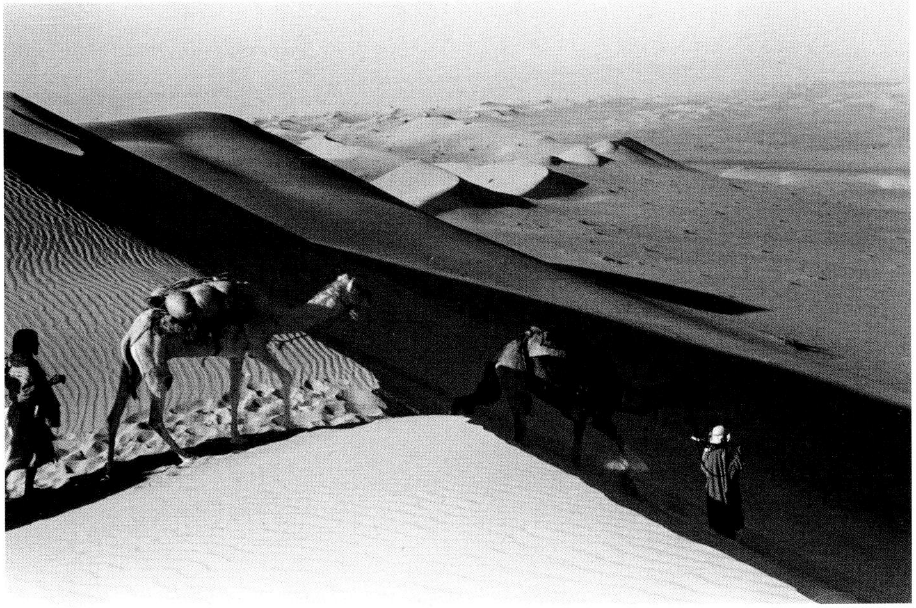

Wilfred Thesiger
The Empty Quarter (Rub' al- Khali) in the Riyadh Province, January 1948
Courtesy of the Pitt Rivers Museum, University of Oxford

Thesiger wrote that "*each dune was three to four hundred feet in height, and the highest peaks were built up round deep crescent-shaped hollows. It took us an hour or more to cross each range. [...] Now for the first time the dunes were a lovely golden-red and, although I was tired, hungry, and thirsty, their shapes gave me great pleasure.*"

Otto Pilny
Towards Mecca, not dated
Oil on canvas
82.5 × 130.5 cm
The Shafik Gabr Collection, London

Religion was one of the favored themes among Orientalist painters. Many Orientalist painters produced genre scenes depicting the interiors of mosques, prayers, calls to prayers, or caravans heading to Mecca.

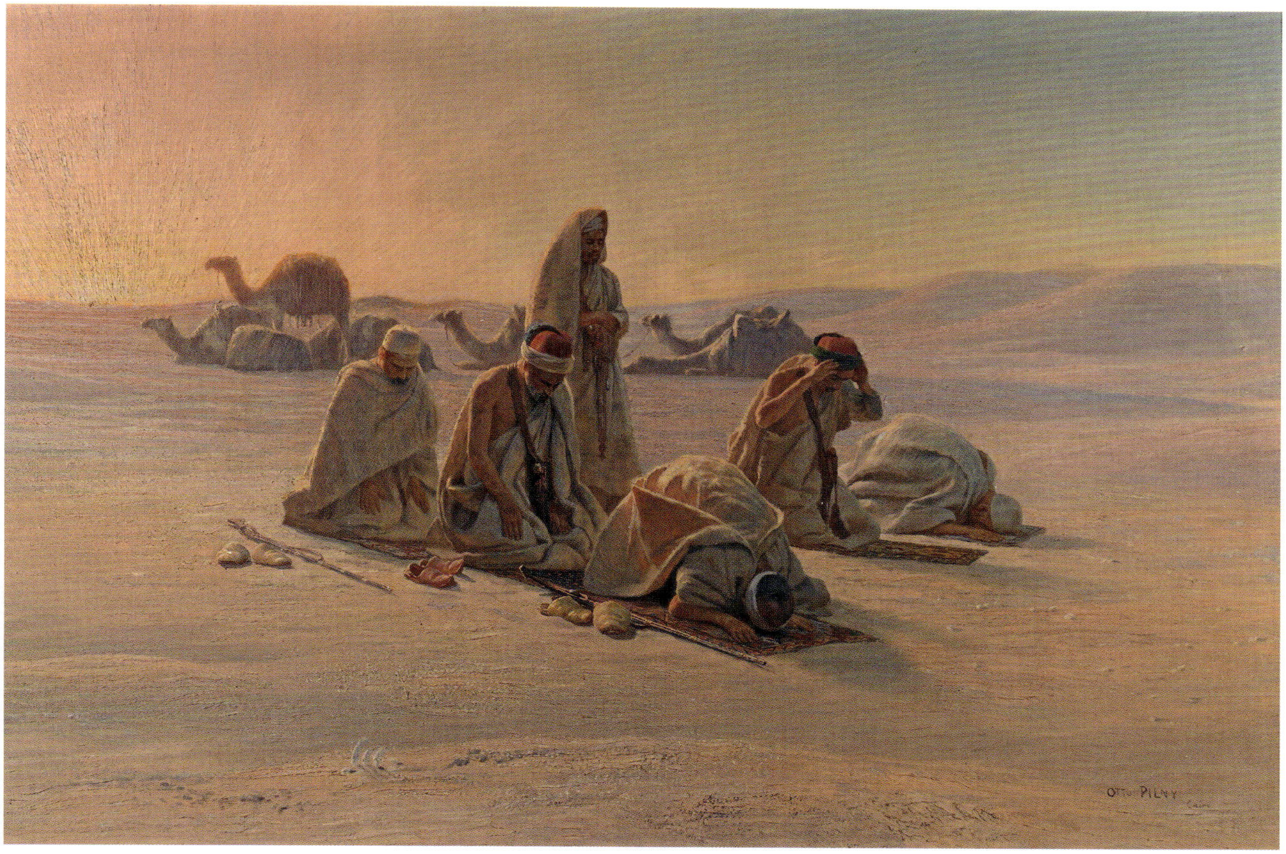

aristocratic British couple, Anne and Wilfrid Blunt (1878), also horse breeders; and the French epigraphist, Charles Huber (1880).

They narrated the memorable experience of crossing the Nafud desert in the many texts they produced. For Anne and Wilfrid Blunt, the Nafud seems to have represented a sort of graal: "The Nafud has been the object of our dreams all through this journey, as the *nec plus ultra* of desert," wrote Lady Blunt in her account of their trip, which began in Damascus. She describes their approach to the Nafud, after departing from Al-Jawf: "These sand dunes are not really the Nafud and are much like what may be seen elsewhere in the desert, in the Sahara for instance, or in certain parts of the peninsula of Sinai. They are very picturesque, being of pure white sand, from fifty to a hundred feet high, with intervening spaces of harder ground, and are covered with vegetation."

Eventually Anne and Wilfrid Blunt left the last village behind before facing the unknown spaces they had come to seek there, crossing "a flat black expanse of gravelly soil covered with small round pebbles, extending southwards to the horizon." Then, "we saw a red streak on the horizon before us, which rose and gathered as we approached it, stretching out east and west in an unbroken line. It might at first have been taken for an effect of mirage, but on coming nearer we found it broken into billows, and but for its red colour not unlike a stormy sea seen from shore, for it rose up, as the sea seems to rise, when the waves are high, above the level of the land. Somebody called out 'the Nafud'," wrote Anne Blunt. Here, they had really reached "the object of [their] dreams," this Nafud which "we hear wonderful accounts of it here, and of the people who have been lost in it."

By mentioning these "wonderful accounts," Anne Blunt implicitly evoked the account of Palgrave's adventures and his book *Personal Narrative of a Year's Journey Through Central and Eastern Arabia*, in which he narrated the details of the many episodes of his quite eventful, dramatic, and risky crossing of the Great Nafud. The works of Wallin and Guarmani had also been published; they both referred to the crossing of the Nafud, and the Blunts had read them too. Nonetheless, familiarity with these two last books had remained limited to the small world of Orientalists and travel enthusiasts. Palgrave's work, on the other hand, had been widely discussed. It benefited from huge publicity because of its sensational character and the numerous dangers that the author, on each page of his book, claimed to have escaped. Thus, on several occasions, the Blunts made corrections to that trait of Palgrave's book, rectifying an assertion,

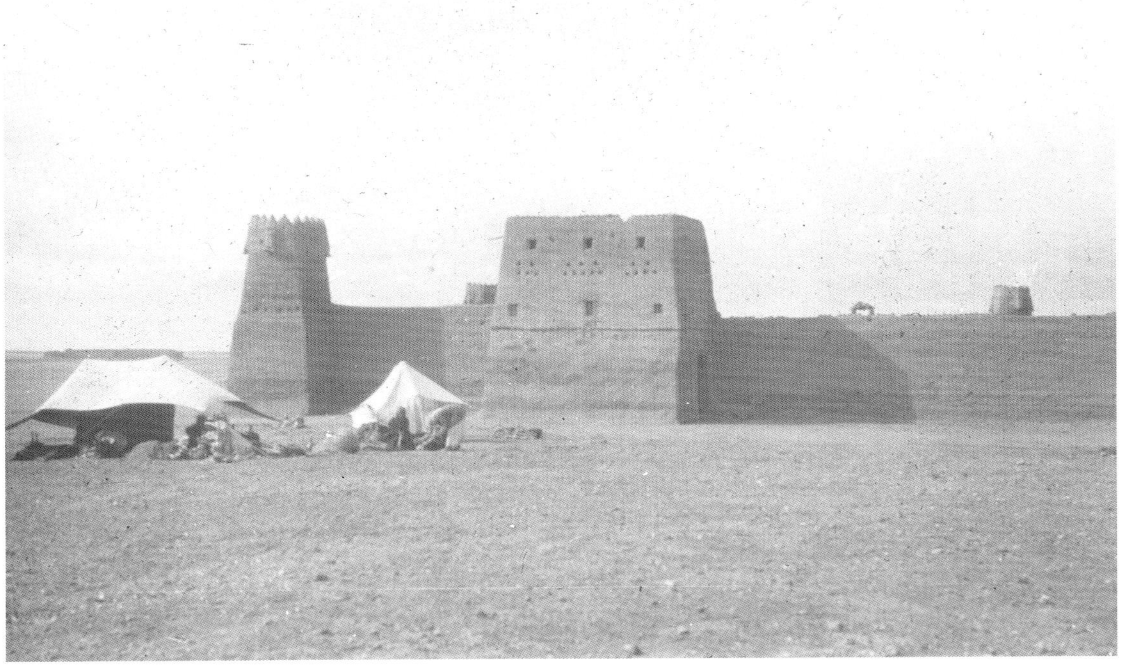

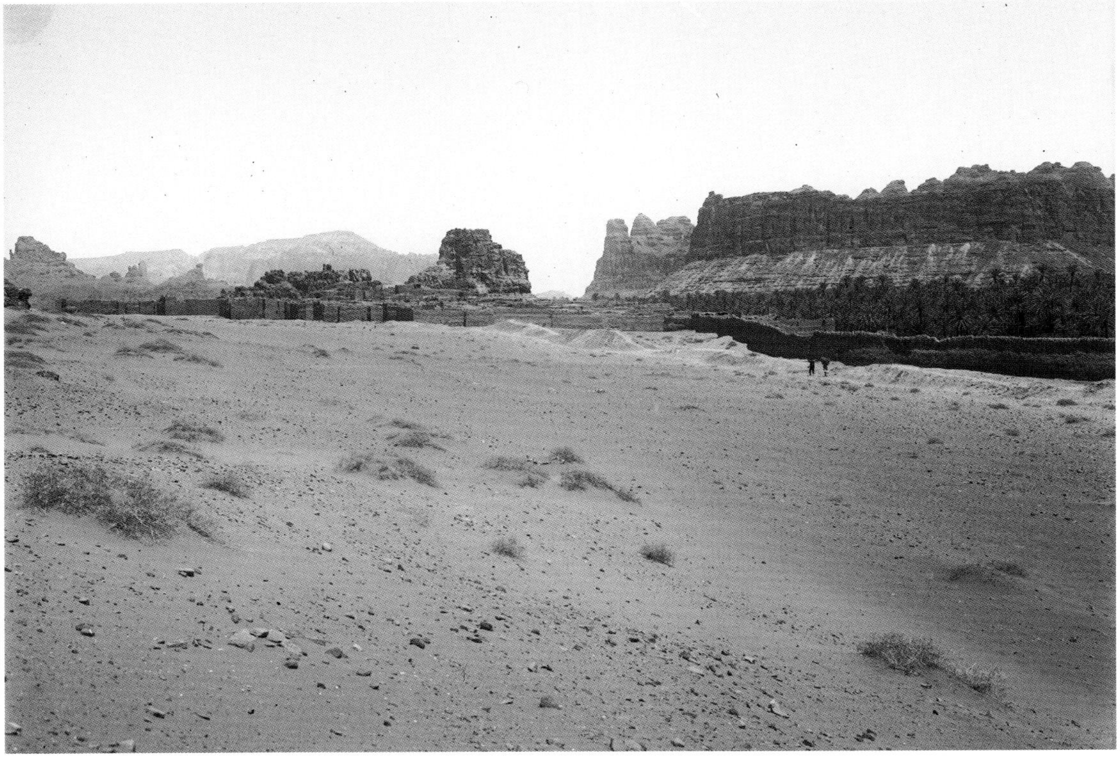

Harry St John Bridger Philby
Adobe fort and camp scene in Wadi Dawasir, 1930
Courtesy of the Royal Geographic Society, London

In *Heart of Arabia*, Philby wrote that he was the first European to ever set eyes on the "great mysterious valley of Dawasir". He and his men sojourned as guests, for seven days, in Barzan, the palace of the governor of Wadi Dawasir.

Jaussen and Savignac
The fortress and the wall of the oasis of Al-Ula (Dedan), viewed from south-west, March 1909
Courtesy of the French Biblical and Archeological School of Jerusalem

Joseph Elmer Yoakum
Sand Dunes in Arabian Desert, Saudi Arabia, 1962–65
Blue ballpoint pen, watercolor, and colored chalks on tan wove paper
22.7 × 30.4 cm
The Art Institute of Chicago, Courtesy of the Art Institute of Chicago / Art Resource New York

"It is this blending of two colours which gives such depth and richness to the Sands: gold with silver, orange with cream, brick red with white, burnt brown with pink, yellow with grey—they have an infinite variety of shades and colours," wrote Thesiger.

George Steinmetz
Across the star-shaped dune-chains of Uruq al-Mutaridah, 2002
Courtesy of the artist

The Rub' al-Khali has always been described as resembling the sea with its wave-like lines of dunes (*uruq*). Wilfred Thesiger, who crossed it in the late 1940s, described in *Arabian Sands* its void beauty: *"I was exhilarated by the sense of space, the silence, and the crisp cleanness of the sand."*

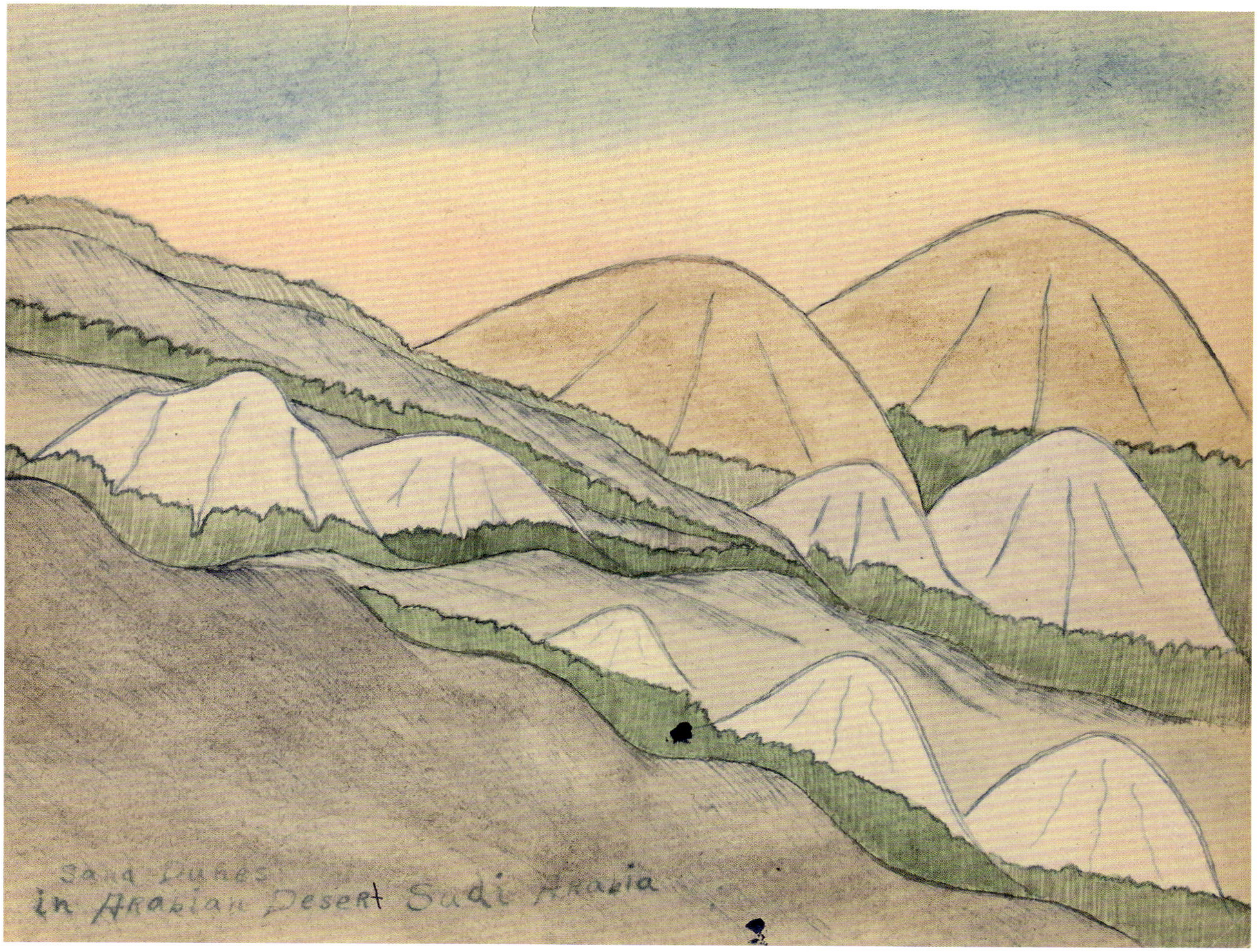
Sand Dunes
In Arabian Desert Sudi Arabia

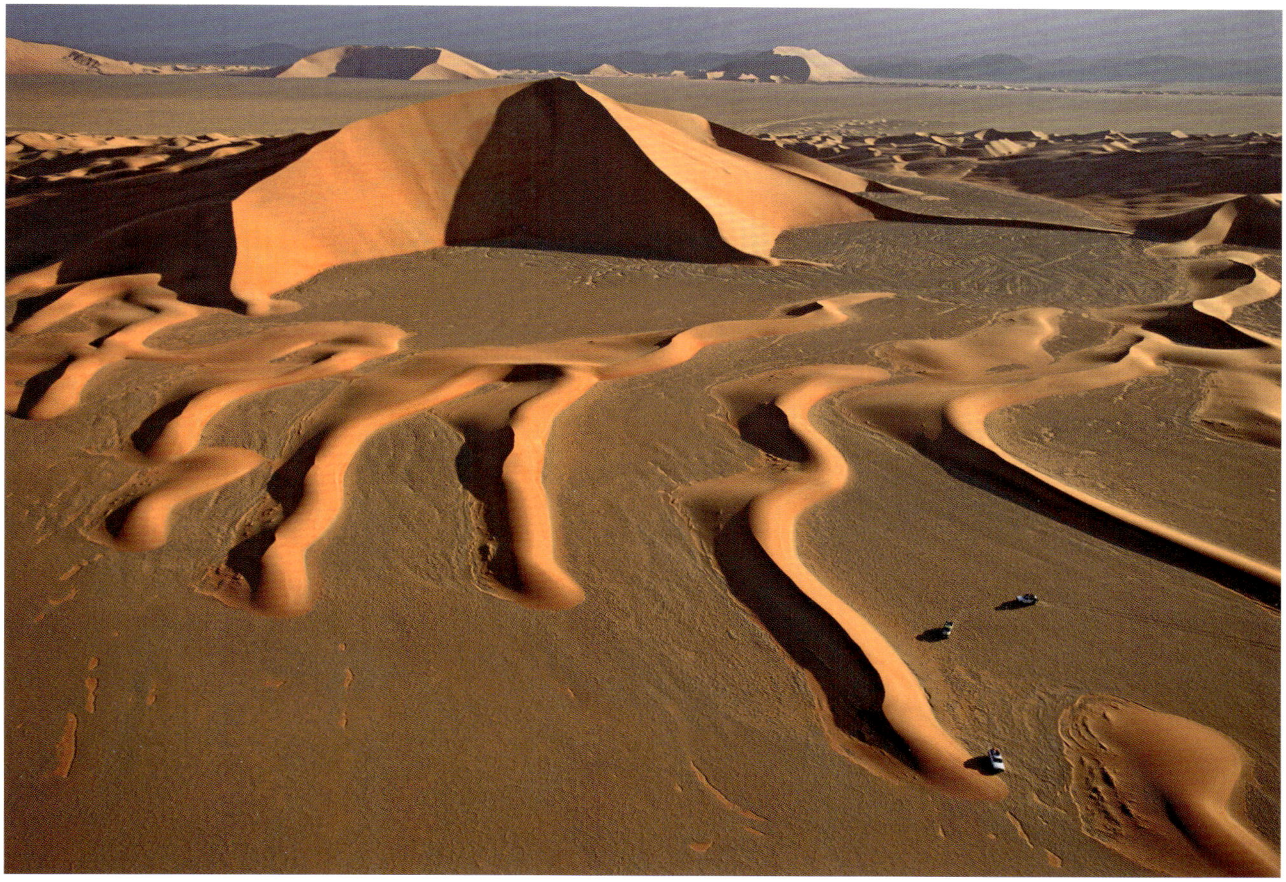

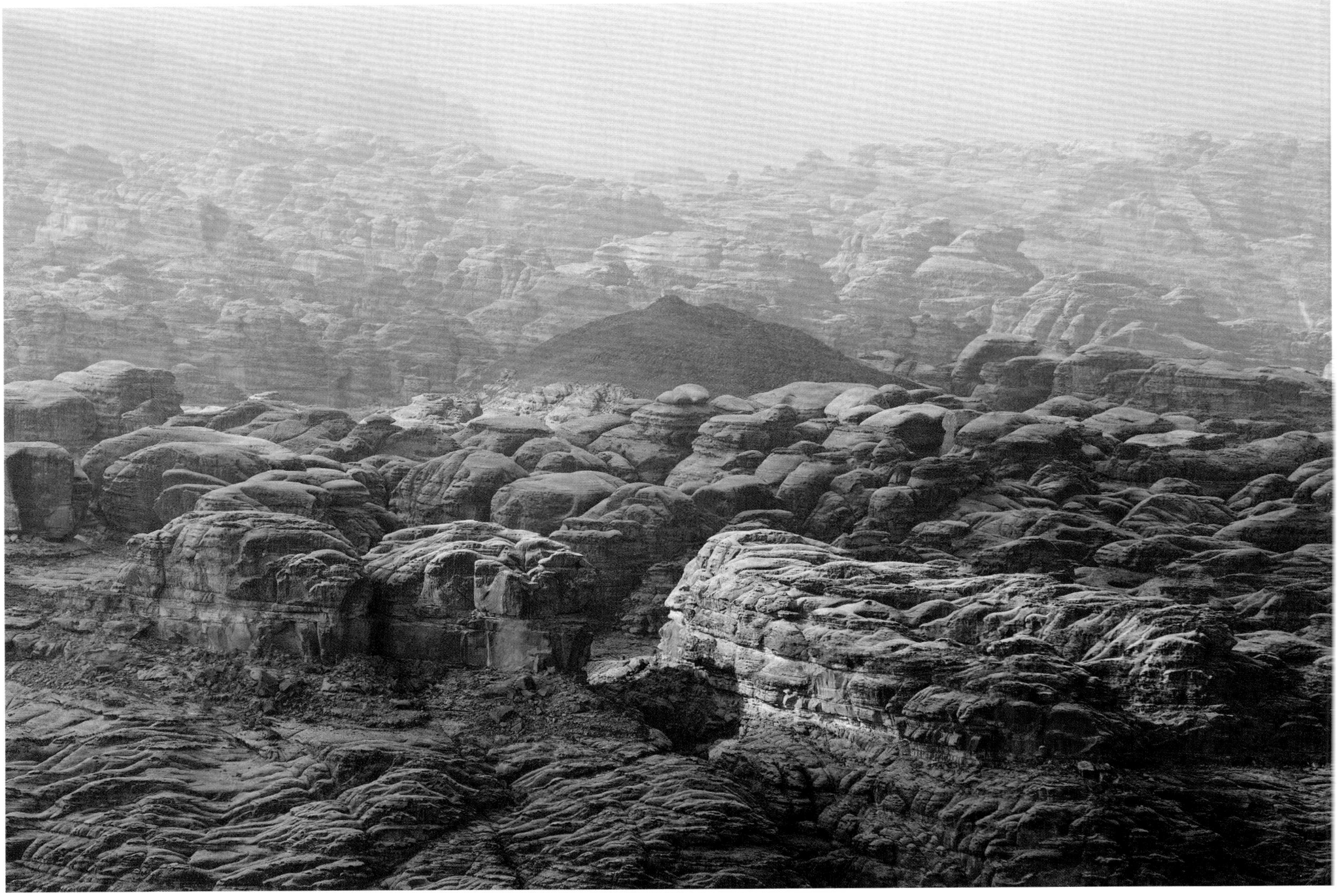

Yann Gayet
Somewhere between Dhouba and Tabuk, 2017
Courtesy of the artist

tempering or toning down another, as many other travelers would do after them, irritated by the exaggerations and the vanity of the adventurer.

For his part, this is how Palgrave approached the Nafud: "We were now traversing an immense ocean of loose reddish sand, unlimited to the eye, and heaped up in enormous ridges running parallel to each other from north to south, undulation after undulation, each swell two or three hundred feet in average height, with slant sides and rounded crests furrowed in every direction by the capricious gales of the desert. In the depths between, the traveler finds himself as if imprisoned in a suffocating sand-pit, hemmed in by burning walls on every side; while at other times, while labouring up the slope, he overlooks what seems a vast sea of fire, swelling under a heavy monsoon wind, and ruffled by a cross-blast into little red-hot waves." It is as if we were in the real Gehenna!

At the start of the twentieth century, the German Carl Raswan, a great enthusiast of Arabian horses, had developed friendships with many members of the famous Bedouin tribe, the Ruwallah, and had traveled extensively with them in these regions. His view, when he "had his first sight of the Nafud," revealed a more subdued realism, without suppressing spontaneous amazement: "And what a sight! The waves of the red desert, rising and falling evenly, seemed to extend to infinity. Crescent-shaped crests and twisted cones; a contrast of light and shade; dark red levels which rose to banks against flanks aflame with the sun. In gorges between the red walls, sixty to a hundred and sixty feet deep, a shimmer of silver and green; scattered low bushes and small trees with straight milk-white trunks and supple drooping branches, bearing feathery twigs and greyish green needles. I held my breath, overwhelmed with amazement and admiration."

For Anne Blunt, "The thing that strikes one first about the Nafud is its colour. It is not white like the sand dunes we passed yesterday, nor yellow as the sand is in parts of the Egyptian desert, but a really bright red, almost crimson in the morning when it is wet with the dew." And, elsewhere: "Yet the Nafud it was, the great red desert of central Arabia." And, again: "Nothing can be more bright and sparkling than the winter's sun reflected from these red sands."

What the Blunts quickly learned was that the Nafud "is better wooded and richer in pasture than any part of the desert we have passed." Actually, "It is tufted all over with ghada bushes, and bushes of another kind called *yerta* [...]. There are, besides, several kinds of camel pasture, especially one new to us called *adr*, on which they say sheep can feed for a month without wanting water, and more than one kind of grass." Charles Huber explained this profusion: "In winter, a few hours of rain are sufficient to germinate the seeds that the sands of Nafud are full of; fifteen days later the ground will be covered like a green tapestry of different types of plants, all with thick leaves full of sap." From then, he says the Nafud "is provided with a relatively dense and vigorous vegetation that provides the camels with fodder for almost the entire journey." And he concluded: "The Nafud is the camels' paradise." For his part, as reported by his wife, Wilfrid Blunt remarked that "Nafud has solved for him at last the mystery of horse-breeding in Central Arabia. In the hard desert there is nothing a horse can eat, but here there is plenty." All this meant that "Instead of being the terrible place it has been described by the few travellers who have seen it," continued Lady Blunt, the Nafud "is in reality the home of Bedouins during a great part of the year." The great lady traveler also issued a quick reserve: "The want of water alone limits the pastoral value." Charles Huber formulated all these things more or less in the same terms: "It has so many qualities that I don't believe there exists a single Bedouin who does not prefer the Nafud to any other desert," although "the lack of water is the only disadvantage of the Nafud, but this one drawback makes the crossing very tough."

This very astonishing desert has another distinguishing and quite specific characteristic that the Frenchman Huber described as follows: "The characteristic of the Nafud, beyond being a desert of absolutely pure sand, without any traces of earth, gravel, or other extraneous materials, consists of its *felq* (pl. *fulûq*). In the Nafud, the *felq* is an excavation in the form of a semi-oval, much deeper in the sand at the centre of the curve, it resembles the print that the hoof of a gigantic horse would leave." Anne Blunt painted them, remarking at the start that "the *felqs* follow each other in strings, not always in straight line, winding gently about," then adding: "these, though varying in size from an acre to a couple of hundred acres, are all precisely alike in shape and direction."

These sorts of coombs (narrow valleys), some of which are extremely vast and can have some very high slopes, are practically immutable; although they consist of loose sands, neither the winds nor bad weather modify them significantly, as the Bedouins who accompany travelers attest. "Some of these *felqs*," Huber also reported, "are crowned on one of their slopes by a hillock of sand, itself crowned by a high crest of white-coloured sand." This red sand crowned by white sand was certainly very striking; the key to its fascination "was its colour, that of rhubarb and magnesia," commented Anne Blunt tersely, who had never seen anything of the sort before!

Traveling among these dunes that cover the entire surface of the Nafud is exhausting because progression proceeds extremely slowly, which is precisely what Carlo Guarmani deplored: "It is necessary to make dozens of detours in all directions and to stray from a straight course very often; later, it is very difficult to return to the principle direction." As Huber pointed out, this was a difficult exercise even for the nomads themselves "because the many detours they were forced to make to follow the outlines of the *felq*s, or of the crests, made them lose their orientation, set them on false tracks, thus causing loss of time and much fatigue." And Huber added: "One is always turning around the *felqs*: some are aligned in zig-zag, rising and falling." Carl Raswan also described in similar terms, "the tortuous slopes" of the Nafud, "which led from trough to crest and, past deep chasms, to the next slope. Impossible to steer a straight course as in the Hamad or Harra," he wrote, thereby demonstrating his knowledge and familiarity with other desert territories of Arabia, "in endless spirals and twists we wound our way, up hill and down dale. [...] Sometimes we took more than half an hour to get from one dune to the next."

Charles Huber made countless peregrinations in the Nafud. During a second journey to Arabia—which he made in 1883–84, the journal of which would be published only after his death—Huber arrived at the conclusion that in the Nafud each crease or earth movement, each slope or mound, was designated by a generic name, which varied according to type and size.

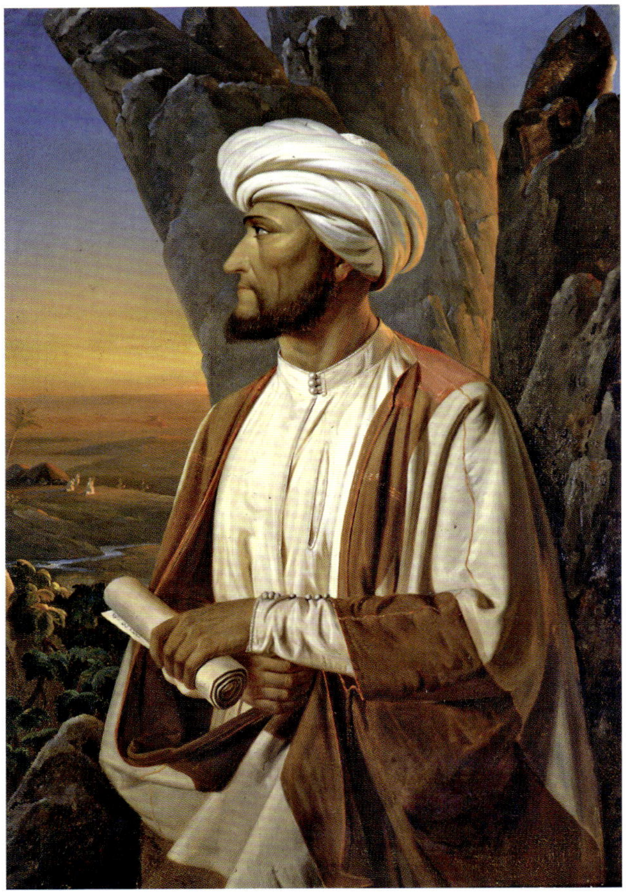

Even more, each of the *felqs* of the Nafud has a name of its own that belongs to no other. Huber made the acquaintance of a Bedouin of the Shammar tribe who had such a detailed knowledge of the desert that he served as the guide for the emir of Ha'il when launching a *ghazu* that would have to cross through the Nafud. It was this man who explained to him that "from Al-Jawf to Jobba, there are one hundred ninety *felqs*, which he knew all by their proper names," reported the French author in amazement. During his first voyage and his first crossing of the Nafud, Huber had already taken note, during the passage, of the names of many of these *felqs* that might refer to a peculiar form or an event of the past, or in another case because it was "still linked to a love story of a thousand years earlier" as his guide at the time had confided to him.

This meticulous comprehension of the desert inculcated exclusively through usage, and the profusion of the toponyms that accompanied it, seems to have fascinated Huber, who devoted himself to the task of writing lexicons and glossaries in the evening, while camping. Ironically enough, it would also be a guide, a few months later, who would be responsible for the death of the young epigraphist during his thirty-seventh year. His notebooks have given us a better comprehension of how the world of the desert, which may seem at first view to be, more than anything else, uniform and unequivocal, instead offers evidence of a proliferation of meanings and an abundance of appearances. Thanks to him, we are perhaps able to better comprehend another, even more subtle universe, that of the oldest poem of this land, certain verses of which provide the better part of these same toponyms:

"Let us stop and pause to weep over the remembrance of my beloved, here was her abode on the edge of the sands, between Dakhul and Hawmal,

Tudith and Miqrat, where winds from South and North, interweaving their breaths, have not remove her trace."

In the creases of the Nafud, the prince-poet would have immobilized his mount... On the scarlet sands, he would have bent down... Imru al-Qays would later have left, riding his mare from *felq* to *felq*, in search of his beloved... Or perhaps, vowing inevitable revenge ...

And these same traces would have quickly disappeared, as Carl Raswan corroborated: "But where were the tents and the herds that at midnight had covered the whole neighbourhood? Far and wide, no other tent. Silently, the Bedouins had broken camp and they—their women, their children, and their animals—had melted away like a mirage. Beside them was a heap of dead ashes and the three soot-blackened stones on which last night the cook-pits had stood."

Here are the dramatic terms that Palgrave used to describe his entry into the desert: "Much had we heard of them from Bedouins and countrymen, so that we had made up our minds to something very terrible and very impracticable. But the reality, especially in these dog-days, proved worse than aught heard or imagined." A crescendo of frightful episodes would follow throughout his crossing: "We muffled our faces, and now with blows and kicks we forced the staggering animals onwards," he began, as he described being overtaken by a sandstorm. "The gusts grew hotter and more violent, and it was only by repeated efforts that we could urge our beasts forward. The horizon rapidly darkened to a deep violet hue, while at the same time a stifling blast, as though from some enormous oven opening right on our path, blew steadily under the gloom; our camels too began, in spite of all we could do, to turn round and round and bend their knees preparing to lie down," he wrote. The ordeal would last for hours, practically a whole day: "each

Robert Wilhelm Ekman
Portrait of Georg August Wallin as Abd Al-Wali, 1853
Photo by Matti Ruotsalainem
Courtesy of the Helsinki University Museum

A Finnish Orientalist, Wallin traveled to Arabia. He died young and was unable to record the whole body of his travels. The account of his journeys is in the Proceedings of the Royal Geographical Society.

Édith Ortoli
Sables rouges 3 (Red sands 3), 2007
Mixed media
26 × 56 cm
Courtesy of the artist

Édith Ortoli
Dunes bleues (Blue dunes), 2006
Mixed media
50 × 70 cm
Courtesy of the artist

The Finnish writer Georg August Wallin, whose first trip to Arabia was in 1845, wrote: *"The monotony of the desert engenders patience. A desert journey is like a sea voyage."*

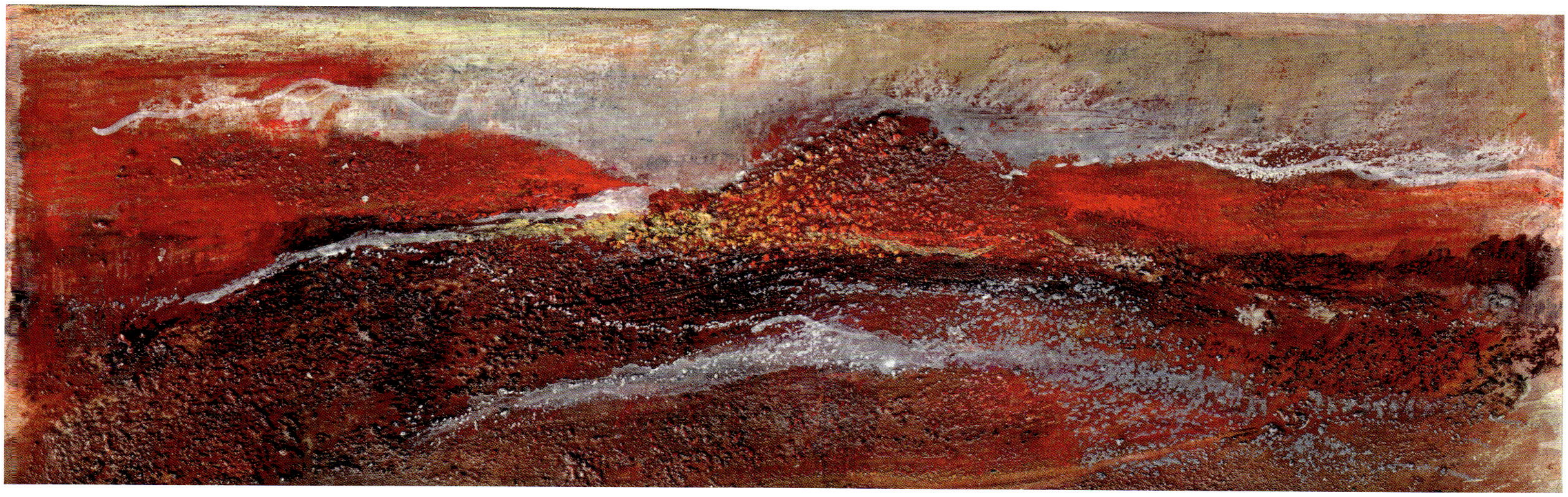

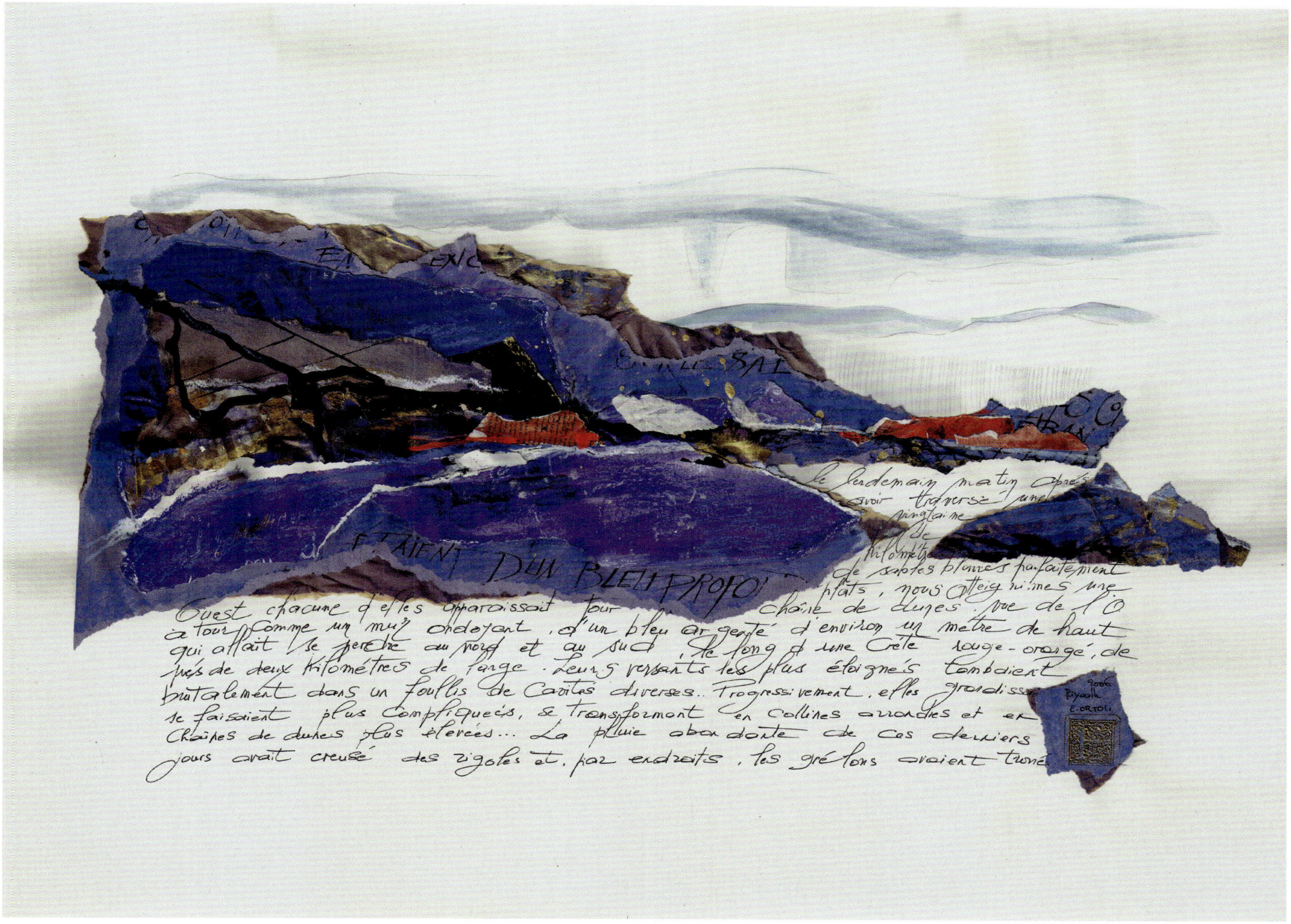
ETAIENT D'UN BLEU PROFO
Le lendemain matin après
avoir traversé une
vingtaine
de
kilomètres
de sables blancs parfaitement
plats, nous atteignîmes une
chaîne de dunes. Vue de l'O
Ouest chacune d'elles apparaissait tour
à tour comme un mur ondoyant, d'un bleu argenté d'environ un mètre de haut
qui allait se perdre au nord et au sud. Le long d'une crête rouge-orangé, de
près de deux kilomètres de large. Leurs versants les plus éloignés tombaient
brutalement dans un fouillis de cavités diverses. Progressivement, elles grandiss
se faisaient plus compliquées, se transformant en collines arrondies et en
chaînes de dunes plus élevées... La pluie abondante de ces derniers
jours avait creusé des rigoles et, par endroits, les grêlons avaient troué
2006
Riyadh
C. ORTOLI

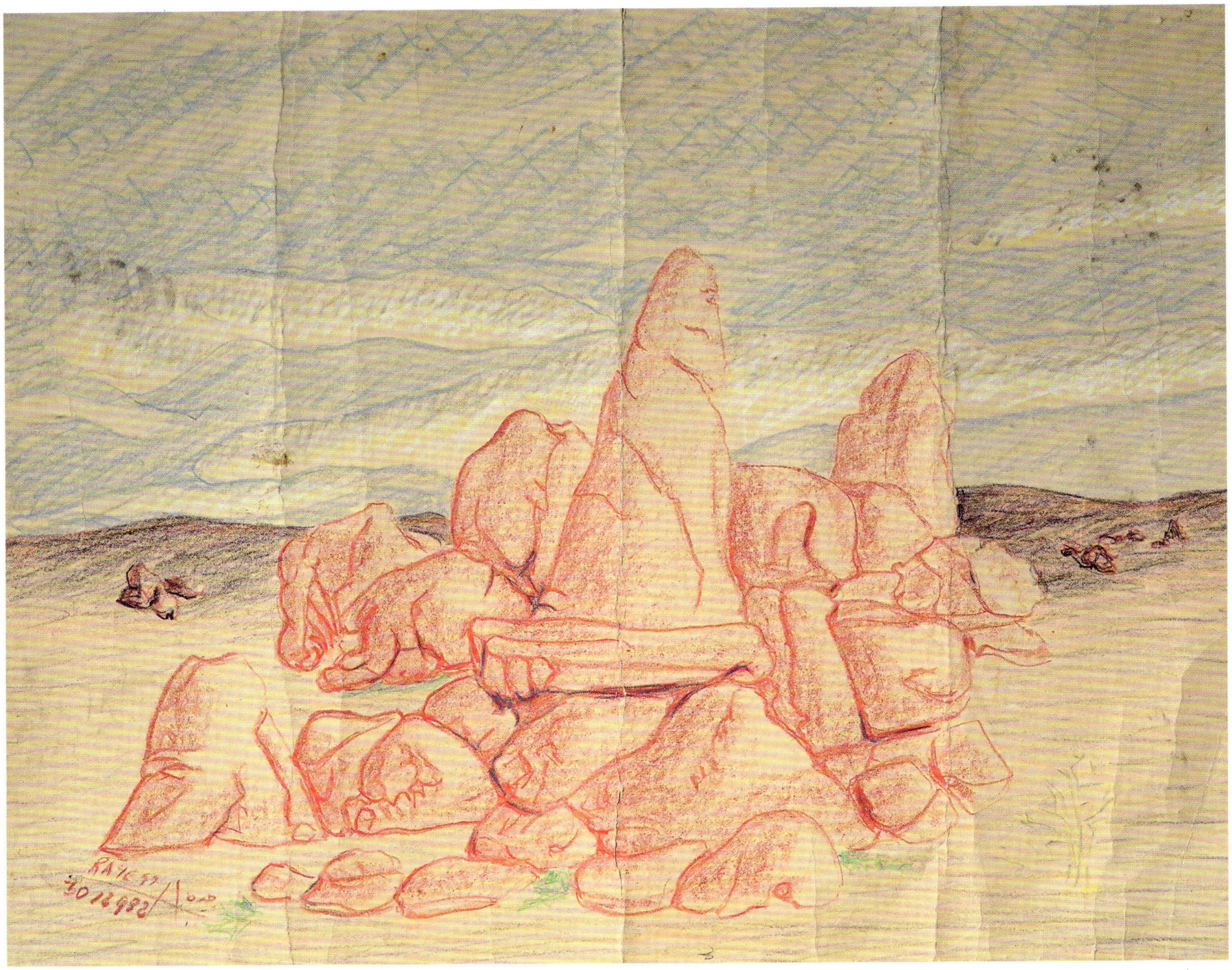

Aref Al Rayess
Untitled, 1982
Pastel on paper
55 × 70 cm
Courtesy of Saleh Barakat, Beirut

Charles Doughty wrote: *"This high droughty country is plain for some days' journeys; mostly sand soil and sand-stone gravel, without furrows of* seyls or wadies."

one of us without more words, threw themselves flat on the ground." Men endured the suffering—"it was better not to breath than to receive these gusts of fire in the chest"—but the animals were suffering just as much—"while our camels lay without moving, like dead, their long necks stretched out on the sand."

It seemed that the whirlwind surrounding them would never end: "a still heat like that of red-hot iron slowly passing over us was alone to be felt." To make matters worse, darkness suddenly overtook them, "so that I hardly know how to account for its singular obscurity." They had to resist this furnace-like heat. Finally, "the semoom had gone by." It was thus that Palgrave commented on his own misadventure: "Many have thus perished; even whole caravans have been known to disappear without a vestige!"

The Blunts also experienced a storm during their crossing. In the evening at the camp, Anne Blunt asked their guide if such circumstances could lead to death. She was assured that no fatality had ever occurred before. She also quoted him remarking that "the sand never buries any object deeply, as we can judge by the sticks and bones" that mark the Nafud. Nonetheless, the end of the crossing would be quite tough: "A terrible day for camels and men," she noted when Jobba was no more than two days away. Many camels were exhausted and could no longer carry their loads, "being too thirsty to eat," and "the whole pace of the caravan has been little over a mile an hour." The men were hardly doing better, exhausted, beyond fatigue. Finally, the small troupe, at the limit of its energies, struggled into Jobba.

The end of the route would be difficult for Charles Huber too after his first crossing through the Nafud. Two days before reaching Jobba, the young man and the few Bedouins accompanying him reached the last watering place, which was almost dry and gave off "an unbearable stench of sulphuric acid," he wrote before commenting that "even the camels winced." The goatskins were empty. Thus, the men had to decide to drink that water too. Huber fell ill immediately, "even though I had boiled it with charcoal and mixed it with tea," wrote the young Frenchman. His traveling companions, "who had suddenly fallen silent," must have been suffering the same illness, he observed.

Aref Al Rayess
Untitled, 1982
Oil on canvas
56 × 71 cm
Courtesy of Saleh Barakat, Beirut

Carlo Guarmani wrote in 1866 in *Northern Najd, A Journey from Jerusalem to Anaiza in Qasim*: *"In the desert the most dangerous foe is man; on hearing or seeing him one takes to flight until in a safe enough place to ascertain if he is alone or in company, in order to reckon whether meeting with him would be risky or not."*

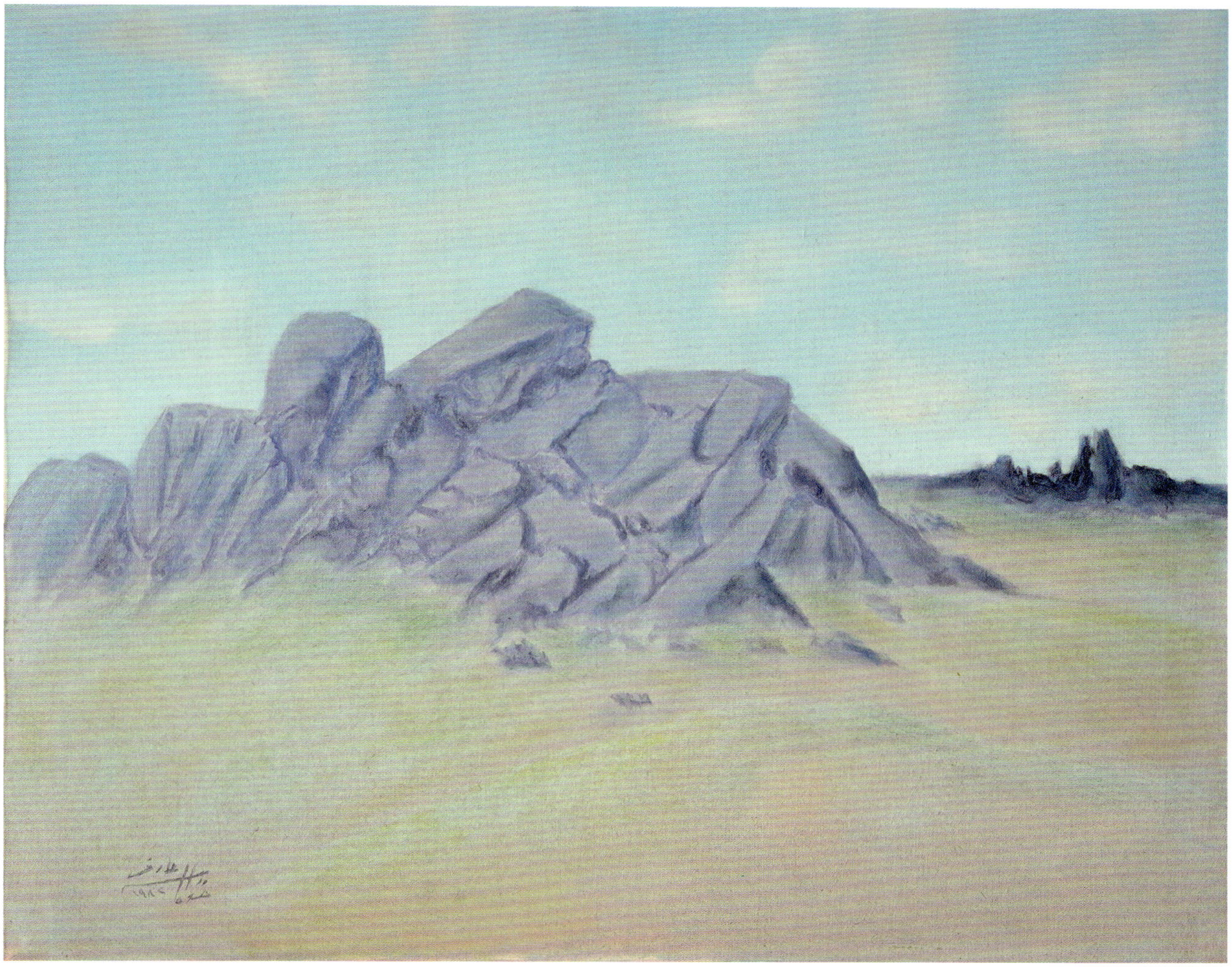

The small group completed its crossing without other impediments but Huber still regretted, before pulling through those who would seek to tarnish the reputation of the Nafud, by casting it as a place of all hazards: "I was pleasantly surprised to see that all that had been greatly exaggerated," he concluded. He preferred, at the time when he reached Jobba and its palm groves, to celebrate the splendor the site had offered him: "When, after having had the uniform pink tint of the Nafud before your eyes, all of a sudden you dominate this immense basin of opaque silver where the beautiful green of the palm groves stands out, all illuminated by the afternoon sun, you are completely dazzled by such a magical scene."

One would have to wait five decades after this episode before some travelers would undertake the crossing of the fearsome Rub' al-Khali.

Three men, hardened to evil as only the British can be. Three men with very different profiles, but in the end quite similar. The first, Bertram Thomas, was born in the United Kingdom, but would die in Cairo. The second, Harry St John Bridger Philby, was born in Ceylon (now Sri Lanka) and would pass away in Beirut. The third, Wilfred Thesiger, was born in Addis Ababa in Abyssinia (now northern Ethiopia) and would die in the United Kingdom. These were three exceptional lives packed with extraordinary adventures, too many to summarize in words.

However, they were also three men who came too late. All three of them realized this. And wrote about it. All three of them regretted it. There were a few months between the crossings of Thomas and Philby of the Rub' al-Khali in 1930–31 and 1932, respectively. The competitiveness between them was so powerful that they say that when Philby learned of Thomas' exploit, he stayed closed in his room for a week without ever coming out. For his part, Thesiger explained in *Visions of a Nomad*, that when he, in turn, undertook the same crossing, it was because "much of it was unexplored. It was one of the very few places left where I could satisfy an urge to go where others had not been. [Reaching] the Empty Quarter would be to answer a challenge, and to remain there for long would be to test myself to the limit," wrote Thesiger, who spent four years of his life there from 1946 to 1950. A spirit of competition undeniably motivated these men, although it did not alter in them the desire to understand the "precise nature of this great void," as Philby elegantly put it.

Above all else, it was evidently the quest that motivated them. In the words of Thesiger: "In the desert I had found a freedom unattainable in civilization; a life unhampered by possessions, since everything that was not a necessity was an encumbrance. I had found, too, a comradeship inherent in the circumstances, and the belief that tranquility was to be found there." He went on to say: "No man can live this life and emerge unchanged. He will carry, however faint, the imprint of the desert, the brand which marks the nomad, and he will have within him the yearning to return, weak or insistent according to his nature."

Such a return would become impossible. Soon this immutable world would no longer exist. When, half a century earlier, Georg A. Wallin, Carlo Guarmani, William G. Palgrave, Anne and Wilfrid Blunt, and Charles Huber crossed the Great Nafud, they probably truly believed that this world would still exist for a thousand years, just as it had been there for a thousand years before. As for Thomas, Philby, and Thesiger, when they crossed the Rub' al-Khali, they sensed that they were both the first and the last witnesses of a way of life on the verge of disappearing.

It was to bid farewell that these men traveled there, undertaking without actually knowing it, the most difficult of all expeditions. All the same, it was a farewell, and the motive for the grave tone that Wilfred Thesiger adopted to salute the desert for the last time in this passage: "All that is best in the Arabs has come to them from the desert: their deep religious instinct, which has found expression in Islam, their sense of fellowship; which binds them as members of one faith; their pride of race; their generosity and sense of hospitality; their dignity and the regard which they have for the dignity of others as fellow human beings; their humour, their courage and patience, the language which they speak and their passionate love of poetry."

Malin Basil
Windswept Desert, 1979
Acrylic on canvas
50 × 70 cm
Private collection

Charles Doughty wrote:
"Commonly the Arabian desert is an extreme desolation where the herb is not apparent for the sufficiency of any creature."

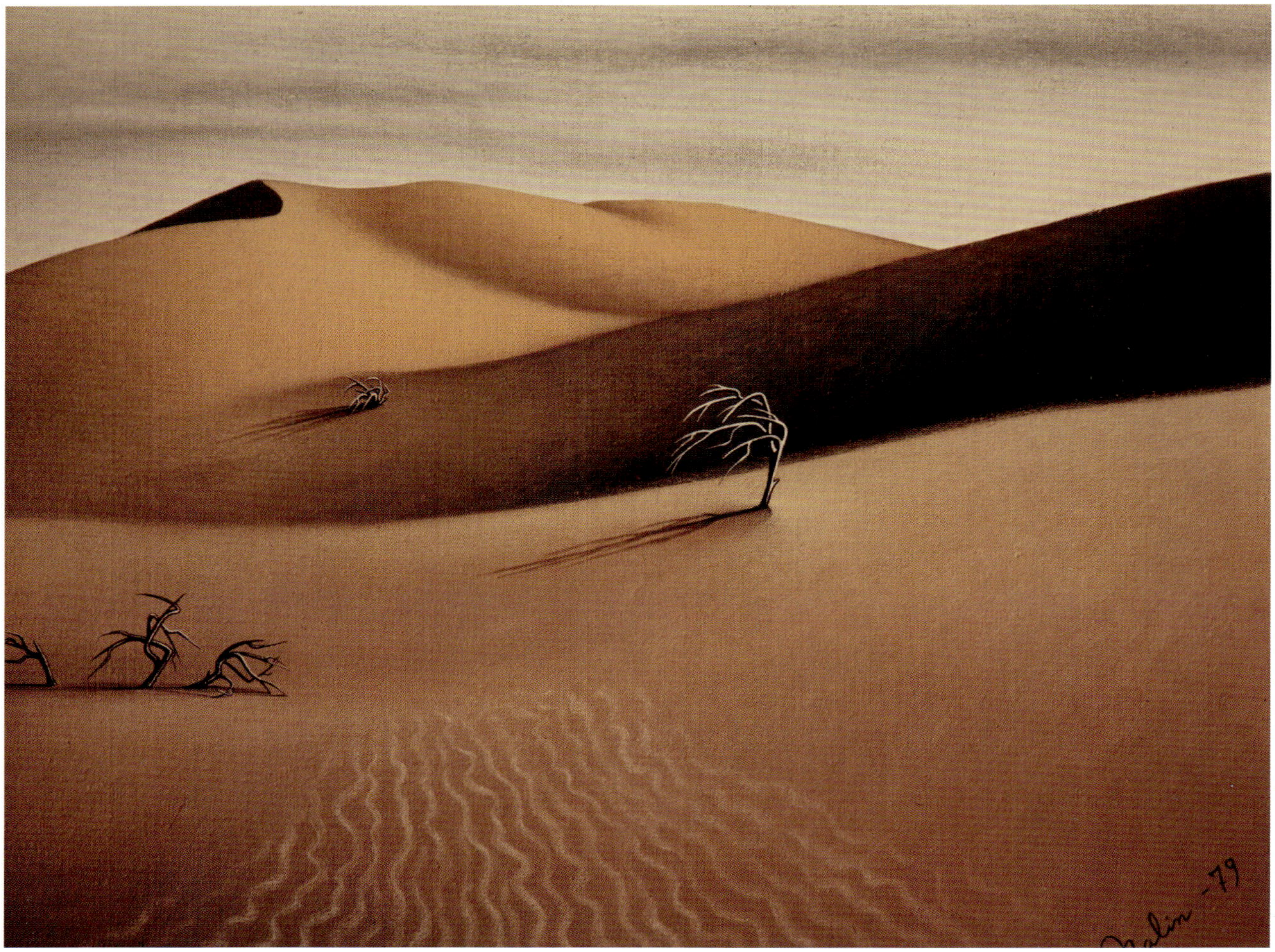

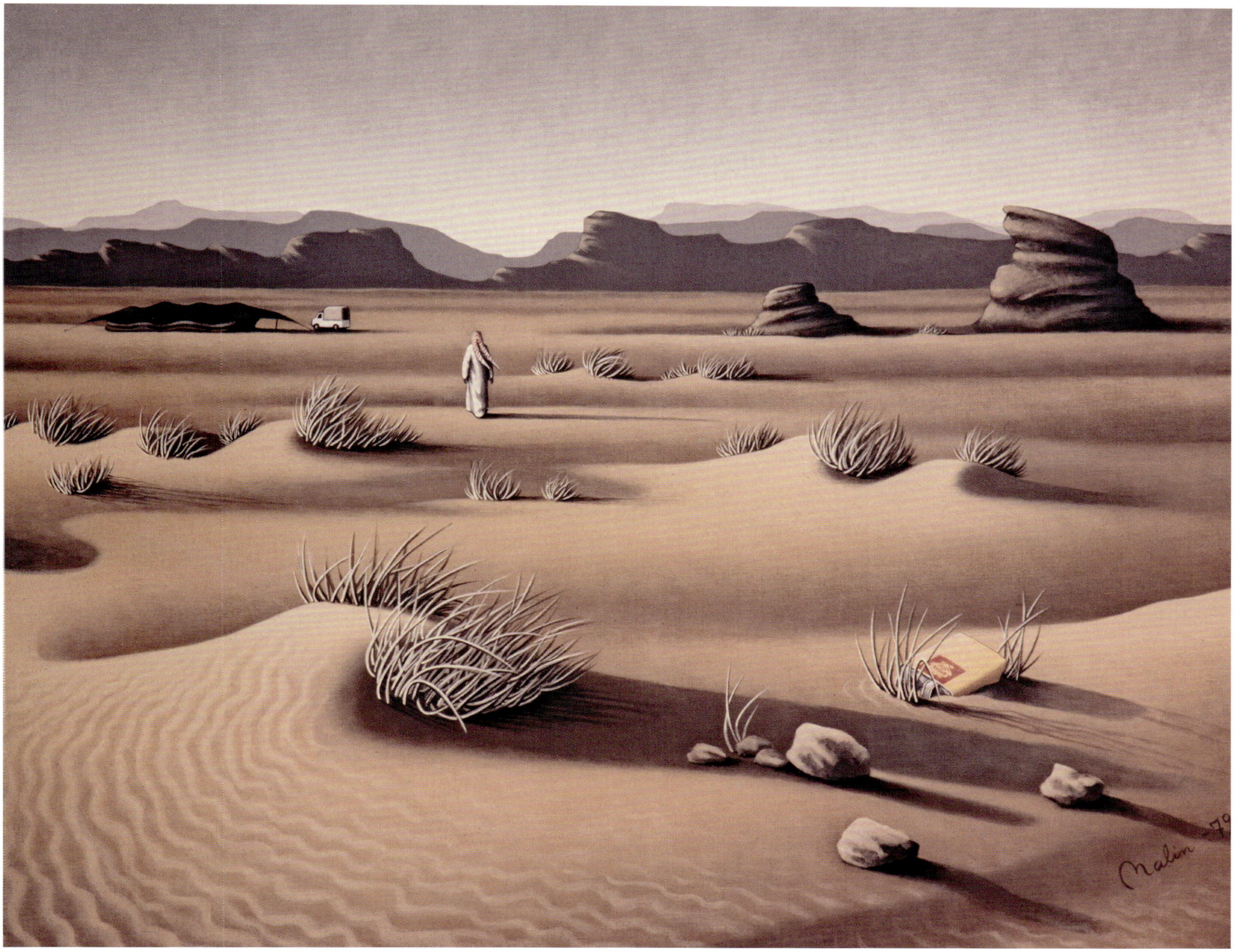

Malin Basil
Desert debris, 1979
Acrylic on canvas
75 × 100 cm
Private collection

Arabia, wrote Philby,
is "*rich in desolate places*".

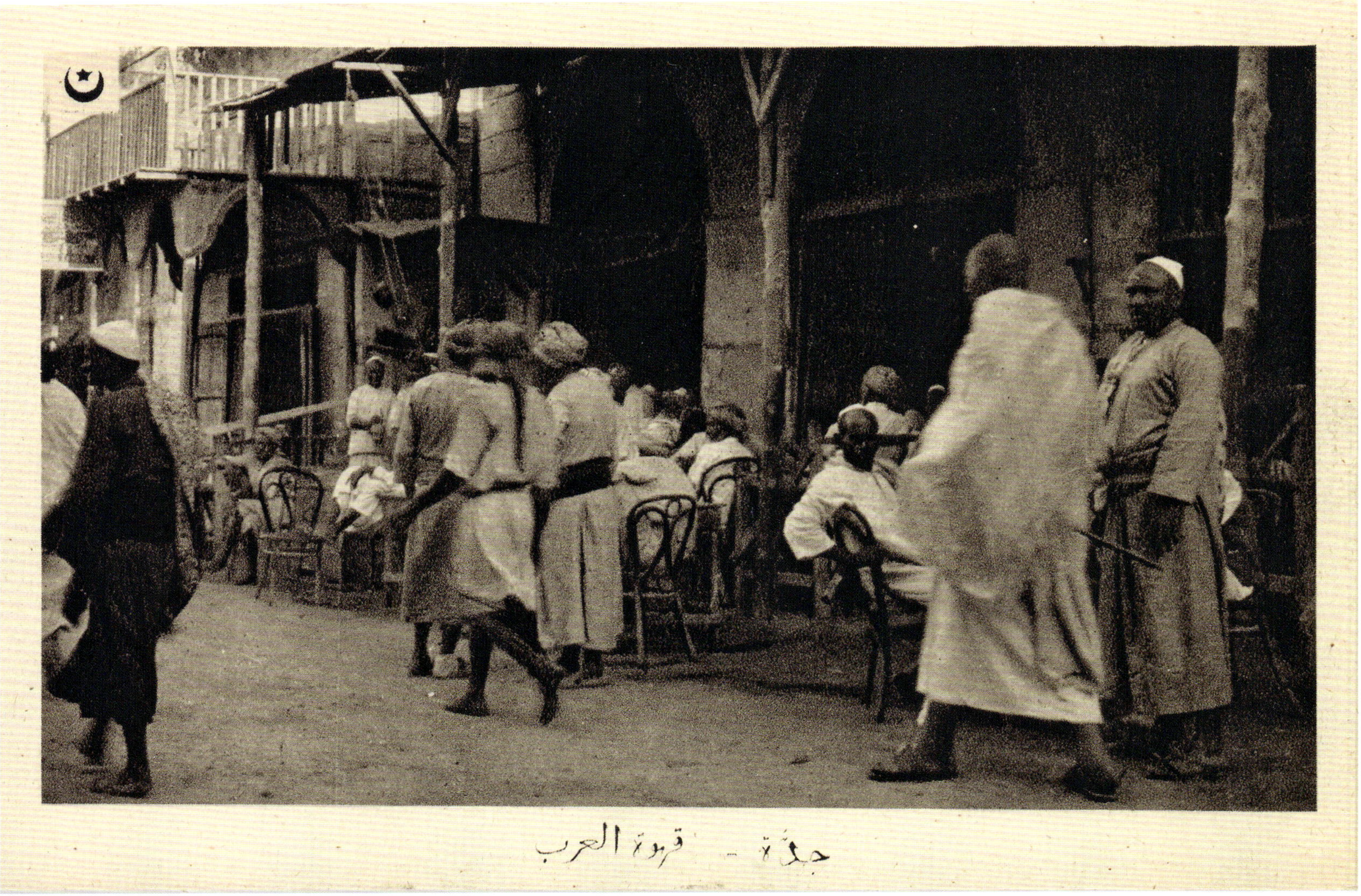
جدة - قهوة العرب

Where else could one find the spirit of a city if not in its cafés, where poets live? What better place to meet up with friends and also encounter strangers?

In a city like Paris where the intersection of two streets guarantees the existence of a corner café, it seems difficult to imagine the city without them.

However, coffee did not appear in Paris until 1657. On the other hand, the city of Marseille had already grown accustomed to it fifteen years earlier. French traveler Jean de Thévenot returned from Cairo with a large package of necessary equipment for the preparation and presentation of coffee, and shared it with his friends from the world of arts and letters in Marseille. The French aristocracy was the first to acquire the taste for coffee. Traders in Marseille set up businesses and supplied the capital. Soon, the high society wanted to taste coffee propelling individual shops to serve the drink. And this is how the first cafés came into existence.

Within thirty years, and before the seventeenth century came to an end, at least three hundred cafés had opened their doors in Paris! What most people do not know is that at that time cafés were already a long-standing tradition—and had existed for over two centuries—in Mecca, where they first appeared during the fifteenth century.

Postcard
Arab café in Jeddah
Nasser D. Khalili Collection of Islamic Art, London

Henry Rooke, a Major in the Infantry, made a brief stay in Jeddah in 1782, which he described: "*There are several coffeehouses which are always full; the common people there drinking their dish of coffee together, as ours would their pot of beer at an alehouse.*"

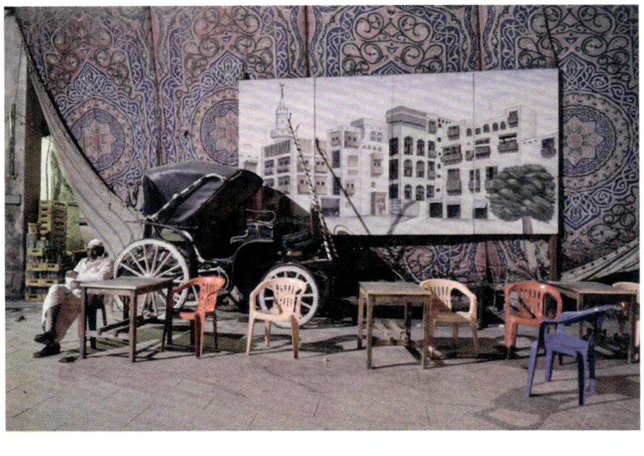

Anne de Henning
Café in Jeddah's Bab Makka in Al-Balad, 2011
Courtesy of the artist

Danish geographer and mathematician Carsten Niebuhr (see chapter *The Flora of the Peninsula*), said, in his *Voyage*, something very obvious—"The coffee plant is the most remarkable tree that Arabia produced"—specifying that it had its origin in the "land of Habbesch," then Abyssinia and modern-day Ethiopia.

In fact, it was from near Ethiopia where the coffee tree ("coffee-plant") grew in the wild that it was then imported to southern Arabia, probably toward the end of the thirteenth century. Initially, only the fruit from the plant was consumed before it was used as a drink. Some five centuries later, Niebuhr described the preparation process as, "They (inhabitants) roast the beans in an open oven, pound them in a wooden or stone mortar, boil them in a well-tinned copper pot."

It is said that the first people to have adopted coffee as a drink were the Sufis, who appreciated it because it not only allowed them to remain alert longer during their nocturnal devotions, but also gave them a sense of elation, an exhilaration that was not induced by alcohol, and consequently was not in contradiction with the principles of Islam. It is not known whether they were the ones who chose to call it by the name *kahwa*, a word that was chosen from the lexicon of ancient classic poetry where it used to refer to wine, liqueur, or any intoxicating drink. Regardless, the word was then used to refer to coffee in all its forms—the beverage, tree and the fruit.

The cultivation of the tree spread throughout the southwest of the peninsula, in Yemen and the Asir region, up to the latitude of the city of Taraba near Ta'if, always at an altitude between one and two thousand meters, where "the soil in the mountains, and the terraces of the gardens where the coffee grows, are partly supported by walls, to keep the earth horizontal," Niebuhr added. The drink soon became popular and was soon consumed all over Arabia. The first cafés—or rather, the first "coffee houses" (*buyût al-kahwa*)—opened in Mecca as early as the fifteenth century!

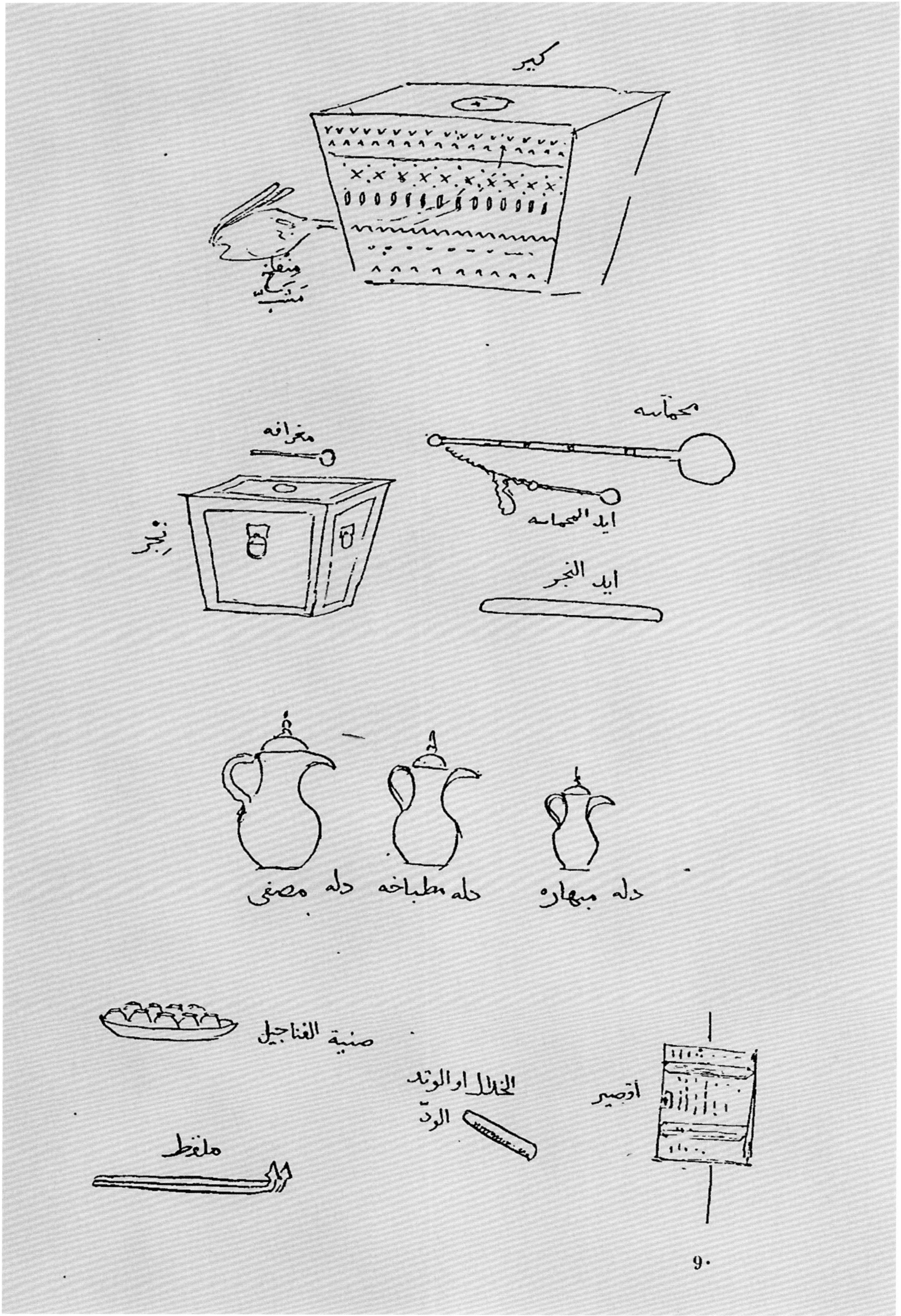

Charles Huber
Sketch from *Journal d'un voyage en Arabie* (1883–84)
Ernest Leroux, Paris, 1896

From top to bottom and right to left: blower, coffee roaster, coffee roaster handle, mortar handle, ladle, mortar, *dallah* (coffee kettle), boiler dallah, strainer dallah, stick, coffee cup tray, tongs.

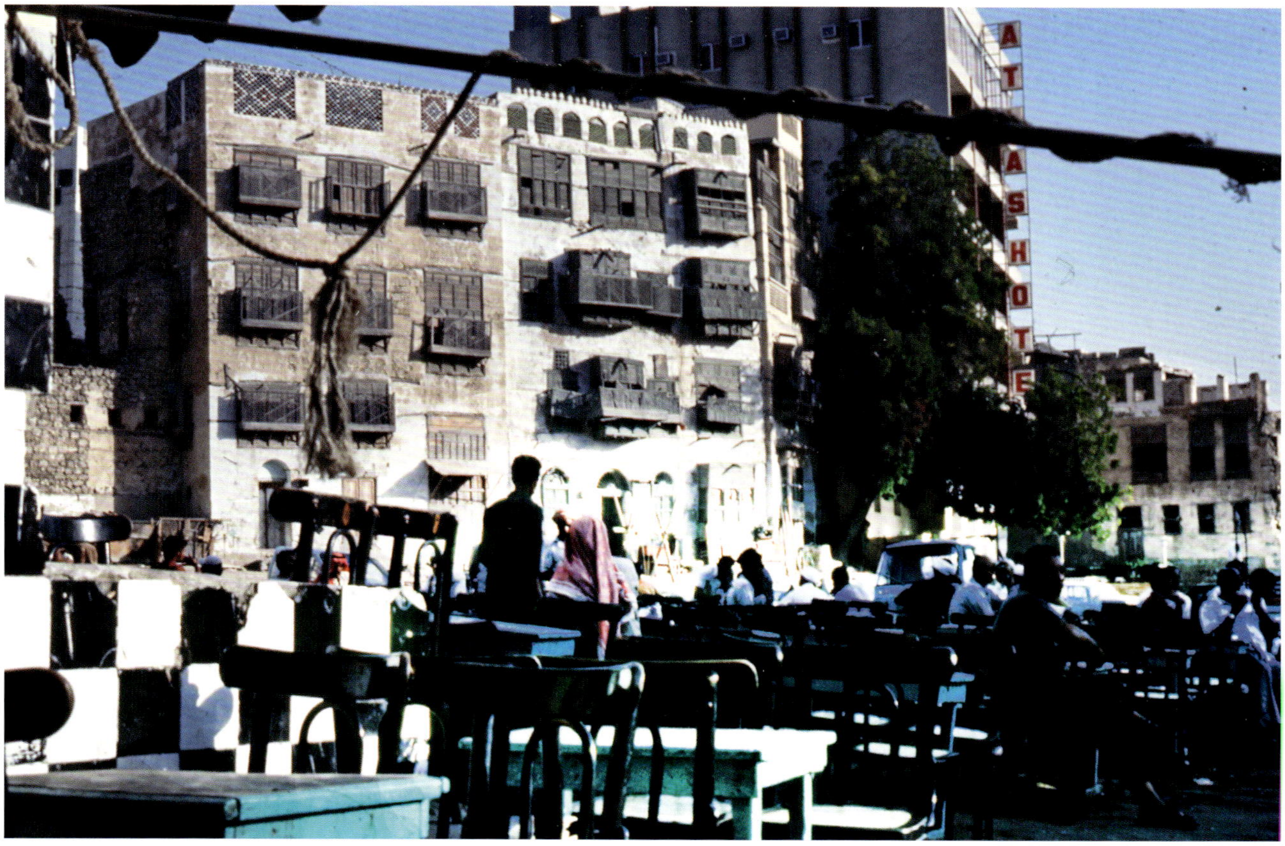

Fouad Elkoury
A café in a square in downtown Jeddah, 1973
Courtesy of the artist

Carsten Niebuhr wrote in *Travels through Arabia and other Countries in the East* (1774) that in Jeddah he and his companions *"went freely to the coffeehouses and markets"*.

Travelers who visited Arabia were all impressed by the numbers of these "coffee houses" and also by the fact that they were on every corner of the road.

In a detailed description that Johann Ludwig Burckhardt gave of the souk in Jeddah in 1814 (see chapter *The Gates of Arabia*), he counted "twenty-five coffee-shops where coffee is served." He also observed that "the coffee-houses were filled with people during the whole day," where they played tric-trac, "the Mangal and the Dama," although they "never play for money," as Niebuhr commented in his time, adding that "orators" were also frequent in the cafés. "There is extraordinary movement," commented the French writer Charles Didier in turn when he discovered the souk of Jeddah, where "everyone rushed into cafés." Maurice Tamisier observed a similar situation. He noted, "All along the bazaar, there are numerous cafés where both local people and foreigners convene."

Cafés were present everywhere. In the cities, of course. Appointments were set there. Étienne Dinet, the Orientalist painter, wrote: "Our guide (*metouaf*) was waiting for us in a café at the entrance to Mecca." But they were also to be found in villages. Even the smallest of them. When Tamisier brought his boat into Aouech, a tiny hamlet of twelve houses with fifty inhabitants on the Red Sea coast, he was amazed to find "a café built from tree trunks covered in algae." Dinet observed "agglomerations of shanty cafés scattered along the way and located near wells." Thanks to their presence, stopovers were more pleasant, as Tamisier admitted: "We found a café in the middle of the mountains where camel riders and travelers usually stopped. Be it an Arab or a foreigner traveling through the region, the resting point was as enjoyable as it was for the taverns at the edge of our main roads."

On the plain of Arafat where pilgrims camped overnight waiting for the sermon of the following day, cafés were set up near the tents and were always full. Burckhardt noted: "The coffee-houses were crowded the whole night with customers." Niebuhr recounted that he "made the acquaintance of a Turk who travelled seven or eight times from Damascus to Mecca to earn his living as a coffee peddler," accompanying the pilgrimage caravan and transporting on "donkeys, mules, horses, or camels, all his equipment, including the wood" needed to light his fires, and "when the caravan stopped to camp, everyone clustered around him, in the same manner as people gathered in a public café in a city."

Except the "Turkish or Persian tobacco pipe" served to customers, these cafés offered nothing other than "coffee without milk or sugar," commented Niebuhr. He

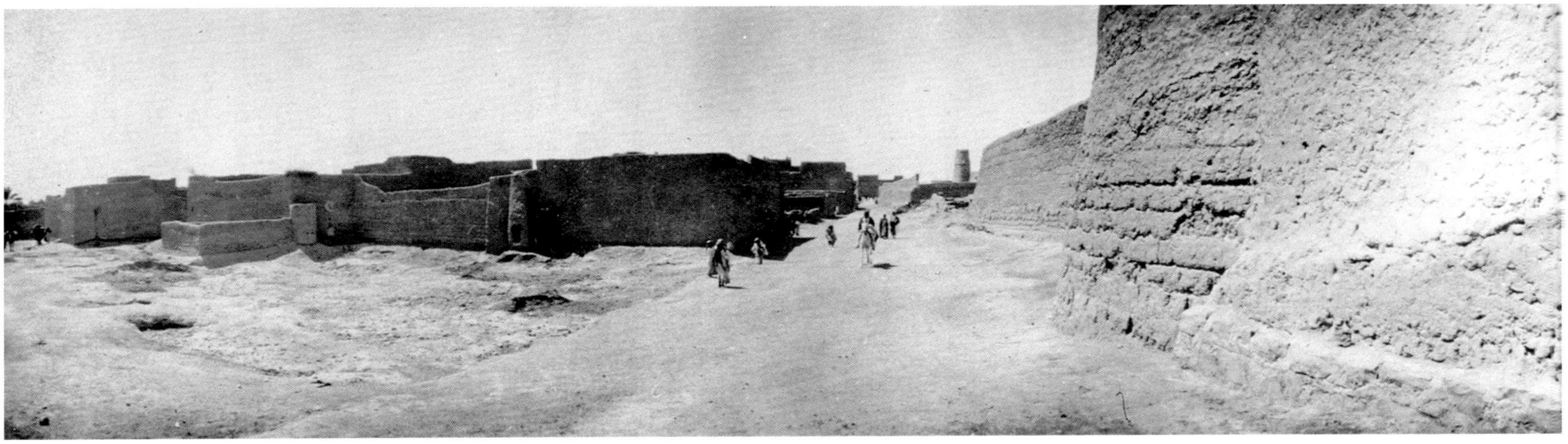

William Henry Irvine Shakespear
Beginning of Al-Thumairi Street in Riyadh. On the right, we see the old mud wall of the city, 1914
Courtesy of the King Abdulaziz Public Library, Riyadh

The city of Riyadh was surrounded by a thick wall of sunbaked mud-bricks with bastions and guard turrets at its corners.

Samer Mohdad
Al Dar'iya, the first capital of the Saudi Royal family, 2000
From *Assaoudia*, Actes-Sud, 2005
Courtesy of the artist

Located some 20 kilometers northwest of Riyadh on the banks of the Hanifah, Dar'iya, was the capital of Nejd in the first Saudi state from 1744 to 1818. The oldest buildings in Dar'iya date to the middle of the eighteenth century. In 1818, on behalf of the Ottoman sultan, Mohammed Ali Pasha sent his son Ibrahim Pasha to attack Dar'iya. The town was captured and razed and its inhabitants left for Riyadh.

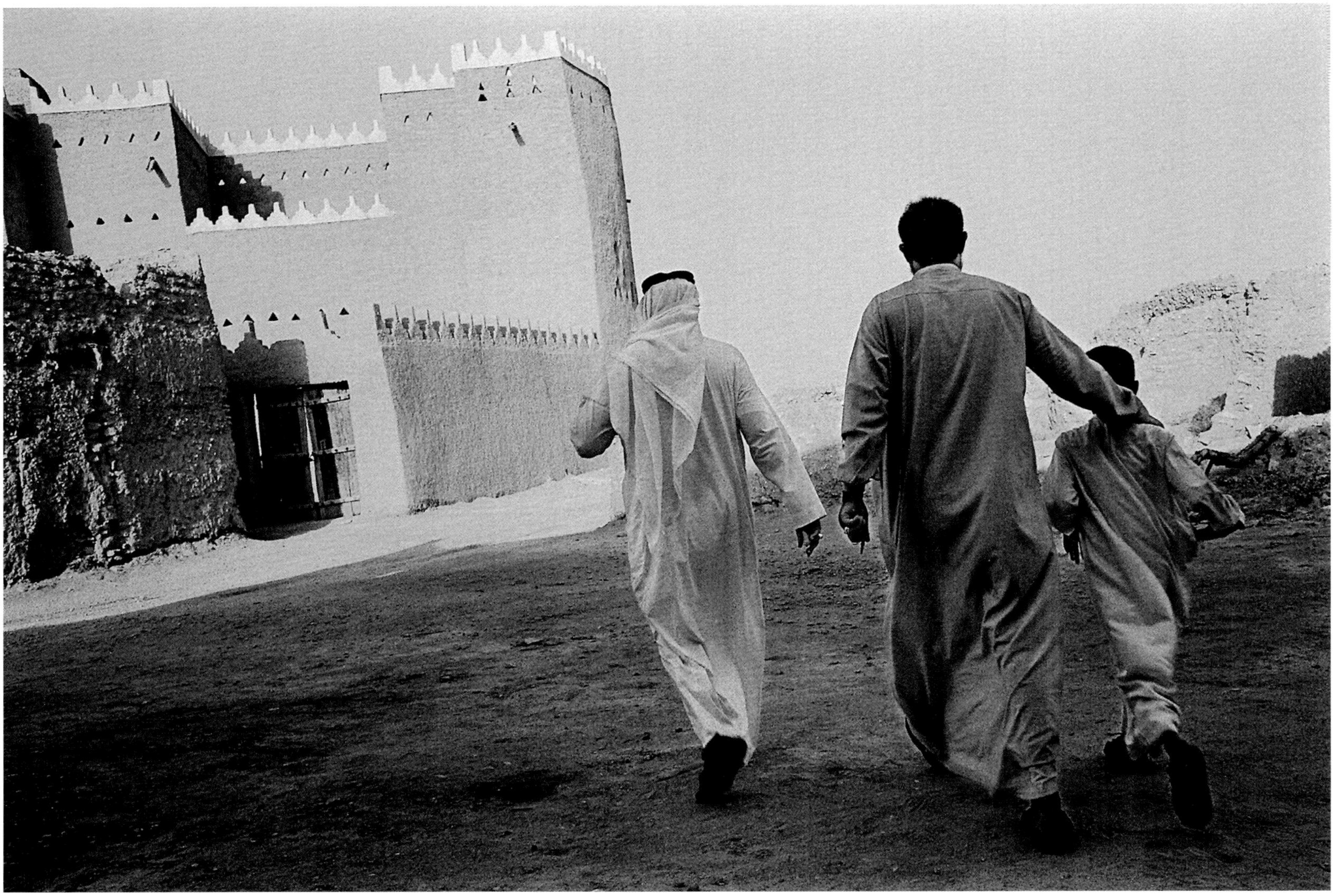

Abbas
Al Dar'iya, the old monuments and the restored wall, 2002
Courtesy of Abbas/Magnum photos

In 1818, after a long siege, Dar'iya was seized by Ibrahim Pasha. Captain G. F. Sadleir, an English officer, visited Dar'iya just after the Turco-Egyptian withdrawal. He recorded in *Diary of a Journey Across Arabia*: *"The palm plantations had been cut down to ensure that there would be a shortage of food and the town stood empty as most of the population had headed south to Riyadh. The ruinous state of many of the old buildings and walls of Dar'iya reflect the effect of bombardment and the repeated destruction that the town suffered at Ibrahim Pasha's hands."* With time, the town was rebuilt alongside the old vestiges and the palaces, walls, and watchtowers were restored.
In 2010, the district of Al-Turaif in Dar'iya was listed as a UNESCO World Heritage Site.

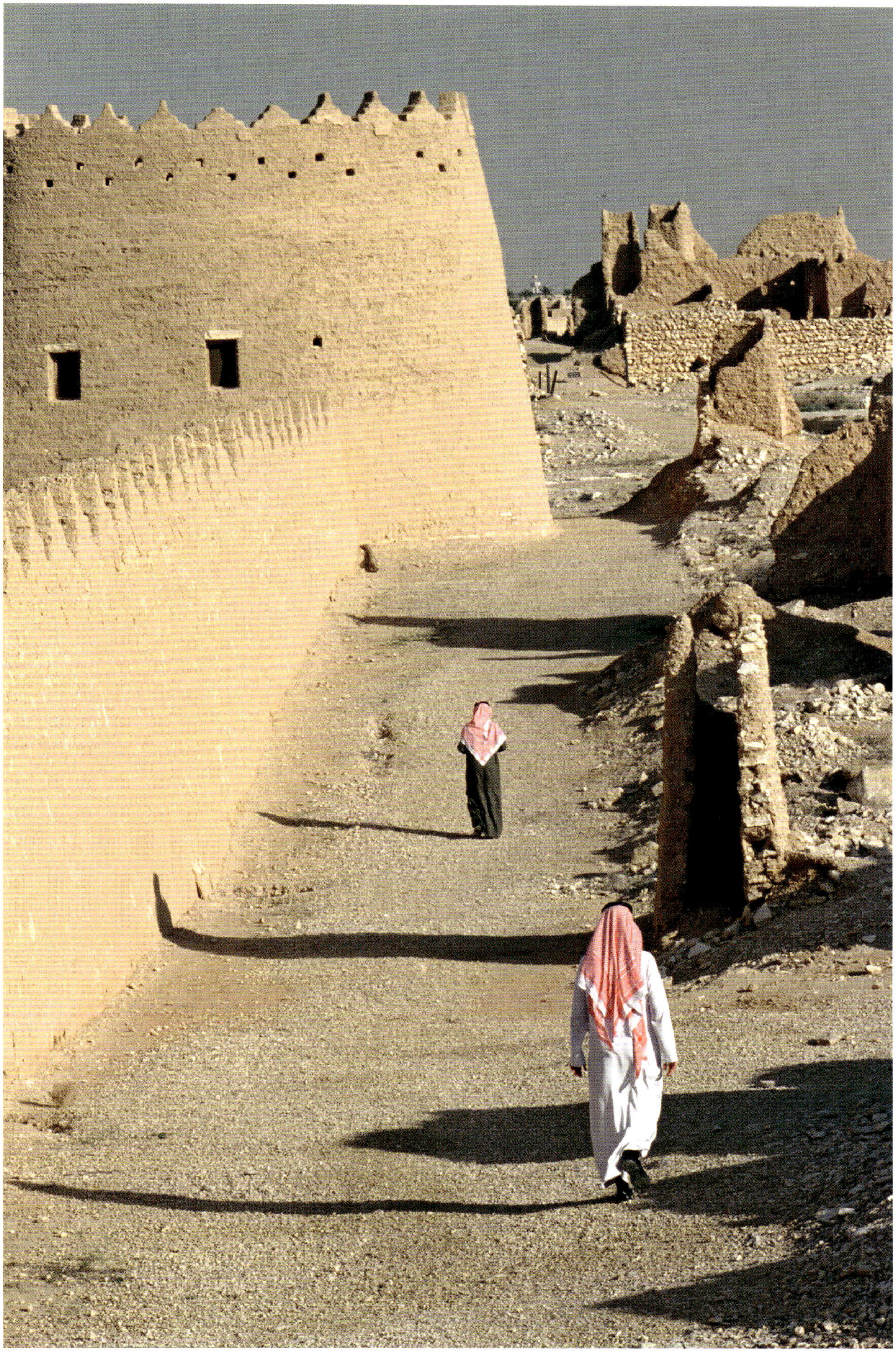

very logically deduced, "so there is no occasion to go to any expense or to be intoxicated, Arabs being as sober in these taverns as they were in ancient times when only water was drunk." However, Niebuhr went on to say that these establishments did offer another drink that was also a derivative of the coffee plant, which they called *kahwa*, or more commonly *kishr*, "It is prepared in the same manner as that from the bean. They start with roasting the husk a little, pounding it moderately, so that it does not take up too much space in the vessel, and boiling it in an earthen pot."

This *kishr* that Niebuhr considered "resembling tea very much in taste and colour", was popular mainly in the southern part of the peninsula and rarely found elsewhere, although Burckhardt observed that "in a few [cafés], *keshre*, an infusion made from the skin of the bean," could still be found in some cafés in Jeddah.

The first Europeans to have ever tasted coffee on the Arabian peninsula are more likely to have come across *kishr* than any other form of drink. During the last decade of the sixteenth century, two Portuguese Jesuits, Fathers Paez and Montserate, were traveling to Ethiopia when their ship was captured. Taken to Yemen—where the two priests would live for several years as prisoners before being ransomed—they were offered a drink that consisted of "water boiled with the husk of a fruit that they call *bun*," as confirmed in *Histoire d'Éthiopie*, by Paez. Discovered in the Jesuits' archives, this work was finally published at the beginning of the twentieth century. Obviously, it was *kishr* that the two Jesuits drank, the word "bun" being the Ethiopian word for coffee, that circulated to Arabia and Egypt where it is still used today.

If the inhabitants of the south at times preferred the white *kishr* to the black *kahwa*, it is because they believed that the latter had the unfortunate property of "heating" the blood, as Niebuhr reported. It is true that coffee "is consumed in excess in the Hidjaz; it is not uncommon for people to drink twenty or thirty cups in one day," as reported by Burckhardt. During a visit to a café on the road from Ta'if to Mecca, Burckhardt observed that "coffee is not served in single cups, as it usually is in most parts of the Levant; but whoever asks for it has a small earthen pot of hot coffee set before them equivalent to ten to fifteen cups; that the traveller often drinks three or four times a day."

The consequence of this "immoderate use," as Burckhardt wrote, is that "they are so much accustomed

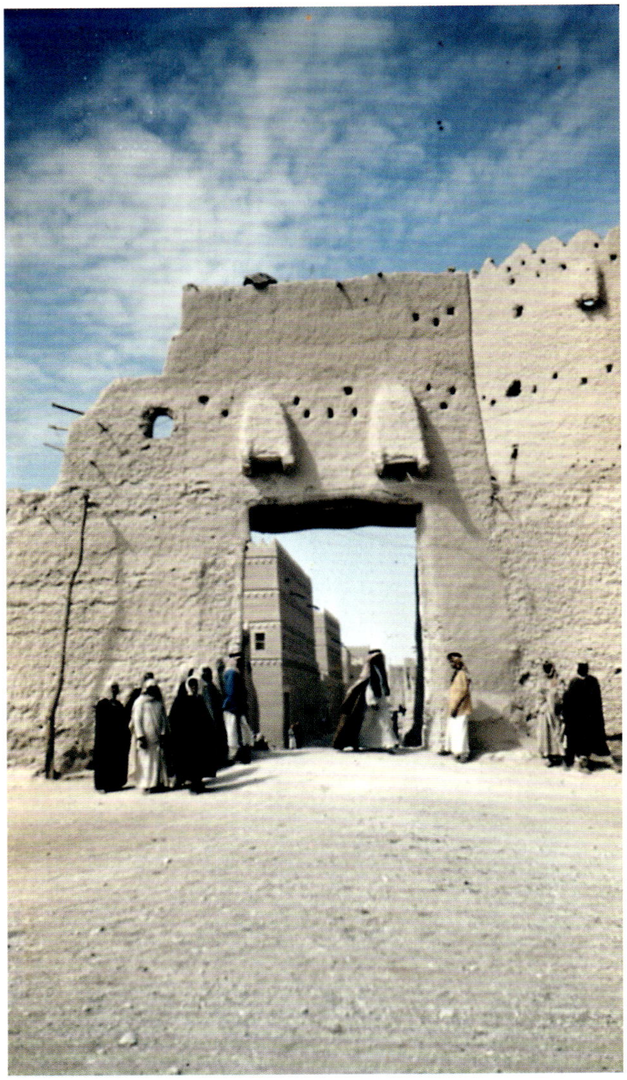

Princess Alice
The Thumairi city gate of Riyadn, 1938
Courtesy of the King Abdulaziz Public Library, Riyadh

This photo is one of the earliest color photographs of the city of Riyadh.
It features the famous main gate of Riyadh, Al-Thumairi. Until the 1920s, Riyadh was enclosed within its ancient walls, and was only accessible through its nine gates: Bab Madhbah to the west, Al Suwaylim to the northwest; Bab Budai'a leading towards the Batin; Bab Shumaysi facing north; Bab Dakhna, Bab Manfuhah, and Bab Muraiqib to the southwest; Bab Dhuhairi to the northwest; and Al-Thumairi on the eastern side. Al-Thumairi was named after a hero who was in the raiding party of the Masmak battle. The gate and a portion of the adjacent wall were torn down in 1950 when construction in the old city started. It was reconstructed at its original location using the same designs and materials.

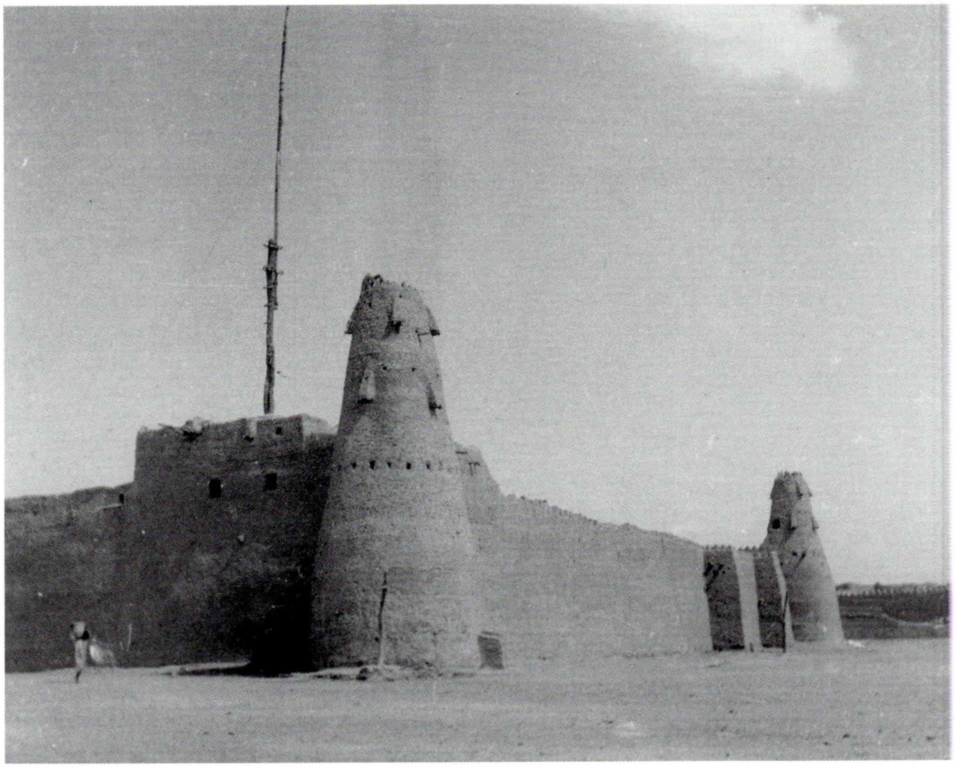

Gerald de Gaury
Fort in Al-Jawf, c. 1934–35
Courtesy of the Royal Geographic Society, London

Al-Jawf is an oasis town located on the Syrian caravan route.

Philip Bouchard
Masmak at Dusk
Oil on canvas
155 × 127 cm
Courtesy of the Mathaf gallery, London

Built around 1860, Masmak is the famous fortress that was seized by King Abdulaziz in the winter of 1900–01. Its historical importance lies in the fact that it was around its entrance that the battle between King Abdulaziz and Al-Rashid, the governor of Riyadh took place. The seize of the fort allowed Ibn Saud, then twenty-two, to restore the rule of Al Saud dynasty. The fortress was neglected and used as an arsenal for a long time. Later it was restored, and today it houses a museum.

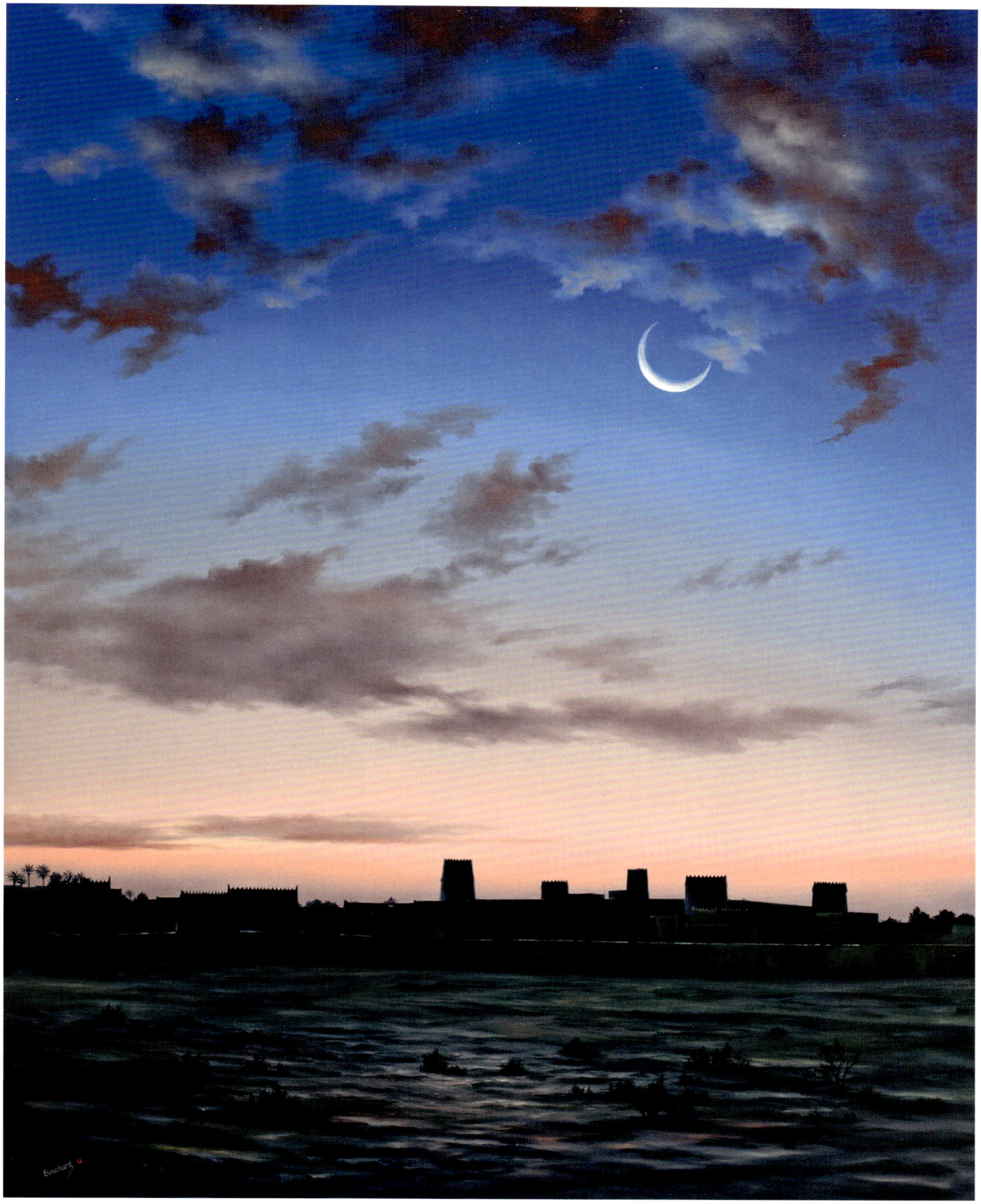

to it from their earliest youth that they would feel great inconvenience in discontinuing the use of it." Consequently, "for an Arab to see coffee-making, and not to put himself in the way of getting a share, would be an act of self-restraint totally unheard of," said the English adventurer William G. Palgrave. This is undoubtedly the reason why Arabs "may be seen assiduously frequenting the public cafés," where "sometimes they gather in hundreds," and where narrators occasionally came to tell their stories, as Niebuhr reported. During his visit to Mecca in 1671, Ottoman traveler Evliya Çelebi noticed the presence in the city of "Ethiopian slave girls, actually singing girls who set hearts aflutter," and reported this in his famous book

MALIN BASIL

Self-taught artist Malin Basil moved to Riyadh, Saudi Arabia, in 1968 and lived there until 1982. She is the perfect example of a cross-cultural citizen. Her journalistic training did not come to use in Riyadh because of the restrictions on women at that time, which prevented her from working as a journalist. One could say that it is the best thing that could have happened to her given the artistic career she developed instead.
Timing was an absolute key to Basil's experience. Her stay in Saudi Arabia took place at a time of extraordinary changes in the Kingdom, which allowed the artist to familiarize herself with the country and its traditional culture. The changes introduced Western influences to the region for various reasons. One was the oil crisis in 1973–74. Another reason was that the Saudi Arabian oil company Aramco integrated an American community into the east coast of the country and developed embassies on the west coast, increasing the number of non-native inhabitants. However, only a few foreign companies were based in the country's capital city, Riyadh, which invited only a handful of non-natives to live in the city. For that reason, Basil was surrounded by locals, demonstrating the fact that timing was an essential pillar in affording the artist a local experience.
Basil's journey as an artist began in Saudi Arabia. Her exhibitions gained press recognition, and the locals' support gave her a sense of fulfillment.

Malin Basil
Morning Village, 1979
Acrylic on canvas
100 × 125 cm
Collection of King Carl XVI Gustaf of Sweden

Malin Basil wrote that she was lucky to arrive in Saudi Arabia when she did, before the major oil crisis of 1973–74, which brought with it many changes.

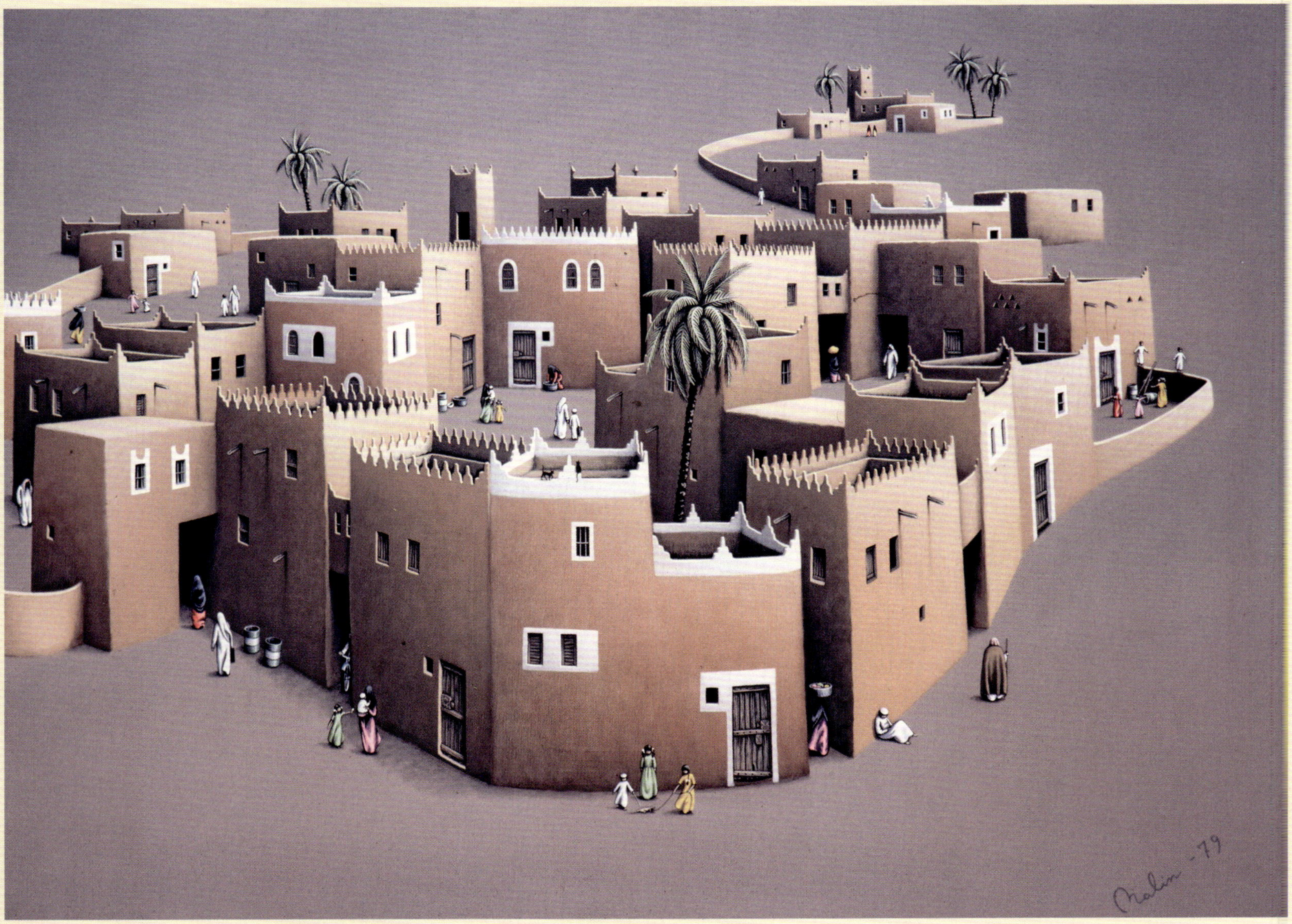

Malin Basil
Detail of *Morning Village*, 1979
Acrylic on canvas
100 × 125 cm
Collection of King Carl XVI Gustaf of Sweden

Crenellated walls, projected wooden tubes, and plaster framing doors and windows are among the typical features of the traditional architecture in Nejd.

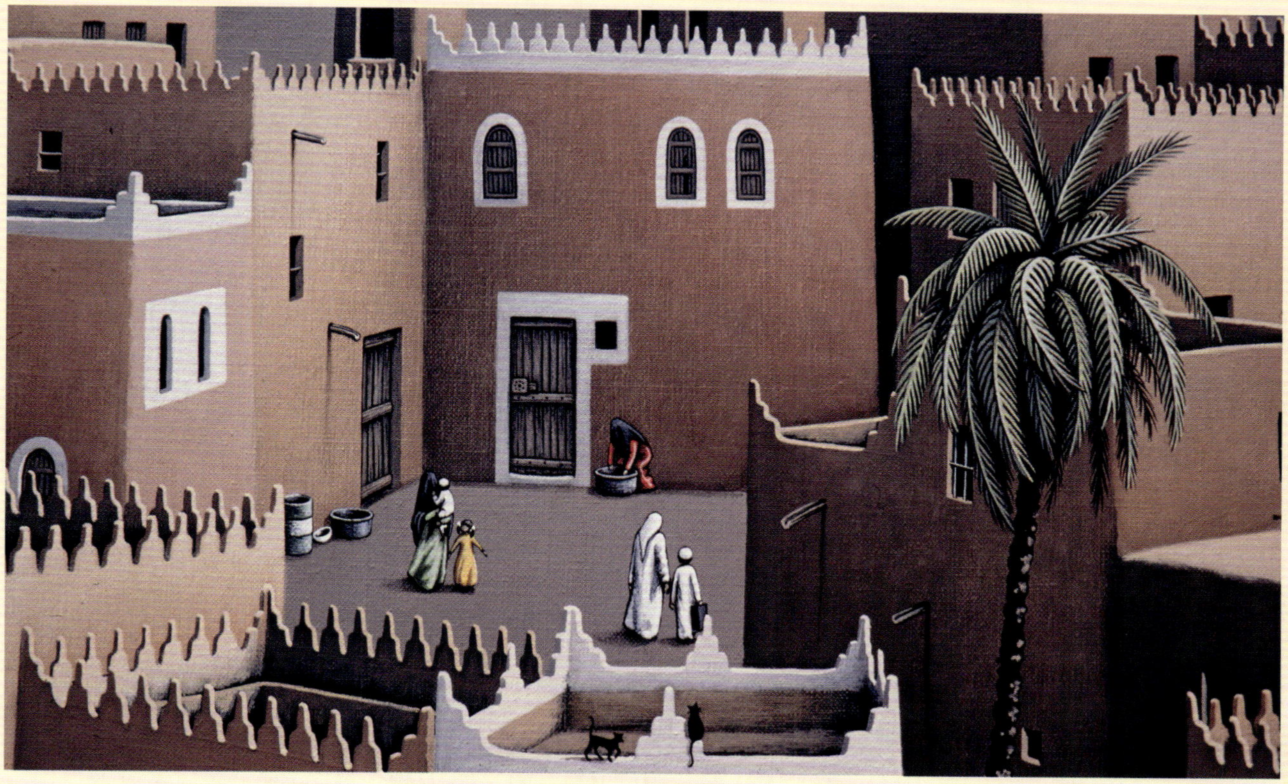

This support strengthened her connection with the local scene, which probably came naturally to her as a result of the appreciation she felt living in the Kingdom. Basil introduces herself as "an artist who has never set foot in an art school, and who has made no attempt at being systematic or objective—neither in the choice of subjects nor in the treatment of them. I know, because I am, that artist." She had a wealth of expressions to share. After she failed to publicize Saudi Arabia through written articles, she refocused her energy on painting. In her words: "I had to give some sort of artistic expression to my experiences in this far-away land." She used her paintbrush to voice her journalistic opinions. Acrylics replaced ink, and a brush replaced her pen. Her first painting depicted a Bedouin camp across the street from her house. The subjects of many of Basil's paintings were the captivating lifestyles of the nomads encountering the changes brought by oil money in the early 1970s. The changes were progressive and positive. However, the artist had concerns that these rich traditions and nomadic lifestyles were fading away undocumented. She was documenting a vanishing civilization that she was sadly trying to capture, fearing it might never be archived. The artist felt "amazement and alarm over the changes," so she decided to avoid the documentation of the refined modernistic side of the country, what she called "wonderful signs of what is to come". Instead she unfolded the aesthetics of the Bedouin tents and mud houses. Basil's layered artistic expression illustrates Saudi's deserts, villages, and the city of Riyadh, including the active locals living their daily lives. She subtly incorporates symbols of changes that are being introduced into a traditional society. By integrating technology into the desert in some of her paintings, the observer could see a powerful sign of change. The composition of earthy tones mixed with inky black illustrates both a sense of warmth and sadness, mirroring the genuine emotions and concerns the artist had. Her artistic use of shadows manifests the element of time that the artist's concern derives from. Her accurate perspective carries a sense of movement, which draws the viewer into her work while the captivating figures convey a lively spirit. Her work coupled both an "emotional content" and a "documentary accuracy," which in her opinion compliment each other. She further developed her opinion, stating that "the documentary aspect justifies the book". Her storytelling subjects astonished her, and her way of depicting them connects any spectator to a simpler time in life—a time when people paid considerable attention to their everyday physical practices, their connection to the land they walked on, and how they are an extension of the sand they sat and worked on. Basil took the deepest look into the nostalgic details of the lives around her, which mirrored her love for the country. She yearned to search for past lives she was not able to experience. Her personal need to help her painted subjects survive is the reason the book *Saudi Arabia Through the Eyes of An Artist* came about, a book in which she humbly gives credit to Saudi Arabia for nurturing her into a painter.

THIERRY MAUGER

It takes an open mind to approach the obscure land of Saudi Arabia and to unfold this remote kingdom takes a dedicated soul. Intrigued by nomadic lifestyles, Thierry Mauger traveled to the Kingdom of Saudi Arabia searching for the diminishing Bedouin culture. For more than ten years he lived in Saudi Arabia, where after a journey across the kingdom, he concentrated on the province of Asir, located in the southwest of the kingdom. *Impressions of Arabia: Architecture and Frescoes of the Asir Region* was published in 1996, after the author gained intimate knowledge of the country. In it, Mauger examines the architectural structures and their materials highlighting the artistic themes depicted on the colorful frescoes that cover the walls of Asir.

Thierry Mauger explores and mines Asir by looking deep into its architecture, landscape, and aesthetics as they correspond to the region's traditions. In response to the conservative ways of life among Asir's inhabitants, the architectural layout of the household had to conform to each household's particular conservative characteristic, starting from the privacy of the home's entrance to the private domain of women, and how they communicated with female neighbors through rooftops built mainly for that reason. The architecture of Asir presents various faces, one of which is a militant façade for protective reasons, which explains why fortified granaries are built as well as hilltop watchtowers.

Thierry Mauger mainly analyzes the

Thierry Mauger
Mud house with striped decoration in Bilad Qahtan, Sinhan (Arabian Tableland)
Courtesy of the artist

In this very colorful village in Bilad Qahtan, the men build the houses and the women paint them. The windows and doors are framed in blue lines and outlined in red on three sides. Thierry Mauger wrote *"decorative frame of the door symbolically recalls the function of an area of transition between exterior and interior"*.

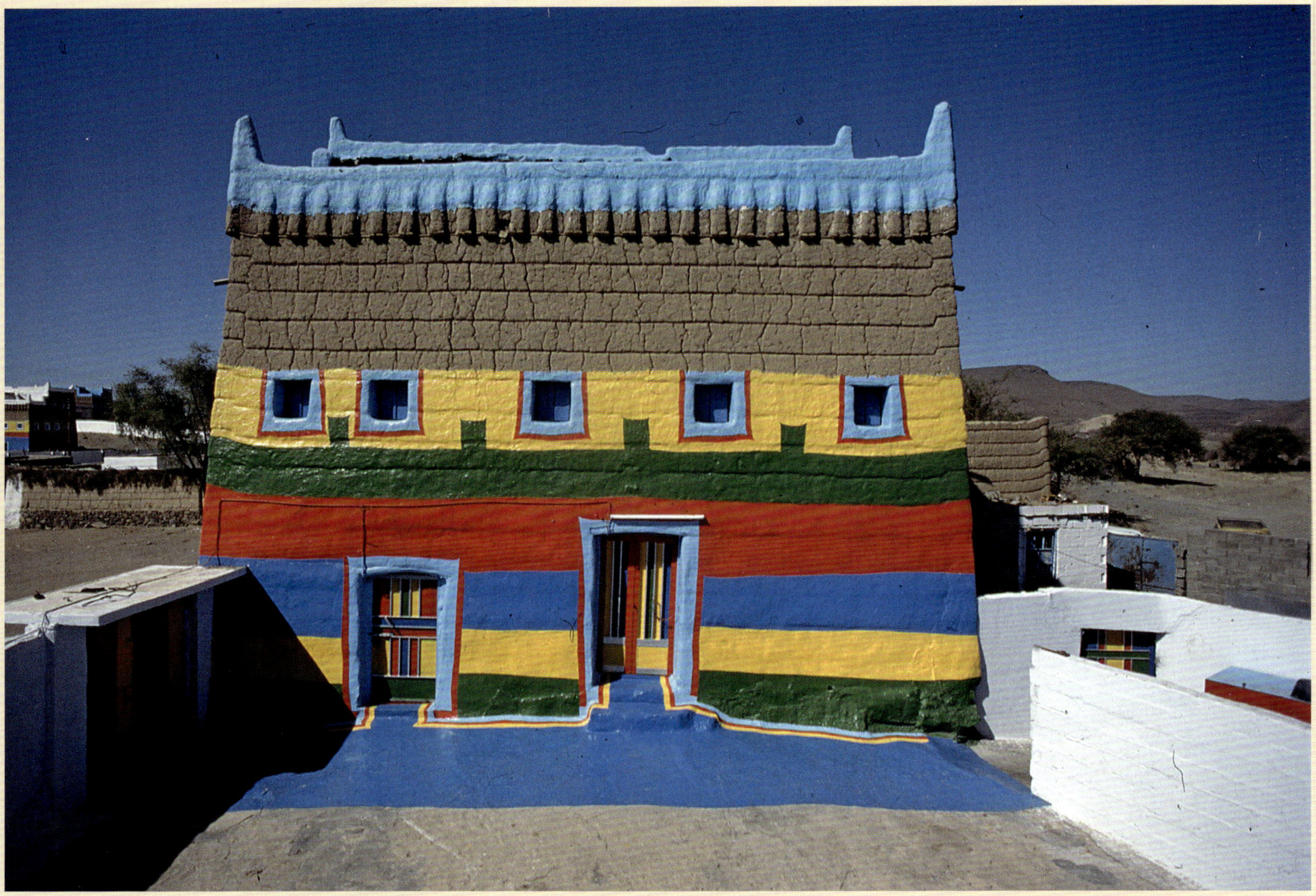

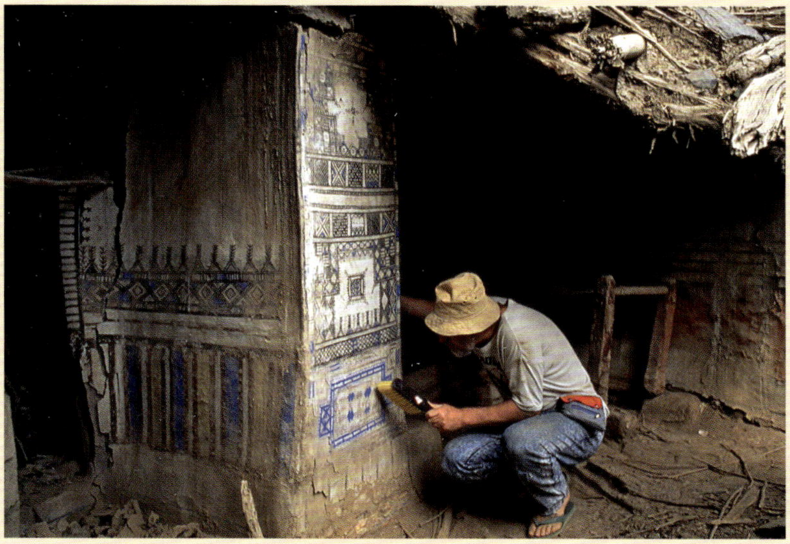

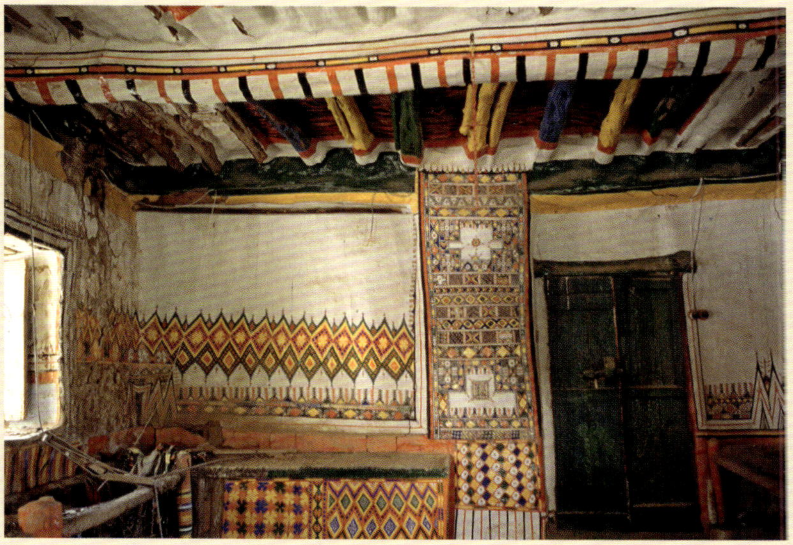

Thierry Mauger
Thierry Mauger restoring a "batarah" (masonry pillar) decorated with natural pigments in Rijal Alma'
Courtesy of the artist

A few examples of the better-preserved houses featuring "Al-Qatt" art are found in the town of Rijal Alma'; a mountainous province located in the southwest of Saudi Arabia. Thierry Mauger, who published several books on Saudi Arabia, provided a blueprint of its landscapes, architecture, and tribal culture. "Al-Qatt" is a geometrical abstract art inherent to the visual and cultural identity of the region of Asir. It is produced by women to decorate the interiors of the houses and is transmitted from generation to generation. The art of "Al-Qatt" was included on UNESCO's Intangible Cultural Heritage of Humanity list in 2017.

Thierry Mauger
Usually the most ostentatious decoration was applied in the majlis *(reception room). The other rooms were simply decorated with bands of color.*
Courtesy of the artist

In the past, the dyes used in "Al-Qatt" murals were extracted from local plants and pigments. The green color, for example, was produced from the clover plant; white pigment was obtained from gypsum; blue pigment was made from the indigo leaves.

traditional murals that cover the façades of houses and their interior decoration, called *Al-Qatt Al-Asiri*. The colors used to create these murals required obtaining pigments from caves hidden in the region's mountains.

This land conveys "architecture without architects," indicating an expressive, talented community. In Mauger's opinion, "The vertical architecture may also be seen as expressing the civilization of a region of builders, a brilliant demonstration of their skill in mastering construction in the third dimension." The skillfulness was carried out by both genders, according to Mauger: "The decoration impulse is a commonplace of human nature, and in this case competition to own a beautiful house plays a major role. The skills and personalities of the women are invested in this task. Previously reserved for the decoration of the *majlis* (reception room), the frescoes gradually spread throughout the house, before appearing on the façade. The frescoes are appreciated not as works of art but as a symbol and proof of the skill of the painter—the wife of the host—and it is the latter who accepts the honor." The murals that decorated the homes carry bold geometrical patterns that correlate with the region's traditions and customs and as such are "social and economic indicators".

Mauger takes personal pride in the access he was permitted and delivers a substantial social and architectural archive to the people of the region and beyond the country's borders. In the author's words, "I decided to use this opportunity to pioneer a documentary method that would both convey and conserve the authenticity of this Arab culture." He humanizes the architecture by depicting its cultural influences which shadow the people of the region and their daily practices, domestic lifestyle, and social statuses.

Mauger's excessive knowledge of the tribal culture shows his close relationship with the locals of Asir, although, at first, the inhabitants had a skeptical impression of his visit. The visual narrative of Asir during the time of Mauger's documentation was unfamiliar. However, his committed work and passion drew attention to a form of traditional art that is facing extermination. Due to his efforts, the expressions of Asir, namely *Al-Qatt Al-Asiri*, have been recognized and were inscribed in UNESCO's Representative List of the Intangible Cultural Heritage of Humanity in 2017. The ramifications of his work are apparent evidence that Mauger's devotion to the Saudi Arabian aesthetic casts much-needed attention to the preservation of national identity, which he actively took part in and which proves to be necessary because some of his documented houses have already been demolished.

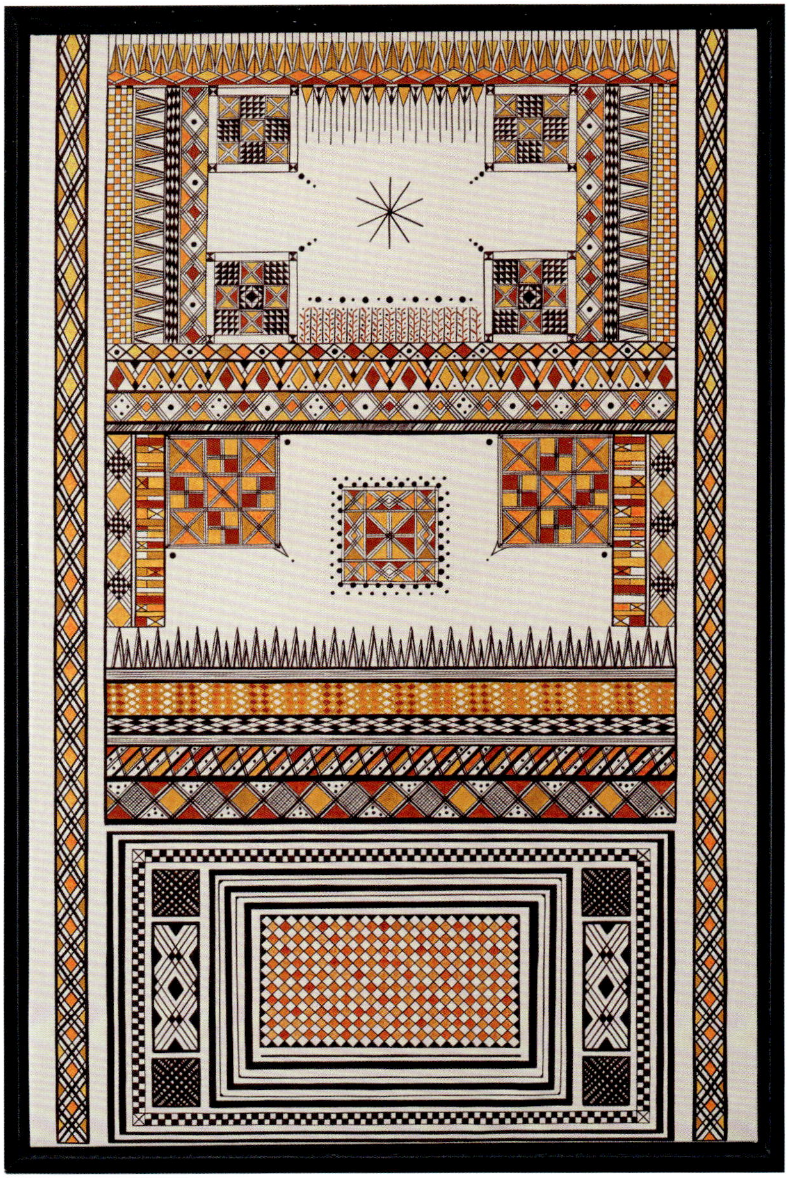

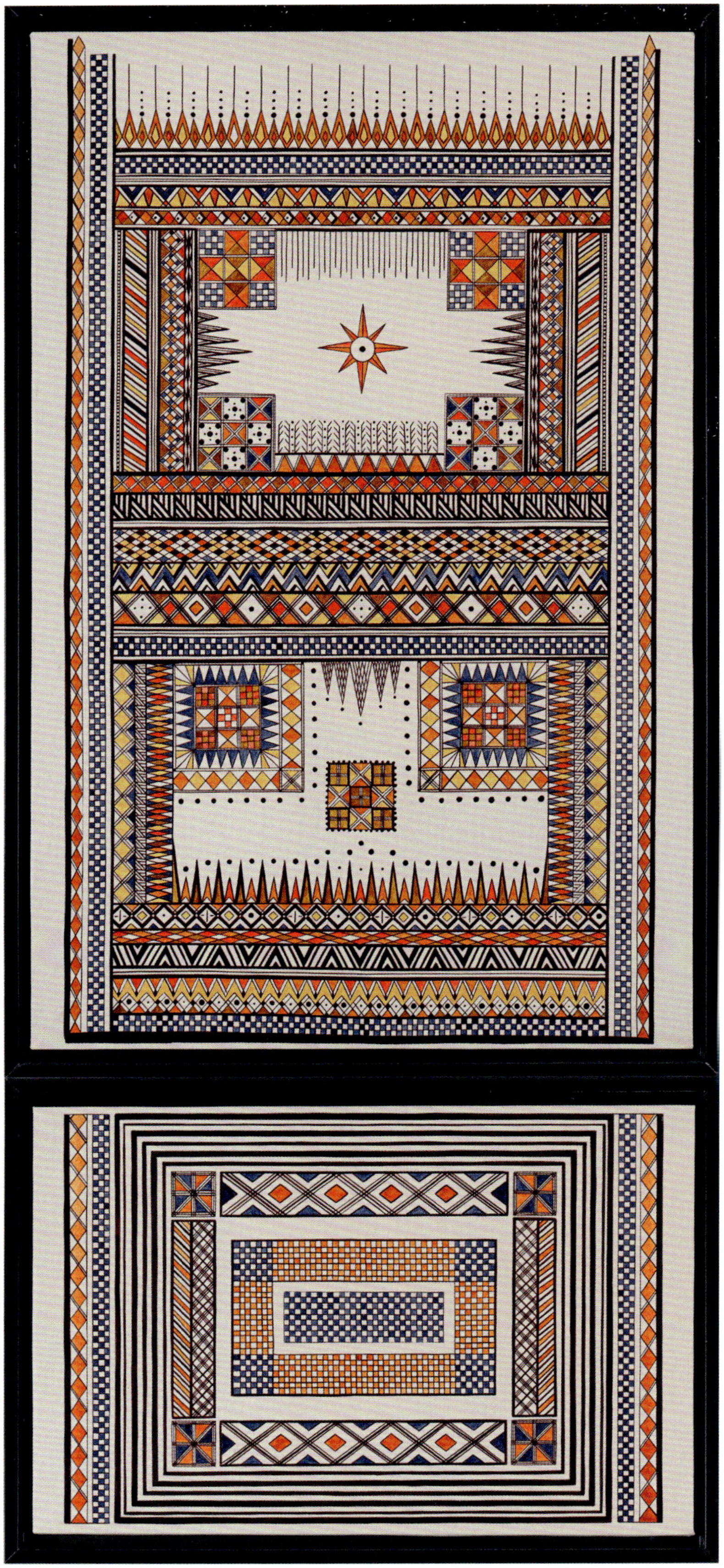

Magali Jeantelot
Riyadh series, 2018
Acrylic on canvas
92 × 65 cm
Photo Aref Alnomay
Courtesy of the artist

In this series, produced during the time the artist was living in Riyadh, Magali Jeantelot revisits the art of "Al-Qatt". In Magali's paintings however, the floral motifs, recurrent sometimes in the Qatt murals, are absent.

Magali Jeantelot
Riyadh series, 2018
Acrylic on canvas
131 × 60 cm
Photo by Aref Alnomay
Courtesy of the artist

The art of "Al-Qatt" requires a great deal of skill, precision, and time. The design is first outlined in black and afterward the motifs are highlighted with a special brush made from goat's tail.

Magali Jeantelot
Riyadh series, 2018
Acrylic on canvas
82 × 255 cm
Photo by Aref Alnomay
Courtesy of the artist

Thierry Mauger's research and books on the art of Asir gained attention of artists such as Magali Jeantelot, who used the art of the murals of Asir as a source of inspiration for many of the paintings she produced during her sojourn in Arabia.

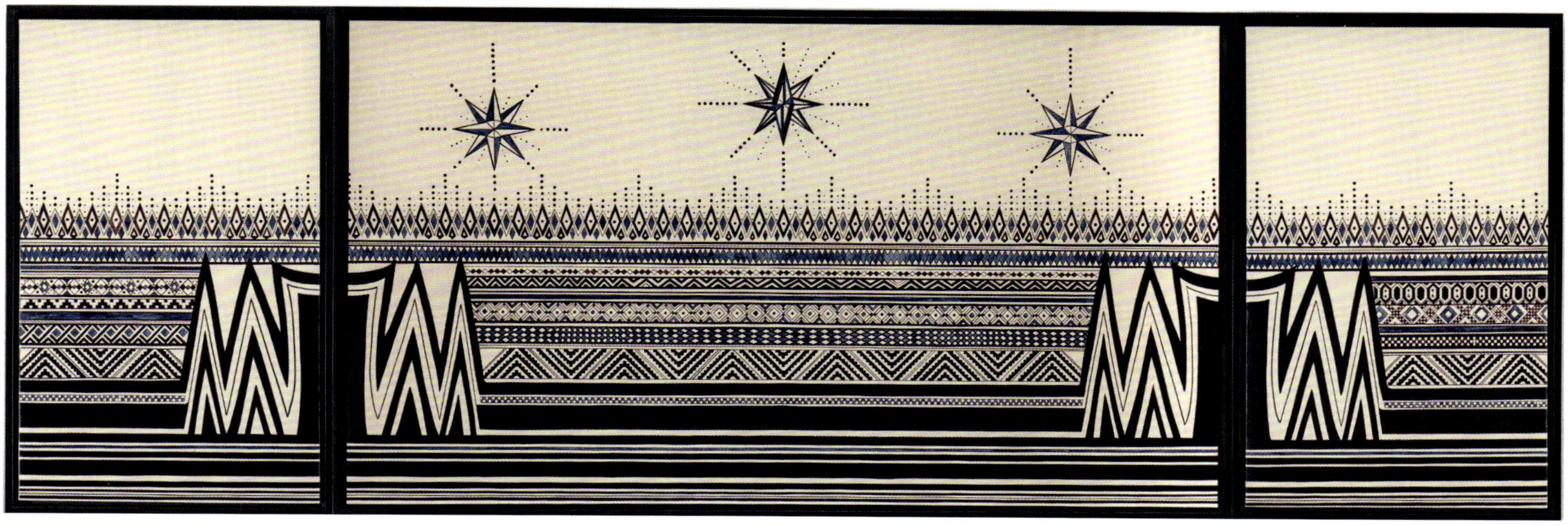

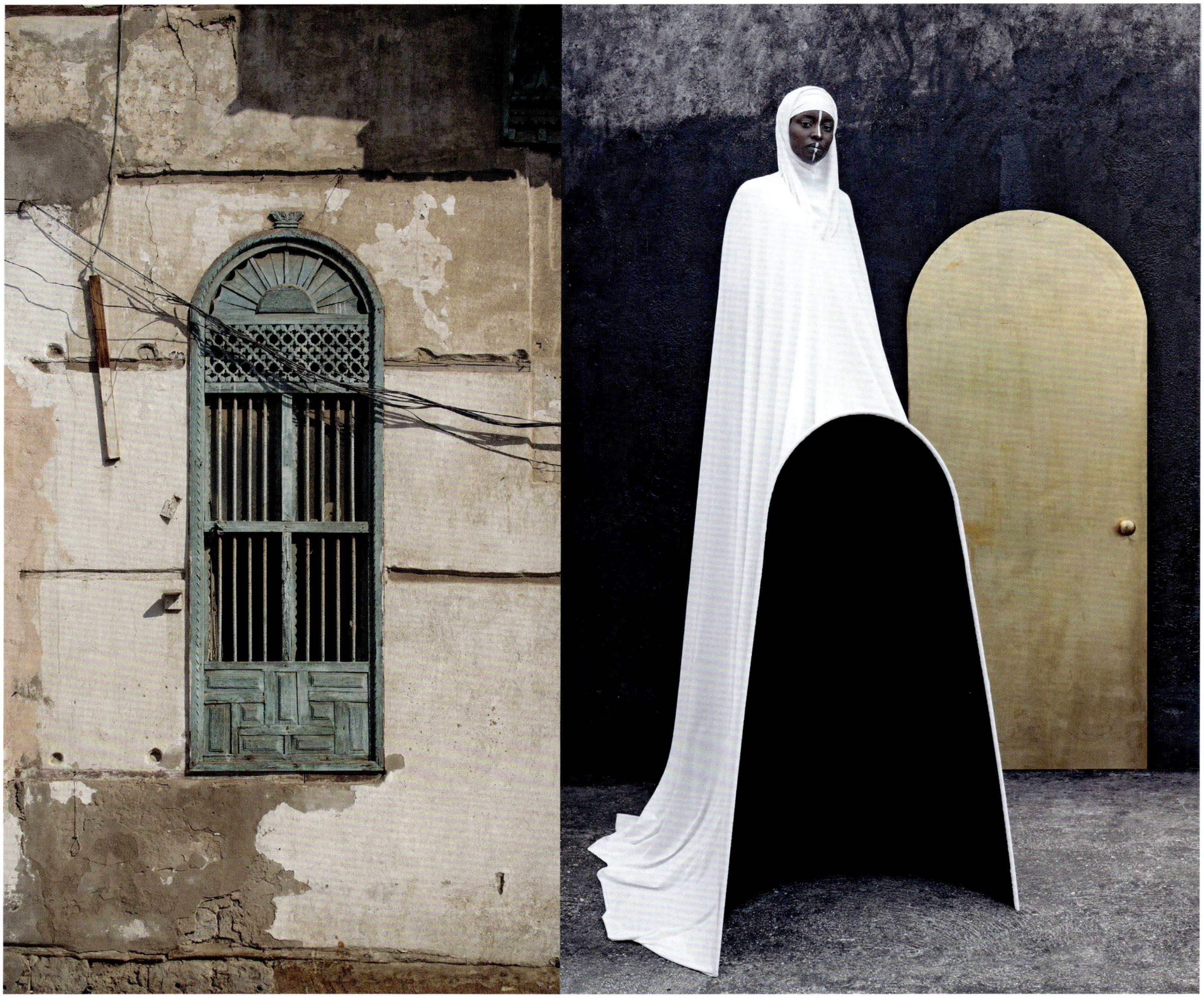

Maimouna Guerresi
Jeddah's door, 2016–18
Courtesy of the artist

Earlier, the few Europeans who were allowed to enter Saudi Arabia were confined to Jeddah. Diplomats and the commercial community lived there. Carsten Niebuhr wrote in *Travels through Arabia and other Countries in the East* (1774): "*We entered this city under strong apprehensions of ill treatment from its inhabitants. Recollection with what contempt Christians are regarded at Cairo, and how our companions have been insulted by the Arabs at Jambo, we feared that, we might experience still more of the inhospitable insolence of the Mussulmans, as we approached nearer to their holy cities. […] The inhabitants of Jidda, who are much accustomed to Christian merchants in the European dress, were not struck with any thing strange in our appearance, and did not seem to take much notice of us.*"

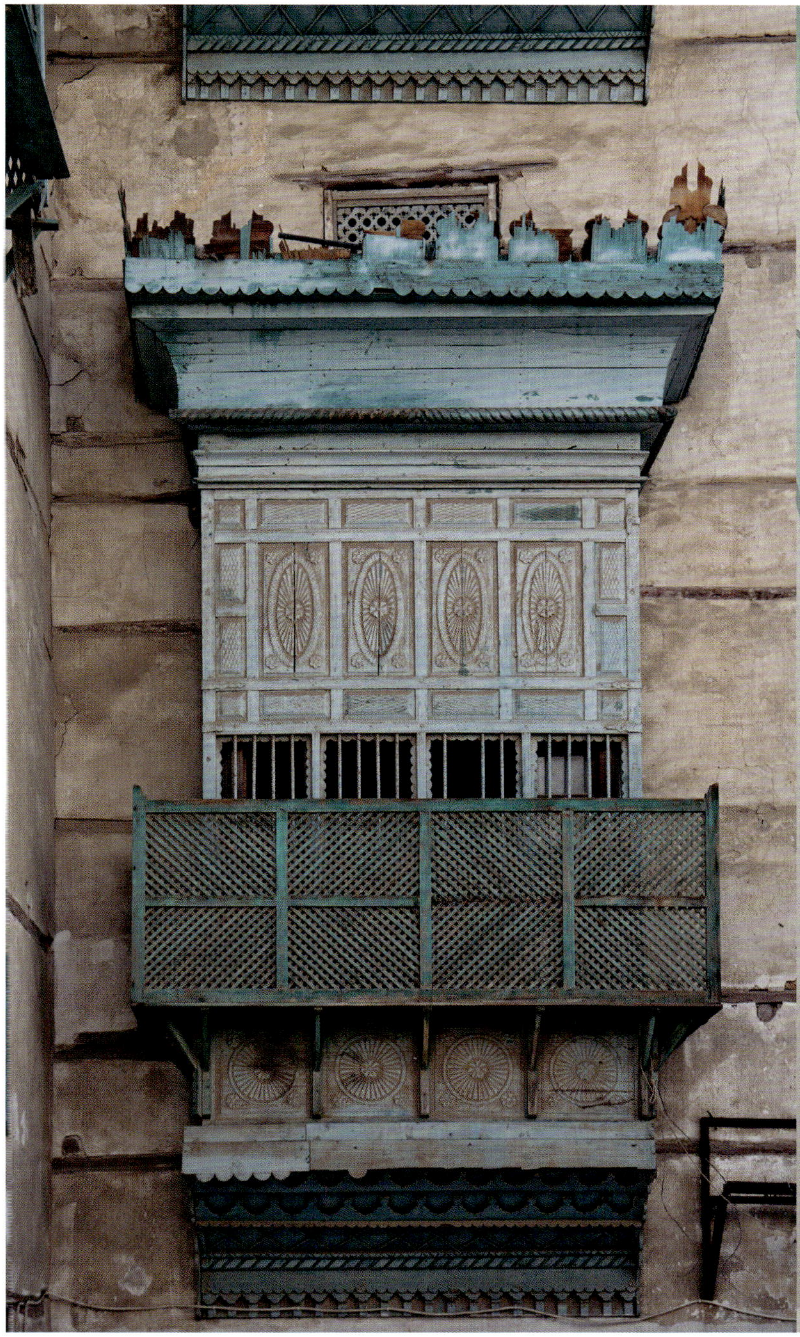

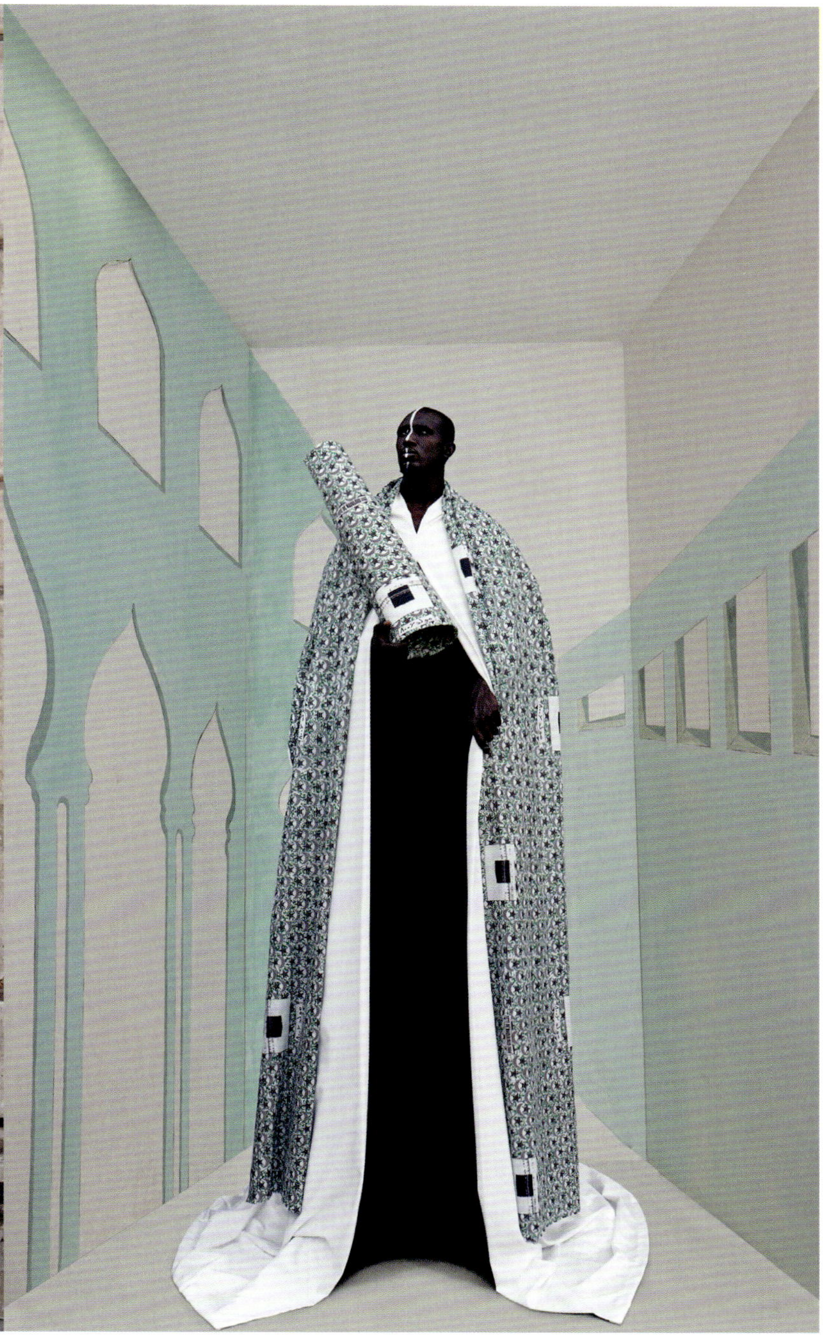

Maimouna Guerresi
Green architecture, 2016–18
Courtesy of the artist

Ali Bey El Abbassi, who sojourned in Jeddah in 1807, described its architecture: "*The houses are fine, built of stone, and are two or three stories high, but are not very solid. They all have a great number of windows, and flat roofs*".

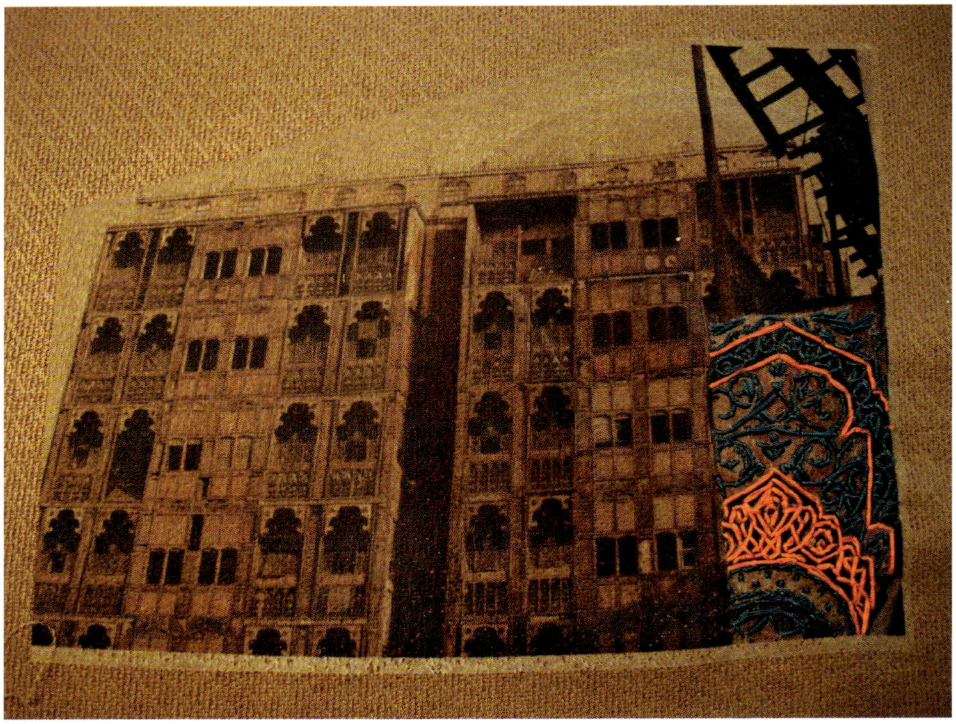

Aya Haidar
Al Balad I, 2010
Screen-printed awning
with embroidery
33.8 × 27 cm
Courtesy of Faisal Tamar
and Sarah Ali Reza, Jeddah

In this series, artist Aya Haidar chooses certain details of the architecture of Jeddah, which she embroiders with brightly colored thread. The artist wrote: "*I discovered Jeddah's old town, subsequently leading to my avid exploration of such a timeless site of true national heritage and pride [...] and leading to the development of* Al Balad, *a body of work merging modern-day printed digital photography on linen with the more traditional practice of hand stitched craft.*"

him to add a large amount of sugar to the drink: "'*Chai* (tea), is the coffee-drink of the *Nasâra* [Christians],' Zeyd said. 'And, good Khalîl, since the sheykhs would taste thy chai, look thou put in much sugar.' 'And how likes you the *kahwat* of the *Nasâra*?' Zeyd cried to them. They answered, 'The sugar is good, but as for this which Khalil calls *chai*, the smack of it is little better than warm water.' A man amongst them inquired saying, 'Khalîl, is not this *el-khamr*, the fermented wine of the *Nasâra*?' And for conscience sake he would not drink; but the company sipped their sugar-drink to the dregs, and bade the stranger pour out more..."

Barely two years later, in Ha'il, Anne Blunt and her husband were not surprised to be offered tea, but this time in the private reception room of the Emir: "Coffee, and a very sweet tea, were handed round in thimblefuls," she wrote. Tea, in Arabia, was first used by the upper classes of society, just as had been the case in Europe.

Everything happened very quickly after that. Frenchman Jules Gervais-Courtellemont, who had completed a pilgrimage in 1896, did not appreciate the routine to which he was subjected during his stay in Mecca. "All day long, when appropriate and even when it was not, we were forced to drink tea, more tea, and always tea. Courtesy requires that you are offered three cups, one after another, and courtesy also required that three cupfuls be religiously absorbed." Gervais-Courtellemont thus concluded, "This is evidently a consequence of Indian influence—to drink nothing but tea!"

However, he was not finished with his disappointments. "It is true that if, as an exception, you are offered coffee, your fate will not be any happier: actually, this excellent mocha from Yemen—what a profanation!—is slightly burnt, ground and infused with cloves, ginger, or cinnamon! They will generally serve

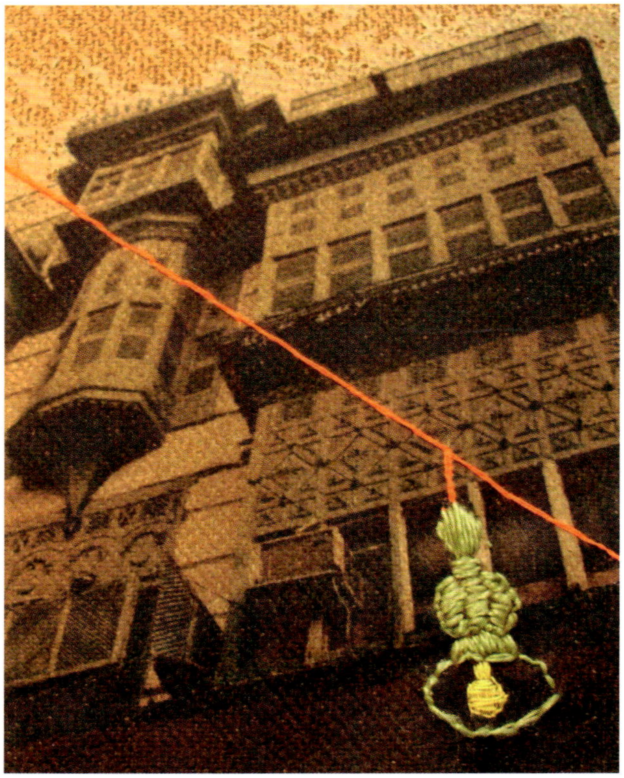

Aya Haidar
Al Balad V, 2010
Screen-printed awning
with embroidery
33.8 × 27 cm
Courtesy of Faisal Tamar and
Sarah Ali Reza, Jeddah

Al Balad is the name commonly used to designate the historic downtown area of Jeddah and of many cities in the Arab world.

Roger Grasas
Faisaliah Tower, Riyadh
From the series *Min Turab*,
2007–16
Courtesy of the artist

Designed by British architect Sir Norman Foster and built in 2000, Al Faisaliah Tower was the first skyscraper in Saudi Arabia.

Roger Grasas
Olaya Street, Riyadh
From the series *Min Turab*,
2007–16
Courtesy of the artist

Olaya Street is one of the main arteries of Riyadh.

Roger Grasas
King Abdullah Financial City, Riyadh
From the series *Min Turab*,
2007–16
Courtesy of the artist

Launched in 2006, once completed the Financial city will provide a new economic zone in the heart of Riyadh with direct connection to the airport.

Roger Grasas
King Fahd Road, Riyadh
From the series *Min Turab*,
2007–16
Courtesy of the artist

Entertainment parks are very popular in Saudi Arabia's major cities.

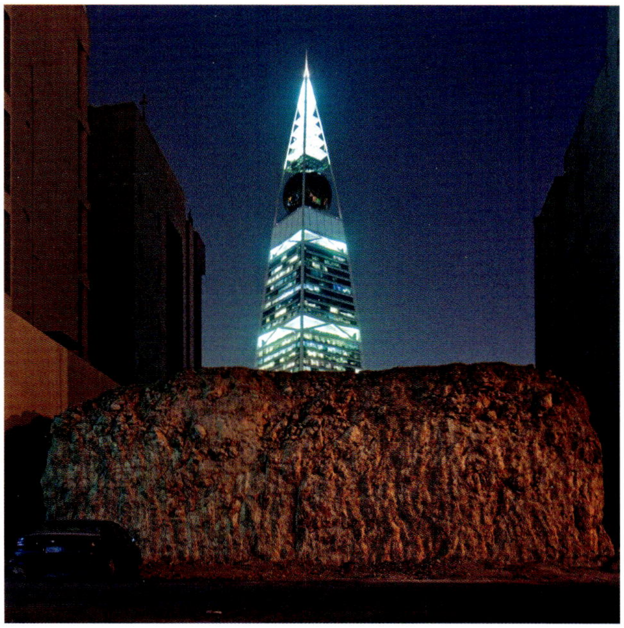

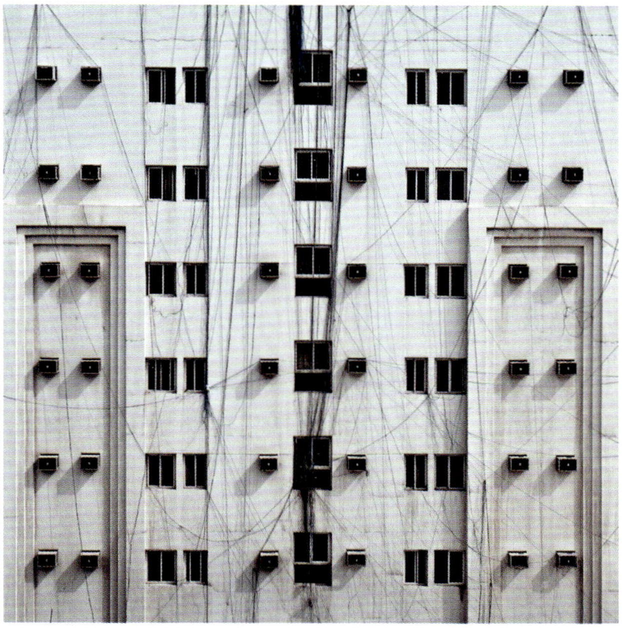

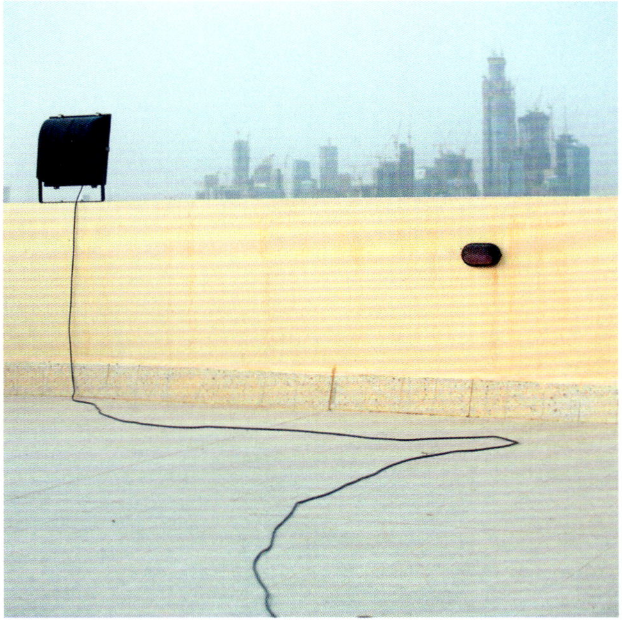

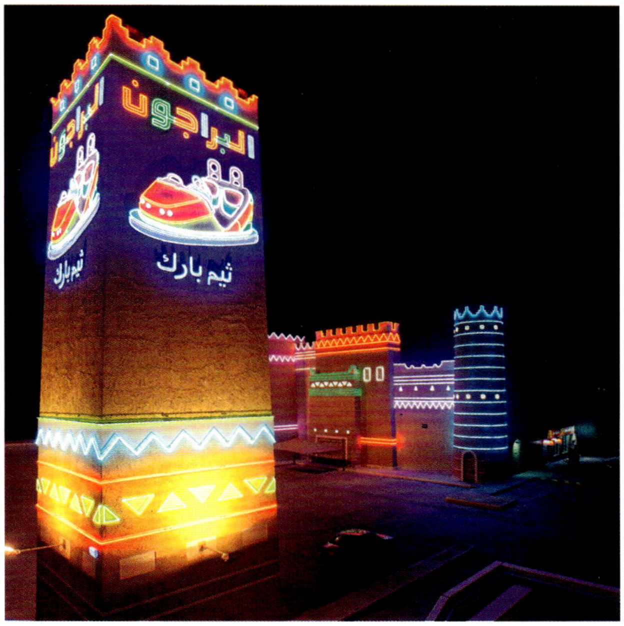

it to you without sugar and as thick as Spanish chocolate: it is very discouraging. The alternative is water," he concluded, "which very happily is limpid and good in Mecca."

Three decades later, the Orientalist painter Étienne Dinet was able to draw this conclusion: "As for coffee, it has been almost completely replaced by the preference for chaï (tea), black or green, of which an infinite number of glasses are consumed." Thus ended a hegemony that had lasted more than five centuries…

ZIAD ANTAR

The photographs and videos of Ziad Antar are quite distinctive to his unique style. He defies the classical standards of fine art photography and follows his experimental instincts. Antar's controversial way of thinking is evident in his work, in which he skilfully combines the traditional and the contemporary. He utilizes very diverse photographic materials, from expired negatives to archives images to question the medium of photography and ask what are the limits of a photographic device in capturing or preserving. Antar explains, "Due to these restraints, I was able to question the medium—in this case, 'What is photography?' The question is at the core of my work. Even when I make one-minute videos, I would always put constraints on myself. Inspired by the first film of the Lumière brothers, I produced a video in one shot. This technical constraint raises the question 'What is a video?'" This experimental spirit frees him, and his interest in constraints liberates him. The artist's questioning of the medium reflects strongly in his work, resulting in productions that project his interrogation.

Vilém Flusser stated in 1991, "Ziad is not a 'functionary'; he does not bind himself by the rules the apparatus sets. He refutes predictable accounts and chooses to create new uncertain narratives through the abruption of various vital photographic elements: time, light, lens to name a few." Ziad Antar's educational background was not related to art nor was he exposed to contemporary art. When his interest in photography peaked, he felt the need to work with basic elements of the medium. At the start of his artistic career, he always relied on the medium, and the need to gain "know-how" experience. He would begin by questioning the medium, then he simplifies and deconstructs. He followed the advice of his mentors and fellow artists but never felt the need to follow guidelines. Antar's projects are not by any means planned. As he goes about life, he stumbles upon a camera or a film which then evolves into an artistic production. His projects always start with experiments, and with no prior planning. This artist learns during the process and adapts while constantly trying to teach himself.

He explained one of his projects—see chapter *The Center of the World*—: "*Expired* is about the disintegration of images. It's a project I started in 2000 and it's one of my first books. That year, I began working and experimenting with expired film negatives and questioning the medium

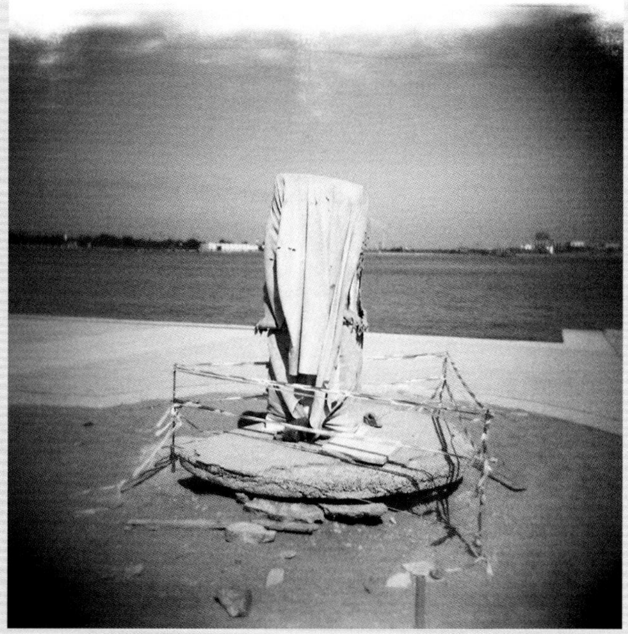

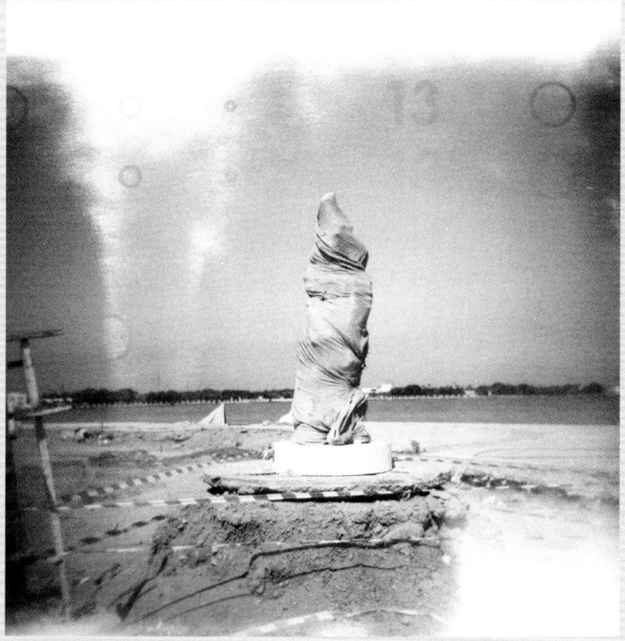

Ziad Antar
Axiom 6, Jeddah
From the series *Derivable*, 2012
Silver print mounted on dibond
120 × 120 cm
Courtesy of the artist

Located on Jeddah's corniche, many of Jeddah's sculptures were produced by renowned artists in the 1980s.

Ziad Antar
Axiom 2, Jeddah
From the series *Derivable*, 2012
Silver print mounted on dibond
120 × 120 cm
Courtesy of the artist

In this series, Ziad Antar chose to photograph Jeddah's sculptures covered, almost disguised, with the sculptures set atop transfer crates. The sculptures become a new body of work with a different aesthetic.

Ziad Antar
Axiom 4, Jeddah
From the series *Derivable*, 2012
Silver print mounted on dibond
120 × 120 cm
Courtesy of the artist

In *Derivable*, Ziad Antar emphasizes the importance and the role of public art in shaping the identity of the city.

Ziad Antar
Axiom 8, Jeddah
From the series *Derivable*, 2012
Silver print mounted on dibond
120 × 120 cm
Courtesy of the artist

Cesar Baldaccini's bronze *Fist*, wrapped before being transferred for restoration.

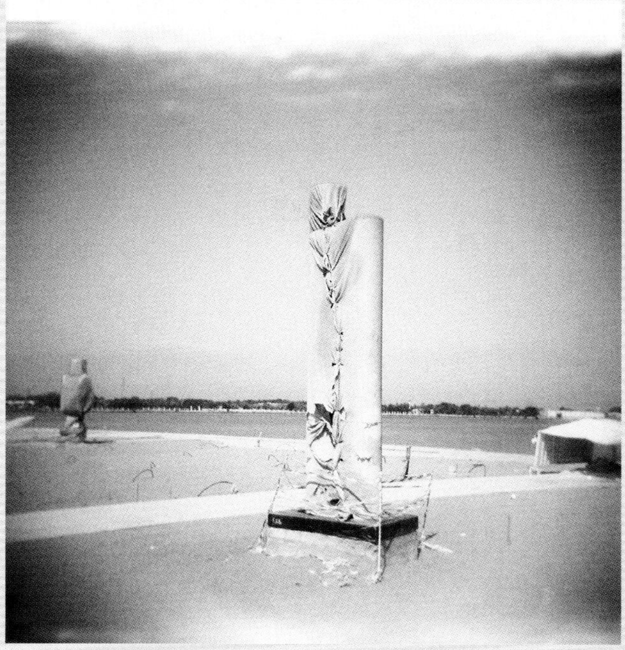

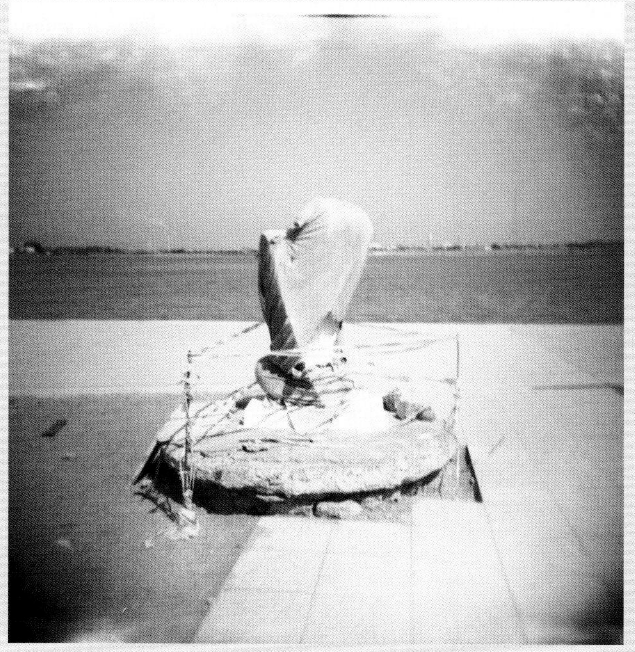

of photography, how to document and what role archives play. The films I worked with had not been exposed and had expired in 1976. They stayed in multiple storage and lived through all the ordeals of Lebanon: fifteen years of war, flood, humidity, theft, and fire."

Antar's photographic experimental process is evident both aesthetically and conceptually. He never allows guiding principles of aesthetics to lead him. During a shoot, he does not follow a photographic timetable for capturing the so-called finest time to photograph, which are the first and last hours of daylight. Antar would photograph all day and as much as he could, ignoring the conventional approach. This led him to produce problematic images that he welcomed, allowing him to express his abstract work and expose images that the viewer can relate to poetically. The blurred images tend to obscure the locations and figures while the dazed colors render a sense of ambivalence, forcing the observer's eye to examine and question.

Antar's work engenders a particular relationship between artworks and perceptions. His chosen subjects transmit his analytical approach to photography and film. This is clearly represented in Antar's corpus titled *Derivable* (see chapter *Cities of Yesterday and Tomorrow*). The monumental sculptures in Jeddah's corniche—commissioned in the 1980s and produced by world-renowned artists Joan Miró, Henry Moore, and César, among others—were wrapped in cloth before being transferred for restoration. Antar chose to capture them in an uncommon manner: the sculptures were covered, almost disguised in a different character, while standing on the transfer crates. The strange shapes suggested a new discourse to these sculptures, from the sculptor, to the employee who wrapped the cloth, himself for capturing the photograph, and the spectators building their interpretations. His photographs do not merely represent still moments but are ongoing narratives that cater to the notion of ambivalence, offering an unexpected possibility of freedom. For Antar, "aesthetics and ethics form an inseparable whole, and this enables another kind of documentary approach in which the photographer's mission to inform is accompanied by a quality of the image that lies beyond its realism, yet that does not make it for this reason a 'picture'."

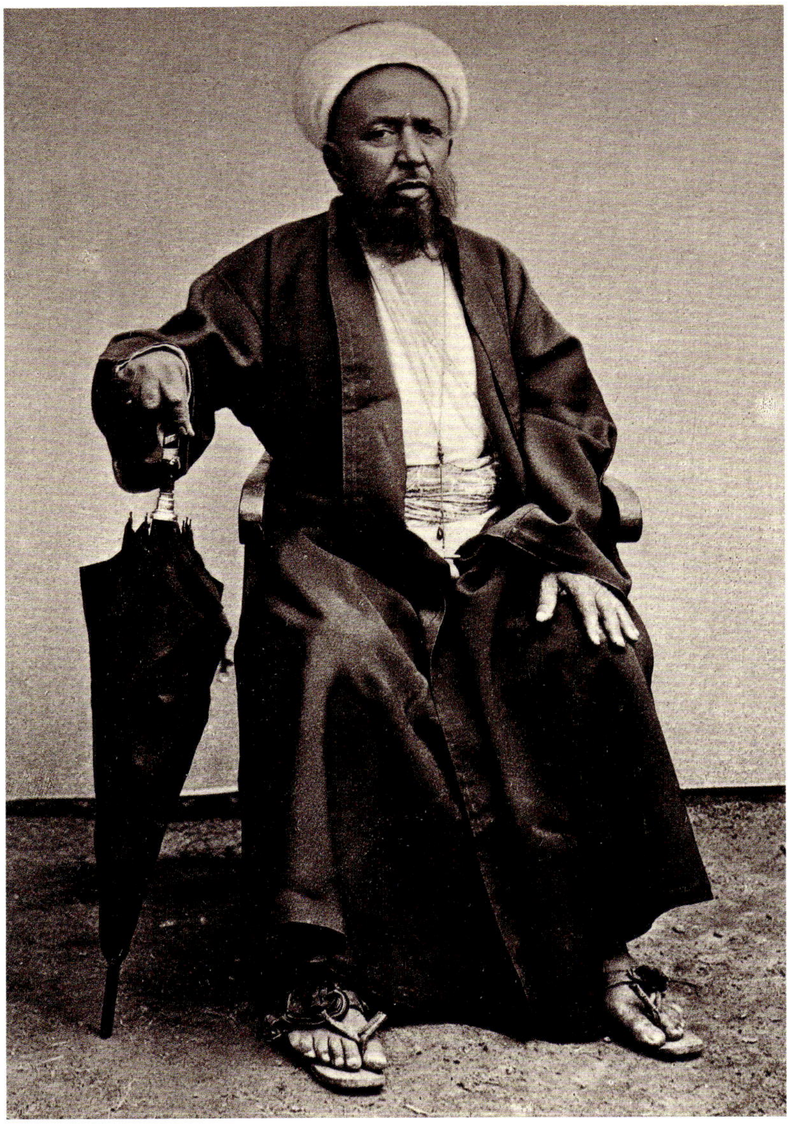

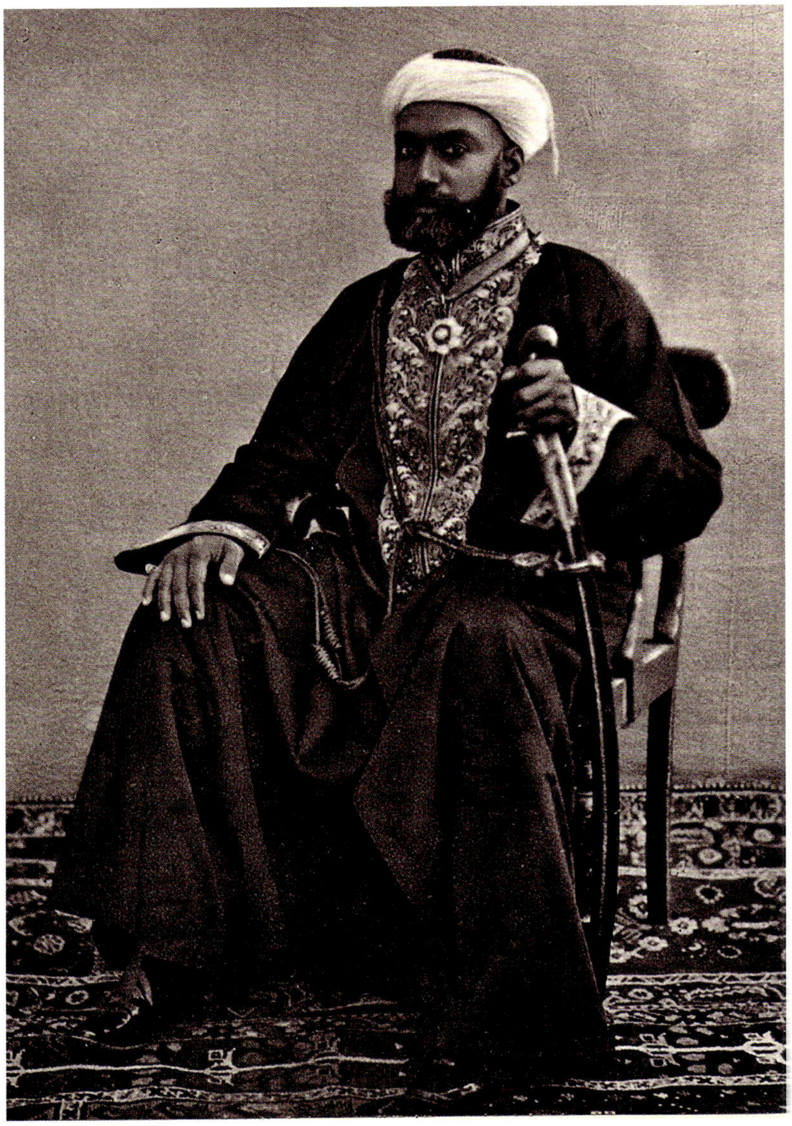

Christiaan Snouck Hurgronje
A doctor from Mecca, 1885
Gelatin silver print
Courtesy of the King Abdulaziz Public Library, Riyadh

During his stay in Mecca, Snouck Hurgronje undertook a social study of the holy city. He took studio portraits of important religious and secular figures from the city as well as of pilgrims from different origins, which were reproduced in *Bilder aus Mekka*. This book contributed largely to the knowledge of Mecca at the end of the nineteenth century.

Christiaan Snouck Hurgronje
Eminent Sayyid, *head of a clan of Mecca*, 1885
Gelatin silver print
Courtesy of the King Abdulaziz Public Library, Riyadh

Ali Bey El Abbasi sojourned in Arabia in 1807. He wrote in his *Travels: "There is a great deal of luxury in the costume and apartments of the rich."*

Christiaan Snouck Hurgronje
Two merchants from Mecca and from Jeddah, 1885
Gelatin silver print
Courtesy of the King Abdulaziz Public Library, Riyadh

Jeddah was always known as a merchant city and its people as traders. As early as 988, Ibn Hawqal wrote of Jeddah in *Kitab Surat al-Ard* (Configuration of the Earth): *"Jeddah was prosperous, rich in commerce and very affluent, and there was not in the Hejaz, apart from Mecca, a city possessing more wealth and more merchandise."*

Christiaan Snouck Hurgronje
Sons of Sheybah family, guardians of the Ka'ba, 1885
Gelatin silver print
Courtesy of the King Abdulaziz Public Library, Riyadh

The Sheybah family was entrusted with the keys of the Ka'ba for fourteen centuries. They are in charge of opening the door of the Ka'ba, at fixed dates, and of changing the *kiswa* every year. Richard Burton described them as "the true-blue blood of Hijaz".

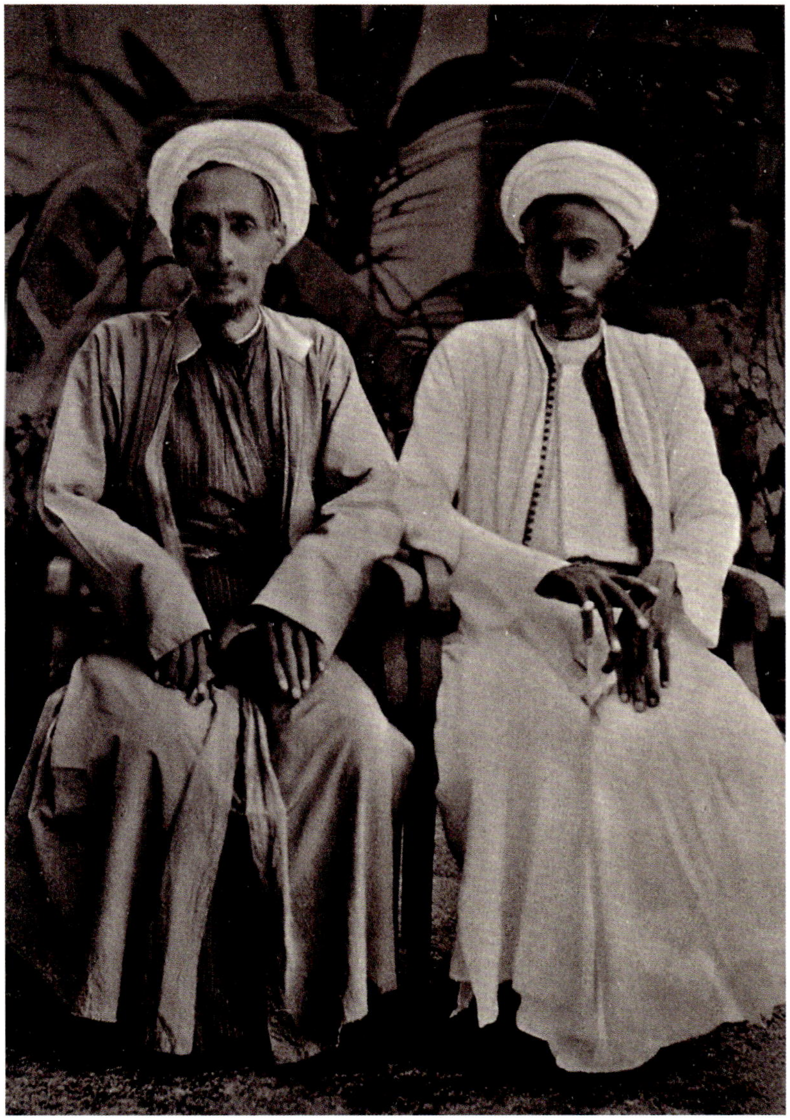

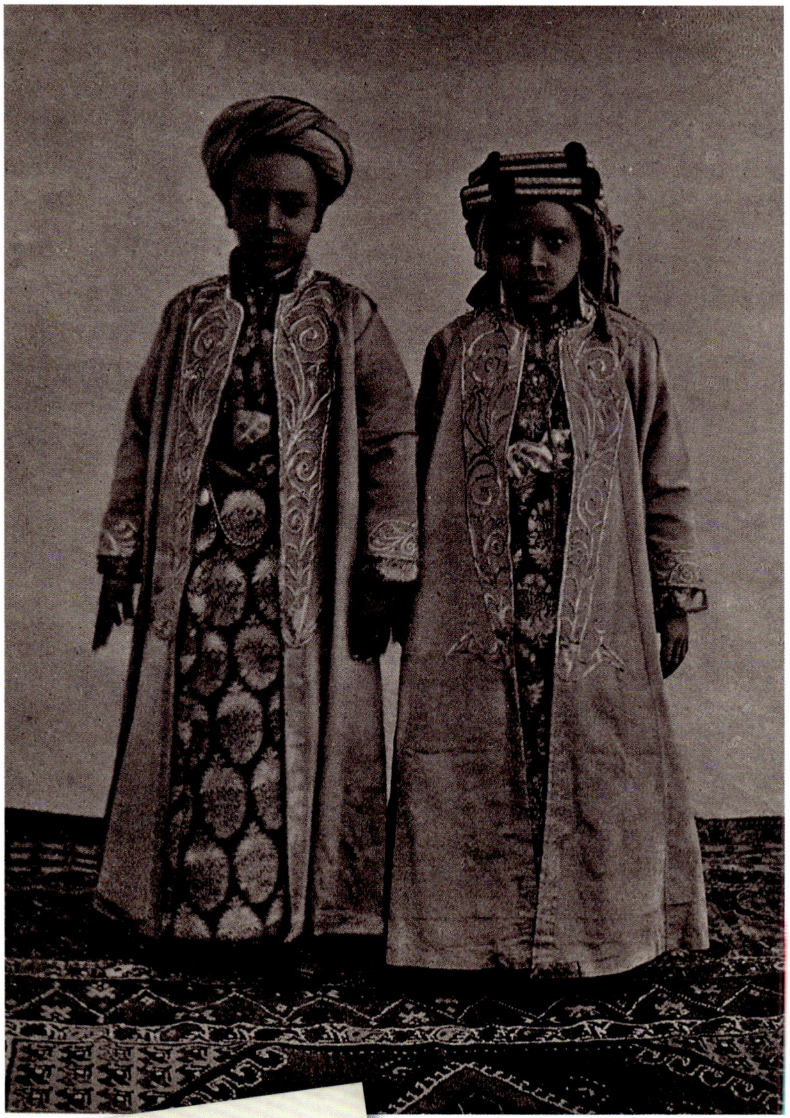

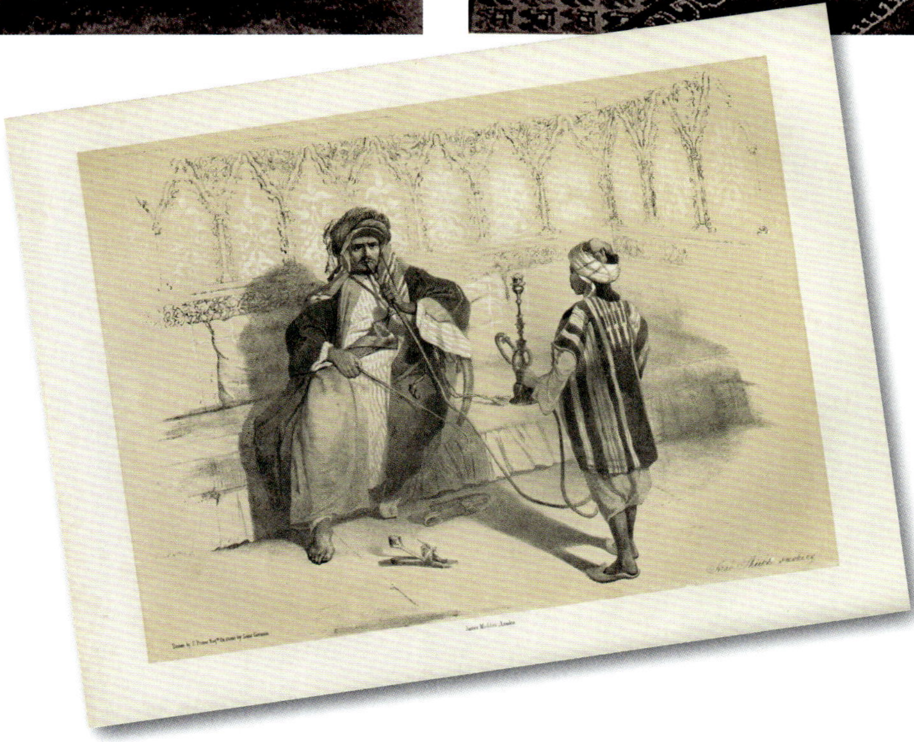

Émile Prisse d'Avennes
Arab Sheikh from the coast of the Red Sea, 1851
Color lithograph
Courtesy of the New York Public Library

John Keane, in *Six months in the Hijaz, Journeys to Makkah and Madinah 1877–1878*, recounted how, in Mecca, he became "*very fond of the hookah; the smoke passes through a chamber full of water which takes up the more solid particles and condenses the steam from the tobacco and cools the smoke, which is always inhaled right into the lungs and has a very soothing effect, though somewhat painful to a beginner.*"

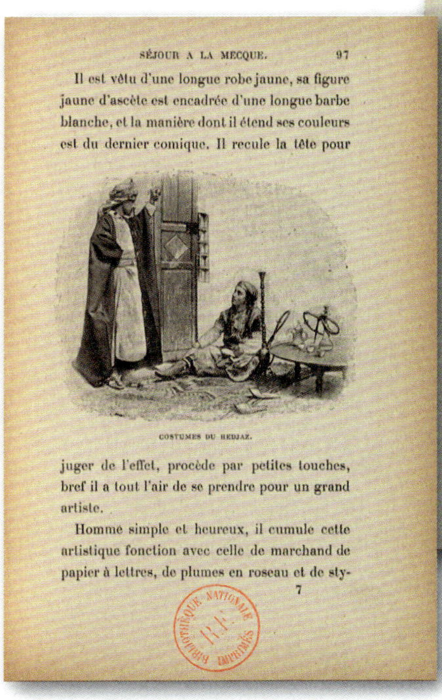
SÉJOUR A LA MECQUE. 97

Il est vêtu d'une longue robe jaune, sa figure jaune d'ascète est encadrée d'une longue barbe blanche, et la manière dont il étend ses couleurs est du dernier comique. Il recule la tête pour

COSTUMES DU HEDJAZ.

juger de l'effet, procède par petites touches, bref il a tout l'air de se prendre pour un grand artiste.

Homme simple et heureux, il cumule cette artistique fonction avec celle de marchand de papier à lettres, de plumes en roseau et de sty-

7

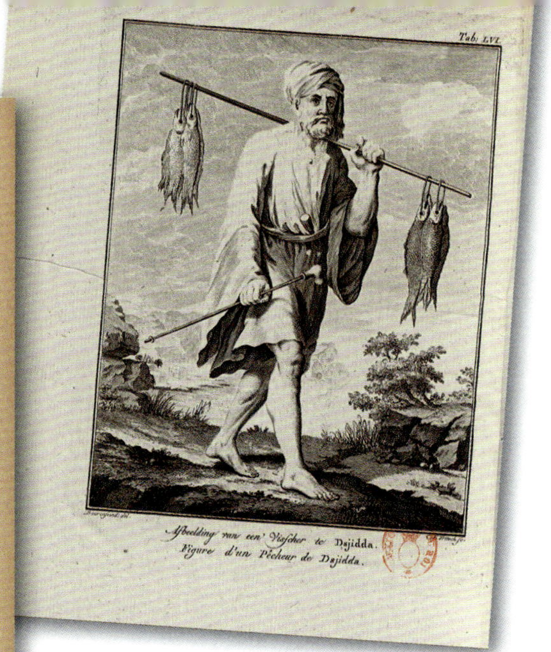

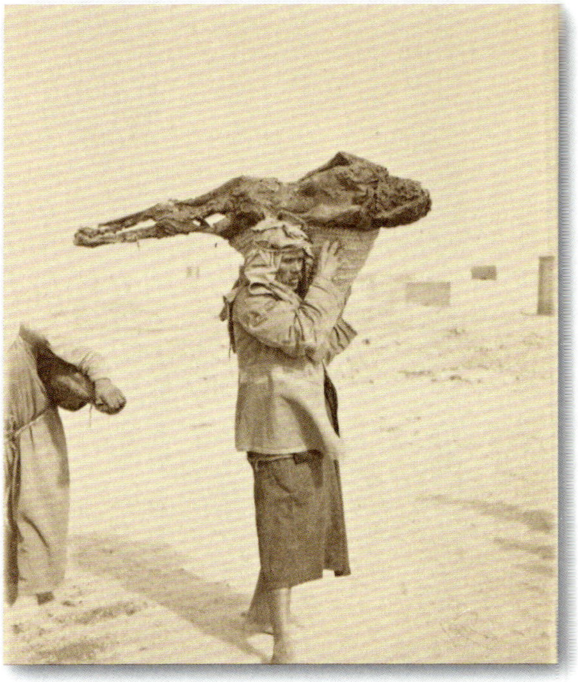

Jules Gervais-Courtellemont
Costumes of Hijaz
From *Mon Voyage à La Mecque*, 1896
Engraving from a photograph by the author
Bibliothèque nationale de France

Henry Rooke, who sojourned in Jeddah for a brief period in 1782, described the way of life of its people in *Travels to the Coast of Arabia Felix*: "*They sit cross-legged at the ground on their meals, wash, pray, drink coffee, and smoke hookah five times in the day.*"

Georg Wilhelm Baurenfeind
Portrayal of fishmonger in Jeddah, 1762
From *Voyage en Arabie*, Niebuhr, 1776
Engraving
19 × 29 cm
Amsterdam: S. J. Baalde, J. Van Schoonhoven
Bibliothèque nationale de France

Baurenfeind was a member of the Danish expedition to Arabia. Carsten Niebuhr, the only survivor of this expedition, published the narrative of the voyage between 1774 and 1778 in which this engraving is reproduced. Niebuhr wrote about Jeddah "*many of the poorer people are employed in fishing, by which they seem to earn but a scanty living*". In his *Bibliotheca historica* (Library of History), Diodorus Siculus of Sicily wrote that in Jeddah, when the flood tide of the sea sweeps over the land, it carries with it an incredible multitude of fish of every kind. "*The women and children seize the smaller fish which are near the shore, and the men of bodily vigour lay hands upon the fish which are hard to overcome because of their enormous size. […] They bake the fish upon the rocks which are red-hot because of the very great heat. They leave the fish there for only a short time and then turn them over, and then, they shake them. The meat, which has become tender because of the warmth, falls away.*"

Postcard
Meat carrier in Hijaz
Printed from a photograph by Muhammad Ali Sa'udi
Nasser D. Khalili Collection of Islamic art, London

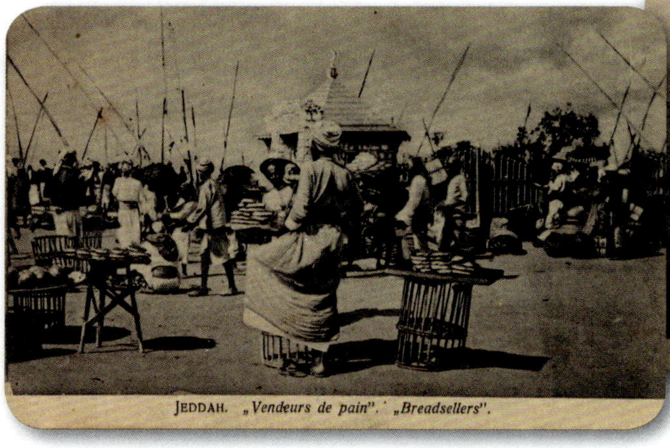

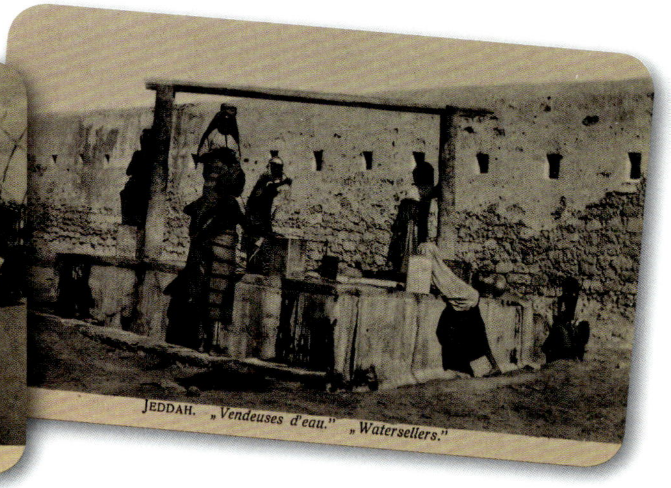

Postcard
Bread sellers in Jeddah
Nasser D. Khalili Collection of Islamic art, London

Lord Valentia undertook a mission to explore the west coast of the Red Sea. He stayed in Jeddah between the end of 1805 and the beginning of 1806. In his *Voyages*, he described the bread he ate in Jeddah in his host's house, a rich Jeddah merchant, as being "*in small cakes, but very good. Jelani [his host] gave us some of a finer sort, it was a little perfumed with carraway seed…*"

Postcard
Water sellers in Jeddah
Nasser D. Khalili Collection of Islamic art, London

Most of the travelers and writers of different origins who visited Jeddah from all times wrote about the scarcity of fresh water in the city and that it had to be fetched from outside on camelbacks. Ibn Battuta, who performed the pilgrimage several times between 1325 and 1354, and visited Jeddah, wrote in his *Travels* that outside "*there are antique cisterns, and in it are pits for water, bored in the solid rock. […] This year was one of little water, so water was brought to Jeddah from the distance of a day's journey, and the pilgrims used to beg for water from the owners of the houses.*"

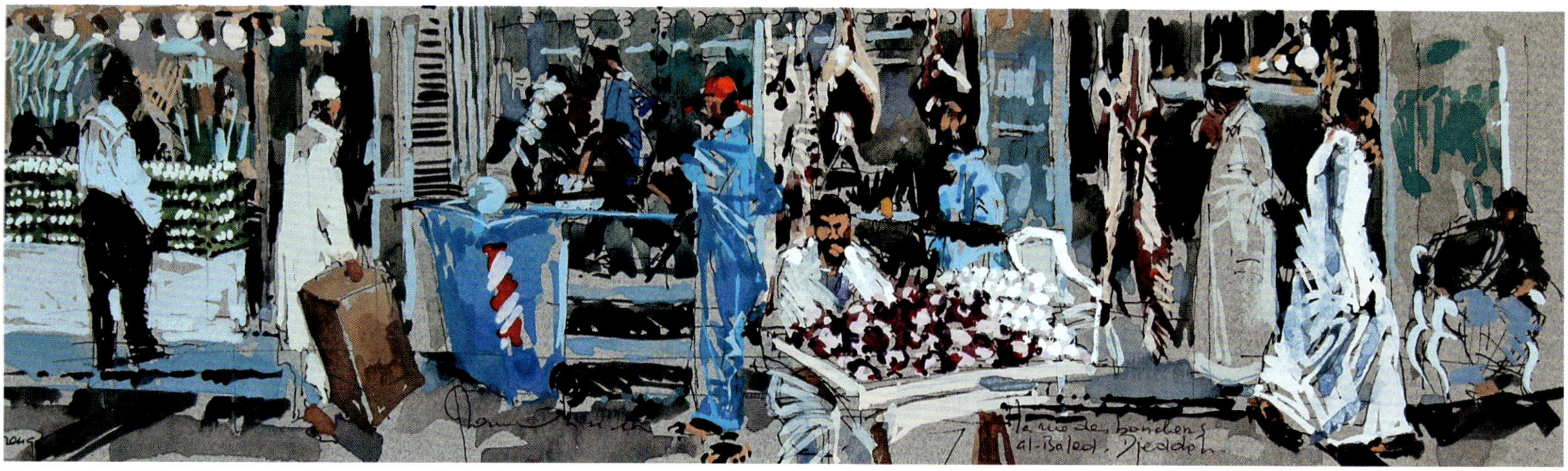

Ronan Olier
Butcher's Street in Jeddah's downtown, 2010
Gouache on paper
15 × 50 cm
Courtesy of the artist

Doughty wrote in *Travels in Arabia Deserta: "We see in the Arabs' life that those which need most are of most hospitality. Famine is ever in the desert, it is therefore in men's eyes a noble magnanimity to set meat before the wayfaring man."*

which they fasten upon their forehead: when they go abroad, they put over all this a large muslin veil that covers their head, face, neck, and shoulders, and falls down below their girdle."

A man who is lucky to encounter these delightfully garbed women will also have "his brain suffused with the perfumes of musk and ambergris and civet," stated Çelebi, who observed with a certain astonishment that in Mecca, "the men are in thrall to their wives: whatever their wives tell them to do, they do!" One hundred fifty years later, traveler Ali Bey, a self-styled Abbasid prince, commented in turn: "The women enjoy more liberty at Mecca than in any other Mussulman city."

Swiss explorer Johann Ludwig Burckhardt, the discoverer of Petra and a contemporary of Ali Bey El Abbassi, also registered his observations as "The women of Mecca dress in Indian silk gowns, and very large blue striped trowsers, reaching down to the ankles, and embroidered below with silver thread; over these they wear a blue and white striped silk *mellaye* of Indian manufacture. The face is concealed by a white or light blue *borko*; on the head, they wear a cap around which a piece of coloured muslin is tightly twisted in folds [...]; they have, at least, one string of sequins tied round it; many have gold necklaces, bracelets and silver ankle-rings." Carsten Niebuhr, the sole survivor of the famous Danish expedition, penned his impressions of the face covered by the veil as "The circle of the eyes, and even the eye-lashes, they paint black, with a preparation of lead called *kochhel*. They stain their hands and

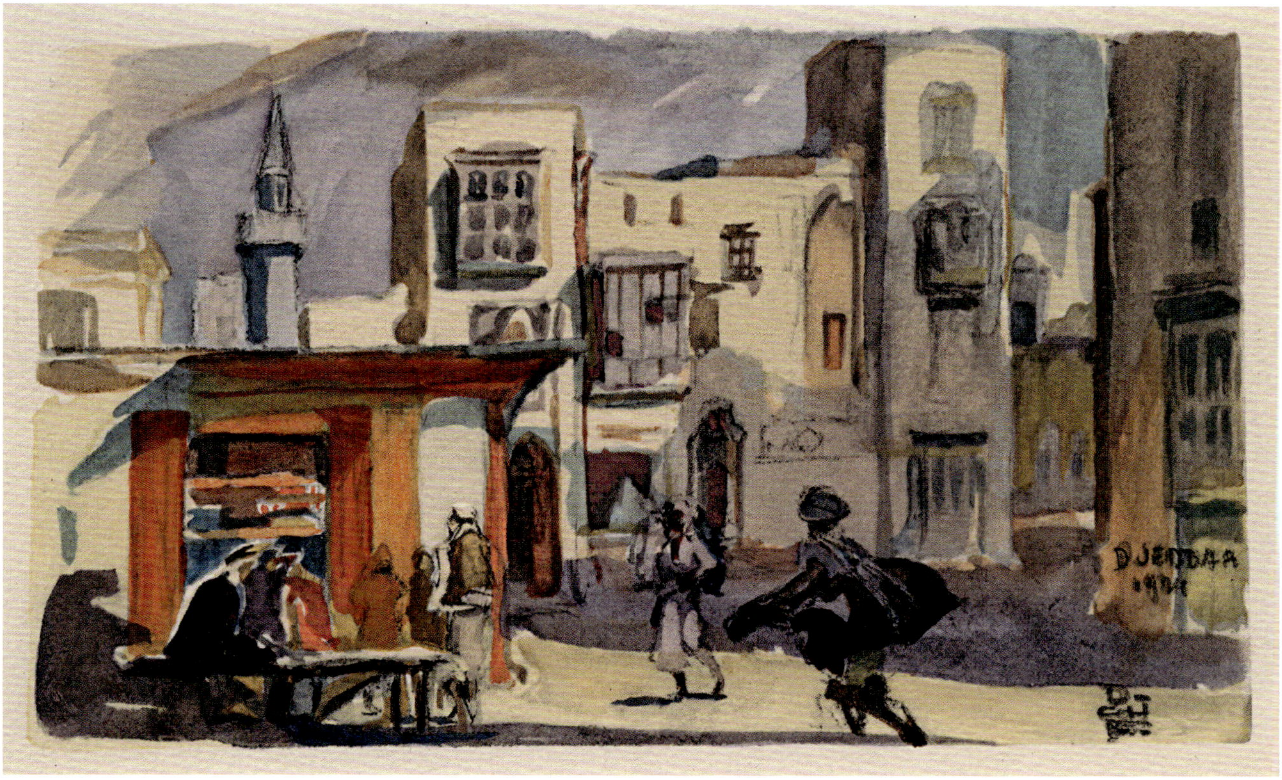

Charles Dominique Fouqueray
Square in Jeddah with a water-carrier, 1921
Lithograph
11 × 18.5 cm
From *Escales d'Asie*, Claude Farrère
Laborey, Paris, 1947
Courtesy of the Musée national de la Marine/A. Fux

Charles Jacques Poncet spent several weeks in Jeddah in 1700. In *The Red Sea and Adjacent Countries at the close of the Seventeenth Century as described by Joseph Pitts, William Daniel and Charles Jacques Poncet*, Sir William Foster wrote that Poncet noted: *"Everything is dear at Jeddah, even as much as water. One pint of water, of our measure of Paris, wou'd cost two pence or three pence, because 'tis brought four leagues off."*

feet of a brownish yellow colour, with the juice of the plant *el-henne*. They make black punctures in their face to improve their beauty and stain the skin of a brown colour. They fancy that when the whole body is brown, the peculiar darkness of the countenance will escape observation."

At the end of the nineteenth century, French traveler and photographer Jules Gervais-Courtellemont was the only one, it seems, who was not sensitive to these feminine charms. He said, "The women of Mecca have the most unsightly costume that can be imagined. On the street, their silhouette resembles that of the sort of grasshoppers that we call the praying mantis. [...] A dark veil that often falls as far as the knees hangs from their strange headdress to complete their resemblance to the ridiculous insect with which I must compare them," he wrote sourly, nevertheless adding "In all fairness, I must however say that this unattractive appearance must often conceal some very beautiful ladies."

In Mecca, weddings are celebrated when pilgrims have left the city. "In the month of *Moharram*, as soon as the Hajj is over, and the greatest part of the pilgrims have departed, it is customary to celebrate marriage," Burckhardt reported. He specified that these ceremonies were conducted "in a very splendid style" and that they involved considerable expense: "A man that has not more than three hundred dollars to spend in the year will then throw away half the sum in the marriage of his child."

On these occasions, "rich clothes and furniture are displayed," continued the Swiss traveler. "The feasting is sumptuous, and often lasts for three or four days." Burckhardt knew that "the price paid for virgins among the respectable classes, in Mecca varies from forty to three hundred hard piastres," he noted. "Half the sum only is usually paid down; the other half is left in possession of the husband, who pays it in case he should divorce his wife."

"On settling a marriage," he continued, "the money to be paid for the bride is carried in procession from the house of the bridegroom to that of the girl's father; it is borne through the streets upon two tabourets, wrapped up in a rich handkerchief, and covered with an embroidered satin stuff." In Mecca, he added, "Weddings are attended by professional females, who sing and dance; they have, it is said, good voices, and are not of that dissolute class to which the public singers and dancers belong in Syria and Egypt."

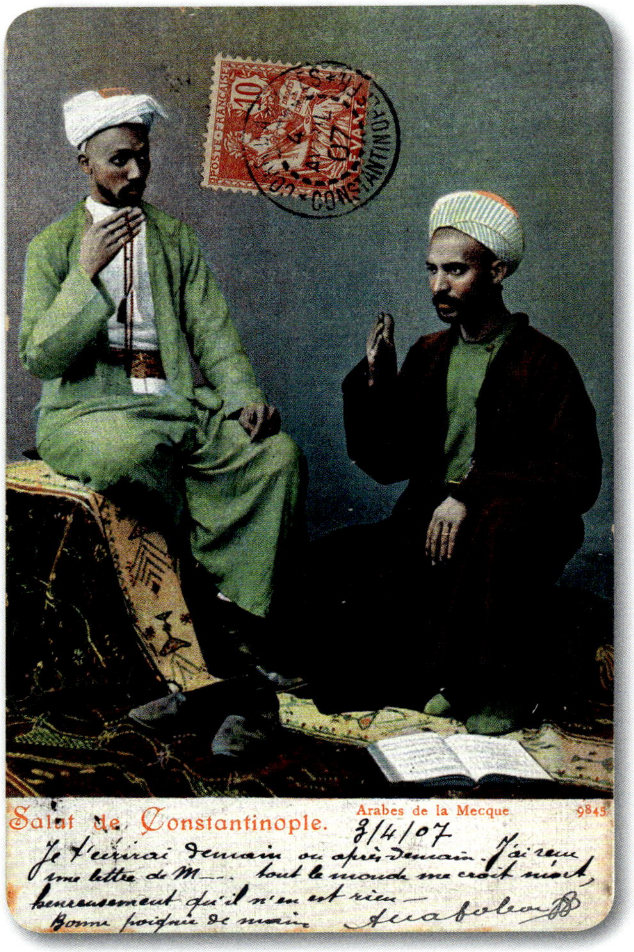

Postcard
Arabs from Mecca
Nasser D. Khalili Collection of Islamic Art, London
Autograph postcard inscribed in French and dated 3/4/1907. The postcard reads: "*I will write to you tomorrow or after tomorrow. I received a letter from Mr. …everyone thinks I died, fortunately this is not the case. Warm handshake.*"

Joseph Pitts, who traveled to Mecca in the late seventeenth century, described the religious men there as "*leading a devout life devoted to reading and studying. They wear a white woollen garment, and a long woollen cap, with a sheep or a goat-skin on their back to lie on. When they read they usually sit down, putting their legs across, and keeping their knees above the ground. They carry their beads about their arms or necks, while others carry them in their pockets.*"

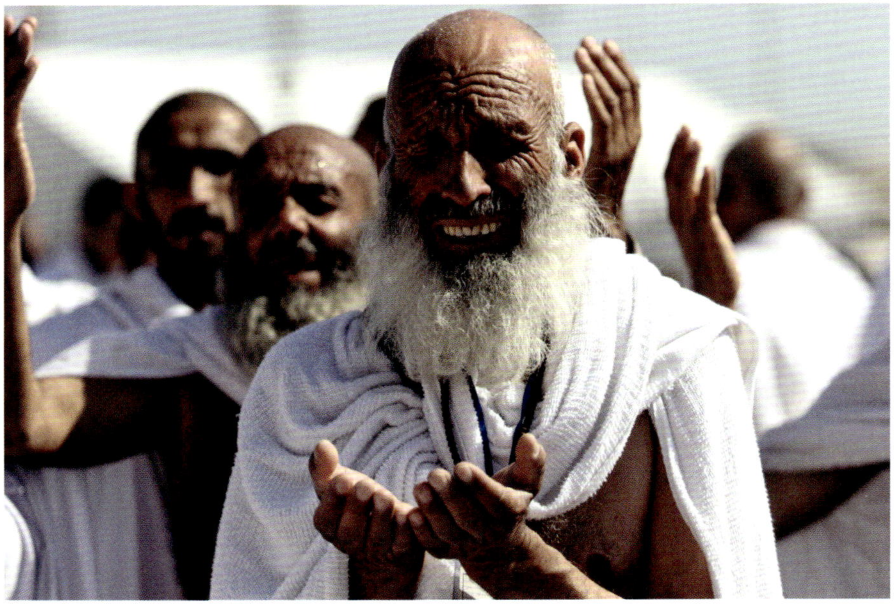

Newsha Tavakolian
An old man cries as he prays at Mount Arafat, 2008
Courtesy of the artist

Joseph Pitts was so moved when he arrived in Arafat. He wrote: "*It was a sight indeed, able to pierce one's heart, to behold so many thousands in their garments of humility and mortification, with their naked heads, and cheeks watered with tears; and to hear their grievous sighs and sobs, begging earnestly for the remission of their sins, promising newness of life, using a form of penitential expression, and thus continuing for the space of four or five hours.*"

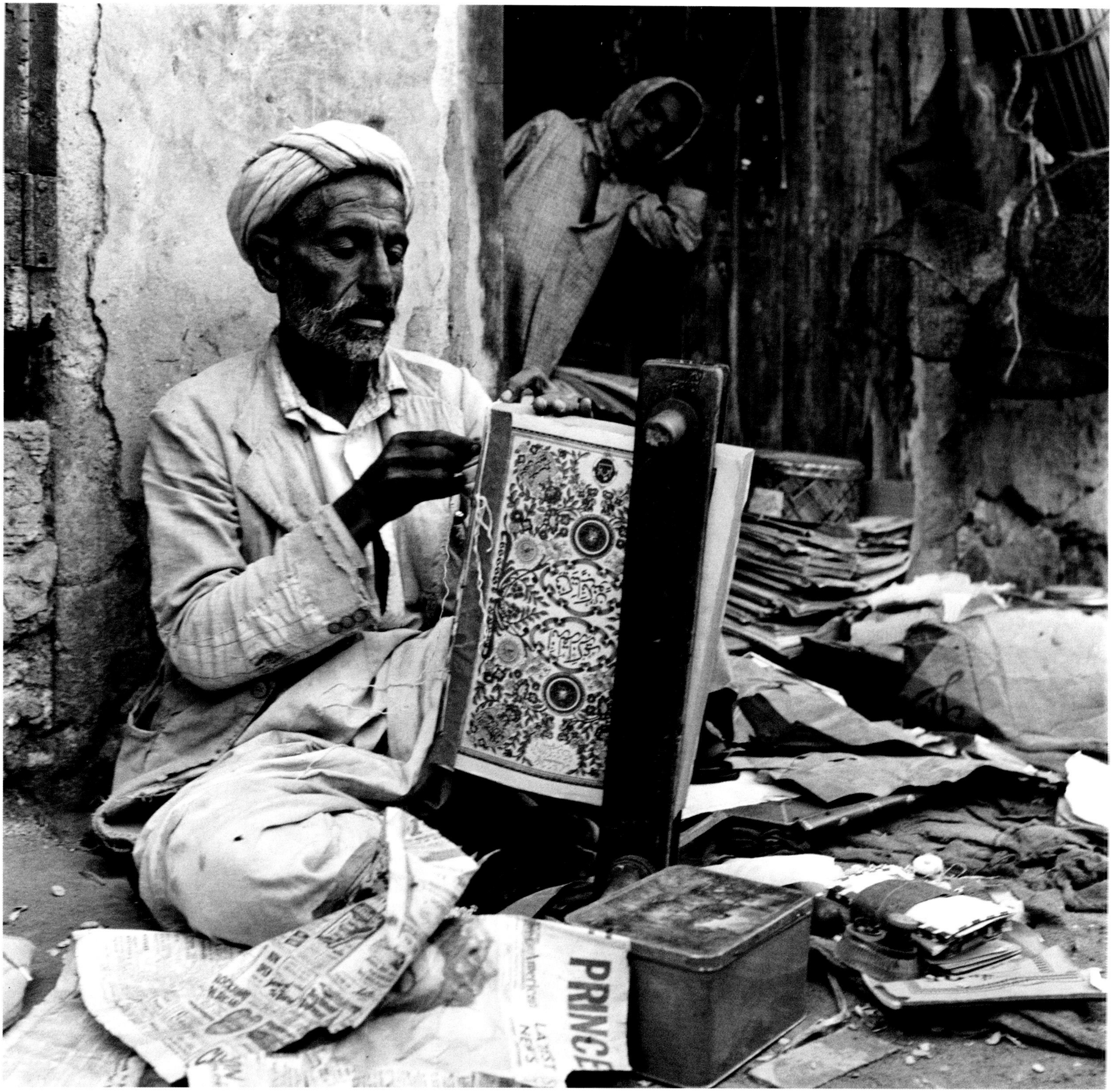

Ilo Battigelli
A binder of Korans, forties–fifties
Courtesy of Pitt Rivers Museum,
University of Oxford

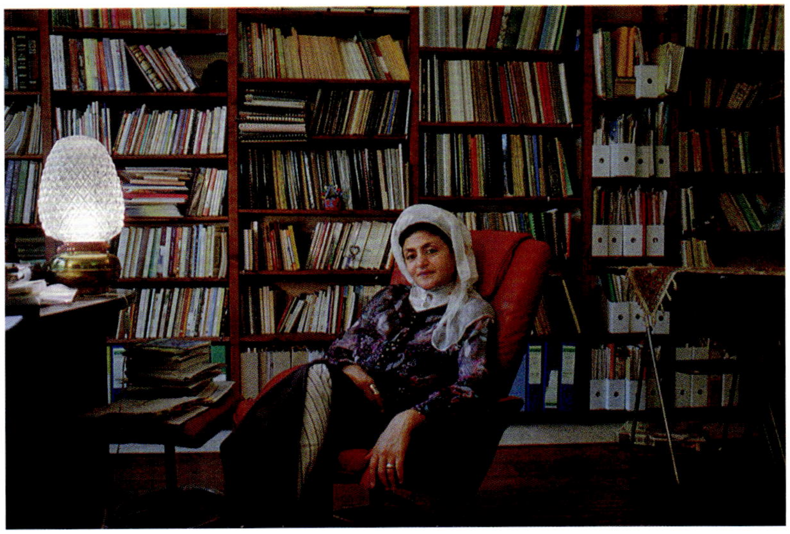

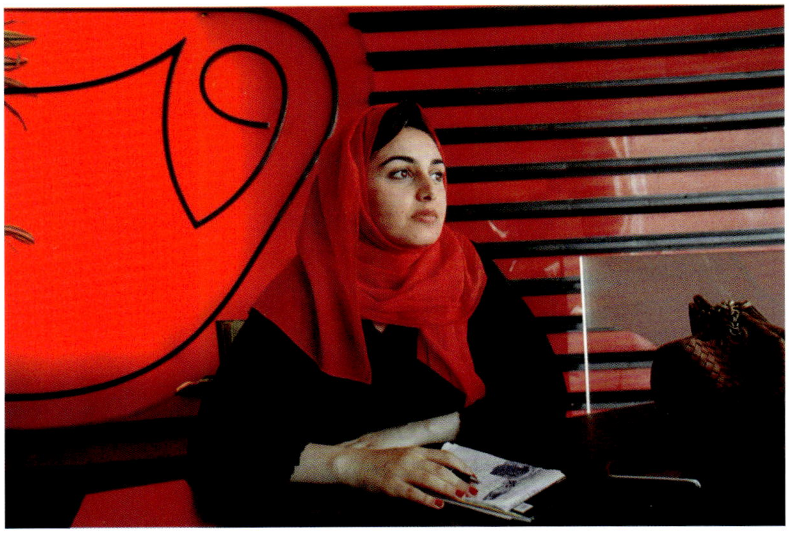

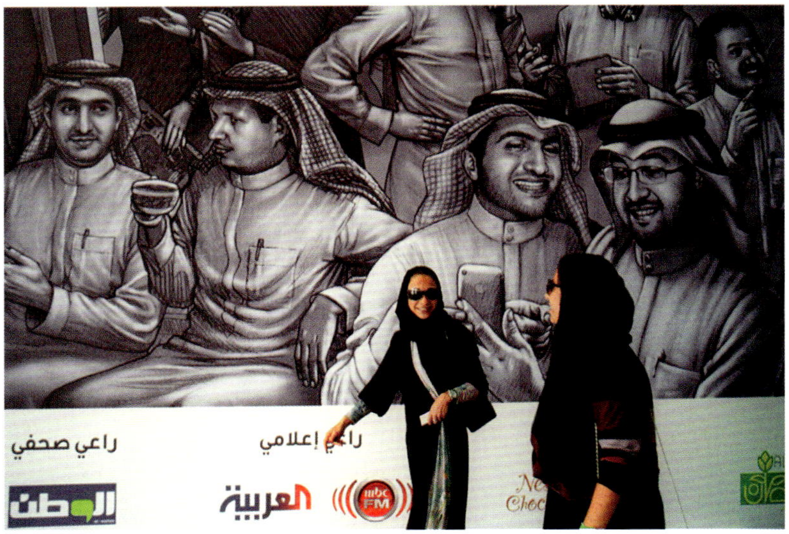

Isabelle Eshraghi
Columnist and associate professor in history Hatoon Al-Fassi dressed in the traditional Meccan style, November 2008
Courtesy of the artist

Isabelle Eshraghi
Maha Taher, co-founder and chairwoman of the board of the "Young Initiative Group," October 2010
Courtesy of the artist

Isabelle Eshraghi
Saudi women in front of the billboard of "The Young Business Expo" in Jeddah's International center for exhibitions, October 2010
Courtesy of the artist

Isabelle Eshraghi
Haifa Mansour, the first Saudi female movie director, January 2011
Courtesy of the artist

In 2012, Haifa Mansour produced *Wajda*, a film in which she praises the courage of a young girl who dreams of owning a bicycle and enters a Koran recitation competition hoping to earn enough money to buy it.

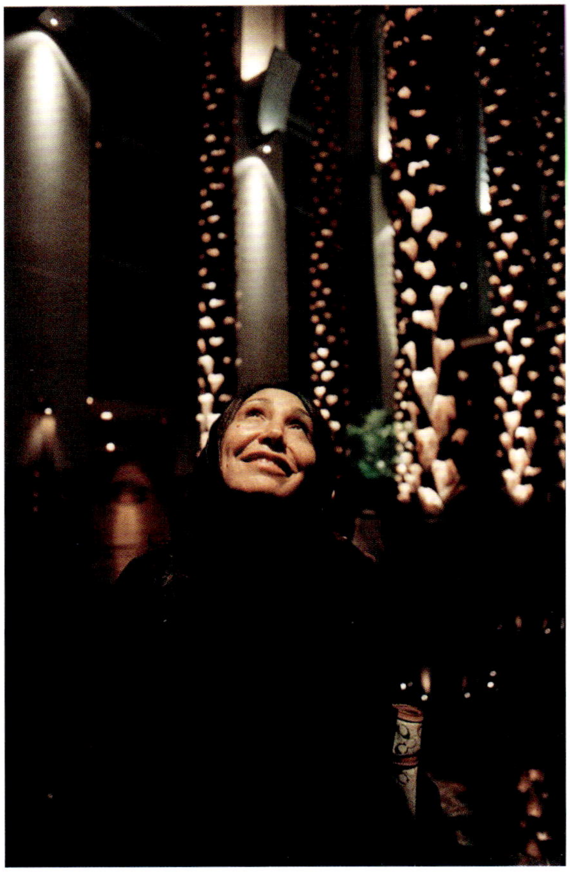

Outside of Mecca things are done very differently. Bedouin women wear simpler attire, as described by Burckhardt: "The ladies' dress is a wide cotton gown of a dark colour, blue, brown, or black; on their heads they wear a kerchief, the young females having it of a red colour; the old, black." Burckhardt added that "the Bedouin ladies half cover their faces with a dark-coloured veil which is so tied as to conceal the chin and mouth." In any case, he assured that "their features are good, their persons extremely well formed."

The women of Hijaz like to wear their hair in plaits, notes Burckhardt, "women's hair-dress varies in almost every tribe," as was also the case of the different tattoos that they make and may appear on their faces—lips, temples, cheeks or forehead—on the bust, the arms, ankles, and feet, depending on the tribe they belonged to.

"The male Bedouins care little about their own appearance," he added, "but love to decorate their wives." Burckhardt said: "All Bedouin women are fond of ear-rings, nose-rings, finger-rings, ankle-rings, and bracelets. The poor have their ornaments made of horn: some wear common glass beads; but the richer use articles of silver, amber, coral, or mother-of-pearl."

The following observation is found among the many remarks made by Louis d'Arvieux during his several months stay in a Bedouin camp during the second half of the seventeenth century: "As the Arabs have no manner of conversation with any women, old or young, but their own, they cannot possibly be in love but by imagination." In fact, the young men "never come near 'em, nor see 'em even in public but by chance, and at a distance". He continues, "the young women's faces are always cover'd with a veil." Because of those hindrances, "the young men take a fancy for 'em from the usual graces of gait, size, voice, and whatever else they can observe from the outside of their person, as they are passing by," wrote d'Arvieux. What to do in such circumstances? The young men are forced to find "a way of seeing 'em without being seen. They hide themselves in some tent or elsewhere, at places they are to go by, or behind the bushes near some springs; when they come for water; for there they commonly chat with their companions bare-faced," explained d'Arvieux.

Sometimes, these efforts were successful. "When the girls have some inclination for the young fellows that court 'em, they give 'em a sufficient opportunity of seeing 'em, by dropping the corner of the veil which they hold in their teeth, just as they pass by 'em, and catching it up again as quick as possible, as if the

Isabelle Eshraghi
Jeddah United basketball team, 2008
Courtesy of the artist

"Jeddah United" was founded in 2003 by Leena Al-Maeenah as a women's basketball team.

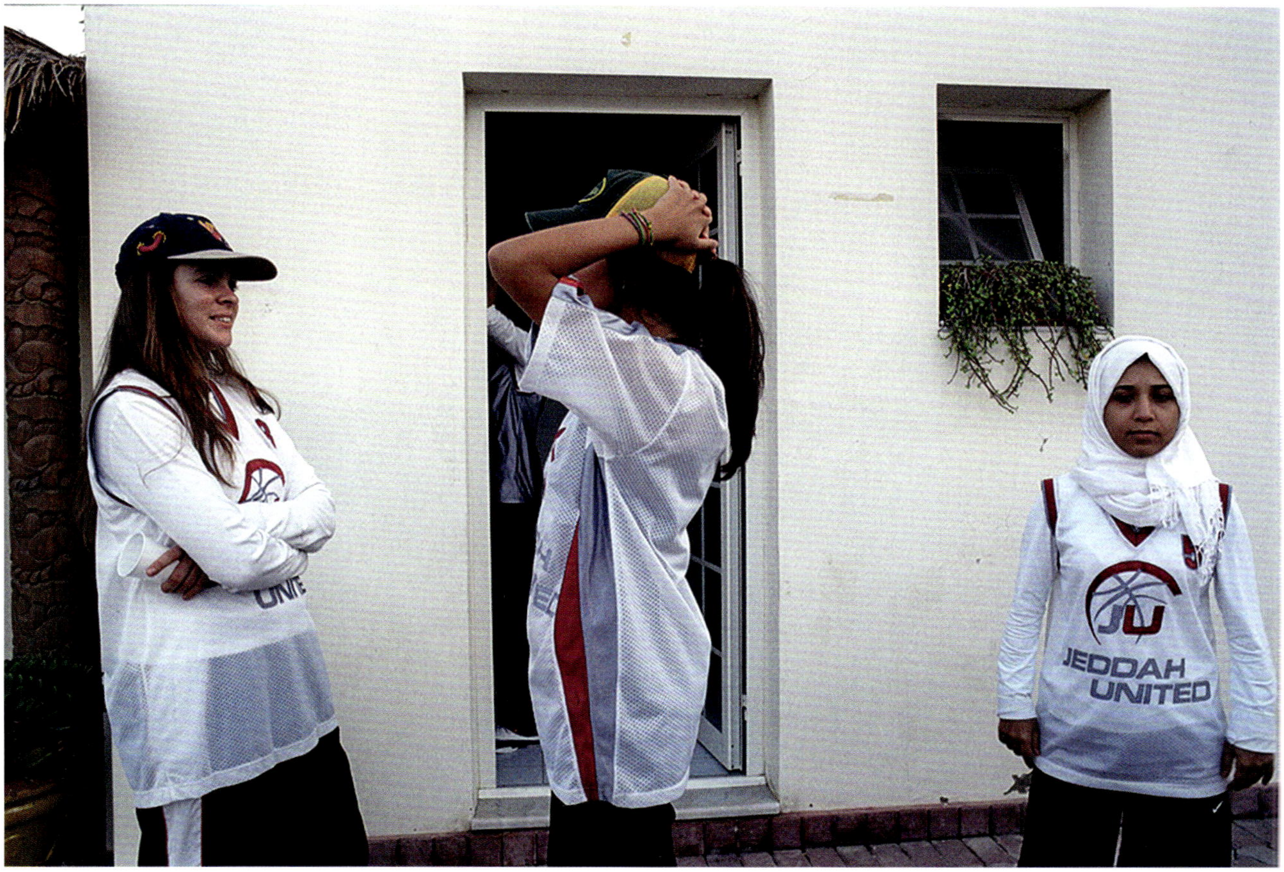

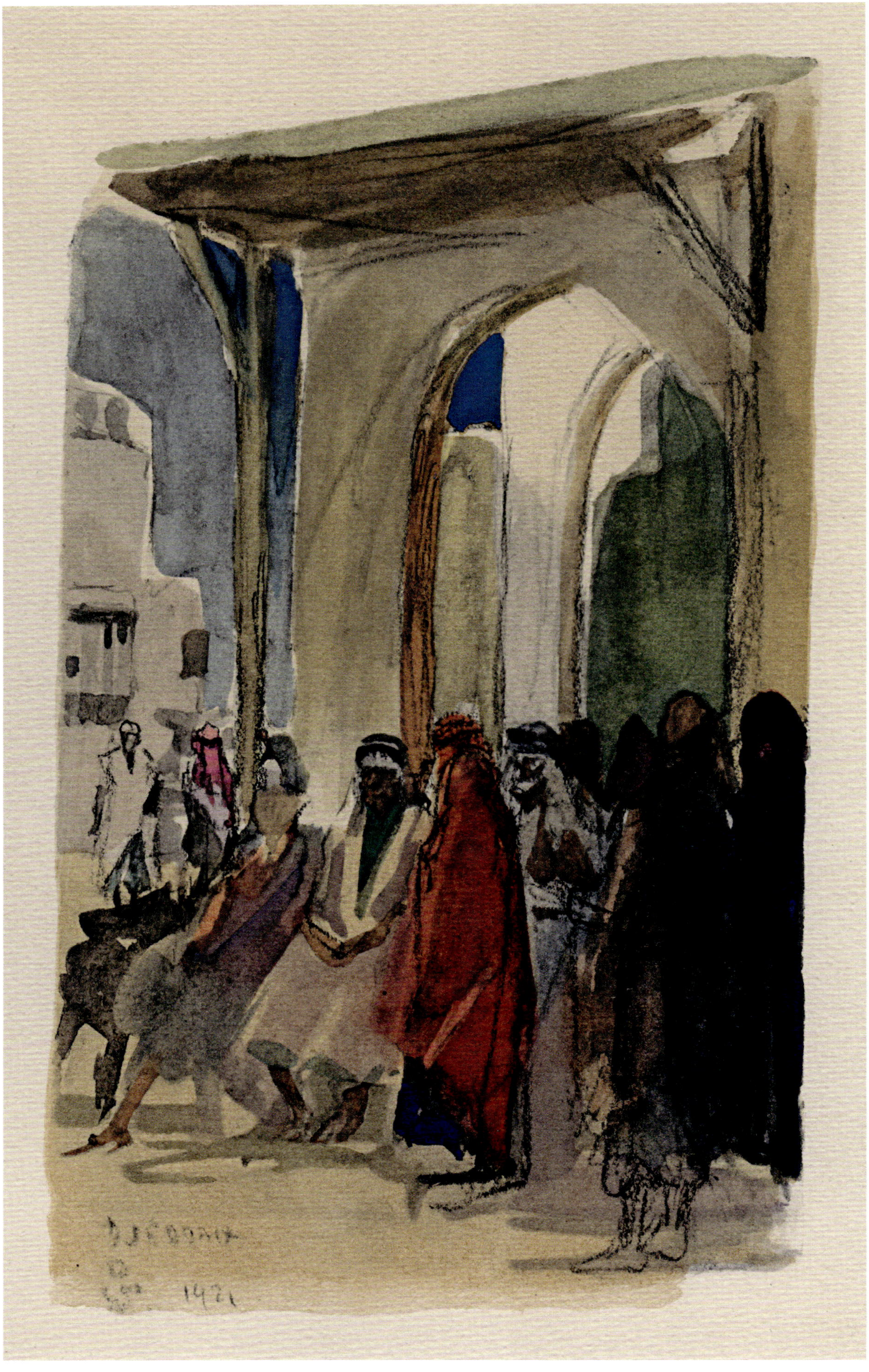

Charles Dominique Fouqueray
Exiting the mosque after the prayer, 1921
Lithograph
21 × 12.5 cm
From *Escales d'Asie*, Claude Farrère
Laborey, Paris, 1947
Courtesy Musée national de la Marine/A. Fux

Maimouna Guerresi
Old Jeddah, 2016–18
Courtesy of the artist

Jeddah was and remains the most visited city in Arabia. Ibn al-Mujâwir wrote in *Tarikh al-Mustabsir: "It is a small city on the seashore and it is the port of Mecca; during the pilgrimage season it is impossible to inhabit this city because of the large crowds of people converging on it from the far corners of the world… from Egypt, from the West, from India and from Yemen."*

Maimouna Guerresi
Column, 2016–18
Courtesy of the artist

Yann Gayet
African woman in Jeddah, 2010
From the series *Contresens*
Courtesy of the artist

Yann Gayet
Men's assembly in Jeddah, 2010
From the series *Contresens*
Courtesy of the artist

Thesiger unfairly wrote in *Arabian Sands: "When moved, Arabs break easily into poetry. I have heard a lad spontaneously describe in verse some grazing which he had just found: he was giving natural expression to his feelings. But while they are very sensible of the beauty of their language, they are curiously blind to natural beauty. The colour of the sands, a sunset, the moon reflected in the sea: such things leave them unmoved."*

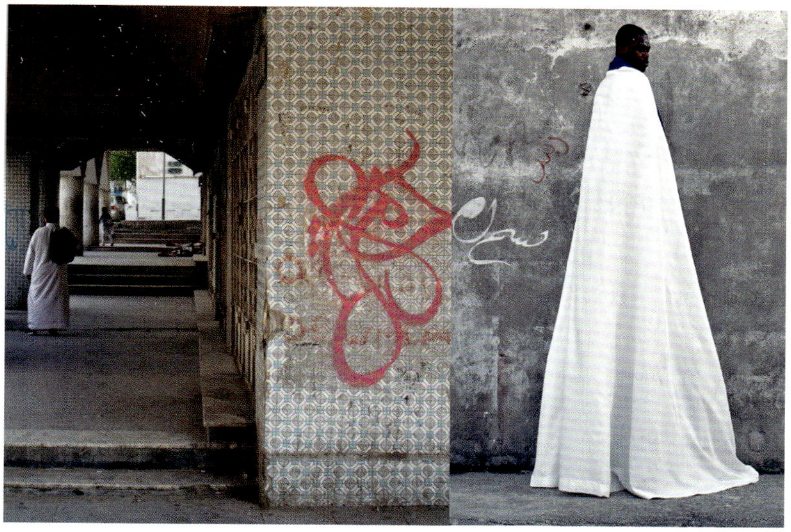

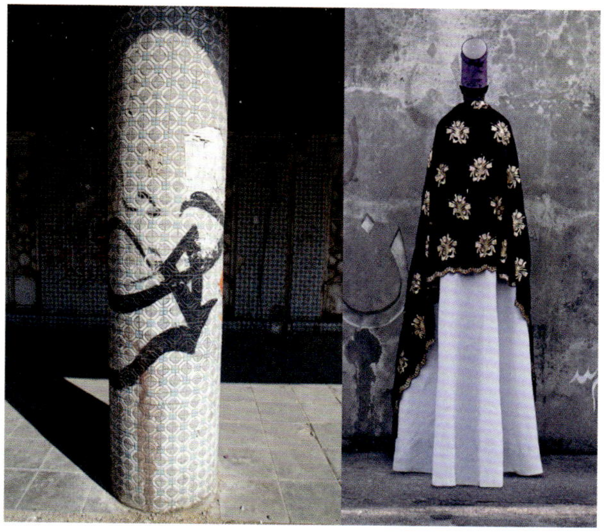

discovery of their face had been from the accidental slip of their veil." Afterwards, if the young man "likes her, he gets some of his relations to ask her father's consent," continued d'Arvieux. "They bargain about the price of the daughter; which the son-in-law is to pay his new father in camels, sheep, or horses," because "the Arabs keep no ready money by 'em".

Afterwards, "they get the contract drawn up by the person the Arabs have chosen among 'em to do the office of *Cadee* or judge," d'Arvieux noted. Regarding this, Carsten Niebuhr also mentioned an occasional usage, not so frequent in general, that allows a father to protect his daughter, especially when rich men "give their daughters to poor young men." In such a case, a father would "even provide his son-in-law with the required sum of the dowry specified in the contract and which will be paid in front of the *cadi* and the witnesses. The marriage is made out by the *cadi* and signed in his presence; and in it not only is the dowry secured to the wife, but also a separate maintenance, in case of a divorce. The wife is then mistress of all property and need not fear a change of situation." Quite often, d'Arvieux confirmed that the Bedouins are "poor folks who can't be at the expense of an instrument, only take witnesses and marry by word-of-mouth, paying upon the spot what was agreed for."

If the future bride is just a simple shepherdess, it may happen that she is not informed of the agreement until the last minute. Burckhardt says, "The young maid comes home in the evening with the cattle. At a short distance from the camp she is met by the future spouse, and a couple of his young friends, and carried off by force to her father's tent. If she entertains any suspicion of their designs, she defends herself with stones, and often inflicts wounds on the young men, even though she does not dislike the lover; for, according to custom, the more she struggles, bites, kicks, cries, and strikes, the more she is applauded even after by her own companions."

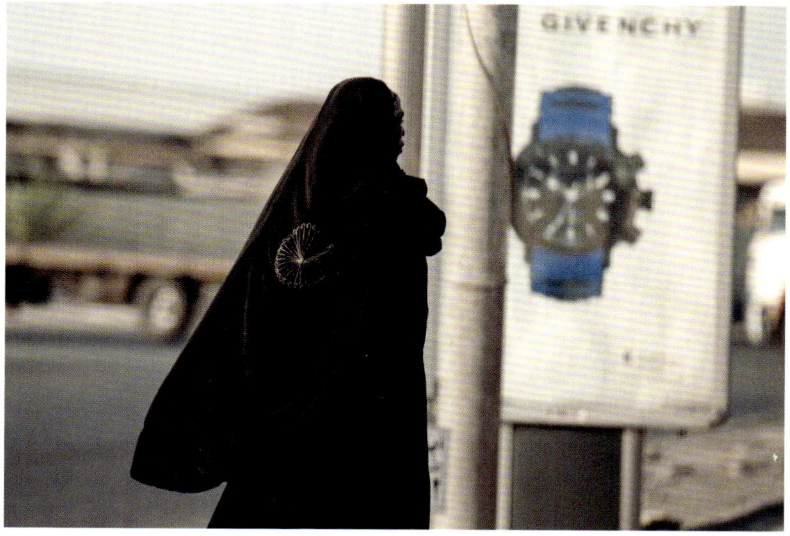

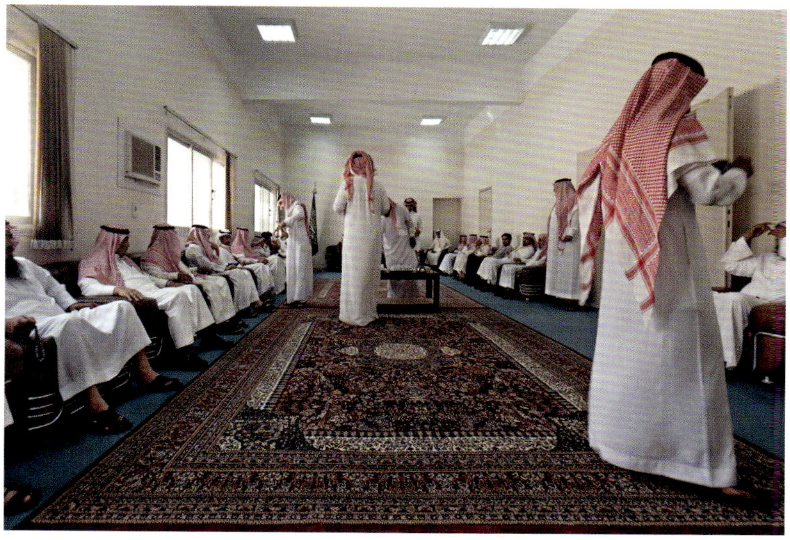

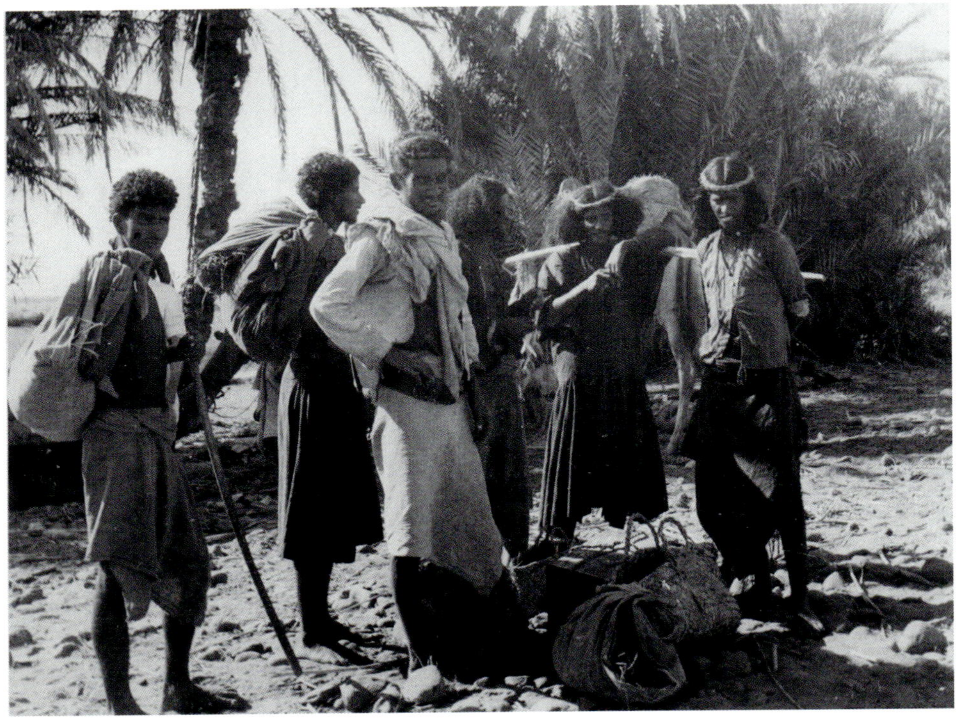

Gerald de Gaury
Asiris, 1942
Courtesy of the Royal Geographic Society, London

For more than 2,000 years, the "flower men" who have been living in the mountainous region of Asir continue today to wear colorful floral garlands in order to look good and smell nice. They also use them for medicinal purposes such as treating headaches.

Thierry Mauger
Flower men of the Tihama region in Saudi Arabia's southwestern Asir province
Courtesy of the artist

A tradition that dates back two millennia, men of this region wear wreaths of dried herbs and flowers on their heads.

Thierry Mauger
Flower men of the Tihama region in Saudi Arabia's Asir province
Courtesy of the artist

Men fetch flowers and herbs such as wild basil from the mountains for their garlands every morning.

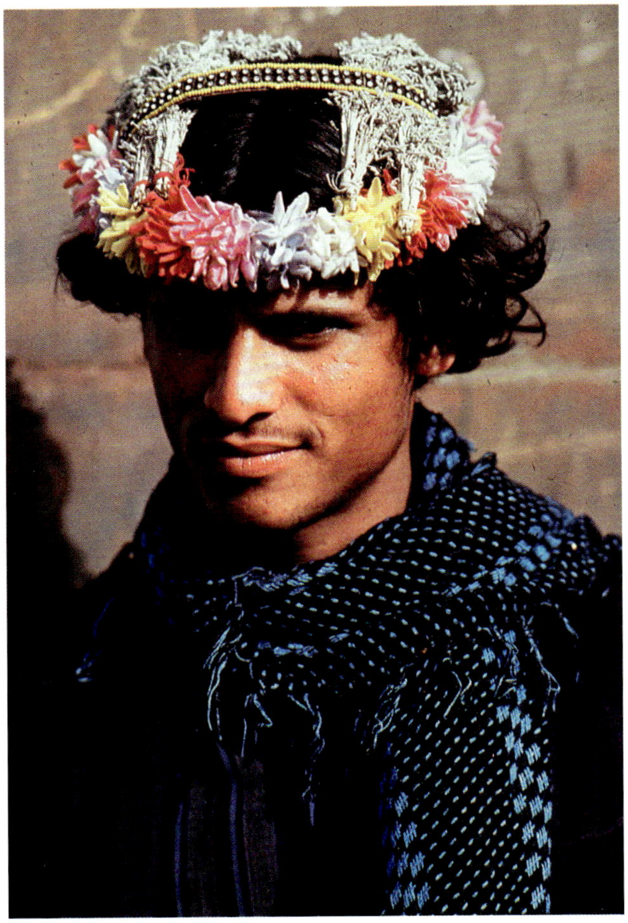

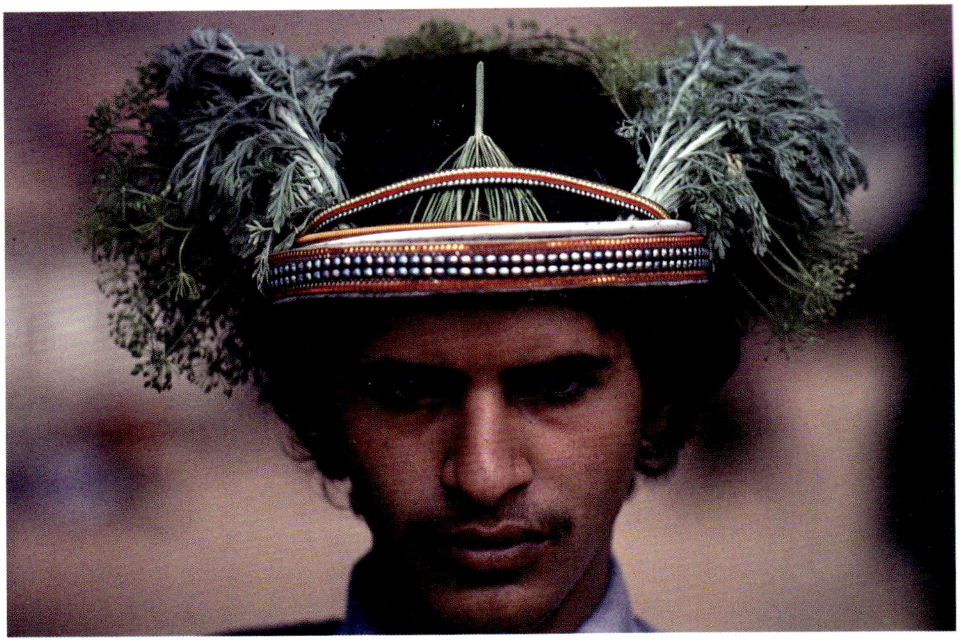

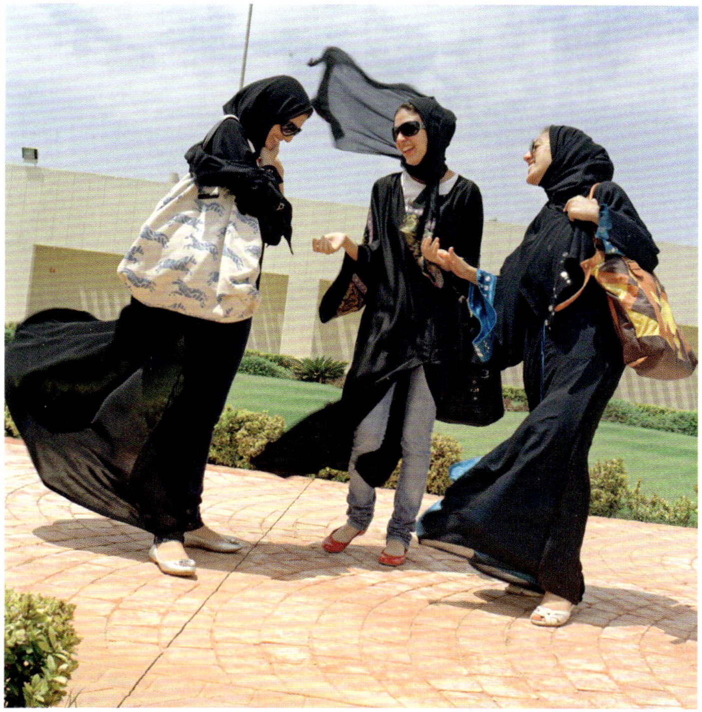

Olivia Arthur
Students at Effat's University for girls in Jeddah, 2009
Courtesy Olivia Arthur / Magnum Photos

Founded in 1999, Effat University is a private institution of higher education for girls in Jeddah.

Ronan Olier
Three Silhouettes, 2010
Sketch
25 × 15 cm
Courtesy of the artist

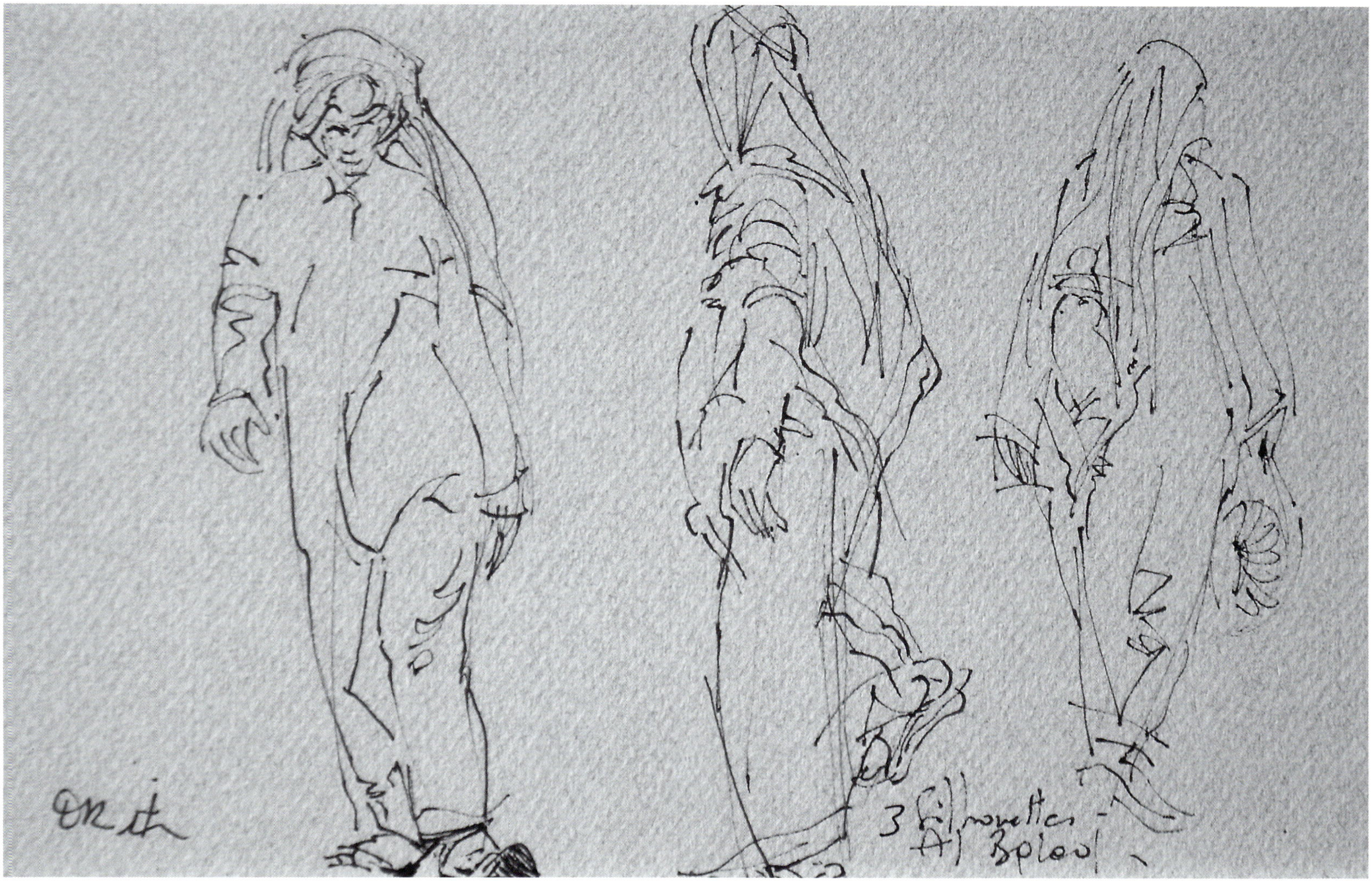

In her father's tent, she is eventually told which of the young men among those who escorted her to the tent wants her for his wife. The women then dress her "in the new clothes provided for her by the bridegroom, and a camel is brought before the tent, ornamented with tassels and shreds of cloth, according to the wealth of the husband. Upon this camel she is mounted, although still continuing to struggle in a most unruly manner, and held by the bridegroom's friends on both sides. Thus she is led three times round his tent," continued Burckhardt. "She is led to the husband's camp, attended by women: during this procession decency obliges her to cry and sob most bitterly."

When the preparations are made with a little more consideration and planning, "the women carry the bride to the first village where there are any hot-baths, where they wash her, put her on her finest clothes and perfume her hair with storax, benjamin, musk, and such other sweets, black the edge of her eyelids and eyebrow, put ground colours upon her face that is already greas'd with essence, upon which they throw gold dust," wrote Louis d'Arvieux, among many other details about the treatment that the women of the tribe reserve for the young bride. "With a certain ink they draw out figures, flowers, fountains, houses, cypress's, antilopes, and other animals upon every part of her body. They dress her up likewise with plain and stone rings and all sorts of gold and silver money according to her quality and circumstances."

"In the meantime," according to Burckhardt, "several sheep have been killed, and the guests who flock to the feast eat bread (for this is a circumstance absolutely necessary on such nuptial occasions) and meat." When the celebrations are conducted with a little more formality, "the men and the women sit down at table in different huts, where they have a wedding entertainment, and receive people's compliments, which are only wishes of a handsome family, abundance of children, and all the happiness and prosperity in the world," notes d'Arvieux. "Men are merry without noise, behaving with great gravity and moderation," while "the women, on the contrary, sing, scream, and tabor it away, bawling out the beauty and advantages of the bride."

Then comes the moment when she is brought into the tent of the "future spouse, who waits for her alone," writes d'Arvieux. "He looks at her as she comes to him without stirring or saying anything to her, nor

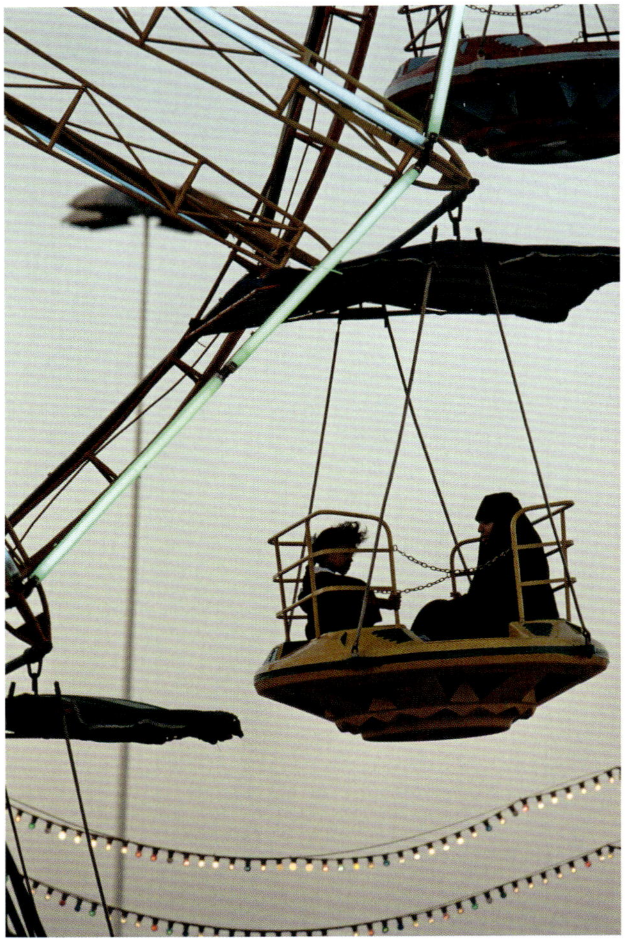

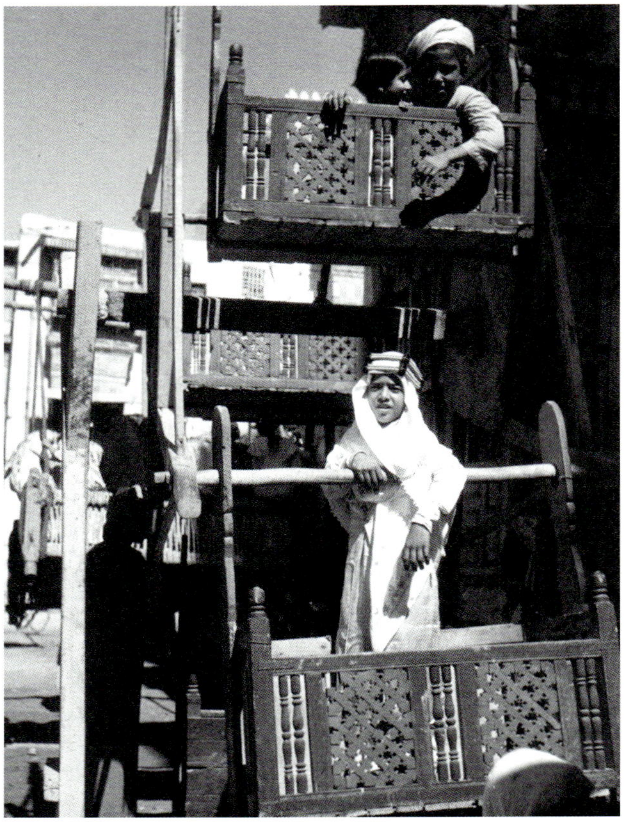

Abbas
Big Wheel in an amusement park in Dhahran, 1990
Courtesy Abbas / Magnum Photos

Gerald de Gaury
The great wheel during holiday in Jeddah, circa 1940s
Courtesy of the Royal Geographic Society, London

The Aid vacation is the occasion for children to go to amusement parks where they spend the money they received as presents from their families.

Roger Grasas
Mecca road in Riyadh
From the series *Min Turab*, 2007–2016
Courtesy of the artist

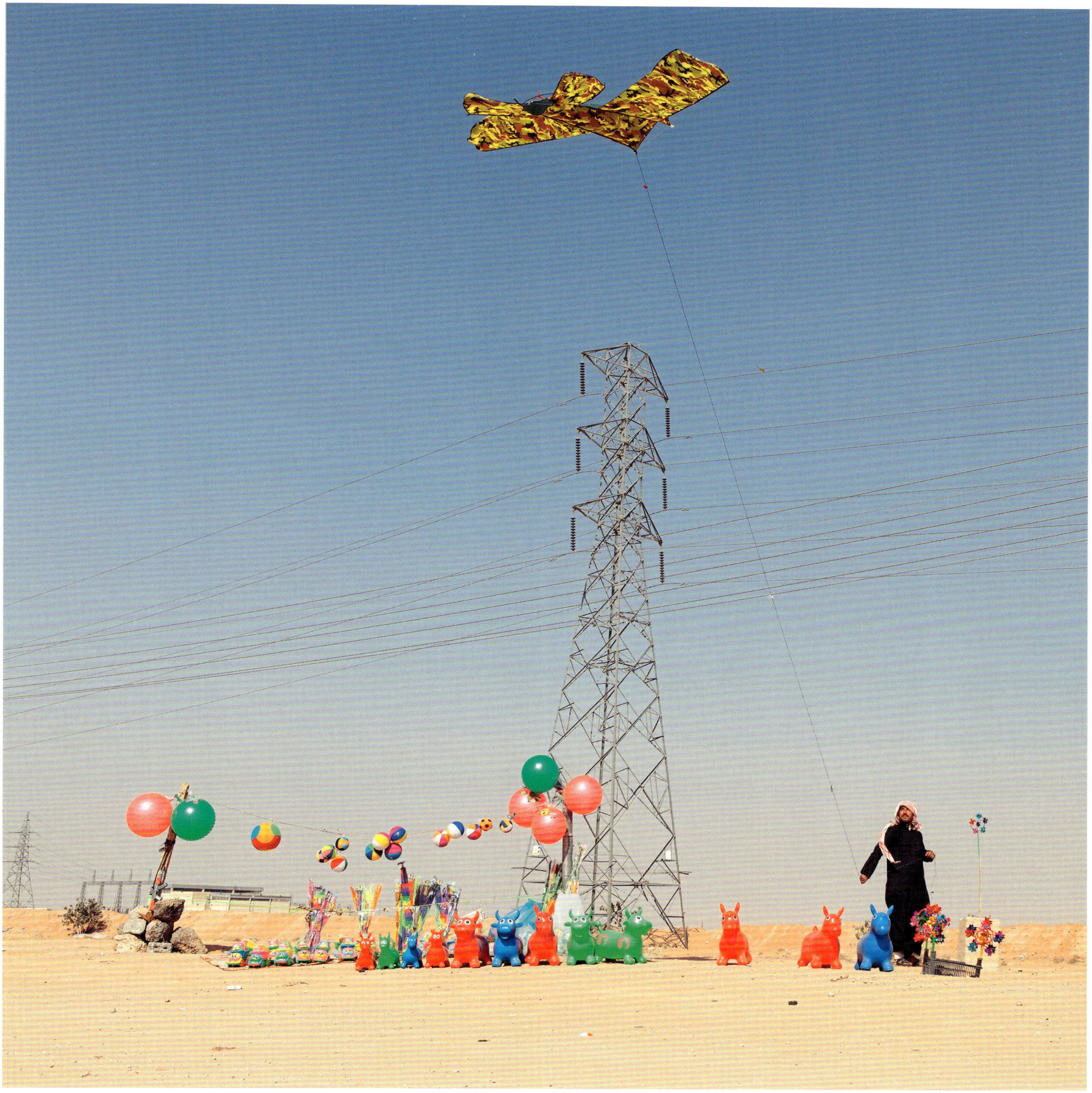

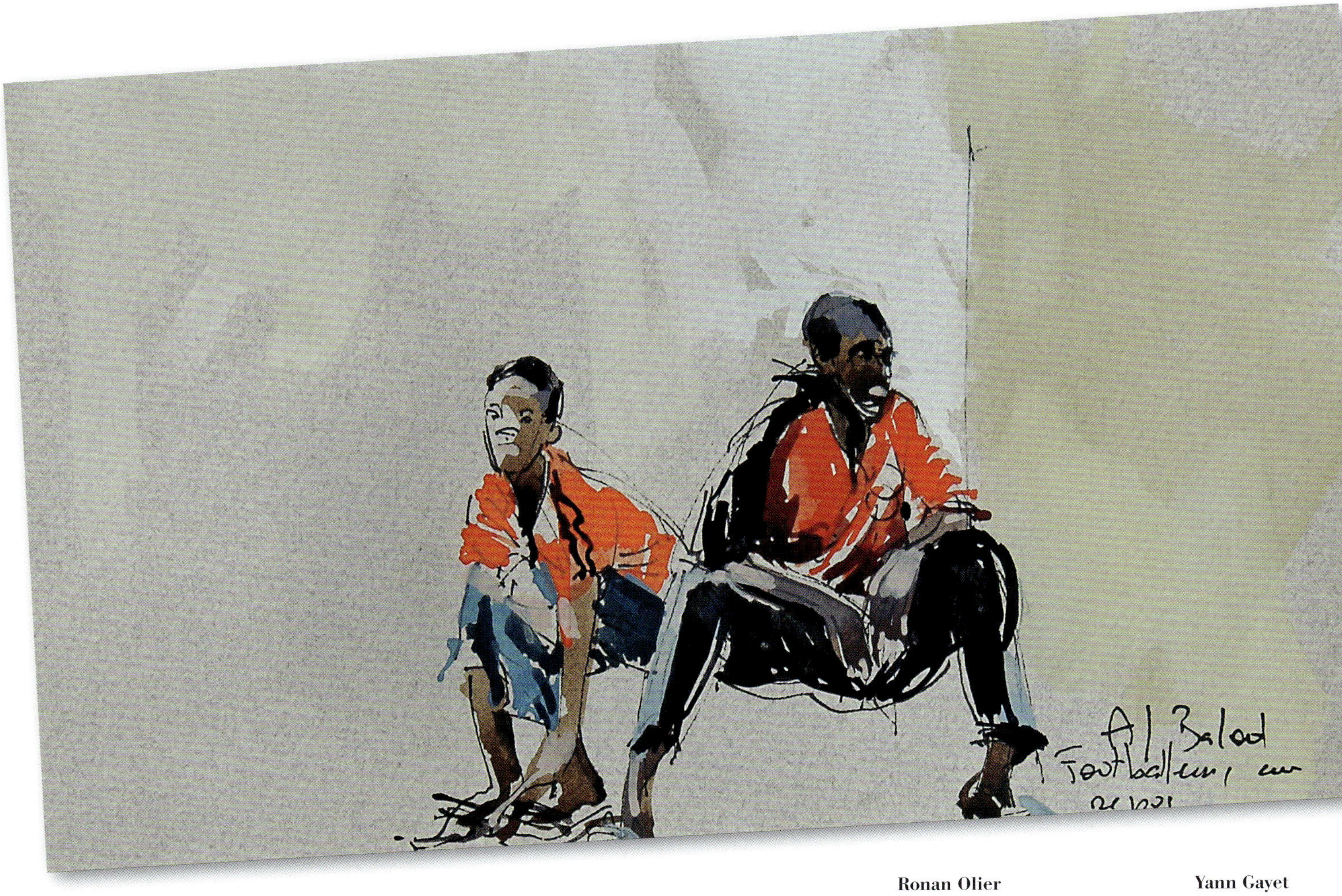

Ronan Olier
Football players at rest, 2010
Gouache
15 × 25 cm
Courtesy of the artist

Yann Gayet
Two Brothers, 2010
From the series *Contresens*
Courtesy of the artist

does she say one word to him." At that same moment, wrote Burckhardt, "the other females assemble before the tent, singing in praise of the young couple." D'Arvieux notes that the future spouse remains "sitting just as he did before with a grave and serious aire and without the least motion, 'till the bride throwing herself at his feet he claps a piece of gold or silver upon her forehead," as d'Arvieux noted.

"This ceremony," he continued, "is over'd three times that very evening; and as they change the bride's [clothes] they present her to the bridegroom, who receives her in the same manner and with the same gravity." D'Arvieux described this particular ceremony as "a kind of magnificence in the East to undress the bride frequently, and to dress her in one day in all the cloaths that have been made for her for her wedding," and "the women at the feast make it their diversion." The decisive moment arrives. Around the third time when "the bride is presented, the bridegroom rises, embraces her, and carries her himself to the tent where

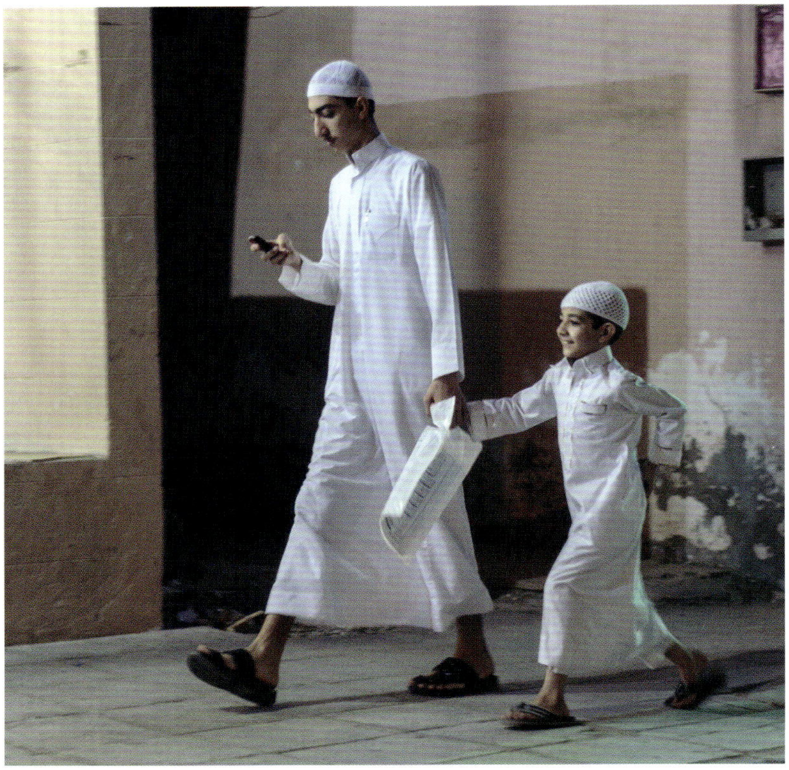

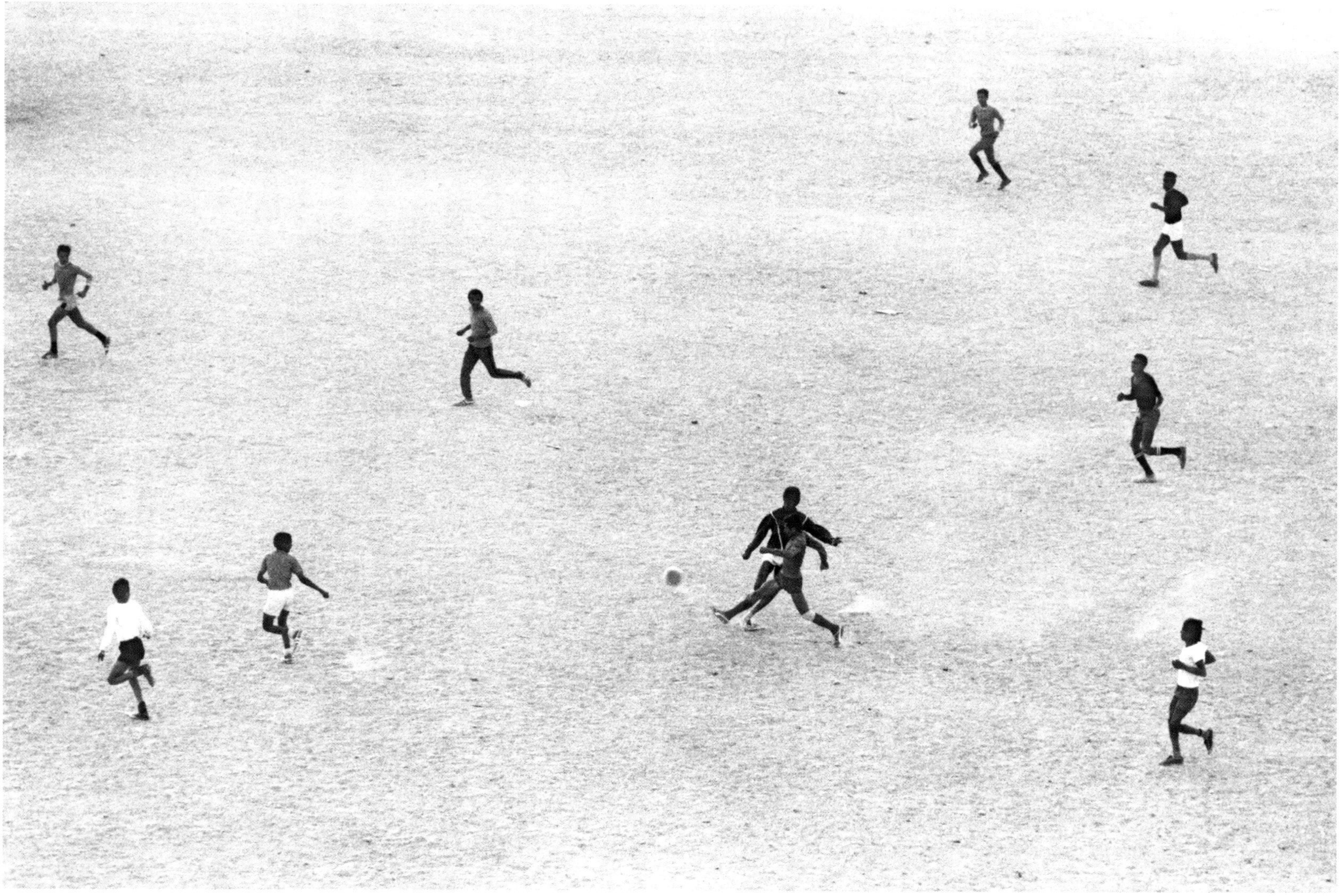

Marc Riboud
Football match in Riyadh, 1974
Courtesy Marc Riboud / Magnum Photos

they are to lie. The women leave her then, and let her go with her husband," wrote d'Arvieux.

That is when the marriage is consummated. "On the next morning every father of a family in the encampment brings a goat as a present to the bride; two or three goats are killed," and then "a plentiful dinner" is organized, Burckhardt reported. "The feast," observed d'Arvieux, "lasts all the rest of the day, and afterwards everybody retires home, and the young married couple begin to mind their family affairs."

It can happen—if it be God's will!—that the young bride is not at all satisfied with the destiny that fortune has assigned her. "If the girl has been married wholly against her inclination, she is allowed on the following morning to take shelter in her father's tent," Burckhardt continues, "neither he nor anybody else can prevent her from doing it."

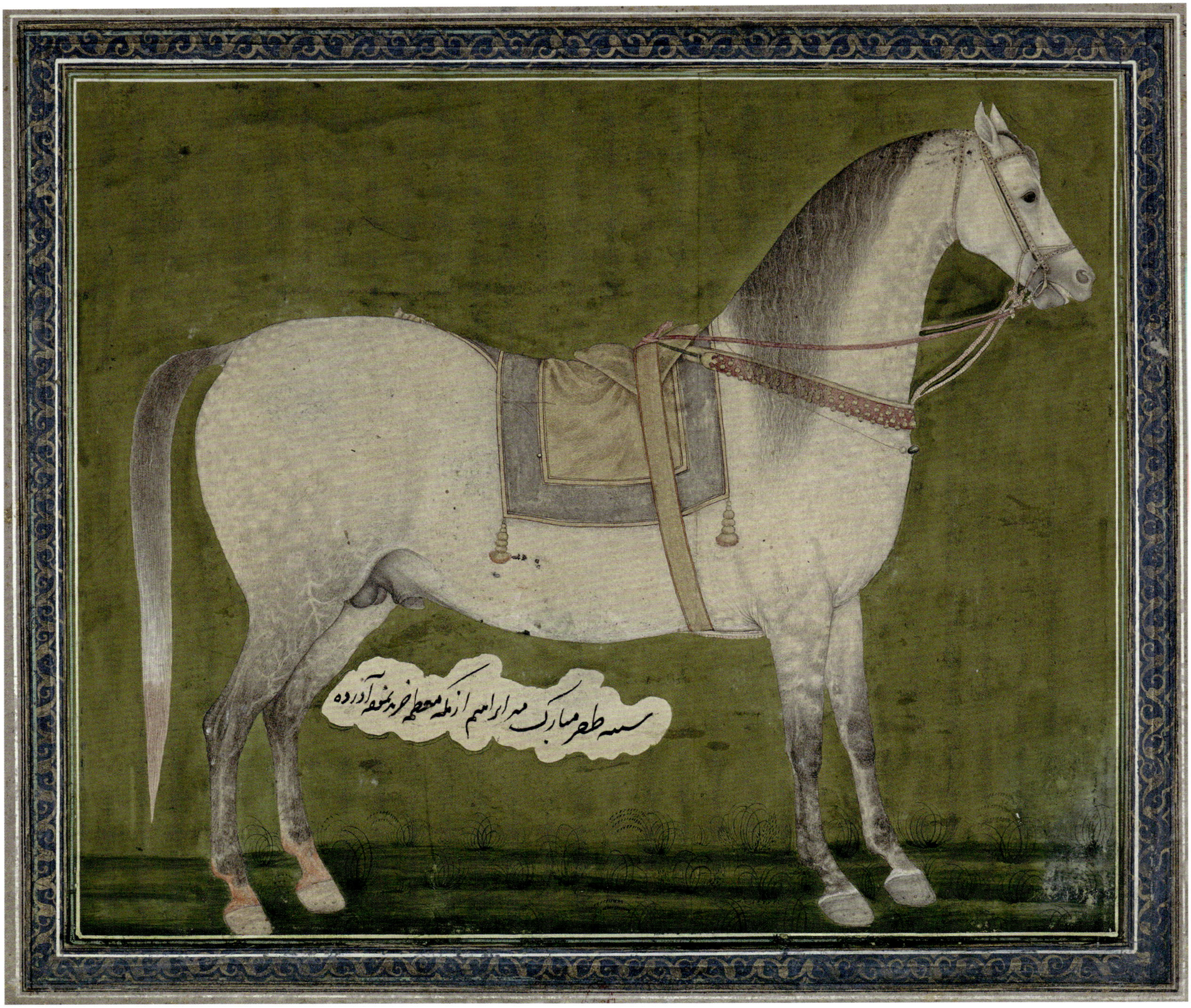

The Arabian Horse

Moghul School
The stud brought from Mecca to India by Mir Ibrâhim, second half of the seventeenth century
Opaque watercolor on paper
Inv. Smith-Lesouëf 247, fol. 34b
Courtesy of the Bibliothèque nationale de France

Several Moghul paintings dating from the seventeenth century depict Arabian horses with their saddles. The inscription on this painting indicates the name of the stallion, Zafar Mubarak, acquired by Mir Ibrahim, an officer of the Emperor Awrangzeb, during a voyage to Arabia.

Most of those whose traveled to Arabia were disappointed they did not encounter Arabian horses, whose fame was such that they expected to find them almost everywhere. Yet it is easy to understand their disappointment because most only visited Hijaz, the unique and ultimate goal for most visitors to Arabia.

"The Hijaz can scarcely be called a country of horses at all, as there are few to be found other than those of the Turkish mounted troops," wrote John Fryer Keane, following his stay in 1877–78. Ali Bey El Abbassi had arrived at more or less the same conclusion seventy years earlier: "At Mecca, there are none to be found. It is true that the soldiers of the guard of the Sultan Scherif possess about a hundred, and that there are about six the property of private individuals." Johann Ludwig Burckhardt, the Swiss author, wrote less than a decade later: "The people of Mecca, in general, have very few horses; I believe that there are not more than sixty kept by private individuals. The Sherif has about twenty or thirty in his stables." And he added: "The Bedouins [...] have also their horses, but none of the merchants or other classes keep any."

"The few horses kept at Mecca are of noble breed, and purchased from the Bedouins; in the spring they are usually sent to some Bedouin encampment, to feed upon the fine nutritious herbage of the desert." Burckhardt went on to comment that "the Bedouins of that country, and those especially around Mecca, are very poor in horses; a few sheikhs only having any, pasture being scarce." However, if there were not many horses at Hijaz, it was certainly because "the great heats of the parts near the Red Sea appear prejudicial to animal generation," rightly claimed Richard Burton, the British writer and explorer, who went on to say that "the lofty table-lands and the broad pastures of Nejd, combined with the attention paid by the people to purity of blood, have rendered it the greatest breeding country in Arabia."

Thus, there was no point in looking for Arabian horses in Hijaz, but elsewhere, specifically in Nejd. Even if a fine mount were found in Mecca, they undoubtedly would have come from Nejd: "The sharif's horses were all pure-bred and small; one in particular, a Nejd horse, brown with black spots, seemed to me to represent the perfection of the Arabian horse," Burton continued, who believed that Nejd supplied the holy cities "with its choicest horses and camels."

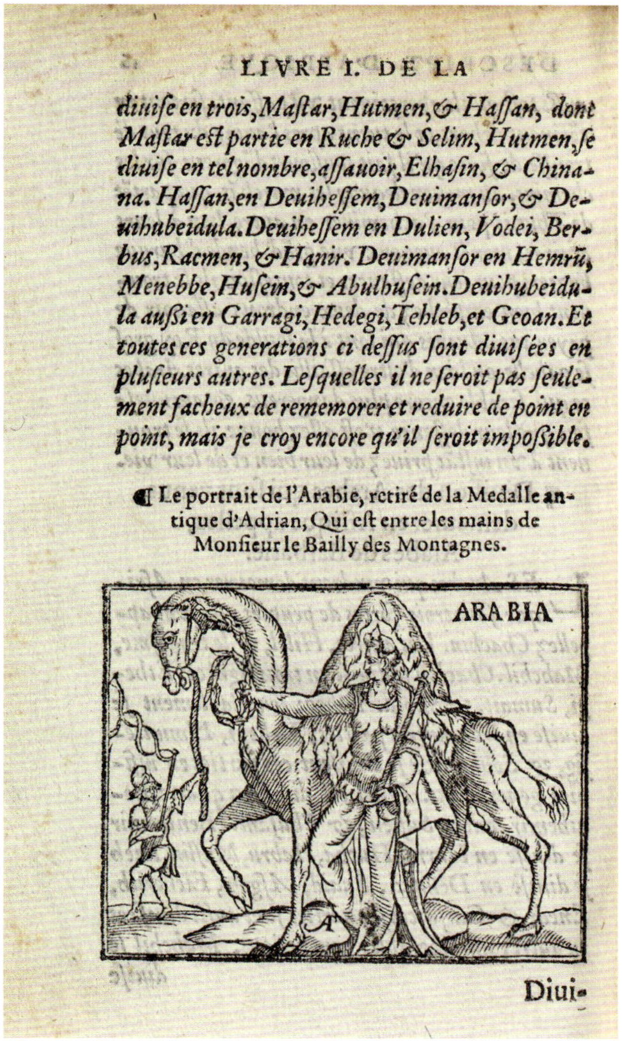
LIVRE I. DE LA

diuise en trois, Maſtar, Hutmen, & Haſſan, dont Maſtar eſt partie en Ruche & Selim, Hutmen, ſe diuiſe en tel nombre, aſſauoir, Elhaſin, & Chinana. Haſſan, en Deuiheſſem, Deuimanſor, & Deuihubeidula. Deuiheſſem en Dulien, Vodei, Berbus, Racmen, & Hanir. Deuimanſor en Hemrũ, Menebbe, Huſein, & Abulhuſein. Deuihubeidula auſsi en Garragi, Hedegi, Tehleb, et Geoan. Et toutes ces generations ci deſſus ſont diuiſées en pluſieurs autres. Leſquelles il ne ſeroit pas ſeulement facheux de rememorer et reduire de point en point, mais je croy encore qu'il ſeroit impoſsible.

Le portrait de l'Arabie, retiré de la Medalle antique d'Adrian, Qui eſt entre les mains de Monſieur le Bailly des Montagnes.

Diui-

Al-Hasan ibn Mohammad al-Wazzan, known as Leo the African
Allegorical figure representing Arabia
From *Description of Africa*, 1556
Engraving
6.7 × 5 cm
Paris, C. Plantin
Courtesy of the Bibliothèque nationale de France

This portrait of Arabia is drawn from an antique medal of Adrian.

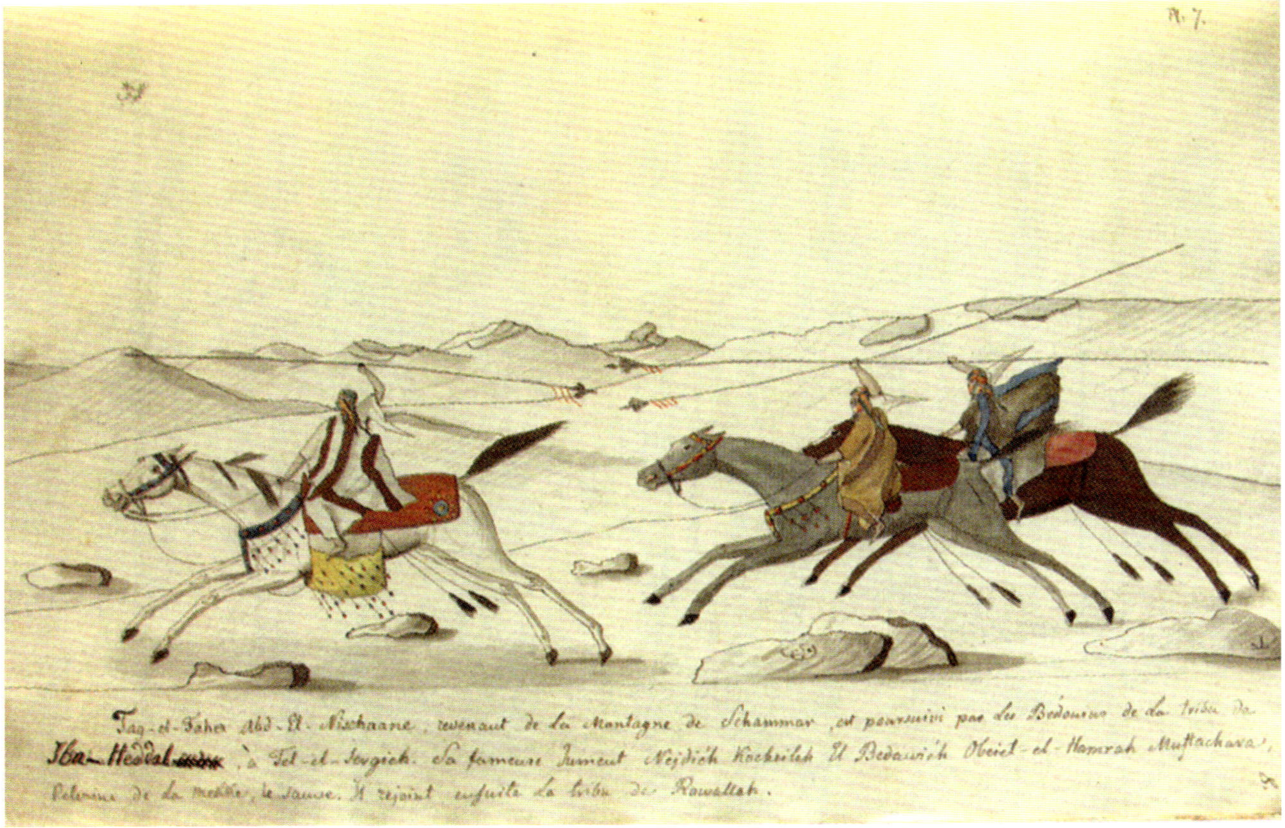

Count Waclaw Seweryn Rzewuski
Tag-el-Faher Abd-El-Nischaane, returning from the Shammar mountain, is chased by the Bedouins of the tribe Ibn-Hedbal, at Tel-el-Seugieh. The famous mare Nejdieh Kockeileh El Bedawieh Obeiet-el-Hamrah Muftachara, Pilgrim of Mekke, saves him. He later joins the tribe of Rowallah.
Color plate in *Impressions d'Orient et d'Arabie. Un cavalier polonais chez le Bédouins, 1817–1819*, 2002
Courtesy of José Corti / Muséum national d'histoire naturelle

When Count Rzewuski returned to Poland, he wrote *Concerning Oriental Horses and Those descended from Eastern Breeds*, an 800-page account of his sojourn in Arabia, its tribes, its horse breeds, and their descriptions.

Travelers who really wished to encounter the Arabian horse had to search, not in Jeddah, nor in Mecca or even in Medina, because none of these were its home. They had to go deep into Nejd, in the heart of Arabia, the home territory of the Arabian horse. It was in the cities of the center of the peninsula where one could first admire it: in the stables of princes and emirs, in Al-Jawf, in Ha'il and in Riyadh; and then, naturally, in the steppe and the desert and in the great Nafud. And farther to the north, in the immense territories where the nomads live, as far as the vicinity of Damascus; and, to the east, to the outskirts of Baghdad.

These were the places where one encountered this superb animal of such noble origins, this horse around which so many legends and traditions are entwined. "God took a fistful of wind from the north and created the horse," wrote the great Polish horseman, Waclaw Seweryn Rzewuski—whose exploits we will examine below—quoting the words of his Bedouin friends. It was in the land of Arabia that Ishmael was the first to tame a horse, according to legend. According to another, the ancestors of this superb steed were to be found on the stables of King Salomon. Rzewuski also reports the echo of another tradition that links the five favorite mares of the Prophet of Islam to the illustrious breed of Nejd horses, notably the Koheilan strain. The Prophet himself had lined the eyes of his mounts with kohl; they would later conserve the memory of this episode in the name of the strain, of the eyes circled with black.

These few examples which could be multiplied by a hundred-fold illustrate the glory and prestige that were associated to this admirable animal. For a very long time, its fame spread around the world, especially to the courts of European monarchs, whose stables and stud farms were eager for Arabian horses. During the seventeenth and above all eighteenth centuries, when light cavalries dominated the battlefields of the European wars, the quality of horses became a determining factor for success, more than previously. Given their geographic proximity to the Ottoman Empire, the Polish and Russian horse breeders had a greater facility to procure Arabian horses. However, the states of central and western Europe also expended great effort, with variable success, to acquire large quotas.

Consequently, toward the end of the seventeenth century, England's King Charles II, for example, sent his royal equerry (Master of the Horse) to the East, to acquire some stallions, as recorded in the royal registries. In Egypt, a little more than a century later, the future emperor Napoleon became a passionate champion of the Arabian horse and subsequently took care to ensure it was always well-represented in his personal stables and that it was bred at the national stud farms. Much later, his favorite mount, Le Vizir—a gift of sultan Selim III—would accompany him to his captivity on the island of Saint Helena.

It is apparent that the envoys of many European courts and wealthy aristocrats rushed to Istanbul with the intention of acquiring horses for their masters toward the end of the eighteenth and the start of the nineteenth centuries. Some, unsatisfied by the choices presented to them, went as far as Aleppo and even to Damascus in the hope of being able to negotiate the purchase of a magnificent charger, "a fine breed, and from among which purchases are made every now and then by European princes, peers, and commoners, often at astounding prices," so spoke William Gifford Palgrave, with the benefit of experience, in the book that describes his journey, *Personal Narrative of a Year's Journey through Central and Eastern Arabia*.

Palgrave had effectively crossed the Great Nafud, stopped in the cities of Al-Jawf and Ha'il, and resided for some time in Riyadh during the winter of 1862–63. In each of these cities, he entered the stables of the princes and, in Riyadh, he had visited those of Faisal, the Saudi sovereign of Nejd. "The Nejdean horse is considered no less superior to all others of his kind in Arabia than is the Arabian breed collectively to the Persian, or Indian. In Nejd is the true birthplace of the Arab steed, the primal type, the authentic model. Among all the studs of Nejd, Feysul's was indisputable the first; and who sees that has seen the most consummate specimens of equine perfection in Arabia, perhaps in the world. The genuine Nejdean breed, so far as I have hitherto found, is to be met with only in Nejd itself; nor are these animals common even there. None but chiefs or individuals of considerable wealth and rank possess them. Nor are they ever sold, at least so all declare." Palgrave added: "When I asked how then one could be acquired, 'by war, by legacy, or by free gift'."

"In this last manner alone," Palgrave continued, on the mention of a gift, "is there a possibility of an isolated specimen leaving Nejd, but even that is seldom, and when policy requires a present to Egypt, Persia, or Constantinople (a circumstance of which I witnessed two instances and heard of others), mares are never sent, and the poorer stallions, though deserving to pass elsewhere for real beauties, are picked out for the purpose!" In these conditions, attempting to acquire a few—or even just one!—of these horses, the jewels of the stables of the masters of Nejd, was like squaring the circle or the Quest for the Holy Grail!

Some European travelers did nonetheless succeed in negotiating the purchase of similar horses. William G. Palgrave was not among them. He was much more concerned about politics than about the chargers of the Nejd, in which his interest was only incidental. He was, in fact, not really a horseman. It was necessary to be one to the ends of one's fingertips, and even beyond, to accept the challenge that a foreigner in those years faced to successfully acquire these exceptional horses while visiting the tribes.

Let us begin with the remarkable personality of Count Waclaw Seweryn Rzewuski, born in 1784 in eastern Poland into a rich and influential family. From his childhood, he became an expert rider, with the advantage of riding the horses from the family's stud farm. He also demonstrated a special gift for languages and, in addition to Polish and French, he soon mastered Russian and German. Following the various partitions of Poland at the end of the eighteenth century, the family possessions were divided among Poland, Russia, and Austria. It was in the latter state, in Vienna, that his parents took up residence when he became an adolescent, and it was also there that he became acquainted and befriended his uncle, Jan Potocki, a great traveler, knowledgeable Orientalist, and famous writer who would later author an internationally renowned book, *The Manuscript found in Saragossa*. It was from Potocki, whose influence he absorbed, that young Waclaw received his first lessons of Oriental culture and languages, which continued to fascinate him throughout his life. He later perfected his knowledge of Turkish and Arabic with the best professors.

An only son, his father was anxious for him to pursue a military and diplomatic career; Waclaw joined a prestigious Austrian cavalry unit and fought brilliantly against Napoleon's army. His mother, intent on his marriage, wedded him to a very young woman of higher nobility. However, Waclaw Rzewuski developed a friendship with one of the greatest Orientalists of that period, Baron Joseph von Hammer-Purgstall, who introduced him to the circle of the greatest specialists. Together with them he published, at his own expense, beginning in 1809, what would be the first leading Orientalist review of Europe, entitled *Mines de l'Orient, exploitées par une société d'amateurs*.

After the death of his father in 1811, Waclaw Rzewuski lived on his properties in Poland with his wife and their four children. In a Europe put to fire and the sword, he managed his stud farm and dreamed only of traveling in the Orient. His financial position was nevertheless unstable. His mother, who had remained in Vienna, lived in great style and contracted debts that the family fortune was no longer able to pay off after the death of the head of the family. Waclaw himself was anything but a good manager. He spent much on horses and, above all, for all of his Oriental passions. Some of his properties began to be seized.

The defeat of France incidentally allowed Rzewuski to reach his goals and realize his dreams of the Orient. The armies of the great powers of the period had been considerably weakened by the Napoleonic Wars and they were engaged in reconstituting themselves, notably by procuring a supply of horses. So it was that Rzewuski persuaded the tsar of Russia, Alexander I, and Queen Catharina of Württemberg, to finance a project for an expedition to Arabia, to be guided, obviously, by himself. He had everything needed to inspire their confidence as an aristocrat of the nobility, a former cavalry officer, owner of a horse-breeding farm and, in addition, an expert on the Orient.

It would take two years, after the monarchs gave their approval to prepare the expedition, to gather a small group of about fifteen to accompany him, including a physician, an equerry veterinarian, servants, and eight young Cossacks. They departed with him in 1817, following the route through Constantinople, then Aleppo to Damascus, which would become the base of the expedition, the city from which Rzewuski would depart, most often alone, for the desert, to meet the tribes.

It was those same tribes who conferred on Rzewuski the authority and legitimation that were his in the desert and that he clearly deserved. This is understood after reading his remarkable book of some eight hundred pages, a masterwork written in French, full of notes in Arabic, that he entitled, *On Oriental Horses and Those Descended from Eastern Breeds*, which would not be integrally published in its entirety until the beginning of the twenty-first century with the title, *Impressions d'Orient et d'Arabie*. The impressive name of Rzewuski in the Orient was Tag el-Faher Abd el-Nîshân, which might be loosely translated as Wreath of Fame, Servant of the Sign, or instead as servant "of the Symbol," a denomination that may denote a Masonic association; as for Tag el-Faher, that is simply the translation of his first name—Waclaw or Wenceslas—from the Slavic *vienetz*, "crown," and *slava*, "glory".

He ascertained that the Bedouins considered him "equal to a grand emir of the tribes from the

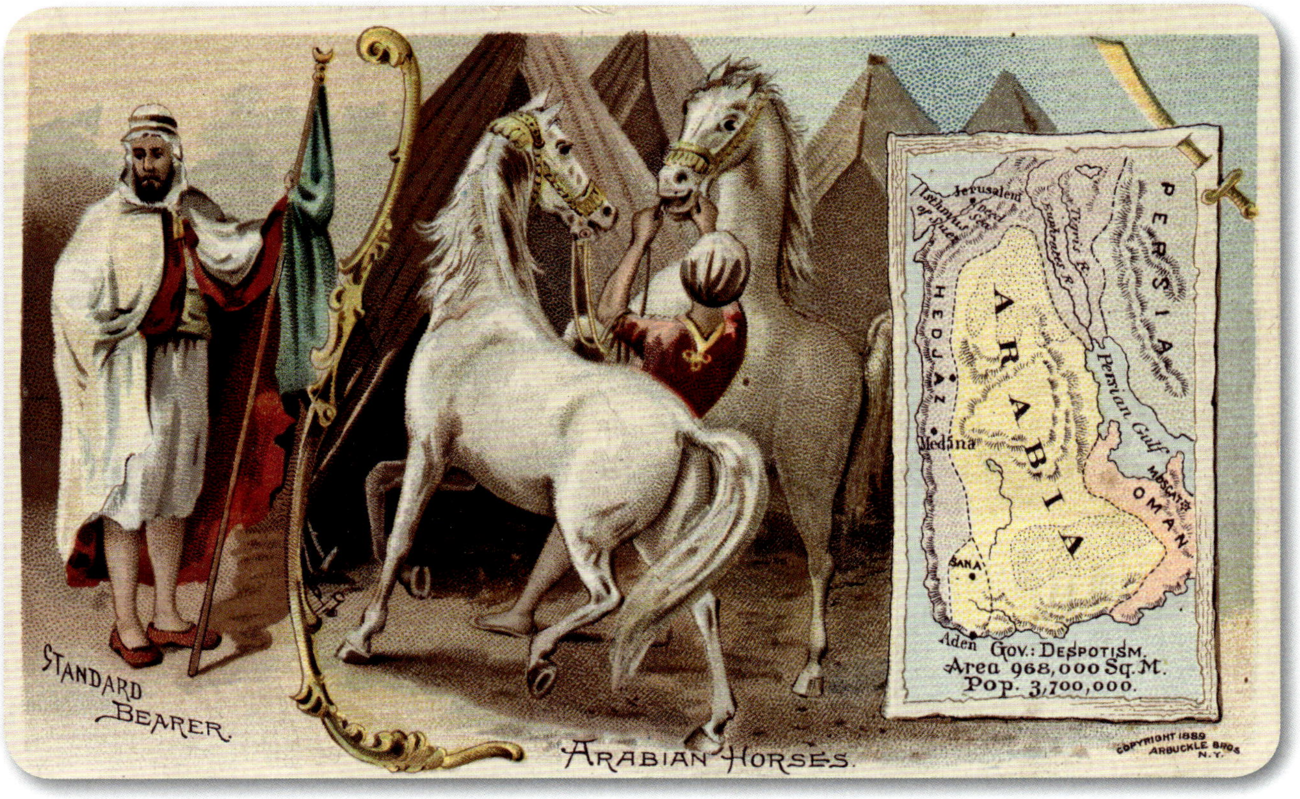

Advertising Card
Arabia, 1889
Series of advertising cards issued by Arbuckle Bros. Coffee Company (New York). Each consists of a map of a country of the world with related illustrations.
Courtesy of the New York Public Library

In the nineteenth century, Arabian horse trade developed in Europe and Istanbul. Pedigrees sometimes stated: "*This horse has drunk the sweet milk of camels and breathed the pure desert air.*"

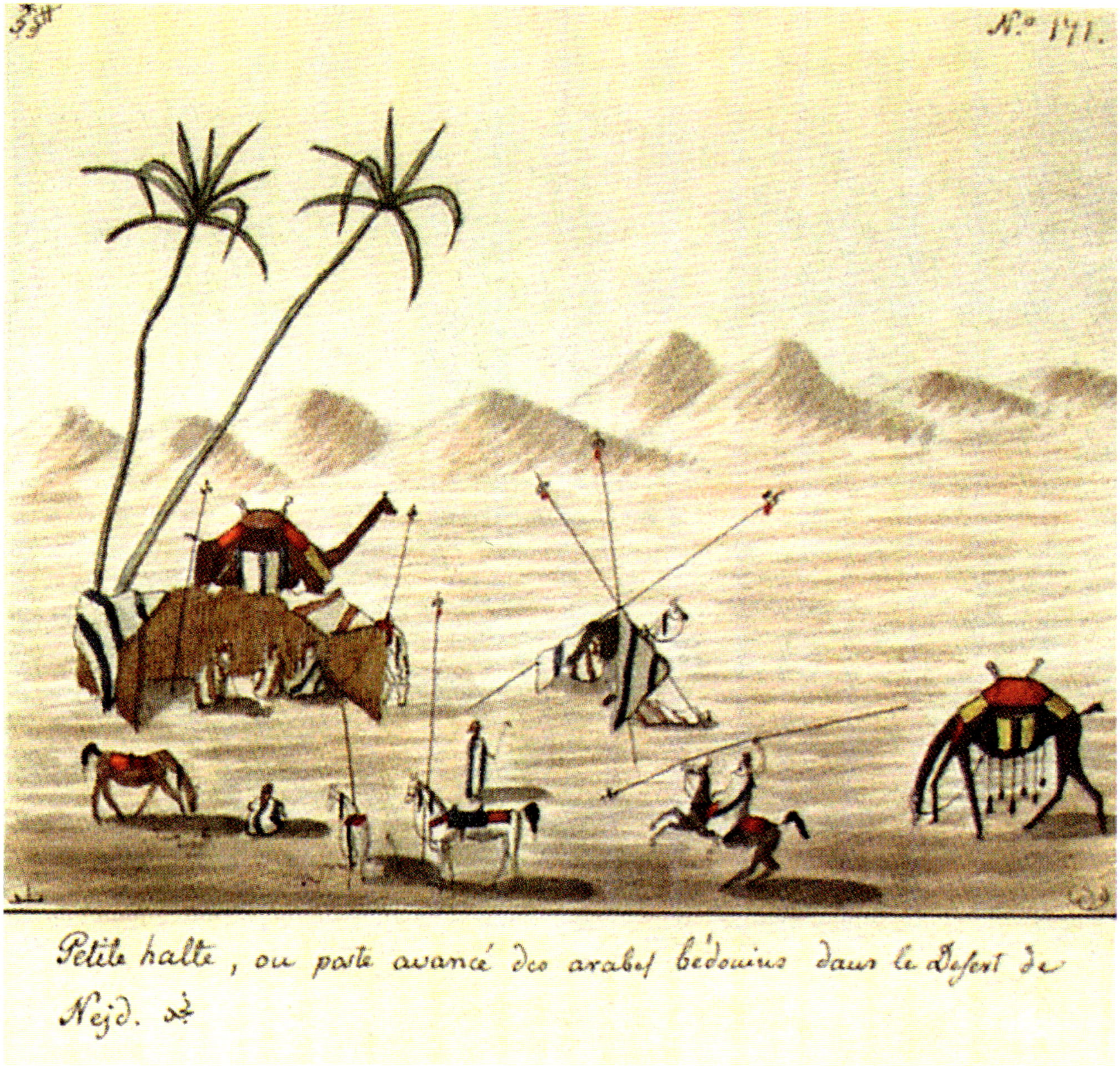

Count Waclaw Seweryn Rzewuski
Short stop, or advanced post, of the Bedouin Arabs in the desert of Nejd
Color plate in *Impressions d'Orient et d'Arabie. Un cavalier polonais chez le Bédouins, 1817–1819*, 2002
Courtesy of José Corti / Muséum national d'histoire naturelle

In the opening of his book, *Concerning Oriental Horses and Those descended from Eastern Breeds*, Count Rzewuski wrote: *"A glance at Arabia is necessary to understand this work. Knowledge of the land and climate provides an essential background to the organization and qualities of the Arabian horse."*

North, in the reign of Skander," the latter being none other than Alexander I, tsar of Russia and king of Poland. Again, according to the text of his book, here is how another emir, Dûhahî ibn Ghbein, presented Rzewuski to his guests: "This is the noble and famous Tag el-Faher Abd el-Nîshân, Emir and sheikh of the Arabs, attached to the allied command of the thirteen tribes. He is my friend, he is my brother, he is my bread and salt ally. The Bedouin tribes of the North who travel the deserts toward the North Star, in the reign of the powerful Skander, king of the entire North, are his subjects. He descends from the four Anazeh tribes who left the Nejd, there are two thousand years with their horses."

Clearly, Rzewuski enjoyed exceptional prestige among the tribes, although one might undoubtedly suspect that he had somewhat exaggerated his merits: "They compare me to the favourite heroes of the Arabs, to the famous Antar. Verses were sung in my praise by the tribes. That is how my name was spread across the desert and soon, as I later learned, arrived in the heart of Arabia, where everything is new and where everyone, swept along by the charms of the language, adds all that is marvellous that a fervent imagination can offer to the truth."

While living with the Bedouins, while sharing their bread and salt, Rzewuski quickly became convinced of the superiority of the *Nejdi Koheilan*, as he called them, above all other equine breeds. In his book, Rzewuski dedicated more than one hundred pages to the description of this famous breed, its strains, and the care that

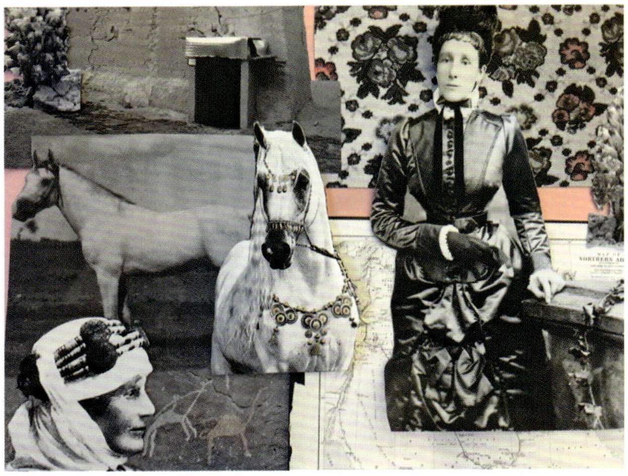

Jackie Leger
Blunt, 2017
Collage-photographs
Courtesy of the artist

Reproduced on the upper left side of this photocollage is the mud house where Lady Anne and Wilfrid Blunt lived during their stay in Ha'il. In the bottom left corner of the photo are representations of Jobba's prehistoric rock art. Anne Blunt described the site of Jobba as either the strangest place in the world or one of the most beautiful. She wrote in *A Pilgrimage to Nejd* (1881) that *"on one of the rocks I noticed an inscription, or rather pictures of camels and horses, cut on a flat surface about five feet across. We could not, however, under the circumstances, copy it."*

the Bedouins dedicated to it. According to Rzewuski, it was practically impossible to draw a succinct portrait of the Nejdi Koheilan; if one follows his description, it "must never be confused with the Koheilan of Mesopotamia and neighbouring countries," as he insisted with an abundance of details and illustrations of minutiae to support his contention.

"The eye," he began, "is large, protruding, black, and lively, with a sweet and intelligent glance that is characteristic of the Nejdi." This was only the start. He continued: "The narrow, elongated, upright pupil is dark blue." And then he elaborated: "Near the top of the pupil, the eyeballs are rather pronounced and irregular." Then Rzewuski added: "The rest of the eye tends to black or brown. The darker it is, the more the Arabs love it." That is, "the darker the eye, the better the vision of the horse," he revealed, confirming that this was "a constant comment among the Bedouins." Further on, he reiterated: "The pupil is always lighter in colour." Rzewuski went deeper and deeper into detail. He then examined the forehead of the horse, which "should be wide and slightly rounded, from eye to eye," noting that "the Bedouins consider it the organ of intelligence and that horses with a flat forehead are stupid." Then he came to the nostrils, which "must be well split, oblong and leave the pituitary membrane in full view; external walls that are not fleshy," adding that "the interspace of the nostrils must be flattened, somewhat concave, wrinkled, with prominent lean cartilage in each nostril." And he was just getting started. Rzewuski expanded at length about the muzzle, the mouth, the lips, the beard, and the mandible. Then it is the turn for the ears, "elegant, long and open—not the usual definition of pretty," as the text instructs. "You can recognize a desert horse by its ears," he noted. "They compensate for their lack of grace by the way the horse places and plays with them, while mounted."

So far, we are still at the head of the animal, about which Rzewuski makes this curious remark: "The Arabs model the head of a horse on that of a gazelle. The closer the former is to the latter, the more it obtains approval," and so it will be for each part of the body—the legs, the rump, the breast, the back, the neck...

"Crossed for millions of years among them without any mixing with a foreign blood line, they have distinct personal and general traits in all the individuals," wrote Rzewuski about the Nejdi Koheilan, mentioning in passing that the size of these "is not as small as self-proclaimed European experts claim it is." He continued: "The Nejd charger has a surprisingly sweet temperament and great intelligence." Then Rzewuski added: "This sweetness depends on the nobility of the blood from which it descends." As for intelligence, "it depends on the great perfection of all the organs, a felicitous result of the race and the climate." As it happens, "the organs of the Nejdi are extremely sensitive. It has sharp eyes, keen ears, and a refined sense of smell. Its nervous sensibility (in other words, its sense of touch) is very refined," concluded the Polish count.

"The Nejdi Koheilan enjoy very good health," he stated clearly before abundantly developing this point. Their lifetimes and years of service were especially long: "Tamed at the age of two and a half years, because in this blazing zone, everything is precocious, they arrive at quite an advanced age," he wrote, assuring that he had seen "many from eighteen to twenty-six years of age and more, according to the Arabs, still providing fine service in war and following the expeditions." On the other hand, "the Nejdi Koheilan eat little [because] the hot climate does not allow the same appetites that one sees in Europe," commented Rzewuski, who also observed that "the same reason makes men tend toward frugality."

The Nejdi Koheilan never lose their sense of orientation, Rzewuski assured, noting that "they have excellent night vision, they are long-winded in the gallop," swim admirably, and "leap across the widest channels with the ease of a stag." This noble charger could be compared, again in the words of Rzewuski, to "a dog, for its intelligence and its fidelity;" with "the lion for its courage and strength" and with the gazelle "for the extraordinary levity of its racing!"

Kazimierz Żwan
Portrait of Count Waclaw Rzewuski, known as the Emir, 1825
32 × 26 cm
Oil on canvas
Courtesy of the National Museum of Warsaw

Count Rzewuski was known in Arabia as *Emir Taj al-Faher* (Crown of Glory) and *Abd el-Nîchân* (Servant of the Sign). His Arabic name, *Taj al-Faher*, is the translation of his Polish name, Waclaw or "Crown of Glory". In Poland, he continued to be known as *Emir* long after his return from Arabia.

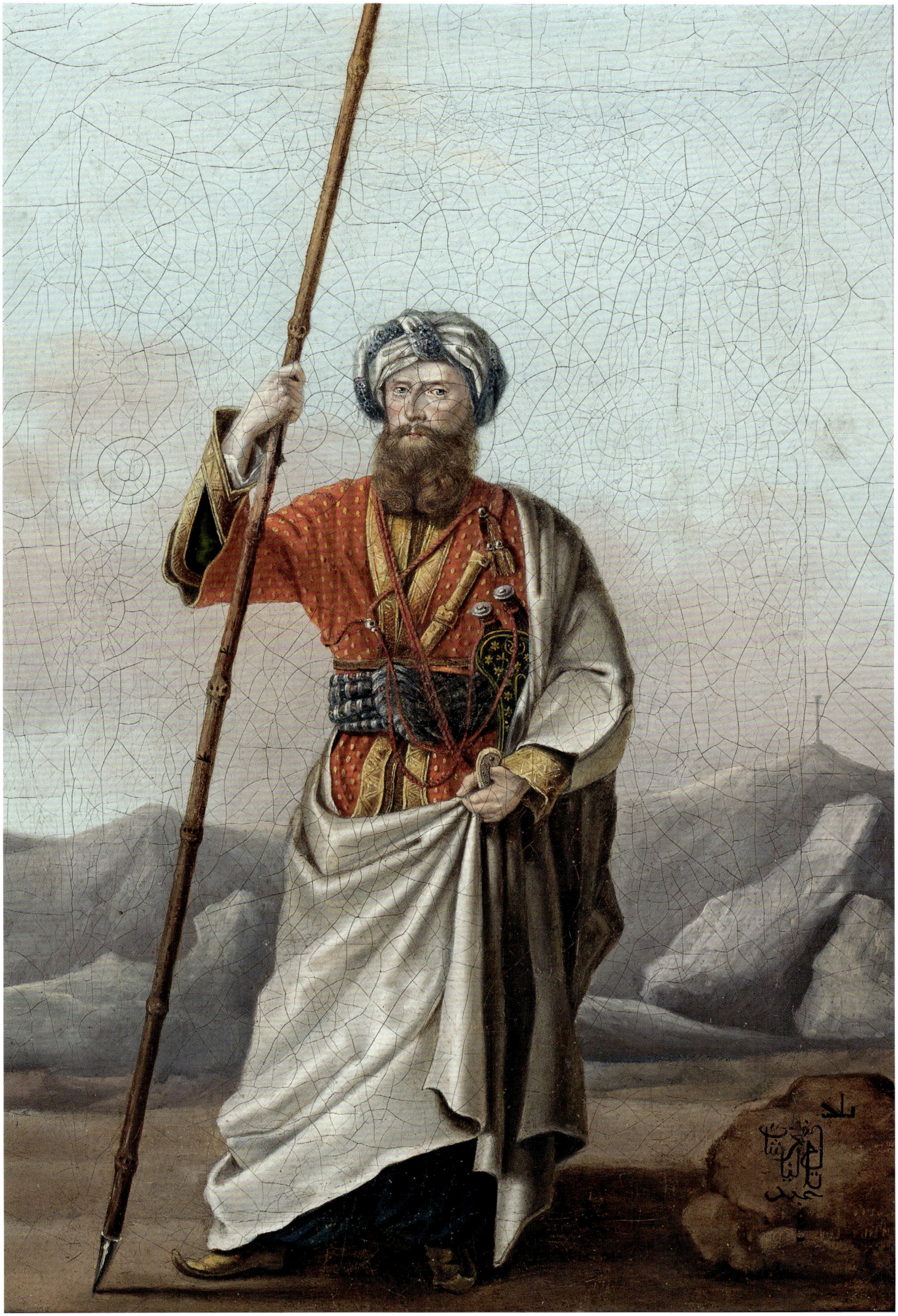

But how can one become the buyer of these marvelous horses? "Very few city people would run the risk of going to the desert to buy horses," reasoned Rzewuski at the outset. "In my time there was just one in Aleppo." At the same time, "there were two in Damascus," he noted before assuring his reader that "they knew nothing about horses." In general, he wrote that "horse traders are nothing more than beasts in their stables." Consequently, "it is at the source, from the Bedouins, that one must attempt to purchase them."

Whatever the fame of count Waclaw Seweryn Rzewuski, better known as Emir Tag el-Faher Abd el-Nîshân in the Bedouin milieu, nonetheless he was still a foreigner who wished to become a buyer of something that was considered the bedrock of the wealth of each tribe. The fact was that each "tribe is judged mighty and rich from the abundance of horses they possess, which is always a criterion of the opulence and power of Bedawies," wrote the Finnish Orientalist Georg August Wallin, after having made two voyages to central Arabia, specifically to Ha'il, in 1845 and 1848. Many times, Rzewuski would recall, a deal had been struck and the money counted when the seller had retracted because he was incapable of separating himself from his horse.

We will attempt here to summarize the methods Rzewuski developed to buy horses in the desert and some of the difficulties he encountered. "Before throwing oneself into the undertaking," he wrote, "it is necessary to take the indispensable measures, in one or more cities near the desert, to have funds available there," which would require the contributions of consuls and bankers. Later, it would be necessary to be very cautious and to pay drafts "only in hard piastres, the only money Bedouins accept." It would also be necessary, in this regard, to take care that these coins "are intact and, as far as possible, without profound scratches because the Arabs do not accept them." Naturally, "before leaving the city, it is necessary to prepare a depot, rent a stable with stable hands, buy the blankets, the barley feed bags, the fetters, the iron posts, stable utensils, the ropes, etc."

Finally, one may set off, accompanied by a guide who belongs to the tribe to be encountered. The latter, however, "will not be able to prevent an attack by roaming horsemen and strangers to his tribe, which may well compromise the mission or lead to the loss of the sum carried along." In addition, one must also make allowance for the difficulties represented by "the scorching climate, the desert wind, hunger, thirst, the quality of

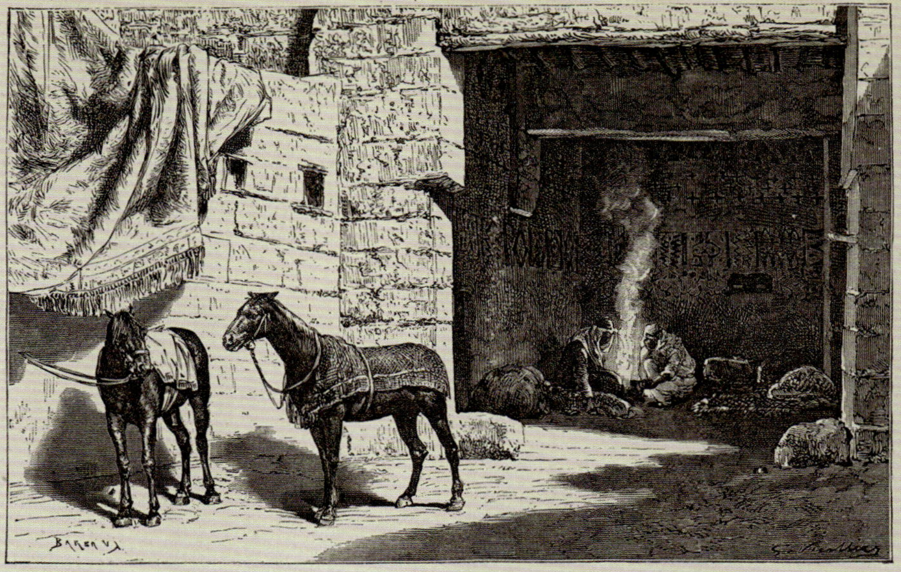

Notre maison, à Haïl

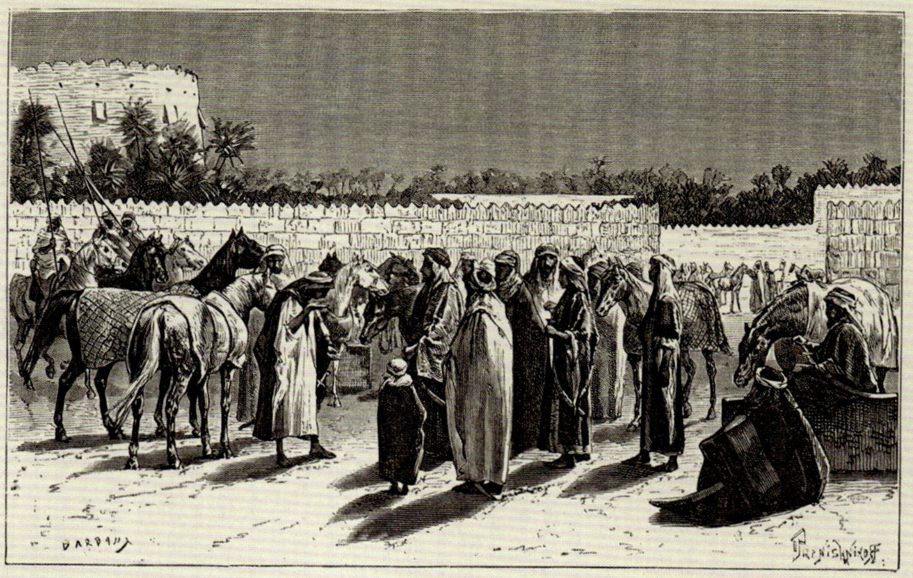

Les écuries d'ibn Rashid.

Anne Blunt
Our House, Ha'il
From *Voyage en Arabie. Pèlerinage au Nedjed*
(A Pilgrimage to Nejd)
Woodcut by Gaston Vuillier
after a watercolor
by Anne Blunt, Paris, 1882
Courtesy of the British Library

Anne Blunt described their house in Ha'il in *A Pilgrimage to Nejd* (1881): *"We found a double house provided for us in the main street of Ha'il, and not two hundred yards from the* kasr*—a house without pretense, but sufficient for our wants, and secure from all intruders, for the street door could be locked, and the walls were high. It consisted of two separate houses, as I believe most dwellings in Arabia do, one for men and the other for women. In the former there was a* kahwah *and a couple of smaller rooms, and this we gave over to Mohammed and the servants, keeping the* harim *for ourselves. This last had a small open court, just large enough for the three mares to stand in."*

Anne Blunt
Ibn Rashid's stables
From *Voyage en Arabie. Pèlerinage au Nedjed* (A Pilgrimage to Nejd)
Woodcut by Gaston Vuillier
after a watercolor by Anne Blunt,
Paris, 1882
Courtesy of the British Library

Anne Blunt wrote in *A Pilgrimage to Nejd* that she was told that there was nothing in Arabia to compare with Ibn Rashid's stud. It had become the most celebrated in Arabia and *"has taken the place in public estimation of that of the stud of Feysul ibn Saoud's"*, which Palgrave saw and described sixteen years earlier.

the foods, the ever-present weariness, the total absence of cleanliness, the very lightweight garments, the very cool and slimy dew."

Let us suppose then, together with Rzewuski, that "the buyer arrives at the tribe with his money." That is the beginning of a tiresome ordeal. The buyer will be "assailed with questions, to fathom his knowledge about horses." It will be better not to make mistakes in the answers provided. The moment will come when the Bedouins will propose a horse which is not a first-class choice. It is with "great tact," says Rzewuski, that the buyer should "propose a well motivated refusal of the horse being presented to him," because otherwise, "the Bedouins will be shocked and there will be no hope for the project after that." It is therefore necessary to exercise "a quick fertile imagination to provide a plausible reason for the refusal, and to concentrate on what is happening in the immediate vicinity." Because there will be one "among the horses that was not presented; while walking around the tribe, one that will be necessary to choose to buy, without having much time to examine it. The Arabs don't like that. A quick look and a great deal of experience are needed to make a decision."

It is then, and only then, that one will be able to perhaps, if not make a great deal, at least open a

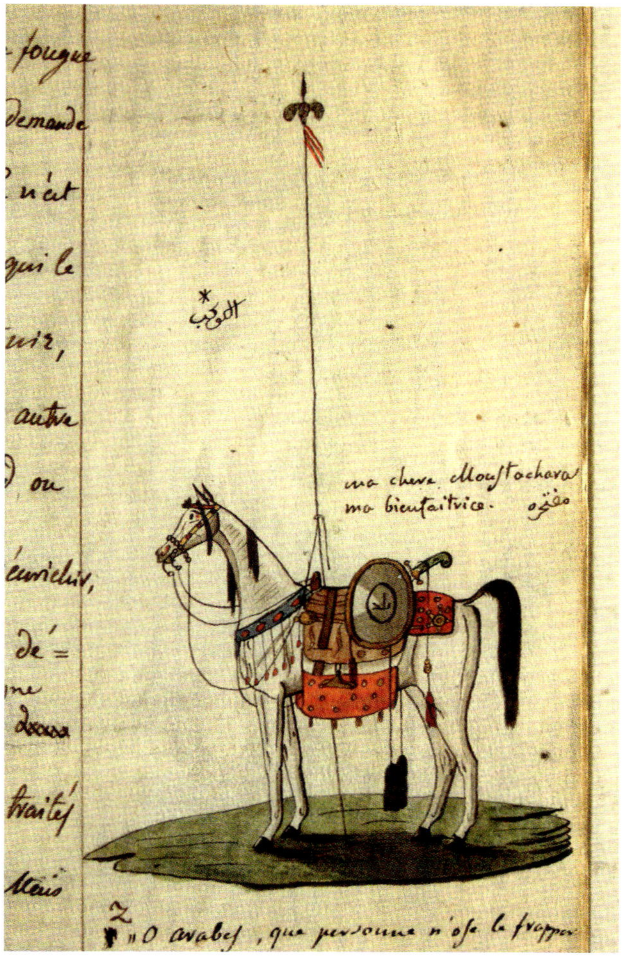

Count Waclaw Seweryn Rzewuski
My dear Mouftachara, my benefactress
Color plate in *Impressions d'Orient et d'Arabie. Un cavalier polonais chez le Bédouins, 1817–1819*, 2002
Courtesy of José Corti / Muséum national d'histoire naturelle

After his Arabian journey, Count Rzewuski returned to Poland dressed in Bedouin robes and mounted on "Mouftachara". In Arabic, this name means "Proud".

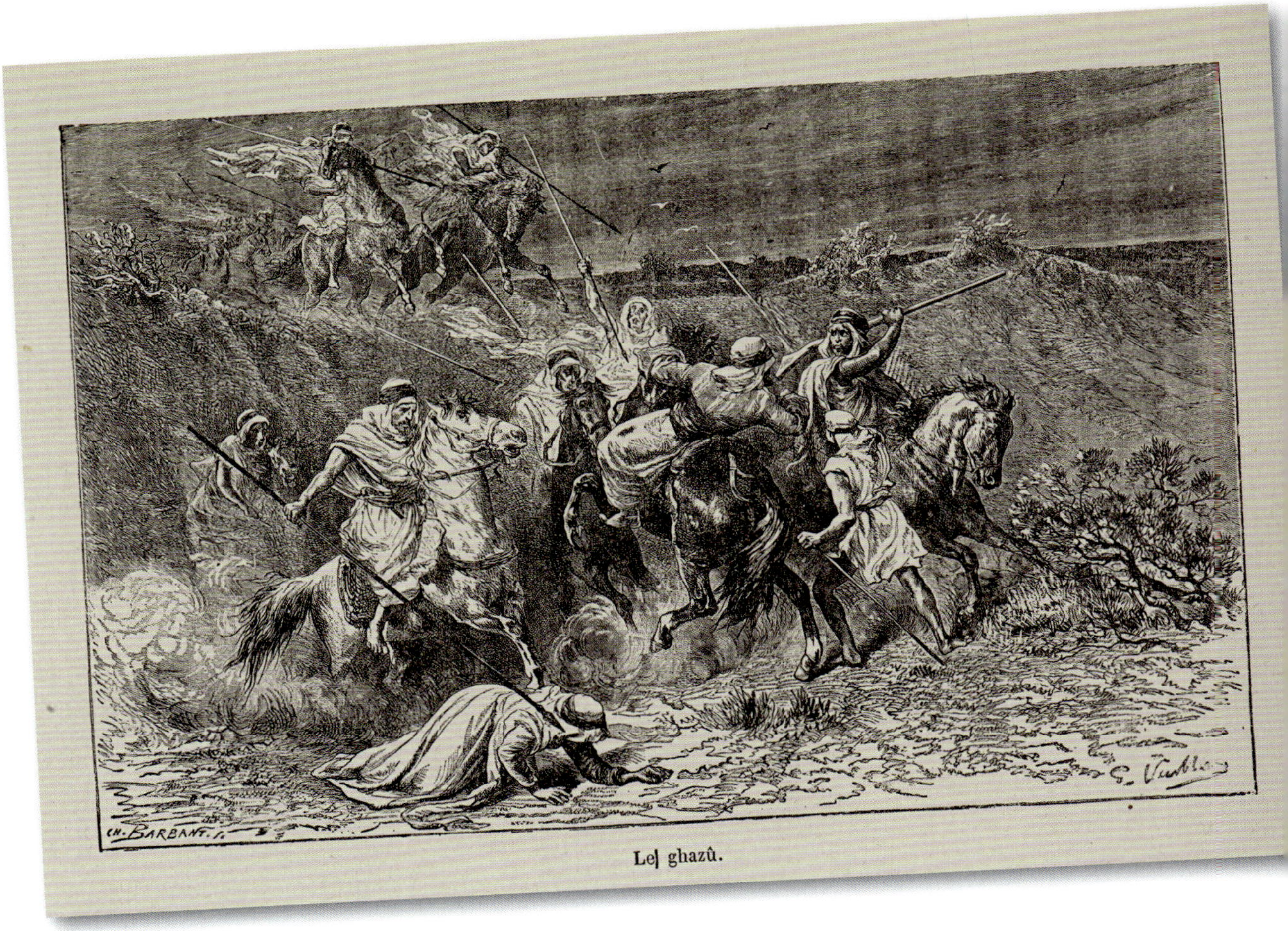

Anne Blunt
Ghazu in the Wady Sirhan, 1882
From *Voyage en Arabie. Pèlerinage au Nedjed* (A Pilgrimage to Nejd)
Woodcut by Gaston Vuillier after a watercolour by Anne Blunt, Paris, 1882
Courtesy of the British Library, London

Ghazu, by definition, is when the enemy is taken by surprise. Anne Blunt and her husband were victims of a *ghazu* attack when they were encamping near wells. She described this incident in *A Pilgrimage to Nejd*, writing that their mares were tied to the bushes and their camels behind them when suddenly they heard thuds on the sand and the sound of galloping. A troop of men with lances galloped toward them, took Wilfrid's gun from him, and broke it over his head. Anne surrendered, shouting "*ana dahilak*" (I am under your protection). The horsemen asked them who they were, and when they discovered that they were under the protection of Ibn Shaalan, they released them and gave them back their mares and gun, lamenting their bad fortune in finding them friends and hence having to return their "*beautiful mares*" and "*the beautiful gun*".

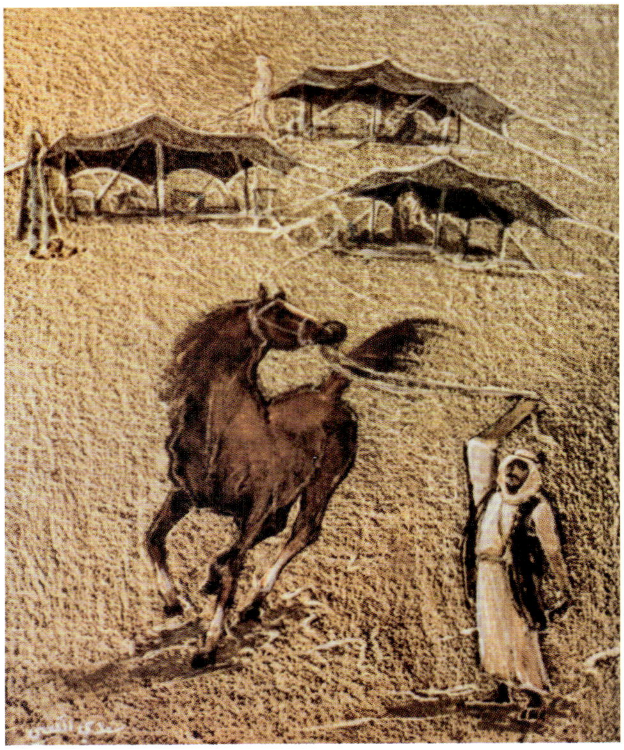

Saadi Al-Kaabi
Desert, 1964
Mixed media
70 × 80 cm
Courtesy of the artist

Carlo Guarmani, after his stay in Nejd, wrote in 1864 a book on the thoroughbred Arabian horse. *El Khamsa* "The Five", devoted to the five strains of the most noble of Arabian horses: the Kuhaylan, Ubayyan, Saqlawi, Hamdani, and Hadban.

Saadi Al-Kaabi
Untitled, 1964
Mixed media
70 × 80 cm
Courtesy of the artist

The famous thoroughbreds in Arabia were fed dates and water, camel's milk, and desert herbs.

negotiation: "Having thus determined the horse or mare that one wants to buy, this is the moment to act," according to the Polish rider. "An Arab," he explained, "is never offended if one asks to buy his mount. Actually, it flatters him. He will not answer yes or no, but will ask: 'What will you give?'" That is the moment when negotiation can begin: "It requires great tact not to offer too little, which would reveal ignorance about the value of the horse and spoil everything," observed Rzewuski. "Knowing something about the price of horses," he continued, "it is easy to make a first proposal, which is never accepted." Because the seller "never reveals the price he wants, he lets the amount grow by a head movement of refusal, until the offer has reached the price fixed inside his head," in the words of the Polish aristocrat, who also affirmed: "The Bedouin Arabs never lie about the races of their horses; their good faith about this matter is a question of religious scruple."

Complications of another sort may arise because it often happens that a handsome horse "has several owners," Rzewuski continued, adding that "a mare almost always belongs to several Bedouins." In such a case, it will certainly be wise "to obtain unanimous consent" from all the owners. It will be just as "important to ascertain whether the womb of the mare is free," because if it is not, "the agreement of the owners to sell the mare would be of no value if its womb is bound to an engagement."

Now suppose, Rzewuski wrote, "that all difficulties have been resolved, the price has been fixed, the history of its races, exploits, and ancestors has been told, and that the only thing left to do was to make payment." That is the moment "when a new scene opens that can, in an instant, annul all the previously overcome difficulties." Rzewuski narrates this scene with humor, where one sees the buyer at first, seated on the ground as he counts out his coins on his mantle. "No one will interrupt him," he points out. Then, "when he has finished, the sellers and their friends sit down around the coins and pass each piastre from hand to hand, examining them meticulously to ensure their complete integrity." Rzewuski points out that this "takes a lot of time, because they contest their perfection and one sees the same piece passing several times at different moments under the eyes of the same individuals."

"When the verification is completed," Rzewuski continues, "the unsatisfactory pieces having been replaced by others, the Bedouins begin to count them." And the Pole goes on: "Arithmetic was born with their ancestors but has been so neglected by the descendants that it takes them considerable time to reach an agreement. One counts on his fingers, another uses a different calculating device, they interrupt and make mistakes. A difference of more or less one piece strikes everyone with astonishment. They begin the entire calculation once again!" All of this certainly takes a very long time: "The Bedouins' slow method of counting money, aside from the inherent difficulties, is a great threat to the sale," concluded Rzewuski on this matter. "If there is an alarm while these calculations are going on, the Arabs will leave the money on the ground, mount their horses, and it may happen that the horse involved is never seen again." This remark says a lot about the climate of permanent insecurity that prevails in the desert!

When the deal is done, then it is necessary "to quickly send the acquisition back to the depot because in a moment of enthusiasm for the Nejdi chargers, the seller can recover the sale and return the money," as Rzewuski commented earlier. Care must be taken to ensure that the horse arrives in good conditions at its destination, put it in the care of a man to guide it through the desert and back to the city, and provide him with enough money to free the horse from an eventual ransom, if necessary. Other difficulties might arise in the city, where handsome horses attract attention,

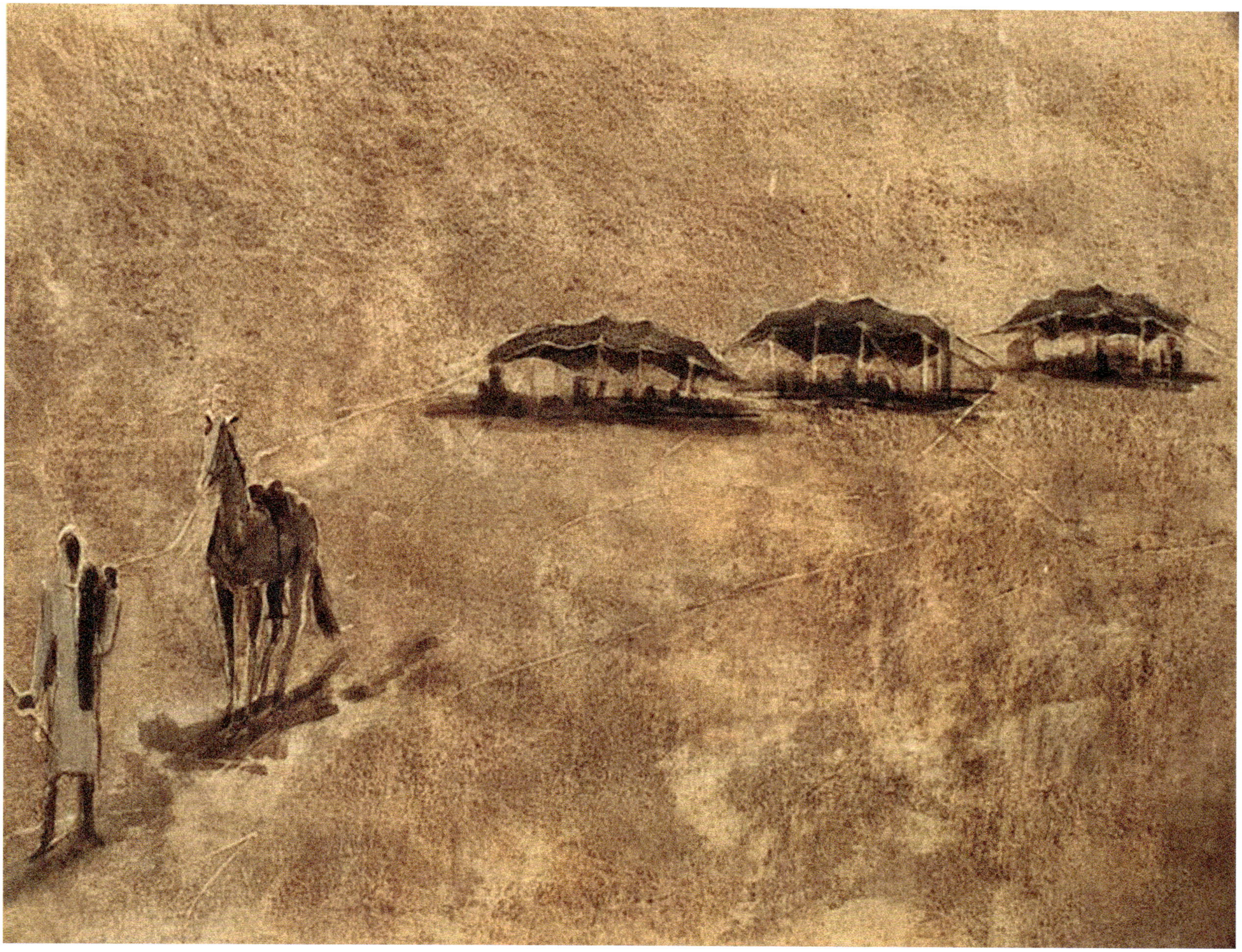

"because as a Christian, one could not refuse to show the Koheilan horses to true believers." Other difficulties came up when it was time to send the horses to Europe: "Arranging their transport out of the city was another moment of difficulties," Rzewuski recalled. "Sometimes crowds would gather and oppose the departure," he noted. "It could be a nasty fellow blocking the traffic in the street, saying that one or another of the horses was stolen from him and he wanted it back. All to rake in some money," wrote Rzewuski, disheartened. "One must pay and pay," he complained. There were more taxes to pay, in each city. Customs fees to be settled. Then the transportation costs to Europe by sea.

"I myself," concluded Rzewuski, "Emir of the Bedouin Arabs, dressed like them, speaking their language and familiar with their customs, I encountered difficulties in Damascus with the horses for the queen of Württemberg. What would happen to a poor Christian who comes to Arabia to buy horses, without knowing the language, the customs, or the breeds! Would he be the most knowledgeable equerry of Europe; he would lose his Latin in Arabia." It is easy to believe him. One can only admire his extraordinary prowess in acquiring, as he did during his two-year journey, precisely one hundred thirty-seven horses, mares, and stallions, for the stables of Queen Catharina of Württemberg and for the stables of the tsar of Russia, Alexander I, as well as his own stables.

In the end, there were not many who undertook the trip to Arabia moved by their passion for horses. Beside Waclaw Rzewuski, there was an Italian by the name of Carlo Guarmani, with origins in a noble family of Tuscany, who lived in Beirut and was an agent for the French imperial mails. He would put his deep understanding of the Near East at the service of a horse-buying project for the imperial stables of Napoleon III and

Peter Upton
Salam Alaikum
Oil on canvas
50 × 80 cm
Courtesy of the artist
and Mathaf Gallery, London

Peter Upton, author of *The Classic Arab Horse*, wrote that the *"purity of the* kuhailan *(purebred horses from the Arabian Peninsula) is well-established, because the desert of the Arabian Peninsula was geographically isolated."*

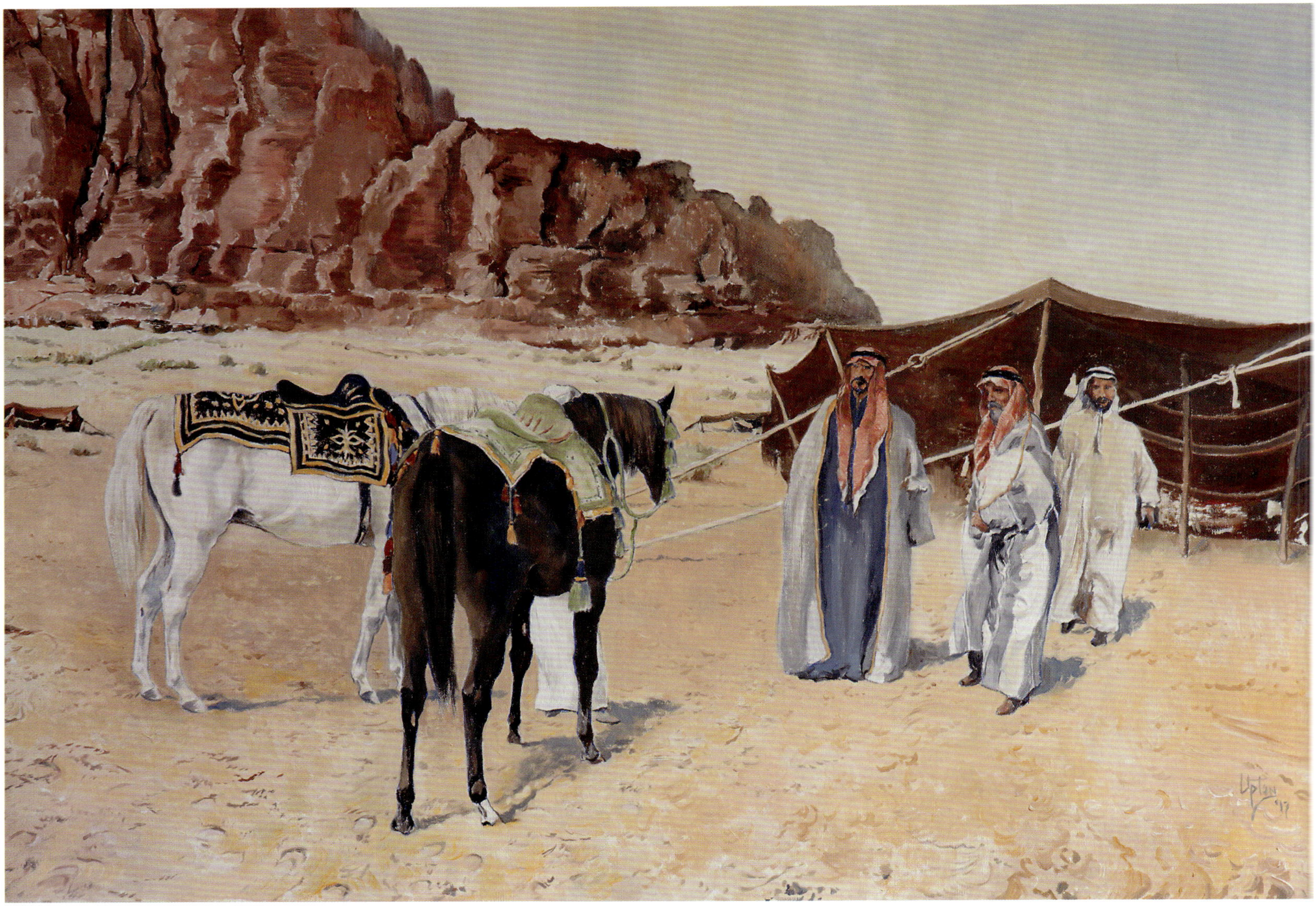

Anne Blunt
Untitled, January 31, 1900
Watercolor
Courtesy of the British Library and the artist

Purebred horses from the Arabian Peninsula were valued for being light and swift and possessing enormous endurance.

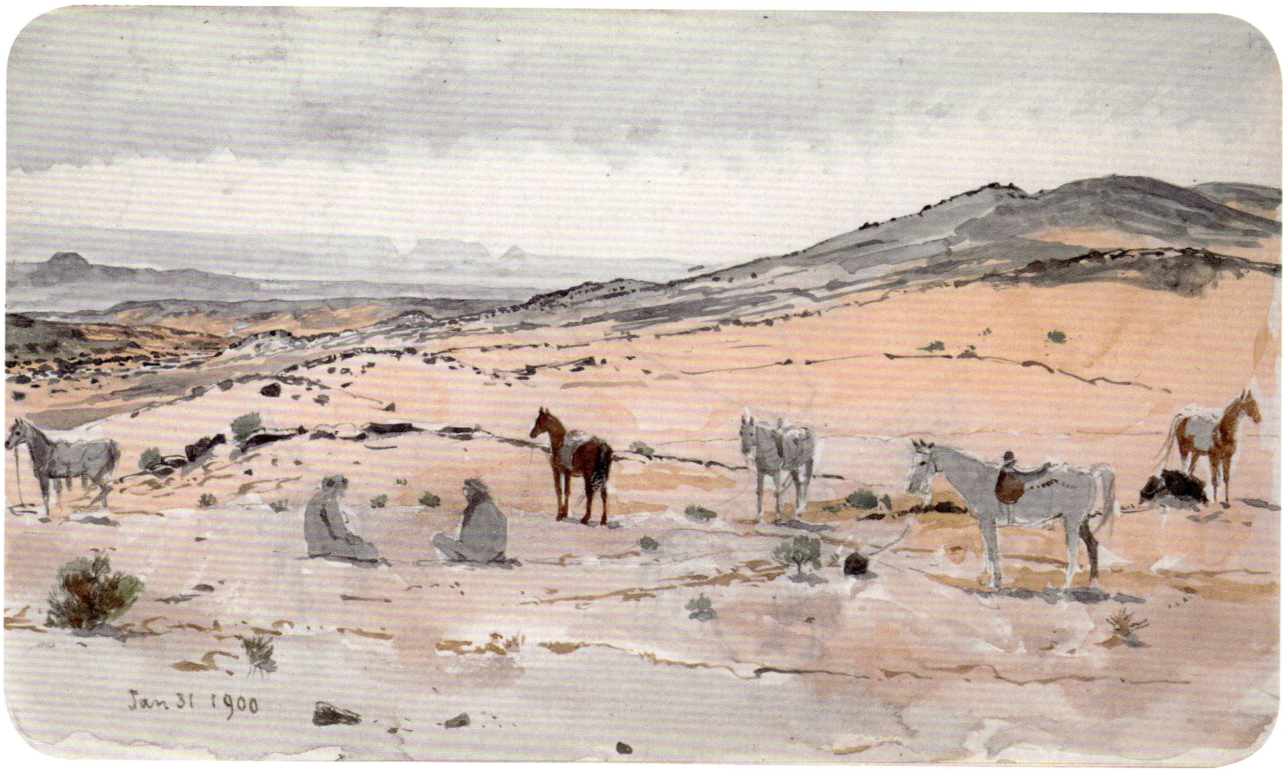

the stables of the King of Italy, Victor-Emmanuel II. Through intercession of the emir of Ha'il and the Anazeh tribe, Guarmani was able to acquire a large group of horses that was sent to France and Italy in 1864.

Guarmani, too, was the author of a travel book, *Northern Najd; A journey from Jerusalem to Anaiza in Qasim*, published in 1865, but more importantly, a book entitled *El Khamsa, the Thoroughbred Arabian Horse*, published in Jerusalem in 1866, which constituted one of the very first dedicated to the Arabian horse. Two books by an Englishman, Major Roger Dawson Upton, *Newmarket and Arabia* and *Gleanings from the Desert of Arabia*, published in England in 1873 and 1881, respectively, can also be classified in this category. Major Upton, after having served in the Indian army, made several voyages to the Arabian desert in the 1870s, assisted by J. H. Skene, British consul in Aleppo from 1855. Upton had been able to purchase a number of horses that had subsequently found their way to prestigious English stables.

During this same period, Anne and Wilfrid Blunt—already mentioned in this book (see chapter *The Desert of Deserts*)—also traveled in the desert, especially in the Nejd region, where they were able to visit the stables of the Al-Rashid princes, whose reputation was such that Ibn Rashid's stud "has become the most celebrated in Arabia," wrote Anne Blunt, noting that it "has taken the place in public estimation of that stud of Feysul ibn Saoud's which Palgrave saw and described sixteen years ago at Riad."

This British couple, descendants of aristocrats and intellectuals, attracted by the East, cultivated a profound interest in the Arabian horse. Anne Blunt happened to be the granddaughter of the great Lord Byron; she wrote travel books, such as *A Pilgrimage to Nejd, The Cradle of the Arab Race*. Having studied painting with Ruskin during her adolescence, she was also the author of beautiful watercolors. Wilfrid was a poet and a writer. Through the intercession of consul Skene, Anne and Wilfrid made the acquaintance of Upton, so one might suppose that the latter suggested the idea to them, mentioned in his books, to found a stud farm in England, where horses of the finest Arabian bloodlines would be bred.

This is how they became buyers, of the finest stallions and mares and, having sent them to England, Anne and Wilfrid Blunt created the Crabbet Arabian Stud in 1878 at one of their properties in Sussex. The undertaking aimed, as Wilfrid Blunt wrote, "to keeping the breed pure and developing the peculiar qualities of the Arab," and rapidly enjoyed a brilliant success. "By the beginning of the twentieth century"—that is, just over twenty years' time—"Crabbet was recognised both at home and abroad as the major source of pure-bred Arab horses. Sales to Arabian studs throughout the world had further extended the influence of Crabbet and

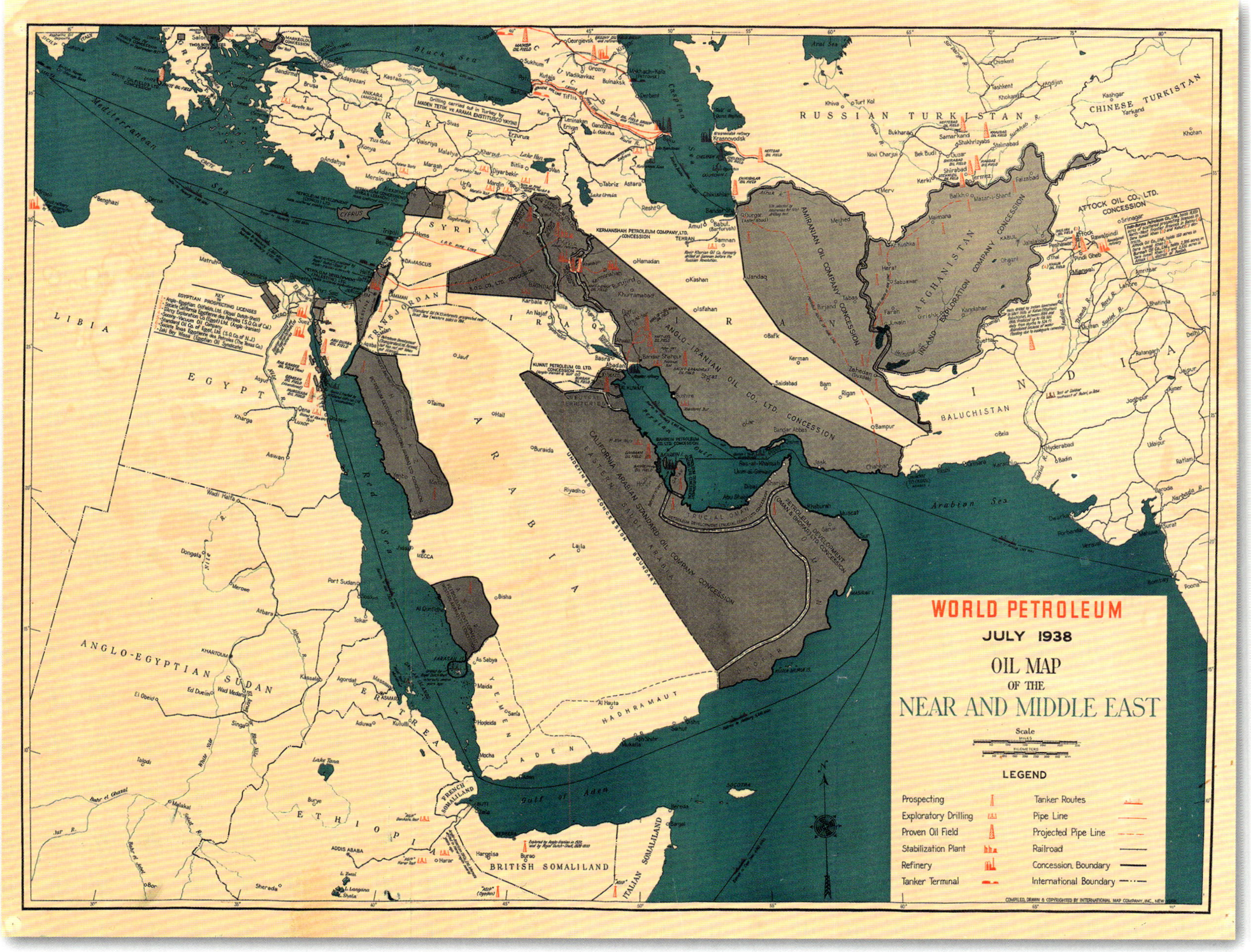

the Bedouin's fragile economy, that is exclusively based on the breeding of camels, completely obsolete. Oil and its revenues, if anything, arrived just in time to offer a real alternative to a people whose livelihoods—which had assured their survival for thousands of years—were now completely obsolete.

Hence Philby was able to quickly make the following observation: "Since hydrocarbons have been mined in the country, a great many Bedouins have been absorbed into the oil industry." Certainly, he would have to wait a long time before the Bedouins, or rather their sons, and then their grandchildren, were able to hold positions of responsibility within the oil industry. Initially, these roles were filled, for the most part, by foreigners. But the evolution was certainly faster than it had first been thought.

Philby continued: "One of the most rugged human adventures is coming to an end on the oil rigs." Without a doubt. Oil wells were appearing in Arabia just when the Bedouin lifestyle was already condemned. And these wells, whose numbers continued to increase, appeared on the horizon like beacons of salvation that would allow these men to soon become masters of this same modern world that had caused the loss of their traditional lifestyle. All it took was one or two generations.

Thesiger was wrong to see things only through the small end of the telescope and to sympathize with disdainful pity, as he did, about the fate of the Bedouins who would sell themselves to the oil industry: "On the oil fields the Bedu could find the money of which they dreamt. They could earn large sums by sitting in the

International Map Company Inc.
Oil map of the Near and the Middle East, July 1938
Chromolithographed map
57 × 75.5 cm
New York International Map Company
Courtesy of Sotheby's

This map shows the principal companies operating in the Near and Middle East, plus international boundaries, concession boundaries, railways, prospecting oilfields, producing oilfields, refineries, pipelines, and tanker routes.

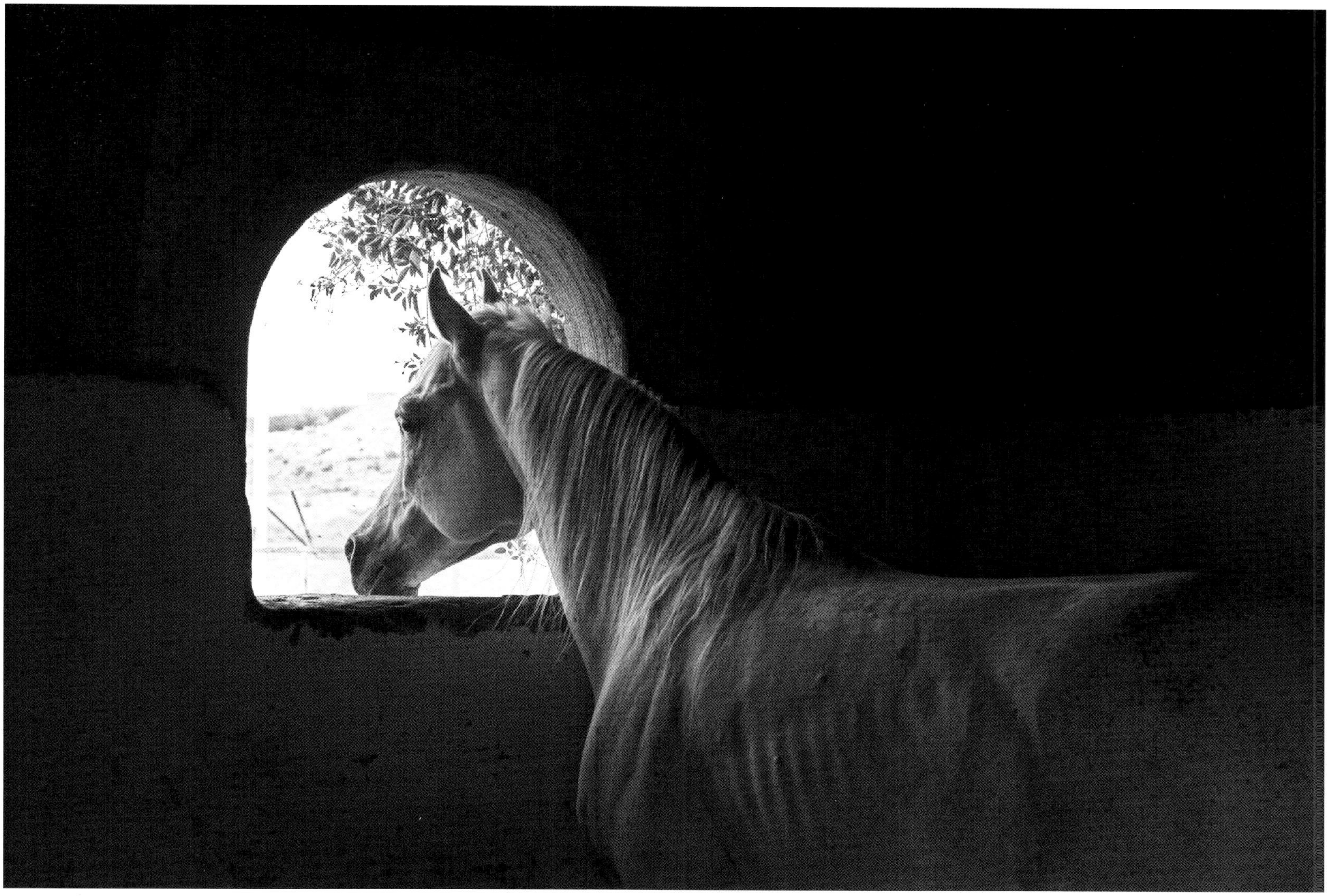

Olivier Couppey
In the stables

Burton wrote that the Bedouins say: *"Honourable to the rider is the riding of the horse; But the mule is a dishonour, and a donkey is a disgrace."*

written by the French general Eugène Daumas in 1851, *The Horses of the Sahara:* "Could it not be that the Arabs, because of their intimate association with the horse, have known how to develop in him faculties unknown to us?"

This Bedouin way of life may well be the origin of the horse's character, "exceptionally sweet, without tantrums, capable of affection and gratitude," Rzewuski commented. Before him, Palgrave wrote: "It is well known that in Arabia horses are much less frequently vicious or refractory than in Europe." Louis d'Arvieux did not say otherwise when he added these words to his observation cited above: "Those mares are so us'd to live in that familiarity, that they bear any kind of toying with."

The timeless Bedouin way of proceeding, remarked Cynthia Culberson in *A Gift from the Desert*, is perfectly similar to the most recent methods of imprinting as defined by equine behavioral scientists. This "imprinting training," implemented by the breeder from the birth of the colt and through its infancy, can profoundly modify their future relations. It is satisfying to see how ethology of the twenty-first century matches the oldest traditions of Arab horse breeding, across the centuries.

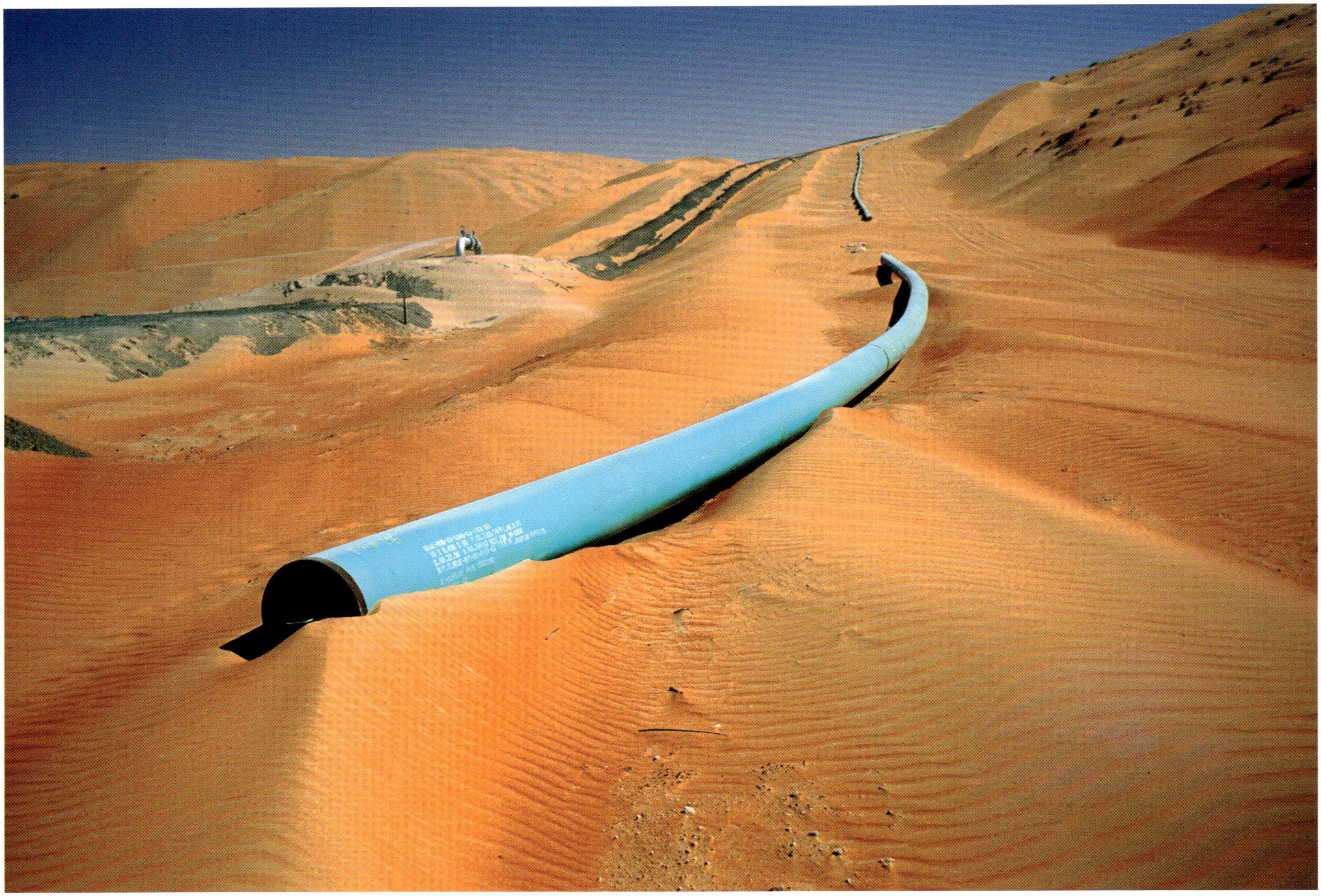

Fortune in Fossils

Stuart Franklin
Pipeline in Shaybah, 2000
Courtesy of Stuart Franklin and Magnum Photos

Shaybah's oil field lies at a distant of about 400 kilometers from the closest highway. The construction of its oil installation required enormous logistics. All the materials used and needed for its construction were transported from Dhahran, including the sand because the sand of the Rub' al-Khali is not suitable for cement. In a period of three years, Saudi Aramco was able to construct 400 kilometers of asphalted road, drill hundreds of wells, construct a pipeline of about 650 kilometers reaching the coastal oilfield of Abqaiq, and build a private airport, housing facilities, and administrative offices for exclusive use of Saudi Aramco.

"The oil story was very different: a veritable romance, surpassing the most improbable tales of the *Arabian Nights* in its astonishing evolution from the first laborious steps of the American geologists in the desert to the discovery and exploitation of a liquid Eldorado, far down in the bowels of the earth," wrote Harry St. John Bridger Philby, who, as a British advisor to the Saudi monarch Abdulaziz ibn Abderrahman Al Saoud, experienced this evolution first-hand.

The beginning of this venture can be traced back to 1922 and to the Conference of 'Uqayr, which took its name from the small port of Al-'Uqayr in the Arabian Gulf close to where the conference was held. This conference allowed the Arab sovereign, who at the time held the title of Sultan of Nejd since he had not yet fully completed the reunification of his country, to meet with representatives of the British Crown and to discuss various issues pertaining to regional policy. Among the attendees of the conference was a strange character who was not a member of any official delegation: Major Frank Holmes from New Zealand, mining engineer and former officer in the British Army. The major was convinced that Arabia, and particularly the region of the oasis of Al-Hasa, near the shores of the Arabian Gulf, contained oil.

Here, we will not recount all the twists and turns that finally led to the discovery of oil in huge quantities, precisely where the major said it was to be found. Suffice to say that Holmes was able to stir the interest of the sovereign, who allowed him to conduct research, even though Major Holmes himself found no oil. The Saudis nevertheless continue to remember him with the affectionate nickname of "Father of Petroleum" (*Abu an-Naft*). Apart from the anecdote, this episode is also recalled in the reflections and remarks of the sovereign's interpreter at the Conference of 'Uqayr, the Lebanese writer Ameen Rihani, who later dedicated various works to Saudi Arabia and its monarch.

Ameen Rihani, in fact, described the sovereign as a man who was constantly concerned for the future of his nation and all of its people. The Bedouins, toward whom he felt particularly close, were also a real challenge for him when it came to creating a unified nation. "The Bedu robbed Ibn Saoud of many a night's sleep," wrote the Lebanese essayist, describing a ruler for whom one of the major concerns was that the tribes were resistant to settling in one spot.

Oil would offer the country the financial means required to undertake the considerable and important changes that, otherwise, would not have even been considered. It was in 1937 that oil deposits were finally discovered in the province of Al-Hasa, near the Arabian Gulf—exactly where Major Holmes had suggested, fifteen years earlier, that oil would be found. The drilling that began in 1938 would soon transform the country.

"The discovery of oil has brought enormous wealth into Arabia," wrote Wilfred Thesiger, a British national who is considered the "last" traveler, or rather overseas explorer, to set out to discover Arabia. Having lived with the nomads for more than four years, from 1946 to 1950, and having crossed the most formidable of all deserts, the Rub' al-Khali, several times, Thesiger developed a fascination for the Bedouin people and their world. He committed himself to the substantial task of paying homage to the culture of these people, with even greater urgency given that he saw that it was at risk, in the context of the transformations Saudi Arabia was experiencing. "In Arabia," wrote Thesiger, "the changes which occurred in the space of a decade or two were as great as those which occurred in Britain between the early Middle Ages and the present day."

However, Thesiger realized that he was mistaken in blaming oil for the inevitable end of the Bedouin lifestyle. Oil was not to blame for this unavoidable disappearance: it was the advancement of science and technology. Steamboats, railways, cars, and planes had made

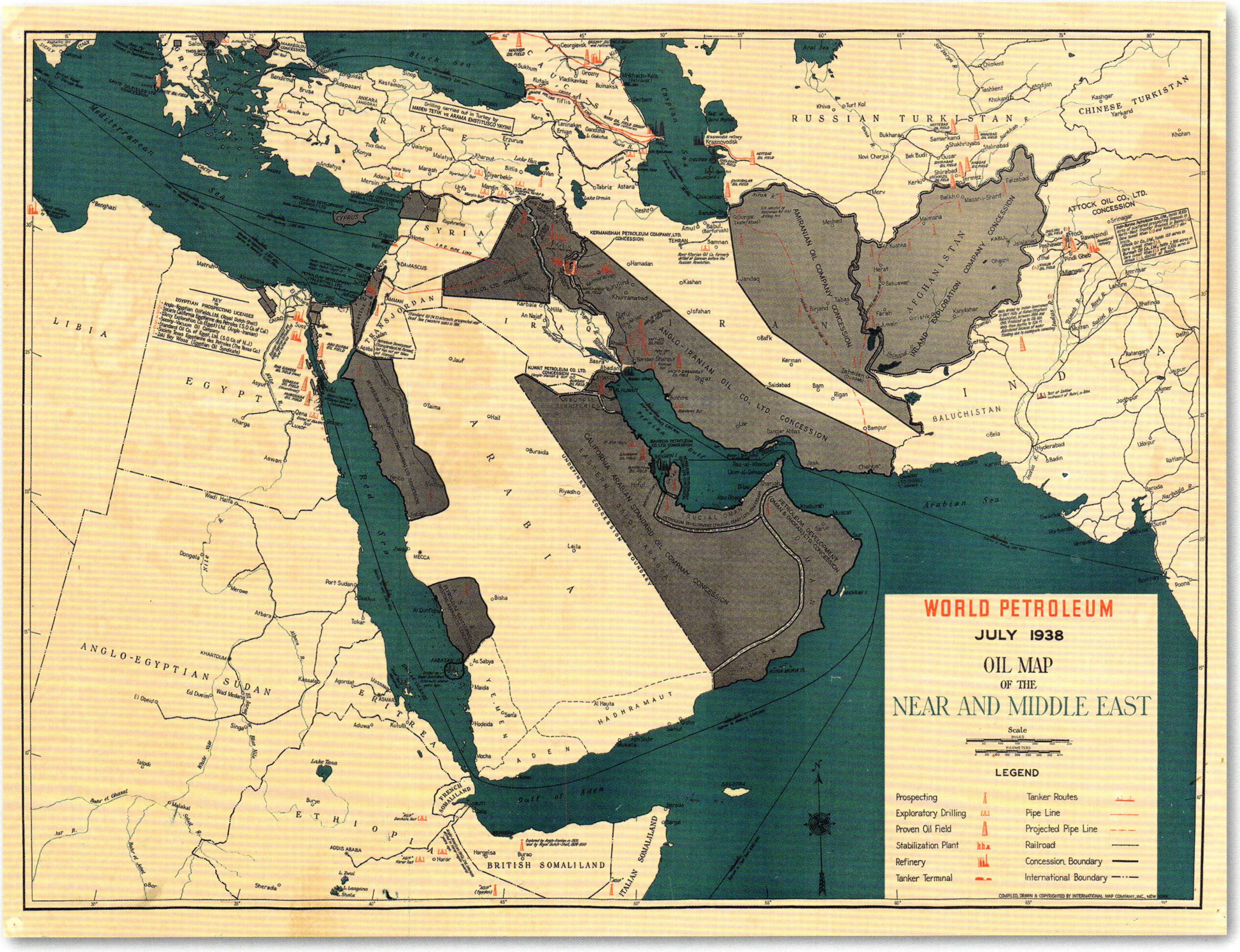

the Bedouin's fragile economy, that is exclusively based on the breeding of camels, completely obsolete. Oil and its revenues, if anything, arrived just in time to offer a real alternative to a people whose livelihoods—which had assured their survival for thousands of years—were now completely obsolete.

Hence Philby was able to quickly make the following observation: "Since hydrocarbons have been mined in the country, a great many Bedouins have been absorbed into the oil industry." Certainly, he would have to wait a long time before the Bedouins, or rather their sons, and then their grandchildren, were able to hold positions of responsibility within the oil industry. Initially, these roles were filled, for the most part, by foreigners. But the evolution was certainly faster than it had first been thought.

Philby continued: "One of the most rugged human adventures is coming to an end on the oil rigs." Without a doubt. Oil wells were appearing in Arabia just when the Bedouin lifestyle was already condemned. And these wells, whose numbers continued to increase, appeared on the horizon like beacons of salvation that would allow these men to soon become masters of this same modern world that had caused the loss of their traditional lifestyle. All it took was one or two generations.

Thesiger was wrong to see things only through the small end of the telescope and to sympathize with disdainful pity, as he did, about the fate of the Bedouins who would sell themselves to the oil industry: "On the oil fields the Bedu could find the money of which they dreamt. They could earn large sums by sitting in the

International Map Company Inc.
Oil map of the Near and the Middle East, July 1938
Chromolithographed map
57 × 75.5 cm
New York International Map Company
Courtesy of Sotheby's

This map shows the principal companies operating in the Near and Middle East, plus international boundaries, concession boundaries, railways, prospecting oilfields, producing oilfields, refineries, pipelines, and tanker routes.

Geological Survey
Arabian Peninsula, 1958
121 × 133 cm
Published in Washington, D.C., under the joint sponsorship of the Kingdom of Saudi Arabia Ministry of Finance and National Economy and the US Department of State.
Courtesy of Sotheby's

This color-printed geological map of the Arabian Peninsula shows oilfields, pipelines, and terminals. In the 1950s, the Saudi Ministry of Finance, the United States Geological Survey (USGS), and Aramco worked together to produce a series of geographic and geologic maps of the country. In addition to mapping, the USGS launched, over a period of nearly fifty years, technical surveys for the purpose of developing the Saudi mineral sector.

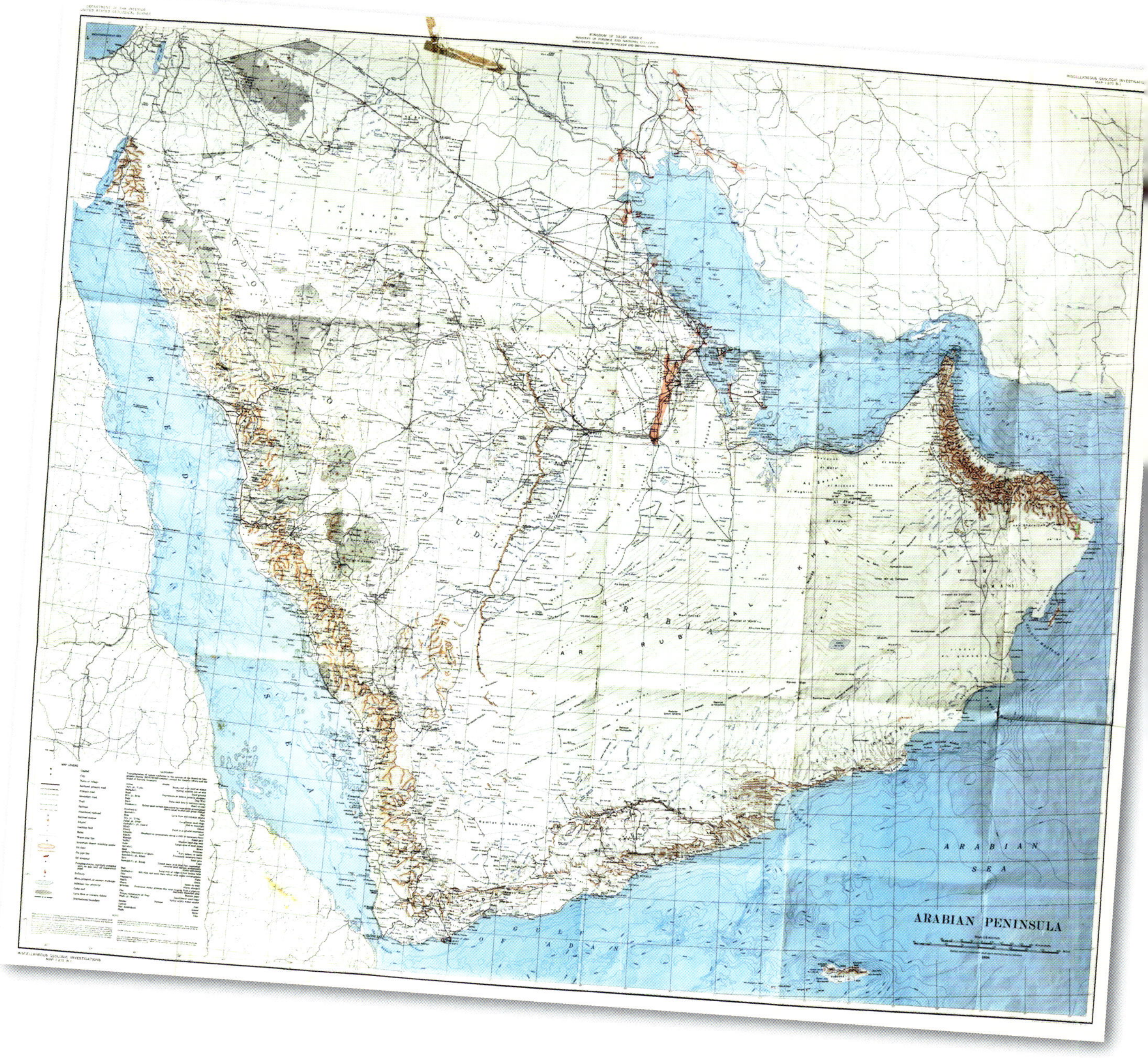

shade and guarding a dump, or by doing work which was certainly easier than watering thirsty camels on a nearly dry well in the middle of summer. There was plenty of good food, abundant sweet water, and long hours for sleep. They seldom had these things before, and now they were being paid into the bargain." It seems ironic—when we read the above—that Thesiger also agreed to be paid by an oil company. Before he wrote his books—the first of them in particular, *Arabian Sands*, would go on to be a real best seller—he had none of the royalties that the stories of his wanderings would later bring him and so he made do with being paid by one of these companies on the pretext that he had to finance his expeditions in some way. In exchange, he offered the oil company the exclusive information he had gleaned during his journeys in the desert!

Life in the desert, which Thesiger would later idealize in his many books, could be incredibly difficult. Nassir Ajmi confirms this in his book, *Legacy of a Lifetime*, published in 1995, three years after he left his duties as vice-president of the national Saudi hydrocarbons company, Saudi Aramco: "For Bedouins, life could be brutally harsh. This was especially true during drought years, when livestock perished and some members of the tribes, weakened by continuous hunger, fell prey to disease." It should be noted that the author of this statement, a Bedouin himself, was born in 1935, in a tent of a nomadic camp which was situated at the time in the western end of what would later become the Ghawar oil field—in other words, the largest terrestrial oil deposit in the world. Furthermore, Nassir Ajmi's role as vice-president of the

PIERS SECUNDA

Piers Secunda's work can be briefly summarized by the superposition of two lines of inquiry, one visual and the other symbolic. His visual research is an inquiry into form, sculpture, and medium. Piers Secunda has always tried to research new mediums or find innovative processes to shape common mediums. His symbolic research, tied to the visual inquiry, is about representing, through form and texture, the political and geopolitical borders and dynamics, as well as the forces exerted by history, that define mankind in present times. Therefore, it was essential to fuse the two separate lines of inquiry into a single set of processes and techniques. He has said: "A great deal of my studio and research time was dedicated to finding a material which could be made to behave like paint, but which would bring the noise and activity of daily life in the twenty-first century into my abstract studio practice." These lines of thought on practice led him, in 2009, to use crude oil as an artistic medium. He considered it to be the perfect melding of process and meaning into one medium, and a way to ground his artworks in the current century. In his words, "Crude oil is the primary material of our time. Not unlike bronze in the Bronze Age, or iron in the Iron Age. The Petrochemical Age will inevitably be acknowledged in a similar way. This means that, in my opinion, crude oil may be a contender as the ultimate artist's material today." Crude oil has the advantage of acting like paint, which makes it a perfect candidate for Secunda's textural research. In addition, he found another way of integrating history in the process, by finding and procuring crude oil from historically significant wells, as opposed to any crude oil. Thus, his first work with this process was made from a sample of crude oil from Drake's Well in Pennsylvania, which was the first commercial oil well, drilled in 1859, and the beginning of what Secunda calls the "Petrochemical Age."

In the artworks featured in this book, Secunda uses oil from Well n° 7, the first commercially successful oil well in Saudi Arabia that blew in—which is the moment at which oil first spews out of a well—in the spring of 1937. Given Saudi Arabia's importance in global oil commerce, it is no stretch to say that this moment was of utmost importance in geopolitics to this day and it also drastically transformed the kingdom and its inhabitants' lifestyles. In *Dammam N° 7 blowing in*, Piers Secunda found an archive photo of the well and used it to produce the silkscreen. It then took him two years to finally find a sample of the well's crude oil, which he used to achieve the silkscreen transfer and printing. With such a piece, Secunda was able to fold

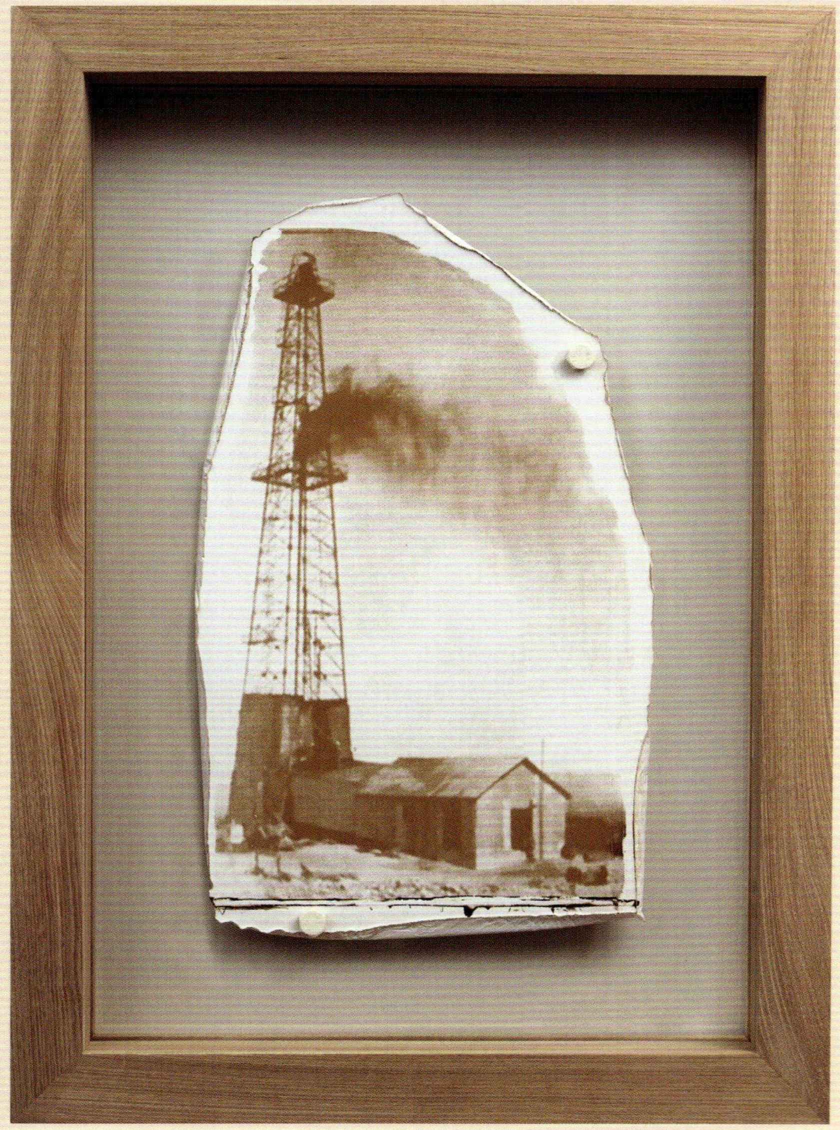

Piers Secunda
Dammam N° 7 blowing in, 1938
2017 Dammam well No. 7
Crude oil and varnish on industrial floor paint, with cast-paint nuts and bolts
69 × 51 × 6 cm
Courtesy of the artist

Discovered in 1938, "Dammam n° 7" produced oil for several decades.

Piers Secunda
Aramco's first office, 1939
2017 Dammam well N° 7
Crude oil and varnish on industrial floor paint, with cast-paint nuts and bolts
51 × 73 × 6 cm
Courtesy of the artist

Established in 1933, CASOC's (California Arabian Standard Oil Company's) first office was housed in Jeddah's "Beit Baghdadi" featured in this photo. Today Saudi Aramco, officially the Saudi Arabian Oil Company, the world's largest petroleum company, is based in Dhahran.

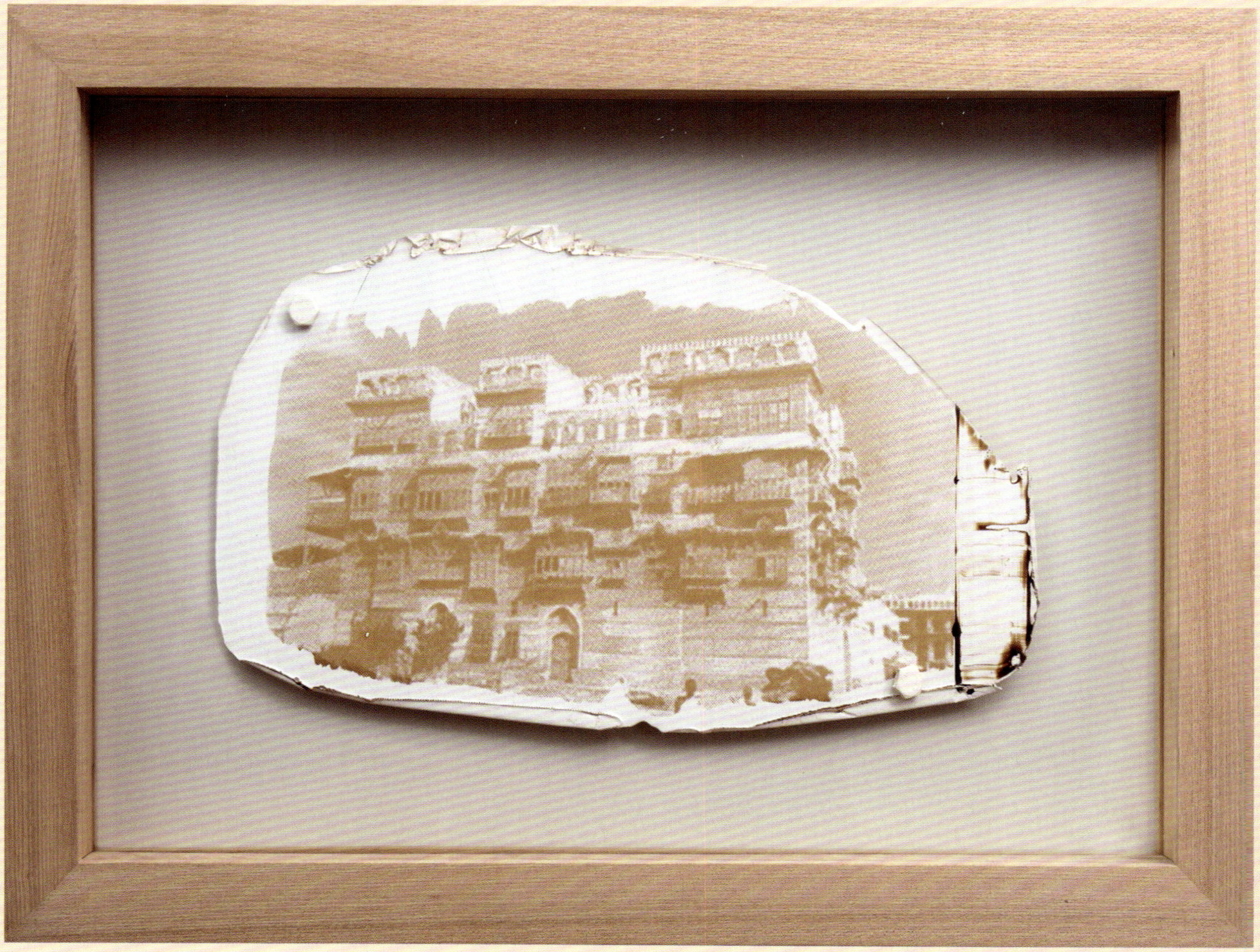

a historical moment, a narrative, and its contemporary consequences onto a single plane.

Despite the numerous political messages which could be ascribed to his work, Secunda is steadfast in describing his crude oil works as apolitical: "Crude oil plays a fundamental role in every aspect of 21st century living, from energy and transport to agriculture and medicine, and is the main component of the world's most frequently used material—plastic. The incredible thing about crude oil is that it's absolutely and totally inseparable from everything we do. It facilitates everything—if you remove it, you'd have mayhem." Secunda does not refute the fact that crude oil in itself has a political dimension, but claims it is not his aim, with this series, to comment on this aspect. His artworks function more as a historical and geopolitical observation on the impact that oil has had on the past and current century. By recording these different times and places that were relevant to the history of crude oil exploitation, Secunda depicts the shifts in the balance of power and the rhythm of human progress. That he was able to master the use of crude oil as the medium to record this evolution is a testament to this resources' importance in all aspects of life.

Leaving the conclusion to Piers Secunda, we can undoubtedly affirm: "If crude oil is the world's ultimate facilitator, it must therefore be a contender as the ultimate artist's material."

Harold Corsini
An oil derrick amid the sand dunes of the desert north of Abqaiq in eastern Saudi Arabia, summer 1947
Courtesy of the Library of Congress Prints and Photographs Division

Abqaiq oil wells are located halfway between Dhahran and Hofuf.

Harold Corsini
Drilling floor crew slipping elevators over drill pipe during a pipe change on an Aramco drilling rig in the Abqaiq field in eastern Arabia, summer 1947
Courtesy of the Library of Congress Photographs and Prints Division

Drilling in Abqaiq started before World War II, but the pace of construction and production increased substantially after the war.

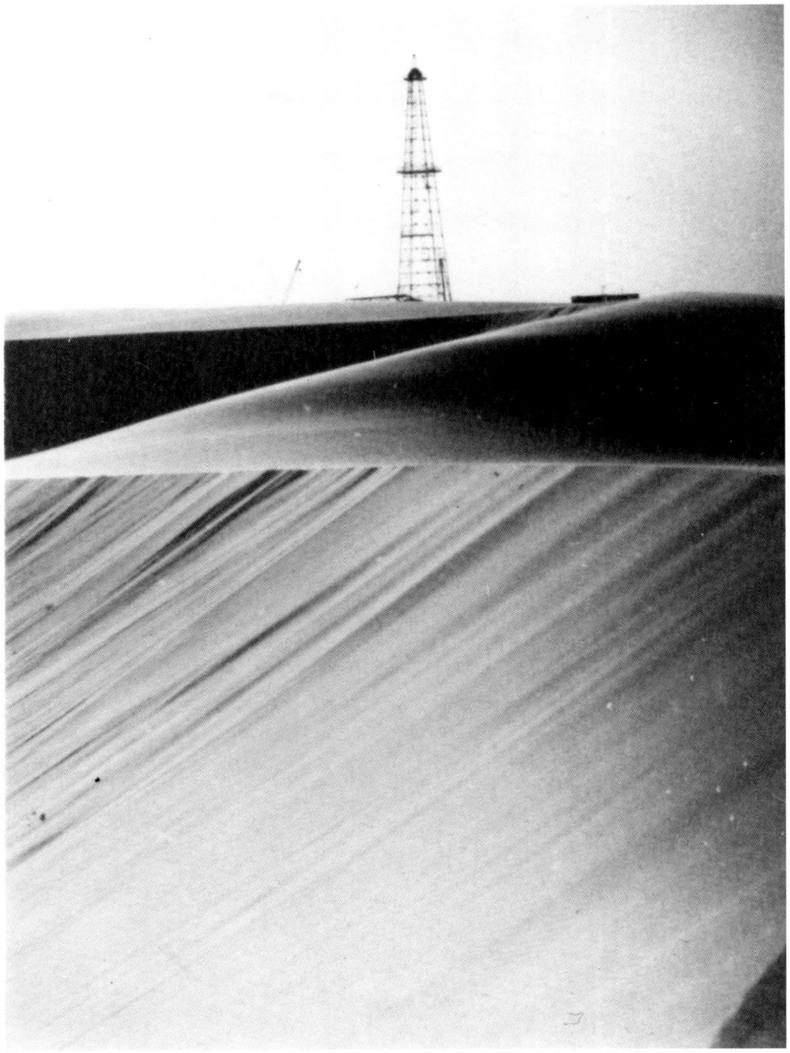

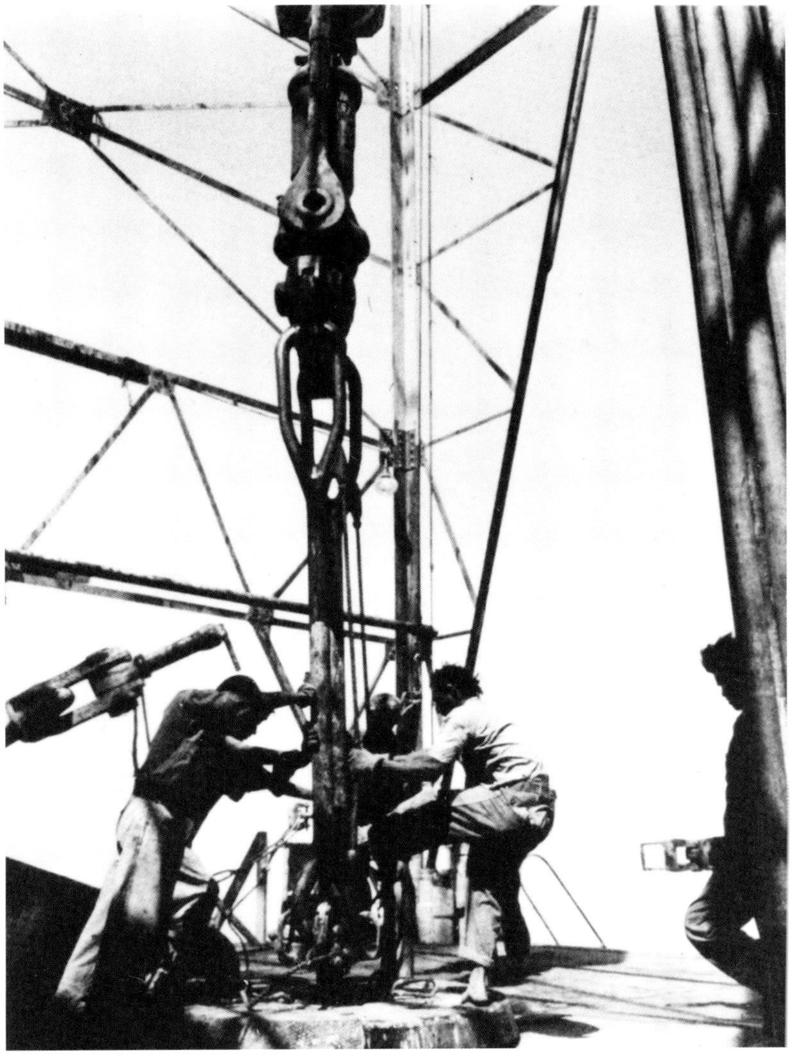

Marc Riboud
Praying in the Rub' Al-Khali, 1974
Courtesy of the Centre Pompidou-MNAMM-CCI/RMN, Paris

The search for oil began after the signature of the 60-year concession agreement between Saudi Arabia and Standard Oil of California on May 29, 1933. At that time no one imagined that Saudi Arabia's oil reserves would produce more oil than any other country on earth.

Raymond Depardon
Ghawar oil well located in Al-Hasa governorate, 1968
Courtesy of Raymond Depardon and Magnum Photos

The Ghawar field, discovered in the mid-1950s, is the world's largest onshore field.

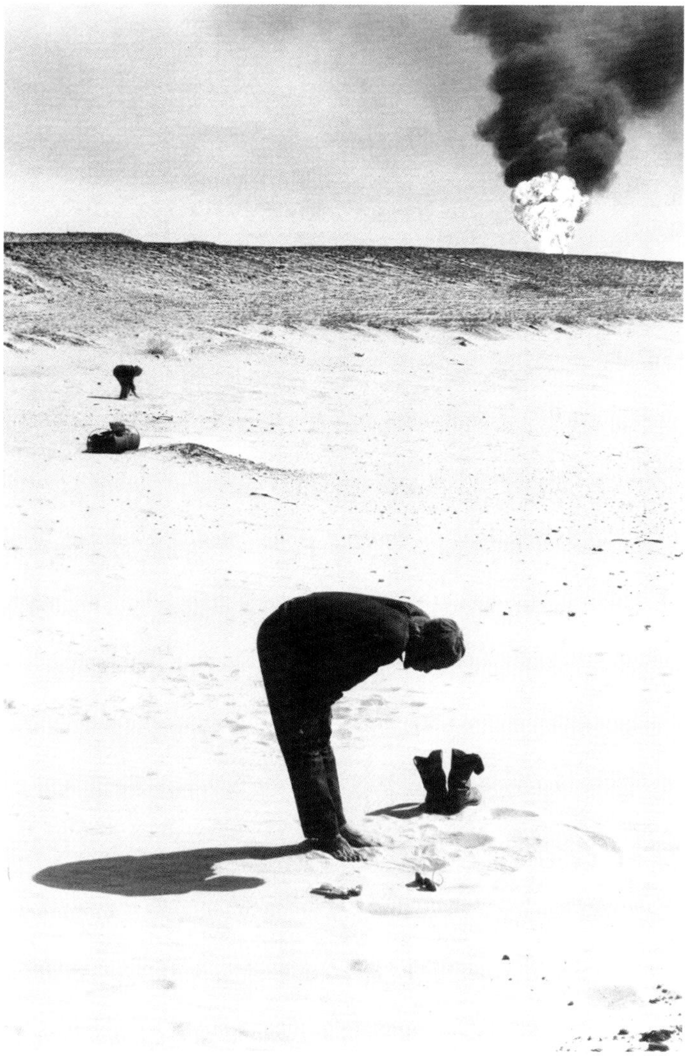

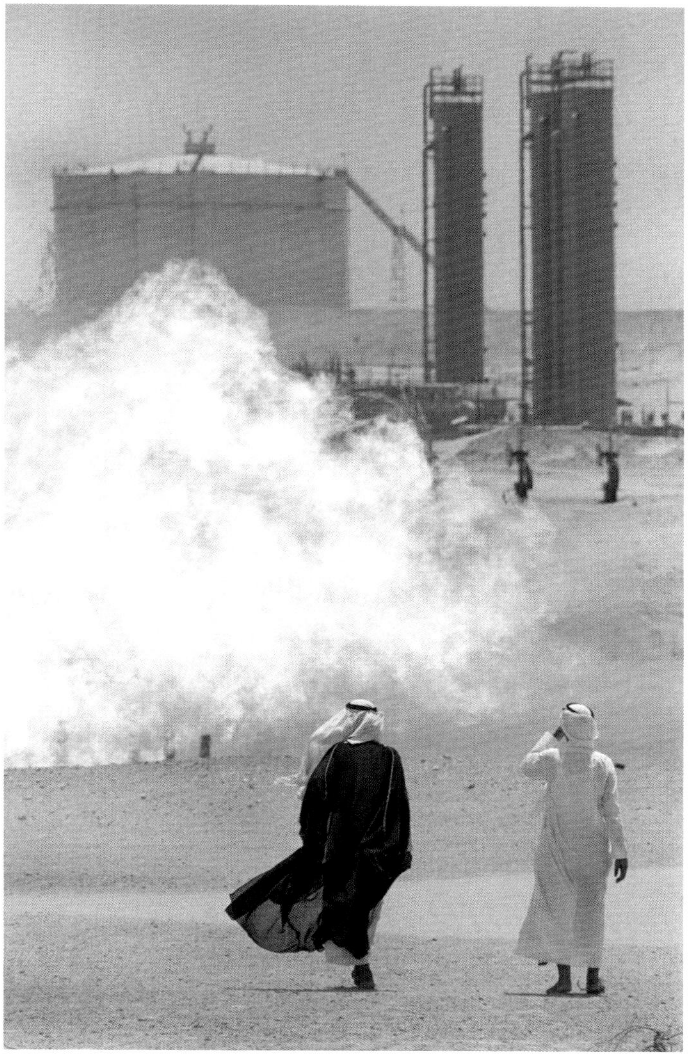

Abbas
Oil Pump in Dhahran, 1990
Courtesy of Abbas and Magnum Photos

Thesiger wrote in *Arabian Sands* that as a result of the discovery of oil in Saudi Arabia, the life described in his book disappeared forever. The changes which occurred in the space of a decade or two were as great as those which occurred in Britain between the early Middle Ages and the present day.

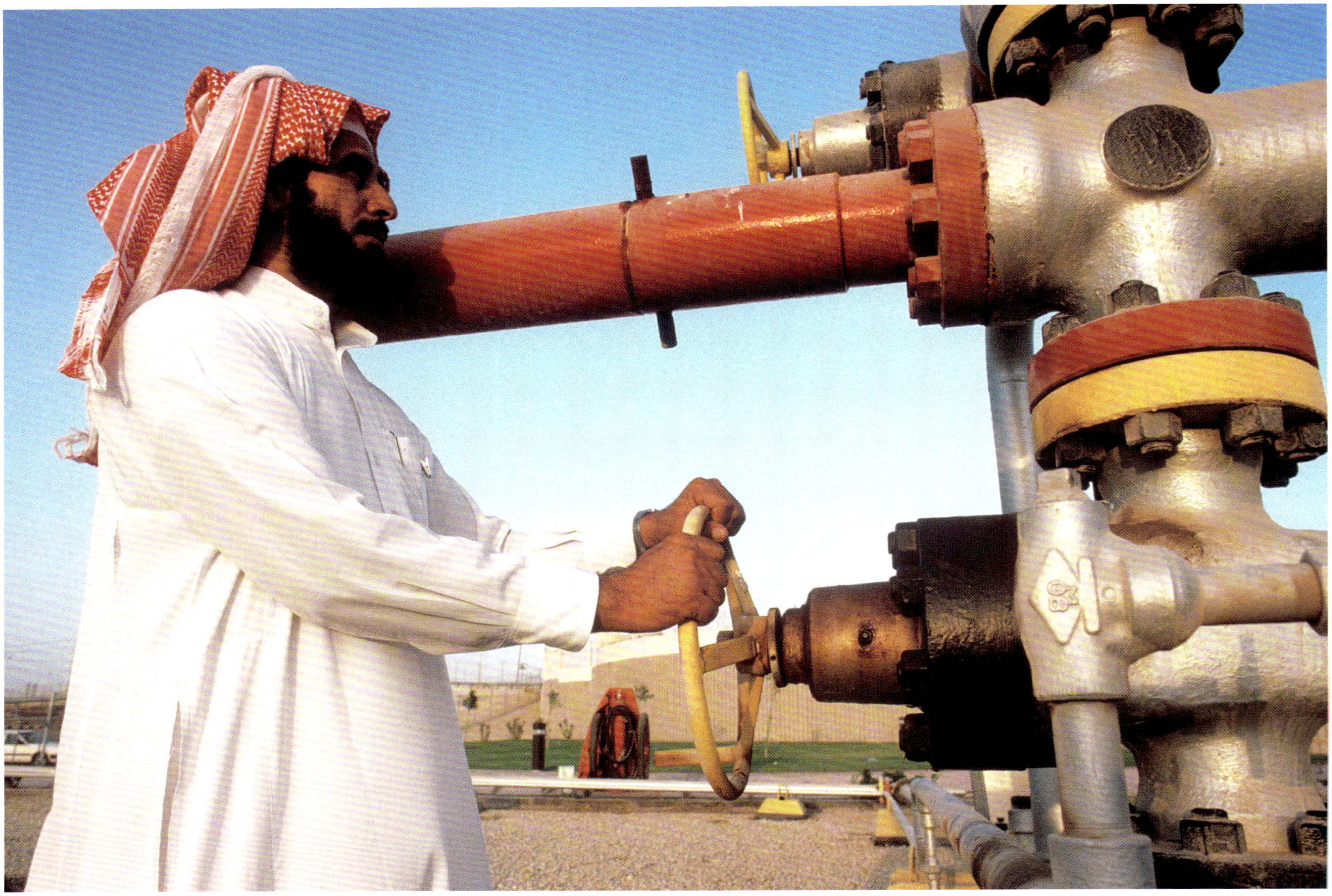

Colbert Held
Aerial view looking north to gasoil separation plant no. 4 (GOSP 4), at Ain Dar, 1958
Courtesy of the Middle East Institute and Colbert Held Archive, Washington, D.C.

Feeder lines from several producing wells bring crude to this GOSP for separation of gas and oil, and the gas (surplus and unusable at this stage) is flared in the burners shown at the bottom of the photo.

Colbert Held
Mid-oblique aerial view looking up the natural sand spit on which Aramco has established its Ras Tanura oil loading terminal. On the right are two loading piers, 1958
Courtesy of the Middle East Institute and Colbert Held Archive, Washington, D.C.

Aramco started the construction of the Ras Tanura refinery in 1943.

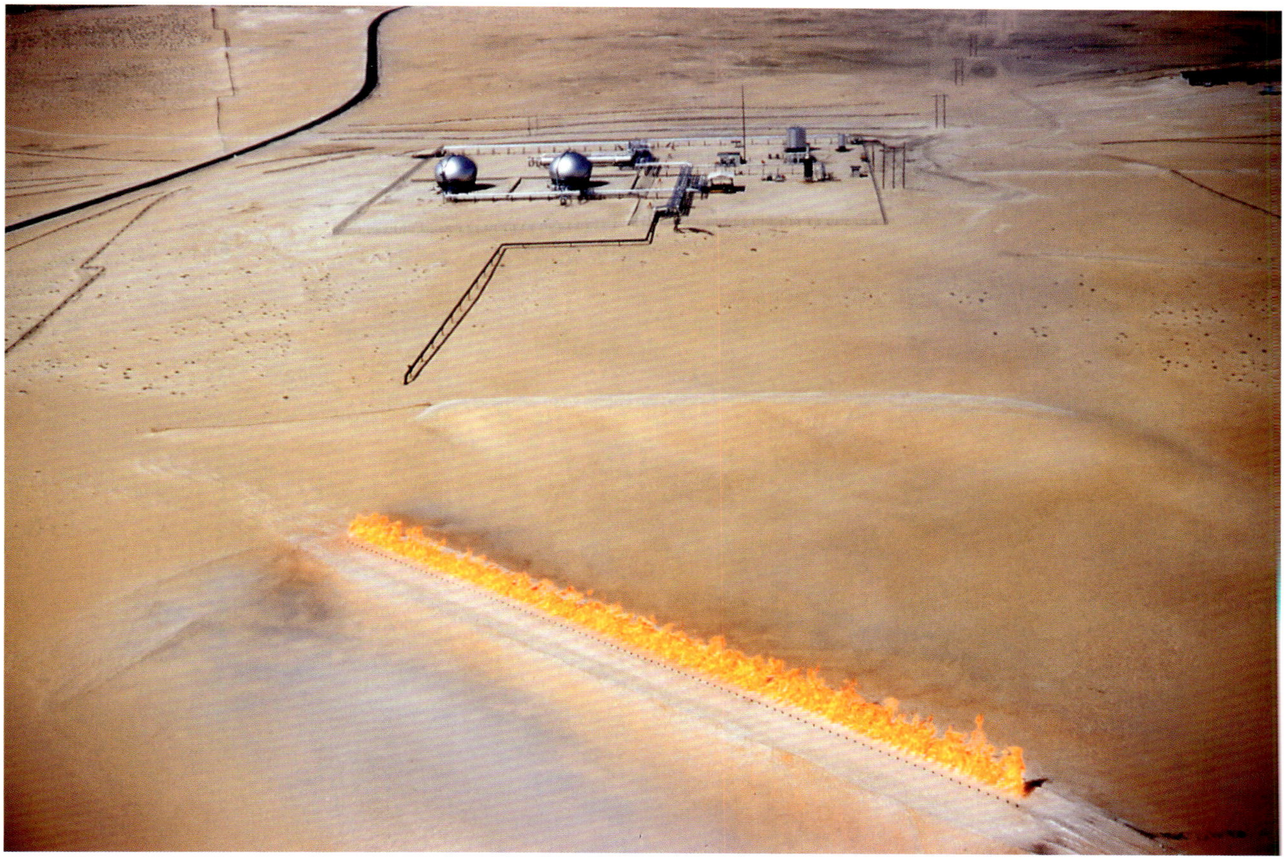

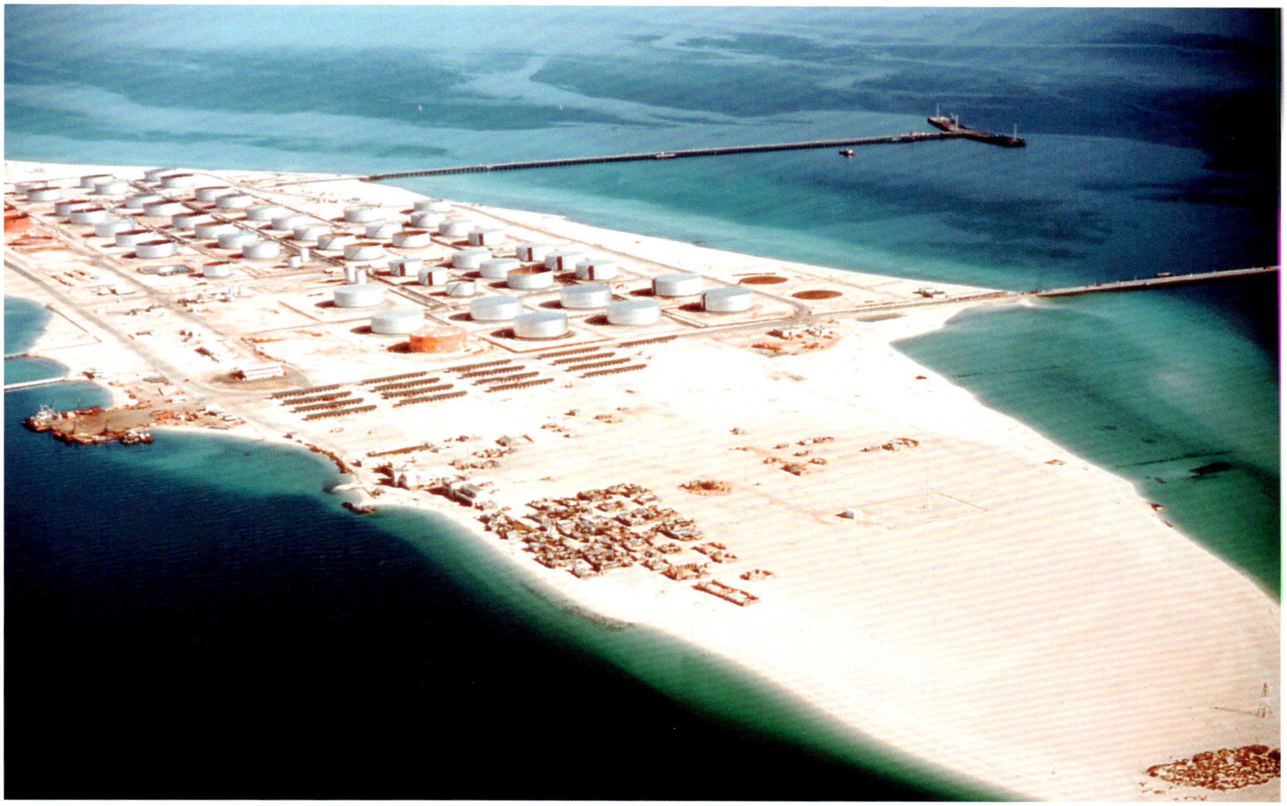

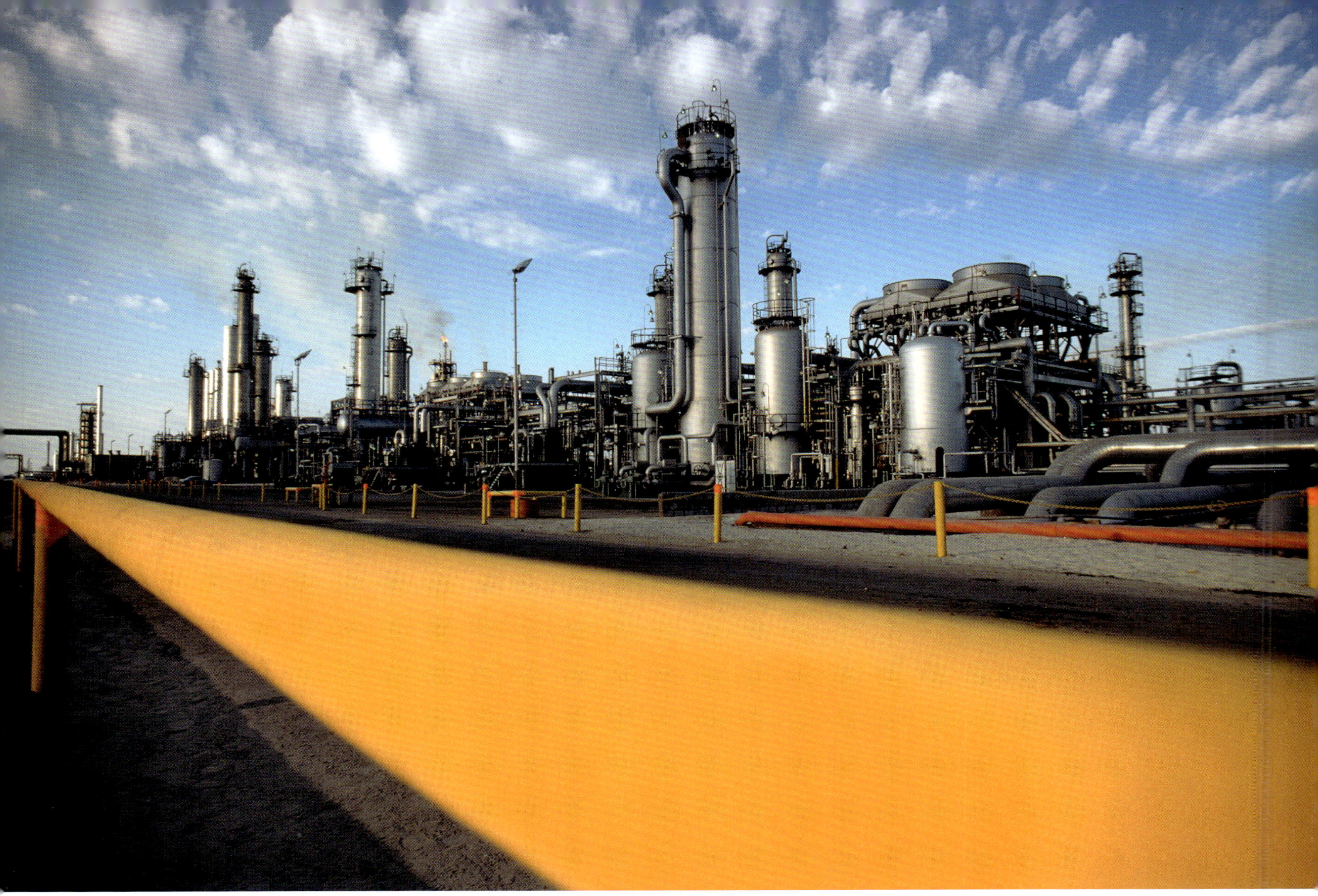

national company proved that the Bedouins were not doomed, as Thesiger implied, to hold minor positions in this industry.

If this was indeed the case during the first years, the situation rapidly changed afterwards. Thus, less than twenty years after oil of the famous "Well Seven," in Dammam, began to be exploited in 1938, 70 percent of the employees in the national hydrocarbon company were Saudi. Ten years later, in 1967, 57 percent of the 1,373 employees occupying positions of responsibility or management were Saudis.

Nassir Ajmi makes it clear in his book why this new industry attracted these men: "Nomadic life was a continuous struggle," he wrote, "but the alternatives were few—limited to subsistence farming, fishing and pearl diving—and just as arduous. Animal rearing was the most lucrative, but nomads looked down on farming because it would force them to settle and restrict their freedom of movement." Obviously, the other alternatives were not as thrilling: "Fishing and pearl diving were similarly despised, for the nomads disliked and feared the sea, to the point of actually starving before eating fish," noted Nassir Ajmi.

As previously mentioned, the widespread use of modern means of transport had dealt an irreversible blow to the nomads' economy, which was based on camels. While Bedouins's revenues were in free fall, those of the pearl fishermen were also hard hit, first by the 1929 crash and then by the world economic crisis—the Great Depression—that ensued and that affected the number of pearls sold considerably. More importantly, the appearance on the market of cultured pearls was the final blow to a sector which would never completely recover. Here again, oil had appeared in a timely and providential way allowing those who were left to fend for themselves to find new jobs in the oil business, leaving behind the

René Burri
Refinery, 1974
Courtesy of René Burri
and Magnum Photos

As early as 1947, Wilfred Thesiger wrote in *Arabian Sands* about the enormous wealth that was pouring into Saudi Arabia from the American Oil Company. In October 1992, Saudi Arabia became the world's top oil-producing nation, eclipsing Russia. Saudi Aramco is also the world's number-one exporter of crude oil and natural gas liquids.

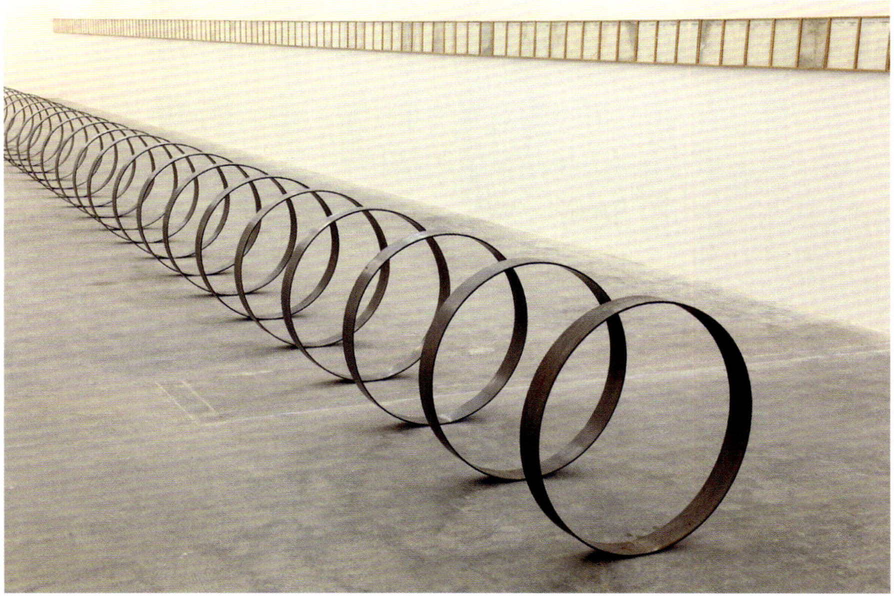

Rayyane Tabet
Steel Rings
From the series *The Shortest Distance Between Two Points*, 2013
Rolled engraved steel with unique location details
80 cm diameter, 10 cm deep, 0.6 cm thick
Courtesy of the artist and Sfeir-Semler Gallery, Beirut/ Hamburg

Steel Rings replicates, in the same diameter and thickness, the pipeline belonging to the Trans-Arabian Pipe Line Company, constructed after World War II to transport oil from Saudi Arabia to the Mediterranean Sea over land. The pipeline was abandoned and its infrastructure left in the sand due to the sociopolitical transformations in the region in 1983.

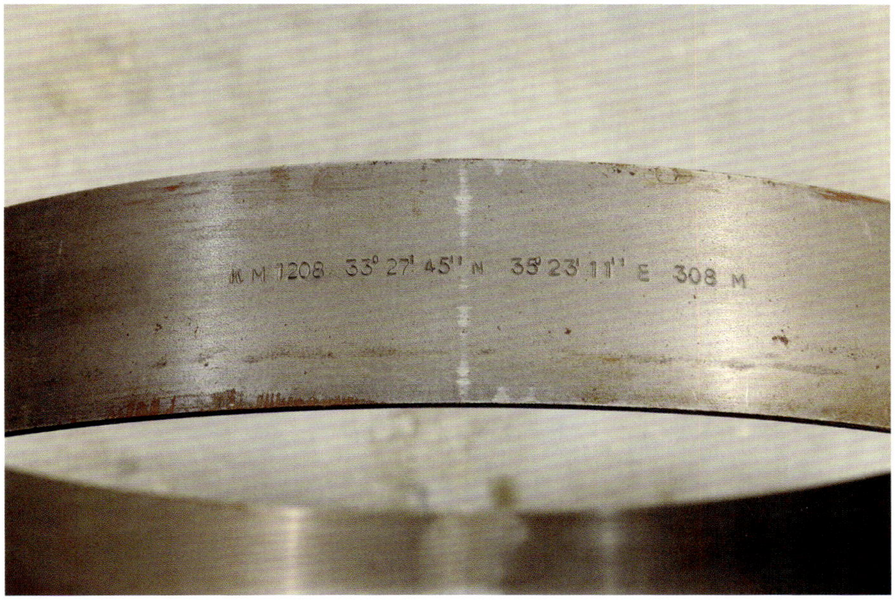

Rayyane Tabet
Steel Rings
From the series *The Shortest Distance Between Two Points*, 2013
Rolled engraved steel with unique location details
80 cm diameter, 10 cm deep, 0.6 cm thick
Courtesy of the artist and Sfeir-Semler Gallery, Beirut/ Hamburg

Detailed view of the rolled engraved steel with kilometer, longitude, latitude, and elevation markings of a specific location on the Trans-Arabian Pipe Line, known as Tapline. Initially Tapline ran north and west across Saudi Arabia and then through Transjordan and Palestine to the port of Haifa. After 1948, Aramco redirected the pipeline through Transjordan, Syria, and to the port of Sidon in Lebanon.

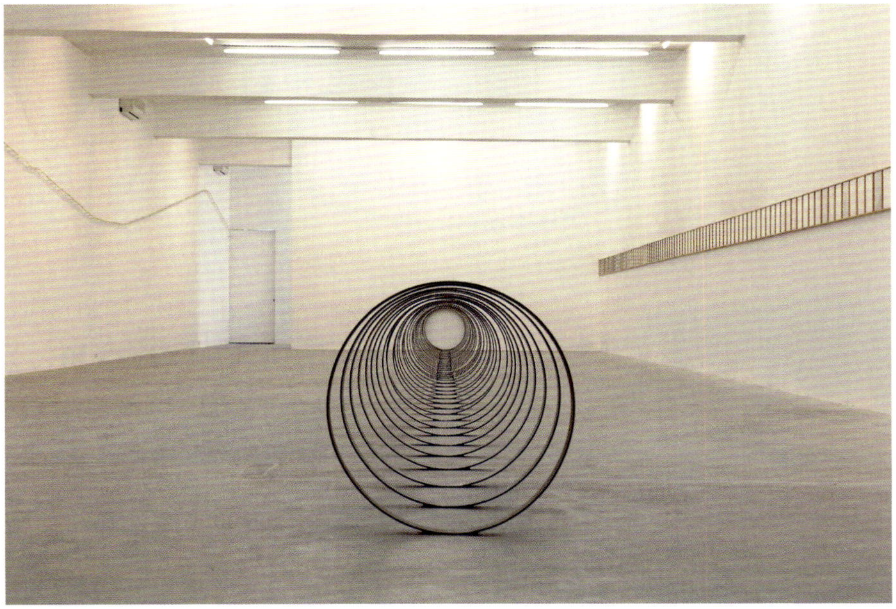

Rayyane Tabet
Steel Rings
From the series *The Shortest Distance Between Two Points*, 2013
Rolled engraved steel with unique location details
80 cm diameter, 10 cm deep, 0.6 mm thick
Courtesy of the artist and Sfeir-Semler Gallery, Beirut/ Hamburg

Steel Rings is composed of forty steel rings that run in a straight line, corresponding to the 40 kilometers of pipeline that cut through Lebanon.

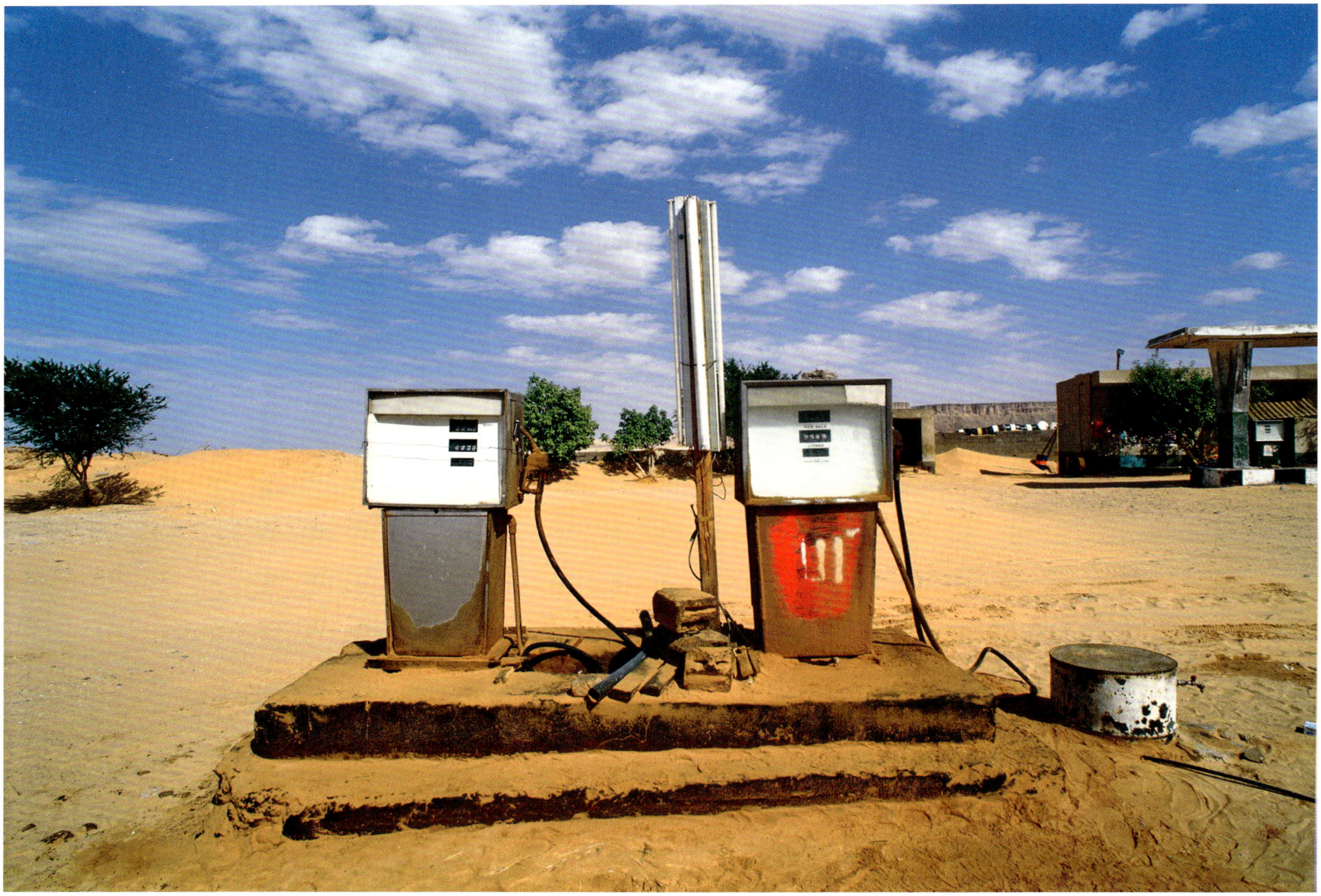

George Steinmetz
Out of order petrol pumps in Al-Fau, 2002
Courtesy of George Steinmetz

George Steinmetz
Flare from the gasoil separation plant (GOSP) in Shaybah in the Rub' al-Khali desert, 2002
Courtesy of George Steinmetz

Located in a remote zone in the northern edge of the Rub' al-Khali, the oil field of Shaybah was not considered profitable when it was discovered in 1968.

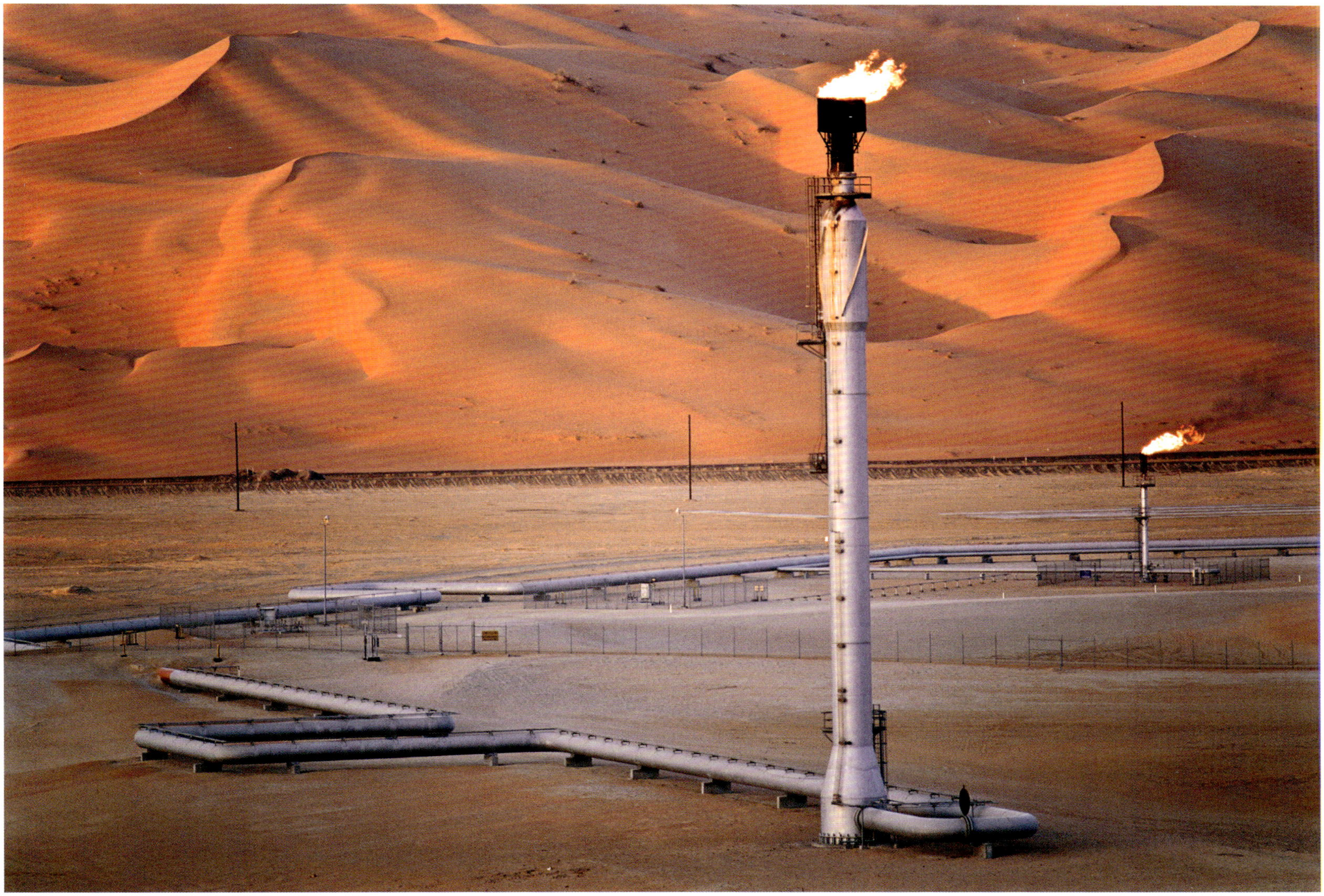

ancestral pearl fishing which had been practiced in the Arabian Gulf for many centuries.

These men—divers, sailors, merchants, and brokers—would form the core of a strictly local work force that would contribute to the rapid development of the oil industry from the very beginning. And this is how the son of a pearl diver, a native of Al-Khobar on the coast of the Arabian Gulf, Abdallah S. Jum'ah, went on to become the CEO of the Saudi national oil company, from 1995 to 2008.

Born in the Bedouin world, as we have already stated, Nassir Ajmi evokes the life of his ancestors with tenderness and nostalgia: "Despite constant hardships, the simple nomadic life was full of joy and laughter. The Bedouin considered themselves superior to farmers and townsmen because of their perceived genealogical and linguistic purity, their courage, resourcefulness, hospitality, and generosity. Their distinctive way of life made them self-reliant, proud, extremely loyal to the tribal heritage, and lovers of freedom. Their integrity, courage, friendship, and hospitality were beyond reproach." The senior officer of the hydrocarbon company concluded: "And it was among the Bedouin that the poets, tellers of epic stories, sportsmen, and hunters were to be found."

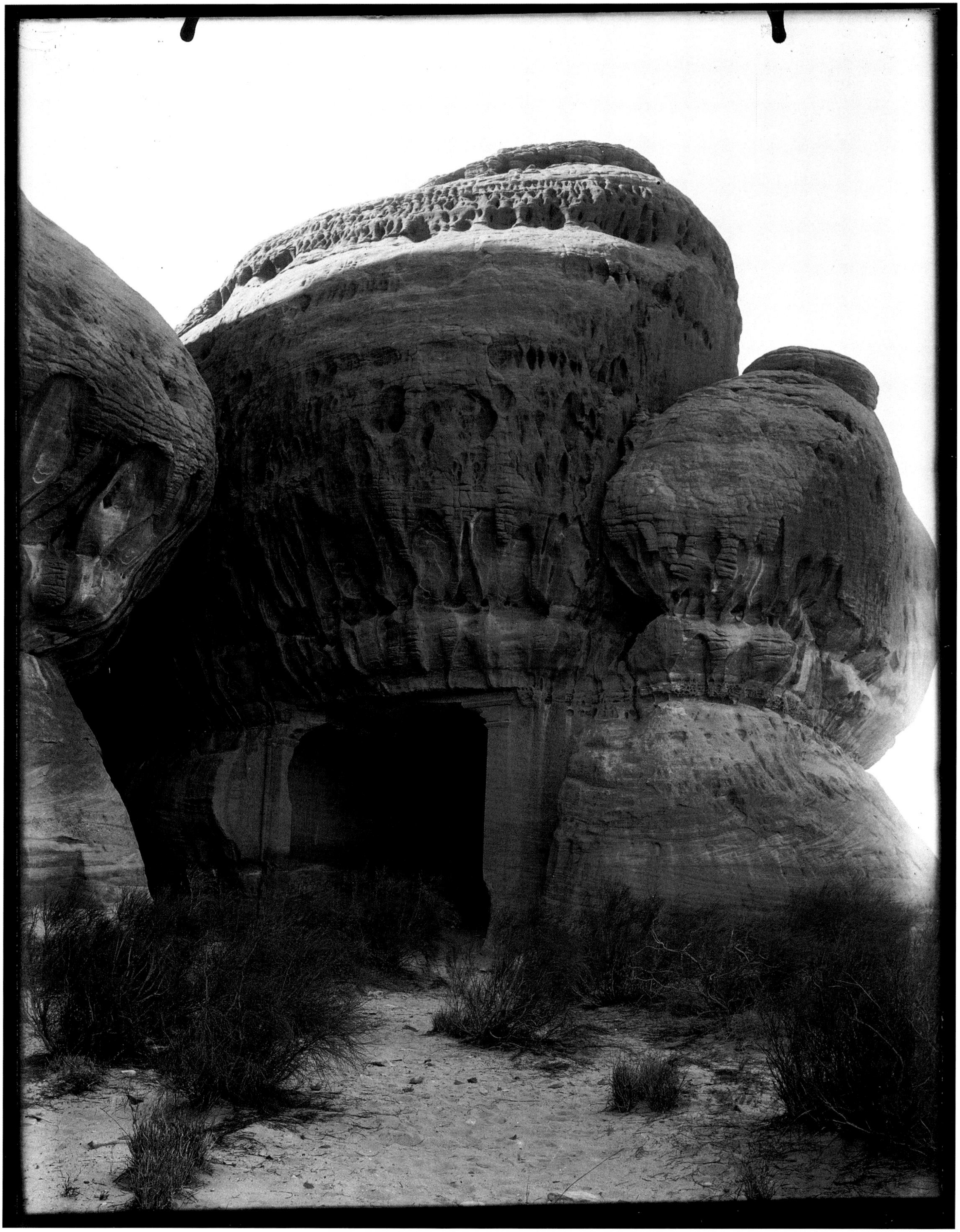

Jaussen and Savignac
The banquet hall "Al-Diwan" at the entry of Jebel Ethlib in Mada'in Saleh (Hegra), 1907
Courtesy of the French Biblical and Archaeological School of Jerusalem

Situated in a passage in Mount Ethlib, the Al-Diwan "hall or council chamber" is the only non-sepulchral monument at Hegra. The Diwan, wrote Doughty in *Travels in Arabia Deserta*, is *"an open chamber: the front is of excellent simplicity, a pair of pilasters to the width of the hewn chamber, open as a nomad tent. [...] In the passage, which is fifty paces long, the sun never shines, a wind breathes there continually, even in summer: this was a cool site to be chosen in a sultry country."*

Shortly after entering Hijaz, pilgrims journeying with a caravan from Damascus to the holy cities of Arabia passed through Al-Hijr. This was little more than a small village, a caravan stop where they could catch sight—as you can still do today—of the extraordinary façades of the ancient rock monuments hewn in the mountains by the Nabataeans. These were described by Ibn Battuta, at the beginning of the fourteenth century, as the homes of the Thamud people: "They are cut in the hills of red rock and have carved thresholds. Anyone seeing them would take them to be of recent construction. Their decayed bones are to be seen inside these houses."

This ancient city, on the southern edge of the Nabatea, was once well known to the Greeks and Romans by the name of "Haegra" or "Egra," derived from the Nabataean "Hijra". The Arabic name Al-Hijr "is the exact equivalent of the Nabataean toponym, the prefixed Arabic article *al-* being the translation of the suffixed Nabataean article *-a* that ends the word 'Hijra'," wrote Laïla Nehmé, Daifallah Al-Talhi, and Jacques Villeneuve, in the chapter entitled *Hegra of Arabia Felix*, in the collective publication *Roads of Arabia: Archaeology and History of the Kingdom of Saudi Arabia*, published in 2010, in Paris, on the occasion of the eponymous exhibition at the Louvre.

Al-Hijr is mentioned repeatedly in the Koran, which reports how a prophet named Saleh was sent to the polytheistic residents of the Thamud city in order to convert them to the worship of the one God, and how their refusal led to their sudden extermination. It is in reference to this episode that Al-Hijr gained the name of Mada'in Saleh (literally "*The Cities of Saleh*"), a name which apparently appeared only later, in the Ottoman era.

In his *Sketch of the Countries*, and in a note dedicated to Al-Hijr, the renowned Syrian geographer Abu Al-Fida, a contemporary of Ibn Battuta, writes that "the pilgrims of Syria stop there on their way to Mecca" and highlights the dreadful fate of the Thamud people. The Kashmiri pilgrim Abdul-Kerym, on the occasion of his stopover in Al-Hijr in 1741, recalls the same destructive circumstances: "In the vicinity of this town are the ruins of another, once very important, but destroyed from the inside out by order of God, who wanted to punish the tribe for its disobedience." In this regard, another pilgrim, the Turk Mehmet Edib Mehmet, in his *Route from Constantinople to Mecca*, written in about 1680, explained that this punishment took place "879 years after the flood of Noah" and that the monuments of the city, "partly formed by sculpted stones, are now uninhabited."

For traveler Ludovico di Varthema—a Mameluke officer, hailing from Bologna and who was part of the escort accompanying the caravan in the year 1503—a terrible punishment of this sort, inflicted on the entire population of a city, was obviously reminiscent of the punishment exacted upon the inhabitants of Sodom and Gomorrah, as recorded in the Bible. We can perceive therefore how he mistook Al-Hijr for the two cursed cities, located near the Dead Sea. He thus wrote when he was passing through Al-Hijr: "We found the valley of Sodom and Gomorrah. Verily the Scriptures do not lie, for one sees how they were destroyed by a miracle of God." The Bolognese adventurer continued: "Of a truth, I believe, upon what I have seen, that they were wicked people, for all around the entire country is desert and barren. The earth produces no one thing, nor water; and they lived upon manna."

Varthema clearly mixed his own recollections of the Bible with the Koranic knowledge of his traveling companions, when, referring to the ancient city and its inhabitants, he wrote: "for not acknowledging the benefits they received; and by a miracle everything is still seen in ruin." Therefore Varthema passed through Al-Hijr, "believing that what he saw was Sodom and Gomorrah, but not suspecting that there was an ancient

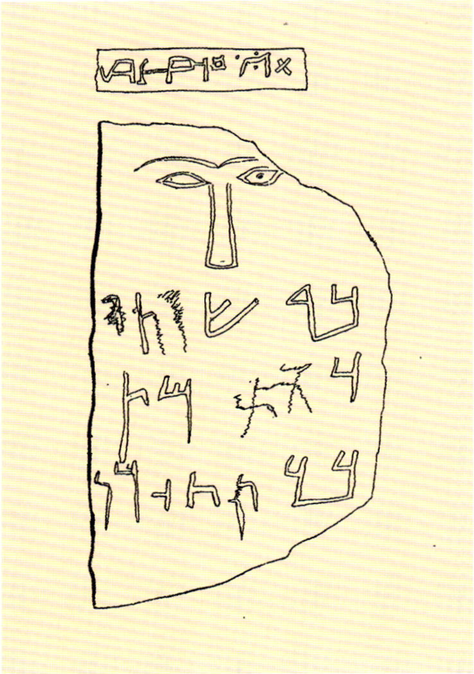

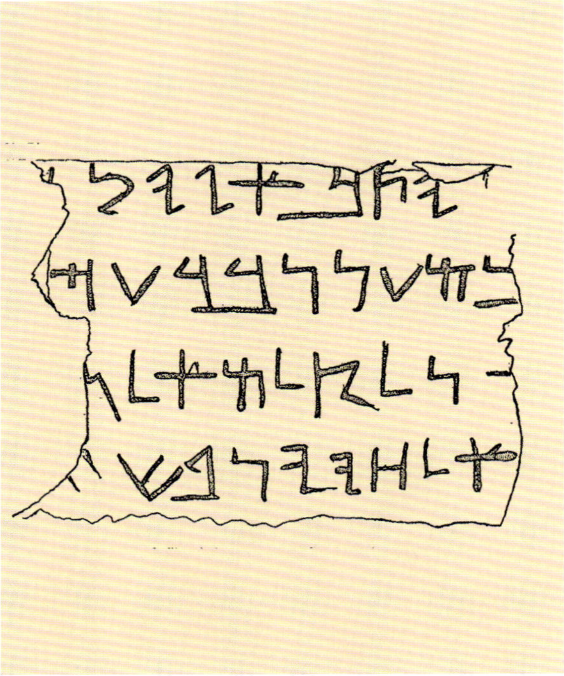

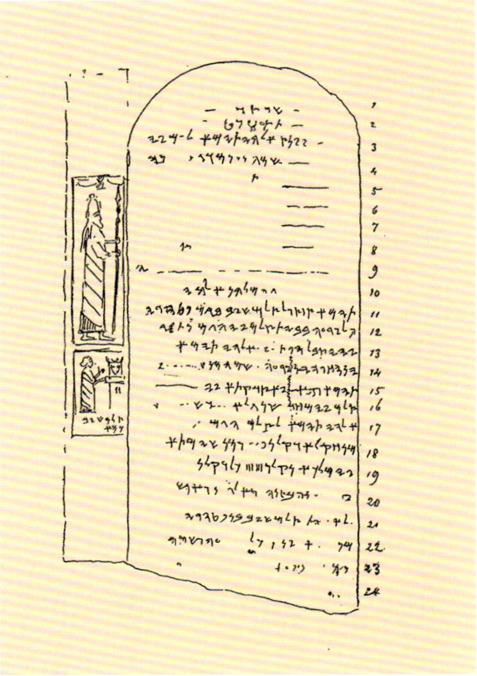

civilization there to be discovered," that of the Nabataeans, as historian Jacqueline Pirenne wrote in her book, *Discovering Arabia*.

Other foreign travelers, after Varthema, committed—or replicated—this same error and showed relatively little interest in Al-Hijr, which is nevertheless one of the most exceptional ancient sites in northern Arabia. In this regard, one must be careful not to attribute to these men interests that could not have been theirs, given both the historical period and cultural context in which they lived. In this manner, and although he had passed through Cairo many times during his numerous travels, and notwithstanding his inquiring mind, Ibn Battuta never mentioned the pyramids—known in the Islamic tradition as the "granaries of Joseph"—and it is very likely that he did not bother to visit them. In the same vein, the English explorer Charles M. Doughty—who, as we will see later, would be the first surveyor of the site of ancient Hegra—was surprised by "the astonishing indifference" of the pilgrims whose caravan stopped a stone's throw from the great Nabataean tombs. Not one of them attempted to get close enough to inspect these monuments despite their repeated mention in the Koran.

Let us also follow the German geographer Carsten Niebuhr who, in 1763, during his trip to the south of the peninsula, made a considerable effort to find the ancient dam of the Sabeans and finally reached the site: "The wall was 40 to 50 feet in height, was built of very large blocks of cut stone, and the ruins of it still remain on either side. But it no longer retains the water which flows at once into the plain." Displeased, Niebuhr concluded, "So the great reservoir near Marib was nothing marvellous."

The disappointment of the traveler can be explained thus: the building is completely ruined. There are also no inscriptions! "Here Niebuhr, who had lavished his interest on so many things, passed by an exciting discovery without noticing its importance," Pirenne noted correctly, before going on to give the reason: "It is true that spotting a datum of fact is of no help, if you do not understand the interest it presents and the knowledge that can be drawn from it. But it is not only Niebuhr but his entire century that had not yet realized that you could discover, simply by analyzing the ancient stones of the ruined monuments, information about their history. Archaeology had not yet been conceived. So they only paid attention to the inscriptions, because they could treat their text like a written document they strove to read. This is why ruins without inscriptions, a dam that no longer even retains water, were the most insignificant things for Niebuhr."

Thus Niebuhr reached Marib and saw with his own eyes, without understanding its importance, the famous dam, historically important for the entire Arabian peninsula. Similarly, over the centuries millions of men, traveling with the caravan from Damascus to Mecca, passed by the rock façades of the Nabataean tombs of ancient Hegra without understanding what they represented from a historical point of view.

Charles Huber
Inscription found on a stone in Tabuk
From *Journal d'un voyage en Arabie* (1883–84)
Paris, Ernest Leroux, 1891

During his two expeditions in Arabia, Huber copied many inscriptions, thus contributing to elucidating the languages spoken in pre-Islamic northern Arabia.

Charles Huber
An Aramaic inscription
From *Journal d'un voyage en Arabie* (1883–84)
Paris, Ernest Leroux, 1891

Christian Robin noted in *Roads of Arabia* (2010) that "*Aramaic script was used in northern Hijaz from the 6th century BC.*"

Julius Euting
The Tayma stele
From Charles Huber, *Journal d'un voyage en Arabie* (1883–84)
Paris, Ernest Leroux, 1891

An important artefact, the "Tayma Stele" was found by Charles Huber and Julius Euting in the 1880s. Doughty had gone to Tayma and found inscriptions, among them—but he did not copy them—the old Aramaic text known as the "Tayma Stele". It was his report that brought Huber to this spot two years later. The "Tayma Stele" is exhibited in the Louvre museum.

Édith Ortoli
Graffiti
From *Esprit du désert*, 2017
Artist book
Mixed media
Single copy
26 × 32 cm
Courtesy of the artist

Epigraphic documents on stone or bronze prove that many languages and scripts existed in Ancient Arabia. Among them is this famous inscription of the Himyarite king Abīkarib As‘ad à al-Ma’sa, found 200 kilometers west of Riyadh. It commemorates the annexation of Central Arabia by Himyar around 430 or 440.

All this would change over the course of the nineteenth century, during which archaeology and epigraphy became sciences. Between the end of the Middle Ages and the early Renaissance period, an interest in art and ancient works had begun to take hold in Europe. Thus the palaces of kings and princes were gradually adorned with botanical gardens, libraries, *studioli*, and cabinets of curiosities, which were drawn up with inventories, catalogues, and other *thesauri*. However, it would take the spirit of the eighteenth century, that of the Enlightenment and Encyclopedism, to transform what had before been a simple curiosity of the mind to be organized into various human sciences, such as anthropology, archaeology, and epigraphy.

This is how European travelers, this time aware of the historical significance that could be found in ruined buildings of ancient civilizations, traveled east from the beginning of the nineteenth century with a real appetite for discovery. In addition to the practical difficulties they would encounter during their quests, they were often confronted with hostile natives, who perceived them as treasure hunters coming to rob them.

The animosity of the inhabitants, nomadic or sedentary, living near ancient sites was not to be taken lightly. Many intrepid explorers lost their lives in these expeditions. This was the case with Ulrich Jaspar Seetzen, a Geman pioneer of South Arabian epigraphy. He was the first to record Himyaritic inscriptions, but was poisoned in Taiz in 1811 on suspicion of having stolen treasure. Similarly, in 1884, the Frenchman Charles Huber, who was among the first, after Doughty, to record the inscriptions on the site of ancient Hegra, was shot to death by his guides near Jeddah.

Going back to Seetzen, he had become convinced, after a long stay in Damascus, that he could find the ancient city and capital of the Nabataean Kingdom, which had been lost to the world—in other words, Petra. In 1806, and in the company of a trusted guide, he was traveling through the region located between the Dead Sea and the far reaches of Arabia when he came face-to-face with locals who, as always, tried to turn him away. He passed very close to Petra but never reached it, and ended up abandoning his search. This prize was to become that of the Swiss explorer Johann Ludwig Burckhardt just a few years later, in 1812.

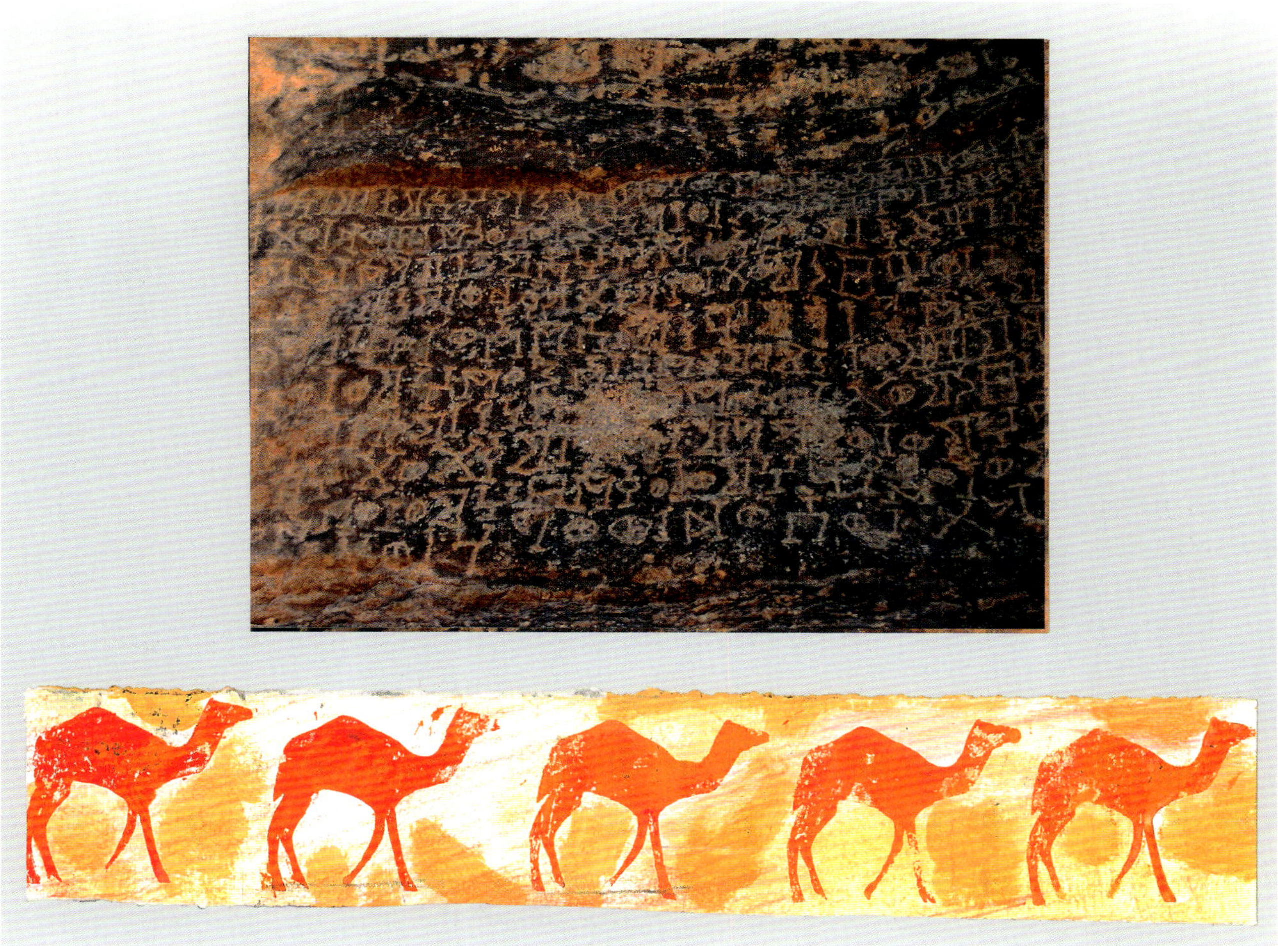

At this starting point, Burckhardt believed that Petra was located in the rocky cliffs of the Wadi Moussa valley, situated in the west of modern-day Jordan. He also knew that on Mount Hor, one of the mountains overlooking the Wadi Moussa Valley, there was a monument which was said to be the grave of the brother of Moses (Moussa), Aaron, and was the subject of frequent religious visits by believers who went there to offer sacrifices. After several days of hiking, Burckhardt did indeed come close to the *wadi*, intentionally from the side opposite the grave. He then went into a nearby village to buy a goat and, above all, to find a guide who would lead him to the tomb of Aaron, to which he claimed he was bound because of a promise and where he wanted to sacrifice the animal. "With this ploy, I thought that it would be possible to see the site," hoped Burckhardt, persuading himself that the Bedouin who had agreed to lead him "would have nothing against this for fear of attracting the wrath of Aaron."

The two men set off. After long hours of walking on particularly steep terrain, they reached a place from which the dome of the tomb of Aaron could actually be seen in the distance. Burckhardt's Bedouin guide insisted then that he proceed to sacrifice the animal there, pointing out that this place was littered with a small pile of rocks as proof of previous sacrifices. Burckhardt countered, saying that his promise was to sacrifice the animal on the tomb itself, and not only from where it could be seen. However, he was deeply worried: "I knew well the character of the people around me; I was without protection in the midst of a desert where no traveller had ever before been seen."

The guide, carrying the goat, agreed to continue. Burckhardt followed, bearing a goatskin filled with water, along the dry *Wadi*. And soon, the incredible discovery, that of the amazing defile—the only one in the world to carry its own name, the *Siq*—and the Treasure, hundreds of tombs, the theatre, Qasr al-Bint... "It was there," wrote Burckhardt soberly, "that the ancient site was located," this inaccessible place, forgotten by the world. Petra! The extraordinary capital of the Nabataeans.

We can imagine the irony of the scene. Burckhardt was overwhelmed, fascinated. However, he could not show his turmoil, his delight, in the presence of his guide, for whom all this was the work of infidels and who pressed him to move forward, claiming that there were jinns in the area. Burckhardt knew that "a close examination of these works of the infidels, as they are called, would have excited suspicions that I was a magician

Charles Montagu Doughty
Beyt Akhreymat
Sketch from *Arabia Deserta*, 1888
Volume 1, New York, Dover Publications Inc., 1979

Intending to study its inscriptions, Doughty decided to stay in Mada'in Saleh, which he reached with the Syrian pilgrim's caravan. He remained there for a period of two months during which he visited its monuments, recorded his observations, and carefully impressed their superscriptions. The French philologist Ernest Renan depicted the Nabataean inscriptions, in 1884, using Doughty's transcriptions.

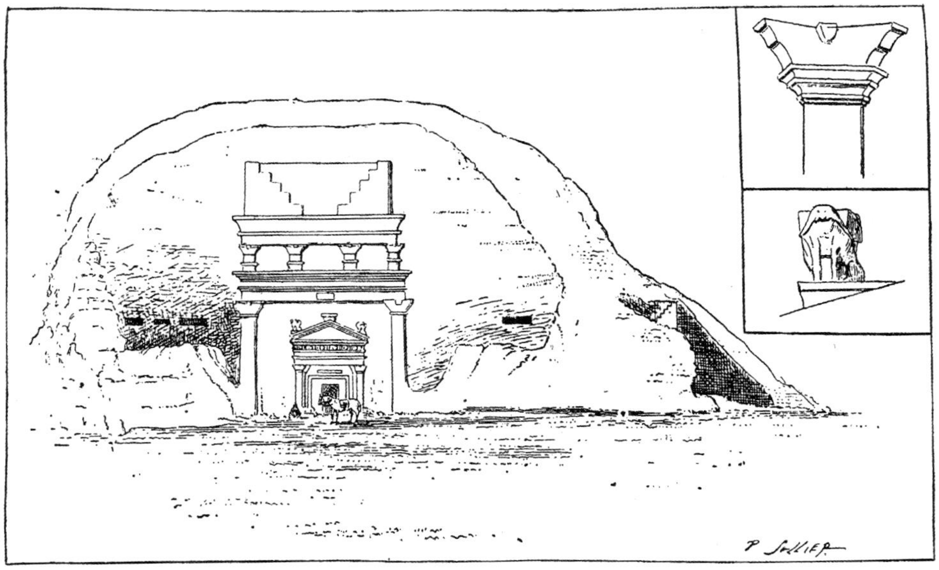

Charles Montagu Doughty
Frontispieces
Sketch from *Arabia Deserta*, 1888
Volume 1, New York, Dover Publications Inc., 1979

Doughty wrote describing these frontispieces that they *"represented four-footed beasts, seen nowhere else. The ornaments on the side pedestals are also singular. As for the tablets he wrote, they are adorned with a fretwork flower (perhaps pomegranate) of six petals."*

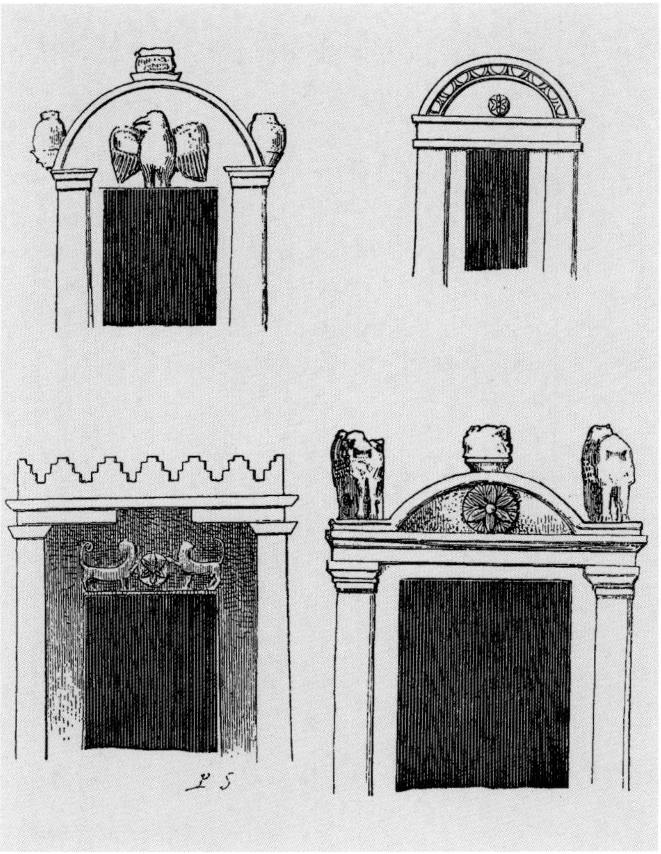

Jaussen and Savignac
Rock-cut Minaean tomb "A 1" featuring beasts in the form of lions carved into the rock to protect the tomb—myth of "The Genie, Protector of the Dead"—in Al-Ula (Dedan), March 1909
Courtesy of the French Biblical and Archaeological School of Jerusalem

Jaussen and Savignac
An eagle atop an obelisk, south of Ethlib mountain in Mada'in Saleh (Hegra), 1907
Courtesy of the French Biblical and Archaeological School of Jerusalem

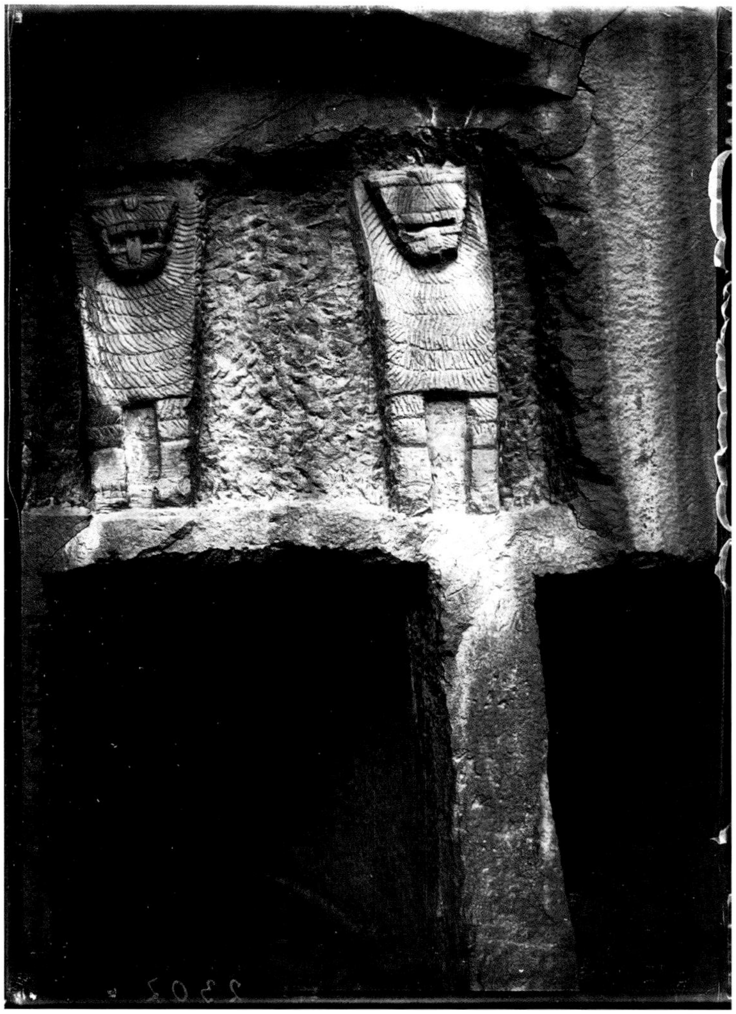

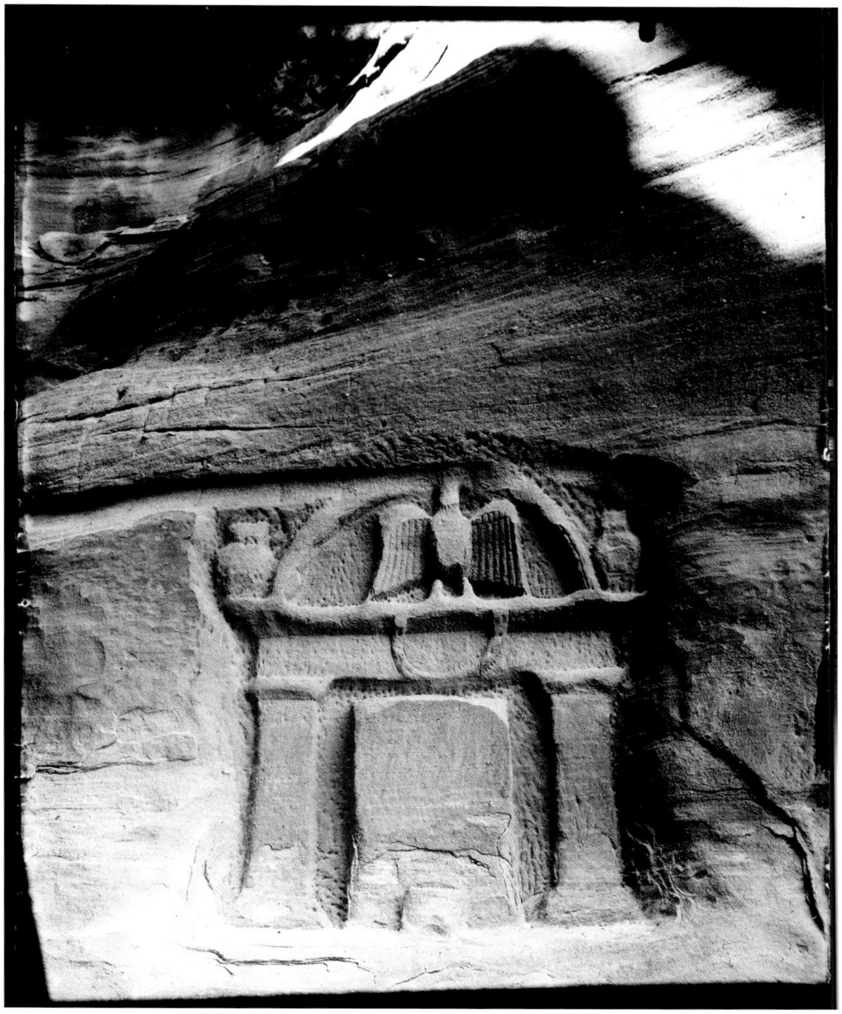

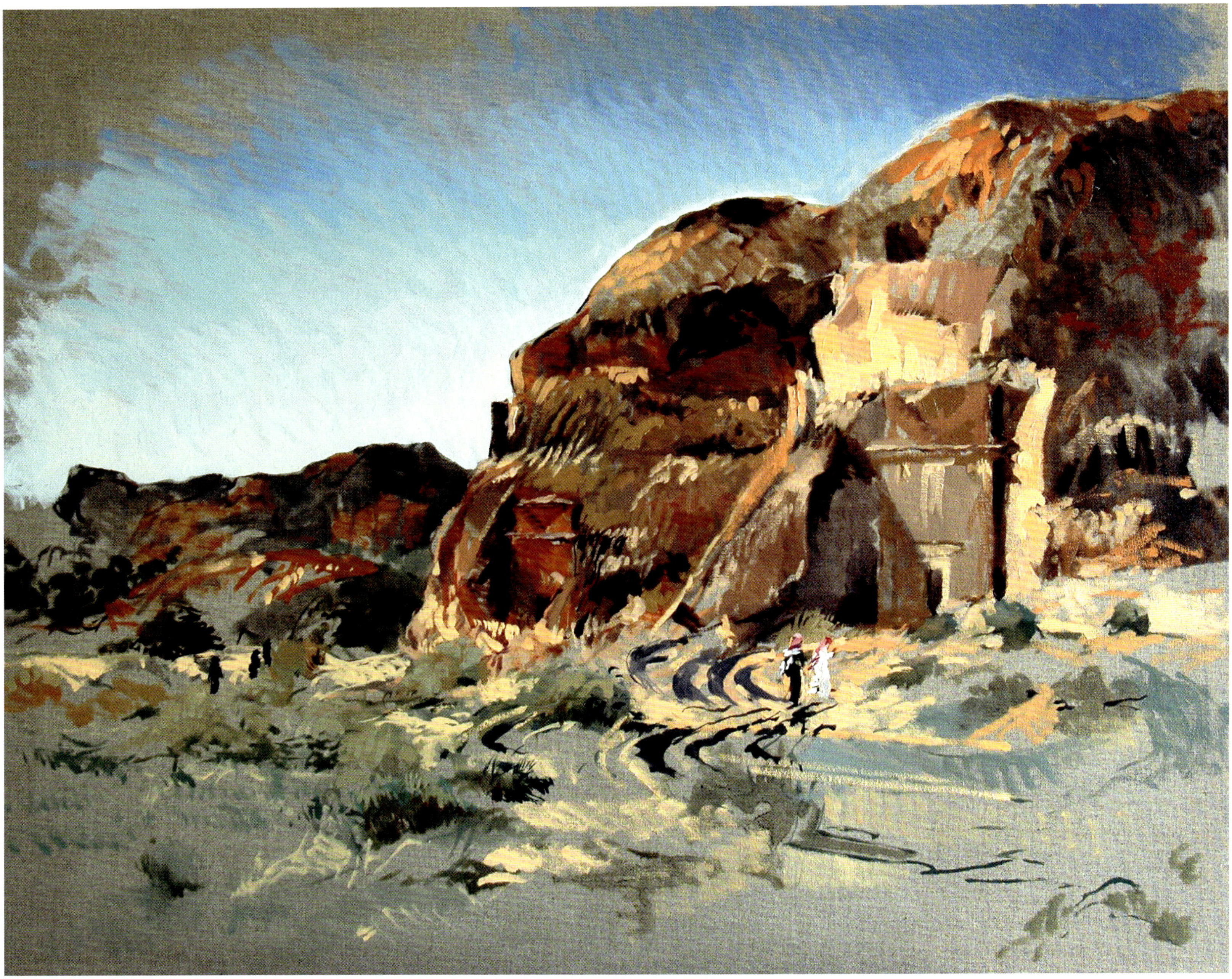

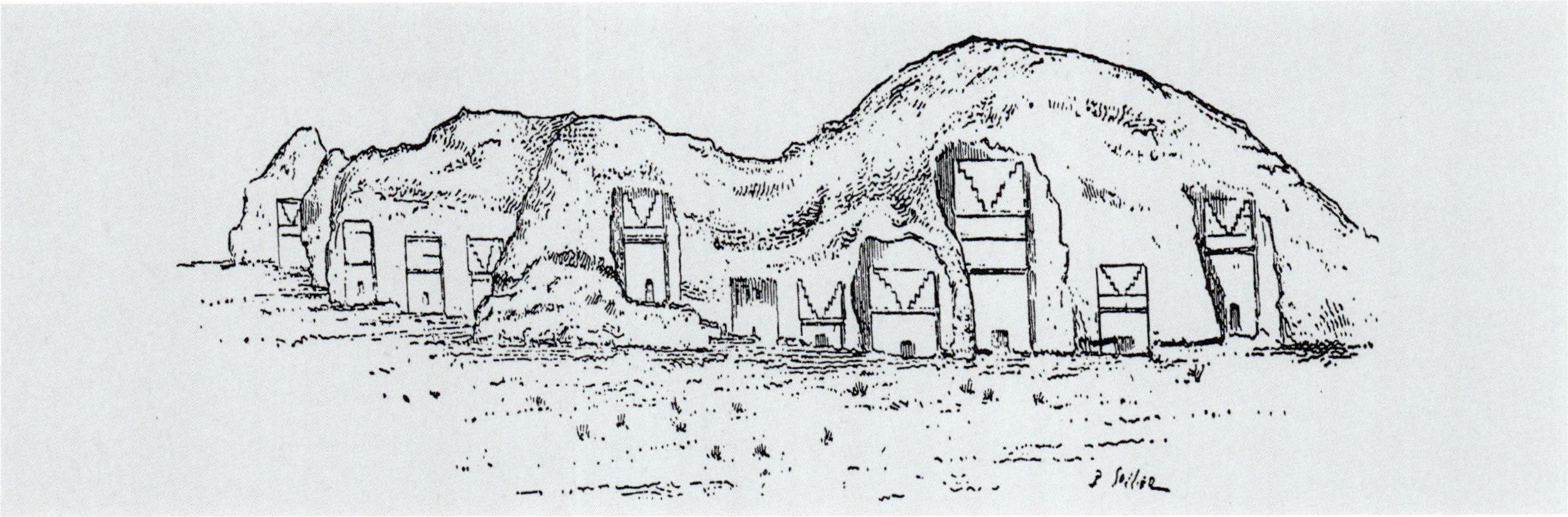

Ronan Olier
Djebel Al-Khuraymat in Mada'in Saleh, 2010
Oil on canvas
50 × 65 cm
Courtesy of the artist

Inhabited by the Nabataeans about 2,000 years ago, Mada'in Saleh was a crossroad for the people of other ancient civilizations who passed through it on their incense route and left vestiges of their own. The Nabataeans themselves traded in incense and spice. Later, Mada'in Saleh became a stopover for pilgrims going to Medina.

Charles Montagu Doughty
Western Rocks
Sketch from *Arabia Deserta*, 1888
Volume 1, New York, Dover Publications Inc., 1979

Charles Doughty, the first Westerner to describe the site of Hegra in 1876, recorded and sketched its hewn tombs and landscapes.

Yann Gayet
Two policemen throwing stones in the water near Mada'in Saleh
From the series *Contresens*, 2010
Courtesy of the artist

in search of treasures; I should have at least been detained and prevented from continuing my journey, if not stripped of the little money I had—as well as my journal, which was infinitely more valuable to me." So he continued along his way, but could not help but go into a tomb or two, claiming mere curiosity.

Burckhardt moved ahead, suffering all the while, the result of parting from where he wanted to be. Then, when he once again stopped to contemplate the site, he incurred the wrath of his guide: "I see now clearly that you are an infidel, who has some particular business amongst the ruins of the city of your forefathers; but depend upon it that we shall not suffer you to take out a single para of all the treasures hidden therein, for they are in our territory, and belong to us."

Burckhardt, however, managed to convince his guide of his innocence and calm his fury. Once again he set off, following his guide and, sick at heart, left Petra behind him. The two men went to slay the goat.

Later, reflecting upon these almost insurmountable difficulties, the Swiss explorer explained: "It is very unfortunate for European travellers that the idea of treasures being hidden in ancient edifices is so strongly rooted in the minds of the Arabs and Turks; nor are they satisfied with watching all the strangers' steps; they believe that it is sufficient for a true magician to have seen and observed the spot where treasures are hidden (of which he is supposed to be already informed by the old books of the infidels who lived on the spot) in order to be able afterwards, at his ease, to command the guardian of the treasure to set the whole before him. It was of no avail to tell them to follow me and see whether I searched for money. Their reply was, of course you will not dare to take it out before us, but we know that if you are a skillful magician you will order it to follow you through the air to whatever place you please. If the traveller takes the dimensions of a building or a column, they are persuaded that it is a magical proceeding."

It was not until almost sixty years after the discovery of Petra by Burckhardt that the other great city of the ancient Nabataeans, Hegra, was identified. The merit for this went to the English explorer and writer Charles M. Doughty. In 1876, having heard about the existence of façades and monuments hewn in the rocks only a few days' walk to the south of Maan, and close to the caravan station of Al-Hijr, or rather Mada'in Saleh as it was more often called then, he decided to go there.

Doughty joined the departing pilgrims' caravan from Damascus to Mada'in Saleh, where he stayed behind while the caravan continued on to Medina and

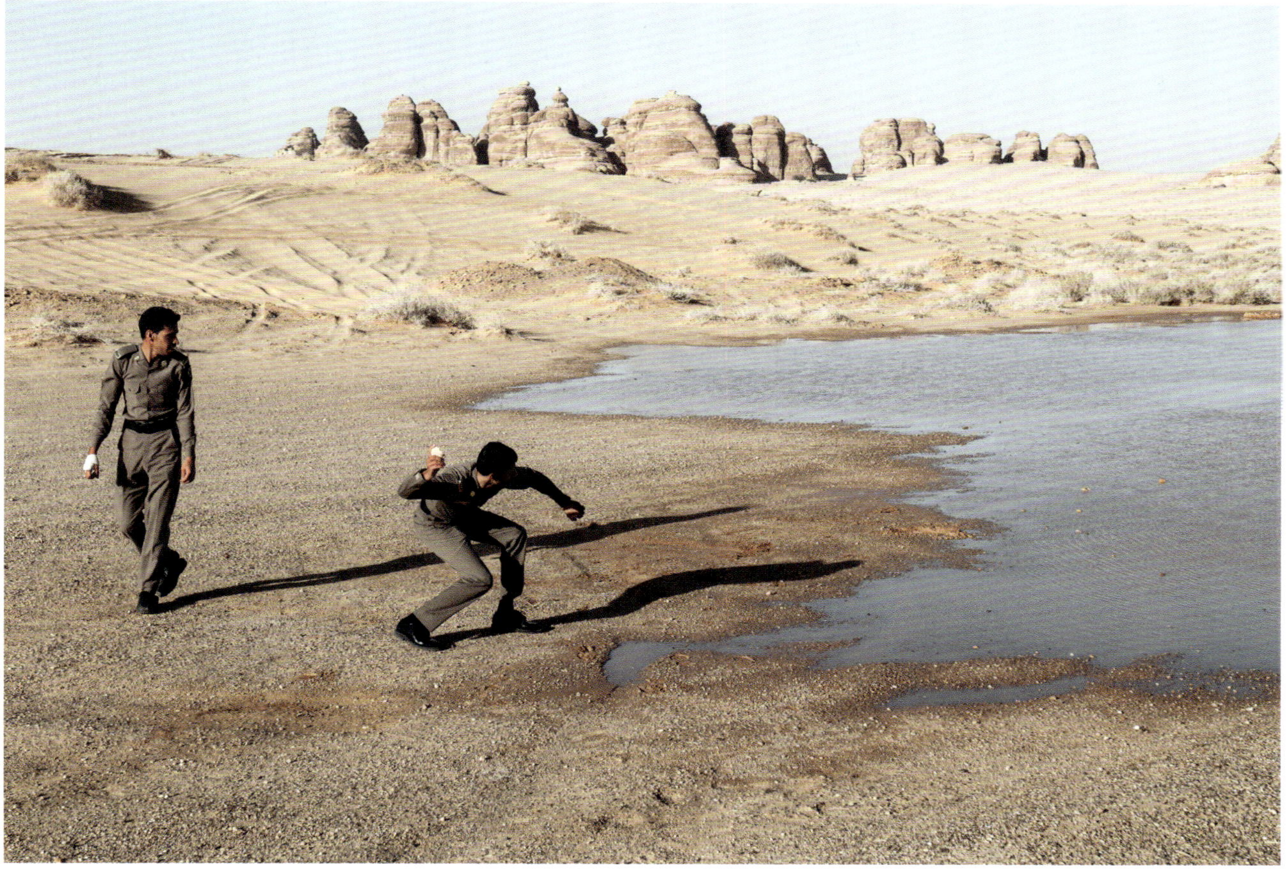

Jaussen and Savignac
Statue "1" of a Lihyanite temple in Al-Ula (Dedan) in Al-Khereibeh, March 1909
Courtesy of the French Biblical and Archaeological School of Jerusalem

The discovery of quarries near Mada'in Saleh proves, noted Laïla Nehmé, a member of the French team of archaeologists in Saudi Arabia, in an article published in *Saudi Aramco* ("New Pieces of Mada'in Salih's puzzle"), that in addition to being renowned as carvers of rock-hewn necropolises, Nabataeans were also builders. This life-size stone statue of a man was discovered by Jaussen and Savignac. It is typical of the art of Lihyanite sculpture and reflects influences of ancient Egypt.

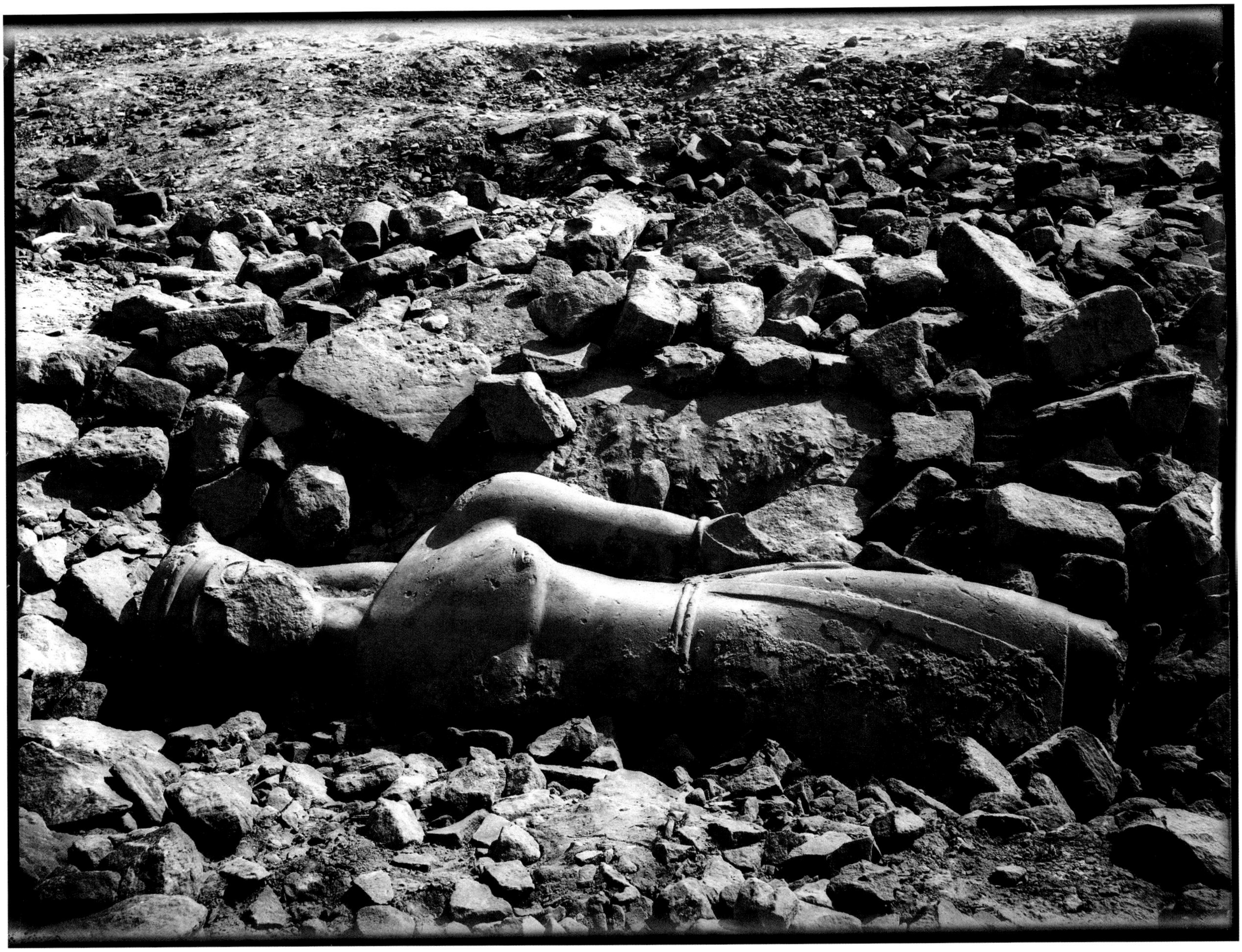

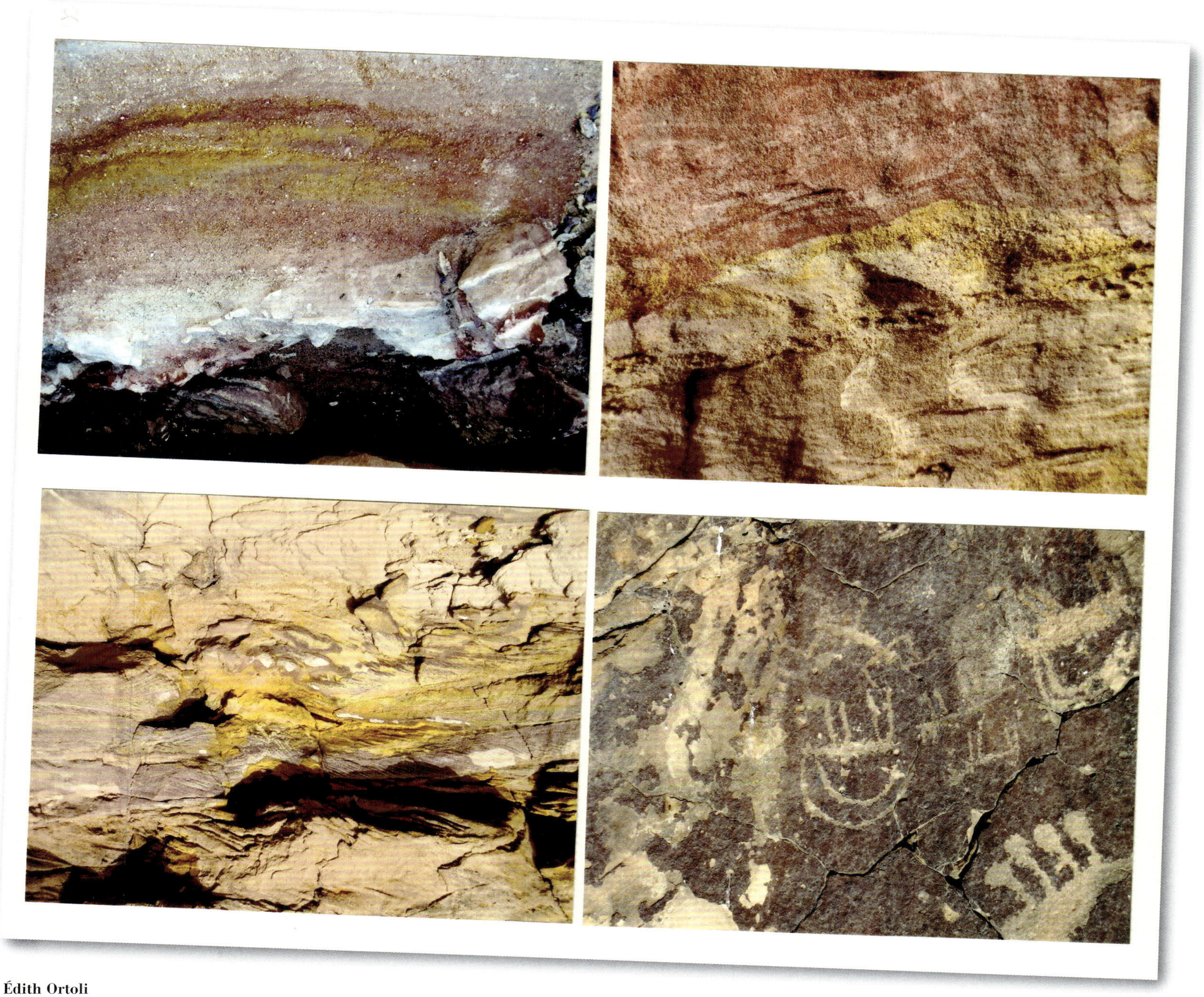

Édith Ortoli
Rochers
From *Esprit du désert*, 2017
Artist book
Mixed media
Single copy
26 × 32 cm
Courtesy of the artist

The earliest examples of rock art discovered in the Arabian Peninsula date from the early Neolithic, around 12,000 BC.

هذه صورة ديار العرب بكاملها التي سنذكر في موضعها في كتابنا هذا خريدة العجائب

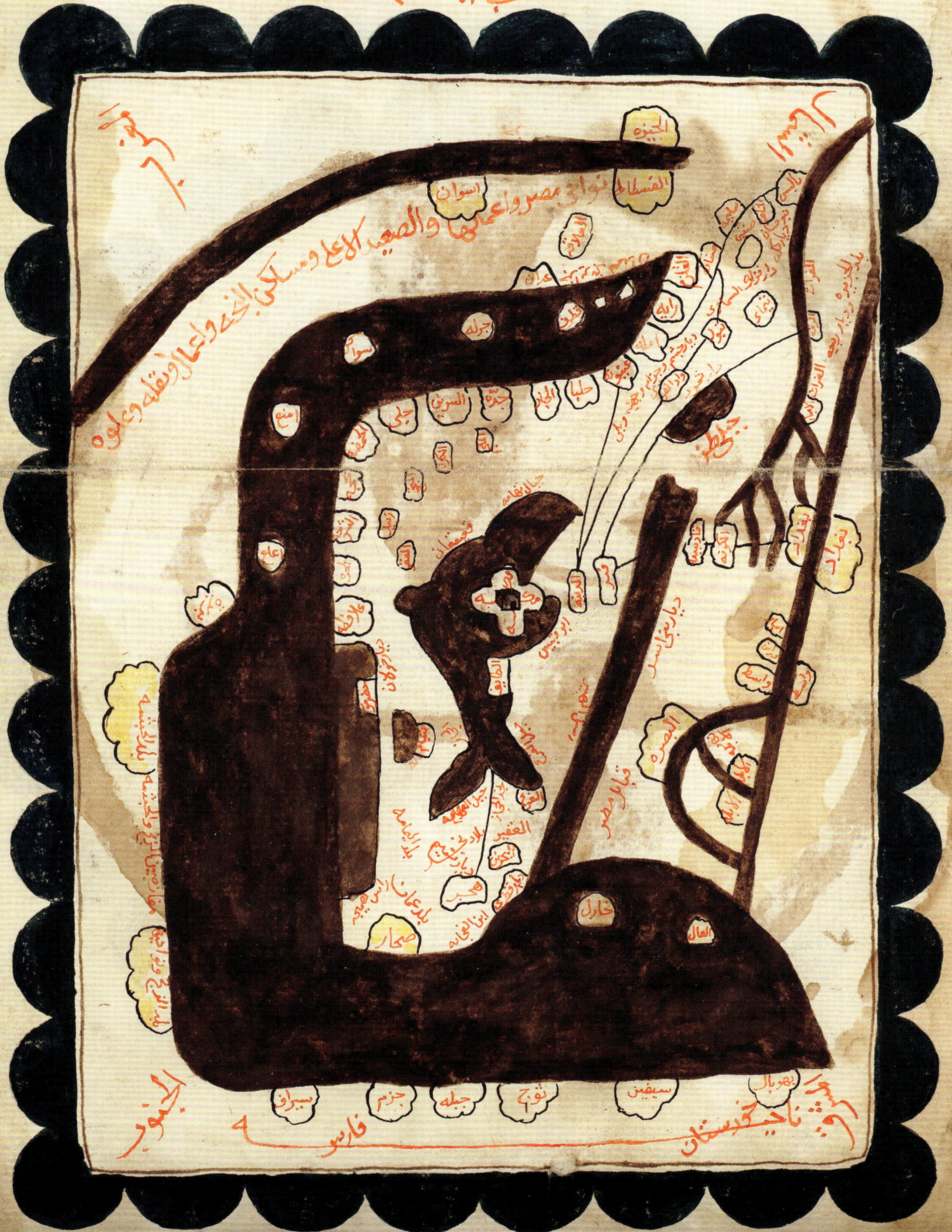

Al-Marrakshi ibn al-Wardi
Kitab Kharida Al-'Aja'ib wa Farida Al-Ghara'ib (The Pearl of Wonders and the Uniqueness of Things Strange), 1575
Ink and opaque watercolors on paper
28.5 × 19 cm
Courtesy of the Museum of Islamic Art, Doha

Copied by Abd Al-Rahman Ibn Al-Surur Ghamadi, who might have been an Indian or Malaysian pilgrim, the text's original author is named "al-Marrakshi". Mounia Chekhab-Abudaya and Cécile Bresc wrote in *Hajj – The Journey through Art* (2013): *"In the tradition of 'sacred geography', many legends developed around the history of the composition of the world. Among them, one recorded in texts, such as in the Mu'jam al-Buldan (Dictionary of Countries) of Yaqut al-Rumi, is that the earth is supported on the horns of a bull, which itself is supported by a stone on the back of a whale. On this map, the brown part represents the seas, and the 'encircling ocean' forms the border of the map. Mecca is in the center, inside a shape recognizable as a whale."*

Ludovico di Varthema, a Mameluke soldier, was the first European to enter Arabia and to provide an account of his travel, undertaken in 1503. In a chapter of his book dedicated to the Red Sea and the difficulties it presented, he wrote: "It will be understood that this sea is not red, but that the water is like that of any other sea."

How is it then that this sea has had this name since time immemorial? It seems that the ancient Greeks had first designated *Erythra Thalassa* (Red Sea) as the entire Indian Ocean, including the two seas that border Arabia to the west (the Red Sea) and to the east (the Arabian Gulf). Later, this denomination was used to refer to the Red Sea only. While Erythra does indeed mean "red" in Greek, it seems—according to Agatharcides, a Greek historian and geographer of the second century BC—that this name had been chosen with reference to the legendary figure of a Persian monarch by the name of Erythras, and not due to the colour of the streams. This confusion—if there is one—has lasted until our time.

However, Agatharcides' explanation is somewhat unsatisfactory. This method of naming the seas seems to have in fact proceeded from an ancient manner of apprehending the world—or at least, its cardinal points—later adopted by the Turks. It made use of a traditional "color code": North denoted black, South was red, East yellow (or gold), and West white. Hence the names of the Mediterranean Sea (in Arabic, the White Sea, *bahr al-Abyad*), the Black Sea, and the Red Sea.

If the seas surrounding Arabia were, in the beginning, described by Greek geographers, various data pertaining to the land was also provided by historians of the antiquity. For example, in the fifth century BC, during his passage through Egypt, the renowned Herodotus collected information about the then famous Arabian spices: incense, myrrh, cassia, cinnamon, laudanum, etc.

"A century later, it was Theophrastus, Aristotle's follower, a philosopher who included scientific observation of all things in philosophy, who when writing his *Enquiry into Plants*, examined the famous spices of Arabia," noted the French historian Jacqueline Pirenne in her book, *À la découverte de l'Arabie* (1958). In his book, Theophrastus extended his survey to the trade and culture of these spices. He also related the customs of the inhabitants of southern Arabia, the Sabaeans, describing them as warriors, farmers, and traders. Regarding the latter, he specified that "their most lucrative activity consisted of transporting the *larimna* plant (aloes plant)," which has the strongest aroma of all spices, "to neighbouring countries."

Other Greek authors, during the course of the first century BC, such as Diodorus of Sicily, and Strabo, native of Pontus, wrote extensively about the prosperity of the inhabitants of southern Arabia. Thus, for Diodorus, the Sabaean people "surpass not only the neighbouring nations but also all other men in wealth. [...] They have never for ages suffered the ravages of war because of their secluded position," he specified, before adding that "both gold and silver abound in the country," and "they live in luxurious houses."

It seems, according to Strabo, and as cited by Jacqueline Pirenne, that "In Sabae, by selling their spices they amassed fortunes. They have embossed goblets of every description, made of silver and gold, couches and tripods with silver feet. Their ceilings and doors they have partitioned by means of panels and coffers made of silver and gold, set with precious stones and placed close together, others of ivory and the most showy precious stones." It would seem quite natural that such extraordinary wealth would arouse envy, and Strabo himself related that the expedition sent against Arabia from Egypt at the orders of the Roman emperor Augustus aimed to take over the caravan trade. We know for a fact (see chapter *The Desert of Deserts*) that the Roman

Abu Abdullah Muhammad Al-Idrisi
World Map, twelfth century
52 × 50 cm
Courtesy of the Bibliothèque nationale de France

In addition to *Kitab nuzhat al-mushtaq fi ikhtiraq al-afaq*, considered one of the greatest works of medieval geography, Al-Idrisi produced a silver planisphere on which a map of the world was depicted. The planisphere was lost but the maps and the book survived.

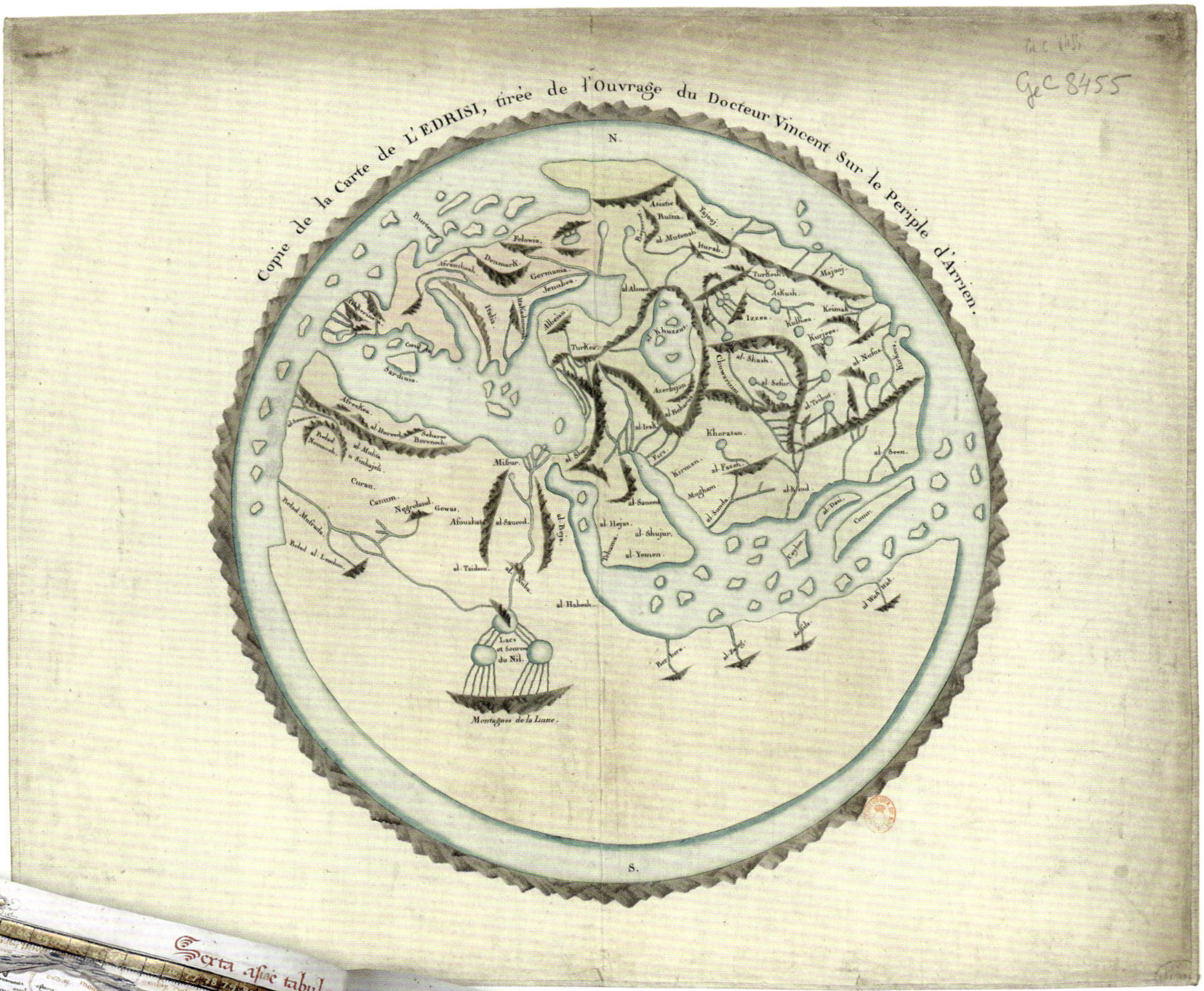

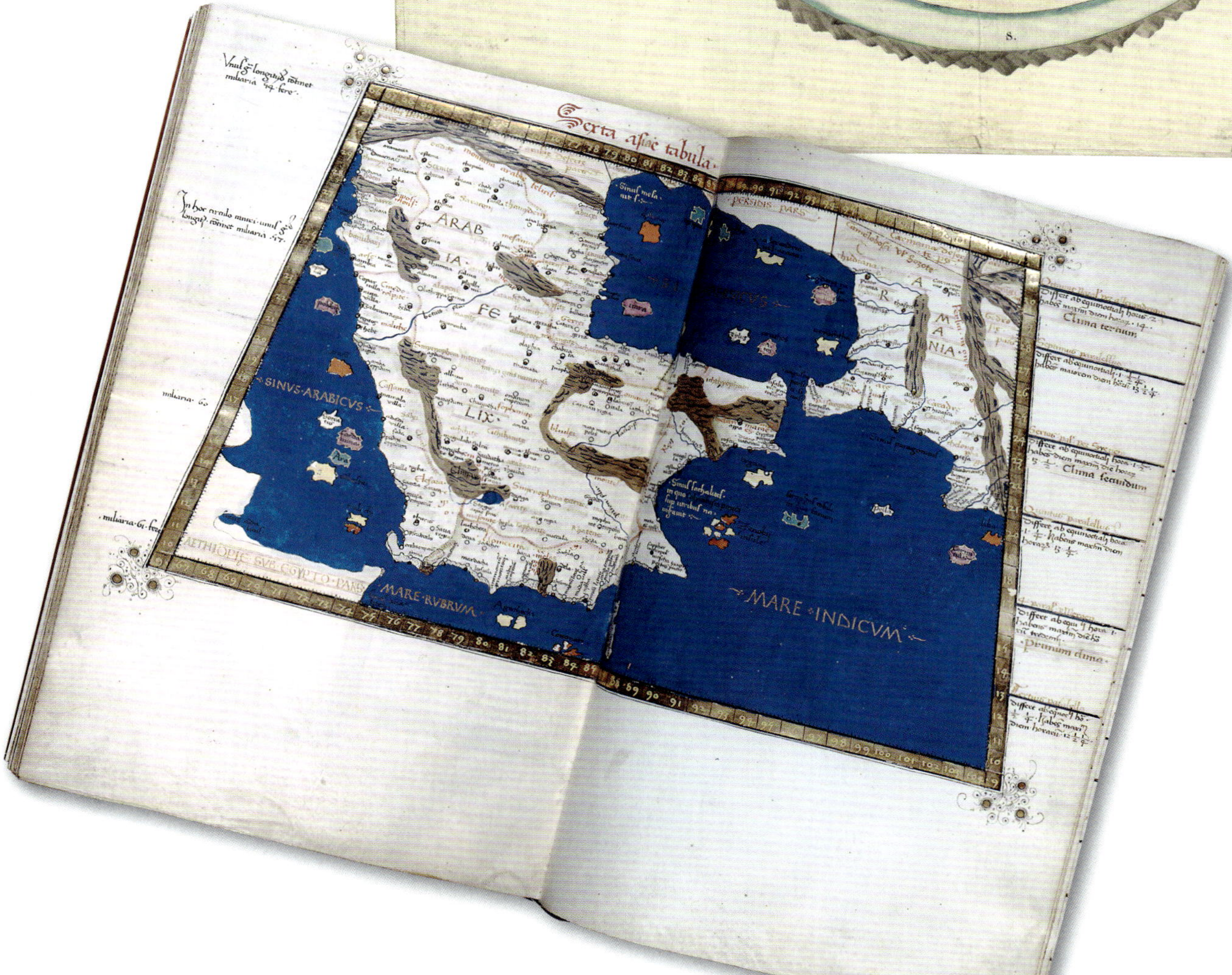

Nicolaus Germanus
Sixth map of Asia (Arabian Peninsula), c. 1477
Ptolemy, author
26 × 47 cm
Courtesy of The New York Public Library

Several editions of Ptolemy's *Geographia* were published in Europe in the fifteenth century. Ptolemaic atlases included twelve maps of Asia. The *Sixth map of Asia* covered the Arabian Peninsula. Ptolemy, in his map, exaggerated the width of the southern part of Arabia as well as the size and shape of the Arabian Gulf. Also, there is no mention of *Arabia Petraea* or *Arabia Deserta*; *Arabia Felix* is applied to the whole of the Arabian Peninsula.

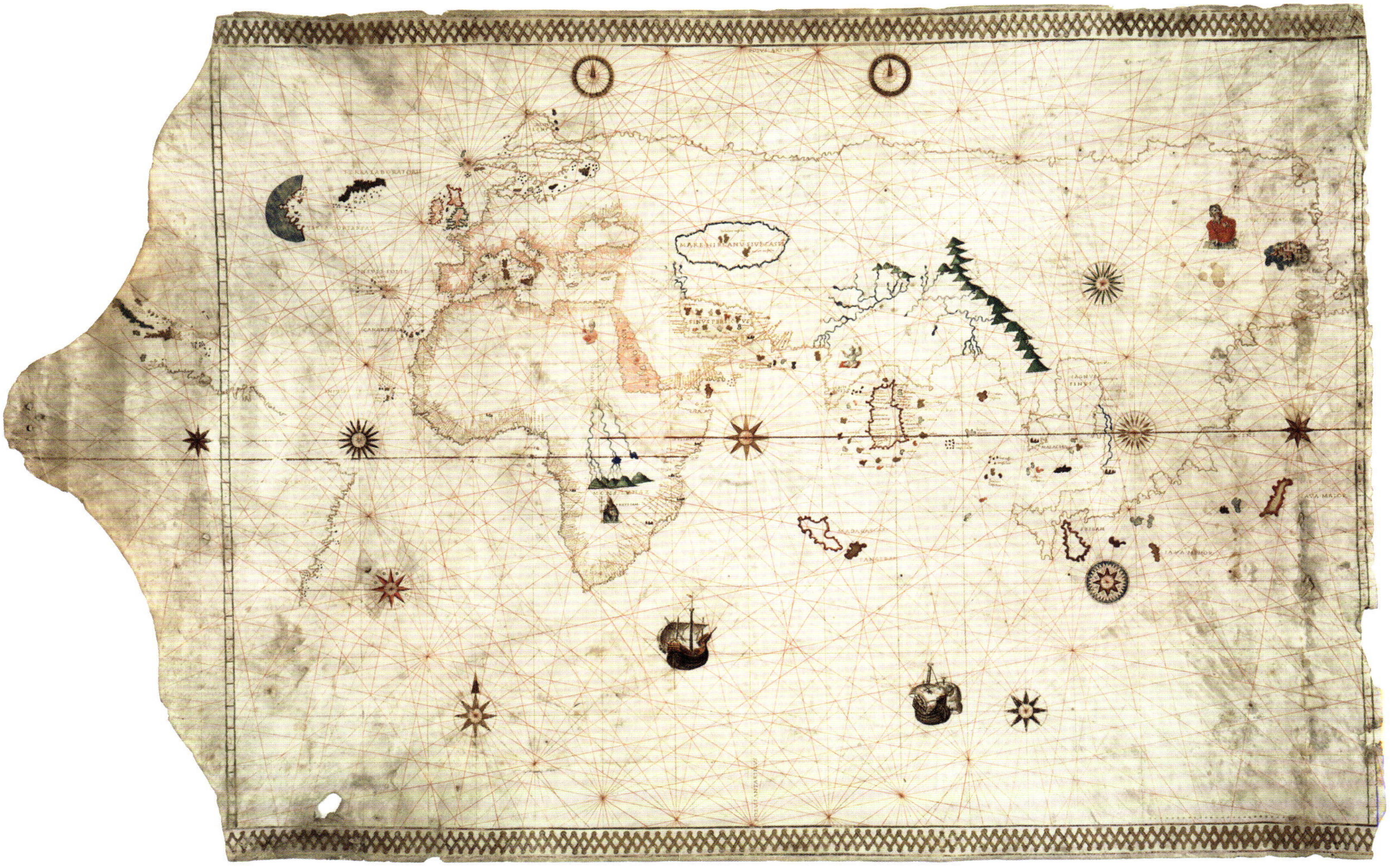

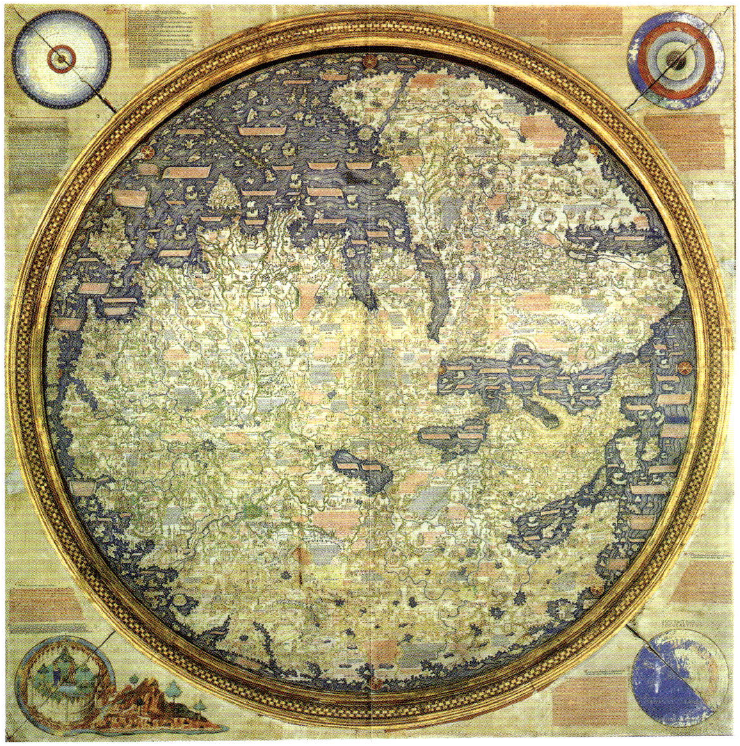

Anonymous
King Hamy Chart, c. 1502
Ink on parchment
53 × 77.2 cm
Courtesy of the Huntington Library, California

The King Hamy chart is attributed to Amerigo Vespucci, probably made in Italy after a Portuguese prototype. The chart is based partly on Ptolemaic and partly on *portolano* traditions. However, it includes portions of Brazil, Venezuela, Antibes, and Newfoundland. By placing the Indian Ocean in the center of the chart, the cartographer made it possible to construct a world map encompassing all of Europe, Asia, Africa, and the Americas. The King Hamy chart was named after its discoverer and first publisher, as its original maker's name is unknown.

Fra Mauro
The Fra Mauro Map, c. 1450
Pigments on parchment
240 × 240 cm
Courtesy of the Museo Correr, Venice

An Italian cartographer, Fra Mauro was a monk who lived in the Republic of Venice and maintained a cartography workshop. He created a detailed and accurate map of the world, the "Fra Mauro Map," which is among the most important maps of medieval cartography. The map reproduces Asia, the Indian Ocean, Africa, Europe, and the Atlantic Ocean. The Asian portion shows the Arabian Peninsula, Persia, the Indian subcontinent, and the islands of Java and Sumatra, as well as Burma, China, and Korea. This map was probably influenced by Al-Idrisi because it is oriented from the south and consequently shows Arabia at the top. It was made for the rulers of Venice and Portugal, two of the main seafaring nations of the time.

army—exhausted, thirsty, and sick—was forced to retreat, causing the operation to fail miserably in 24 BC.

However, an important discovery made during the course of the second century BC resulted in better knowledge of the Arabian coastlines and consequently of the peninsula itself. This was that of the monsoon (from the Arabic *mawsim*, or season), a phenomenon which a Greek sailor by the name of Hippalus was, it seems, the first to comprehend. From then on Greek sailors were able to frequently undertake the voyage to India by regularly sailing along the coastlines of Arabia while seeking to avoid monsoons.

Later, various texts at the beginning of the Christian era reveal that knowledge of the geography of the peninsula was growing deeper. Hence, Pliny the Elder, the Roman historian of the first century AD, was able to list cities and villages, and the names of tribes, stating that the population of Arabia was composed of nomads and settlers. During the same period, the anonymous author of the *Periplus Maris Erythraei*—most likely a Greek in Alexandria—pointed out the multiplicity of tribes in Arabia, and drew up the caravan routes linking the kingdom of the Nabataeans to that of the Sabaeans, and the latter to Hadhramaut and Oman.

Another Greek in Alexandria, Claudius Ptolemy, succeeded in creating a great leap forward in the scientific knowledge of Arabia and many other parts of the world known in his time, initially by systematically taking into account all the data gathered before him (before the second century AD), and above all by taking this data into account in a true atlas.

The great work of Ptolemy, his *Geography*, consisted of an essay accompanied by twenty-seven maps which were among the first documents that the Renaissance man was eager to print, at the end of the fifteenth century, in the years that immediately followed the

Lopo Homem
The nautical atlas of the world, known as the Atlas Miller, 1519
42 × 59 cm
Courtesy of the Bibliothèque nationale de France

This Portuguese atlas is a joint work of the cartographers Lopo Homem, Pedro Reinel, and Jorge Reinel, and illustrated by miniaturist Antonio de Holanda. The atlas was acquired by librarian Bénigne Emmanuel Clement Miller of the National Library of France in 1897, hence the name *Atlas Miller*. This part of the chart shows the Horn of Africa and part of the Red Sea, Arabia, Persia, and India (including Sri Lanka/Ceylon). *Sinus Arabicus* is used to refer to the Gulf of Aden and *Rubrum Mare* for the Red Sea. The *Atlas Miller* also depicts Mecca, represented by a temple.

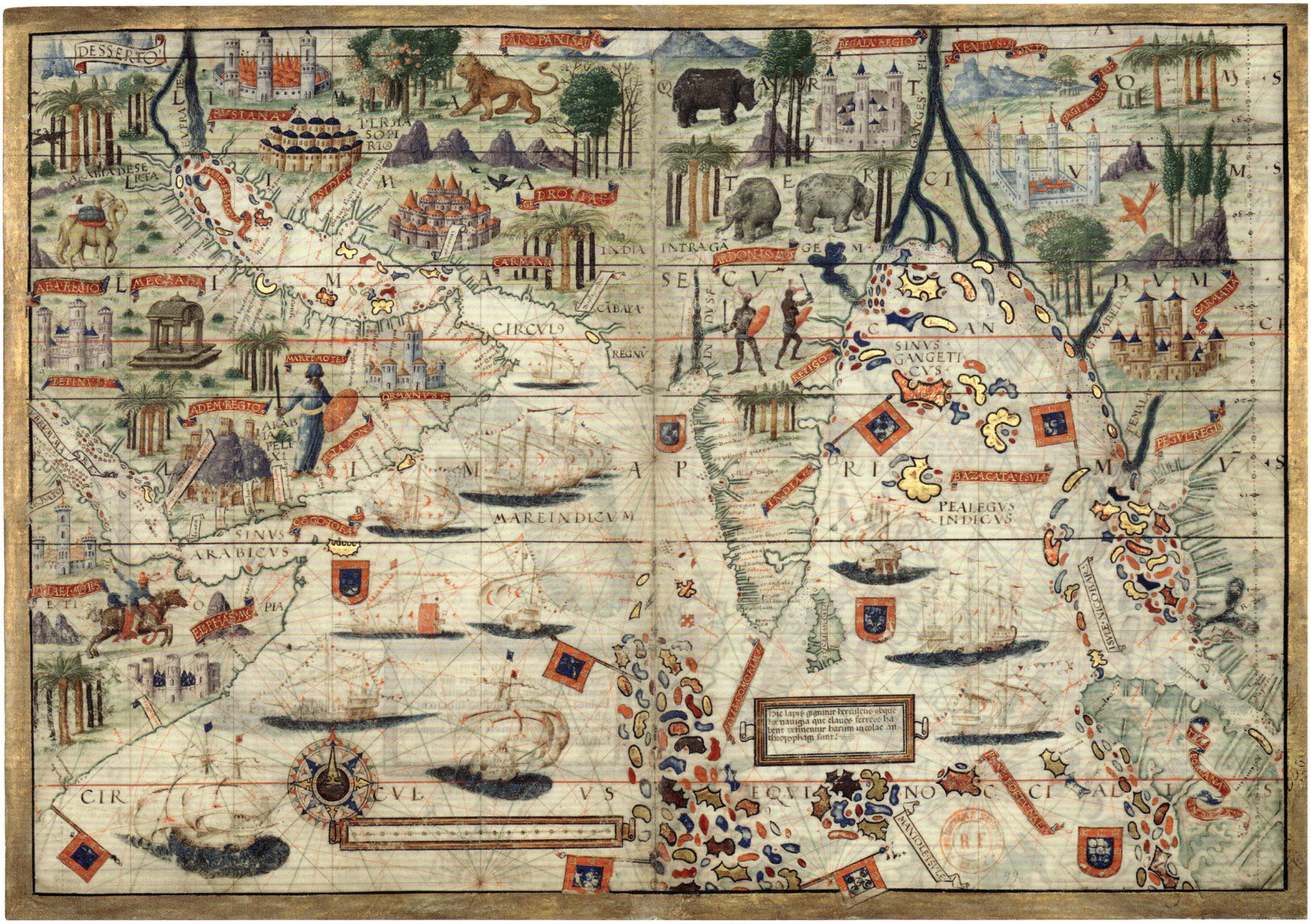

invention of the printing press. Before that, Ptolemy's work was lost for a long time in Europe. However, the Greek text had been translated into Arabic at the start of the ninth century, by the great philosopher Al-Kindi, and at the request of the Abbasid caliph Al-Ma'mun. A second translation of the same text was completed only a few decades later by the astronomer and mathematician Thābit ibn Qurra, which demonstrates how important this work was considered.

Ptolemy's text would serve as the foundation for the works of numerous Arab geographers, particularly for one of the most renowned among them, Al-Idrisi, raised in Cordoba at the beginning of the twelfth century. A geographer and explorer, as well as a botanist and physician, Al-Idrisi built a terrestrial planisphere for the Norman King of Sicily, Roger II: a massive disc of solid silver, two meters in diameter. He also wrote a book, *Kitab nuzhat al-mushtaq* (A Diversion for the Man Longing to Travel to Far-Off Places), sometimes known as *Kitab Roger* (Roger's Book), which was a long commentary, with illustrations, of the planisphere.

The Arabic version of Ptolemy's text would be retranslated from Arabic to Greek in the thirteenth century, into Latin at the start of the fifteenth century, and eventually into various European languages. Based on the distances indicated in the text, and taking into account the eight thousand toponyms it contains, it has been possible to reconstruct Ptolemy's maps with a reliable degree of precision.

The first printed edition of Ptolemy's text was published in 1475 in Vicenza, and the first to include maps in 1477 in Bologna. The Arabian Peninsula as represented on these maps is overly stretched in breadth toward the bottom, and the Arabian Gulf has mistakenly rectangular dimensions, as is the case, for example, on the map by Nicolaus Germanus. When

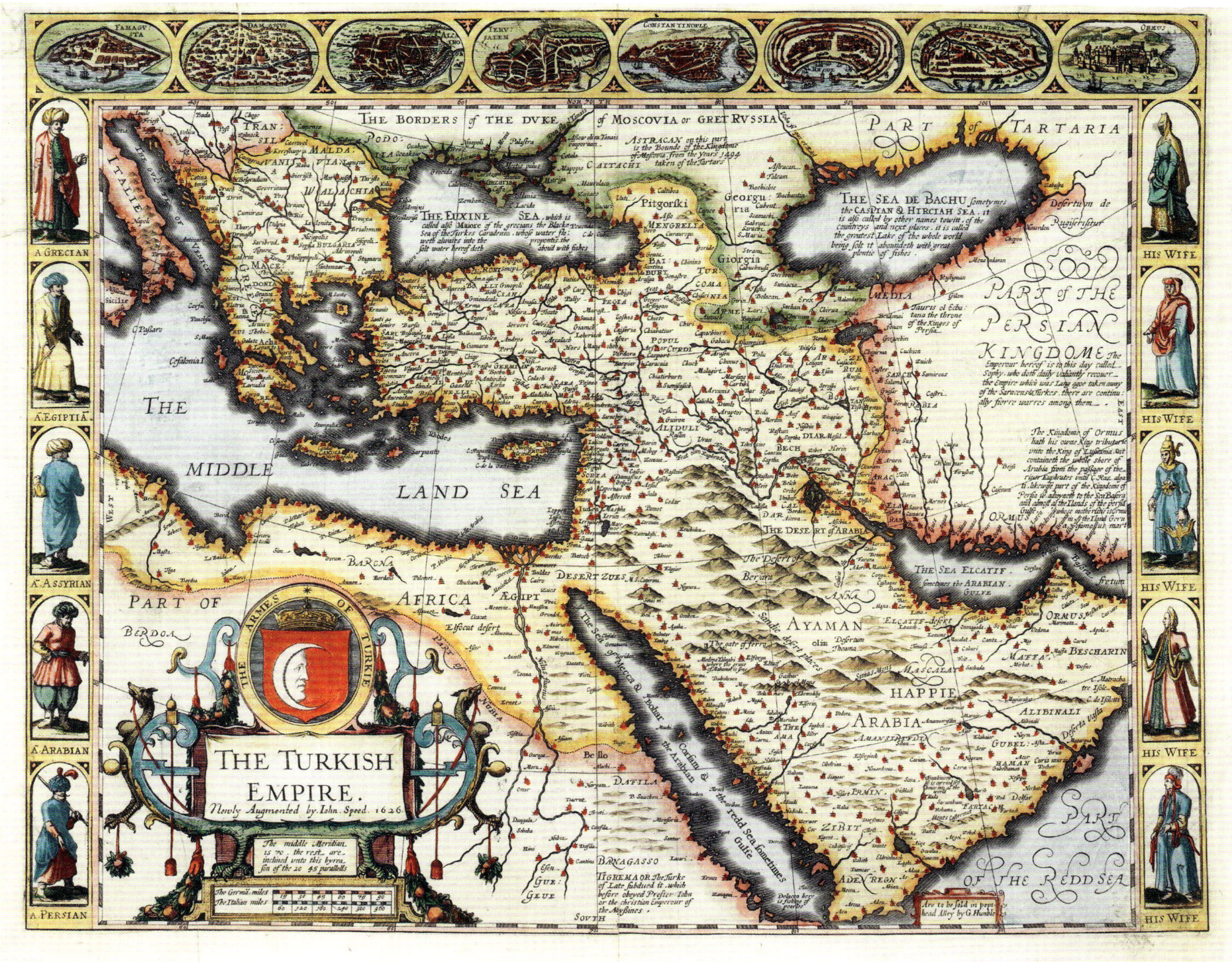

John Speed
The Turkish Empire, 1627
Hand-colored copper-plate engraved map from John Speed's *Theater of the World*
London, John Humble
39 × 52 cm
Courtesy of the Nasser D. Khalili Collection of Islamic Art, London

This is one of the most decorative maps of the region produced in the seventeenth century and the first of the region to be published in England. There are ten costumed figures in the side margins, including an Arabian and his wife. For commercial purposes, cartographers in the seventeenth century introduced local exotic customs in the maps' vignettes.

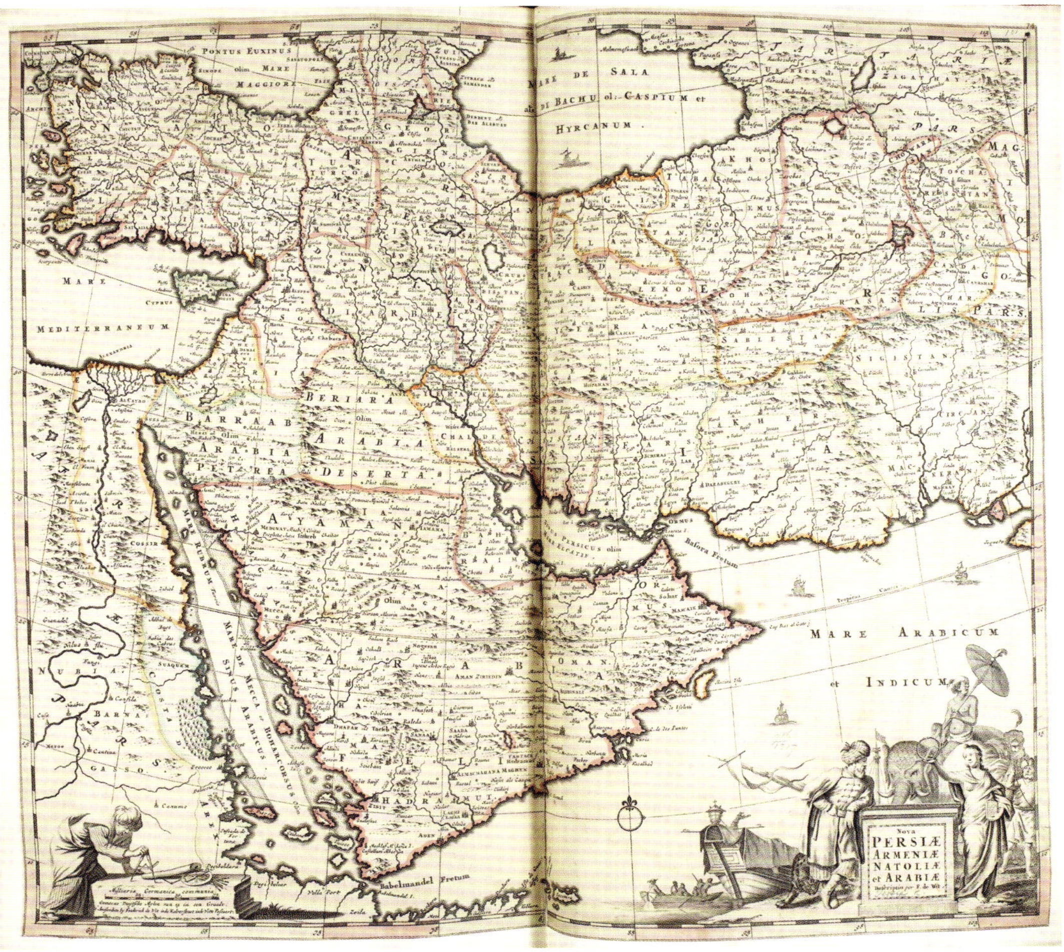

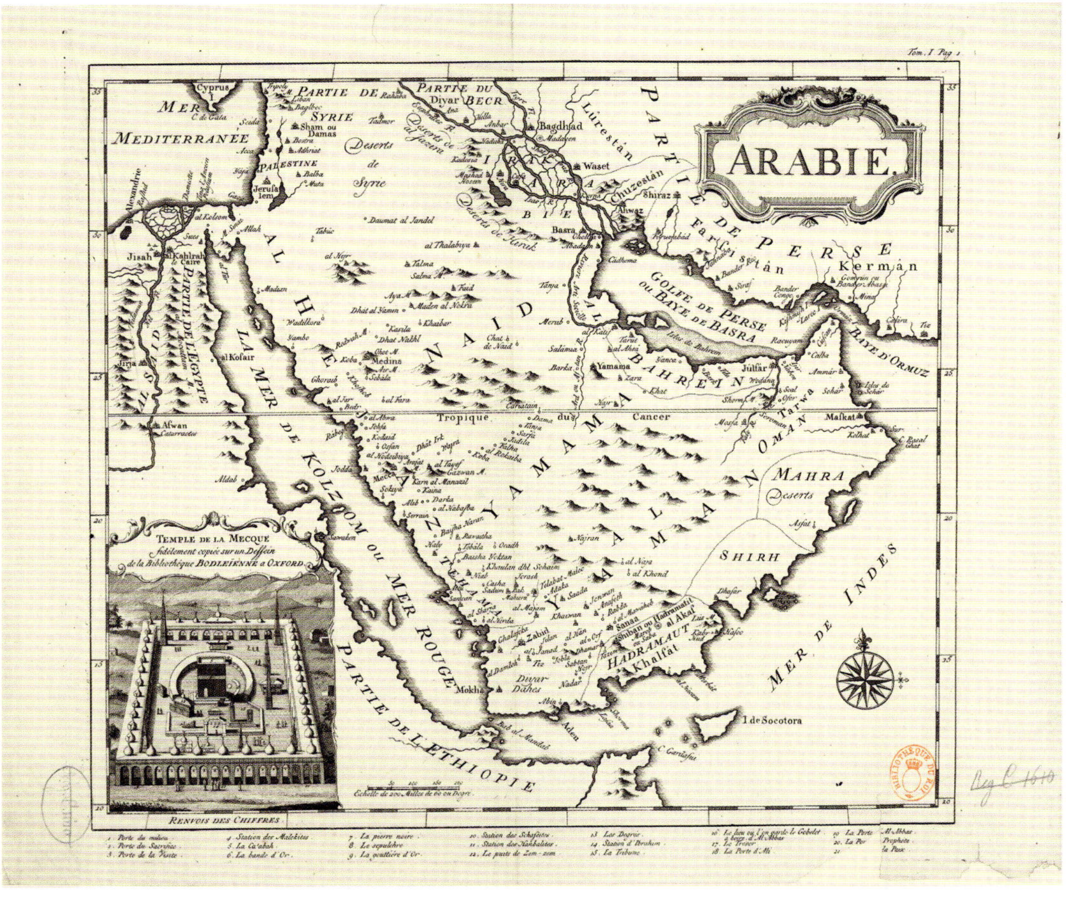

Philippe de La Rue
Ancient Assyria Divided into Syria, Mesopotamia, Babylonia, and Assyria, 1651
Jan Somer, engraver
Hand-colored
38 × 52 cm
Pierre Mariette, Paris
Courtesy of the British Library

This map, showing the ancient kingdoms of the Middle East, is an addition to the atlas Philippe de la Rue published in 1651, *La Terre sainte en six cartes géographiques* (The Holy Land in six maps).

Anonymous
Arabie, seventeenth century
37 × 44 cm
Courtesy of the Bibliothèque nationale de France

This anonymously drawn map of Arabia has an inset featuring the "Temple of Mecca" and was reproduced from a drawing kept in the Bodleian Library at Oxford.

Herman Moll
Arabia Agreeable to Modern History, 1715
Hand-colored engraved map
23 × 18 cm
Thomas Bowles and John Bowles, London
Courtesy of the British Library

This detailed map covers the Red Sea, part of east Africa, the Arabian Peninsula, the Arabian Gulf (labeled "Gulf of Bassora"), and northward to present-day Syria, Iraq, and Iran. The map shows physical features, settlements, caravan trails, and tribal affiliations.

Pieter van der Aa
L'Arabie, 1729
From the *Galerie agréable du monde, où l'on voit en un grand nombre de cartes très exactes et de belles tailles douces, les principaux empires, roïaumes, républiques, provinces, villes, bourgs et forteresses…les îles, côtes rivières, ports de mer…les antiquitez, les abbayes, églises, académies…comme aussi les maisons de campagne, les habillements et mœurs des peuples…dans les quatre parties de l'univers.*
Divided in LXVI (66) volumes, the etchings were drawn and printed by Luyken, Mulder, Goerée, Baptist, Stopendaal, and other renowned masters
Peter Boudewyn, engraver and publisher, Leyden, The Netherlands
40 × 6.5 cm
Courtesy of the Bibliothèque nationale de France

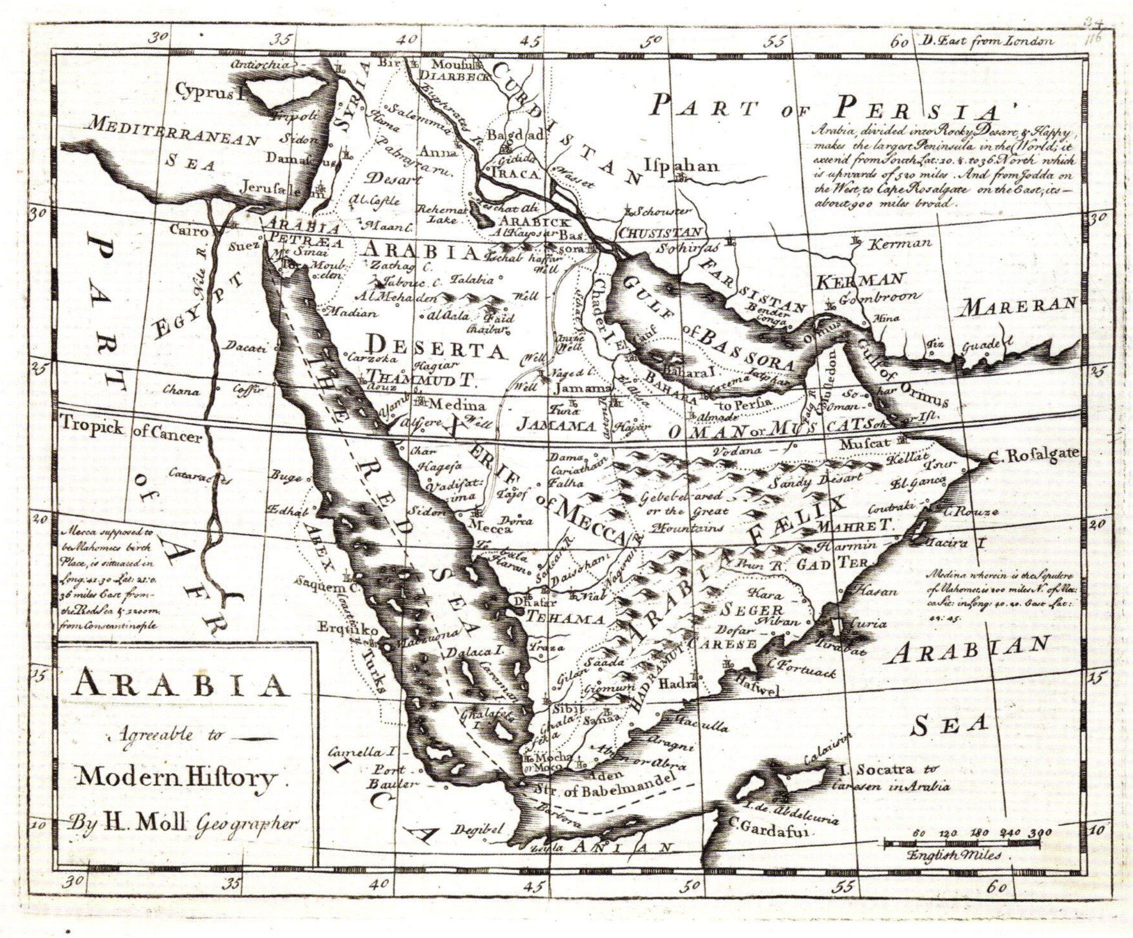

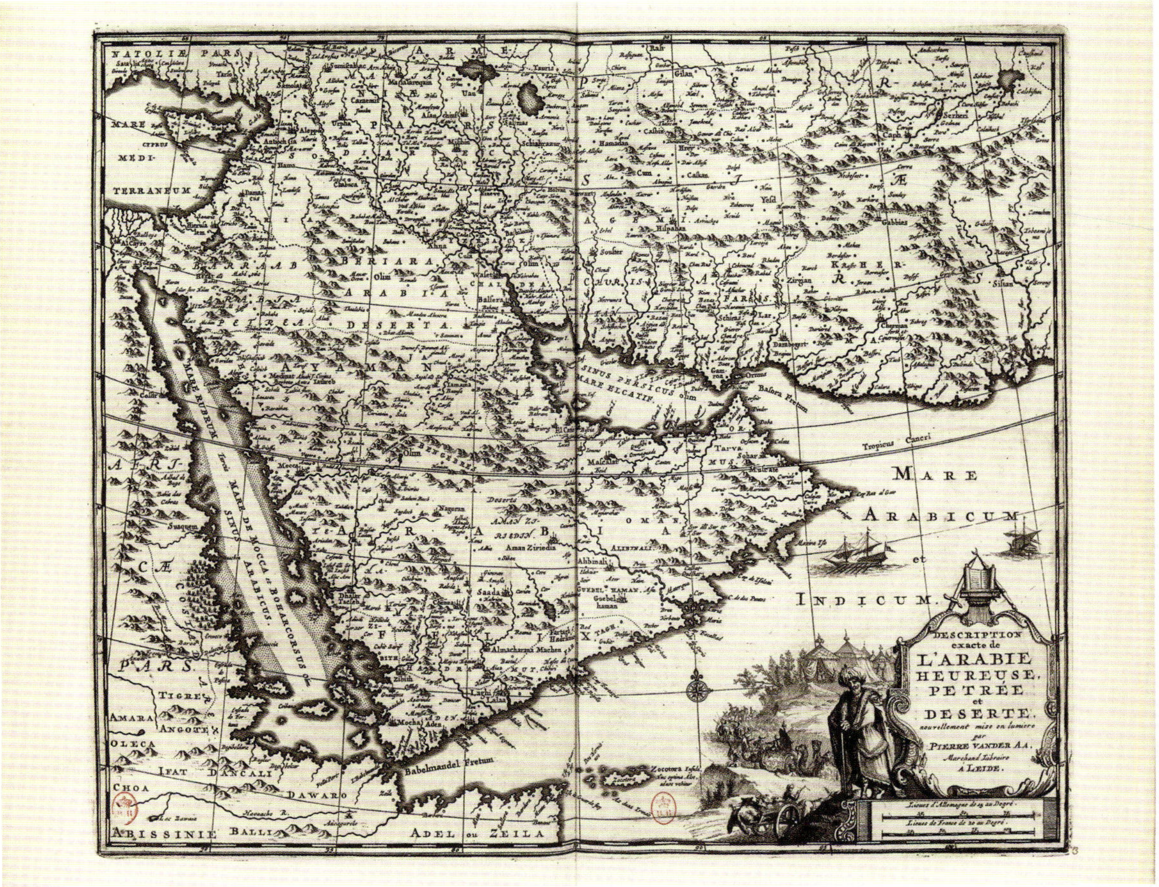

Arabia was represented on the first universal maps—or planispheres—such as that of the Venetian monk, Fra Mauro, it was once again based on the work and indications of Ptolemy.

While the outline of the Arabian coasts was gradually improved by the information gleaned by sailors, the inland remained little known. The earliest maps offered very little information in this regard, often fantasized to include mountain chains, lakes, and rivers arbitrarily distributed in the hinterlands. However, travelers, including those who are the subject of this book, headed off to explore the country and wrote books that expanded the extremely limited knowledge Europeans had of Arabia at that time. It is the Frenchman, Jean-Baptiste Bourguignon d'Anville, geographer and cartographer of King Louis XV, to whom "the merit goes for having published in 1755 the first approximately exact map of Arabia," wrote Jacqueline Pirenne.

This was the map that the members of the famous Danish expedition took with them. It was this map to which Carsten Niebuhr, the sole survivor of that expedition, rendered honors: "Among the maps of Arabia hitherto known there is none which deserves more attention than that which Mr. d'Anville had engraved." Although it still had many omissions and inaccuracies, it presented an image of the country that would not drastically change in the future, an image in which we immediately recognize Arabia.

Jean-Baptiste Bourguignon d'Anville
Première partie de la carte d'Asie contenant la Turquie, l'Arabie, la Perse, l'Inde en deçà du Gange et de la Tartarie, 1751
Engraved by Guillaume-Nicolas Delahaye, Paris
One map on two sheets
79 × 82 cm
Courtesy of the Bibliothèque nationale de France

This map includes, in the north, Turkey—through the Black and Caspian Seas—to Tibet, and in the south, the Arabian Peninsula to eastern India and the Maldives.

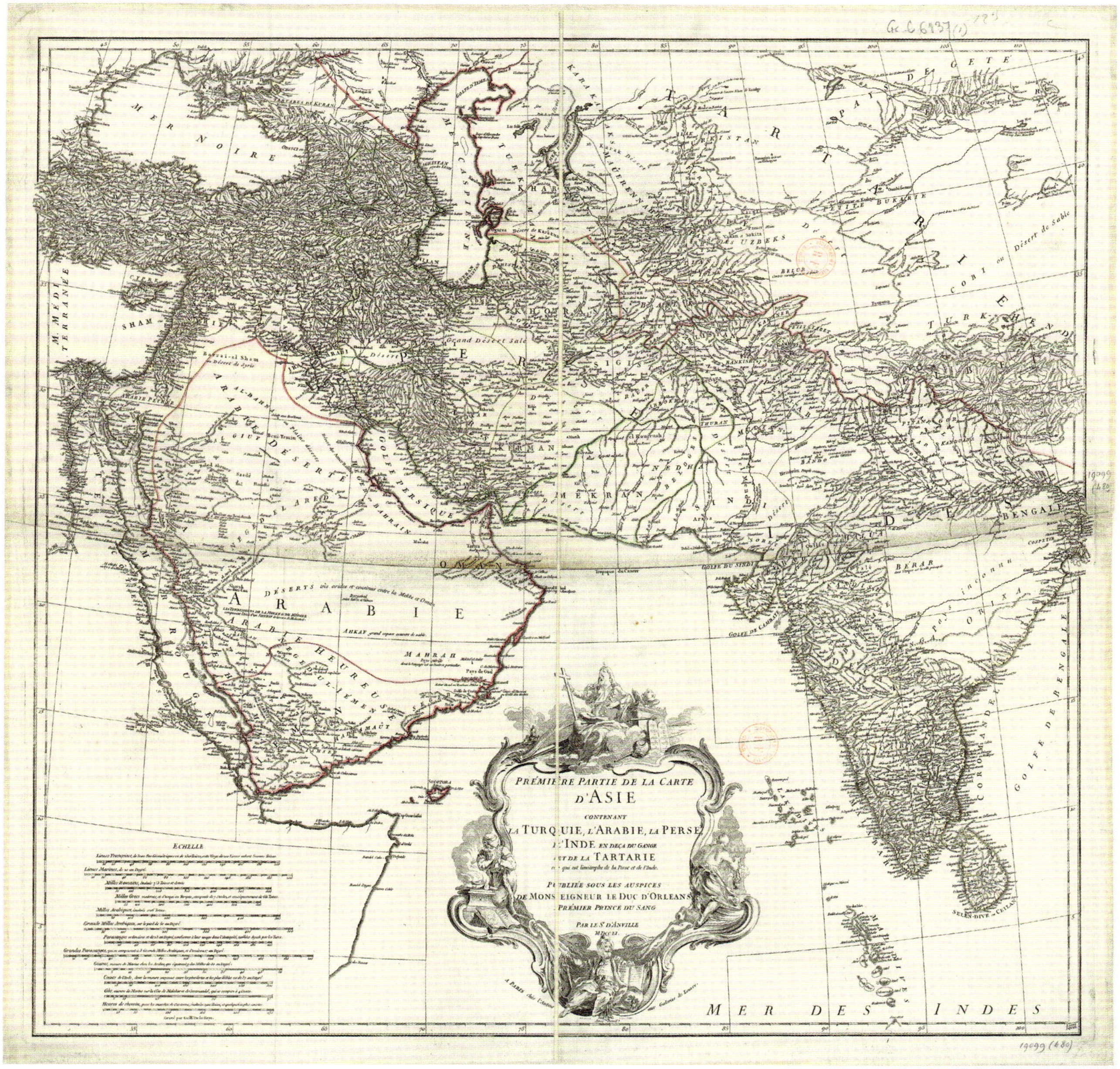

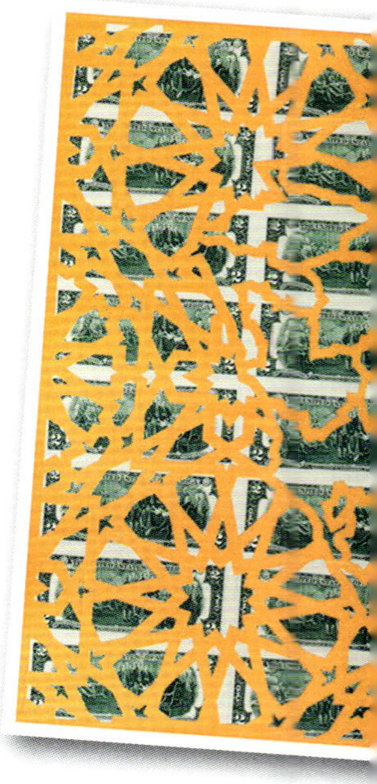

John Cary
A new map of Arabia, including Egypt, Abyssinia, the Red Sea &c. &c. from the latest Authorities, 1819
Hand-colored
London
47 × 52 cm
Nasser D. Khalili Collection of Islamic Art, London

Published in John Cary's new universal atlas containing maps of all the principal states and kingdoms of the era throughout the world, this map is centered on the Arabian Peninsula and the Red Sea. It shows the caravan routes, including several to Mecca, maritime routes, desert wells, and oases.

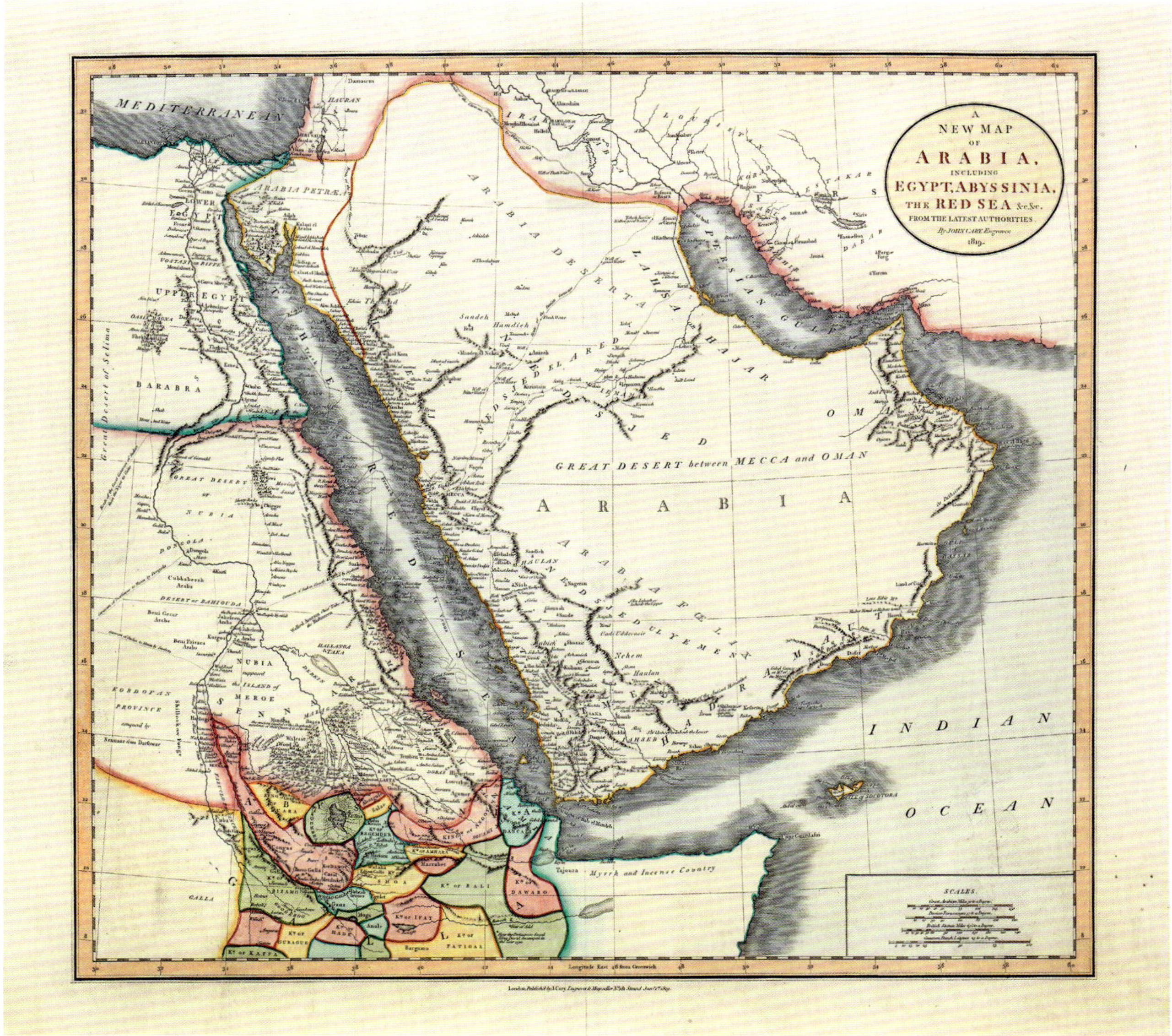

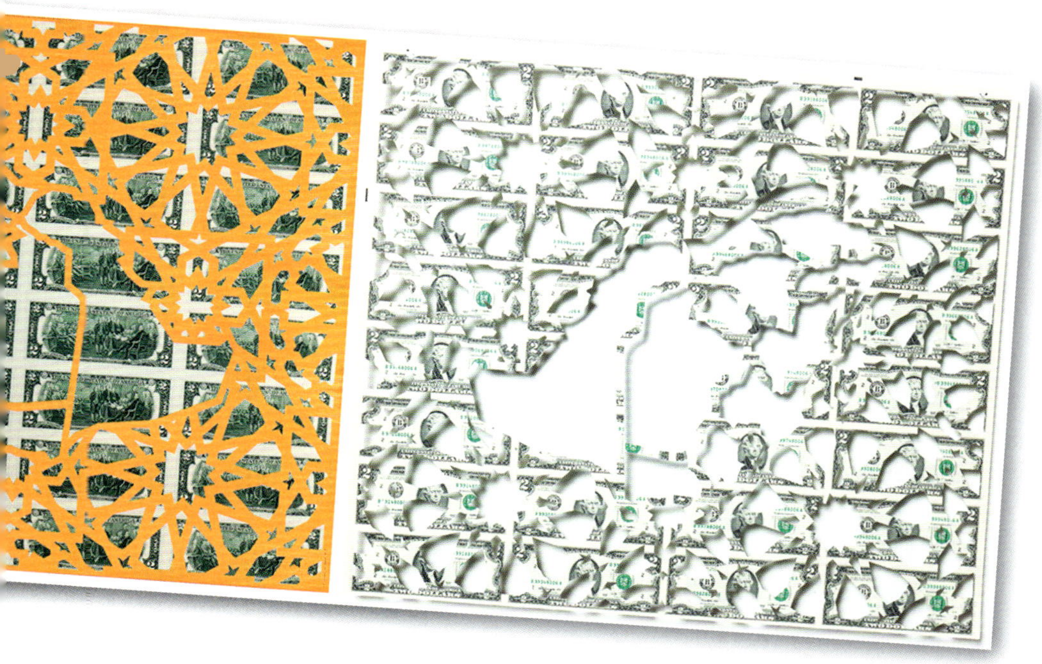

Abdullah Syed
Mapping Investments – Saudi Arabia, 2017
Hand-cut U.S. two-dollars banknote sheet and banknote collage with acrylic on gold-inked hand-made paper (wasli)
Diptych, 20.25 × 50.25 cm (each)
Courtesy of the Aicon Gallery, New York

In this series, Abdullah Syed superimposes different geographical maps of Middle Eastern and South Asian countries on Islamic geometric patterns. The design is first drawn on gold-inked hand-made paper and then superimposed on an uncut sheet of U.S. two-dollars banknotes. The pattern is then hand-cut and the detritus is laid over the inked paper like a veil. The result, states the artist, is a mesh of "geo-design" that evokes *mashrabiyas*.

Biographical Notes

Pieter van der Aa
(Mechelen, Belgium, 1659 – Leiden, The Netherlands, 1733)

A son of a stonecutter and a native of Holstein, Pieter van der Aa settled in 1682 in Leiden, where he established a printing house in which he worked with his two brothers. He started his business by printing books on botany as well as Latin texts in medicine and science. He later specialized in producing maps and geography publications, and printed a compilation on the history of Italy and Sicily that was met with great success. In 1694, he was made printer to Leiden University and in 1715, he was appointed the official printer to the town of Leiden.
His seminal publication was an innovative sixty-six volume illustrated atlas of the world, titled *Galerie Agréable du monde*. Published in 1728, it was then the largest book of prints ever published. Only 100 copies were printed and it featured 3,000 plates of native peoples, architecture, and history from around the world.

Abbas
(Kash, Iran, 1944 – Paris, 2018)

Abbas' family left Iran and settled in Algeria when Abbas Attar, his birth name, was then a child. It is there that, during the Algerian war of independence, he taught himself the art of photography. He chose self-exile in Paris, where he published his first photographs on Biafra, Vietnam, South Africa, and the Middle Eastern wars. He became a member of the French news photo agencies SIPA and Gamma. He covered for the latter the Iranian revolution. In 1981, Abbas joined Magnum Photos.
From 1987 to 1994, Abbas photographed the resurgence of Islam, from social and political perspectives, from China to Morocco. His book *Allah O Akbar, a journey through militant Islam* is the result of his journeys in twenty-nine Muslim societies, torn between the past and the desire for modernization. Abbas is known for his photographic work on religions.
He has also published *Faces of Christianity*, *Les Enfants du lotus: voyage chez les bouddhistes* (Children of the lotus: journey among the Buddhists) and *Gods I've Seen: Travels among Hindus*.

Khedive Abbas Hilmi II
(Alexandria, 1874 – Geneva, 1944)

The great-great-grandson of Mohammed Ali, Khedive Abbas Hilmi II ruled from 1892 to 1914, and attempted to lessen the influence of British control in Egypt. He devoted much attention to agrarian and irrigation projects. In 1914, the British deposed him due to his support of the nationalist movement. Abbas Hilmi II led the Hajj in 1909–10 and took photographs during the pilgrimage.

Hamra Abbas
(Kuwait, 1976)

Hamra Abbas shuttles between Boston and Pakistan, where she is an advisor to postgraduate students at the National College of Arts in Lahore. She has frequently exhibited in Germany, Turkey, Azerbaijan, China, and South Korea. She has been awarded several prizes, including the Sharjah Jury Prize (2009) and the Abraaj Group Art Prize (2011), and she was nominated for the Jameel Prize (2009).
Hamra Abbas works in a variety of media, including paper, plastic, and stained glass. In her artwork *Kaaba Picture as a Misprint*, she conveys the notions of diversity and difference. She explains that "difference in religion can and is often treated as a form of error". It is thus interesting to note that the Kaaba is depicted always in black. "Black is the composition of all colors, and a slight shift in our sense of sight can create an 'error' or 'misprint' to reveal the presence of colors that constitute black."

Ali Bey El Abbassi
(Spain, 1766 – Syria, 1818)

The origins of Ali Bey El Abbassi are obscure. He probably came from a Spanish family carrying the name Badia y Leblich, and his first name was Domingo. However, other ancestries were attributed to him. From 1801, he was known only under the name of Ali Bey El Abbassi, a distant descendant of the Abbasid

princes and caliphs. It is unclear how he gathered his considerable wealth. He published an account of his travels in the Arab world in a three-volume book series published in English in 1816, titled *Travels of Ali Bey, Morocco, Tripoli, Cyprus, Egypt, Arabia, Syria and Turkey between the years 1803 and 1807*. The book included the account of his pilgrimage to Mecca as well as the first circumstantial description of the city, from which he was able to determine its position by astronomical observations and by establishing various plans.
The book enjoyed great success. He returned to Europe to live for a time in Andalusia as governor of Cordova and then of Sevilla, then under French administration. When the French administration came to an end, he settled in France. He returned later to the Middle East, where he died near Aleppo, in circumstances that remain mysterious.

Princess Alice
(Windsor Castle, England, 1883 – London, 1981)

When Princess Alice, the youngest granddaughter of Queen Victoria (her father, Leopold, duke of Albany, was the fourth son of the queen), visited Saudi Arabia in 1938, she was not only the first British royal to visit the country, but also the first European royal to travel to Saudi Arabia. Although her visit was not political, it contributed to consolidating the diplomatic relations between the two countries.
The visit was planned after Princess Alice met Prince Saud at Ascot racecourse. George V, who fell sick, asked his cousin, Princess Alice, to replace him at the racecourse. She was seated next to the young Prince Saud, the crown prince and eldest son of King Abdulaziz. In her memoirs, Princess Alice wrote: "Out of politeness I said how sorry I was that I had never visited Arabia. He at once asked: 'Why not come to Arabia?' He said if I did not mind sleeping in tents, it was easy. I replied that I had often slept in camps without tents at all and accepted right away."
Two years later, Princess Alice's three-week journey through Saudi Arabia took place. She was accompanied by her husband, the Earl of Athlone. Princess Alice was the first member of the British royal family to meet King Abdulaziz. During her voyage, Princess Alice took 322 photographs. These photos, which document Saudi Arabia's architecture and way of life before the oil boom, are held at the King Abdulaziz National Library in Riyadh.

Ziad Antar
(Sidon, Lebanon, 1978)

The year after Ziad Antar received a bachelor's degree from the American University of Beirut in Agricultural Engineering in 2000, he participated in a workshop run by Lebanese filmmakers Mahmoud Hojeiji and Akram Zaatari. Henceforth, he focused entirely on his artistic career. Antar's interests revolve mainly around the relationships between mythology and history, as well as problems linked to geography and borders. He questions the notion of photography and the camera as a medium and developed an original aesthetic derived from rejecting the strict standards of fine photography. Antar's main exhibitions resulted in published books, including *Beirut Bereft: The Architecture of the Forsaken and Map of the Derelict* (with Rasha Salti), published by the Sharjah Art Foundation (2009); *Portrait of a Territory* (Actes Sud, 2012); *Expired*, published by the éditions des Beaux-Arts in Paris (2014); and *After Images.Stories from the Mountains of Asir* (Kaph Books, 2016). His work is also part of prominent public collections, including the British Museum in London and the Centre Georges Pompidou in Paris.

Olivia Arthur
(London, 1980)

Olivia Arthur has mostly focused in her photographic works on the representation of women in relationship to the divide between East and West. She studied mathematics at Oxford University but changed course and entered a program in photojournalism at the London College of Printing. She started working as a photographer in 2003, when she moved to Delhi. In 2006, she moved to Italy for a one-year residence at Fabrica. There, she started working on her series about women, which led her to travel to India, Saudi Arabia, Iran, and Turkey.
Olivia Arthur has published two books to date. *Jeddah Diary*, published in 2012, depicts the lives of young women of Jeddah. *Stranger*, published in 2015, views Dubai through the eyes of the survivor of a shipwreck. Olivia Arthur has been a full member of Magnum Photos since 2013. Her work has been exhibited internationally and included in institutional collections in the UK, USA, Germany, and Switzerland.

Kader Attia
(Dugny, France, 1970)

Kader Attia was raised in Algeria and in France, where he studied at the École Supérieure des arts appliqués Duperré and at the École nationale supérieure des arts décoratifs in Paris. He has lived in Congo and in South America, and currently lives and works in Berlin and Algiers.
An artist working in different mediums—painting, photography, sculpture, and video—as well as installations, Kader Attia's practice is inspired by and deals with history and sociology; memory, colonialism, violence, repair, and multiethnic societies are recurrent themes in his work.
Kader Attia's artwork has been exhibited worldwide at major art institutions and is held in many public

and private institutions, including the MoMa, the Tate Modern, the Musée d'art moderne de la Ville de Paris, and the Centre Pompidou (Paris).
He participated in the 57th Venice Biennale (2017) and in documenta K13 (2012) in Kassel and received many awards, including the Leica Special Prize (Paris, 1997), the Prize of the Cairo Biennial (Cairo, 2008), the Abraaj Capital Prize (Dubai, 2010), the Marcel Duchamp Prize (Centre Georges Pompidou, 2016), the Joan Miró Prize (Barcelona, 2017), and the Yanghyun Art Prize (Seoul, 2017).

Malin Basil
(Sweden, 1944)

Swedish self-taught visual artist Malin Basil is a graduate of the University of Stockholm, with degrees in Russian and political science. She lived in the United States for a few years and married Rodney Basil, an American who had a career waiting for him in Riyadh, where the couple relocated and lived for many years. In Saudi Arabia, Malin Basil witnessed continuous progressive changes, which impacted the entire society. The couple lived in the heart of the city, allowing the artist to interact with the local population on a daily basis. Malin Basil's husband worked at a company that was maintaining water wells across the country, and she would often venture off with him through the deserts while he worked, giving her an extra lens to view the country through. Her curiosity and love of exploring helped her form a broad view of the county.
Basil's artistic career began in Saudi Arabia with her first solo exhibition in 1972 at the Al-Yamama hotel lobby in Riyadh. For the next ten years, she regularly exhibited in Riyadh and in Al-Khobar, a city located on the east coast of the country. The artist showcased her work in London in 1977, the same year she published her first book, *Saudi Arabia Through the Eyes of An Artist*. In 1979, her second book, *Saudi Arabia-Past and Present*, was published. During the 1980s and 1990s, she staged several solo exhibitions in the United States, Sweden, and London, until she opened her own gallery in the English countryside. Her work is held in the collection of the King of Sweden, as well as in several private collections in Saudi Arabia.

Ilo Battigelli
(San Daniele del Friuli, Italy, 1922–2009)

Italian photographer Ilo Battigelli was among the workers recruited by Aramco after the end of World War II to help build the Ras Tanura refinery. He arrived from the former Italian colony of Eritrea with a large group of Italians who had been interned by the British during the War. Battigelli was hired in 1946 to document the building of Aramco's refinery construction. He set up a studio on the beach near his tent, learned Arabic, and with his Rolleiflex 3.5 camera, he photographed people and local scenes, making a name for himself as "Ilo the Pirate". He also photographed King Abdulaziz's official visit to Ras Tanura.
He left Aramco in 1954 and moved to Rhodesia, where he opened a studio. He retired in 2000, returning to Italy. Battigelli's photographs were exhibited in the USA, England, Saudi Arabia, Italy, and Rhodesia. After his death, his family donated his important photo collection to the Pitt Rivers Museum at the University of Oxford.

Georg Wilhelm Baurenfeind
(Nuremberg, 1728 – at sea near Bombay, 1763)

Son of a calligrapher, German draftsman, and engraver, Georg Wilhelm Baurenfeind took an apprenticeship with a copper engraver in Nuremberg and later followed him to Copenhagen, where he received, in 1759, the Royal Danish Academy of Fine Arts' gold medal for his engraving work. He was appointed drawing master of its academy in 1760.
The same year, under the aegis of King Frederick V of Denmark was assembled a team of northern Europe's best scholars to set out on an expedition to Arabia. This expedition, known as the "Danish Arabia Expedition," included German mathematician, cartographer, and explorer Carsten Niebuhr; Swedish natural scientist Pehr Forsskål, a student of Linné; philologist and linguist Frederick Christian von Haven; physician Christian Carl Kramer; and orderly Lars Berggren. Baurenfeind's task was to depict the findings of the members of the expedition in drawings. All members of the expedition except for Carsten Niebuhr died during this difficult voyage. However, Baurenfeind's drawings and sketches were included in the expedition reports by Niebuhr and Forsskål in the seminal *Travels through Arabia and other Countries in the East*, and Forsskål's posthumous *Descriptiones animalium, Flora Aegyptiaco-Arabica*.

Gertrude Bell
(County Durham, England, 1868 – Baghdad, 1926)

The first woman to earn first-degree honors in Modern History at Oxford University, Gertrude Bell was an explorer, diplomat, and archaeology specialist in Mesopotamia. Bell's fascination with the Middle East began when she visited her uncle, who was the British ambassador to Iran at that time. She studied Persian and later learned Arabic.
From 1900 until the Great War, Bell was a member of the Arab Bureau of the British Intelligence Division in Cairo. During the war she applied her knowledge in the service of the British government. In the 1920s she was nominated to serve as the Oriental secretary to the British high

commissioner in Baghdad.
In 1913, accompanied by five local guides and twenty camels, Bell traveled to Ha'il, a town in northern Arabia. When she reached Ha'il, the Rashids, who were governing the town, were suspicious and put her under house arrest in the royal complex. For about a week, Bell was entertained by the women in the palace and was able to take photographs of the palace and the city with her 4x4 Kodak and her panoramic camera. She wrote several books, including accounts of her travels in the desert. In 2000, private dairies containing details of her trip to Ha'il were published under the title *The Arabian Diaries, 1913–1914*.

Léon Belly
(Saint-Omer, France, 1827 – Paris, 1877)

Belly studied painting and joined the artists of the School of Barbizon. From 1850–51, he accompanied a scientific expedition led by the archaeologist L. F. J. Caignart de Saucly, with a mission to study the historic geography of the Dead Sea basin. On the occasion of this journey, he visited Lebanon and Egypt and produced paintings representing Baalbek and the Dead Sea. Belly returned to Egypt twice, from October 1855 to November 1856, in the company of the painter Jean-Léon Gérôme and the sculptor Auguste Bartholdi, and the second time from October 1857 to May 1858 with the Orientalist painter Narcisse Berchère. During this second trip, he visited the Sinai and the Nile valley. In the 1861 Salon, Léon Belly presented four Oriental paintings, including his imposing *Pèlerins allant à La Mecque*, which was awarded the "First Class" medal.

Lady Anne Blunt
(United Kingdom, 1837 – Cairo, 1917)

Anne Blunt, the granddaughter of Lord Byron, also known as "the noble lady of the horses," was an avid violin player and learned drawing from John Ruskin. Later, on the occasion of her travels, she produced remarkable sketches and beautiful drawings.
She visited Arabia, accompanied by her husband Wilfrid Blunt, in search of thoroughbred Arabian horses. Lady Anne Blunt and her husband, after crossing the Nafud desert, stayed with the Emir of Ha'iI, whose stables were the most celebrated in Arabia.
Anne Blunt delivered an interesting account of that stay in her book, *A Pilgrimage to Nejd*.
In 1878, Anne Blunt and Wilfrid Blunt created in Sussex, on the family's estate, "England's Crabett Arabian Stud". Devoted to the conservation of the Arabian horse, the stud encountered immense international success, which continued after they both passed away.

Philip Bouchard
(Cairo, 1952)

Self-taught artist Philip Bouchard lived during his childhood in the Middle East, where his father was a diplomat. He returned to the Middle East in the 1970s and had the occasion to live for two years in Saudi Arabia, where he accompanied a group of archaeologists to the deserts and mountains of southwest Arabia. During his three-month stay, he sketched the landscapes which inspired him to write the following comment: "Up until then, most of my work had been totally from my imagination. Now, however, I was discovering a kind of surrealism in the stillness of the vast desert [...]. All I had to do was to copy what I saw." His book *From Surrealism to Orientalism* (London: Immel Publishing, 1985) is a testimony of his fascination with Saudi Arabia's landscapes and deserts. Bouchard's artwork has been exhibited regularly since 1974, his Arabian paintings were presented in 2003 in England, and in 2016, his Orientalist paintings were exhibited at the Arab-British Chamber of Commerce in London.

Jean-Baptiste Bourguignon d'Anville
(Paris, 1697–1782)

A geographer and cartographer, Jean-Baptiste Bourguignon d'Anville started drawing maps inspired by the descriptions of Latin authors at the age of twelve. His first map was published when he was fifteen. D'Anville contributed to the reform of French cartography initiated by Guillaume Delisle. Instead of copying older maps, he deliberately left unknown areas blank. He thus corrected numerous maps, including a map of Arabia.
In 1754, d'Anville became a member of the French Académie des Inscriptions et belles-lettres and in 1773 he was appointed first geographer to the king of France and was elected to the Académie des Sciences.

Gaspar Bouttats
(Antwerp, c. 1640 – c. 1695)

Born into a family of famous engravers, Gaspar Bouttats trained with his father Frederick. Later, in turn, Gaspar trained his son Pieter Balthazar. Gaspar Bouttats mainly etched, using burin. In 1668, following the footsteps of his father, he became a member of the famed Guild of Saint Luke, an association of painters, engravers, sculptors, and printers active since the fourteenth century, in Italy, France, Holland, and Rhineland. He even became its dean from 1690 until his death. Bouttats worked for prominent publishers who commissioned him to print designs by famous artists such as Jan Peeters, his contemporary and also a native of Antwerp, whose drawings he used for a volume of city views of Jerusalem and its surroundings entitled *Views of Jerusalem, and the surrounding Country* (1674).

Pierre-Joseph Buc'hoz
(Metz, France, 1731 – Paris, 1807)

After completing classical studies in Metz, Pierre-Joseph Buc'hoz settled in Pont-à-Mousson, where he went to study law before becoming a lawyer there in the beginning of the 1750s. He abandoned his legal career to study medicine and showed a special interest in natural history. One of his first books was *Histoire des plantes de la Lorraine* (History of the Plants of Lorraine), which was published in 1762. He later published *Histoire naturelle de la France* (Natural History of France) in fourteen volumes before undertaking *Histoire universelle du règne vegetal* (Universal History of the Vegetal Reign), according to the nomenclature of Linné. Although the first volumes were published in 1773, he was unable to complete this publication. He authored many books on botany and also studied zoology. His interest extended to birds and minerals. As a demonstrator at the Collège Royal des Médecins (Royal College of Physicians) of Nancy, Pierre-Joseph Buc'hoz also published books on medicine and *Mémoire sur la manière de guérir la mélancolie par la musique* (Thesis on how to use music as a therapy for treating melancholy). As a polygraph, Buch'oz published more than three hundred books during his long and fruitful lifetime.

René Burri
(Zurich, 1933 – Paris, 2014)

Graduated from the Zurich University of the Arts, René Burri quickly became one of the most well-known photojournalists of his time. A member since the 1950s of the photo agency Magnum, he covered the Korea and Vietnam wars, as well as the Cuban Missile Crisis. His striking wartime photos, although very riveting, show no casualties. They were featured in the most prestigious publications, such as *Life*, *Look*, *Stern*, *Paris-Match*, *Réalités*, *Epoca*, and *The New York Times*. His portraits of Picasso and Che Guevara became iconic, contributing to his significant renown. It was in 1974 that he undertook his reportage on Saudi Arabia.
His photographs were exhibited in the most prestigious institutions worldwide, including the Art Institute (Chicago), the Kunsthaus Zürich, the Musée des arts décoratifs (Lausanne), the International Center of Photography (New York), the Palais de Tokyo (Paris), and the Fotografie Forum International (Frankfurt).
In 2004, the Maison Européenne de la photographie in Paris organized a retrospective of fifty years of his work. This retrospective later traveled to Lausanne, Basel, Milan, and Zurich.

Richard Francis Burton
(Torquay, Devon, 1821 – Trieste, 1890)

Born to a well-to-do family from the west of England, in his childhood, Richard Francis Burton accompanied his parents wherever they settled in France or Italy. The young Burton learned and spoke fluent French and several Italian dialects, proving that he was particularly talented in languages. Later, during his studies at the Trinity College in Oxford, he learned Arabic. At the age of twenty, he joined the English army and was stationed in East India, where he started his career as an officer in Bombay. He overcame the boredom of life in a garrison by quickly mastering Hindustani, and later Gujarati and Marathi, while also pursuing his studies of Arabic and Persian. During his life, Burton learned to speak thirty languages and acquired a rich knowledge of the cultures where they were spoken. Aside from his military career, which lasted around ten years, and then his diplomatic career—when he held the post of consul in Fernando Po (Equatorial Guinea), Santos (Brazil), Damascus (Syria), and finally Trieste—he led the life of an adventurer, an explorer, a writer, and a translator, which made him quite famous. Among the places he explored were the interior of Somalia; the discovery of the city of Harar, which he was the first Westerner to visit; the discovery of Lake Tanganyika; and the discovery of the secret sources of the Nile. Burton also performed the pilgrimage to Mecca and wrote an account of his voyage, *Personal Narrative of a Pilgrimage to Al-Madinah and Mecca*, which was published near the beginning of his renown. To illustrate the extent of his curiosity, knowledge, and accomplishments, suffice it to note that he authored around forty books in addition to hundreds of articles. Among the books he wrote were *Goa and the Blue Mountains* (1851), *Sindh and the Races That Inhabit the Valley of the Indus* (1853), *A Complete System of Bayonet Exercise* (1853), *The Lake Regions of Central Africa* (1860), *The City of the Saints, Among the Mormons and Across the Rocky Mountains to California* (1861), *The Nile Basin* (1864), *Explorations of the Highlands of Brazil* (1869), *Letters From the Battlefields of Paraguay* (1870), *Zanzibar* (1872), *Ultima Thule or a Summer in Iceland* (1872), *Etruscan Bologna* (1876), *Two Trips to Gorilla Land and the Cataracts of the Congo* (1876), *To the Gold Coast for Gold* (1883), and *The Book of the Sword* (1884). To this list we can add several remarkable translations Burton completed, including *The Kama Sutra of Vatsyayana* (1883) and *The Book of the Thousand Nights and a Night* (1885). Burton's translation of the latter is the first not to be expurgated and remains, until today, the best translation in English.
Awarded Knighthood by the queen, Sir Richard Francis Burton lived the prodigious life of one of the most accomplished great travelers of the end of the nineteenth century, in addition to being a prolific and talented writer.

John Cary
(Corsley, England, 1754 – London, 1835)

John Cary started his career as an engraver in London and established his own business on the Strand in 1783. In 1787, he published *The New and Correct English Atlas*, which quickly become a standard point of reference and brought him fame for the quality of his maps and globes.

Ali Cherri
(Beirut, 1976)

Ali Cherri received a Bachelor of Arts in graphic design from the American University in Beirut and a Master of Arts in performing arts from DasArts in Amsterdam.
Cherri's artworks focus on current affairs as well as ancient history and archaeology.
Trembling Landscapes (2014–16) is an ongoing series in which Ali Cherri pursues—through film, video, drawing, printmaking, and performance—an investigation into the effects of catastrophe, both man-made and geological, on his native Lebanon and neighboring territories.
Ali Cherri's artwork was shown in the Jeu de Paume in Paris (2017), the Guggenheim in New York (2016), the Tate Modern in London (2013), the Museum of Modern Art in New York (2012), and the Centre Georges Pompidou in Paris (2011).

Christian Clot
(1972)

Christian Clot has, for the last twenty years, been leading scientific explorations to the most extreme environments of our planet: very high mountains, jungles, deserts, seas, and underwater. He has carried out around thirty expeditions without motorized transport, alone or with others. With a life-long passion for comics, in 2010 he created a series on the Great Explorers for Éditions Glénat. These then became part of the Explora collection in 2012. He is also the author of stories such as *Ultima Cordillera* (Arthaud, 2007) and children's books such as *Moi, Explorateur* (Glénat 2017).

Harold Corsini
(New York City, 1919 – Pittsburgh, 2008)

Harold Corsini's professional career began in the early 1940s, when he worked briefly for *Life* magazine. He was hired as a photographer for Standard Oil in 1943 and was able to document the oil company's operations worldwide, including the Pacific and Saudi Arabia.
Corsini later became the official photographer for US Steel. Much later, he retired from commercial photography and joined Carnegie Mellon University (Pittsburgh), where he taught photography and design.
Corsini's photographs were displayed in museums worldwide and are currently held in various prestigious collections, including the George Eastman Museum in Rochester, New York, and the Carnegie Museum of Art in Pittsburgh.

Olivier Couppey
(Cherbourg, France, 1968)

From a very early age, Olivier Couppey was interested in nature and especially birds, which he observed and painted. He discovered photography and familiarized himself with the specialties of black-and-white prints and the audiovisual arts. He started his career as the director of video production for a company outside Paris and as freelance video editor in Paris.
In 1995, he seized the occasion to begin work for an organization whose mission was the conservation of nature in Saudi Arabia. Responsible for the production of multimedia tools for education and information, his activities were diverse: production of documentary films, reportage, and graphic creation. Video filming and photography led him to travel across the Kingdom. In addition to this work, his personal interest in a multifaceted culture allowed him, during the twenty-three years he lived in Saudi Arabia, to deeply discover the country and its people. Since his return to France and still today, he pursues his passion for images, be it in the nature field or others.

Charles Cousen
(Yorkshire, England, 1819–1889)

Charles Cousen served an important function as a printmaker during the second half of the nineteenth century in England. He is mainly known for illustrating books focusing on the Middle East, such as *The Christians in Palestine*, by Henry Stebbing; *The Beauties of the Bosphorus*, by Julia Pardoe; and *The Nile Boat* or *Glimpses of the land of Egypt*, by W. H. Bartlett.

Raymond Depardon
(Villefranche-sur-Saône, France, 1942)

Raymond Depardon took photographs of the family farm at the age of 12 with a 6x6 medium-format camera. Upon completing his primary education, he started an apprenticeship at a photography shop in Villefranche-sur-Saône. He moved to Paris in the early 1960s, where he joined the Dalmas Agency reporting on conflict zones such as Algeria, Vietnam, and Biafra. In 1966, he cofounded his own photojournalism agency, Gamma, and became its director in 1973. In 1977, he received a Pulitzer Prize for his reports on Chad. Raymond Depardon left Gamma and joined Magnum Photos in 1978. During that time, Depardon pursued a concurrent career as a documentary filmmaker, starting with short documentaries in the 1960s and advancing to feature-length documentaries in the 1980s.
His photographs have been featured in many publications and he received numerous awards for both his photos and his documentaries. His

photographs have been presented in two large-scale retrospectives: at the Maison Européenne de la photographie, Paris, in 2000, and later at the Mucem, Marseille, in 2014.

Charles Montagu Doughty
(Saxmundham, England, 1843 – Sissinghurst, England, 1926)

Poet, writer, and traveler Charles M. Doughty is mostly known for his two-volume account of his travels, *Travels in Arabia Deserta*. Written in a very mannered and flamboyant English, the book records the discoveries of Doughty in the deserts of Arabia and demonstrates his deep knowledge of geology, a discipline Doughty had studied, as well as archaeology and anthropology.
After setting out from Damascus with the pilgrims' caravan, Doughty left them midway to become the first Westerner to visit the Nabatean tombs of the antique site of Hegra, near Mada'in Saleh, where for two months he was able to record its inscriptions and produce many drawings. Doughty would send from there his drawings, created with a brush and a sponge on absorbent paper to copy the inscriptions, to Ernest Renan and to the Marquis de Vogüé in Paris, which earned him great fame with all Semitic scholars. Doughty also visited Tayma, Ha'il, Khaybar, and Boreyda before reaching Jeddah. When he returned to England, he wrote his one-thousand-page account, which he published in 1888. In that book, Doughty painted Arabia and the life of its Bedouins with great sincerity.

Robert Wilhelm Ekman
(Uusikaupunki, Finland, 1808 – Helsinki, Finland, 1873)

A painter and teacher, Robert Wilhelm Ekman first studied in Finland before pursuing his studies at the Royal Swedish Academy of Arts in Stockholm. He specialized and excelled in the art of portraits, and when he graduated in 1836, he was granted a traveling scholarship which allowed him to work in the Netherlands, France, and Italy from 1837 to 1844. He then returned to Sweden, where he became a member of the Academy of Arts and was nominated for "court painter".
In 1854, Ekman returned to Finland, where he was commissioned to paint the frescos of the Cathedral of Turku, located in the southwest, on the Baltic Sea. He also painted some thirty frescos and altarpieces in different churches in Finland. In 1846, a school of drawing was established in Turku, and Ekman was appointed its director until his death in 1873. His artwork, representative of Finnish romanticism, is held in several museums.

Fouad Elkoury
(Paris, 1952)

Photographer and filmmaker Fouad Elkoury lives in both Paris and Beirut. After earning a degree in architecture in London in 1979, Elkoury turned to photography, documenting daily life during the civil war in Lebanon.
He photographed many cities in the Middle East, including Jeddah, where he was able to capture images of its authentic architecture.
In 1989, Elkoury joined the Rapho photo agency, and after winning the Prix Medicis Hors les Murs, he spent a year in Egypt retracing the steps of Gustave Flaubert and Maxime Du Camp.
In 1997, Elkoury cofounded the Arab Image Foundation, whose mission is to archive and preserve photographs of Lebanon as well as other countries in the Middle East.
Elkoury authored many books, including *Beyrouth aller-retour* (1984), *Palestine, l'envers du miroir* (1996), *Liban Provisoire* (1996), *Suite Égyptienne* (1999), *Sombres* (2002), and *La Sagesse du photographe* (2004). He also produced several videos, including *Jours tranquilles en Palestine* (1998), *Lettres à Francine* (2002), *Moving Out* (2003), *Welcome to Beirut* (2005), *Civil war* (2012), and *Re: Visiting Tarab* (2013). His photographs have been presented in numerous exhibitions worldwide and his work is found in various museums in Europe and the Middle East.

Isabelle Eshraghi
(Isphahan, Iran, 1964)

Isabelle Eshraghi was born to a French mother and Iranian father. Her family left her native country when she was three years old. She later discovered her passion for photography while travelling in the Algerian desert at 17 with a small Kodak Instamatic and has since then made this passion her career.
Her recent work is mostly focused on the depiction of women in the Arab and Muslim world. Her projects *Women in the Arab World* and *Women on the Move* had her travelling to Saudi Arabia several times. Eshraghi's photos have appeared regularly in prestigious newspapers and magazines worldwide. Her work has also been included in group and solo exhibits worldwide and she has won prestigious awards including the Kodak Critics' Photographic Prize for her work on Women of Isfahan in 1997, the Villa Médicis Hors les Murs/AFAA award for her photographic work titled *Being twenty in Tehran* in 1999, and the FIACRE Program award for her photographic work on Iranian men in 2001.

Osama Esid
(Damascus, 1970)

Osama Esid studied photography at the Technical Institute of Damascus while working in his father's tailor shop. In 1994, he decided to leave Syria and traveled to Paris. In 1996, he moved to the United States, where he lived and worked in Minneapolis, Minnesota. Esid gained recognition for his mastery of hand-coloring black-and-white prints. This

technique, introduced and practiced in the Middle East in the early twentieth century by Armenian photographers, is disappearing today.
Esid's photographs focus mainly on the themes of "Orientalism" and the "exotic" while questioning issues pertaining to identity and the otherness. His body of photographs includes his iconic series on imagined Parisian brothels, "Workers of Cairo" and "Orientalism and Nostalgia".
In 2017, Esid traveled to Turkey, where he photographed the Syrian Refugee Camp in Adana. This series of photographs, titled *STILL/ LIFE/ SYRIA*, was presented during the Northern Spark Festival in Minneapolis.

Julius Euting
(Stuttgart, 1839 – Strasbourg, 1913)

After studying theology and Semitic languages, the philosopher and Orientalist Julius Euting was appointed professor at the University of Strasbourg as well as director of its Library. He traveled to Arabia in 1883–84. Funded by King Charles of Württemberg, his expedition was motivated by archaeology and epigraphy. He studied and copied the inscriptions of its pre-Islamic monuments.
The accounts of Professor Euting's travels were translated into English in *Diary of a Journey to Inner Arabia* (1896); the second volume was printed in 1914.

Charles Fouqueray
(Le Mans, France, 1869 – Paris, 1956)

Son of a Le Mans baker, Charles Fouqueray was admitted in 1887 to the École des Beaux-Arts of Paris, where he was the student of Alexandre Cabanel and Fernand Cormon. Fouqueray was unable to enter the naval school due to weak mathematics. Instead, from 1890 onward, he collaborated with a variety of newspapers and magazines, including *Le Monde illustré*, *L'illustration*, *The Sphere*, *The Graphic*, and *The Illustrated London News*. In addition, he illustrated many novels and literary works, mainly the books of the novelist Claude Farrère, an officer in the navy and a member of the Académie française, including the *Album historique de l'Armée et de la Marine* (Historic Album of the Army and the Navy). Enthralled by the maritime life, his paintings are largely inspired by this theme. After several requests, he finally obtained the title of Official Artist to the Navy, which allowed him to embark on the most beautiful ships of the French Navy and paint faraway horizons. This tradition still prevails today.
Fouqueray studied in the École des Beaux-arts from 1887 to 1893. Later he worked with Pierre Puvis de Chavannes to produce decorative paintings. He was also appointed Artist to the Army and Artist to the Air Force.
Charles Fouqueray traveled three times to Saudi Arabia, in 1917–18, 1921, and 1924. He was thus able to paint and sketch the ports, the inhabitants, the architecture, and the dhows of Al-Wejh, Yanbu, and Jeddah. He also produced several paintings showing pilgrims disembarking in Jeddah and the French Navy commissioned him to produce three murals representing Arabia. These paintings are hung inside the *Cercle Naval* in Toulon. Today, Fouqueray's artworks are found in national museums in France and abroad.

Stuart Franklin
(London, 1956)

After studying photography at the West Surrey College of Art and Design, Stuart Franklin first worked for *The Sunday Times* and the *Sunday Telegraph Magazine* in London before joining the Sygma Press Agency in Paris from 1980 to 1985. During that time, he covered for Sygma the 1983 Nigerian military coup, the Heysel Stadium disaster, the Beirut bombing of the French and American bases, the civil wars in Lebanon and Sri Lanka, the conflict in Northern Ireland, and finally, the 1984–85 famine in Sudan. He was invited to become a Magnum associate member in 1985 and became a full-fledged member in 1989. He would go on to being elected president of Magnum from 2006 to 2009.
In 1989, while in China, he captured the iconic photo, *Tank Man*, of a man standing in the middle of an avenue blocking the path of a tank column during the Tiananmen Square protests. In 1990, Franklin started working for *National Geographic* and contributed to more than twenty reports for the publication, with wide-ranging subjects. It is in this capacity that he traveled to Arabia in 2000, to the Rub' al-Khali desert. To further his understanding on the subjects he aimed to capture, he resumed his studies at the University of Oxford, where he received a doctorate in geography in 2000. He has been a professor of documentary photography since 2016.

Gerald de Gaury
(London, 1897–1984)

Arabist, explorer, historian, diplomat, and officer, Lt. Col. Gerald de Gaury served in World War I, notably in the Gallipoli campaign, and was wounded several times. During times of convalescence, he taught himself how to speak Arabic.
His command of the Arabic language, as well as his knowledge of Muslim culture and religious lore, put him at the forefront of the British diplomatic relationship with the nascent Kingdom of Saudi Arabia. During this time, he formed a personal relationship with Ibn Saud, thanks to their common fondness for hunting.
In 1935, he was tasked with presenting Ibn Saud with the robes and insignia of the Order of the Bath and with reading in Arabic an address from King George to the royal court. He

published several books on Saudi Arabia, among them *Arabian Phoenix: An Account of a visit to Ibn Saud* (1946), *Arabian Journeys and Other Desert Travels* (1950), *The Ruler of Mecca* (1954), and *Faisal, King of Saudi Arabia* (1965).
Gerald de Gaury was a talented photographer, watercolorist, and sketch artist, and his depictions of the kingdom's life and landscapes on various media form a rare outsider's vision of Saudi Arabia at its beginnings.

Yann Jules Gayet
(Paris, 1981)

Yann Gayet began studying Arabic language and literature in Paris, then in Damascus, and later in Aix-en-Provence. He undertook research on the French translations of the old Arabic poetry when he was offered a post at the French Consulate in Jeddah. He went to Saudi Arabia in the autumn of 2007.
It is in Jeddah that he met a fellow Frenchman, Olivier Couppey, who had been working for the NWRC (National Wildlife Research Centre) for fifteen years and who guided him on his first hike on Djebel Shada, a mountain in the Al-Baha region. Two weeks later, Yann Gayet returned to explore the mountain alone.
The few days that he spent walking and meeting the locals made him decide to resume photography, which he had abandoned after a period of intense practice in adolescence.
From then until May 2010, he traveled tens of thousands of kilometers, many of which were off-road.
In 2013 and 2014, he participated in the Franco-Saudi archaeological missions in Mada'in Saleh and Dumat al-Jandal, allowing him to extend his photographic research. And in 2017, he returned to carry out technical photographic surveys on historical buildings along the north coast of the Red Sea.

Nicolaus Germanus
(c. 1420 – c. 1490)

Cartographer Nicolaus Germanus was a monk from Reichenback Priory, Germany, where he lived in the fifteenth century. Nicolas Germanus participated, with other cartographers, in revising the famous *Cosmographia*, produced in the second century AD, by the Roman geographer Claudius Ptolemy. In 1467, he re-created a version of Ptolemy's atlas, covering the total known areas from Greenland to India.

Jules Gervais-Courtellemont
(Seine-et-Marne, France, 1863 – Coutevroult, France, 1931)

A journalist, writer, and photographer, Gervais-Courtellemont grew up in Algeria, where he developed a passion for the Orient and converted to Islam. In 1894, he performed the pilgrimage in the company of an Algerian merchant named Haji Akl, who had previously performed the Hajj twenty times.
On that occasion, Gervais-Courtellemont took numerous photos in Arabia which he used to illustrate his book *Mon Voyage à La Mecque* (1896).
Gervais-Courtellemont returned to Hijaz in 1908, when he was invited by Sultan Abdulhamid II to attend the inauguration of the Hijaz railway station.
Gervais-Courtellemont took color autochromes of his travels to Turkey, Palestine, Egypt, Tunisia, Spain, India, Morocco, and China. He covered World War I, and after the war, worked for *National Geographic*. Between 1923 and 1925, he published *La Civilisation-histoire sociale de l'humanité*, a three-volume book illustrated with his photographs.

Roger Grasas
(Barcelona, 1970)

After studying photography and philosophy, Roger Grasas produced photo documentaries for several NGOs as well as UNESCO. He taught photography and cofounded the Phototroupe Studio photography agency.
Roger Grasas' photographic work focuses on the contradictions and transformations in our environment caused by modernity and technology. Beginning in 2005, he developed a passion for societies in the Gulf and created two important projects on these societies, to which he gave the Arabic names *Min Turab* (From the Earth) and *Inshallah*. These photography projects focused on changes in the desert and the broader landscape in the Gulf countries. Grasas also showed in his photo reportages the consequences of changes to societies which, less than two or three generations ago, were governed by the very austere lifestyle nomadic life.
"What I am interested in", says Grasas, "is the ability of photography to convert the ordinary into extraordinary."
The photographic work of Roger Grasas has been exhibited in various countries around the world, including Spain, France, Mexico, and Saudi Arabia.

Ezio Gribaudo
(Turin, 1929)

Ezio Gribaudo trained at the Accademia di Brera as an architect. Chromatic precision and historical determination pervade his work as a painter, sculptor, and graphic artist. His artwork has been recognized with various international prizes, among them the IX Rome Quadrennial in 1965, the XXXIII Venice Biennale Prize (for graphic arts) in 1966, and the São Paulo Biennale in 1967. Gribaudo's prolific production and diverse activities made him a highly

significant figure in contemporary Italian art. He has worked with Lucio Fontana, Francis Bacon, Giorgio de Chirico, Peggy Guggenheim, and the Cobra Group's Pierre Alechinsky and Jean Dubuffet, to mention only a few artists and personalities with whom he crossed paths. Through his committed activity as an art publisher, he has mentored and promoted many artists since the 1950s.
Gribaudo's experimentations with materials, paper, and print allowed him to develop a new approach by representing archeological remnants in the context of intense chromatic studies. His use of a manual press renews the function of an old and noble instrument, now incorporated with craft and ability in his daily practice.

Maïmouna Guerresi
(Pove del Grappa, Italy, 1951)

A multimedia artist working with photography, sculpture, video, and installation, Maïmouna Guerresi converted to Islam after living in Senegal. She presents in her work a very personal perspective on the spirituality of human beings and their relation to their inner mystical dimensions.
Maïmouna's work is a hybrid embrace of her spirituality and her mixed African, Asian, and European heritage. Her work has been exhibited in solo and group shows in Europe, Africa, the United States, Asia, and the Middle East. She participated in the Italian pavilion at the Venice Biennale in 1982, 1986, and 2011, as well as in documenta K18 (1987) in Kassel, Germany. Her work is included in private and public collections worldwide.
Maïmouna Guerresi visited Saudi Arabia (Jeddah and Mecca) in 2017. She lives in Italy and Senegal.

Aya Haidar
(Houston, 1985)

After graduating from the Slade School of Fine Art in London, Aya Haidar completed an exchange program at the School of the Art Institute of Chicago. She then earned an MSc with Merit from the London School of Economics and Political Science.
Aya Haidar has always been involved with humanitarian, education, and social issues, and has worked with NGOs. Her multimedia practices include crafts such as knitting and embroidering.
Subsequent to her discovery of the architecture of Jeddah's downtown, Aya Haidar produced in 2012 *Al Balad*, a body of work combining printed digital photography on linen with hand-stitched craft. In this series, the artist chose details of the facades of the buildings in her photographs and embroidered them using brightly colored thread, hence merging the practice of the modern media of digital photography with the traditional practice of hand-stitching.
Aya Haidar's artwork has been exhibited worldwide and she has participated in various international art fairs.

Caroline Havers
(The Netherlands, 1959)

After studying museology at the Reinwardt Academy of Amsterdam, Caroline Havers worked as a fair-trade importer of quality handicrafts from Third World countries.
Havers trained in painting, drawing, etching, photography, and printmaking. In the early 1990s, she started working as a freelance illustrator and since then has pursued a career as a full-time professional artist.
Caroline Havers lived in many cities worldwide: Manila, Washington, D.C., Prague, Brussels, London, Riyadh, and Cairo. In each of the countries where she has lived, local culture, nature, and her experiences have been a source of inspiration for her.
During her stay in Riyadh from 2012 to 2016, Havers produced an important collection of paintings depicting the environment and the colors of Arabia. In her series *Sands & Serendipity* (2014), Havers worked on a traditional tent canvas, purchased from a tent souk, on which she applied sand and other organic materials such as dried bits of palm tree to create a coarse, uneven texture evoking the desert's temperament.

Colbert Held
(Stamford, Texas, 1917 – Waco, Texas, 2016)

A foreign service officer and a professor of political and cultural geography, Colbert Held photographed the Middle East between 1957 and 2005. In 2014, he donated about 20,000 of his color slides to the Middle East Institute in Washington, D.C.
The collection comprises photographs of topography, landscape, portraits, and cityscapes that demonstrate the enormous changes the Middle East underwent in the second half of the twentieth century. Held also took numerous aerial photographs, including some of offshore oil infrastructures.
Colbert Held joined the Army Air Corps in 1942, where he attended the Air Photographic School. He later taught at the University of Nebraska before serving mainly in Lebanon, Saudi Arabia, and Iran.
His book, *Middle East Patterns: Places, Peoples, and Patterns*, coauthored with John Thomas Cummings and published in 1989, is now in its fifth reprint. Accompanied by more than one hundred photos and sixty maps, Held's book remains an important reference for the geography of the region.

Anne de Henning
(Paris, 1946)

Anne de Henning started her photography career in 1969, at the age of 23, when she crossed the USSR on the Trans-Siberian Railway on her way to Vietnam. A Vietnam War

photojournalist based in Hong Kong, she traveled around Southeast Asia and photographed in the Philippines the nomads of the sea in Sulu Archipelago. In Sarawak, she stayed with the Dayaks of Borneo.
Her photographs and articles were published frequently in the most illustrious newspapers and magazines worldwide and were often presented in exhibitions.
In 2005, while working on a story about women in the French army, which took her to Djibouti after passing through the Suez Canal and the Red Sea, Anne de Henning reached the Arabian Peninsula. She decided then to photograph the diversity of the countries in that region (Saudi Arabia, Oman, Yemen, Bahrain, Qatar, Kuwait, United Arab Emirates), aiming to show their traditions and modernity, while also capturing the relationship that the inhabitants maintain within the framework of urban life and their natural environment. Her artwork has been exhibited in galleries in Paris and Munich, as well as in the National Navy Museum in France as part of a joint exhibition on Henry de Monfreid. Her two photographic projects on Yemen were awarded the "Aga Khan Prize for Architecture".

Hergé
(Etterbeek, Belgium, 1907 – Woluwe-Saint-Lambert, Belgium, 1983)

Known by the pen name Hergé, Georges Remi was without doubt one of the most popular European cartoonists of the twentieth century—to the extent that he was often referred to as "the Father of the European Comic Strip". He was mainly famous for *The Adventures of Tintin*, which he created in 1929. Long before the advent of the television, it succeeded in introducing readers to new countries, landscapes, and cultures.
Hergé started his career as an illustrator for a boy scouts magazine. He was hired later by the conservative Catholic newspaper *Le Vingtième Siècle*, in which its youth supplement included the first comic strips of *Tintin*.
The launching in 1946 of *Tintin* magazine, where he served as artistic director, was a success. By the mid-1960s, *Tintin*'s sales reached 600,000 per week. *The Adventures of Tintin* have been translated to more than seventy languages and sold more than 250 million copies since 1929.
In 1986, following Hergé's death, the Hergé Foundation was created, and in 2009, the Hergé Museum opened in Louvain-la-Neuve. In 2016–17, an important exhibition on Hergé was organized in the Grand Palais in Paris.
Hergé's cartoons, notable for the clarity of the drawings, the well-researched plots, and the universal themes, contributed to the success of Franco-Belgian cartoons. They are the subject of numerous essays and university research papers and were adapted for radio, television, cinema, and computer games.
Hergé's characters became iconic and appeared in every conceivable marketing material.

Sheila Hicks
(Hastings, Nebraska, USA, 1934)

It seems that Sheila Hicks has traveled for most of her life. After finishing her studies at Yale University, she received a Fulbright scholarship and went to Chile, where she studied Pre-Inca textiles, the subject of her PhD thesis. She later traveled, worked, and lived extensively in Mexico, France, Morocco, India, Chile, Sweden, Japan, South Africa, and Saudi Arabia. In all of these countries, Hicks led extensive studies on indigenous weaving techniques and investigated local craft practices. In most, she also organized workshops dedicated to transformative textile. Her work, which is characterized by her distinguished dexterity and great sensibility to colours, was presented and is held in the world's most prestigious collections, including the Metropolitan Museum of Art and the Museum of Modern Art (New York City); the Museum of Fine Arts (Boston); the Art Institute of Chicago; the Victoria & Albert Museum (London); the Stedelijk Museum (Amsterdam); the Centre Pompidou (Paris); the Museum of Modern Art (Tokyo); and the Museo de Bellas Artes (Santiago).

Lopo Homem
(1497-1572)

Portuguese cartographer and cosmographer Lopo Homem joined forces, around the year 1526, with a team of cartographers, Pedro (father) and Jorge (son) Reines, considered the best cartographers of their time. Together they produced the Lopo Homem-Reines Atlas, also known as the Atlas Miller. The illustrations of Arabia and the Indian Ocean are very intricate and detailed, and although there is a clear lack of accuracy, their charts of this region are considered to be the most beautiful in the atlas.

Charles Huber
(Strasbourg, 1847 – near Jeddah, 1884)

Charles Huber studied chemistry and medicine before embarking on a trip to North Africa in 1874. He traveled afterward to Damascus to study both the classical and the dialectal Arabic language. In 1880, having earned a sponsorship from the French Ministry of Education, he crossed the Syrian desert, then the Nafud, and visited the cities of Al-Jawf and Ha'il. His diary revealed the variety of his interests: geodesic determination, hypsometric observations, and meteorological statements in addition to geological, ethnographical, archaeological, and linguistic studies. In March 1881, he reached Baghdad,

where he participated in the archaeological excavations of Babylonia. He traveled later to Damascus and from there returned to France.
Awarded the Gold Medal by the Geographical Society of Paris, Huber was assigned another time by the Commission of the Missions of the Ministry of Education to undertake a new trip to Arabia in May 1883. In July he was in Damascus, which he left to travel once again to Al-Jawf and Al-Ula. He arrived in Jeddah in May 1884 and left that city at the end of July 1884. He was assassinated by his guides a couple of days later near Rabigh. Ernest Renan, with the support of the Geographical Society and the Asian Society, published his notes in 1891 under the title *Journal d'un voyage en Arabie* (Diary of a travel in Arabia).

Mahmud Husayn Malik Al-Shu'ara'
(Tehran, 1813 – 1893/94)

A Qajar painter who belonged to the Kashan school of painting, Mahmud Husayn was known for his meticulously drawn landscapes.
An intellectual as well, he studied literature, religious law, prosody, rhyming, poetry, history, mathematics, and philosophy. He was given the post of *malik al-shu'ara'*, or poet laureate, and also held the posts of chief financial officer of the government newspaper and the national printing house. Mahmud Husayn was also a talented calligrapher and he took a series of photographs of royal palaces and gardens. A skilled painter, he mastered both the old and new style of painting. He is known for his architectural paintings, including two that are held in the Gulistan Palace Museum in Tehran.

Abu Abdallah Muhammad al-Idrîssî
(Ceuta, Morocco, 1100 – c. 1165)

A geographer and cartographer, Al-Idrîssî studied in Cordoba before traveling extensively in Europe, Africa, and Central Asia.
He settled later in Palermo, where the court of Roger II of Sicily commissioned him to produce a book on geography. After more than fifteen years of research, Al-Idrîssî's *Kitab nuzhat al-mushtaq fi ikhtiraq al-afaq* (The Pleasure Excursion of One who is eager to traverse the regions of the World), known as The Book of Roger, was completed in 1154. Written in Arabic and Latin and accompanied by maps, it presented the world as a sphere and divided the world into seven climatic zones. Considered one of the most important scientific works of that period, Al-Idrîssî's book was destroyed during the civil unrest before the end of the twelfth century. The abbreviated version of his second book, "Little Idrîssî" is all that remains of Al-Idrîssî 's cartography. It was printed in Vicence in Arabic in 1475 and in Latin a few decades later. Muhammad Al-Idrîssî was the first to claim that the earth was round and surrounded by a blanket of air.

Fathers Jaussen and Savignac
Antonin Jaussen
(Sanilhac, France, 1871 – Jonquière-Saint-Vincent, France, 1962)

Raphaël Savignac
(Cajarc, France, 1874 – Bethlehem, 1951)

Founded in 1890 in the Saint-Étienne convent, the École pratique d'études bibliques, which became in 1920 the École française archéologique et biblique de Jérusalem, was the first permanent institute dedicated to archaeological and biblical research in the Holy Land. Antonin Jaussen, then aged 19, joined the school the year it was created. He undertook theology studies there, was ordained priest, and stayed there until 1928, when he joined a new institute created in Cairo. His research activity was intense: he was an ethnologist, explorer, epigraphist, and photographer. He taught Arabic, Nabatean, and Sabaean. Raphaël Savignac arrived at the school in 1893, when he was 18, and settled in Jerusalem after his ordination. He taught biblical geography and Aramaic. At the beginning of the twentieth century, Father Jaussen was the director of the school; he was also the director of the expeditions that the school organised, in Palestine and beyond, to visit the Bedouin and Christian Arab tribes of the Moab country (1905), to Petra (1906), around the Dead Sea (1908–09), and to the desert fortresses in the east of Amman (1912). Fathers Jaussen and Savignac went on three missions to Arabia (1907, 1909, and 1910), mainly to Mada'in Saleh, Khereibeh, and Al-Ula, taking the Hijaz Railroad several times on their voyages. It is in the context of these expeditions that Father Savignac developed his remarkable photographic talent. These expeditions resulted in the publication of important publications, mainly the five volumes of *Mission archéologique en Arabie*, published from 1909 to 1919, and reissued by the French Institute for Oriental Archaeology of Cairo in 1997.

Magali Jeantelot
(Paris, 1958)

After graduating in sociology and anthropology, Magali Jeantelot specialized in African studies. She first visited Jeddah in Saudi Arabia in 2011 and lived there for three years. In 2017 she moved to Riyadh.
During her various travels, Jeantelot searched for ways to connect with the different cultures she encountered. Jeantelot painted her whole life, and on every trip during her travels, she gained a technical skill. She picked

up the daring composition of colors from Morocco, and Greece taught her how to add gold to a canvas. So naturally, upon her arrival in Saudi Arabia, the artist investigated the local visual heritage and was introduced by Thierry Mauger's book to Al-Qatt Al-Asiri, a geometrical abstract art originating from the region of Asir. The artist was instantly attracted to Al-Qatt's colorful aesthetics and was inspired to paint in the same style. The difficulties she faced with the design encouraged her to deconstruct and further develop. What drives Jeantelot's fascination is both the practice of this art form and the theory behind it, which in her opinion compliment and clarify one another. Jeantelot's work was published in Thierry Mauger's book *Rijal au fil du pinceau*.

Saadi Al-Kaabi
(Najaf, Iraq, 1934)

Saadi Al-Kaabi graduated from Baghdad's Institute of Fine Arts in 1960. Six years later, he accepted a job offer as an art teacher in Saudi Arabia, where during four years he taught in different institutions. His influence, as well as that of other Iraqi artists, would be significant on several representatives of the first generation of Saudi artists. Upon his return to Baghdad, he was appointed director of the Department of Planning at the Iraqi Ministry of Culture and Information. Later, he occupied several important posts in the administration of culture in his country while establishing himself as an important artist in the art scene.
A member of the modernist movement, Saadi Al-Kaabi was among the artists who sought to forge an authentic Iraqi artistic identity by borrowing elements from the heritage and the history of the country. Numerous exhibitions of his artwork were organized in Baghdad and in the Arab world, as well as in Rome, New York, Moscow, Stockholm, Berlin, Prague, Beijing, and Ankara.

Bob Landry
(Pennsylvania, 1913–1960)

The photojournalist Bob Landry was on a cruiser in the Pacific when the Japanese attacked Pearl Harbor. His photos were the first to show the aftermath of the event in *Life* and *Time* magazines. From then on, he covered World War II for *Life* in several theaters of battle, from the Egyptian desert to the Normandy landing.
Bob Landry's photograph of King Abdulaziz was published on the cover of the March 5, 1945 edition of *Life*, on the occasion of the King's meeting with Franklin Roosevelt. Other photographs by Landry featured the royal palace in Riyadh, camel caravans, cemeteries in Riyadh and Jeddah, Prince Faisal's tent in Arafat, and pilgrims in Jeddah.

Philippe de La Rue
(seventeenth century)

Active during the seventeenth century, little is known of cartographer Philippe de La Rue excepting the fifteen maps or so he produced.
We know, however, that he worked with another cartographer, Nicolas Sanson, with whom he produced in 1651 a series of maps of the Holy Land, *La Terre sainte en six cartes géographiques* (The Holy Land in six maps). By organizing these maps in chronological order, La Rue's intention was to trace the history of the world from its origin.

Jackie Leger
(Boston, 1947)

After graduating from the Massachusetts College of Art and Design, Jackie Leger obtained an MFA from Yale University School of Art. She works primarily with black-and-white traditional photography documenting vernacular architecture, historic ruins, heritage and landscapes. Using her background in photography, she makes uses of mixed media techniques in her artwork to include alternate photographic processes, photo collage and photo silkscreen.
Jackie Leger arrived in Saudi Arabia for the first time in 1999. She has been teaching photography, graphic arts, and Saudi heritage in Riyadh for the last fifteen years. Fascinated by Lady Anne Blunt and Gertrude Bell, two female travelers and adventurers who visited Saudi Arabia in the end of the nineteenth century and beginning of the twentieth century, Jackie Leger followed and photographed their respective paths in the Kingdom.
She published in 2012 a small book destined for tourists visiting the region: *Riyadh Point of View*. She held several exhibitions of her Saudi-inspired artwork inside the Kingdom and abroad, including one at the Brunei Gallery of London, entitled: *History Lessons, Mada'in Saleh*.

Prosper Marilhat
(Vertaizon, France, 1811 – Paris, 1847)

Prosper Marilhat, a banker's son, left his native province to study painting in Paris, in the ateliers of Pierre-Luc-Charles Cicéri and later with Camille Roqueplan. In 1831, Baron Karl von Hügel, an Austrian aristocrat, noticed his outstanding talent as a draughtsman and invited him to join a scientific expedition he was leading in the Middle East and India.
Fascinated with the architecture of Cairo and Alexandria, Marilhat decided not to pursue the trip with his companions to India and instead stayed in Egypt for two years. He had the opportunity during his stay to produce portraits of Mohammed Ali and Prisse d'Avennes, and also to create many drawings that he showcased after his return to France in 1834, and which earned him the respect of painters, such as Corot and Fromentin. He was also lauded by writers, such as Théophile Gautier and Fromentin. Later, Marilhat traveled to Italy, and afterwards, to Provence. However, Egypt continued to dominate his work. In France,

he created paintings such as *La Place de l'Esbekieh* and *Souvenir de la campagne de Rosette*, and also *Ruines de la mosquée du Khalife Hakem*, which collectively resulted in his being considered one of the pioneers of Orientalism. Marilhat had always suffered from physical ailments and as his health deteriorated, he became incapable of undertaking new trips, to his dismay. His paintings, though very scarce, continued to circulate, thanks to lithography by around forty printers. He died at the age of thirty-six without being able to return to the Orient.

Thierry Mauger
(Nice, 1947 – France, 2017)

Writer, photographer, and ethno-photographer Thierry Mauger graduated from the École des Hautes Études en Science Sociales (EHESS) of Paris. He was a member of the Royal Geographical Society, as well as an active member of the International Cooperation for the Preservation and Protection of Traditional Architectural Heritage (CICAT). His doctoral dissertation in social anthropology and ethnology focused on the vernacular architecture of Asir (EHESS, 1995). Having lived in Saudi Arabia for more than ten years, he devoted himself, on one hand, to preserving the architectural treasures of the region using the honest medium of photography—which according to Mauger, "shows rather than describes"—and on the other hand, to providing a survey on this threatened and non-accessible terrain, shedding light on the danger of losing a rich culture. He dedicated several publications to this subject: *In the Shadow of the Black Tents* (Tihama, 1986), *Bedouins of Arabia* (Souffles, 1988), *Flowered Men and Green Slopes of Arabia* (Souffles, 1988), *The Ark of the Desert* (Souffles, 1991), *Undiscovered Asir* (Stacey, 1993), and *Impressions of Arabia: Architecture and Frescoes of the Asir Region* (1996).

Lionel Marty
(1971)

First he published *Mort Linden*, a science fiction series, then *Le Rêve de Jérusalem*. Even though he does not have a particular style or genre, he admits his love for science fiction films as well as his admiration for great artists, such as Frazetta, Mignola, and Wendling.

Fra Mauro
(Venice, c. 1385 – c. 1459)

Fra Mauro delivered a unique piece of history, a world map that reflected geographical knowledge of his time. In 1450, Mauro composed the great *Mappa Mundi*—world map. The map at that time was extremely accurate and a result of extensive research. It took several years to complete. The thorough mapmaker assembled a copious amount of knowledge and produced it in text and illustrations, all included with the map. The map is today known as the "Fra Mauro map" and it featured tales by travelers and explorers gathered by Mauro from around the globe.

Samer Mohdad
(Bzebdine, Lebanon, 1964)

After finishing his studies in the art of photography in 1988 at the École supérieure des arts Saint-Luc in Liège in Belgium, Samer Mohdad worked for the photo agency Vu in Paris until 2002. In 1997, he cofounded with Fouad Elkoury the Beirut-based Arab Image Foundation, an organization that seeks to archive and preserve photography from the Middle East and North Africa. Mohdad authored five photography books: *War Children, Lebanon 1985-1992* (1993), *Return to Gaza* (1996), *Mes Arabies* (1999), *Assaoudia* (2005), and *Beirut Mutations* (2013). A retrospective of his work was shown in 2013 at the Submarine Base in Bordeaux in its "Photographers for the History" cycle and during the summer of the same year at the "Rencontres d'Arles in Black" in France. Samer Mohdad's photographs have been exhibited at the FotoFest Biennial in Houston, Texas (2014), the Blue Sky Center for Photographic Art in Portland, Oregon (2015), and the Sol Mednick Gallery in the University of Arts in Philadelphia, Pennsylvania (2016).

Herman Moll
(Bremen, c. 1654 – c. 1732)

Born in Germany, Herman Moll emigrated very early in his life to England and should therefore be considered a London cartographer. He opened his own book and map enterprise in London and was considered one of the most influential individuals in the English map trade. Moll studied the work of other cartographers, whom he used as sources for creating his own maps. He worked as an engraver for several map publishers in London, which allowed him to gain his own clientele, propelling his individual work.
In 1709, he published an engraved map of Arabia that was colored by hand. The title of the map was *Arabia Agreeable to Modern History*. It was published in *Atlas Manuale – A New Set of Maps of All Parts of the Earth*, one of the first small-format atlases created by Moll. His atlases were popular for their affordability and their revisions in follow-up editions. Despite its small size, *Arabia Agreeable to Modern History* is rich in details, including physical attributes of the area, caravan trails, and tribal alliances and settlements.

Henry de Monfreid
(Franqui, France, 1879 – Paris, 1974)

Henry de Monfreid's writings, paintings, and photographs document his thirty-five years of wanderings in the Red Sea. A tireless adventurer, he undertook all trades and dealings: coffee, leather, pearls, arms…
During World War I, he was entrusted

with an espionage mission. He later published his first novel in 1931, *Les secrets de la mer Rouge* (Secrets of the Red Sea). He also worked as a correspondent covering the wars in Yemen (1934) and Ethiopia (1936).
After the outbreak of World War II, de Monfreid refused to leave Ethiopia and consequently was accused of espionage for the enemy, arrested by the British, and deported in Kenya, where he was placed under house arrest.
Henry de Monfreid returned to France after the end of World War II, where he pursued writing and painting.
He wrote more than seventy books.

Bernhard Moritz
(Guben, Germany, 1859 – Berlin, 1939)

After finishing his studies in Protestant Theology and Oriental languages at the University of Berlin, where he received a doctorate in 1882, Bernhard Moritz received a grant from the German Archaeological Institute, enabling him to travel to Syria and Mesopotamia, between 1883 and 1885.
After his return to Germany, Moritz worked as a research assistant at the Egyptian Department of the Royal Museums in Berlin, as well as a librarian and Arabic teacher at the University of Berlin. During that period, he continued to travel frequently to the Middle East, where he took numerous photographs.
From 1896 to 1911, Moritz headed the Egyptian National Library in Cairo. During that period, he undertook several research trips to the Sinai and to Hijaz.
Upon his return to Berlin, he pursued his university career and published several books on the Middle East, among them *Bilder aus Palästina, Nord-Arabien und dem Sinai* (Pictures from Palestine, North Arabia and the Sinai), which includes numerous photographs Moritz took of Mecca, Medina, Jeddah, Meda'in Saleh, and Yanbu, as well as the construction of the Hijaz Railroad.

Mohamed Naghi
(Alexandria, 1888–1956)

Mohamed Naghi studied law in Lyon from 1906 to 1910. He was the first Egyptian to study visual arts in Florence, from 1910 to 1914. Naghi continued his studies at the School of Fine Arts in Cairo, where he was later appointed its first Egyptian director.
As a diplomat, he traveled extensively during his life and lived in Brazil and in different European countries.
In 1918, he spent several months in Giverny in the company of Claude Monet, whom he admired.
In 1932, Naghi founded the Atelier, an artist collective in Alexandria, and three years later he participated in the creation of the Cairo Atelier, which included artists and writers.
He was appointed director of the Museum of Modern Art in Cairo from 1939 to 1947 and was director of the Egyptian Academy in Rome from 1947 to 1950. In 1952, he established the Cairo atelier.
A painter, a poet, a thinker, Mohamed Naghi was a free artist in all his expressions. He was familiar with all the artistic movements. He succeeded, however, in elaborating on a perfectly personal and original style. In 1962, the Egyptian Ministry of Culture converted his studio in Cairo into a museum.

Ahmad Nawar
(Gharabiya, Egypt, 1945)

Nawar is a dry-point artist, master etcher, painter, and draftsman.
Following his graduation from the Helwan Faculty of Fine Arts in 1967, Nawar was called for service in the Egyptian army and was deployed to Suez during the October 1973 War.
His sculptures produced from objects from the battlefields and his etchings that showed dismembered figures on dark backgrounds reflect this experience, which deeply affected him.
Ahmed Nawar was granted a scholarship to study at the Real Academia de Bellas Artes de San Fernando in Madrid, where he received a degree in mural painting in 1974.
In the 1980s, Nawar founded, with three other Egyptian artists, the "Mihwar" (Axis) group. In 1982, he was commissioned to create the Faculty of Fine Arts at Minia University, where he served as dean and chair of its graphics department.
From 1988 to 2006, Nawar held the position of director of the Fine Arts Sector in the Ministry of Culture, and also headed the Museums Sector of the Supreme Council of Antiquities in Egypt from 1994 to 1999.
In the series *Hijaz, Inspiration from the Holy Land*, Nawar depicts scenes that fluctuate between the past and the present. The composition of his drawings is theatrical. The artist produces with brio a multitude of layers of shadow and light reminiscent of the chiaroscuro technique.

Carsten Niebuhr
(Lüdingworth, Germany, 1733 – Meldorf, Germany, 1815)

After completing his studies in mathematics and cartography, Carsten Niebuhr, then 28, was asked to participate in an expedition to Arabia organized by the Danish government.
Commissioned by King Frederick V of Denmark, the mission included, in addition to Niebuhr, Pehr Forsskål, a botanist and former student of Linné; Christian Karl Cramer, a physician and zoologist; Friedrich Christian von Haven, a philologist and linguist; and Georg Wilhelm Baurenfeind, an artist and engraver.
The mission came to be remembered as the "Danish Arabia expedition"; Niebuhr was its only survivor.
During the expedition, Niebuhr produced important maps that were used for more than one hundred years, in addition to charts and plans for towns. Upon his return, he published the narrative of his travels,

Travels through Arabia, and other countries in the East, as well as Forsskål's work, the naturalist of the expedition, under the title *Flora Aegyptiaco-Arabica*.

Alex Nikolavitch
(1971)

Alex Nikolavitch has dedicated his entire career to comic books.
A translator of American comics since the late 1990s, he has written the French versions of more than 350 comic books, including stories by Alan Moore, Grant Morrison, and Warren Ellis. As a comic book story writer, he has a clear preference for historical subjects. We owe thanks to him for *La Dernière Cigarette* (Vertige Graphic), *Spawn Simony*, and more recently, *Tengu-Do* and *Crusades* (Les Humanoïdes Associés). He also wrote the essay *Mythe & Super-Héros* ((Les Moutons électriques). For Glénat, he collaborated with Christian Clot on the scenario of the two *Burton* comics in the Explora collection.

Kazuyoshi Nomachi
(Kochi prefecture, Japan, 1946)

Nomachi began studying and practicing photography when he was a teenager,. He began his career as a freelance advertising photographer. When he made his first trip to the Sahara, at twenty-five, he discovered the strength of its people, who lived in difficult conditions, and decided to devote his career to photojournalism. Since then and for the last forty years, Nomachi has been photographing various populations living in harsh areas, highlighting their strength. He has photographed the Nile, the Ganges, Uganda, Ethiopia, China, Peru, and Bolivia.
From 1995 to 2000, Nomachi traveled to Saudi Arabia, photographing its annual pilgrimage. He was the first Japanese to extensively document the pilgrimage. His photographs of Mecca and Medina were published in a book titled *Mecca the Blessed, Medina the Radiant*. Nomachi's photographs have been published worldwide and he has won numerous awards, including the Annual Award of the Photographic Society of Japan in 1990 and 1997, and the Medal of Honor with Purple Ribbon in 2009.

Ronan Olier
(Douarnenez, France, 1949)

He studied at the École des Beaux-arts in Quimper and then at the École nationale supérieure des arts décoratifs in Paris. In 2001 he was appointed "Official Painter of the Fleet". This allowed him to sail to distant seas on board French navy vessels.
In 2008, en route to Djibouti, he stayed for four days in Jeddah and produced several paintings of the Red Sea. In 2010, he was invited to Jeddah for a residency. There he organized painting workshops as well as an exhibition of his paintings inspired by his stay in Arabia.
During this residency, he traveled 3000 kilometers around the western region of Arabia and visited and painted the cities of Ta'if, Al-Baha, Dhee Ayn, Al-Ula, Meda'in Saleh, and Yanbu.
The works of this painter and traveler have been featured in many exhibitions in France and abroad, and he has illustrated several books, including *À la poursuite du rayon vert*, which received the Cercle de la Mer prize. Ronan Olier lives and works in Brittany.

Georg Emanuel Opiz
(Prague, 1775 – Leipzig, 1841)

Opiz studied law for a short period before finding his calling at the Academy of Arts in Dresden. He later moved to Vienna, where it seems that he was a pupil of Francesco Giuseppe Casanova, a painter of battle pieces. In the beginning of his practice, Opiz concentrated on portraiture, later becoming a skilled miniaturist, watercolorist, and engraver. Beginning in 1807, he specialized in everyday life and satirical genre scenes. He traveled to Paris after the fall of Napoleon, where he produced one of his major artworks, *Scènes de caractère de la vie Parisienne*, and composed twenty-four aquatint prints. He later traveled extensively in Europe, Russia, England, and Turkey. In the 1980s, he settled in Leipzig where he became a professor in its Academy of Arts. His paintings are held in numerous museums, including the Carnavalet Museum in Paris, the Wien Museum in Vienna, and the Royal Collection Trust in England. Opiz wrote novels published under the pseudonym "Bohemus".

Édith Ortoli
(Mayenne, France, 1949)

Édith Ortoli graduated from the École des beaux-arts in Paris. Her artistic production includes works in acrylic, mixed media, collages, and drawings, and she has won several prizes at exhibitions in France.
Édith Ortoli lived in Riyadh from 2005 to 2008 and brought back to France a wealth of visual impressions and a rich palette of pastels and ochres. Her artistic vision of Arabia is represented in paintings, drawings, photographs, and, above all, in her artist's book *Esprit de désert* (Spirit of the Desert), in which architectural motifs, calligraphy, and Neolithic graffiti remind us of the continued human presence in these deserts for thousands of years.

Alberto Pasini
(Busseto, Italy, 1826 – Cavoretto, Italy, 1899)

One of the most famous Italian Orientalists, Alberto Pasini enrolled in the Academy of Fine Arts of Parma, where he studied landscape painting and drawing. He next traveled to Paris,

where he joined the School of Barbizon. In 1853, he was admitted to the Salon de Paris and to the workshop of Théodore Chassériau. In 1855, the French diplomat Prosper Bourée invited him on an official mission to Nasser-al-Din's court in Persia. He spent eighteen months in Persia, where he made many trips in the company of the Shah, who commissioned him a number of paintings. In subsequent trips, Pasini visited Egypt, the Red Sea, and Arabia. In 1865, he spent some time in Cannes, where he painted landscapes of the Riviera. He visited Istanbul in 1868–69 and traveled to Syria and Lebanon in 1873.
Pasini was enthralled by the light of the East, which he reproduced in landscapes bathed in shadow and sun. His quasi-hyperrealistic style sets him apart from the exotic paintings of the early Orientalists.

Jan Peeters
(Antwerp, 1624–1678)

Born in Antwerp in 1624, Jan Peeters studied painting with his two elder brothers, Gilles and Bonaventura. In 1645, he became, like them, a member of Antwerp's Guild of St. Luke. He specialized in seascape paintings and especially in paintings depicting, under dark skies, ships during storms. Peeters traveled a great deal throughout Europe, especially in France, to paint its cities and ports. His drawings were later copied and commercialized as prints. It seems that his travels led him as far as Libya, Egypt, and Palestine, which he also depicted in his drawings.

Harry St John Bridger Philby
(Ceylon, 1885 – Beirut, 1960)

British Arabist, explorer, and colonial office intelligence officer Harry St John Philby studied oriental languages at the University of Cambridge. In 1917 and 1918, he headed the British political mission to Central Arabia. He sojourned in Riyadh on three occasions and was the first European in 1917 to visit the southern provinces of Nejd. He converted to Islam in 1930, adopted an Arab identity as Shaykh Abdullah, and became adviser to King Abdulaziz, helping him to negotiate with the United Kingdom and the United States after petroleum was discovered in 1938. He later settled in Jeddah.
In 1932, Philby was the second European, a year after Bertram Thomas, to cross the Rub' al- Khali. He mapped on camelback what is now the Saudi-Yemeni border on the Rub' al-Khali; his road tracing is still valid today. Philby is the author of several books on Saudi Arabia including *The Heart of Arabia* (1922), *Arabia of the Wahhabis* (1928), *The Empty Quarter* (1933), *A Pilgrim in Arabia* (1943), *Arabian Highlands* (1952), and *Saudi Arabia* (1955).

Otto Pilny
(Budweis, Bohemia, 1866 – Zürich, 1936)

Otto Pilny studied art in Prague. His first trip to Egypt was in 1875, where he spent two years. On the occasion of that trip he followed the caravan road between Cairo and Tripoli, with his dog as his sole companion. It was during his second trip, from 1889 to 1892, that the khedive Abbas Hilmi II discovered and admired his work and decorated him with the Order of the Medjidie. Pilny was a prolific artist who produced many paintings featuring the desert, its landscapes, and people. He often traveled to the desert with the Bedouins and depicted their entertainment as well as their prayers.

Émile Prisse d'Avennes
(Avesnes-sur-Helpe, France, 1807–1879)

Artist, writer, scholar, engineer and linguist, Émile Prisse d'Avennes studied at the École des arts et métiers in Chalons, France, where he acquired skills in drafting and engineering. From an early age he dreamt of exploring the Orient, and at the age of nineteen he traveled to Greece to participate in the war for independence from the Ottoman Empire. Afterward, he traveled to India, Palestine, and then Egypt, where he settled and worked at first on civil and hydrological projects.
He developed a great interest in Egyptology, embraced Islam, took the name Edris-Effendi, and decided to abandon his career as a lecturer in fortifications at the School of Infantry at Damietta to dedicate himself to archeological research.
He settled in Luxor and from there, during a seven-year period, he embarked on numerous journeys, including travels to Nubia, Abyssinia, Syria, Palestine, Persia, Turkey, and Arabia. Émile Prisse d'Avennes spoke Arabic, Turkish, Greek, Coptic, Amharic, Latin, English, Italian, and Spanish, and had a marked ability to decipher hieroglyphics. He sketched many inscriptions and bas-reliefs on temples, palaces, and tombs in Karnak.
He published *Les Monuments égyptiens* in 1847 and *Oriental album* in 1848. Both publications included chromolithographs and woodcuts of his Egyptian drawings. From 1869 to 1877, he published *L'Art arabe*, which contained two hundred plates. Finally, in 1877, Émile Prisse d'Avennes published *L'Histoire de l'art égyptien*, containing one-hundred sixty plates.

Aref El Rayess
(Aley, Lebanon, 1928 – Beirut, 2005)

Self-taught painter and sculptor Aref El Rayess started painting at the age of eleven using his mother's paints and brushes. His first exhibition took place in 1948 in the West Hall of the American University of Beirut. That same year, the artist moved to Paris, where he studied painting in the

studios of Fernard Léger and André Lhote, etching with Friedlander and sculpting with Ossip Zadkine while studying at the famous Académie de la Grande Chaumière.
In the 1980s, Aref Rayess traveled regularly to Saudi Arabia, where he lived during the years of the civil war in Lebanon. He was appointed art consultant for the city of Jeddah and was commissioned to produce a number of public sculptures for the country, the most ambitious of which is a twenty-seven-meter-tall aluminum sculpture representing the name of "Allah". It stands in an important square in Jeddah.
A prolific artist, during his stay in Saudi Arabia, Aref Al Rayess produced, using bold colors in his almost abstract style, many paintings representing the country's landscapes.
El Rayess exhibited internationally and received numerous awards for his work. The Aref El Rayess Foundation was created in 2015.

Marc Riboud
(Saint-Genis-Laval, France, 1923 – Paris, 2016)

Marc Riboud was given his first camera, a Kodak Vest Pocket, for his fourteenth birthday in 1937, and took his first photos at that year's World's Fair in Paris. After the war, he studied engineering at the École Centrale de Lyon. He embarked on a career in engineering but abandoned it after three years to devote himself to photography.
His first published photo appeared in *Life* magazine in 1953. The same year, he became a member of the Magnum Photo agency on the invitation of Henri Cartier-Bresson and Robert Capa. From then on, his numerous assignments cemented his reputation for arresting war photography.
In the 1960s, he covered the struggle of the Algerian people for independence. In 1967, during a protest against the Vietnam War outside the Pentagon, he captured his most iconic photo, *Flower Child*, depicting a protester holding a flower in front of the bayonets of National Guardsmen.
Two large-scale retrospectives of his work were organized in Paris, at the musée de la Vie Romantique in 2014, and at the musée Guimet in 2010.

Claire Rivier
(Lyon, 1948)

Claire Rivier works today in France after residing in many countries in the Arab world, in particular in Algeria, Lebanon, Yemen, United Arab Emirates, and Saudi Arabia. She participated in several exhibitions, especially during her stays in Riyadh from 1993 to 1999 and 2005 to 2009. She set up and led a wood-painting workshop in Riyadh.

Waclaw Seweryn Rzewuski
(Lwów, Poland, 1784 – 1831)

Count Waclaw Rzewuski, Polish nobleman, officer in the Australian army, and writer, developed a twin passion for horses and Orientalism. As a child, he rode horses on the family stud ranch. He was initiated to Oriental languages by his uncle, Jan Potocki, a great traveler, learned Orientalist and famous writer who influenced him greatly and who later authored a world-renowned book, *The Manuscript found in Saragossa*.
In 1817, Rzewuski succeeded in convincing the Tsar Alexander I and Queen Catherine of Württemberg to finance an expedition to Arabia. He traveled to Aleppo and from there to Damascus before finally reaching the Arabian desert. After many adventures, Rzewuski purchased one hundred thirty-seven horses, mares, and stallions for his stables as well as for his patrons.
He returned to Poland where he lived in his family's estate, dressed in Bedouin robes among his Arabian horses and his rich collection of Oriental manuscripts and weapons. He then wrote an 800-page, exquisitely illustrated account of his travels. Titled *On Oriental Horses and Those Descended from Eastern Breeds*, it was published in its original form only in 2002.
Count Rzewuski was killed in in 1831 in the battle of Daszow during the Polish Uprising.

Muhammad Sadic Bey
(Cairo, 1822–1902)

Muhammad Sadic Bey was one of the first Egyptians educated in France, where he studied at the École Polytechnique in Paris and learned photography and drawing. When he returned to Cairo, Sadic worked as an engineer in the army. He was commissioned to take journeys to Mecca and Medina, where he took photos that were displayed in the Egyptian pavilion at the Universal Exhibition of 1876 in Philadelphia. He also showed his images of the two holy cities of Mecca and Medina at the Third International Geographical Congress in Venice in 1881, where he was rewarded with a gold medal for the exhibition. Muhammad Sadic was later elected president of the Khedival Geographic Society in Cairo. He was conferred the title of "bey" and published several books on the pilgrimage.

Piers Secunda
(London, 1976)

A British visual artist residing in London, Piers Secunda studied painting at the Chelsea College of Arts in London. Among his main lines of artistic inquiry is the way materials and textures can express the lines, divides, and dynamics that arise from politics, geopolitics, and the urgency of climate change. He started by using paint as a sculptural material and then developed other innovative mediums for his work, stemming from a will to use materials not usually thought of as artistic mediums. One such process is working from casts he took of bullet holes and bombing damage in Kabul, Afghanistan; in gang-controlled neighborhoods of Kingston, Jamaica; and in Iraqi Kurdistan after fights between ISIS and the Peshmerga. Piers Secunda also worked with crude oil to create arresting works of art, such as his *Dammam No 7* series, which spark reflections and debates on the intersecting narratives of geopolitics and environmental politics.

Ursula Schulz-Dornburg
(Berlin, 1938)

Born in 1938, Ursula Schulz-Dornburg lives and works in Düsseldorf. After studying journalism in the early 1960s, she started a career in journalism focusing immediately on dwellings as fundamentally human elements. She traveled from the secret city of Kurchatovia, Kazakhstan, to Kroonstad, Russia; from the border that separates Georgia and Azerbaijan to Iraq and Syria; and from Armenia to the Hijaz railway in Saudi Arabia, to photograph the strong ties between industrial and architectural structures, the landscape, and the people who inhabit them. Schulz-Dornburg's artwork is a critical exploration of the construction of power and its impermanent character. Since 1975, her work has been featured in more than forty exhibitions—including recently in the Tate Modern in London and in the Giorgio Mastinu Gallery in Venice.

William Henry Irvine Shakespear
(Mumbai, 1880 – Al Majma'ah, Saudi Arabia, 1915)

William Henry Irvine Shakespear joined the British Foreign Office in 1904, becoming the youngest vice-consul in British India. A remarkable linguist, he spoke fluent Urdu, Pashto, Persian, and Arabic. While in his post in Kuwait from 1909 to 1915, Shakespear undertook seven expeditions into the Arabian Peninsula. On his return to Kuwait from his second expedition in 1910, he met Ibn Saud, then the Emir of the Nejd. They were both then in their mid-thirties and quickly became close friends.
In each of these expeditions, Shakespear took with him the necessary photographic equipment. It was Shakespear who in 1911, at Thaj, took the first-ever photographs of Ibn Saud, who had never seen a camera before.
The account of that meeting, which Shakespear recorded in his diary, is believed to be the earliest description of King Abdulaziz with European eyes. "Ibn Saud was a fair, handsome man, considerably above-average Arab height and of very courteous manner," he wrote.
In March 1914, Shakespear began a 2,900-kilometer journey from Kuwait to Riyadh and on to Aqabah via the Nafud Desert, which he mapped. The data he collected was destined for the geographical department of Britain's War Office.
In 1914, Sir Percy Cox, the British political agent in Kuwait, sent William Henry Shakespear to protect Ibn Saud, whose army was attacked by Ibn Rashid. During the Battle of Jarrab in January 1915, Ibn Saud asked Shakespear to retreat to a safe location before the fighting began. He declined to do so and was struck by a bullet and killed. Shakespear was buried in Kuwait.
Captain Shakespear owned two cameras: a small Ensignette, a foldable camera introduced in 1909 by the British company Houghton, and a Kodak panoramic camera, a wooden device with a spring-mounted lens. Shakespear carried with him tanks of chemicals, developing his negatives in a blacked-out corner of his tent.

Ali ibn Ahmad ibn Mohammed al-Sharafi al-Safaqusi
(sixteenth century)

Al-Safaqusi belonged to a family of cartographers living in the city of Sfax, Tunisia. He wrote in 1571 *The Mediterranean Sea atlas,* held in the Bodleian Library and published in Manchester in 2003 by W. C. Brice.

Humberto da Silveira
(Poxoréo, Brazil, 1954)

Humberto da Silveira studied photography with Roberto Maia in Rio de Janeiro and later at Parson's School of Art and Design in New York. He worked as a professional photographer in Brazil, the USA, and France.
In 1985, an invitation to attend the opening of the Islamic Art Gallery of the King Faisal Foundation in Riyadh allowed him to discover the Kingdom. Since then, da Silveira has been spending much of his time in Saudi Arabia where, for the last thirty-five years, he has been documenting the country's people and heritage.
In 1992, Humberto da Silveira published *Najd,* a photographic study on the central region of Saudi Arabia. In 1994, he published *Bedu*, in which he documented the nomadic way of life in Saudi Arabia. In 2013, he published *Hegra*, a comprehensive photographic album on the Nabatean civilization in Arabia including the Dedanite and Lihyanite cultures.
In 2017, he published *Madinah* in which he documented the holy city's architectural heritage. In addition to his books devoted to Arabia, Humberto da Silveira published in 2013 a photographic study on Al Aqsa Mosque in Jerusalem.

Walid Siti
(Duhok, Iraqi-Kurdistan, 1954)

Walid Siti graduated in 1976 from the Institute of Fine Arts in Baghdad

and pursued his studies in Ljubljana, Slovenia. Fleeing the turmoil in his home country, he settled in the United Kingdom and was granted political asylum in 1984, where he still resides. Siti trained in printmaking, but works extensively in a variety of mediums including installation, 3-D works, work on paper, and painting.
He is strongly influenced by his experience of war, exile, memory, and loss. His works often question the notions of collective identity and interdependence and the way they are shaped by culture, tradition, borders, and nations. Siti's work is held in prestigious collections such as The British Museum, The Imperial War Museum, and the Victoria & Albert Museum in London; The Metropolitan Museum, in New York; and the World Bank in Washington, DC.

Christiaan Snouck Hurgronje
(Oosterhout, Holland, 1857 – Leiden, Holland, 1936)

The Dutch Christiaan Snouck Hurgronje was sometimes considered, alongside the Hungarian Ignac Golziher and the German Theodor Nöldeke, as one of the founders of modern Orientalism. After completing his doctoral thesis at Leiden University in 1880, on the history of the Hajj and its customs, he was granted a scholarship which allowed him to travel to Arabia, starting with Jeddah, where he converted to Islam, and afterwards to Mecca, where during six months he pursued his Koranic studies and observed the habits and customs of all the classes of the society.
On his return, Snouck published his two-volume work *Mekka*, accompanied by a volume of plates, *Bilder Atlas zu Mekka*. It contained 75 loose photographs of the inhabitants of Mecca and Jeddah—Mecca's important families and pilgrims from Java, Sumatra, and other islands in the Dutch East Indies. A second portfolio, *Bilder aus Mekka*, was published in 1889. Snouck's book provided a valuable description of Mecca's society, its daily life, and its customs, guilds, and festivals.
The publishing of the book in 1888 granted him impressive renown. He was offered a professorial chair by Leiden University as well as by Cambridge. He declined both positions as he preferred pursuing his research, this time in Indonesia, where he sojourned for a long period. Henceforth, he advised the Dutch government on issues pertaining to Islam. It was in the framework of this advisory function that his role was largely controversial. In this same manner, and upon his return, he advised several European governments on questions relating to Muslim colonies. In 1906, he joined Leiden University, where he provided instruction in the field of Arabic, Indonesian, and Islamic studies, and regularly published, until his death in 1936, scholarly books in various fields.

John Speed
(Cheshire, England, c. 1551 – London, 1629)

A cartographer and a historian, John Speed started his career working in his father's tailor's business. He received an allowance from patrons, enabling him to dedicate time to research. At about the end of the 1580s, he worked on publishing *A Concent of Scripture*, a study on the chronology of the Bible, which included several maps. Queen Elizabeth granted him the use of a room in the Custom House where he could undertake his research. In 1595, John Speed published a map of biblical Canaan. His atlas, *Theatre of the Empire of Great Britaine*, was published in 1611–12. In 1627, Speed published *Prospect of the Most Famous Parts of the World*, the first world atlas produced by an Englishman. Known for his very colorful and decorative maps, often including inserts with costumed figures and panoramas of their cities, Speed's maps were very much sought after.

George Steinmetz
(Beverly Hills, California, 1957)

George Steinmetz graduated from Stanford University with a degree in geophysics. He then started his career as a professional photographer by hitchhiking through Africa for eighteen months, then received his first assignment for *National Geographic* in 1987. For this publication, he has examined subjects ranging from global oil exploration to the innermost stretches of the Sahara and Irian Jaya, Indonesia.
George Steinmetz has also worked for the French and German editions of *GEO*, producing reports on the Great Salt Desert of Iran and the Empty Quarter of Saudi Arabia. His first book, *African Air*, presents ten years of his aerial photography in Africa, much of it done with a motorized paraglider. His second book, *The Empty Quarter*, documents three expeditions into the heart of Saudi Arabia, where he traversed the world's largest sand sea.

Abdullah Syed
(Karachi, 1974)

Artist and designer Abdullah Syed grew up and lived several years in Saudi Arabia, where his father worked for Saudi Arabian Airlines. He studied painting in Pakistan and afterwards he completed a PhD in Art, Design, and Media from the University of New South Wales in Sydney.
He currently splits his time among Karachi, New York, and Sydney. Abdullah Syed uses various techniques and mediums in his artworks, including print screening,

sculpture, video installations, drawing, and performance. In his series *Mapping Investment*, he examines the relationships among art, economy, and politics using drawing, hand-cut bank notes, and collages.

Rayyane Tabet
(Achkout, Lebanon, 1983)

Rayyane Tabet received a bachelor's in architecture from The Cooper Union in New York and a master's in fine arts from the University of California in San Diego. His art practice focuses mainly on the use of objects which he treats as sculptures and archaeological artifacts that explore memory and history. His artwork *The Shortest Distance between Two Points* is a conceptual and aesthetic investigation of the history of the Trans-Arabian Pipe Line (TAP Line), initiated in 1946 by the companies Caltex, Esso, and Mobil to transport Saudi oil to the port of Haifa and afterwards to Sidon in Lebanon. *The Shortest Distance between Two Points* explores the interrelation between geopolitics, history and oil circulation in the Middle East.
Important exhibitions presenting Rayyane Tabet's artworks were organized in Sharjah (2011), Amsterdam (2014), Florence (2016), Rotterdam (2017), Hamburg (2017), and Berlin (2017).

Newsha Tavakolian
(Tehran, 1981)

A self-taught photographer, Newsha Tavakolian began taking photos at the age of sixteen, and covered the 1999 student uprising in Teheran.
In 2002, she started working internationally, covering the war in Iraq and natural disasters, and filming social documentary films in Iraq, Lebanon, Syria, Saudi Arabia, Pakistan, and Yemen.
In 2008, Newsha Tavakolian received a press visa for the Hajj and was one of the few photographers permitted to photograph during that year's Hajj. Her photographs were published in *The Fifth Pillar, Hajj Pilgrimage* (Gilgamesh Publishing House, 2012). In 2009, she was one of the four photographers who created the female collective "Rawiya" whose main aim was to produce endogenous visions that contribute to breaking down Western stereotypes and clichés about the Orient.
Her work ranges from reportage of political events and socially engaging topics to portraits and art photography. Her photographs and projects have been published in newspapers and magazines worldwide, and she has exhibited in international institutions such as the Victoria & Albert Museum, the Los Angeles County Museum of Art (LACMA), the British Museum, and the Boston Museum of Fine Art. Newsha Tavakolian became a Magnum Associate in 2017.

Wilfred Thesiger
(Addis Ababa, Ethiopia, 1910 – London, 2003)

His birth in Abyssinia, Ethiopia, where his father was serving as the head of the British legation, gave Wilfred Thesiger a taste for the elsewhere. As soon as he finished his education at Eton and Oxford, he accepted a job as a colonial administrator in Darfur (west of the Anglo-Egyptian Sudan), and throughout the rest of his life, he sought the most remote missions. Hence, he readily accepted a proposal from the Food and Agriculture Organization (FAO) of the United Nations to travel to the Empty Quarter of Arabia to collect information on locust movements. Thesiger crossed several times the terrible desert of the Rub' al-Khali, where he spent five years with the Bedouins. He traveled later to Kurdistan, to the marshes of Iraq, to the Hindu Kush, to the Karakorams, to Morocco, to Abyssinia, to Kenya and Tanganyika. He continued traveling until the age of 70. His numerous books, illustrated with his own outstanding photographs, are a testament to his great talent and his travels.

Samuel Thornton
(1670–1715)

After the death of his father—chart-maker, engraver, publisher, and English sea captain John Thornton—in 1708, Samuel Thornton continued his father's work by reprinting it and producing new charts. His *Sea Atlas* contained 172 hand-colored charts, making it one of the most comprehensive collections of printed charts of the era.

Abu Subhi Al-Tinawi
(Damascus, 1888–1973)

Abu Subhi Al-Tinawi came from a family of glass painting and tapestry. He had a small housewares shop in Damascus, where he produced tapestries and paintings depicting folk tales, legends, and heroes. Hung in coffee shops, the stories of these tapestries were narrated by professional storytellers. Al-Tinawi also painted in reverse on the back of glass panels, a technique known as reverse painting, which first developed in Europe before spreading to Turkey and then to the Middle East. After the Azem Palace Museum in Damascus commissioned Al-Tinawi to paint some glass paintings for its museum, he gained fame in Syria and abroad. Subsequently, and to satisfy the large number of commissions he received from dealers in Beirut and galleries abroad, he produced numerous glass paintings. He even held an exhibition of his reverse paintings in Paris.
Al-Tinawi was known for the vivid and bright colors of his paintings. He prepared his own colors using colored earths, plant dyes, ground malachite, and lapis lazuli mixed in

egg white or Arabic gum. After his death, his sons and daughters continued to paint on glass using their father's name. In Damascus and in the Middle East, the "school" of Al-Tinawi is renowned; his reverse paintings are very much sought after, and several researchers and filmmakers have documented his artwork.

Peter Upton
(England, 1937)

Peter Upton, a leading expert on Arabian horses, authored several books on the subject, among which were *The Arab Horse*, republished numerous times; *Royal Heritage, The Story of Jordan's Arab Horses* (with Princess Alia Al Hussein); and *Out of the Desert*. Upton visited Saudi Arabia and Jordan several times with the aim of perfecting his knowledge of Arabian horses. In addition to the books he authored, he has specialized in representing Arabian horses in paintings. His paintings of horses are sought after by horse lovers and were showcased several times in the Mathaf Gallery in London.

Safi ibn Vali
(Gujarat, India, seventeenth century)

Probably a native of the region of Gujarat, Safi ibn Vali was a scholar who authored a commentary on the Koran which he dedicated to Zebunnisa, daughter of the Mughal emperor, who sponsored his pilgrimage trip of 1676–77. During the pilgrimage he wrote, in Persian, a Hajj guidebook titled *Anis al-Hujjaj* (Pilgrims' Companion) in which he proffered to future pilgrims plentiful advice pertaining to different aspects of the pilgrimage.

Gaston Vuillier
(Perpignan, France, 1845 – Gimel, France, 1915)

Gaston Vuillier studied drawing at the École des Beaux-Arts in Marseille. From 1878 onward, he worked as an illustrator for the two most illustrious Parisian illustrated magazines at that time: the *Magasin pittoresque* and *Le Tour du Monde*, published by Hachette.
Gaston Vuillier loved traveling, especially to Mediterranean countries. He published books on Sicily, Tunisia, Corsica, Sardinia, and Tripoli. He also produced woodcut prints, drawings, sketches, and watercolors from works by other artists. In *A Pilgrimage to Nejd* (1882), Vuillier produced sixty prints from Anne Blunt's watercolors. Towards the end of his life, Vuillier gave up traveling, devoting himself to illustrating books, including Prosper Mérimée's novellas, *Carmen* (1911) and *Colomba* (1913), as well as Chateaubriand's *The Last of the Abencerrajes* (1912).

Al-Marrakshi ibn al-Wardi
(c. 1400–1457)

A historian, Ibn al-Wardi authored a geographical treatise, *Kitab Kharida al-'adjaïb wa farida al-ghara'ib* (The Pearl of wonders and the Uniqueness of strange things), that included sections on natural history. Ibn al-Wardi compiled, in this book, not only the known geographical facts of the Arab world of his time, but also information on climates; topography; fauna and flora; and people and their way of living.
His book included a world map and a map of Mecca which, it was written, was copied from Yaqut al-Rumi's *Mu'jam al-Buldan* (Dictionary of Countries). In the latter map, as in that of Ibn al-Wardi, the earth is represented as being supported by the horns of a bull.

Al-Hasan ibn Mohammad al-Wazzan, known as Leo the African
(Grenada, 1494 – Tunis, 1554)

An Andalusian explorer and diplomat, Leo the African's family sought refuge in the city of Fes after Andalusia was conquered by Isabella of Castile and Ferdinand of Aragon. He studied theology in several *madrasas* and trained to be a diplomat. His travels, which he undertook at a young age, led him to explore the entirety of Morocco, as well as all regions of the Maghreb, the Arabian Peninsula, Saharan Africa, Egypt, and Constantinople. In 1518, as he returned from the pilgrimage, he was captured by Sicilian sailors who delivered him to a knight from the Order of Saint-John, who in turn delivered him to Pope Leo X.
The Pope forced him to convert and gave him a new Christian surname, his own name, John-Leo. He then became John-Leo Medici, known as "Leo the African".
In Bologna, where he was then residing, he wrote, at the behest of the Pope, his famous *Description of Africa*. This book was the only source on the culture and customs of Africa at the time. Its maps and illustrations made it the only reference book for explorers set to travel to Africa and the Arabian Peninsula.

Joseph Elmer Yoakum
(Missouri, 1889 – Chicago, 1972)

The young Joseph Elmer Yoakum, of African-American and Cherokee descent, left his family at the age of nine and worked as a stable boy for several circuses, all over the United States. His early life was quite nomadic, and he eventually traveled to Europe with the circuses. He returned to Missouri and married in 1908, but was later drafted and sent to France for the last year of World War I. The record of his life afterwards is quite incomplete but marked by his remarriage in Chicago in the 1940s. He started drawing, in Chicago, first to preserve the memory of the places and landscapes he visited in his life, but later he started illustrating locations he would dream, hear, or read about. Having little, if any formal training, he quickly found his one-of-a-kind style, marked by very dreamy and colorful drawings that nonetheless resembled anatomical or biological cross-section drawings. It was only in 1967, at the age of 77, that his work started being acknowledged by the public, and only in 1972 that he was given his first solo exhibition at the Whitney Museum of American Art in New York City, just one month before his death.

Kazimierz Żwan
(Mikitycze, Poland, 1792 – Warsaw, 1858)

A Polish colonel and painter, Kazimierz Żwan was, by his mother, the grandson of Polish King Stanislaw August Poniatowski. He joined the army in 1809, but left it in 1831 after the defeat of the Polish uprising against invading Russian forces. He had already shown an interest in paintings during his military service and trained himself by copying Dutch painters. When he left the army, he chose to focus solely on his art, mainly painting landscapes and military scenes, but also portraits of diplomats and members of Polish high society.

Bibliography

Edward Abbey, *Désert solitaire* (Paris, 2010)

Abdoul-Kérym, *Voyage de l'Inde à la Mekke*, translated by L. Langlès (Paris, 1797)

Ismael Abulféda, *Description Générale de l'Arabie*, edited by M. de La Roque (Amsterdam, 1718)

Abu-l-Fida, *Géographie*, translated by M. Reinaud (Paris, 1848)

Ali Bey, *Travels of Ali Bey in Morocco, Tripoli, Cyprus, Egypt, Arabia, Syria and Turkey, between the Years 1803 and 1807* (London, 1816)

Ali Bey, *Voyages d'Ali Bey El Abbassi en Afrique et en Asie, pendant les années 1803, 1804, 1805, 1806 et 1807*, 2 vol. (Paris, 1814)

Khaled Al Ankary, *La Péninsule Arabique dans les cartes européennes anciennes. The Arabian Peninsula in Old European Maps* (Paris, 2001)

George Annesley Mountnorris, *Voyages and Travels to India, Ceylon, the Red Sea, Abyssinia and Egypt in the Years 1802, 1803, 1804, 1805 and 1806* (London, 1809)

Laurent d'Arvieux, *Voyages dans la Palestine. Vers Le Grand Émir, Chef Des Princes Arabes Du Désert, Connus Sous Le Nom De Bédouins* (Amsterdam, 1718)

Laurent d'Arvieux, *The Travels of the Chevalier d'Arvieux in Arabia the Desert* (London, 1732)

Adolphe d'Avril, *L'Arabie contemporaine, avec la description du pèlerinage de La Mecque* (Paris, 1868)

Taylor Bayard, *Travels in Arabia* (New York, 1892)

Jacques Benoist-Méchin, *Ibn Séoud, la naissance d'un royaume* (Paris, 1955)

Lady Anne Blunt, *A Pilgrimage to Nejd*, 2 vol. (London, 1881)

Anne Blunt, *Voyage en Arabie. Pèlerinage au Nedjed, Berceau de la Race-Arabe*, translated and presented by Léoplod Derôme (Paris, 1882)

Wilfrid Blunt, *The Bedouin Tribes of the Euphrates* (1879)

Johann Ludwig Burckhardt, *Notes on the Bedouins and Wahabys* (London, 1830)

Johann Ludwig Burckhardt, *Travels in Arabia* (London, 1829)

Johann Ludwig Burckhardt, *Travels in Syria and the Holy Land* (London, 1822)

Johann Ludwig Burckhardt, *Voyages en Arabie. Suivis de Notes sur les Bédouins et d'un Essai sur l'histoire des Wahhabites*, translated by J. B. B. Eyriès (Paris, 1835)

Sir Richard Francis Burton, *Personal Narrative of a Pilgrimage to Al-Madinah and Meccah* (London, 1893)

Richard Burton, *Voyage à la Mecque*, translated by H. Loreau (Paris 1881)

Le Café en Méditerranée (Aix-en-Provence, 1980)

Evliya Çelebi, *An Ottoman Traveller* (London, 2011)

Mounia Chekhab-Abudaya and Cécile Bresc, *Hajj – The Journey through Art* (Milano, 2013)

Sylvia Chiffoleau, *Le Voyage à La Mecque. Un pèlerinage mondial en terre d'Islam* (Paris, 2015)

Lady Evelyn Cobbold, *Pilgrimage to Mecca* (1934)

Louis Alexandre Olivier de Cortancez, *L'Histoire des Wahabis depuis leur origine jusqu'à la fin de 1809* (Paris, 1810)

Charles Didier, *Séjour chez le Grand-Chérif de La Mecque* (Paris, 1857)

Charles Didier, *Sojourn with the Grand Sharif of Makkah*, translated by Richard Boulind (London, 1985)

Étienne Dinet, *Le Pèlerinage à la maison sacrée d'Allah* (Paris, 1930)

Diodorus of Sicily, *The Historical Library of Diodorus the Sicilian*, translated by C. H. Oldfather (London, 1946-1953)

Charles Montagu Doughty, *Travels in Arabia Deserta*, 2 vol. (Cambridge, 1888)

Charles Montagu Doughty, *Documents épigraphiques recueillis dans le Nord de l'Arabie* (Paris, 1874)

Alexandre Dumas, *Pèlerinage de Hadji-Abd-El-Hamid, Médine et La Mecque* (Paris, 1857)

Alexandre Dumas, *L'Arabie heureuse. Souvenirs de voyage en Afrique et en Asie* (Paris, 1860)

Claude Farrère, *Escales d'Asie* (Paris, 1947)

Henry Field, "Camel Brands and Graffiti from Iraq, Syria, Jordan, Iran and Arabia", in *Journal of the American Oriental Society*, 15 (1952)

Giovanni Finati, *Narrative of the Life and Adventures of Giovanni Finati*, edited by William J. Bankes, 2 vol. (London, 1830)

Elian-Joseph Finbert, *La Vie du chameau, vaisseau du désert* (Paris, 1938)

Pehr Forsskål, *Flora Aegyptiaco-Arabica* (1775)

Sir William Foster, *The Red Sea and Adjacent Countries at the close of the Seventeenth Century* (London, 1949)

Julien-Claude Galland, *Recueil des rites et des cérémonies du pèlerinage à La Mecque* (Paris, 1754)

Jules Gervais-Courtellemont, *Mon Voyage à La Mecque* (Paris, 1897)

Carlo Guarmani, "Le Nejd Septentrional", in *Bulletin de la Société de Géographie* (Paris, 1865)

Carlo Guarmani, *Northern Nejd, A Journey from Jerusalem to Anaiza in Qasim*, translated by Lady Capel-Cure (1938)

Carlo Guarmani, *El Khamsa, le cheval arabe de pur sang* (Jérusalem, 1866)

Abdellah Hammoudi, *Une Saison à La Mecque* (Paris, 2005)

Peter Harringan, "New Pieces of Mada'in Salih's puzzle", in *Saudi ARAMCO*, 58 (2007)

John Hayman (edited by), *Sir Richard Burton's travels in Arabia and Africa, Four Lectures from a Huntington Library Manuscript* (2005)

Charles Huber, "Voyage dans l'Arabie centrale, Hamâd, Shammar, Qaçîm, Hedjâz", in *Bulletin de la Société de Géographie* (Paris, 1884)

Charles Huber, *Journal d'un voyage en Arabie (1883-1884)* (Paris, 1891)

Christiaan Snouck Hurgronje, *La Mecque* (1889)

Christiaan Snouck Hurgronje, *Mekka in the Latter Part of the 19th Century* (Leiden, 1931)

Ibn Battuta, *The Travels of Ibn Battuta 1325–1354*, translated by H.A.R. Gibb, vol. 1 (London, 1954), vol. 2 (London, 1962), vol. 3 (London, 1971), translated by C. F. Beckingham, vol. 4 (London, 1994)

Ibn Batutah, *Voyages* translated by C. Defreney and B. R. Sanguinetti, 5 vol. (Paris, 1853-1859)

Ibn Fadlan, Ibn Jubayr, Ibn Battuta, *Voyageurs arabes* (Paris, 1995)

Ibn Jubayr, *The Travels of Ibn Jubayr*, translated by R. J. C. Broadhurst (London, 1952)

Ibn al-Mujawir, *Tarikh al-Mustabsir*, in *Descriptio Arabiae Meridionalis*, edited by O. Löfgren (Leiden, 1951)

Idrisi, *Géographie*, translated by P. A. Jaubert (Paris, 1836-1840)

Antonin Jaussen and Raphaël Savignac, *Mission archéologique en Arabie* (Paris, 1919)

Antonin Jaussen and Raphaël Savignac, *Coutumes des Fuqarâ* (Paris, 1914)

John Fryer Keane, *Six months in the Hijaz, Journeys to Makkah and Madinah 1877-1878* (Manchester, 2006)

Nassiri Khosrau, *"Sefer Nameh", Relation du Voyage de Nassiri Khosrau*, translated by Charles Schefer (Paris, 1881)

Naser-e Khosraw, *Naser-e Khosraw's Book of Travels (Safarnama)*, translated by W. M. Thackston Jr (New York, 1986)

Farid Kioumgi and Robert Graham, *A Photographer on the Hajj: The Travels of Muhammad 'Ali Effendi Sa'udi* (Cairo, 2009)

Thomas Edward Lawrence, *Seven Pillars of Wisdom* (London, 1926)

Thomas Edward Lawrence, *The Letters of T. E. Lawrence*, edited by Malcolm Brown (London, 1988)

Albert Londres, *Pêcheurs de perles* (Paris, 1931)

Mehmet Edib Mehmet, *Itinéraire de Constantinople à La Mecque* (Istanbul, 1816)

Johann David Michaelis, *Recueil de Questions Proposées à une Société de Savants, qui par ordre de Sa Majesté Font le Voyage de l'Arabie* (Amsterdam, 1774)

Guillaume de Monfreid, *En mer Rouge* (Paris, 2005)

Henry de Monfreid, *Les Secrets de la mer Rouge* (Paris, 1931)

Robert Moresby and T. Elwon, *Sailing Directions for the Red Sea* (London, 1841)

Alois Musil, *The Northern Hegaz* (New York, 1926)

Carsten Niebuhr, *Description of Arabia made from Personal Observations and Information collected on the spot* (1775)

Carsten Niebuhr, *Travels through Arabia and other Countries in the East*, translated by R. Heron, 2 vol. (Edinburgh, 1792)

Carsten Niebuhr, *Voyage en Arabie et en d'Autres Pays Circonvoisins* (Amsterdam, 1773)

Carsten Niebuhr, *Description de l'Arabie d'après les Observations et Recherches faites dans le Pays Même* (Paris, 1779)

Sandra L. Olsen and Cynthia Culbertson, *A Gift from the Desert* (Lexington 2010)

William Gifford Palgrave, *Personal Narrative of a Year's Journey through Central and Eastern Arabia* (London, 1865)

William Gifford Palgrave, *Une année dans l'Arabie Centrale (1862-1863)*, translated by Émile Jonveaux (Paris, 1866)

Lewis Pelly, "A visit to the Wahabee Capital, Central Arabia", in *The Journal of the Royal Geographical Society*, 35 (1865)

Jean-Jacques Pérennès, *Le Père Antonin Jaussen, o.p. (1871-1962). Une passion pour l'Orient musulman* (Paris, 2012)

Angelo Pesce, *Jiddah. Portrait of an Arabian City* (London, 1974)

Harry St. John Bridger Philby, *The Heart of Arabia, a record of travel and exploration*, 2 vol. (London, 1922)

Harry St. John Bridger Philby, *Sa'udi Arabia* (London, 1955)

Harry St. John Bridger Philby, "Palgrave in Arabia", in *The Geographical Journal*, 109 (1947)

Jacqueline Pirenne, *À la découverte de l'Arabie* (Paris, 1958)

Joseph Pitts, *A true and faithful account of the religion & manners of the Mohametans* (Exeter, 1704)

Venetia Porter et al., *Hajj: Journey to the heart of Islam* (London, 2012)

François Pouillon, *Bédouins d'Arabie: Structures anthropologiques et mutations contemporaines* (Paris, 2017)

Augustus Ralli, *Christians at Mecca* (London, 1909)

Carl Raswan, *Au pays des tentes noires. Mœurs et coutumes des Bédouins* (Paris, 1936)

Ibrahim Rif'at Pasha, *Mir'at al-Haramayan* (1925)

Ameen Rihani, *Ibn Saoud of Arabia* (London, 1928)

Ameen Rihani, *Around the Coasts of Arabia* (London, 1930)

Roads of Arabia: Archaeology and History of the Kingdom of Saudi Arabia (Paris, 2010)

Léon Roches, *Trente-Deux Ans à travers l'Islam (1832–1864)*, 2 vol. (Paris, 1884–1885)

Henry Rooke, *Travels to the Coast of Arabia Felix* (London, 1783)

Routes d'Arabie. Archéologie et Histoire du Royaume d'Arabie Saoudite (Paris, 2010)

Stanislas Jules Marie Russel, *Une mission en Abyssinie et dans la Mer Rouge* (Paris, 1884)

Eldon Rutter, *Holy Cities of Arabia* (1928)

Waclaw Seweryn Rzewuski, *Impressions d'Orient et d'Arabie* (Paris, 2002)

Muhammad Sadik Pacha, "Summary of the Exploration of the Wajh-Madinah Hijaz Route and its Military Cadastral Map", in *The Egyptian Military Gazette* (Cairo, 1877)

Muhammad Sadik Pacha, *Guide to the Hajj for its Universal Arriving Visitors* (1896)

George Forster Sadlier (Sadleir), *Diary of a Journey Across Arabia (1819)*, (Bombay, 1866)

Soubhy Saleh, *Pèlerinage à La Mecque et à Médine* (Cairo, 1894)

Ulrich Jaspar Seetzen, *Notes sur les Bédouins et les Wahhabis* (1810)

Maurice Tamisier, *Voyages en Arabie, séjour dans le Hedjaz, campagne d'Assir* (Paris, 1840)

Newsha Tavakolian, *The Fifth Pillar: the Hajj pilgrimage* (London, 2011)

Wilfred Thesiger, *Arabian Sands* (London, 1959)

Wilfred Thesiger, *Le Désert des déserts* (Paris, 1978)

Wilfred Thesiger, *Visions of a Nomad* (London, 1987)

Wilfred Thesiger, *Visions d'un nomade* (Paris, 1987)

Bertram Thomas, *Arabia Felix* (1932)

Peter Upton, *The Arab Horse* (Ramsbury, 1989)

Major Roger D. Upton, *Gleanings from the Desert of Arabia* (London, 1881)

Major Roger D. Upton, *Newmarket and Arabia* (London, 1873)

Ludovico di Varthema, *The Travels of Ludovico di Varthema in Egypt, Syria, Arabia Deserta and Arabia Felix, in Persia, India, and Ethiopia, A.D. 1503 to 1508*, edited by G. P. Badger (London, 1863)

Ludovico di Varthema, *Les Voyages de Ludovico di Varthema*, translated by J. Balarin de Raconis (Paris, 1888)

Georg August Wallin, "Journey from Cairo to Medina and Mecca, by Suez, Araba, Tawila, al Jawf, Jubbe, Hail, and Nejd in 1845", in *The Journal of the Royal Geographical Society*, 24 (1854).

Georg August Wallin, *Travels in Arabia (1845 and 1848)*, (London, 1979)

Arthur J. B. Wavell, *A Modern Pilgrim in Mecca and a Siege in Sanaa* (1913)

Johann Gottfried Wetzstein, *Les Déserts de la Syrie et l'Arabie septentrionale* (1865)

Michael Wolfe, *One Thousand Roads to Mecca* (New York, 1997)